A Practical Guide to Legal Writing and Legal Method

ASPEN COURSEBOOK SERIES

A Practical Guide to Legal Writing and Legal Method

Fifth Edition

John C. Dernbach
Widener University School of Law

Richard V. Singleton II
Blank Rome LLP

Cathleen S. Wharton
University of Georgia School of Law

Joan M. Ruhtenberg
Indiana University Robert H. McKinney School of Law

Catherine J. Wasson
Elon University School of Law

Wolters Kluwer
Law & Business

Published by Wolters Kluwer Law & Business in New York.

Wolters Kluwer Law & Business serves customers worldwide with CCH, Aspen Publishers, and Kluwer Law International products. (www.wolterskluwerlb.com)

To contact Customer Service, e-mail customer.service@wolterskluwer.com, call 1-800-234-1660, fax 1-800-901-9075, or mail correspondence to:

Wolters Kluwer Law & Business
Attn: Order Department
PO Box 990
Frederick, MD 21705

Printed in the United States of America.

Text is printed on 50% post consumer recycled paper.

1 2 3 4 5 6 7 8 9 0

ISBN 978-1-4548-2699-6

Library of Congress Cataloging-in-Publication Data

A practical guide to legal writing and legal method / John C. Dernbach, Widener University School of Law, Richard V. Singleton II, Blank Rome LLP, Cathleen S. Wharton, University of Georgia School of Law, Joan M. Ruhtenberg, Indiana University School of Law at Indianapolis, Catherine J. Wasson, Elon University School of Law. — Fifth edition.
      pages cm. — (Aspen coursebook series)
   Includes index.
   ISBN 978-1-4548-2699-6
   1. Legal composition. 2. Law—United States—Language. 3. Law—United States—Methodology. I. Dernbach, John C., 1953-
   KF250.P72 2013
   808.06'634—dc23

                                                              2013013316

About Wolters Kluwer Law & Business

Wolters Kluwer Law & Business is a leading global provider of intelligent information and digital solutions for legal and business professionals in key specialty areas, and respected educational resources for professors and law students. Wolters Kluwer Law & Business connects legal and business professionals as well as those in the education market with timely, specialized authoritative content and information-enabled solutions to support success through productivity, accuracy and mobility.

Serving customers worldwide, Wolters Kluwer Law & Business products include those under the Aspen Publishers, CCH, Kluwer Law International, Loislaw, Best Case, ftwilliam.com and MediRegs family of products.

CCH products have been a trusted resource since 1913, and are highly regarded resources for legal, securities, antitrust and trade regulation, government contracting, banking, pension, payroll, employment and labor, and healthcare reimbursement and compliance professionals.

Aspen Publishers products provide essential information to attorneys, business professionals and law students. Written by preeminent authorities, the product line offers analytical and practical information in a range of specialty practice areas from securities law and intellectual property to mergers and acquisitions and pension/benefits. Aspen's trusted legal education resources provide professors and students with high-quality, up-to-date and effective resources for successful instruction and study in all areas of the law.

Kluwer Law International products provide the global business community with reliable international legal information in English. Legal practitioners, corporate counsel and business executives around the world rely on Kluwer Law journals, looseleafs, books, and electronic products for comprehensive information in many areas of international legal practice.

Loislaw is a comprehensive online legal research product providing legal content to law firm practitioners of various specializations. Loislaw provides attorneys with the ability to quickly and efficiently find the necessary legal information they need, when and where they need it, by facilitating access to primary law as well as state-specific law, records, forms and treatises.

ftwilliam.com offers employee benefits professionals the highest quality plan documents (retirement, welfare and non-qualified) and government forms (5500/PBGC, 1099 and IRS) software at highly competitive prices.

MediRegs products provide integrated health care compliance content and software solutions for professionals in healthcare, higher education and life sciences, including professionals in accounting, law and consulting.

Wolters Kluwer Law & Business, a division of Wolters Kluwer, is headquartered in New York. Wolters Kluwer is a market-leading global information services company focused on professionals.

To our families and friends—
for their love, support, and patience.

Summary of Contents

Contents   xi
Acknowledgments   xxi
Introduction   xxiii

Part A   Introduction to Law

1   Rules and Policies   3
2   Sources of Law   11
3   Case Analysis and Case Briefs   23
4   Precedent and *Stare Decisis*   43

Part B   Basic Concepts of Legal Method

5   Understanding Legal Rules   57
6   Identifying and Selecting Issues for Analysis   73
7   Common Law Analysis   99
8   Statutory Analysis   115
9   Reaching a Conclusion   131

Part C   Basic Concepts of Legal Writing

10   Organization   143
11   Describing the Law   169
12   Applying the Law   187
13   Signposting   199
14   Drafting the Analysis   213
15   Revising and Editing   243

Part D   The Office Memorandum and the Opinion Letter

16   Elements of an Office Memorandum   259
17   Objective Writing   267
18   Statement of Facts for a Memorandum   277
19   Questions Presented   291
20   Opinion Letters   297

Part E   Briefs and Oral Argument

21   Elements of a Brief   311
22   Structure of an Argument   323
23   Persuasive Writing   337
24   Point Headings   357
25   Statement of Facts for a Brief   367
26   Briefs to a Trial Court   381
27   Briefs to an Appellate Court   399
28   Preparing and Presenting an Oral Argument   409

Appendices

Appendix A   Memorandum Concerning Tyler's Possible
Fraud Claim   443

Appendix B   Opinion Letter to Tyler   453

Appendix C   Defendant's Brief to the Trial Court   457

Appendix D   Plaintiff's Brief to the Trial Court   465

Appendix E   Trial Court's Decision   471

Appendix F   Appellant's Brief   477

Appendix G   Appellee's Brief   491

Appendix H   Selected Books on Style and Grammar   503

Bibliography   Sources of Law   505

Index   515

Contents

Acknowledgments — xxi

Introduction — xxiii

Part A Introduction to Law

1 Rules and Policies — **3**
Legal Rules — 3
Law and Policy — 4

Exercise 1-A — 8
Exercise 1-B — 8

2 Sources of Law — **11**
The Hierarchy of Laws — 11
The Hierarchy of Jurisdictions — 13
The Hierarchy and Jurisdiction of Courts — 13
Source Material for Researching the Law — 16
   Primary Authority — 17
   Secondary Authority — 18

Exercise 2-A — 20
Exercise 2-B — 21

3 Case Analysis and Case Briefs — **23**
1. Read the opinion carefully. — 26
2. Identify the holding. — 26
3. Identify the issue. — 28
4. Identify the rule. — 30
5. Identify the facts. — 32
6. Identify the disposition of the case. — 35
7. Identify the reasons and policies. — 35
8. Check for congruency. — 36
9. In multiple-issue cases, analyze each issue separately. — 37

Exercise 3-A — 40
Exercise 3-B — 40
Exercise 3-C — 41

4   **Precedent and *Stare Decisis***   **43**
         Exercise 4-A   49
         Exercise 4-B   50
         Exercise 4-C   51
         Exercise 4-D   52

         Part B   Basic Concepts of Legal Method

5   **Understanding Legal Rules**   **57**
         How Rules Are Constructed   57
             Elements of a Rule   58
             The Result and Its Relationship to the Elements   59
             Exceptions in a Rule   59
             Sub-Elements   60
         Developing a Rule from Multiple Sources: Synthesis   61

         Exercise 5-A   69
         Exercise 5-B   69
         Exercise 5-C   70
         Exercise 5-D   70

6   **Identifying and Selecting Issues for Analysis**   **73**
         1.   Focus only on questions within the scope of the
              problem.   76
         2.   Identify all relevant questions.   77
         3.   Exclude "givens" from detailed discussion.   85
         4.   Separate issues and sub-issues.   86

         Exercise 6-A   89
         Exercise 6-B   91
         Exercise 6-C   94

7   **Common Law Analysis**   **99**
         1.   Determine how the facts of the decided cases
              support your client's position.   105
         2.   Determine how the facts of the decided cases
              support your opponent's position.   106
         3.   Determine how the reasons and policies of the
              decided cases support your client's position.   106
         4.   Determine how the reasons and policies of the
              decided cases support your opponent's position.   107
         5.   Evaluate the strength of your client's case.   109

         Exercise 7-A   110
         Exercise 7-B   110
         Exercise 7-C   111

8   **Statutory Analysis**   **115**
1.   Determine how the language of the statute, and the
      facts of any cases interpreting the statute, support
      your client's position.   120
2.   Determine how the language of the statute, and the
      facts of any cases interpreting the statute, support
      your opponent's position.   121
3.   Determine how the policies of the statute, and the
      policies of any cases interpreting the statute, support
      your client's position.   121
4.   Determine how the policies of the statute, and the
      policies of any cases interpreting the statute, support
      your opponent's position.   122
5.   Evaluate the strength of your client's position.   124

Exercise 8-A   126
Exercise 8-B   126
Exercise 8-C   126
Exercise 8-D   127
Exercise 8-E   128

9   **Reaching a Conclusion**   **131**
1.   A position is stronger to the extent that it involves
      little or no extension of existing law.   132
2.   A position is stronger to the extent that it furthers the
      policies or purposes of the law.   135
3.   When the law does not require a particular result, a
      position is stronger to the extent that it involves a
      fair or just outcome for the parties.   136

Exercise 9-A   139
Exercise 9-B   139
Exercise 9-C   139

Part C   Basic Concepts of Legal Writing

10   **Organization**   **143**
1.   Address "givens" at the outset of your analysis.   144
2.   Discuss each issue separately.   147
3.   Discuss each sub-issue separately.   150
4.   For each issue or sub-issue, describe the applicable
      law before applying it to the factual situation.   153
5.   State the reasons supporting your conclusion on an
      issue or sub-issue before discussing counterarguments.   155

6.   When there is more than one issue, discuss the issues
in a logical order.   158

Exercise 10-A   161
Exercise 10-B   163
Exercise 10-C   165

11   Describing the Law   **169**
1.   Be accurate.   169
2.   Describe only the relevant law.   172
3.   Describe the law in enough detail to enable your
reader to understand the discussion.   173
4.   Summarize the law whenever appropriate.   175
5.   Synthesize the law whenever necessary.   178

Exercise 11-A   184
Exercise 11-B   184
Exercise 11-C   184
Exercise 11-D   184

12   Applying the Law   **187**
1.   Be precise.   187
2.   Show every step in your analysis.   189
3.   Describe every reasonable basis for your conclusion.   191
4.   Explain the context.   194

Exercise 12-A   197
Exercise 12-B   197
Exercise 12-C   197
Exercise 12-D   197

13   Signposting   **199**
1.   Use thesis statements to set out your conclusion
for each issue and sub-issue.   200
2.   Use paragraphs to divide the discussion into
manageable parts.   200
3.   Use a topic sentence to define the purpose of a
paragraph.   204
4.   Use transitions to show the relationship between
ideas.   205

Exercise 13-A   209
Exercise 13-B   210

14   Drafting the Analysis   **213**
Purpose   213

Process   213

Audience   216

1. For each issue, state your conclusion and set up
   your discussion of the issue in an introduction.   217

2. For each sub-issue, state your conclusion in terms
   of the rule and the relevant facts.   219

3. Describe the law relevant to your conclusion for each
   sub-issue.   220

4. Explain why the law supports your conclusion for each
   sub-issue.   222

5. Describe any reasonable counterargument for each
   sub-issue and state why it is unpersuasive.   224

6. Describe how the law supports the counterargument
   for each sub-issue.   226

7. Explain why the counterargument does not change
   your conclusion for each sub-issue.   227

8. Edit the discussion to include signposts.   229

Exercise 14-A   238
Exercise 14-B   242
Exercise 14-C   242
Exercise 14-D   242
Exercise 14-E   242

15 Revising and Editing   **243**

1. Be direct and precise.   244
2. Blend precision with simplicity.   245
3. Use verbs whenever possible to make your writing
   forceful.   246
4. Be concise.   248
5. Edit intrusive or misplaced words and phrases.   253
6. User correct grammar, punctuation, and spelling.   254

Exercise 15-A   255
Exercise 15-B   256

Part D   The Office Memorandum and the Opinion Letter

16 Elements of an Office Memorandum   **259**

1. Heading   260
2. Questions Presented   261
3. Brief Answer(s) (optional)   261
4. Statement of Facts   262
5. Discussion   262

6. Conclusion 262

Special Considerations for Electronic Communication 264

17 Objective Writing **267**
1. Think like a judge. 268
2. State your conclusion on each issue or sub-issue
   objectively and candidly. 268
3. Describe the law objectively. 270
4. Explain the analysis objectively. 271

Exercise 17-A 275
Exercise 17-B 275
Exercise 17-C 275
Exercise 17-D 275

18 Statement of Facts for a Memorandum **277**
1. Identify the legally significant facts. 279
2. Identify key background facts. 281
3. Organize the facts intelligibly. 281
4. Describe the facts accurately and objectively. 282

Exercise 18-A 285
Exercise 18-B 286

19 Questions Presented **291**
1. Be understandable. 292
2. Be objective. 293

Exercise 19-A 296
Exercise 19-B 296

20 Opinion Letters **297**
1. Begin by addressing your client's question or
   concern. 298
2. Summarize the facts upon which your opinion is
   based. 300
3. Explain the law and its application. 302
4. Be objective. 304
5. Adopt a style and tone appropriate for your reader. 305
6. Special considerations for e-mail correspondence. 306

Exercise 20-A 308
Exercise 20-B 308

Part E Briefs and Oral Argument

21 Elements of a Brief   **311**
   1. Caption or Title Page   313
   2. Table of Contents   314
   3. Table of Authorities Cited   314
   4. Opinions Below   315
   5. Jurisdiction   315
   6. Constitutional Provisions, Statutes, Regulations,
      and Rules Involved   316
   7. Standard of Review   316
   8. Introduction   317
   9. Questions Presented   317
  10. Statement of Facts   318
  11. Summary of Argument   318
  12. Argument   319
  13. Conclusion   319
  14. Appendices   320

22 Structure of an Argument   **323**
   1. Present your strongest issues, sub-issues, and
      arguments first.   324
   2. When issues are of equal strength, present the
      most significant issues first.   326
   3. Present your client's position on each issue or
      sub-issue before answering counterarguments.   328

   Exercise 22-A   332
   Exercise 22-B   333

23 Persuasive Writing   **337**
   1. Be professional and honest.   337
   2. Fully argue your client's position.   342
   3. Present arguments from your client's point of view.   346
   4. Craft sentences and choose words to persuade.   350

   Exercise 23-A   355
   Exercise 23-B   355

24 Point Headings   **357**
   1. State your legal conclusions and the basic reasons for
      these conclusions.   358
   2. Structure point headings to be both specific and
      readable.   360

3.   Place headings at logical points in your brief.   361

Exercise 24-A   364
Exercise 24-B   364

25   Statement of Facts for a Brief   367
1.   Describe the facts from your client's point of view.   372
2.   Vividly describe favorable emotional facts and
       neutralize your opponent's emotional facts.   372
3.   Organize your statement to emphasize favorable
       facts and de-emphasize unfavorable facts.   373

Exercise 25-A   377
Exercise 25-B   377
Exercise 25-C   380

26   Briefs to a Trial Court   381
1.   Focus more on the applicability of legal rules than
       on policy.   387
2.   Emphasize that fairness requires a decision in your
       client's favor.   389
3.   Be brief.   391
4.   Write for the court.   394

Exercise 26-A   397
Exercise 26-B   397
Exercise 26-C   397

27   Briefs to an Appellate Court   399
1.   Focus on the claimed errors of the lower court.   400
2.   Base your argument on the appropriate standard
       of review.   402
3.   Emphasize that a decision in your client's favor
       would further the policies underlying the law.   404
4.   Explain how a decision in your client's favor would
       foster harmony or consistency in the law.   406

Exercise 27-A   408
Exercise 27-B   408

28   Preparing and Presenting an Oral Argument   409
Preparing for oral argument   410
1.   Know your case.   411
2.   Know your audience.   411
3.   Plan within the court's time limit for oral argument.   412
4.   Develop a theme when appropriate.   413

5.   Select for presentation your strongest and
      most essential arguments.   415
6.   Plan and practice your argument.   417

Presenting an oral argument   420
1.   Begin with a strong opening.   420
2.   Make your basic arguments as simple and direct
      as the material allows.   423
3.   Make effective use of questions.   425
4.   Manage your time.   430
5.   Present your argument in a professional manner.   431
6.   Close with confidence.   433
7.   Use rebuttal time effectively.   435

Exercise 28-A   438
Exercise 28-B   438
Exercise 28-C   438
Exercise 28-D   438
Exercise 28-E   439

Appendices

Appendix A   Memorandum Concerning Tyler's Possible
                  Fraud Claim   443

Appendix B   Opinion Letter to Tyler   453

Appendix C   Defendant's Brief to the Trial Court   457

Appendix D   Plaintiff's Brief to the Trial Court   465

Appendix E   Trial Court's Decision   471

Appendix F   Appellant's Brief   477

Appendix G   Appellee's Brief   491

Appendix H   Selected Books on Style and Grammar   503

Bibliography Sources of Law   505

Index   515

Acknowledgments

After a hiatus of more than twelve years, we have now published three editions of this book since 2007. That this book is still being used, more than thirty years after it was first published, is a reflection of the support of thousands of teachers and students.

This edition is informed by the teaching and law practice experience of its authors. John Dernbach (government law practice and teaching) and Richard Singleton (private law practice) are again joined by three legal writing directors—Cathleen Wharton, Joan Ruhtenberg, and Catherine Wasson.

At Widener University Law School, the administration and faculty have been consistently supportive of this book. Dean Linda Ammons and Vice Dean Robyn Meadows have always encouraged and supported this project. We are especially grateful to the legal methods and academic support faculty—Anna Hemingway, Dionne Anthon, Ann Fruth, David Raeker-Jordan, Amanda Smith, and Starla Williams—for their suggestions and feedback. Jess Schuller was unfailingly helpful with secretarial support. John Dernbach is also grateful to Palmer Lockard and Tamar Schwartz Eisen.

At the University of Georgia, the writing faculty has contributed valuable insight into both the writing process and the teaching of writing. Dean Rebecca Hanner White and Associate Dean Paul Kurtz have consistently provided support and encouragement. Laura Ivey wrote the first draft of the memorandum in Appendix A.

The students at Indiana University Robert H. McKinney School of Law at Indianapolis and Deborah McGregor, a member of the legal writing faculty, provided helpful comments and suggestions.

At Elon University School of Law, we thank Dean George R. Johnson, Jr. and Associate Dean Catherine Ross Dunham for their support, and the legal writing faculty for their creative teaching ideas and practical suggestions.

We are deeply grateful to the late David W. Craig, former President Judge, Commonwealth Court of Pennsylvania; the Honorable Lynn N. Hughes, United States District Judge, Southern District of Texas; the Honorable Sylvia Rambo, United States District Judge, Middle District of Pennsylvania; Bridget Montgomery, then law clerk to Judge Rambo, who reviewed and commented on many of the chapters in Part E; and Karen Kramer, who reviewed the appendices.

At Aspen, Carol McGeehan and George Serafin helped convince us to publish another edition. Dana Wilson, developmental editor; Julie Nahil, copy editor; and Jan Cocker, proofreader, provided editorial support.

Fred B. Rothman, who passed away in 1988, believed in this book from the beginning. His decision to publish the first edition made all the rest possible.

Our greatest debt is to our students, both past and present, at six different schools over more than thirty years. We hope they have learned as much from us as we have learned from them.

Introduction

A good lawyer is much more than a professional. A good lawyer is a craftsperson, applying his or her talents with imagination, diligence, and skill. Although the practice of law requires a combination of negotiation, counseling, research, and advocacy skills, there is one skill upon which all others depend: The good lawyer, the craftsperson, must be able to write effectively.

Effective legal writing combines two elements—legal method and writing. Legal method is the process of applying legal rules to specific, factual situations and drawing justifiable and well-organized conclusions. Law school, it is often said, is designed to teach you to "think like a lawyer." The myriad legal rules presented in torts, civil procedure, property, and other courses are important, but law school courses should also instill the logic or method of law. A good lawyer knows how to resolve a particular problem, even though he or she may not yet know the relevant legal rules.

A thorough understanding of the legal problem-solving process is of little value, however, unless the analysis can be communicated on paper. Good legal writing is in many ways the same as good writing in general. Legal writing should be clear, precise, and complete, yet fully understandable to a layperson. Although it may be surprising, good legal writing is not a legalistic style of Latin phrases and archaic words.

Effective legal writing is hard work. Nothing is included without good reason, and nothing of significance is omitted. Each word and each sentence is chosen or structured with care. If the document reads smoothly and intelligently, it is not usually because it was easy to write. The reverse is more often true; the document that was easy to write is often muddled. The beauty of well-crafted writing is that the final product masks the painstaking and difficult process by which it was created. The good writer—the craftsperson—makes it *look* easy.

The good writer also understands his or her audience. Not surprisingly, the audience is most often lawyers. It includes friendly or supportive lawyers, lawyers for the opposing side, lawyers who are judges, and lawyers who are clerks. They have different experiences and legal skills, but you should assume that they understand legal method and legal writing and that they bring certain expectations to what they read. They don't necessarily know the law relevant to a particular problem, so they expect that a memorandum or brief will explain it. They have good noses for the strengths and weaknesses of legal conclusions, so they expect conclusions to be explained and counterarguments answered. They are sensitive to the real-world consequences of decisions based on legal documents, so they take these documents seriously. And they are busy—often extremely busy and working under a deadline—so they expect memos and briefs to be as direct, easy to read, and understandable as the material will allow.

This book is designed as a legal writing text, primarily for first-year law students. Its value as a learning tool is based on two classroom-tested premises. First, the fundamental principles of legal writing and legal method can be reduced to a series of fairly simple guidelines. Second, these guidelines can best be learned by practice, particularly by working through highly focused exercises. Nearly thirty years with the first three editions of this book have confirmed these premises.

This book provides practical guidance in the basic skills of legal writing and legal method.[1] Each chapter covers a specific topic, such as organization or precedent. Most chapters set out a short series of principles or guidelines. These guidelines are explained, justified, and then illustrated with hypothetical legal problems. The book shows good and bad ways of applying these guidelines to the problems and explains why one way is better than the others. Exercises of varying complexity, which afford an opportunity to learn and apply the rules, are provided at the end of each chapter (except Chapters 16 and 21). The illustrations and exercises are based on altered or abridged versions of real cases and statutes, citations to which are set out in the Bibliography.

Because legal writing and legal method are skills, they are best learned and improved through the type of practice provided here. Because many different skills are involved, you need to master each one of them, and you must be able to use many of them in a single document. While mastery of basic knowledge about writing and legal method is also essential, simply memorizing that information will not do. If you cannot apply that information on your own in a particular problem, you do not know it.

Learning new skills is often difficult, particularly at first. This is true of all skills, such as riding a bicycle, keyboarding (or typing), driving, playing a musical instrument, or participating in a sport. The more you practice these legal writing and legal method skills, the better you will get, and the more you will enjoy using them.

The book is divided into five parts. The first three parts focus on analytical and writing lessons that are common to most legal documents. These three parts introduce the law (Part A) and explain basic concepts of legal method (Part B) and legal writing (Part C). Although the examples used in these parts tend to be based on legal memoranda, the guidelines in these

---

1. Legal research, basic grammar, and citation form are not discussed. These subjects are covered in detail elsewhere, and there is little value in summarizing them here.

parts also apply to briefs and other legal documents. The last two parts of the book show how these guidelines apply to the writing of memoranda and opinion letters (Part D) as well as briefs (Part E), and give additional guidelines for writing these types of documents.

In addition, Appendices at the end of the book show examples of a legal memorandum and client letter, as well as trial court briefs and appellate briefs. These appendices are intended to be helpful models of the kind of writing taught in this text—not only for class but afterwards in the practice of law.

Although the book offers a step-by-step approach to legal writing and legal method, you need to be aware that legal writing is a recursive process. You may outline a memorandum or brief, begin writing, and then find you need to change your outline. You may find, as you revise your explanation of how a particular statute is applicable to your case, that the statute actually is *not* applicable. The steps in this book do not, in other words, move inevitably from "earlier" to "later" because you will often find yourself going back to "earlier" steps.

The book integrates and synthesizes many of the fundamental lessons of other law courses. It explicitly states the basic principles of legal method and provides a way of learning this method by explicating the thinking and writing necessary to analyze specific legal problems.

The materials in this book are intended to be straightforward, manageable, and easy to understand. After the guidelines are understood in this context, they can be applied to legal writing assignments and to more complex situations. With time and practice, the finer points of legal writing and legal method can be mastered. Ultimately, this book provides tools that will be helpful wherever you go in the practice of law.

A Practical Guide to
Legal Writing and
Legal Method

Introduction to Law

1

Rules and Policies

Defining law is a difficult philosophical problem, but law can generally be understood as the rules and underlying policies for guiding or regulating behavior in society. Rules describe what behavior is permissible or impermissible, what procedures must be followed to achieve certain ends, and what happens to those who do not follow them. Legal rules are intended to provide a means of resolving disputes peaceably, predictably, and, more or less, efficiently. They define relationships among individuals and groups, and help people arrange or conduct their business with greater security.

Legal Rules

Legal rules come about when the legislature enacts a statute, when a court resolves a dispute, when the president ratifies a treaty with another nation after the Senate has given its advice and consent, or when a government agency promulgates administrative regulations. Legal rules differ from other rules because their creation and enforcement require the participation of government. The police, courts, and other governmental bodies are responsible for ensuring compliance with these rules.

Rules vary considerably in their scope, clarity, and precision. Common law rules are created one case at a time. Although they may apply to more situations than just the case at hand, they may be so narrowly tailored that they have little application beyond the particular case from which they arose. Some rules are phrased in broad or general language. Many federal constitutional rules, for example, prohibit persons from being denied "freedom of speech" or "equal protection of the laws." Much tort law turns on what is "reasonable" in particular cases. Rules with such broad terms offer attorneys and judges considerable freedom for interpretation. Other rules are much more specific. Statutes tend to be more detailed than constitutions, and administrative regulations tend to be even more detailed. An administrative regulation, for example, may require a person who uses explosives to be certified by the state after paying a $300 fee and passing a competency test. Such regulations offer less room for interpretation than rules defined by concepts like "freedom of speech." Common law rules, such as those involving estates in land, can also be quite specific.

This range reflects, at each extreme, contrasting approaches to the creation and application of law. Common law is made on a case-by-case basis when a court fashions or applies a rule to the case before it. The common law thus develops cautiously and is premised on the view that problems are best understood and analyzed in light of the facts of each particular case. Other laws, such as statutes and administrative rules, confront problems in groups. This approach is bolder, relies on the premise that problems can be understood in categorical terms, and makes law about particular situations in advance. Each approach works to solve certain problems, but neither approach works for all problems.

Law and Policy

Policies are the specific underlying values or purposes for legal rules. Policies reflect varying and sometimes inconsistent views about what is socially good. Much property law survives from feudal times primarily because of the convenience of adhering to custom. More recent lawmaking, on the other hand, is often directed toward the achievement of specific political goals. Policies also vary greatly in abstractness, even for the same rules. A building code provision requiring a certain kind of fire extinguisher for apartment buildings will probably be premised on technical judgments concerning the safety or efficiency of certain products or materials. These technical judgments, in turn, will be premised on certain moral or value judgments about the degree of protection that ought to be afforded tenants of apartment buildings. Sometimes policies are articulated clearly, but frequently they are stated unclearly or not at all. Often, a single rule is buttressed by several policy considerations.

Because legal rules are based on social judgments, they tend to act as a shorthand way of deciding what is just in a specific factual situation. Instead of simply asking what is right, for example, a court will first apply the relevant legal rule. The Twenty-Sixth Amendment to the United States Constitution provides that a United States citizen who is 18 years of age or older cannot be denied the right to vote simply because of the person's age. The answer to the question, "Can Isaac vote in the national presidential election?" depends on whether Isaac is a United States citizen and is 18 years of age or older. There are good reasons for restricting the national voting privilege to United States citizens, but we all know of 10- and 12-year-olds who could vote more intelligently than some adults. Could we fairly select and include these children while excluding certain adults? Probably not. The age of 18 is simply a reasonable place to draw a line. Line drawing is one of the most important policy considerations in creating and applying legal rules.

Because legal rules are often created to achieve socially desirable goals, they are not etched in stone for eternity, nor do they necessarily reflect the "natural" order of things. Change in underlying values or policies will often be followed by change in the legal rules.

The evolution of the law regarding sex-based discrimination is illustrative. The Fourteenth Amendment to the United States Constitution, which went into effect in 1868, provides in part that no state shall "deprive any person of life, liberty, or property, without due process of law." In 1872, the United States Supreme Court decided in *Bradwell v. Illinois* that this provision of the Constitution did not prevent Illinois from refusing to license an otherwise qualified woman to practice law in that state. The legislature had said, in effect, that only men could be lawyers. Justice Bradley, writing for himself and two other justices, commented:

> The paramount destiny and mission of woman are to fulfil the noble and benign offices of wife and mother. This is the law of the Creator. And the rules of civil society must be adapted to the general constitution of things, and cannot be based upon exceptional cases. . . . I am not prepared to say that it is one of her fundamental rights and privileges to be admitted into every office and position, including those which require highly special qualifications and demanding special responsibilities.[1]

Although the Court's sex discrimination decisions leave open some important questions about equality, there can be little question that its outlook has undergone a marked change. It is difficult to imagine the Court drawing the same conclusion today as it did in 1872. As Justice Brennan, referring to the *Bradwell* case, wrote in a 1974 opinion:

---

1. Bradwell v. Illinois, 83 U.S. (16 Wall.) 130, 141-42 (1872) (Bradley, J., concurring).

> There can be no doubt that our Nation has had a long and unfortunate history of sex discrimination. Traditionally, such discrimination was rationalized by an attitude of "romantic Paternalism" which, in practical effect, put women, not on a pedestal, but in a cage.[2]

This change in the Court's attitude, and ultimately in the law, came as a direct result of changing public views about the role of women. This is not to suggest that judicial (or even legislative) decisions are made only after a poll is taken; the point is rather that public attitudes and values influence the environment in which these decisions are made.

The law, in turn, is a source of social norms and expectations. What the law requires, permits, or prohibits often comes to be associated with what is good or right. Just as the Supreme Court's early decisions helped maintain or create patterns of sex discrimination, so its more recent opinions can be credited with helping to lessen it.

The conclusion that rules are created to carry out socially desirable goals has an important corollary: Rules should never be applied to a factual situation without consideration of the consequences. This may seem like a paradox. If the rule is thoughtfully designed to achieve a particular goal, after all, then every application of that rule to a factual situation ought to further that goal; there should be no need to examine its fairness in each case. The practical difficulty with this proposition, however, is the impossibility of knowing in advance the full range of situations to which the rule might ultimately apply. As a result, the rule may not achieve the desired result in all cases and may even achieve exactly the opposite of what was intended.

The old legal adage "hard cases make bad law" is rooted partly in the tremendous difficulty that lawyers and judges have when a rule is clearly applicable to a factual situation in which it would work a manifestly unjust result. Sometimes the rule is flexible enough that the problem can be solved by interpretation. Sometimes the rule provides for exceptions. Sometimes it is more important to maintain the integrity of the category than it is to work justice in all cases. And sometimes it is necessary to change the law.

Suppose, for example, the rule is that the named beneficiary in a will inherits the property of the deceased. The rule respects the wishes of the deceased and provides a way for the orderly distribution of the dead person's property. But what if the beneficiary murders the person who wrote the will to collect the inheritance? The rule contains no exceptions or room for interpretation. If it is applied as written, the beneficiary will collect the inheritance. Although the basic purposes of the rule would be served, applying the rule seems terribly wrong. A

---

2. Frontiero v. Richardson, 411 U.S. 677, 684 (1974) (footnote omitted).

court's best alternative in this situation is to change the rule: A beneficiary may not inherit property from a person he has murdered.[3]

Other hard cases require a judge to reconcile competing policy considerations. At what point, for example, does a criminal defendant's right to a fair trial limit the public's right to full media reporting of that trial? To what extent can a person's right to run her own business as she sees fit be limited by society for the protection of her employees? You will constantly be probing the cases you read for the justness of their rules and policies.

Law practice and legal education tend to focus on hard cases. Easy cases do not necessarily require a lawyer at all. One does not need a law degree to know that a person who drives seventy miles per hour in a residential neighborhood is breaking the speeding law. Lawyers are most necessary when hard cases arise. Their training and experience help them solve problems that others cannot resolve.

The importance of recognizing that value choices support legal rules cannot be overstated. You will need to explain and weigh competing policies in your office memos. As an advocate, moreover, you will be writing briefs to explain why certain policies outweigh others, and you will have to understand and be responsive to the values of your audience to do so.

Value choices are important in the practice of law. Lawyers have obligations to their clients, but they also have obligations to society. When these obligations are in tension with one another, the tension is not always easy to resolve. If you successfully help a company develop a shopping mall near a city, for instance, you will have a significant effect on local land use, transportation, and housing patterns. If you successfully represent a landowners' group seeking to block that development, you prevent those effects but cause others. Whichever side you represent, you will be arguing for the social good your clients ostensibly seek. "Justice" and "the social good" have many meanings, and you will develop and refine your own understanding of these concepts as you study law.

---

3. Riggs v. Palmer, 22 N.E. 188 (N.Y. 1889).

EXERCISES

The following exercises are intended to show you some of the difficult problems judges and legislators face. As you answer the questions in the exercises, ask yourself where your policy or value judgments come from, whether other judgments might be more appropriate, and what consequences your judgments would have.

Exercise 1-A

1. Assume you are a state legislator voting on the following bills. State whether you would vote for or against these bills and explain your decisions.

    (a) A bill requiring persons who ride motorcycles to wear protective helmets.
    (b) A bill requiring companies that produce food or beverages for public consumption to place warning labels on products known to contain cancer-causing agents.
    (c) A bill requiring couples applying for a marriage license to undergo twelve hours of psychological counseling and testing before the license is granted so they can better determine whether marriage is appropriate for them.
    (d) A bill prohibiting any person from smoking tobacco.

2. Are your decisions consistent with one another? Explain.

3. Do you think it is important that your decisions be consistent? Is it more important that judicial decisions be consistent? Explain.

Exercise 1-B

1. Assume you are a trial judge. Decide each of the following cases according to your idea of a just result and explain the reasons for your decision. Do not refer to any of the other cases in making your decision and do not invent additional facts.

    (a) Dale Price was arrested and charged with armed robbery shortly after three men stole $20,000 from Crabtree National Bank. Two of the men escaped. Price objected to his prosecution on the ground that he should not be tried unless the other two were tried with him. Does Price have a valid defense?
    (b) Jennifer Fong was arrested for driving sixty-four miles per hour in a fifty-five mile-per-hour zone. She objected to her prosecution because she had just been passed by two trucks and a car, all traveling five to

ten miles per hour faster than she. Most of the other vehicles were traveling at the speed limit. Does Fong have a valid defense?

(c) Sally Hyde was arrested and charged with possession of marijuana at the annual "Hash Bash," an unofficial celebration of spring that drew 2,000 people. She objected to her prosecution because most of the other people there also possessed marijuana. There were no other arrests for drug possession, and the police said she was arrested at random "as an example to others." Does Hyde have a valid defense?

(d) Denise Gilman was arrested for cohabitation with a male friend. She is an outspoken and militant critic of the Motor City police department's practice of random traffic stops in poor, primarily African-American neighborhoods. The cohabitation law had not been enforced for years. She objected to her arrest on the ground that she was being unfairly singled out. Does Gilman have a valid defense?

2. Using your decisions and your stated reasons for those decisions in these four cases, frame a rule that will reconcile your conclusions. Remember that your statement of the rule should be clear and precise. Justify your rule.

Diff b/w riding a motorcycle & marriage is intimacy of the decision

2

Sources of Law

The United States has many sources of law because of our federal system. Power is divided between the federal government and the fifty states. The United States Constitution is the nation's charter and the source of authority for federal laws and the federal courts. The Constitution delineates the limits of federal power and reserves considerable authority to the states. Each state has authority over persons and activities within its boundaries. State governments, in turn, delegate some authority to local governments.

The federal government, state governments, and many local governments are divided into three branches. The legislative branch writes laws, the executive branch carries out those laws, and the courts interpret them. Thus, each of these governmental units may, within certain constraints, make law.

Understanding how laws arise and how they affect our activities requires an understanding of two key concepts: (1) the relationships among laws within a single jurisdiction, and (2) the relationships among federal, state, and local governments in the system. This chapter describes these two concepts and briefly describes resources for legal research.

The Hierarchy of Laws

Four basic kinds of laws exist: constitutions, statutes or ordinances, administrative regulations, and judge-made law.[1] These sources form

---

1. This summary is limited to the basic internal laws of the United States. International agreements and laws of other countries are not described here.

a hierarchy with constitutions at the top and judge-made laws at the bottom. Within a jurisdiction, the constitution is the highest authority; statutes, regulations, and common law must not conflict with the constitution.

Statutes create categorical rules to address particular problems. The Food, Drug, and Cosmetic Act, for example, was adopted by Congress to ensure the safety and healthfulness of the nation's food supply. A statute is controlling as to the subject it encompasses, unless the statute is unconstitutional.

The federal government and most states have many agencies with diverse responsibilities (*e.g.,* labor, veterans' affairs, transportation, commerce, environmental protection). Administrative regulations are rules promulgated by such agencies to help implement specific statutes. For example, the "laws" relating to declarations of nutritional information required on the packages of certain foods are largely administrative regulations promulgated by the Food and Drug Administration under the Food, Drug, and Cosmetic Act. Properly adopted administrative regulations have the same legal effect as statutes, so long as they are consistent with the Constitution and relevant statutes.

Judges often interpret or apply constitutions, statutes, or regulations. At other times, when such law is not applicable, they interpret or apply a body of judge-made law known as the *common law.* In either situation, law is made whenever a court decides a case. Once a constitutional provision, statute, or regulation has been construed by a court, that construction becomes law.

The charts below illustrate the order of authority within the federal government and within a state government:

United States
United States Constitution
Food, Drug, and Cosmetic Act, passed by Congress to ensure the safety and healthfulness of the nation's food supply
Administrative regulations promulgated to effectuate the Act, such as rules relating to the declaration of nutritional information required on the packages of certain foods
Judicial decisions construing the Act or the regulations

California
California Constitution
California Environmental Quality Act, passed by the California legislature to protect and enhance the quality of the environment in the State of California
Administrative regulations promulgated to effectuate the Act, such as the rule that an environmental impact report must be filed before a construction project is approved
Judicial decisions construing the Act or the regulations

The Hierarchy of Jurisdictions

The United States has fifty-three sovereign systems of law: federal law and the laws of each of the states and territories. Although these systems are parallel, they sometimes intersect. Federal law controls when they do. Article VI of the United States Constitution provides that the Constitution and federal laws made pursuant to the Constitution "shall be the supreme law of the land."[2]

Therefore, a state may not act, through its legislature or its courts, in a way that is inconsistent with applicable provisions of the United States Constitution or with federal statutes and regulations. For example, the federal Voting Rights Act restricts or bars entirely devices used to discourage voting by racial and ethnic minorities, such as poll taxes, literacy tests, and voting and registration instructions written only in English. A state whose laws conflict with this Act must change its laws to conform to the federal statute.

Subdivisions of the state, including counties, townships, cities, boroughs, villages, or parishes, may also make laws. These laws, usually called "ordinances," must comply with the applicable provisions of the state and federal constitutions as well as state and federal statutes.

The Hierarchy and Jurisdiction of Courts

The federal court system and most state court systems consist of three tiers: the trial courts, the middle-level court of appeals, and the court

---

2. This is commonly referred to as the "Supremacy Clause."

of last resort. Within each system, the jurisdiction of the courts—that is, the authority of courts to hear a case—is limited by geography and subject matter. In the federal system, the trial courts are known as *district courts* because the jurisdiction of each is limited to cases brought within its geographic district. A district might be an entire state (such as Maine) or a portion of a state (such as Texas, which currently has four federal judicial districts). The jurisdiction of the middle tier, the *federal appeals courts,* is also generally defined by geographic boundaries. The fifty states and the territories are currently divided into eleven judicial circuits, with the District of Columbia Circuit forming the twelfth and the Federal Circuit forming the thirteenth.

The eleven judicial circuits that are geographically limited include the following states and territories:

Circuit	States Included
1st Circuit:	Maine, Massachusetts, New Hampshire, Puerto Rico, Rhode Island
2nd Circuit:	Connecticut, New York, Vermont
3rd Circuit:	Delaware, New Jersey, Pennsylvania, Virgin Islands
4th Circuit:	Maryland, North Carolina, South Carolina, Virginia, West Virginia
5th Circuit:	Louisiana, Mississippi, Texas
6th Circuit:	Kentucky, Michigan, Ohio, Tennessee
7th Circuit:	Illinois, Indiana, Wisconsin
8th Circuit:	Arkansas, Iowa, Minnesota, Missouri, Nebraska, North Dakota, South Dakota
9th Circuit:	Alaska, Arizona, California, Guam, Hawaii, Idaho, Montana, Northern Mariana Islands, Nevada, Oregon, Washington
10th Circuit:	Colorado, Kansas, New Mexico, Oklahoma, Utah, Wyoming
11th Circuit:	Alabama, Florida, Georgia

Each federal court of appeals has jurisdiction to hear appeals from districts within its circuit and may affirm or reverse district court decisions. The final level of appeal is to the United States Supreme Court, which may affirm or reverse federal court of appeals decisions as well as certain decisions by a state's highest court.

The following chart illustrates the hierarchy of courts within three jurisdictions:

Jurisdiction	Federal	Florida	Indiana
Highest Court	United States Supreme Court	Florida Supreme Court	Indiana Supreme Court
Middle-Level Appeals Court	United States Court of Appeals for the First Circuit	Court of Appeals of Florida, Fifth District	Indiana Court of Appeals, Second District
Trial Court	United States District Court for the District of Massachusetts	Circuit Court for Seminole County	Marion County Superior Court

The power of a court to hear certain types of cases is known as *subject-matter jurisdiction.* The subject-matter jurisdiction of the federal courts is limited by the United States Constitution and Congress. Federal courts have no authority to hear cases that fall outside those limitations. As a general matter, the federal courts have subject-matter jurisdiction over (1) civil actions that arise under the Constitution, laws, or treaties of the United States (federal-question jurisdiction); (2) cases involving admiralty or maritime law; (3) civil cases in which the amount in controversy exceeds $75,000 if the plaintiff and defendant are citizens of different states (diversity jurisdiction); and (4) cases involving federal crimes. Congress has also created specialized civil courts, such as federal bankruptcy courts, whose jurisdiction is limited to a particular area of the law.

The jurisdiction of state courts is similarly defined by the state's constitution and legislature. A trial court's jurisdiction ordinarily is limited by geography (usually all or part of a county or municipality), subject matter, and the amount in controversy. The court system in a municipality or county may include criminal courts and civil courts of limited or general jurisdiction. The latter are often called *circuit courts, superior courts, district courts,* or *county courts.*

A state court may hear questions of federal law as well as state law. For example, a defendant who has been charged with violating a local ordinance and who believes the ordinance violates the right to assemble guaranteed by the United States Constitution may raise the constitutional claim in state court. Federal courts may also hear questions of state law, but they must apply the law of the state under whose laws the claim arose. If the law of the state is unclear, the federal court must either make an educated guess about what the highest court of that state would do if confronted with the question before it or, if state law permits, certify the question to the state's highest court.

Within each jurisdiction, the decision of the highest court is binding on the lower courts. A decision of the United States Supreme Court on a federal question would be binding on all courts that entertain the identical federal question. As explained more fully in Chapter 4 (Precedent and *Stare Decisis*), when the question is one of state law, state courts are bound by their court of last resort, but they are free to accept or reject decisions by courts of other states and decisions by federal courts interpreting their state law. Judicial decisions outside the jurisdiction may be persuasive but are never binding.

Source Material for Researching the Law

The sources of law described above—constitutions, legislation, regulations, and judicial decisions—are referred to as *primary authority*. They are "law," and the outcome of legal disputes turns on their applicability and interpretation.

Other resources, in which people write about the law or collect and offer general theories about selected rules of law, are known as *secondary authority*. Included in this category are treatises, restatements of the law, articles in law reviews and other legal periodicals, annotations, and legal encyclopedias. These resources may describe the law in a general way or suggest what the law should be, but they are not sources of law. Although secondary authority may assist in persuading a court that a given result is correct or preferable, it cannot mandate that result. Nevertheless, some secondary authority has greatly influenced the courts, and many courts have adopted various statements in secondary authority as the law of the jurisdiction. Once a court has adopted a rule proposed or stated in secondary authority, that rule becomes primary authority.

The following is a brief overview of the main sources in which primary and secondary authority are located.[3]

---

3. Primary authority and some secondary authority are also published in electronic databases, such as LexisNexis and Westlaw, in addition to the print sources described in this section.

Primary Authority

Federal statutes are published chronologically as they are enacted, first in pamphlet form called *slip laws,* and then in a series of books called *United States Statutes at Large.* They are also published by subject matter in the *United States Code* (U.S.C.), the official version; in *United States Code Annotated* (U.S.C.A.), published by West Publishing Company; and in *United States Code Service* (U.S.C.S.), published by Lawyers Cooperative Publishing Company. The publication of state statutes follows a similar pattern. Recent enactments are first published in pamphlet form and then in books organized by subject matter. U.S.C.A., U.S.C.S., and most, if not all, state codes are annotated, which means that the compilations include the history of successive amendments to a code section, references to analogous statutes, references to secondary authority and finding aids, and brief annotations or descriptions of cases construing a particular section.

Constitutions are published in the same manner as statutes. The United States Constitution is published in U.S.C., U.S.C.A., and in U.S.C.S., for example. State constitutions are also usually published in compilations of state statutes.

Administrative regulations are printed in the *Federal Register,* which is published five days per week by the United States Government Printing Office. The *Federal Register* also contains proposed regulations and various notices. Regulations are then published by subject matter in the *Code of Federal Regulations* (C.F.R.), the official source for United States government regulations. In many states, administrative regulations are published in a state version of the *Federal Register* (*e.g., Pennsylvania Bulletin*) and then codified by subject matter (*e.g., Pennsylvania Code*).

Judicial opinions are published in hardbound volumes, roughly in chronological order, with pamphlet supplements that contain opinions too recent to be published in hardbound. Decisions by the United States Supreme Court are published in *United States Reports* (U.S.), the official version; the *Supreme Court Reporter* (S. Ct.), published by West Publishing Company; and *United States Supreme Court Reports, Lawyers' Edition* (L. Ed.), published by Lawyers Cooperative Publishing Company. West publishes decisions by the federal appeals courts in *Federal Reporter* (F., F.2d, F.3d) and by the federal district courts in *Federal Supplement* (F. Supp., F. Supp. 2d, F. Supp. 3d). Not all federal district court and court of appeals decisions are published.

Most states publish their own court decisions. West also publishes state court decisions by region. It has divided the country into seven regions:

West Regions	States Included
Atlantic (A., A.2d, and A.3d):	Connecticut, Delaware, Maine, Maryland, New Hampshire, New Jersey, Pennsylvania, Rhode Island, Vermont, the District of Columbia
Northeastern (N.E. and N.E.2d):	Illinois, Indiana, Massachusetts, New York, Ohio
Northwestern (N.W. and N.W.2d):	Iowa, Michigan, Minnesota, Nebraska, North Dakota, South Dakota, Wisconsin
Pacific (P., P.2d, and P.3d):	Alaska, Arizona, California, Colorado, Hawaii, Idaho, Kansas, Montana, Nevada, New Mexico, Oklahoma, Oregon, Utah, Washington, Wyoming
Southeastern (S.E. and S.E.2d):	Georgia, North Carolina, South Carolina, Virginia, West Virginia
Southwestern (S.W., S.W.2d, and S.W.3d):	Arkansas, Kentucky, Missouri, Tennessee, Texas
Southern (So., So. 2d, and So. 3d):	Alabama, Florida, Louisiana, Mississippi

Because of the efficiency of the West national reporter system, some states have discontinued the publication of official versions of their decisions. Their published decisions are available only in West's regional reporters.

Secondary Authority

This category includes encyclopedias, annotations, scholarly publications, and restatements.

Encyclopedias. Two encyclopedias, found in virtually every law library, cover the scope of Anglo-American jurisprudence—*American Jurisprudence, Second Series* (Am. Jur. 2d), published by Lawyers Cooperative, and *Corpus Juris Secundum* (C.J.S.), published by West. Some encyclopedias are devoted to the law of a particular state. If a state encyclopedia is published by one of the two national publishers, West or Lawyers Cooperative, topics are arranged to conform to the national encyclopedia. Like other encyclopedias, the topics in legal encyclopedias are arranged alphabetically with cross-references in the index.

Annotations. *American Law Reports* (A.L.R.) publishes selected cases along with annotations that survey the law within a discrete area suggested by a particular case. The cases are selected for their interest to the practicing lawyer. A selected case might represent, for example, a new development in the law or one approach to an issue on which the jurisdictions have split. An annotation on the issue you are researching will give you not only an overview of the law nationwide but also citations to the most useful cases in each jurisdiction.

Scholarly Publications. Scholars and practitioners publish books within their particular area of expertise. These are called *treatises* (multivolume sets) or *hornbooks* (single volumes). In addition, law reviews, law journals, and other legal periodicals throughout the country, most of them run by law students, publish numerous scholarly articles each year on current topics of interest to the legal community. These publications cover subjects in more depth than legal encyclopedias or A.L.R. annotations, and the research is usually comprehensive. They frequently propose solutions to particular legal problems.

Restatements of the Law. At the beginning of the twentieth century, a group of lawyers formed the American Law Institute. In 1932, the Institute initiated a series of publications consisting of black-letter rules that generally reflect the majority view on a given common law issue. For example, the American Law Institute has issued restatements of the law on the following subjects: Agency, Conflict of Laws, Contracts, Foreign Relations Law of the United States, Judgments, Property—Landlord and Tenant, Property—Donative Transfers, Torts, and Trusts. Each rule is followed by a Comment that further explains the rule or the reasons for its adoption, and Illustrations that demonstrate how the rule applies in specific situations. In format, a Restatement resembles a code. It is divided into sections, with each section stating a separate rule.

Here is an example from the Restatement (Third) of Agency:

§ 1.01 Manifestations of consent.

Agency is the fiduciary relationship that arises when one person (a "principal") manifests assent to another person (an "agent") that the agent shall act on the principal's behalf and subject to the principal's control, and the agent manifests assent or otherwise consents so to act.

This code-like structure has led many law students to believe that a restatement is more authoritative than it actually is. Restatements are only secondary authority. They are written by authors who describe what the law is in some jurisdictions or what it ought to be, but who have no authority to make laws. Courts and legislatures, however, sometimes adopt a particular restatement provision. When that occurs, the restatement provision is the law of that jurisdiction.

This description of the origin of laws, the hierarchy of authority in our federal system, and the published sources of laws and commentary about the laws should enable you to put the resources you will find in a law library in the proper perspective.

EXERCISES

The following exercises will test your understanding of the information in this chapter.

Exercise 2-A

You represent Chad Hollister, who has been accused of raping his companion while the two were on a date. Hollister admits that he had sexual intercourse with the victim but claims that she consented. The prosecution has brought charges in state court and has sought to introduce evidence that Hollister has been publicly accused of rape several times in the past and prosecuted for rape once. Hollister would like you to offer a motion to exclude this evidence if you can find sufficient legal authority to support the motion. You have found the following:

1. A section of the code of your state that says evidence of prior wrongs is usually inadmissible but may be admissible to show the accused person's criminal intent.

2. A law review article on the difficulty of proving criminal intent in date-rape cases.

3. A decision by a middle-level appeals court in another state in which the court held that if the accused rapist admits the act, his intent is irrelevant, the only issue being the consent of the victim.

4. A decision by a federal court of appeals, applying the law of another state, in which the court held that prior rapes are irrelevant to both the defendant's intent and the victim's consent, and are therefore inadmissible.

5. A section of the code of your state that defines rape as compelling another person to engage in a sexual act by force or threat of force.

6. A decision by the highest court of another state in which the court held that evidence of prior rapes is relevant to show the defendant's awareness that the victim had not consented and therefore his intent to rape.

7. A decision by the highest court of another state in which the court held that prior acts of rape are not admissible because they are unfairly prejudicial and have no bearing on the defendant's intent at the time of the rape for which he is on trial.

8. A dissent by a judge in the case described in item 7. The judge believed that the prior acts were similar enough to show the defendant's characteristic behavior and thus to rebut the defense that the victim consented.

Divide these sources into three categories: (A) primary authority that is binding, (B) primary authority that is persuasive, and (C) secondary authority. Which source in category (B) is likely to be most persuasive?

Exercise 2-B

Your client is Sarah Berg, who owns an apartment complex. As part of a remodeling project, she hired a paint contractor, Deco, Inc., to strip the paint off the walls of the common areas in the apartment building and repaint them. Several of the tenants became ill after inhaling fumes from the paint remover. They have brought suit against Berg and Deco in state court, alleging that the workers were negligent in using the paint remover without adequate ventilation and without warning the tenants that they should vacate the premises during the paint removal process. Berg has an insurance policy that excludes from coverage damages or injuries resulting from the "dispersal, release, or escape of pollutants." The insurer has denied coverage on the grounds that the pollution exclusion clause applies to indoor releases of pollutants. Thus, the resulting injuries are excluded from coverage. In researching this issue, you have found the following:

1. A law review article discussing whether the standard pollution exclusion clause in an insurance policy applies to indoor releases of contaminants.

2. An A.L.R. annotation on the courts' construction of the pollution exclusion clause.

3. An opinion by the highest court of another state addressing the same issue in a case with similar facts (insecticide sprayed inside an apartment building).

4. An opinion by a federal court of appeals addressing the same issue in a case with similar facts (fumes from house paint) and applying the law of another state when that state's courts had not decided this specific issue.

5. An opinion by a federal district court addressing the same issue in a case with similar facts (fumes from diesel fuel sprayed inside the foundation of an apartment building to eradicate termites) and applying the law of your state when your state's courts have not addressed this specific issue.

6. An article in a national legal periodical on the history of the pollution exclusion clause.

7. An opinion concerning an automobile liability policy, decided by the highest court of your state, in which the court set out certain principles regarding the construction of insurance policies.

8. An opinion by a federal court of appeals addressing the same issue in a case with similar facts (carbon monoxide released by a faulty furnace) and

applying the law of another state, relying on a decision by a middle-level appeals court in that state.

9. An opinion by the same court described in item 8 deciding the same issue but reaching the opposite conclusion based on decisions by the highest court in still another state.

Divide these sources into three categories: (A) primary authority that is binding, (B) primary authority that is persuasive, and (C) secondary authority. Which source in category (B) is likely to be most persuasive?

3 Case Analysis and Case Briefs

As explained in Chapter 2 (Sources of Law), courts often interpret rules that are codified in statutes, regulations, or constitutions. At other times they make their own rules as they decide cases, forming the common law.

Judicial decisions are the result of a great deal of time and hard work on the part of lawyers, judges, and all other participants in the litigation process. Disputes are first heard in trial courts. Whether one party is suing another for breach of contract, or whether the state is prosecuting someone for manslaughter, the trial court hears the case first. The trial court has two responsibilities. First, it decides what actually occurred in the case. For example, where was the defendant on the night of June 25? Sometimes the parties agree on the facts, but often they do not. Different witnesses may have different stories. The court will hear the testimony of these witnesses and it will examine other evidence to determine which version of the facts is correct. Sometimes a jury determines the facts; sometimes that job belongs to the judge. Second, the trial court is required to determine what legal rules should be used to decide a particular case. In light of both the law and the facts, the court then decides which party prevails.

The losing party may challenge the decision in a higher or appellate court if that party believes the trial judge made a mistake in stating or applying the relevant legal rules and the mistake affected the outcome in the trial court. Appellate courts must usually accept the factual record from the trial court; the only remaining issues are legal ones. The appellate court will examine the legal rule or rules at issue, sometimes upholding the trial court decision and sometimes reversing it. Unlike trial courts, whose responsibilities are limited largely to ascertaining what actually happened and doing justice in individual cases, appellate courts must think about a range of situations far beyond the facts of the case and about the broader policy implications of what the trial court has done. Because appellate courts review decisions by many trial courts under them, they also help ensure that legal rules are understood and applied uniformly.

Courts record their decisions in opinions, which describe what the dispute was about and why the court decided the case as it did. These opinions deserve careful study. Because courts rely on earlier cases in resolving disputes, cases have enormous value in predicting what a court might do in a specific situation and in persuading a court to reach a particular conclusion. Your ability to understand what these cases mean is thus a necessary skill in analyzing or writing about any legal problem.

More fundamentally, cases demonstrate the basic methods of legal reasoning that you will use in studying and practicing law. Courts must decide how particular laws apply to factual situations, and they must explain their reasoning. Similarly, the study and practice of law will require you to decide how certain laws apply to certain facts. You, too, must explain your reasoning. You can learn a great deal about legal reasoning by studying the ways that courts analyze problems. At the same time, you should realize that judicial decisions (including the cases in this book) contain both good and bad examples of legal reasoning. Over time, you will learn to recognize the difference.

A case brief is a written summary of your analysis of a case that should help you prepare for class or write an assignment. (Case briefs are not to be confused with trial and appellate court briefs discussed in Part E of this book, which are written to persuade a court to adopt your client's position.) Many formats exist for case briefing, but they all include the elements described in this chapter.

Although judicial opinions can contain many things, six components are critical. These are (1) a description of the facts, (2) a statement of the legal issue or issues presented for decision, (3) the relevant rule or rules of law, (4) the holding (the rule of law applied to the particular facts of the case), (5) the disposition by the appellate court, and (6) the policies and reasons that support the holding. The facts of the case, in turn, can be divided into facts about the legal procedure involved in the case and facts that are relevant to the applicability of the relevant law.

The chart below illustrates these components.

***State v. Jones* (1991)**	
Jones appeals his conviction for possession of marijuana. When the police stopped and searched Jones's van, they found an ounce of marijuana in a backpack in the far rear of the vehicle. Although Jones admitted he knew the marijuana was there, he defended against the charge by claiming that the backpack and drugs belonged to a hitchhiker who had been riding with him and who had accidentally left them in the van. In this state, it is presumed that drugs are in the possession of the person who controls them. The issue in this case is whether the marijuana was within Jones's control even though it was in a backpack in the rear of his van. That the backpack and drugs may have been owned by someone else is irrelevant. Public policy dictates that possession should not be synonymous with ownership because the difficulty of proving ownership would permit too many drug offenders to evade prosecution. It is sensible to assume that anything inside a vehicle is within the control of the driver. We hold that Jones possessed marijuana because the backpack was within Jones's van and thus under his control. Affirmed.	Procedural fact Facts relevant to the legal issue Rule Issue Reasoning and policy that support the holding Holding Disposition

Although few cases lend themselves to such ready analysis, each case should contain these elements.

You should, however, be aware of three major difficulties. The first is learning how to think in reverse. The opinion is the end product of a lawsuit. You have to start with this end product and work backward to unravel what the dispute was about, what happened in the trial court, and what happened on appeal. This process is akin to discovering the secret of a competitor's product through reverse engineering. The second difficulty is understanding the interplay among the basic components of a judicial opinion. All the components of a case—facts, issues, rules, holdings, disposition, and reasons and policies—are related. One element cannot be understood without understanding the others. Case analysis is thus largely a recursive process. You will revise your understanding of the elements as you begin to fit them together. The third difficulty is that not all of the elements may be expressed. Because all six elements should be present in any opinion, you often must read between the lines to pinpoint an element as precisely as you can when you do not see it identified.

The remainder of this chapter is designed to give you a method for analyzing cases. Each component of a case will be discussed separately with an emphasis on identifying and understanding that component. Because of the web-like nature of a judicial opinion, no method will result in instant identification or understanding of the components. As you gain experience at briefing cases, you will develop a format that suits your particular abilities and needs. The following method should prove helpful as a starting point and framework for your analysis.

1. Read the opinion carefully.

Several readings are usually required before you can completely understand a case. During your initial reading you will gain a general understanding of who the parties were, how the dispute originated, and what effect the court's decision had on the parties. You will also form tentative theories concerning the basic components of the opinion that you will test and clarify during later readings. After you have acquired a basic understanding of the facts of the case and the "real-world" implications of the court's decision, you can figure out what the court decided.

2. Identify the holding.

The *holding* is the actual decision in the case. It is the answer to the legal question presented to the court. Identifying the holding requires you to study the opinion and determine what the court *actually decided* in the case. Holdings can be either express or implied. *Express holdings* are easy to identify because they are announced as such. In an express holding, for example, a court might state:

> We hold that driving a car at ninety miles per hour is prima facie reckless driving.

Although identifying express holdings appears easy from this example, there is a hidden danger. Courts sometimes inadvertently state they are ruling one way when, in fact, they are deciding the case a different way, or they identify as a holding something that is really reasoning or policy. To avoid being misled, concentrate on what the court actually did in the case, rather than on what it said.

Implied holdings are usually harder to identify than express holdings because you can rely only on the court's actions. The court gives its ultimate decision and the reasons supporting it, but does not tell you what rule it has formulated or followed. In an implied holding, for example, a court might state:

The trial court found the defendant guilty of reckless driving without any testimony that the defendant was, in fact, operating his car in a reckless manner. Anyone who drives at ninety miles per hour is forced to dodge and weave through traffic at a high rate of speed. This conduct is inherently reckless and endangers the well-being of others. Affirmed.

The court's holding is the same as in the first example, but here the judge did not expressly state it.

Do not confuse implied holdings with the reasons for the decision. Sometimes these two elements are hard to distinguish. Remember that the holding is the actual decision and that the reasons or policies are the justifications given for the decision. The two concepts can be distinguished by a simple but useful idea: Each issue has only one holding, but each holding may be supported by several reasons.

Study the following judicial opinion and the three proposed holdings for the case:

State v. Klein (1979)

Casey Klein appeals his conviction for burglary. Klein was apprehended reaching into a house with ten-foot-long tree snips he had modified into a long pair of tweezers. He admitted to the police that he intended to steal a mink coat lying on a chair near an open window.

Appellant Klein denies that he could properly have been convicted of burglary. The maximum offense, he argues, is attempted larceny, because that crime requires only an attempt to steal the property of another. The prosecutor, however, correctly sought and won a conviction for burglary.

Generally, burglary occurs only if the defendant is physically present in the house; he must actually penetrate the enclosure of the dwelling. Although the defendant in this case never entered the house, he did extend his tree snips through the window. There is no meaningful difference between the snips and his arm because the penetration by the snips was merely an extension of Klein's person. Crime has run rampant in recent decades and this type of activity must be discouraged. Burglary carries a greater penalty than attempted larceny and this penalty will more effectively deter such crimes. We therefore hold that the need to deter such activities renders the defendant's actions burglary. Affirmed.

ANSWER A: A defendant may properly be convicted of burglary during a high-crime period when his conviction will deter similar actions, even if he was not physically present in the building.

ANSWER B: For the purposes of burglary, tree snips are the same as a human arm.

ANSWER C: The protrusion of tree snips held by defendant into a dwelling satisfies the penetration element of burglary even if the defendant's body does not enter the dwelling.

The actual holding of the case is contained in Answer C. It shows how the relevant legal rule was found applicable to the facts of this case. Answer C does not justify the holding; it is simply a statement of what the court decided. This is the rule that subsequent courts will apply or distinguish.

Answer A is what the court said it was holding, but not what it actually held. Deterring crime is a reason the court gave for deciding the case the way it did, but reasons and holdings are different things. Answer A reflects the court's confusing way of stating a policy justification for the decision, but it is not the court's holding.

Answer B sounds more like a holding and less like a reason than Answer A. It does not, however, offer a very useful holding. A tree snips may be the same as a human arm, but that statement fails to explain what legal rule is involved. In addition, the court *reasoned* that there was no meaningful difference between a tree snips and a human arm for purposes of satisfying the penetration requirement. Thus, Answer B is also more like a reason.

3. Identify the issue.

Cases usually develop because the parties disagree over the application of one or more rules of law to a particular set of facts. The *issue* is the legal question that must be resolved before a case can be decided. Notice the interplay between holdings and issues: Holdings are the legal answers to the issues.

The issue in a case, like the holding, can be express or implied. Many times the court will tell you the issue. For example: "The question presented in this case is whether a snowmobile is a motor vehicle within the meaning of the Michigan Motor Vehicle Code." This is an *express issue*. Sometimes a court will tell you the issue is one thing when a close reading of the case will demonstrate that it is something else. Sometimes the court will not tell you the issue; this results in an *implied issue*. When this happens, you must read the case carefully and identify the issue based on the holding and the reasons that support the holding. The holding helps identify the issue because the holding is the answer to the issue. Once you have identified the holding in a case, you should have little trouble spotting the issue.

Study the following opinion and three suggested issues:

Johnson v. Silk (1980)

Alice Silk and Fran Johnson, university students who had recently met, decided to use Silk's small sports car to drive to their hometown for the weekend. Silk told Johnson she would pay all their traveling expenses to repay Johnson for tutoring Silk before the midterm examination in Silk's Chinese philosophy class. Shortly after they started out, Silk lost control of her car and it struck a construction barrel on the side of the road. Johnson suffered severe injuries and brought suit against Silk to recover damages. The trial court granted Silk's motion to dismiss, and Johnson appealed.

The state Automobile Guest Statute bars guest passengers from suing drivers for injuries they sustain in automobile accidents. The statute applies only if the passenger did not confer a substantial benefit on the driver that motivated the driver to provide the ride.

The trial court found that Johnson was barred from recovery because she "paid nothing for the ride." The issue in this case is whether Johnson assumed the risk of her own injury by riding on a busy highway in a small sports car. Johnson tutored Silk, and she did so before the ride with every expectation of repayment. It is not necessary that the substantial benefit motivating the ride be cash. Silk owed a favor to Johnson that she felt obligated to repay, and under general principles of fairness actually was bound to repay. The Guest Statute therefore is inapplicable. Reversed.

ANSWER A: Whether a passenger injured in an accident while riding in a small sports car on a busy highway is barred by assumption of risk from suing the driver of that car for damages.

ANSWER B: Whether a court can disregard the Automobile Guest Statute to reach a just and fair result.

ANSWER C: Whether a passenger's tutoring of a driver before a midterm examination constitutes a substantial benefit that bars application of the Automobile Guest Statute.

The correct statement of the issue is Answer C. The court had to decide whether the Automobile Guest Statute applied to this situation. Application of the statute turned on whether the passenger conferred a substantial benefit on the driver. This is the real issue. The court determined that Johnson's tutoring of Silk constituted a substantial benefit because Silk had an obligation to repay Johnson by providing the ride. The court, therefore, held the statute inapplicable, and this holding provides further evidence of the issue.

Answer A is what the court said the issue was, but it is not what the court decided. Assumption of risk, as you may know, is a defense to negligence. Most of this opinion, however, deals with the Automobile Guest Statute, and this is a good clue that the issue concerns the statute and not assumption of risk. Although few courts will err as obviously as this one did, you must remember that word and deed are not necessarily the same thing in judicial opinion writing.

Answer B may be your first reaction to what happened in this case, but issues must be stated in terms of a legal rule, not policy. Fairness is mentioned in the opinion, but it was a reason for the decision, even though the court mistakenly said it was the holding. This mistake points to an important lesson: You must be very sure you have identified the correct holding before you use it to infer the issue. Answer B does not define the legal issue.

---

4. Identify the rule.

Once you have determined the issue and holding, you should identify the rule. The *rule* is the general legal principle relevant to the particular factual situation presented. It can be a rule fashioned by a court in a previous case, a synthesis of prior holdings in cases with similar facts, or a statutory provision.

Identifying the rule involved in a particular case is relatively easy. The court will usually state what rule it is applying or why it is refusing to apply a certain rule. When the court does not state the rule, and you are unfamiliar with the area of law, you will have to infer the rule from the issues, holdings, and facts of the case.

Rules, issues, and holdings are closely related. The issue is generally how the relevant rule will be applied to the specific facts of the case. The holding is the resolution of the issue—the determination of how the rule should be applied to the case. For example, in *State v. Klein*, the rule is that "burglary occurs only if the defendant is physically present in the house; he must actually penetrate the enclosure of the dwelling." The issue is whether a defendant was "physically present" or "penetrated" the building when he held an object that entered the building rather than entering it himself. The holding is the application of the rule to these particular facts—the defendant satisfied this requirement by penetrating a dwelling with tree snips.

The following examples are illustrative:

Whitman v. Whitman (1997)

James Whitman's will left all of his property to his brother, George. James's wife challenged the validity of the will after James died, claiming that it did not express James's clear intent. She sought to present evidence, including her own testimony that James actually wanted to give a substantial portion of his estate to her. The trial court excluded the evidence, and we affirm. The rule in this state is that an unambiguous will is conclusive as to the testator's intent unless it would contravene law or public policy. All other evidence must be excluded. Because James's wife sought to present precisely such evidence, and the will was not ambiguous, the trial court properly ruled the evidence inadmissible. We find no legal or public policy reason to depart from the intent expressed in the will.

Identifying the rule in this case is simple because the court explained that "the rule in this state" is that an unambiguous will is conclusive as to the testator's intent. But consider this opinion:

Central Credit Co. v. Smith (1989)

Olan Computer Company began to operate as a business before it was properly incorporated. Prior to proper incorporation, the company made sales and incurred debts. Olan's creditors are seeking to hold Smith and Jones, the incorporators and sole shareholders, personally liable for these debts. A corporation does not legally exist until it has been properly incorporated. Once a business is properly incorporated, a creditor must look to the corporate entity to satisfy its claim. The trial court properly found Smith and Jones personally liable for the debts. Affirmed.

Because the precise rule used by the court is not stated here, you must identify it by inference. The legal rules stated by the court and its holding in this case help the inquiry. A corporation's legal existence begins with proper incorporation, the court said. After that time, the corporation's shareholders are not personally liable for its debts. The court also held these shareholders personally liable for debts they incurred before incorporation. The court thus applied a corollary of the rules stated: A shareholder of a corporation can be held personally liable for debts incurred when the company is not properly incorporated.

Sometimes, however, there is no rule in the jurisdiction, and the court must create a rule. These cases are referred to as cases of first impression. The case below is an example.

Morgan v. Davis (2002)

Kevin Morgan hired Sam Davis to construct a gazebo in his backyard. While excavating soil for the foundation, Davis discovered a metal box filled with gold coins dating from 1848 to 1893. Davis kept the box and its contents, and Morgan filed suit against Davis for recovery of the property. The trial court held that the right to possession of the coins belongs to the landowner. Davis appealed, claiming that the coins are treasure trove and possession belongs to the finder.

This is a case of first impression in this state; we have not had occasion to decide who has the right to possess treasure trove that has been found. Treasure trove includes gold or silver coins or bullion concealed in the earth or in a structure. The common law in many other states is that the finder of treasure trove has a right to possess it against everyone but the true owner. Our cases recognize another class of property that is somewhat similar, however. The owner of land on which embedded property (personal property that has become part of the earth) is found has a right to possession of that property as against all but the true owner, even if it was found by someone else.

We agree with Davis that the coins are properly classified as treasure trove, but we find archaic the common law rule that the right to possession of treasure trove belongs to the finder. Giving the right of possession to a trespasser or a hired workman rather than to the landowner does not conform to present day notions of fairness. We also see no reason to distinguish between treasure trove and other personal property embedded in the soil. We hold that, as a matter of law, the right to possession of property classified as treasure trove belongs to the owner of the land upon which it was found. Affirmed.

This case required the court to decide what the rule is. After considering the traditional common law rules regarding found property, the court decided to fashion its own rule because it found the distinctions between certain categories of property artificial and outdated. When you identify the rule for such cases, you will describe the state of the law prior to the court's decision.

5. Identify the facts.

Once you understand the rule, holding, and issue, you will be able to identify the relevant facts of the case. After the initial reading of the case, you have a general knowledge of the facts. Now you are ready to reread them and determine which facts were important to the decision.

Judicial opinions usually contain a lengthy description of the facts because the court wants the reader to understand the situation completely. You should identify two kinds of facts—legally relevant facts and procedurally significant facts.

Legally relevant facts are those the court considered important in deciding the case. Sometimes these facts are events that did occur, and sometimes they are events that did not occur. These facts are outcome-determinative; they affected the court's decision. Because facts are inextricably tied to legal issues and rules, it is impossible to know which facts are relevant without first knowing what the court decided. Sometimes a court will state precisely those facts it thought significant in deciding the case. At other times, you will have to guess those facts from the court's holding and reasons. There is no rule that indicates which facts are outcome-determinative, and no single fact is necessarily legally significant.

Procedurally significant facts describe at what stage in the case an error may have occurred in the lower court. These facts, which are routinely stated in appellate opinions, include the ruling of the trial court on the matter that is the subject of the appeal. They are important because they describe the specific question that the appellate court will address and determine the scope of the court's review. The alleged error might be as narrow as whether the court erred in denying a motion to exclude a certain piece of evidence or as broad as whether the court erred in refusing to grant a motion for a directed verdict at the end of the trial.

Procedural facts are also important because the procedural posture of the case affects what legally relevant facts are available to the appellate court. When the parties agree on the facts, the trial court simply determines and applies the relevant law. If the parties disagree on the facts, a trial is held in which each side presents witnesses and other evidence to support its story. Appellate courts are then confronted with more numerous and less consistent facts than if a case is resolved before trial. The procedural posture of the case also affects what the appellate court can do if it disagrees with the trial court. If the factual record is complete, the appellate court's decision should end the controversy; if the record is not complete, the appellate court will remand the case for more fact finding. In *State v. Klein*, for example, the defendant appealed his conviction for burglary, and the court affirmed his conviction. Because he was convicted, you know that there was a trial and that the evidence concerning the tree snips came out of that trial. Because his conviction was affirmed, you also know that this case (barring a further appeal) is over.

Consider the following opinion and factual statements:

Lost River Ditch Co. v. Brody (1923)

The defendant owns a small riparian tract on Apple Blossom Creek. In the fall of 1922 he began diverting 45,000 gallons of water a day from a pump house on that tract to a nonriparian parcel one-half mile from the stream. The defendant claimed he needed the water because he had just doubled the size of his herd. The plaintiff, who owned another riparian tract downstream on the creek, sued the defendant for damages, claiming that any diversion of water from the watershed was impermissible. Although the plaintiff was unable to prove any actual damages, the jury awarded him one dollar in nominal damages. We reverse. Diversion of water from the creek to a nonriparian tract without some evidence of damage does not provide a basis for recovery of nominal or any other damages.

ANSWER A: The defendant, who owned a small riparian tract on Apple Blossom Creek, diverted 45,000 gallons of water per day in the fall of 1922 to supply water for his recently doubled cattle herd. The plaintiff, a downstream riparian owner on the same creek, sued the defendant for damages, claiming that any diversion of water from the riparian tract was prohibited. A jury awarded the plaintiff one dollar in nominal damages even though he was unable to prove actual damages. The defendant appealed.

ANSWER B: The defendant, who owned a riparian tract on a creek, diverted water from the creek to a nonriparian tract. The plaintiff, a downstream riparian owner on the same creek, sued the defendant for diverting the water. The plaintiff could not show actual damages, but a jury awarded him nominal damages. The defendant appealed.

Answer B is better because it contains only those facts the court used to decide the case and those facts needed to explain what happened in the trial court. Answer B contains nothing else; it is simple and succinct. Answer A is a slightly rewritten version of the facts stated in the case. It includes interesting details, but the name of the creek, the quantity of water diverted, the actual amount of the nominal damages, and some other details are irrelevant to the issue on appeal. Answer A also omits an important fact. Because the rule applies only to water diverted to a nonriparian tract, Answer A should have stated that the water was diverted from the creek to a nonriparian tract.

6. Identify the disposition of the case.

The *disposition* is simply a statement of what the appellate court did with the decision of the court below. When only two courts are involved—the appellate court and the trial court—stating the disposition is straightforward. If the court agrees with the lower court's decision, as was the case in *Whitman v. Whitman*, the judgment is "affirmed." If the court believes the decision was erroneous, as was the case in *Lost River Ditch Co. v. Brody*, the judgment is "reversed." As stated above, if additional facts are necessary for a disposition of the case, the court may also *remand* the case for further proceedings.

Sometimes, more than one lower court is involved. A trial court decision, for instance, might be reversed by an intermediate court of appeals. The supreme court of the jurisdiction might then reverse the court of appeals decision and reinstate the trial court's decision. When that occurs, your brief of the supreme court's decision should describe its disposition of the decisions of both the trial court and the intermediate appellate court.

7. Identify the reasons and policies.

Reasons are the steps in the logical process a court uses in arriving at its holding. Reasons can be simple explanations of how a legal rule or policy is applicable or inapplicable to the case, or they can be more involved explanations of why the analysis from one area of the law is applicable to an entirely different area of the law. When studying cases, you should determine the exact reasoning process the court employed to arrive at its holding on an issue. Only through understanding the reasons behind a court's decision can you understand what the decision actually means or how broadly or narrowly the case might be interpreted.

Chapter 1 (Rules and Policies) defines policies as the underlying purposes of legal rules. They are similar to but broader than reasons. Whether a court is modifying the law in bold strokes to reach certain goals or whether it is carefully limiting the scope of earlier decisions, it will usually advance some policy justification for its decision. Even when a court admits it reached a harsh or unfair result for the parties, it will still try to show how the decision is in the best interest of the public. In other cases, when the law dictates an outcome the court dislikes, the court may complain about the law and even suggest the desirability of legislative change, but it will still explain the policies underlying the law and the outcome. Policies are important because they define the future direction of the law.

The easiest way to identify policies is to first identify the holding. Once you have determined what the court decided, look for the social justifications for the court's decision. The court in *State v. Klein* held that use of tree snips satisfied the penetration element of burglary even though no part of the defendant's body entered the building. The court stated a broad policy in support of its conclusion by emphasizing the high crime rate and the deterrent value of the more severe penalty for burglary.

Some opinions contain no policy justification at all. In the water diversion illustration given earlier in this chapter, for example, the court stated a rule and reversed the trial court without explaining the basis for the rule or its holding. A court is less likely to provide an explanation in cases such as this, when the rule and its application are fairly well settled. Look to earlier decisions, if necessary, to determine the policies underlying the rule.

The close relationship between reasons and policies sometimes makes it difficult to tell the two apart, but the following test is useful: Reasons indicate how the court arrived at its holding; policies tell you why this holding is socially desirable. An opinion can make sense without any policy justifications, but it cannot make sense without reasons explaining how the court arrived at its conclusion.

Sometimes, you will find that the court's explanation is incomplete or ambiguous. When that occurs, say so. If only one interpretation is logical, explain it. If several interpretations are possible, you may want to explain them.

In *State v. Klein*, for example, the court stated that tree snips were an extension of Klein's arm. The court's reasoning is not explained, beyond the statement that there is "no meaningful difference" between the snips and Klein's arm. You might reconstruct the court's reasoning as follows:

> The requirement that the burglar must penetrate the enclosure would mean nothing if a burglar could circumvent the requirement by devices that extend the reach of the burglar's arm. Therefore, we will enlarge this requirement by redefining penetration to include a mechanical extension of a burglar's person.

This reconstruction explains how the court arrived at its holding. The announced policy to deter crime, in addition, helps to justify the court's extension of one of the burglary requirements.

8. Check for congruency.

Once you have some idea of the important facts, the issue, the rule of law, the holding, the disposition, and the reasons and policies, check these elements against one another to make sure they are congruent. There is an interplay among them that should be obvious by now. Such interaction makes the case an interlocking whole and underscores why you cannot understand any one element without reference to the others. Always pause when you have gone this far to make sure the elements are congruent.

You might test for congruency by using the following model:

Facts	What happened?
Rule	The law
Issue	How does the law apply to these facts?
Holding	The result when the law is applied to the facts
Disposition	Did the court agree or disagree with the decision below?
Reasons & Policies	Justification for the result, in light of the law and facts

If you are using the same law and the same facts in each element, and they accurately reflect the court's decision, you have a good case brief. When the court's holding changes the law, however, you will find that the law described in the holding differs from the law described in the rule. In *State v. Klein*, as you know, the court modified the rule that a person must penetrate the dwelling to include penetration by an extension of the person's body. Your case brief should reflect any modifications to the rule.

9. In multiple-issue cases, analyze each issue separately.

A case can contain more than one issue because there may have been several disagreements about the law that the appellate court was asked to resolve. Although an appellate court will frequently dispose of an entire case after resolving only one of these disagreements, many times an opinion will contain a discussion of several issues with a corresponding holding for each issue. If there are several issues, analyze each issue separately. For each issue you must identify the rule, relevant facts, holding, and reasons and policies supporting the court's decision. Although the issues may be closely related, your analysis of each should be distinct. Once you have identified each issue presented in an opinion, follow the steps outlined in this chapter for dissecting each one.

Each of the elements discussed above may be written out in a case brief. As already stated, a case brief is a short summary of a case that may be useful to you in preparing for class or when researching a problem. It gives you a ready reference so you do not have to reread a case to remember what it was about.

Below is an opinion and, following that, a sample case brief.

Roberts v. Zoning Commission (1998)

Appellant Edwin Roberts owns a parcel of land. He applied to the city Zoning Commission to rezone the parcel from R-3 (single-family residential) to O-I (office-institutional). The Commission denied his application, finding that all surrounding parcels are zoned for and contain single-family homes. Roberts produced evidence that the parcel was appraised at between $50,000 and $90,000 under the current zoning, but would be worth $200,000 to $250,000 if rezoned.

Following the denial of his rezoning request, Roberts filed this action, alleging that the Zoning Commission had taken his property without compensation, in violation of the state and federal constitutions. To demonstrate a taking, the challenger to a zoning classification has the burden of presenting clear and convincing evidence that he has suffered a significant detriment.

The trial court properly dismissed the landowner's complaint because Roberts failed to meet his burden. Merely showing a disparity in the market value of property as currently zoned versus its value if rezoned is not, by itself, sufficient to establish a significant detriment. Offers for real estate depend on the method of marketing and the asking price. Because the landowner did not attempt to market the property at an asking price consistent with its value under current zoning, no significant detriment has been shown. We must bear in mind that zoning ordinances exist to ensure the greater good of the community even though specific zoning may not always be in the best interest of an individual. Affirmed.

In the sample brief of this case, the order of the six parts of the case brief is different from the order in which they were described earlier in this chapter. Looking for the holding first, and then the issue, rule, facts, disposition, and reasons and policies, is a good way to study a case. But you may want your written case brief to have the six parts in the order shown in the example below. Case briefs are for your use. You should feel free to adopt a format that works best for you.

Roberts v. Zoning Commission (1998)

<u>Facts</u>: A landowner applied for a rezoning of his property. His request was denied even though his property would have been worth substantially more if it were rezoned. He did not try to market the parcel under the existing zoning classification. The landowner then sued, alleging an unconstitutional taking. The trial court dismissed the complaint.

<u>Rule</u>: The government may not take property without compensation. To show a taking from a rezoning denial, a landowner must demonstrate by clear and convincing evidence that he has suffered a significant detriment.

<u>Issue</u>: Has the landowner suffered a significant detriment?

<u>Holding</u>: No. A landowner cannot show a significant detriment unless he attempts to market the property at an asking price consistent with its value under current zoning.

<u>Disposition</u>: Affirmed

<u>Reasons and policies</u>: A significant detriment does not occur when the landowner is deprived of a potential increase in property value that would result if the property were rezoned. A difference in market value depends on such variables as how the land is marketed. Zoning may not always serve the best interest of the individual, but it serves the greater good of the community.

EXERCISES

The following exercises are designed to introduce you to case analysis. Each opinion contains all of the components discussed in this chapter. Using the format provided above for case analysis, write a brief for each one. The goal is to identify the various components as precisely as possible.

Exercise 3-A

Toad v. Ulrich (2002)

The appellee, Michael Toad, operates a roadside stand where he sells hand-carved, three-legged wooden stools to tourists. Toad's business started slowly, but it has increased substantially in recent years. Toad now derives a modest income from his enterprise. From the start, he has advertised and referred to his stools as "Toad Stools." After Toad operated his stand for one year, the appellant, Bruce Ulrich, began operating a similar stand and selling similar stools, which Ulrich also called "Toad Stools." When Ulrich first opened his stand, Toad asked him not to use the name "Toad Stools," but Ulrich did so for two years. Toad made no further effort to prevent the use of the name until he started this suit.

Toad filed suit alleging that the appellant had infringed on his trademark. Toad requested $45,000 in damages for lost sales and an injunction barring Ulrich from using the name "Toad Stool." The trial court awarded Toad $40,000 in damages and granted his request for an injunction. Appellant Ulrich now contends that the trial court erred in finding a trademark infringement because Toad did not actively defend his use of the name.

Common law trademark principles can protect the name of a business or product, but that protection is not absolute. A person must actively defend that trademark against known infringements. If he or she does not actively defend the name, a competitor is free to use that name after two years. "Actively defend" means making diligent efforts, including lawsuits if necessary, and Toad has not made diligent efforts according to the traditional rule.

We must, however, distinguish between large businesses that have the capacity and the resources to litigate such claims, and small businesses that do not have these resources and should not be held to the same standards. The smaller the business, the easier it should be to satisfy the active defense requirement. When Toad approached Ulrich and asked him not to use the name, he satisfied that requirement. Therefore, Toad is entitled to common law trademark protection. Affirmed.

Exercise 3-B

Bronson v. Road Runner Shoe Co. (1985)

The appellee, Road Runner Shoe Co., is a Maryland corporation that manufactures and sells running shoes. Twenty of the company's 100 employees work at its Maryland headquarters, while the remainder work at offices through-out the United States. The company, which sells to major retailers, has a fleet of trucks for delivering its shoes. The company employed George Granger as a general helper and driver for one of its delivery trucks.

Johnny Bronson filed suit against the company for injuries he sustained when one of the company's trucks, driven by Granger, jumped the median strip and struck him while he was jogging. It is undisputed that Bronson was using extreme care while jogging and was wearing a bright red jogging out-fit. Bronson claimed he would never be able to jog again and that he has had emotional problems since the accident. Granger, who had not received per-mission to use the truck, had visited his girlfriend during his lunch hour. The company gives Granger one hour to eat lunch, and he was speeding back to work when the incident occurred. Granger was nineteen years old at the time and a "hard worker who comes from a reputable family." He had worked for the company for two years and was saving money to go to college and major in business administration. Granger was arrested once when he was sixteen for drag racing on a public highway, but his case was dismissed.

The trial court granted the company's motion for summary judgment. On appeal, Bronson argues that the company should be liable on the theory of *respondeat superior*. We agree.

The general rule is that an employer is liable for the acts of employees when they are acting within the scope of their authority. In this case, Granger did not have permission to use the truck during lunch and did not usually drive it then. However, Granger normally had exclusive possession of the keys during working hours, and the company had never objected to Grang-er's private use of the truck. Employers should be held liable for the torts of their employees. It is too easy for an employer to shrug off legal responsibil-ity by saying the employee was not authorized to commit the act. Very few employers expressly authorize employees to commit tortious acts. Employ-ers, by their position of authority, have control over employees. Employees who do not behave responsibly should be discharged. Reversed.

Exercise 3-C

State v. Phillips (1999)

The appellant set fire to an unoccupied building. The building had been deserted for many years and had been condemned as a "firetrap." The appel-lant poured several gallons of gasoline throughout the first floor of the build-ing and then ignited it. The building burned to the ground in thirty minutes. The trial court found her guilty of arson, a felony in this state. The appellant does not contest that conviction here.

On the way to put out the fire, a fireman was killed when he fell off the back of the fire truck and was run over by a car that was speeding and fol-lowing the truck too closely. There was no way the driver of the car could have avoided the fireman. The driver of the car was charged and convicted of speeding and careless driving.

The appellant was also found guilty of murder under the felony murder rule. She appealed this conviction. The felony murder rule provides that if someone is killed during the commission of a felony, the defendant is guilty of murdering that person. The purpose of the rule is to deter people from committing felonies, particularly those which are inherently dangerous to human life. In this case, there is no doubt the fireman was killed during the commission of a felony.

Fires and arson are inherently dangerous to people in buildings, bystanders, the surrounding neighborhood, and firemen summoned to combat the blaze. The appellant should have known that a fire truck would be summoned to put out the fire, but she could not foresee someone would be following the truck too closely. Public policy dictates that there must be a limit to liability. The felony murder rule borders on strict liability in criminal law. Any expansion should be carefully scrutinized. As with any principle of strict liability, there must be a causal connection. Reversed.

Precedent and *Stare Decisis*

Judges have considerable freedom to modify legal rules and principles in accordance with social norms and their views of justice and common sense. The concepts of precedent and *stare decisis* serve as important checks on this judicial freedom and ensure that the law develops in an orderly fashion.

One of the fundamental principles of our legal system is that courts look to previous decisions on similar questions for guidance in deciding present cases. These decisions are known as precedent, and their usefulness is premised on the idea that an issue, once properly decided, should not be decided again. Reliance on precedent ensures that similar cases are decided according to the same basic principles and helps courts to process cases more efficiently. Durable rules also reinforce the social norms they define, encourage confidence in the legal system, and assist people in planning their activities.

The values that surround the notion of precedent are reinforced by the principle of *stare decisis.* Whereas precedent merely requires that courts look to previous decisions for guidance, *stare decisis* requires that a court follow its own decisions and the decisions of higher courts within the same jurisdiction. A state trial court, for example, must follow the decisions of appellate courts in that state; an intermediate appellate court must follow the decisions of the state's highest appellate court. Federal courts of appeal must follow those of the United States Supreme Court, but decisions of federal district courts or other federal courts of appeal do not bind them.

Precedent, then, can be of two types—binding or persuasive. When the doctrine of *stare decisis* applies, precedent is binding and a court must reconcile the result in a given case with past decisions. Only after explaining why previous cases are inapplicable may a court fashion new rules or modify or expand existing ones; a court may never simply ignore or contradict binding precedent. When the doctrine of *stare decisis* does not apply, as with decisions from other jurisdictions or lower courts in the same jurisdiction, courts are free to follow, or refuse to follow, previous decisions. Although not binding, such decisions may be *persuasive.* The reasoning of other courts often illuminates the issues and suggests solutions to a problem.

The concept of binding precedent may seem absolute. But in practice, *stare decisis* is a flexible concept. Because a judicial opinion may be interpreted in different ways, judges have significant latitude even when dealing with binding precedent. Differing interpretations result from internal tension—on one hand, between the facts and holding of a case, and, on the other hand, its underlying reasons or policies. Viewed most narrowly, a case stands for a particular result regarding that set of facts. Courts often do confine cases to narrow factual categories, but such interpretations give the case relatively little importance. Viewed more broadly, a case stands for the articulated reasons or policies. Because the court was concerned primarily with the facts of the case before it, legal analysis travels on increasingly risky ground the further it ventures from those facts in trying to predict the outcome of future decisions. The best guides in venturing from those facts are the reasons and policies given in the opinion.

The various ways in which a case can be interpreted highlight the fundamental role that *stare decisis* plays in the process of legal analysis. In his well-known book, *The Bramble Bush,* Professor Karl Llewellyn defined this range of interpretation in terms of "strict" and "loose" views of precedent. The *strict* view, applied to "unwelcome" precedent, limits the reach of prior cases to show that they are not applicable to the case at hand. Strict construction of precedent requires careful distinguishing of the facts and policies of the prior case(s) from those of the present case. The loose view, applied to "welcome" precedent, maximizes the reach of these cases to show how they are applicable, or analogous, to the present case. As Llewellyn pointed out, both approaches are "respectable, traditionally sound, [and] dogmatically correct."[1]

Flexibility is necessary to the legal system because it allows the law to adapt to evolving conditions and to accommodate new factual situations. However, the stabilizing effect of *stare decisis* should not be underestimated. When the rules are well defined and the factual situations are clearly similar or plainly different, *stare decisis* mechanically

---

1. KARL LLEWELLYN, THE BRAMBLE BUSH 66–69 (1930).

dictates the result. Even when the rule is ambiguous or the factual situation complex, *stare decisis* at least defines the starting point for analysis. This tension between restraint and freedom, between stability and change, embodies the essence of our common law system.

Determining the precedential value of rules or ideas in a court's opinion requires a close reading of the case. Statements made by a court that do not bear on the issues before it are known as *dicta* (from the Latin phrase *obiter dictum,* literally, "said in passing"). *Dicta* have little precedential value because a court is supposed to decide only the issues before it and *dicta,* by definition, are not part of the reasoning process that led to the decision. Courts sometimes rely on *dicta* nonetheless because *dicta* reflect other judges' concerns and often indicate how a court would rule in the future.

Courts may also rely on the ideas and reasoning of concurring and dissenting judges. Appellate courts consist of a panel of judges who may not agree on how a dispute should be resolved or why a particular decision should be reached. If the court is divided, one of the judges in the majority will write the opinion of the court. Judges who disagree with the decision reached by the majority and refuse to join the court's opinion are said to *dissent.* Judges who agree with the decision but either disagree with the majority's reasons or would have reached the same decision on other grounds are said to *concur.* These judges frequently write separate opinions.

Unlike *dicta,* which may indicate how a court would rule in the future, a concurring or dissenting opinion indicates only that a judge disagreed strongly enough to write a separate opinion. Nevertheless, these opinions can be a valuable resource. Often, a dissenting or concurring opinion sharpens the focus of the debate. It may offer a different interpretation of precedent, emphasize social policies disregarded by the majority, or frame the legal question in a different way. A court that is considering a change in the law of its jurisdiction or facing an issue of first impression will read concurring and dissenting opinions on the issue in question with great interest. Dissenting opinions in an earlier case are sometimes adopted by a majority of the court in later cases.

The following two cases illustrate how precedent and *stare decisis* function. They concern the question whether a landlord should be held liable for negligently exposing tenants to foreseeable criminal activities. After deciding the first case, *Brainerd v. Harvey*, in 1982, the same state appellate court was presented with an opportunity four years later, in *Douglas v. Archer Professional Building, Inc.*, to expand the scope of the rule to cover a different factual situation.

Brainerd v. Harvey (1982)

The plaintiff is an elderly man who lived in a small building in a high crime area. The building had poor lighting on its front porch and a continuously unlocked outer door. As the plaintiff was about to enter the building one night, the outer door was jerked open by an unknown youth who had been hiding inside. The youth struck and robbed the plaintiff. The plaintiff brought suit against the landlord, but the trial judge granted the defendant's motion for a directed verdict of no cause of action.

We reverse. We have from time to time held that persons are liable for negligently exposing others to foreseeable criminal activities, and this is such a case. The inadequate lighting and locks were physical defects in a common area of the building under the landlord's control; this would be a far different case if the building had not contained such defects. The landlord's negligence in failing to repair them made it more likely than not that the plaintiff would be victimized by a criminal attack.

The trial court also erred in refusing to grant the plaintiff's demand for a jury trial. He did not waive that right by waiting until the pretrial conference to make his demand. Remanded for a jury trial.

Douglas v. Archer Professional Building, Inc. (1986)

In 1978, a mental health clinic leased and began occupying an office on the fifth floor of the Archer Professional Building. About two years later, an out-patient at the center stabbed Carol Douglas, a physician with an office in the building, while both of them were riding in the building's elevator. Dr. Douglas brought suit against the owner of the building. At trial, the director of the clinic testified that the stabbing was the first such incident in his ten years of experience with such programs. There was also testimony that before the incident other tenants in the building had voiced concern over use of the elevators and stairwells by the clinic's patients. Dr. Douglas won a jury verdict for $115,000 in damages. We affirm.

We stated in *Brainerd v. Harvey* that landlords are liable for damages caused when they negligently expose others to foreseeable criminal attacks in common areas of buildings they lease. In both this case and *Brainerd*, the attack occurred in an area of the building under the landlord's control and used by all tenants. Just as the landlord in *Brainerd* knew or should have known about the absence of adequate lighting and locks in the apartment building, the defendant here knew or should have known about the potentially dangerous condition in the professional building. When the landlord is informed by his tenants that such a condition exists, he has a duty to investigate and take any possible preventive measures. The jury could properly find that the landlord's failure to do so was negligence.

Fisher, J., dissenting. The court here imposes unwarranted and unreasonable burdens on landlords by vastly extending their potential liability. In *Brainerd v. Harvey*, we expressly limited the landlord's liability to his failure to detect and repair dangerous physical conditions in common areas of leased buildings. Unlike the front door, this professional building had no physical defect that enabled the assault to occur. In *Brainerd*, we also limited liability to foreseeable criminal attacks, rather than those based merely on the subjective fears of some tenants in the building. The majority opinion suggests a medieval fear of persons who receive mental health care and will impede the state's goal of returning mental patients to the community.

Although the majority and dissenting opinions reached opposite conclusions in the *Douglas* case, they both relied on *Brainerd* for the basic principles of decision. Both opinions acknowledged that landlords are liable when they negligently expose their tenants to foreseeable criminal attacks in common areas of buildings they lease. The principle of *stare decisis* requires that the court start from that position, rather than craft new and different rules.

The division of the court in *Douglas* illustrates the flexibility of *stare decisis*. The majority interpreted *Brainerd* broadly as "welcome" precedent. When the landlord is informed by his tenants of their subjective fears of a potentially dangerous condition in a common area of the building, the majority ruled, he has a duty to investigate the situation and take precautionary measures. The court departed from *Brainerd* by refusing to limit the landlord's liability to situations in which there was tangible evidence suggesting the possibility of a criminal attack. The court responded to the different factual situation presented in *Douglas* by pushing the law in a different direction, even as it reasoned that it was merely following the *Brainerd* decision.

The dissenting judge interpreted *Brainerd* more narrowly as "unwelcome" precedent. *Brainerd*, he concluded, conditions the landlord's liability on the presence of physical defects in the building and objective evidence suggesting the possibility of a criminal attack, neither of which were present in *Douglas*. To support its narrow reading of *Brainerd*, the dissent also raised an objection about the effect of the court's decision on landlords in general and outpatient mental clinics in particular. The dissenting opinion is buttressed by *dicta* from *Brainerd* that states the case would be different if the building did not have physical defects. The statement is *dicta* because it was not necessary to the resolution of the *Brainerd* case and was thus disregarded by the majority in *Douglas*.

These two cases illustrate the tension between change and stability that is central to the study and practice of law. Certain factors militate in favor of stability. The *Brainerd* decision altered business expectations and forced landlords to modify their practices to avoid liability. In addition, the corporate owner was found liable in the second case pursuant to a rule that was not articulated until the owner was found to have breached it. After *Douglas*, landlords for other office buildings no doubt made significant changes in their leasing procedures and plans.

Uncertainties would be magnified by any perception that the law was subject to further modification.

Other factors counseled for change. The injury to Carol Douglas underscored the majority's view that landlords should keep their common areas free of foreseeable criminal activity. Even if the risk seemed most apparent after the harm occurred, the court concluded that a subjectively perceived risk of great bodily harm should be sufficient to warrant extra protective measures by the landlord. In addition, liability under the new formulation of the rule is the only realistic incentive for encouraging a plaintiff to seek relief in court. *Douglas* was based on an evolving view of the landlord-tenant relationship. Although the arguments vary somewhat from case to case, the tension between change and stability remains.

Two additional considerations are necessary for a full understanding of the mechanics and policies of precedent and *stare decisis*. First, appellate courts are supposed to decide only as many issues as are necessary for the disposition of a case. As Chapter 3 (Case Analysis and Case Briefs) points out, sometimes this requires courts to decide multiple issues. Each holding on an issue is precedent for later decisions. The court's holding in *Brainerd* concerning the plaintiff's demand for a jury trial, as well as its holding on the negligence issue, are both precedent and will have to be considered by future courts rendering decisions on the same issues.

Second, trial courts are responsible for finding facts and applying the law, while appellate courts have greater authority to modify and expand the law. Appellate courts therefore have greater freedom in treating precedent than trial courts. Appellate courts sometimes find it impossible to use previous cases and still reconcile their decisions with their own values or social norms. When this happens, the court may simply overrule the previous cases and chart a new course rather than show how these cases may be distinguished. Courts usually justify overruling previous decisions by pointing to the outdated principles or poor reasoning that supported them. These decisions are often spectacular, as when the United States Supreme Court, in the 1954 case of Brown v. Board of Education,[2] held that a state could not constitutionally require racial segregation in public schools, overruling its 1896 *Plessy v. Ferguson*[3] decision permitting "separate but equal" accommodations. Cases may also be more subtly overruled; a series of decisions, for example, may chip away at the scope of an earlier rule or undercut its policy basis.

---

2. 347 U.S. 483 (1954).

3. 163 U.S. 537 (1896).

EXERCISES

The exercises that follow are intended to show the stability and flexibility inherent in the concepts of precedent and stare decisis.

Exercise 4-A

Assume that you are a state appellate court judge. Eric Buckler was charged with reckless endangerment under the Motor Vehicle Code after the car he was driving left the road early one morning and struck a tree, killing a passenger. The trial judge instructed the jury that it could return a guilty verdict only if it was convinced beyond a reasonable doubt that the evidence showed Buckler had operated his motor vehicle in reckless disregard of the lives or safety of others. The judge then read a separate provision of the Motor Vehicle Code, which prohibits driving while under the influence of alcohol. Although Buckler was not charged with violating this provision, there was evidence that he had been drinking heavily. The judge told the jury it could use Buckler's violation of this provision to determine his guilt for reckless endangerment. Buckler was convicted. On appeal, he seeks a new trial by challenging the trial judge's instruction that guilt for driving while under the influence of alcohol could be used to establish guilt for reckless endangerment.

There are two relevant cases in the state:

State v. Waterford (1909)

This action began on a criminal complaint charging defendant with reckless endangerment. The complaint charged that defendant recklessly ran his motor vehicle against the decedent and the horse that the decedent was riding, killing both. The defendant filed a demurrer, claiming that the complaint did not indicate the offense with sufficient clarity to notify the defendant specifically for what crime he was to be tried. The trial court overruled the demurrer, and the defendant was convicted. We affirm.

Operators of motor vehicles have a duty to obey the laws regarding the use of motor vehicles. Disregard of or inattention to this duty, as defined in any of the motor vehicle laws, constitutes recklessness. The complaint therefore properly used the words "reckless endangerment" to describe the manner in which the defendant acted, particularly considering his manifest drunkenness. This was not an innocent accident.

State v. Seperic (1975)

A criminal complaint charged the defendant with reckless endangerment in violation of the Motor Vehicle Code. He was convicted after a jury trial. The defendant argues on appeal that the statute violates the state constitution because it does not state with sufficient clarity what it prohibits. We disagree.

> Motor vehicles play such an important role in our lives that reckless driving has come to have a commonly understood meaning—driving with wanton disregard for the lives or safety of other persons. The acts prohibited are sufficiently definite to persons of ordinary intelligence. The standard requires not only reckless operation but also operation that endangers the lives or safety of others. Nothing else is needed to establish reckless endangerment. Affirmed.

1. The court in *Seperic* did not mention the *Waterford* decision. Does the holding in the later case nonetheless affect the validity of the earlier case? Explain.

2. How would you decide Buckler's case? Why? How would you use these cases to explain your decision?

3. Could you use *Waterford* to support a decision contrary to the one you reached in response to questions in item 2? Could you use *Seperic* to support a decision contrary to the one you reached in response to questions in item 2? Explain.

Exercise 4-B

Assume you are a trial judge. In the case before you, Marie Elson, an elderly blind woman, defaulted on the land contract for her home. The real estate company wants to repossess the house and keep $57,000 in payments she has made thus far on the $84,000 contract. Elson does not contest her default, and she is willing to let the real estate company repossess the house. She does, however, insist on the return of the $57,000.

The following case is the only relevant precedent in your state:

Aaron v. Erickson (1960)

> Susan Aaron defaulted on a $30,000 land contract after making $12,000 in payments. The trial court denied Aaron's request for return of the $12,000. We affirm. There is a fundamental difference in our law between land contracts and mortgages. A land contract is an installment plan under which the purchaser does not get title to the property until the last payment. Those who buy property on a mortgage have it financed through a third party and receive title immediately. It may be a hard result, but those who buy property on a land contract take the risk of losing everything for failure to make payments. If this were a mortgage, we would reach a different result.

The following case is from the highest court of another state:

Deal v. Novack (1994)

> In 1980 Samuel Deal entered into a land contract with Larry Novack for $60,000. Deal defaulted in 1990 after making $24,000 in payments. The

court of appeals affirmed the trial court's holding that Novack was entitled to repossess the property and retain Deal's payments. We reverse. Had Deal entered into a typical mortgage arrangement, he would have title to the property and the mortgagee who provided the purchase price would have a lien on the property to secure the loan. Upon his default and the mortgagee's foreclosure, he would lose the property but his $24,000 would be returned. To hold that a land contract is conceptually different from a mortgage is to elevate form over substance. In both cases, the seller gives up possession of the property in exchange for the purchase price. In the case of a land contract, the seller retains legal title to the property as security for the price. In the case of a mortgage, the mortgagee retains a lien on the property as security. It is inequitable to hold that the defaulting buyer under the first arrangement must forfeit 40% of the purchase price while the defaulting buyer under the second arrangement forfeits nothing.

Pearle, J., concurring. A buyer who enters into a land contract must make a clear showing of inequity in order to avoid forfeiture of his payments. Otherwise, the court's opinion can be read as a wholesale repudiation of the land contract as an accepted instrument of commerce.

1. Is Elson entitled to have the money refunded? Justify your decision.

2. Is your answer to question 1 consistent with your sense of a just result? Explain.

3. Could you have used the cases to support a decision contrary to the one you reached in response to question 1? Explain.

Exercise 4-C

Assume you are a judge confronted with the following cases:

1. Jennifer Tubbs and Mark Hoffman negotiated every word of the contract by which Tubbs sold her elaborate stereo system to Hoffman for $4,300. The contract provided that Tubbs would deliver the stereo to Hoffman's house, and that Hoffman would be obligated to accept the stereo and pay the full price even if it was damaged in transit. The stereo was damaged when Tubbs' truck was involved in an accident. Hoffman accepted the stereo, but he insisted on a deduction from the full price. Can Tubbs collect the $4,300 from Hoffman?

   Decide this case according to your idea of a just result, and state a rule that explains your decision.

2. Beth Goldberg insured her house on Louisiana's Gulf Coast for $290,000. The contract was identical in form to all other home insurance policies sold by the company. Goldberg's home was severely damaged by flooding from a hurricane, and she made a claim on her policy. The company denied the claim, stating that a line in the middle of the seven-page contract

specifically excluded hurricane flooding from coverage. Beth Goldberg had never read the contract. Can she recover for damage to her home?

Decide this case in a manner that is consistent with your answer to question 1. State a rule that explains your decision in both cases, and describe the basis for your rule.

3. Justin Graff bought a refrigerator from his neighborhood appliance dealer for $700. Because he could not pay the full purchase price, he agreed in a contract to the dealer's financing scheme, which required a $35 payment each month for five years. Graff has a third-grade education and is not good with figures, so he did not know (nor was he told) that the refrigerator would actually cost him $2,100. After he had paid the dealer $840, a friend explained the contract to him. He made no further payments. Can the dealer collect the remaining $1,260?

Decide this case in a manner that is consistent with your decision in question 2. State a rule that explains your decision and describe the basis for it.

Exercise 4-D

Assume you are a trial judge in a civil action in which Elizabeth Fowler, the defendant, claims the court has no jurisdiction because service was obtained "by trickery and fraud." Fowler, a resident of another state, knew she was the possible subject of two civil actions in your state, one for a $5,000 damage deposit she had not returned to a merchant, and the other for a $200,000 insurance swindle. She wanted to resolve the first potential suit but not the second. To do this, she arranged a vacation in your state so she could pay off the merchant, who said he wanted "to avoid litigation over the deposit." She met the merchant at the airport and paid his deposit. The merchant, who secretly worked for the allegedly defrauded insurance company, then served her with papers for the insurance scheme.

The following case is the only relevant precedent in your state:

Eckersly v. Ramon (1981)

The appellant, Sean Eckersly, a resident of this state, sought to bring an action against Hal Ramon, a nonresident, for breach of contract. To secure service of process on Ramon, Eckersly requested several of Ramon's acquaintances to persuade Ramon that his mother, who also lives in this state, was terminally ill. Ramon agreed to come to this state to visit her. In reality, Ramon's mother was hiking in the Rocky Mountains. Ramon was met at the airport by Eckersly's agent, who served Ramon with papers in the contract action. The trial court rejected Ramon's claim that it lacked jurisdiction because service was fraudulently obtained. We disagree. When plaintiffs resort to such shocking fraud to obtain service of process, the integrity of the entire judicial system is undermined. The trial court had no power to render judgment in this case. Reversed.

1. Decide whether your court has jurisdiction, using the *Eckersly* case as precedent. Justify your decision.

2. Is your answer to question 1 consistent with your sense of a just result? Explain.

3. Could you have used *Eckersly* to support a decision contrary to the one you reached in response to question 1? Explain.

Basic Concepts of Legal Method

5 Understanding Legal Rules

As noted in Chapter 1 (Rules and Policies), legal rules guide and regulate our society and provide a means to resolve disputes. Some rules tell us what kinds of behavior are permitted and not permitted. For example, state statutes will tell you that driving a car is permitted behavior, but driving a car while under the influence of alcohol is not permitted behavior. Other rules define what procedures must be followed in order to achieve certain goals. For example, if you want to be permitted to drive a car, state laws establish the requirements that you must meet in order to obtain a license. Legal rules also tell us what will happen if we follow—or fail to follow—the rules. For example, if a person meets the driver's licensing requirements, he will be issued a driver's license. If a driver's blood alcohol level exceeds the legal limit, she may be fined or jailed.

Legal rules can be derived from a single source, such as a case, a statute, or a regulation. They can also be derived from a combination of sources—a series of cases, or a statute and cases that interpret the statute. Regardless of their source, legal rules are the framework upon which legal discussions and arguments are built. Sound legal analysis depends on your ability to understand the structure and operation of legal rules.

How Rules Are Constructed

A legal rule may contain several parts: elements, sub-elements, results, and exceptions. To understand a legal rule you must find all of its parts, discern how they fit together, and determine what will happen when the requirements of the rule are met.

Elements of a Rule

An *element* of a rule describes a factual condition that must exist for a rule to apply. Each element can stand alone as an independent unit. Consider the following rule regarding driver's licenses:

> A person shall be issued a driver's license if he or she meets all of the following requirements:
>
> 1. The person must complete an application for a license.
> 2. The person must be at least 16 years of age.
> 3. The person must be a resident of the state.
> 4. The person must pass all examination requirements for a license.
> 5. The person must pay the appropriate fee.

This rule has five elements. Notice that each element can stand alone; each can exist without reference to the others. For example, it is possible to complete an application for a license without being sixteen, and it is possible to pass the examinations without paying the fee. But how are these five elements to be combined? The way in which the elements of a legal rule are combined determines how the rule operates.

The elements of a legal rule are commonly combined in one of three ways. First, the rule may require all of the elements to be met. Some lawyers refer to this kind of rule as a *conjunctive rule,* because the elements are often linked with the conjunction "and."

Second, the elements in some rules are linked with the word "or." Some lawyers refer to this kind of rule as *disjunctive.* Disjunctive rules create alternative ways for a rule to be established. If the rule above were a disjunctive rule, a sixteen-year-old from another state, a three-year-old state resident, or a Norwegian tourist who paid the appropriate fee could get a license.

Finally, the elements of a rule might be introduced with a phrase such as "the following are relevant," or "the court shall consider." Such a rule, often called a "factors test," indicates that all of the elements are relevant, but *only some, not all,* are needed. Under a factors test, the licensing bureau could decide that the applicant need only meet most of the elements and issue a license to a twelve-year-old state resident who passed the vision test and paid the required fee. In the alternative, the bureau could decide that a particularly strong showing on one or two elements will be sufficient and issue a license to a sixty-year-old who agreed to pay twice the usual fee.

Thus, the manner in which the elements of a rule are linked together is crucial. As the examples above show, improper connections between the elements of a rule can lead to absurd, and possibly dangerous, results. Here, the introduction to the driver's license rule indicates it is a conjunctive rule by stating that a license will be issued if "*all* of the requirements" are met.

The Result and Its Relationship to the Elements

The *result* of a rule describes what will happen when the elements of the rule are met. For example, the driver's license rule states that a person *"shall be issued a driver's license"* if the elements of the rule are met. The single word "shall" links the result to the elements of the rule and tells you that the result *must* follow if the elements are established. The licensing bureau cannot refuse to issue a license to a person who meets all the requirements of the rule.

Other rules might establish a different link between the elements of a rule and the result. Consider the following examples:

> EXAMPLE A: Any person who is convicted of two or more moving traffic violations within six months may not operate a motor vehicle until the person completes a driver safety course.

> EXAMPLE B: A person who is convicted of driving under the influence of alcohol may be sentenced to imprisonment not exceeding thirty days or required to pay a fine not exceeding $2,500.

Rather than requiring a certain result, the rule in Example A *prohibits* a certain result. If the elements of this rule are established, a certain behavior is not permitted: The person who meets the elements of this rule may not drive. The rule in Example B, however, neither requires nor prohibits a certain result. If the elements of the crime are established, the sentencing judge will decide what penalty, if any, to impose on the defendant.

Exceptions in a Rule

Sometimes legal rules have exceptions. Exceptions are often indicated with words such as "unless," "provided that," or "however." Recall the rule on driver's licenses:

A person shall be issued a driver's license if he or she meets all of the following requirements:

1. The person must complete an application for a license.
2. The person must be at least 16 years of age.
3. The person must be a resident of the state.
4. The person must pass all examination requirements for a license.
5. The person must pay the appropriate fee.

If, however, the person has three or more convictions for driving under the influence of alcohol, from this or any other state, a driver's license may not be issued.

In this example, when a person has three or more DUI convictions, then the usual result does not follow, even if all of the elements of the main rule are established. An affirmative defense such as self defense in criminal law works as an exception; even if the elements of the crime are otherwise proven, a defendant who can show she acted in self defense should not be convicted.

When an exception may be available, the proper approach is to first analyze whether the elements in the general rule have been established. Then, separately, analyze whether the exception applies. If there is a plausible basis for the applicability of the general rule and the applicability of the exception, then the problem has two issues. Do not limit your analysis to the exception alone.

Sub-Elements

Sometimes an element of a rule is defined by one or more *sub-elements.* To understand the role that sub-elements play in a legal rule, consider the tort of battery as defined in the Restatement (Second) of Torts § 13 (1965):

An actor is subject to liability to another for battery if

(a) he acts intending to cause a harmful or offensive contact with the person of the other or a third person, or an imminent apprehension of such a contact, and
(b) a harmful contact with the person of the other directly or indirectly results.

The rule appears to contain two elements, because it is divided into two subsections. But a closer look suggests that more than one major requirement is contained in each of these subsections. Under subsection (a), two requirements are apparent: (1) the defendant must "act," and (2) the defendant must intend to cause a certain kind of contact. The two requirements are different and thus may need separate analysis. Under subsection (b), there also appear to be two requirements: (1) a "harmful contact" must occur, and (2) the contact must be the "result" of the defendant's act—that is, there must be a causal connection between the defendant's act and the harmful contact. Note also that subsections (a) and (b) are connected with the word "and." Thus, these elements are conjunctive; the act, the intent, the contact, and the causal connection must all be present for a battery to be committed. Finally, the consequence of this rule is clear: If all of the elements are established, the defendant is liable for battery.

This big picture view of the rule for battery is accurate, but it is not quite complete. Both the second and third elements contain subelements. In the second element, the defendant can intend to cause either of two things: actual contact or an "imminent apprehension" of actual contact. Moreover, the contact can be either "harmful" or "offensive." Finally, the intent can be directed towards either of two persons: "the other" or "a third person." "Contact" in the third element can be made with either of two people ("the other" or "a third person"), and in either of two ways ("directly" or "indirectly"). Notice that all of the subelements embedded in the rule are disjunctive; they are alternatives, separated by the word "or." Thus, what appeared on a quick first reading to be a simple two-element conjunctive rule becomes, on another reading, a simple four-part conjunctive rule, and, on still another reading, a complex four-element rule with a web of possibilities. A lawyer who does not recognize these nuances and possibilities will have only a superficial understanding of the rule.

Developing a Rule from Multiple Sources: Synthesis

Legal rules do not always appear fully formed in a single case or statute. As you will learn in Chapter 7 (Common Law Analysis), the common law develops over time, as later cases add to or refine the rule. Similarly, as you will learn in Chapter 8 (Statutory Analysis), court decisions often interpret and clarify the meaning of a statute, affecting how the statute is applied in future cases. It is therefore important to be able to derive a rule from a body of law, as well as from a single source. The process of combining sources into a coherent statement of the law is referred to as "synthesis." The following examples illustrate the synthesis process.

Assume that you are defending a client who has been charged with aggravated menacing. You have found the statute and three relevant cases. You need to determine the meaning of the word "knowingly" as used in the statute.

Section 290.30 Aggravated Menacing

No person shall knowingly cause another to believe that the offender will cause serious physical harm to the person or property of the other person, the other person's unborn, or a member of the other person's immediate family. Whoever violates this section is guilty of aggravated menacing.

State v. Rosenby (1991)

Appellant Ronald Rosenby appeals his conviction for aggravated menacing. At trial, Clarice Penn testified that she terminated her relationship with appellant in July 1989 because appellant had physically abused her. Penn also testified that on the evening of October 15, 1989, appellant drove to her home and screamed at her from his vehicle for nearly one-half hour, and then threatened to "take her to the grave with him."

Appellant contends that the elements of aggravated menacing were not met because the statement "take her to the grave with him" was not accompanied by any kind of physical movement or attempt to carry out the threat. The statute, however, does not require that the offender be able to carry out his threat. It is sufficient if the offender "knowingly" causes the victim to believe the offender will carry his threat into execution. The jury could reasonably conclude that appellant "knowingly caused" Penn to believe that he would kill her when he approached her at home and told her that he would "take her to the grave with him." Affirmed.

State v. Wentz (1996)

Defendant appeals his conviction for aggravated menacing, arguing that the evidence was insufficient to establish all elements of the charge.

Fifteen-year-old Nick Hampton testified that Defendant told him to relay a message to his mother, Ronnie Hampton, that "she's messing with the wrong person and if she tries to bust him for anything, she'll be hurting." During a subsequent encounter two days later, Defendant asked Hampton if he had relayed the message to his mother. Ronnie Hampton testified that her son told her what Defendant had said, and that she interpreted the message as a threat of "serious physical harm, like he was going to come after me and shoot me or something."

Defendant argues that there was insufficient evidence to establish that he acted "knowingly" because he did not threaten Hampton's mother personally and therefore did not "knowingly cause her to believe that he would harm her." Defendant knew that Hampton lived with his mother, asked him to take her a message, and then verified that the message had been delivered. We hold that Defendant acted with the requisite knowledge when he directed Nick Hampton to deliver a threatening message to a member of his own family, his mother Ronnie Hampton. Conviction affirmed.

State v. Huffman (2003)

Appellant appeals his conviction for aggravated menacing. We reverse.

The County Child Support Enforcement Agency intercepted Appellant's income tax refund as a result of child support arrearages. Appellant called a caseworker, Josephine Manning, to complain about the amount of money he had been ordered to pay to his former wife and said, "I can't even afford to eat. Maybe I should just kill her, maybe that will end it all." Manning reported this conversation to her supervisor, Ned Turner, who reported the incident to the police and warned Appellant's former wife about the comment Appellant had made. After a bench trial, Appellant was found guilty of Aggravated Menacing and placed on probation.

Appellant contends that it was against the manifest weight of the evidence for the court to find that he acted "knowingly" because it was not probable that his statement to Manning would be conveyed to his former wife. A person acts knowingly when he is aware his conduct will probably— that is, more likely than not—cause a certain result. For appellant to have spoken knowingly, therefore, it must have been "more likely than not" that Manning would relate Appellant's statement to his former wife.

Manning did not know Appellant's former wife. She testified that she did not call the police and did not expect that her supervisor would. In light of this testimony, reasonable minds could not conclude that it was "more likely than not" that Manning would convey Appellant's statements to his former wife. Accordingly, we reverse his conviction.

You have been asked to write a memorandum regarding the meaning of the word "knowingly." Your problem is that the three decisions are each based on different factual situations and different rationales. Which statement of the rule would your supervisor find most helpful?

ANSWER A: To be found guilty of aggravated menacing, the defendant must "knowingly cause another to believe that the offender will cause serious physical harm to the person or property of the other person, the other person's unborn, or a member of the other person's immediate family." State Code § 290.30. The meaning of "knowingly" depends on the manner in which the threat is delivered. *See, e.g., State v. Rosenby; State v. Wentz; State v. Huffman.*

ANSWER B: To be found guilty of aggravated menacing, the defendant must "knowingly cause another to believe that the offender will cause serious physical harm to the person or property of the other person, the other person's unborn, or a member of the other person's immediate family." State Code § 290.30. The "knowingly" element is established if the defendant (1) delivers the threat directly to the victim,

> *State v. Rosenby*; (2) delivers the threat to a member of the victim's family, *State v. Wentz*; or (3) delivers the threat to a third party who defendant believes will "more likely than not" convey the threat to the victim, *State v. Huffman*.

Both answers cite all of the relevant authorities. Answer B is better, however, because it defines the "knowledge" element clearly. The reader knows immediately that the element can be satisfied in three different ways and can easily check the rule against a new set of facts to see if the element is met. Answer B provides a brief summary of each of the three cases in a way that provides considerable precision about how the courts have interpreted the word "knowingly." Answer A is weaker because it conveys much less information about that element. It implies that there is more to the word "knowingly" than meets the eye, but is much too vague to give the reader a clear understanding of the rule and its requirements.

This example shows how one can synthesize a statute and cases to create a comprehensive statement of a rule. In this example, it is relatively clear that the court is developing a definition of the word "knowingly." Sometimes, however, the cases are less clear, and the synthesis process is more difficult.

Many states have hate crime statutes that provide for enhanced penalties if a defendant is motivated by bias when committing certain crimes. Consider the following:

> Section 720.5(a)—A person commits a hate crime when, by reason of the race, color, creed, religion, gender, sexual orientation, physical or mental disability, or national origin of another individual or group of individuals, he commits assault, battery, criminal trespass to residence, criminal damage to property, criminal trespass to real property, or disorderly conduct as these crimes are defined in this Code.

You have been asked to determine what kind of evidence establishes the element of biased motive, that is, that the defendant acted "by reason of" another's membership in one of the classes listed in the statute.

You cannot find a case with a clear definition of biased motive, but you have found four cases where the defendant was convicted of committing a hate crime.

State v. Shugart (1994)

Defendant displayed highly offensive drawings showing violence against African-Americans to Matt Bullis, a Caucasian, while Bullis was with two African-American friends. The drawings included a picture of a Ku Klux Klansman holding a bloody ax above the body of a dark complexioned person and showed other Klansmen wearing robes emblazoned with racist and white supremacist phrases and obscenities. Defendant was found to have committed disorderly conduct by reason of racial bias and was convicted of a hate crime. Defendant argues that his conviction should be overturned because his victim, Bullis, is not a member of a class protected by the statute.

The victim of a hate crime need not be a member of one of the statute's enumerated classes. To require such would constitute an overly restrictive interpretation of the statute. Our entire community is harmed by a defendant's bias-motivated criminal conduct. We conclude that the legislature, aware of this fact, intended that improper bias which motivates certain criminal acts be the component which elevates the conduct to the level of hate crime, rather than the status of a particular victim. The facts presented provide sufficient evidence to support defendant's conviction for a hate crime.

State v. Cortez (1996)

Ben Becker, the victim in this case, is a seventeen-year-old Orthodox Jewish boy. Mr. Becker was assaulted by Respondent, David Cortez, as he walked home from school. Becker was wearing a yarmulke and prayer tassels (tzitzis), both of which symbolize his religious beliefs. Respondent shouted obscene and anti-Semitic comments at Becker, including the comment "I am going to kill you Jew." He then threw a knife at Becker. Respondent testified that he was "bored" and Becker "looked funny." On cross-examination, however, he admitted that he understood the religious symbolism of Becker's dress. After a bench trial, Respondent was convicted of committing a hate crime.

On appeal, Respondent argues that the evidence was insufficient to prove him guilty of a hate crime. We disagree. The statute does not require that bias be Respondent's *only* motive. Immediately after making anti-Semitic remarks, Respondent admittedly committed an assault on Becker, the target of the abuse. The trial judge could properly infer that the assault was motivated, at least in part, by religious animus. The State proved the charge of a hate crime beyond a reasonable doubt. Accordingly, the judgment of the trial court is affirmed.

State v. Nelson (1996)

Defendant was convicted of aggravated battery and a hate crime. Defendant appealed his hate crime conviction, arguing that there was insufficient evidence that he assaulted the victim because of his race. We affirm the trial court.

Beau Sinclair, a Caucasian, and his friend Thad Marks, an African-American, were approached by Defendant, who had just been evicted from a bar and was intoxicated. Defendant shouted "What are you laughing at?" and shouted racial slurs at the men. He then proceeded to beat Marks senseless.

There is no doubt that Defendant perpetrated a battery upon Marks; whether he did so "by reason of" Marks's race is less clear. Defendant had five beers in less than an hour, had just been expelled from a bar, and claims to have believed that Sinclair and Marks were laughing at him. Defendant's question, "What are you laughing at?" suggests that Defendant confronted the men for a race-neutral reason. The trial court, however, specifically found that Defendant attacked, and seriously injured, Marks after uttering a racial slur. Even if Defendant first confronted the men because he thought that they were mocking him, he directed his words and assault at Marks, an African-American, rather than Sinclair, his white companion. Viewing this evidence in the light most favorable to the State, a factfinder could conclude that Defendant assaulted Marks because of his race.

State v. Trinh (1999)

The victim was a server at a pizza restaurant who took Defendant's order. When the victim requested payment, Defendant refused to pay him. Instead, he told the restaurant manager not to let "that faggot" touch his food. The manager was busy when Defendant's pizza came out of the oven, so the victim began to slice the pizza. Defendant came up to the counter and began yelling at the victim and pounding his fist on the counter. He called the victim names, including "Mary," "faggot," and "Molly Homemaker." Defendant continued yelling for more than ten minutes and, when not pounding his fist, shook his finger at the victim, attracting the attention of other customers. Defendant was convicted of a hate crime based on the predicate offense of disorderly conduct.

Defendant contends that the hate crime statute is unconstitutional when the underlying offense is disorderly conduct because it interferes with his right to express unpopular views. The hate crime statute, however, does not punish those who express unpopular views. It applies only if one's conduct is unreasonable and provokes a breach of the peace, thus constituting the crime of disorderly conduct. Defendant is free to believe what he wants regarding people who are homosexual, but he may not force his opinions on others by shouting, pounding on a counter, and disrupting a lawful business. We hold that the hate crime statute is not unconstitutional when the underlying offense is disorderly conduct. Because Defendant does not challenge the sufficiency of the evidence against him or assert any other basis for reversal, we affirm the conviction.

There was sufficient evidence that the defendants in these cases had a biased motive or they would not have been convicted. But, since the court has not clearly defined this term, you must figure out what the cases say about biased motive.

Start synthesizing the cases by looking for common threads. It might help to think about the subject in visual terms. When you read the cases, think about what a biased motive "looks like." What common characteristics are present? In all of the cases above, for example, the defendant used derogatory language about a certain class of people. In *State v. Shugart* the language was written rather than spoken, but derogatory language was used in all cases.

As you continue to study the cases, you might notice two more common threads. First, the derogatory language was used just before or at the same time that the defendant committed the crime. In *State v. Shugart* and *State v. Trinh* the derogatory language was part of the defendants' disorderly conduct. In the other cases the defendants used derogatory language and then immediately threw something at the victim or assaulted the victim. Second, there is sometimes additional, circumstantial, evidence of bias. In *State v. Cortez*, for example, the victim was wearing clothing that identified him as Jewish. In *State v. Nelson* the defendant was angry at two men, but chose to assault the African-American man rather than his white friend.

Thus, by reading the cases carefully one can identify three common threads:

(1)   the defendant used derogatory language about a class of people;
(2)   the defendant used the derogatory language during or just before the crime;
(3)   other circumstantial evidence of bias was present.

These common threads are the elements of the synthesized rule, but how do they fit together? Evaluate the possibilities:

- All three elements are required; they should be connected to one another with the word "and." This is not correct because the courts relied on additional circumstantial evidence in only two of the four cases.
- Only one of the elements is required; they should be connected to one another with the word "or." This is not correct because the court in *State v. Nelson* implied that derogatory language alone was not sufficient to establish biased motive.
- All elements constitute a factors test; the court will consider them all, but no single element is required. This seems like the most reasonable conclusion because the four cases, read together, suggest that at least two of the three elements should be present.

After identifying the elements of the rule and discerning how they are connected to one another, it is easy to finish the description of the rule by stating the result that will follow if the necessary elements are established: The court will likely find that the defendant possessed a biased motive.

Now that you have synthesized the meaning of biased motive based on the entire body of law, you can communicate that understanding to someone else:

> The courts consider three factors when determining whether a defendant possessed a biased motive when he committed a crime: (1) whether the defendant used language that is derogatory toward a particular class, (2) whether the defendant used this language during or immediately before committing the crime, and (3) whether there is additional evidence that supports a finding of bias on the part of the defendant.

Notice that the writer does not overwhelm the reader with details and then force the reader to figure out the rule himself. The paragraph above is a straightforward and understandable description of the end result of the writer's analytical process. As you will learn in Chapter 11 (Describing the Law), after stating the basic rule, the writer will go on to describe and justify the synthesized rule by explaining relevant portions of the cases from which the rule was derived. The writer's deep understanding of the law will give meaning and structure to the rest of the discussion.

EXERCISES

All legal analysis begins with the governing law. Whether the law is simple or complex, the ability to understand the law completely and describe the rule accurately is one of the most important skills that you will need as a lawyer. The exercises below will help you practice this essential skill.

Exercise 5-A

Read the following rule:

> To show undue influence sufficient to void a will, the one who contests the will must establish by clear and convincing evidence that (1) when the will was executed the testator was of weakened intellect and (2) a person in a confidential relationship with the testator (3) receives a substantial benefit under the will.

1. How many elements does this rule contain?

2. Do any of the elements have sub-elements?

3. What type of rule is this—disjunctive, conjunctive, a factors test, or a combination of types?

4. What result if the elements of the rule are established?

5. Is that result mandatory? Prohibited? Optional or discretionary?

6. Are there any exceptions to the rule? If so, when do they come into play? What result if an exception to the rule exists?

Exercise 5-B

> To establish intentional infliction of emotional distress the plaintiff must show that the defendant's conduct was intentional toward the plaintiff, the conduct must be extreme and outrageous, there must be a causal connection between the defendant's conduct and the plaintiff's mental distress, and the plaintiff's mental distress must be extreme and severe.

1. How many elements does this rule contain?

2. Do any of the elements have sub-elements?

3. What type of rule is this—disjunctive, conjunctive, a factors test, or a combination of types?

4. What result if the elements of the rule are established?

5. Is that result mandatory? Prohibited? Optional or discretionary?

6. Are there any exceptions to the rule? If so, when do they come into play? What result if an exception to the rule exists?

Exercise 5-C

Read the following case:

Nicholson v. Carson's Tavern (1979)

Ben Cooper, a minor, went out with his brother and several friends to celebrate his brother's twenty-first birthday. In the course of the evening three bars served alcohol to Cooper. When Cooper and his friends got ready to leave Carson's Tavern, Cooper told his brother that he would drive home and grabbed the car keys. During the drive home, he broadsided a car driven by the plaintiff's husband, Randy Nicholson. Mr. Nicholson was killed in the crash and the plaintiff sued the bars for negligence. The trial court dismissed her suit, citing the legislature's recent repeal of the law which imposed strict liability on tavernkeepers. We reverse and remand for a trial on the merits.

The repeal of the law imposing strict liability on tavernkeepers does not mean that basic principles of negligence do not apply to facts similar to those presented by this case. One is liable for the reasonably foreseeable consequences of his or her acts. An unreasonable risk of harm to a third party is clearly foreseeable if taverns serve alcohol to one who they know, or should know, is a minor, knowing that that person is going to drive. The plaintiff is entitled to attempt to prove that the defendant bars were negligent when they served alcohol to Cooper, a minor.

1. What is the rule? How many elements does this rule contain?

2. Do any of the elements have sub-rules and sub-elements?

3. What type of rule is this—disjunctive, conjunctive, a factors test, or a combination of types?

4. What result if the elements of the rule are established?

5. Is that result mandatory? Prohibited? Optional or discretionary?

6. Are there any exceptions to the rule? If so, when do they come into play? What result if an exception to the rule exists?

Exercise 5-D

Read the following cases. Then create a synthesized rule using *Nicholson v. Carson's Tavern* (Exercise 5-C) and the cases below. In what ways does the synthesized rule change the original rule that you derived from *Nicholson* alone?

Teniel v. Olde Towne Inn (1986)

On October 30, 1984, witnesses saw the plaintiff's husband, James Teniel, drinking at several locations during the morning and early afternoon. He entered the Olde Towne Inn at approximately 3:00 p.m. While there he was served at the bar with two shots of whisky and three beers. At about 4:30 p.m. Mr. Teniel got up to leave, saying that he had to get home "while I can still drive." On the way home, he veered off the road and struck a tree. He died later that day. The plaintiff sued, asserting that the defendant negligently served alcohol to her husband while he was visibly intoxicated. The defendant appealed from a judgment entered in favor of the plaintiff, arguing there was no evidence from which the jury could find that the bartender knew or should have known that the decedent was intoxicated.

Officer Rodriguez testified that when she arrived at the scene of the accident at 4:43 p.m. "there was a very, very strong smell of alcohol" in the car, and there was a damp spot on Mr. Teniel's jacket that smelled of beer. There were no containers in the car. The medical examiner, Dr. Spellman, testified that there was a "strong odor of alcohol" when he examined Mr. Teniel's body approximately 8 hours after the accident. When combined with the defendant's admission regarding the alcohol that they served to Mr. Teniel, this evidence is sufficient to support the jury's finding that the Inn "knew or should have known" that Mr. Teniel was intoxicated. It was reasonably foreseeable that if he continued to be served, Mr. Teniel could harm himself or others if he got behind the wheel of his car. Affirmed.

Valerio v. Glenn (1996)

Anthony Valerio, a nine-year-old child, was riding his bike down the street outside his home when he was hit by a car driven by the defendant, Tanya Jennings. His leg was broken, and he sustained numerous cuts and lacerations. Jennings, who is sixteen, was driving home from a Labor Day barbeque hosted by Ted Glenn, whose daughter attends school with Jennings. Mr. Glenn purchased a keg of beer for the barbeque and allowed the minor guests to serve themselves.

Anthony's parents sued Glenn, asserting that he was negligent when he served excessive amounts of alcohol to Jennings, a minor, while she was a guest at his home, and then permitted her to drive. The court concluded that the rule enunciated in *Nicholson v. Carson's Tavern* is limited to tavern keepers and other sellers of alcohol and dismissed plaintiff's complaint for failure to state a claim.

The issue is whether a person who does not hold a liquor license and who furnishes excessive amounts of alcohol to a minor on a social occasion can be held liable for the negligent acts of a minor which cause injury to a third party. We conclude that such a person may be held responsible where the facts warrant it. There is nothing in *Nicholson* that bars this suit as a matter of law, and the same principles of negligence upon which we relied in that case are equally applicable to private individuals. Defendant Glenn knew that Jennings was a minor and served her excessive amounts of alcohol. It was reasonably foreseeable that she might cause harm to another if she were to drive. Young people are drinking to excess at younger ages than ever before. It would be indefensible to hold social hosts immune from liability under the circumstances presented here.

6 Identifying and Selecting Issues for Analysis

The first step in solving a legal problem is to select the questions that require analysis from the broad range of questions suggested by the facts of the case. Some questions that occur to you will not require analysis because they are not relevant—that is, they are not essential or even helpful in answering the inquiry. Other questions might prove to be relevant, but they are excluded from detailed analysis because they have clear answers. Questions that must be resolved before a legal problem can be solved are known as issues, and they occur whenever there can be some reasonable disagreement about whether, or how, a legal rule should apply to a set of facts.

Selecting issues is a tentative and ongoing process, requiring you to change or sharpen the focus of your inquiry as you think about the problem and the legal authority that will govern the outcome. The process involves four distinct steps, which are best illustrated in the context of a specific problem.

Fred Brookson, a lifelong resident of Klamath Falls, Oregon, contacted your firm to see whether he can file suit against Wendell Carter for injuries sustained as a result of an incident that occurred in southern Oregon. About three months ago, Brookson and his wife, Ellen, from whom he is now separated, participated in a demonstration concerning recent acts of violence against doctors practicing in a local abortion clinic. The demonstration occurred on a wharf extending into the Coos River. A group of people, including Wendell Carter, gathered around the demonstrators and began to heckle them. The two groups exchanged remarks and eventually the hecklers threw rocks and bottles at the demonstrators. When Carter threw a rock that struck and injured Ellen, Fred became angry and approached Carter. Carter said he regretted injuring Ellen because he had been aiming at Fred. The two men exchanged heated remarks. Then, without any provocation, Carter pulled out a knife, screamed, and lunged at Brookson, intending to stab him. As Brookson jumped back to avoid being injured, he almost bumped into an unidentified demonstrator. The demonstrator, who apparently thought he was being attacked, struck Brookson several times and seriously injured him. Both Brooksons required medical treatment, and Fred Brookson required an extended hospital stay. His medical expenses exceeded $128,000; his estranged wife's expenses were approximately $9,000. Both have lost weight, exhibit chronic anxiety, and have periods of severe insomnia.

Your supervising attorney wants you to write a memo assessing Fred Brookson's chances of success in an action against Carter for the damages Carter inflicted on him. Carter grew up in California but has spent the last three years attending college and living with his brother in Oregon. Your supervising attorney believes it best to bring this action in federal district court because of the unpopular nature of the incident that gave rise to the injuries. Can a federal district court exercise jurisdiction in this case? What claims can Fred Brookson raise?

Your preliminary research has turned up two statutory provisions and three cases. The statutory provisions are federal; they are taken from the United States Code. The first case was decided by the United States court of appeals for your circuit. The highest court of your state decided the other two cases.

§ 1332. Diversity of Citizenship; Amount in Controversy; Costs

(a)   The district courts shall have original jurisdiction of all civil actions where the matter in controversy exceeds the sum or value of $75,000, exclusive of interest and costs, and is between—

     (1)   citizens of different States;

     (2)   citizens of a State and citizens or subjects of a foreign state;

     (3)   citizens of different States and in which citizens or subjects of a foreign state are additional parties; and

     (4)   a foreign state . . . as plaintiff and citizens of a State or of different States.

For the purposes of this section . . . an alien admitted to the United States for permanent residence shall be deemed a citizen of the State in which such alien is domiciled.

§ 1333. Admiralty, Maritime and Prize Cases

The district courts shall have original jurisdiction, exclusive of the courts of the States, of:

(1)   Any civil case of admiralty or maritime jurisdiction, saving to suitors in all cases all other remedies to which they are otherwise entitled.
(2)   Any prize brought into the United States and all proceedings for the condemnation of property taken as prize.

Krebs v. Beechwood Aircraft Co. (1986)

Appellant Krebs filed suit in federal district court after the small plane in which he was flying crashed into the ocean off the Washington coast because of a defective engine mount. Krebs claimed admiralty jurisdiction under section 1333 of the United States Code. The district court dismissed for want of jurisdiction and we affirm.

Federal courts are courts of limited jurisdiction. Absent an express grant of jurisdiction by Congress or the Constitution, the federal courts have no power to hear a case. Section 1333 vests the federal courts with jurisdiction over cases that are maritime in nature. Maritime jurisdiction under section 1333(1) is appropriate when a potential hazard to maritime commerce arises out of an activity that bears a substantial relationship to traditional maritime activity. Claims dealing with navigation, shipping, and commerce by sea are typical subjects for maritime jurisdiction. Airplane crashes are not so linked. Although such crashes may present a potential hazard to maritime commerce, aircraft operations do not bear a substantial relationship to traditional maritime activity. Nor is this a case under Section 1333(2) involving a prize, such as a ship seized in wartime or a newly discovered undersea treasure.

Jansen v. McLeavy (1987)

Sandra Jansen brought suit against the defendant for negligence and intentional infliction of emotional distress after the defendant's car ran a stop sign and killed her young son. She witnessed the accident from her front yard. The jury awarded her $175,000 for the defendant's negligence in causing the death of her son and $250,000 for intentional infliction of emotional distress. The defendant appeals only the latter award, and we reverse.

For intentional infliction of mental distress, proof of four elements is required to establish the cause of action: (1) the conduct of the defendant must be intentional toward the plaintiff; (2) the conduct must be extreme and outrageous; (3) there must be a causal connection between the defendant's conduct and the plaintiff's mental distress; and (4) the plaintiff's mental distress must be extreme and severe. On this appeal, the defendant vigorously argues that the first element has not been met. The tort of intentional infliction of emotional distress requires some evidence that the defendant intended to inflict the emotional distress on the plaintiff. Although Jansen's mental distress was great, the driver did not intend to cause that distress. While some jurisdictions have allowed recovery in similar circumstances on a theory that the defendant's conduct made it probable that mental suffering would result, we will continue to require intentional infliction in this state.

Powers v. Locke (1989)

While plaintiff Anthony Powers and defendant James Locke were waiting in line to board a school bus, Locke shoved Powers in an effort to take his place in line. Powers fell through a glass door and suffered multiple injuries. Powers sued Locke for battery. The trial court entered a directed verdict in favor of Powers.

A defendant commits battery when he acts intending to cause a harmful or offensive contact with the plaintiff or a third person and thereby causes a harmful or offensive contact with the plaintiff. Because battery is intended to protect a person's body from intentional and unwanted contact, its protection extends to anything so closely connected with the person's body as to be regarded a part of it, but it does not extend to contact that is legally consented to or otherwise privileged. One who commits battery is liable for no more than nominal damages unless the person contacted proves actual harm.

Locke's argument that the evidence does not support a finding that he intended to cause injury to Powers is without merit. The tort of battery requires only that the defendant intend the contact that caused the harm, not the harm itself. Here, the evidence is uncontroverted that Locke intended to shove Powers. Locke also argues that Powers consented to the battery by agreeing to engage in a "shoving match" with Locke. Because the evidence presented at trial is conflicting on this issue, a directed verdict was improper. Reversed and remanded.

---

1. Focus only on questions within the scope of the problem.

Legal memos and briefs should discuss only those questions necessary to resolve the question presented. Do not discuss questions that were not asked, no matter how interesting or important; they are simply outside the scope of the problem.

Two considerations are especially important in determining what legal questions are within the scope of a particular problem. First, if you have been expressly instructed to address specific legal questions, you should disregard all other questions. If you have not been given express instructions, the scope of your discussion will usually be dictated by the relationship of your client to the other parties, by the relief sought, or by the procedural posture of the case. You should, for example, discuss only questions that concern your client's rights against the named adversary and not consider questions that pertain to additional parties. Second, the questions that should be discussed will vary with the procedural context of the case. Exclude questions that are not important at a given point in the procedural development of a case. For example, potential defenses to a suit would be proper questions in the context of a motion for summary judgment but not in the context of a motion to dismiss. If you are uncertain about the scope of a problem, seek clarification from the person who assigned it.

In the Brookson case, look for legal questions dealing with the encounter between Fred Brookson and Wendell Carter. The diversity jurisdiction question is clearly within the scope of the memorandum because the instructions specifically direct you to consider this issue. Possible questions concerning a cause of action on behalf of Fred Brookson for battery and intentional infliction of emotional distress are within the scope of the memorandum. Both of these issues are dictated by the procedural context of the anticipated case, which requires you to assess the chances of success if Fred Brookson files suit. The law and facts also suggest a possible cause of action by Fred Brookson against the unidentified demonstrator. The questions raised by this potential suit, however, are outside the scope of the memo because you are asked only to examine causes of action against Carter. Likewise, Ellen Brookson's possible cause of action against Carter is outside the scope of the memo. Because Fred Brookson is the party for whom the lawsuit is contemplated, your only concern is with possible avenues of relief for him.

2. Identify all relevant questions.

The next step is to identify potentially applicable legal rules. A legal question arises from the possible application of a legal rule to a set of facts. To identify the issues in a case, you have to ask whether these rules apply or, if there is no question that they apply, what effect they will have on the outcome.

Many rules may seem to apply at first, but only a few are likely to prove useful in analyzing a particular problem. A rule applies to a situation when it so closely corresponds to the situation that it affects the rights and responsibilities of the persons involved. A statutory rule applies when it covers the facts of the case. A common law rule applies when the decided cases are more analogous to the client's case than they are different. Some rules will clearly apply; others will be plainly irrelevant and can be eliminated immediately. Keep under consideration rules that do not fit easily into either category. It is better to weed out an irrelevant rule later than to discard a potentially applicable rule prematurely.

To identify potentially applicable rules, you must first decide what large body of law applies to your problem and do preliminary reading in that area. After you have identified a body of law, such as torts, determine what kind of tort or torts might have been committed and what defenses might be available. Reading background material such as treatises, digests, annotations, and legal encyclopedias will focus your attention on the broad spectrum of rules encompassed by a particular body of law.

When you have gained a general understanding of the large body of relevant law, tighten the focus of your inquiry by examining and comparing primary sources of rules, such as cases, statutes, constitutions, and administrative regulations. You must examine all reasonable sources of legal rules to determine which of these rules, if any, match your factual situation closely enough to have a plausible effect on the outcome. At the simplest level, rules will be applied to the specific situations for which they were created. At a more abstract level, rules may be applied to different situations if it is sensible to do so.

Relevant questions are of two kinds. The first involves legal rules that plainly affect the outcome because there can be little dispute that they apply. The second involves rules that may or may not affect the outcome. Given the value and limits of a lawyer's time, a lawyer cannot explore every question in this second category and must use judgment to determine which are plausible enough to consider. There is a certain threshold of plausibility concerning the possible application of rules to the facts of your problem. Questions that do not reach this threshold are not relevant and should be discarded.

The threshold is not always easy to determine, and there can be reasonable disagreement about whether a problem involves a particular question. For example, suppose that an ordinance imposes on a city a duty to keep sidewalks in good repair, and case law has established that this duty gives rise to a cause of action against the city by pedestrians injured while traveling over sidewalks in disrepair. The rule would clearly apply to a pedestrian who tripped over a broken sidewalk slab, but at first glance does not seem to apply to a person injured while riding a bicycle or roller-skating over a broken sidewalk because that person is not a pedestrian. Further research might reveal, however, that cyclists and skaters could be in the same category as pedestrians because they customarily travel on sidewalks.

In the Brookson case, you need to answer two questions: (1) how can this case be brought in federal court, and (2) what claims can reasonably be brought against Carter? Thus, the bodies of applicable law are civil procedure and torts.

As you research those areas of law, identify the potentially applicable rules and read them carefully. Each word in a rule may be legally significant. That is, each word may form the basis for determining whether the rule applies to the facts of your case. As a practical matter, however, most rules are comprised of elements. As explained in Chapter 5 (Understanding Legal Rules), the elements of a legal rule—whether a common law rule or a statutory rule—are those things that need to be satisfied or met for the rule to apply to a particular situation.

In identifying relevant questions, review the rules and their elements carefully, and decide whether their application to your case is plausible. A good test for determining a relevant question is whether you can make a plausible argument for each side, even though you may not be persuaded by the argument for one side. As indicated earlier, at this stage in your research and thinking, all potentially applicable rules should be included.

Jurisdiction. The jurisdictional rule regarding diversity of jurisdiction appears to be relevant. Section 1332(a) gives the federal district courts original jurisdiction to hear certain cases. Section 1332(a) has three elements: it applies to (1) civil actions (2) where the amount in controversy exceeds $75,000, exclusive of interest and costs, and (3) the parties fall into one of four categories. These categories are (a) citizens of different states, (b) citizens of a state and citizens or subjects of a foreign state, (c) citizens of different states and in which citizens or subjects of a foreign state are additional parties, and (d) a foreign state as plaintiff and citizens of a state or of different states.

Each of these elements is plausibly met in this case. An action by a private citizen to recover damages is a civil action, which satisfies the first element. The term "civil action" distinguishes this potential lawsuit from a criminal case. Fred Brookson's medical expenses exceed $128,000, which satisfies the element requiring that the amount in controversy exceed $75,000. The third element can be satisfied if the parties fall into one of the four categories. It is plausible that Brookson and Carter are citizens of different states and thus fall into the first of these categories. Brookson is an Oregon citizen. Although Carter has attended college and lived three years in Oregon, he grew up in California. This point will require additional legal research and analysis, because Carter's residency in Oregon as a college student for the past three years may make him an Oregon citizen. An elements chart forces you to review the other three categories. Because those elements involve foreign states or citizens of foreign states, however, you would consider them no further after your review.

An elements chart, such as the one below, shows whether the individual elements of a rule are, may be, or are not applicable to the facts of your case:

Diversity Jurisdiction ELEMENTS CHART		
Element	**Facts of Our Case**	**Element Met?**
Civil action	Action by private citizens to recover damages	Yes
Amount in controversy exceeds $75,000	Medical costs exceed $128,000	Yes
Parties fall into one of the following categories:		
a. Citizens of different states	Parties are Oregon resident and person who grew up in California but lived in Oregon for the past three years as a college student	Maybe
b. Citizens of a state and citizens or subjects of a foreign state	Same	No
c. Citizens of different states and in which citizens or subjects of a foreign state are additional parties	Same	No
d. A foreign state as plaintiff and citizens of a state or different states	Same	No

You may have identified the jurisdictional rule regarding admiralty jurisdiction because the incident took place on a wharf over a river. Your research already shows section 1333 to be inapplicable. The *Krebs* case identifies two elements required for jurisdiction under section 1333(1): There must be (1) a potential hazard to maritime commerce (2) arising out of an activity that bears a substantial relationship to traditional maritime activity. It is plausible that the demonstration on the wharf created a potential hazard to maritime commerce. But it is not plausible to state that an abortion demonstration bears a substantial relationship to traditional maritime activity. Nor is it plausible to state, under section 1333(2), that the case involves a prize. Section 1333 is so plainly irrelevant that it should not be mentioned in the memorandum.

In situations like this, when it is fairly easy to discern that a rule is inapplicable, an elements chart may be unnecessary. An elements chart on this question, however, might look like this:

Admiralty Jurisdiction ELEMENTS CHART		
Element	**Facts of Our Case**	**Element Met?**
1333(1) Potential hazard to maritime commerce	Demonstration on wharf over river	Maybe
Arising out of an activity that bears a substantial relationship to traditional maritime activity	Demonstration involved abortion	No
1333(2) Proceeding for condemnation of property taken as a prize	Civil claims arising from a demonstration	No

Tort Claims. The cases indicate that several tort rules potentially apply. The court in *Jansen v. McLeavy* explicitly identified the specific elements necessary for intentional infliction of emotional distress.[1] According to the court, emotional distress has not occurred unless all four elements are met. Go through the elements one by one. Look for corresponding facts in Fred Brookson's case to see whether this rule might apply.

A review of each element shows that Fred Brookson may have a cause of action for intentional infliction of emotional distress. The first element requires that the defendant's conduct be intentional in regard to the plaintiff. At first it may appear that this element has been met because Carter lunged at Brookson with a knife. But the language of the rule is unclear about what must be intended. Although Carter intended to stab Brookson, it is not clear whether Carter intended to cause Brookson emotional distress. At this point, you cannot say for

---

1. The elements and structure of this rule should be familiar to you if you completed Exercise 5-B. Here, you see the rule analyzed in a factual context.

certain whether the element is met. The *Jansen* case does not address this issue, so you will need to find cases that do.

The second element is plainly met. Under that element, the defendant's conduct must be extreme and outrageous. By lunging at Brookson with a knife, Carter engaged in extreme and outrageous conduct.

The third element requires a causal connection between the defendant's conduct and the plaintiff's mental distress. This element may or may not be met. Brookson was beaten up by another man when he moved to avoid Carter's knife. To meet this element, however, you will need to show a causal connection between Carter's action and Brookson's emotional distress. This connection plausibly exists. But the odd chain of events, and the possibility that Brookson's emotional distress could have other causes, means it may not exist. Legal research involving cases that have specifically addressed this element is needed. Factual research on the causes of his distress may also help.

The final element requires the plaintiff's mental distress to be extreme and severe. Brookson's chronic anxiety and severe insomnia meet that element.

Because two of the elements are easily met, and two might plausibly be met, Carter may be liable for intentional infliction of emotional distress. While additional research will be necessary, intentional infliction of emotional distress appears to be a relevant question.

You might use a chart like the following to depict the results of this analysis:

Intentional Infliction of Emotional Distress ELEMENTS CHART		
Element	**Facts of Our Case**	**Element Met?**
The defendant's conduct must be intentional toward the plaintiff	When Carter lunged at Brookson with a knife, he must have intended physical harm to Brookson	Maybe
Conduct must be extreme and outrageous	Carter tried to stab Brookson	Yes
Must be a causal connection between the defendant's conduct and the plaintiff's mental distress	Brookson beaten up by another when he avoided Carter's knife	Maybe
The plaintiff's mental distress must be extreme and severe	Brookson has chronic anxiety and severe insomnia	Yes

Carter may also have committed battery. The *Powers* case defines battery as follows:

> A defendant commits battery when he acts intending to cause a harmful or offensive contact with the plaintiff or a third person and thereby causes a harmful or offensive contact with the plaintiff.

This rule requires an analysis different from the rule in *Jansen* because the court has not divided it into elements. As already stated, each word in this rule may be important, and as you saw in Chapter 5 (Understanding Legal Rules), the rule on battery contains several elements and sub-elements. It is important to appreciate the complexity of a legal rule, but using each word as an element or sub-element when trying to identify the issues in a case can be cumbersome and confusing to both you and the reader. You should therefore try to identify elements by clustering the words into specific concepts or ideas. When the court does not expressly describe individual elements, you can identify them in two ways: You can look at how the court has clustered words or phrases in its decision, or you can cluster the words or phrases yourself (if the court has not done that, or has not done it clearly). Sometimes you may need to do both.

The *Powers* case gives some clues for identifying the elements of battery. The court states that battery occurs if, among other things, the plaintiff intended a harmful or offensive contact. This suggests that intent to cause harmful or offensive contact could be considered one element. It is possible to break this element into smaller pieces (intent, contact, harmful or offensive), but there is no apparent reason for doing so now. An element, again, is a conceptual unit of a rule. The use of elements forces a closer and more rigorous examination of the rule's specific requirements. An element in one situation may be two or more elements in another situation and only part of an element in still another situation.

If intent to cause harmful or offensive contact is one element, then an act by the defendant is another. The *Powers v. Locke* court states that harmful or offensive contact with the plaintiff is an element and that a causal connection between the defendant's act and the plaintiff's harmful or offensive contact is also an element. Divided into these elements, the rule is as follows:

> A defendant commits battery when he (1) acts (2) intending to cause a harmful or offensive contact with the plaintiff or a third person and (3) thereby causes (4) a harmful or offensive contact with the plaintiff.

All four of these elements must be satisfied for a battery to occur. The absence of just one element means that Brookson has no cause of action for battery. Note that several elements include the word "or." As Chapter 5 states, when "or" is used in an element, the element may be met in more than one way; it is not necessary for both requirements to be met. The intended contact, for example, must be harmful or offensive, but it need not be both. The intended contact must be with the plaintiff or a third person, but not necessarily both.

Thus divided, the problem readily lends itself to analysis. The first element—an act—is satisfied because Carter lunged at Brookson with a knife. Trying to stab Brookson also satisfies the element requiring intent to cause harmful or offensive contact with the plaintiff or a third party. The fourth element is met by the unidentified demonstrator's beating of Brookson as Brookson tried to avoid Carter's knife. That surely qualifies as a harmful or offensive contact with the plaintiff. It is plausible that the third element, a causal relationship between Carter's act and Brookson's injuries, is also met. As Brookson was avoiding Carter's knife, Brookson almost bumped into another demonstrator. That demonstrator then struck and seriously injured Brookson. Further research will identify cases that specifically address this issue, and you may or may not ultimately conclude that this element is met. But it is certainly worth pursuing.

You may have noticed that the causation element for battery seems similar to the causation element for intentional infliction of emotional distress. When you see these similarities, be careful not to conclude automatically that the elements are the same. For intentional infliction of emotional distress, for example, you are looking to see whether a causal relationship exists between Brookson's emotional distress and Carter's act. It will be easier to show that Brookson's physical injuries arose from the beating than it will be to show that his emotional injuries arose from the beating. His severe insomnia and chronic anxiety may be caused, at least in part, by separation from his wife or his public participation in a politically charged demonstration.

The following chart outlines the analysis for battery:

Battery ELEMENTS CHART		
Element	**Facts of Our Case**	**Element Met?**
Acts	Carter lunged at Brookson with a knife	Yes
intending to cause a harmful or offensive contact with the plaintiff or third person	Carter wanted to stab Brookson	Yes
thereby causing	Brookson almost bumped into an unidentified demonstrator to avoid Carter, and demonstrator then beat Brookson	Maybe
harmful or offensive contact with the plaintiff	Brookson was severely beaten by an unidentified demonstrator	Yes

3. Exclude "givens" from detailed discussion.

A *given* is a legal question with a clear answer.[2] Some questions, even though relevant and within the scope of the problem, are so easily resolved that they are not genuine issues. Because legal documents must be concise, you should discuss a question at no greater length than it deserves. A memorandum or brief should usually mention givens as necessary to proceed in a logical fashion or to fully describe the context, but givens should not be discussed in detail. Tell the reader in two or three sentences what the rule and relevant facts are and what the result will be. If you are unsure about whether a question is a given, however, discuss it in as much detail as necessary.

The answers in the charts distinguish between givens and issues. The third column contains answers to the question of whether a particular element has been met in the Brookson case. If the answer is "yes," the applicability of the element is given. If the answer is "maybe," the applicability of the element is plausible enough to be an issue. (If

---

2. Use of the word *given* as a noun is not recommended in a memorandum or brief. It is used in this book as a shorthand way of describing a legal question for which there is obviously only one answer.

the answer is "no," as already suggested, the element or rule is clearly not met.)

The diversity jurisdiction rule contains two givens. It is given that the lawsuit would be a civil action because it would be an action by a private citizen to recover damages. The amount in controversy exceeds $75,000 because Fred Brookson's medical expenses alone are more than $128,000. Your discussion of diversity jurisdiction would briefly explain the applicability of these two elements. Because there is some question whether the parties are from different states, however, you should spend your time on that issue. Fred Brookson is an Oregon citizen and it is not clear whether Carter is a citizen of Oregon or California. This uncertainty makes diversity jurisdiction an issue.

The tort involving intentional infliction of emotional distress also involves two givens. Because Carter lunged at Brookson with a knife, it is given that his conduct was extreme and outrageous. Because Brookson has chronic anxiety and severe insomnia, it is given that his mental distress is extreme and severe. When you write your analysis, you should briefly explain why these elements have been satisfied, but you need not discuss them in detail. The harder questions are whether Carter intended to cause Brookson's emotional distress, and whether Carter caused that distress. On these two questions, there may be some dispute about the outcome. The analysis of these two questions, therefore, should be the core of this part of the memo.

Three of the four elements of battery are also given. Carter certainly acted when he lunged at Brookson with his knife, and his intent to cause harmful contact is obvious from his attempt to stab Brookson. Brookson's severe beating by an unidentified demonstrator satisfies the element requiring harmful or offensive contact. (The exception noted in *Powers*, that it is not battery if the contact is consented to or otherwise privileged, need not be discussed at all because no facts indicate that this exception applies.) There is likely to be no dispute regarding the applicability of these three elements. As a result, your explanation of these elements need not be detailed. The more difficult question is whether Carter's actions caused the injuries Brookson suffered after he almost bumped into the unidentified demonstrator. More research and analysis are required before this question can be resolved.

4. Separate issues and sub-issues.

Some issues can only be resolved by first resolving smaller included issues known as *sub-issues*. Sub-issues typically occur when a legal rule includes several elements and the application of at least two of these elements may be disputed. The applicability of the rule is thus the issue, and the applicability of each element that may be disputed is a sub-issue.

There is no particular magic that separates issues from sub-issues; what is an issue in one case might be a sub-issue in another. The status of a question as an issue or sub-issue depends on the extent to which you have eliminated some questions because they are irrelevant, outside the scope of the problem, or givens. The division of questions into issues and sub-issues is simply a useful tool for understanding and stating the relationship among the legal questions in your memorandum or brief.

While sub-issues serve a useful organizational purpose, they should not be fabricated for the sake of convenience. Never divide a question into two parts if the question raises only one issue. Sub-issues must be issues in their own right and they must always be analytically independent of one another.

Issues and sub-issues arise by possible application of the elements of specific legal rules to a factual situation. Issues, therefore, should not be stated in overly general terms, such as whether your client should win the case or whether the court is likely to grant a motion for summary judgment. State issues specifically, focusing on the application of the precise legal rule to the case at hand.

In Fred Brookson's case, intentional infliction of emotional distress depends on whether Carter intended Brookson's emotional distress, and whether he caused it. Thus, intentional infliction of emotional distress is an issue, and there are two sub-issues. Each is independent of the other, and both must be resolved in favor of Fred Brookson for there to be an intentional infliction of emotional distress.

The battery claim, however, involves only one issue: whether Carter caused Fred Brookson's injuries. Similarly, diversity jurisdiction depends solely on whether there is sufficient diversity of citizenship.

This careful screening of the questions that merit analysis in the Fred Brookson case leaves three tentative issues, one of which has two sub-issues. They should be outlined as follows:

Outline of Legal Questions

1. Whether there is diversity of citizenship between the parties for purposes of federal diversity jurisdiction.
2. Whether Carter is liable to Fred Brookson for intentional infliction of emotional distress.
   a. Whether Carter intended to cause Brookson's emotional distress.
   b. Whether Carter caused Brookson's emotional distress.
3. Whether Carter caused Brookson's battery.

This problem has been cut to its bare legal bones. These issues and sub-issues each merit a detailed analysis, and those questions that do not merit detailed analysis have been excluded. (Givens must be included in a discussion, but they do not merit detailed analysis.) Remember that your list of issues will be somewhat tentative until you have finished your research. You may find cases or statutes in your jurisdiction that clearly resolve something you initially identified as an issue, or you may find cases or statutes that open up questions you had thought closed, or raise entirely new questions. Sometimes you will find cases that add to or modify your list of elements. Much will depend on the quality of your research. For example, you may have guessed that Brookson has a potential cause of action against Carter for assault—a possibility you would investigate if you were researching this problem.

Although the four steps discussed above are distinct, they need not be taken in any particular order and some can be combined. The process that you follow will depend upon your knowledge of the relevant law and the nature of the problem. Use these steps as a checklist whenever you are asked to write a document assessing or arguing a client's case.

EXERCISES

The following exercises are designed to let you work through the four steps of issue identification.

Exercise 6-A

Recently, Neil McKay telephoned Hugh Green and, as a joke, offered to sell his $100,000 yacht for $10,000 cash. McKay has a reputation as a practical joker. Although Green knew the true value of the boat, he did not know McKay's reputation. Green said to McKay, "You can't be serious," and then told McKay he needed time to think it over and raise the money.

Three days later, Green telephoned McKay to accept the offer but McKay was golfing. Green told McKay's secretary to tell McKay that he had called concerning the boat. The secretary called the golf course and left a message for McKay: "Green called—something about the yacht." By that time McKay was in the clubhouse and was intoxicated. The bartender took the secretary's message to McKay, who then telephoned Green.

Immediately after he started talking with Green, McKay passed out. While McKay was unconscious, Green told him, "I accept the offer," and added, "but I'd like to see your golf clubs thrown into the deal, too." McKay does not remember the telephone conversation and now refuses to sell the yacht to Green. Is there an enforceable contract?

You have found two cases from your state and some secondary authority.

Derek v. Beir (1985)

The appellant, Morse Beir, was a known eccentric with a reputation for playing practical jokes on his neighbors. One day he approached his neighbor, Bob Derek, whom he disliked. Beir stated, "For five bucks I will build a ten-foot-high wall at my own expense between our lots just so I will never have to look at your ridiculous face again." Derek, who was well aware of Beir's reputation, immediately agreed and paid Beir five dollars. Beir failed to build the wall, and the appellee filed this suit for breach of contract. The trial court awarded Derek $3,000 in damages, which represented the cost of building the wall. Beir appealed.

Although the trial court made several errors in this case, we do not have to discuss most of them here because we find the contract unenforceable. The general rule is that a contract is not enforceable unless there is an effective offer. For an offer to be effective, the offeror must intend to make a binding contract. In this state, the test for intent by the offeror is whether a reasonable person in the offeree's shoes would believe that the offeror intended to make a binding contract. We conclude that Derek knew or should have known that Beir was not serious and did not intend to make a contract. Because there was no offer, we do not have to reach the question of whether the consideration was so grossly disproportionate that it would shock the conscience of the court to enforce the contract. Reversed.

Caldwell, J., dissenting. It is axiomatic that the appellate court will not set aside a jury finding unless it is clearly contrary to the preponderance of the evidence. The jury in the court below heard testimony from both Derek and Beir as to Beir's true intent and Derek's conception of it. After a correct instruction from the judge on the rule of law in this state, which rule the majority has stated correctly and succinctly, the jury decided that the parties intended to make a contract. It is not up to this court to decide whether the contract was nonsensical or absurd or ill-advised. The court below, after consideration of conflicting evidence, found that the parties intended to enter into a contract. Because that finding was not clearly against the weight of the evidence, I would affirm on the issue of intent to make a valid offer.

Although the majority did not reach the issue of adequacy of consideration, having disposed of the case on other grounds, I would remind the court that any consideration, no matter how small, is generally sufficient to support a contract freely entered into by the parties. Lewis J. Holloway, *A Treatise on Contract Law* 10 (2d ed. 1982).

Anselm v. Kinnet Textiles, Inc. (1986)

The appellant, Charles Anselm, offered to sell 200 bales of cotton to the appellee, Kinnet Textiles, Inc. One hundred bales were to be delivered on March 1, and the remaining 100 were to be delivered on April 1. Kinnet sent a messenger to Anselm's office with a written note that stated, "We agree to your offer in all respects if we can instead take delivery on March 5 and April 5." Because Anselm was out of the office, his secretary accepted the note from the messenger and placed it on Anselm's cluttered desk. Anselm did not see it for several weeks and, in the meantime, committed the cotton to another buyer. Kinnet filed suit for breach of contract. The trial court found that the contract was valid and awarded damages to Kinnet. We disagree.

A contract is not formed unless there is a valid acceptance. Because we have not adopted the Uniform Commercial Code in this state, the case is governed by common law. The appellant claims there was not a valid acceptance for two reasons. First, the appellant claims there was no acceptance because he did not see or read the note. We find the delivery and placement of the acceptance on the appellant's desk to be a sufficient communication of the acceptance. Once the offeree has delivered a written acceptance, it would be unreasonable to require the offeree to ensure that the acceptance is read. We do, however, agree with Anselm that the contract is invalid because the acceptance differs from the offer. The rule in this state is that the acceptance must mirror the offer in every respect. If it varies from the offer, it is considered a counteroffer and not an acceptance. Because the dates for delivery in the acceptance here varied from those in the offer, we find there was no acceptance and thus no enforceable contract. Reversed.

Morris, J., concurring. I agree with the majority that there was no acceptance of the offer in this case. However, I disagree that this result must be reached by the application of the mirror-image rule. The creative and regenerative power of the law has been strong enough to break chains imposed by outmoded former decisions. What the courts have power to create, they also have power to modify, reject, and recreate in response to the needs of a dynamic society. The exercise of this power is an imperative function of the courts and is the strength of the common law. It cannot be surrendered to legislative inaction.

Most states have discarded the archaic mirror-image rule and have replaced it with section 2-207 of the Uniform Commercial Code, which treats additional terms in a contract as proposals for additions to the contract unless the acceptance is expressly made conditional on assent to the additional terms. U.C.C. § 2-207. In this case, the acceptance was conditional on Anselm's agreeing to the changed dates. Hence, it was not an acceptance at all but was, instead, a counteroffer. Thus, there was no contract.

Excerpt from Lewis J. Holloway, *A Treatise on Contract Law* 10 (2d ed. 1982)

Generally, an enforceable contract must contain three elements: (1) an offer, (2) an acceptance, and (3) consideration by both parties. Consideration means that each party must incur a legal detriment, *i.e.*, give something of value or a promise to do something one is not already obligated to do. Any consideration is sufficient, no matter how small.

Excerpt from Edna C. Simpson, *Contracts* 37–38 (3d ed. 2006)

A counteroffer is a rejection because it manifests an unwillingness to assent to the offer as made, unless the offeree in making the counteroffer states he still has the original offer under consideration. An acceptance of an offer on condition that the offeror do something more than he has promised in his offer is not an acceptance at all; it is a counteroffer and operates to terminate the original offer. Acceptance conditioned on the seller's delivering additional goods not specified in his offer is a counteroffer and a rejection.

1. As a starting point, what is the question stated in this problem?

2. State the rule and the elements of the rule that will answer this question.

3. Using your answer to question 2, prepare an elements chart to identify any issues and sub-issues in this problem.

Exercise 6-B

Cynthia Mickel, a reporter for the *Star City Banner-Patriot,* was recently assigned to write an investigative series on an organization called Citizens for Law and Order (CLO). She learned from her investigation that CLO is a paramilitary organization whose primary purpose is to arm citizens on behalf of "the Aryan or white elements in our society." The organization is so secretive that its members refused to discuss it with her or even to acknowledge that they were members. Several former members stated that CLO believes that "the whole country is crawling with black, red, and yellow people," that "everybody in power has sold out," and that only "CLO could buck the tide." The organization sponsors target-shooting events for its members, publishes a newsletter discussing different kinds of rifles and handguns, and routinely sends anonymous letters to the *Banner-Patriot.* Mickel recently learned that the Star City Police Department has been investigating CLO for two years. Although the Department has never arrested any CLO members for illegal activities related to their membership, Mickel has reason to believe the police files are extensive and that they contain information primarily concerning the structure, activities, and membership of the CLO. She has learned, for example, that the mayor's wife is an officer of the CLO and that the files describe her involvement in detail.

Pursuant to the state Freedom of Information Act, Mickel filed a request with the Police Department seeking all files concerning its CLO investigation. Three days later the Department denied her request, stating in part that "these records are confidential." Two days later, the mayor phoned her, stating that he would sue the newspaper "for every penny it has" if it published a story about the CLO. Mickel's editors are reluctant to run the story without corroborating information from the police files. The paper has asked you to determine whether it can obtain the information through a lawsuit against the Police Department.

The state Freedom of Information Act, as amended in 1984, provides:

> **Sec. 2.** As used in this Act:
>
> (a) "Person" means an individual, corporation, partnership, firm, organization, or association.
> (b) "Governmental body" means—
>   (i) A state officer, employee, agency, department, division, bureau, board, commission, council, authority, or other body in the executive branch of the state government, but does not include the governor or lieutenant governor, the executive office of the governor or lieutenant governor, or employees thereof.
>   (ii) An agency, board, commission, or council in the legislative branch of state government.
>   (iii) A county, city, township, village, intercounty, intercity, or regional governing body, council, school district, special district, municipal corporation, or a board, department, commission, council, or agency thereof.
> (c) "Public record" means a writing prepared, owned, used, in the possession of, or retained by a governmental body.

Sec. 3.

(a) A person desiring to inspect or receive a copy of a public record may make an oral or written request for a public record to the governmental body.
(b) The governmental body shall grant or deny a request in not more than five business days after the day the request is received.

Sec. 4. If a governmental body denies a request, the requesting person may commence an action in circuit court to compel disclosure of the public records. An action under this section may not be commenced unless the requesting person has allowed the governmental body five business days to respond to the request.

Sec. 5. A governmental body may exempt from disclosure as a public record under this Act:

(a) Records of law enforcement agencies that deal with the detection and investigation of crime and the internal records and notations of such law enforcement agencies which are maintained for its internal use in matters related to law enforcement.
(b) Information or records subject to the attorney-client privilege.
(c) Records of any campaign committee, including any committee that receives monies from a state campaign fund.
(d) Information of a personal nature where the public disclosure of the information would constitute a clearly unwarranted invasion of an individual's privacy [added in 1984].

The highest appellate court in your state has decided the following cases:

Holcombe v. Badger Newspapers, Inc. (1983)

The plaintiff, a rape victim, brought an action for damages for invasion of privacy against the defendant newspaper for publishing a factual article about the crime, including her name and address. The trial court dismissed her complaint and we affirm.

The state Freedom of Information Act provides that every citizen has a right to the disclosure of any public record. Although the Act exempts certain public records from disclosure, none of these exceptions pertains to this factual situation. There can be no liability for invasion of privacy at common law when the defendant further discloses information about the plaintiff that is already public. We are sympathetic to the plaintiff's problem, but our duty ends when we have construed the statute. The legislature may amend the Act, but we cannot.

Wheeler Publishing Co. v. City of Bad Axe (1985)

The Bad Axe Police Department maintains two kinds of records relevant to this case. One is called an "Offense Report," and it includes information concerning the offense committed, the surrounding circumstances, the witnesses, and the investigating officers. The other is called a "Supplementary Offense Report," and it includes information such as the names of potential informants, officers' speculations about a suspect's guilt, and the results of various laboratory tests. The plaintiff, the owner of the *Bad Axe Daily Telegram,* sought to inspect both kinds of reports for its daily newspaper coverage of crime in the Bad Axe area. The Department refused, claiming that the information fit the "police records" exception in section 5(a) of the state's Freedom of Information Act. The plaintiff is challenging that interpretation.

We hold that section 5(a) does not allow the Police Department to withhold the Offense Report. Although the information contained in the Offense Report deals with the detection and investigation of crime, it is not the kind of information that should be solely for the Police Department's "internal use" under section 5(a). The press and the public have a right to information concerning crime and law enforcement activity in the community. In determining the reach of that right in specific situations, however, it is necessary to weigh and balance competing interests. With respect to the Offense Report, the public's right to know about specific crimes is paramount. Access to the Supplementary Offense Report, on the other hand, is protected by section 5(a). To open this material to the press and the public might reveal the names of informants and otherwise jeopardize law enforcement activities. The Department must release Offense Reports but is entitled to retain Supplementary Offense Reports.

1. As a starting point, what is the question stated in this problem?

2. State the general rule and the elements of the rule that will answer this question.

3. Using your answer to question 2, prepare an elements chart to determine what issues, if any, arise from the general rule in this problem.

4. Which of the exceptions might be applicable to this problem?

5. For one plausibly applicable exception chosen by you or your professor, state the rule and the elements of the rule.

6. Using your answer to question 5, prepare an elements chart to identify any issues and sub-issues for the exception.

Exercise 6-C

Flower Hughes, a 25-year-old law student who also holds a graduate degree in business and accounting, recently inherited $500,000 from a rich uncle. To celebrate her good fortune, Hughes decided to have a few drinks at the Blue Goose Inn, a local tavern. Hughes arrived at noon and had several drinks during the course of the afternoon. Soon after her arrival (about three drinks later), she explained to Ron Zoeller, the bartender and sole owner of the Inn, that she wanted to invest her inheritance in some enterprise that would yield a high return.

Zoeller began telling her what a fine business he had in the Blue Goose, and how he was getting old and would like to sell it. He told Hughes that the net worth of the Goose was $400,000 and that she could expect to make a $45,000 net profit each year. He admitted that he had only made $25,000 each year for the three years he had owned the place but assured Hughes that revitalization of the inner city and proposed construction would probably double or triple the Inn's profits in no time. The net worth of the Goose was really only $280,000. Zoeller went to the back room and produced a ledger book that he said contained his business records. The entries in the book had obviously been altered to reflect the figures he had quoted to Hughes. (He had altered them originally for tax and insurance purposes.) Hughes examined the book briefly and expressed some concern about the validity of the figures. Zoeller replied, "Sure there might be some mistakes; I'm not very good with figures." He added, "What good are figures anyway? A good businessman trusts his instincts above all else." Zoeller then offered to sell Hughes the tavern for $340,000. Hughes smiled and said she would think it over.

At about 5 p.m., several of Hughes's friends joined her at the tavern. Hughes continued drinking until 1 a.m., when Zoeller leaned over the bar and said, "Tell you what, because you're such a nice kid, I'll sell you the whole place for $320,000. It's a real steal." Hughes, who was intoxicated by this time, could not hear Zoeller over the noise in the tavern, and asked him to write his statement down. Zoeller then wrote his exact statement on one of the bar's napkins, which had "Blue Goose Inn" printed on it. It said, "Ron Zoeller offers to sell the Blue Goose Inn to Flower Hughes for $320,000." Hughes laughed and said, "Sure, why not? It'll be a good time."

The next day Hughes remembered the conversation and went to Zoeller and said she hoped he was only joking around. Zoeller said that he was serious and intended to hold Hughes to the contract. He also told Hughes that a customer who had been sitting next to Hughes at the bar was toying with his new digital recorder at the time. The customer had accidentally recorded the entire conversation, Zoeller said, and was willing to send him the recording. He also named several other witnesses who heard the conversation and who would confirm the agreement if necessary.

Hughes has come to you for assistance. After some research and thought on the matter, you have discovered the following statute and cases from your state:

State Rev. Laws § 60.1(4) Statute of Frauds

No action shall be brought against any person . . . (4) upon any contract for the sale of lands, tenements, or hereditaments, or any other interest concerning them . . . unless the agreement upon which said action shall be brought, or some memorandum or note thereof, shall be in writing and signed by the person to be charged therewith, or by some other person thereunto by him lawfully authorized.

Treacher v. Plums (1953)

The appellant, Ivan Treacher, entered into an oral contract with the appellee, Roy Plums, whereby Treacher purported to sell Plums a ten-acre tract of farm land. Treacher proposed the deal at 10 a.m. and Plums immediately agreed. They did not put the agreement in writing because Plums was illiterate. Instead, they immediately proceeded to the church, and they both stated the terms of the agreement in front of the minister and two witnesses. Later that day, Plums wanted to cancel the deal. Treacher refused and filed suit. The trial court found that the state Statute of Frauds rendered the agreement of no effect. We agree.

The original Statute of Frauds was enacted in England in the seventeenth century. The statute in our state, which is modeled on the English Statute of Frauds, has been interpreted extensively by the courts. Case law has now clearly established that the statute requires contracts for the sale of land to be in writing. The writing must state with reasonable certainty and accuracy (1) the parties to the contract, (2) the subject matter to which the contract relates, and (3) the terms and conditions of all promises constituting the contract and by whom and to whom the promises are made.

In this case, there is no question that the terms of the contract, the subject matter, and the parties were all described with the requisite certainty. The exact location and size of the property, the purchase price, the conditions of payment, and the names of both parties were all stated. The fact remains, however, that they were not stated in writing. We have recognized two purposes served by the statute. One is evidentiary—putting the agreement in writing ensures that there will be proof of the agreement. The second is cautionary—reducing the agreement to writing requires the parties to think through the proposed transaction carefully and make sure they are serious about going through with the deal. Even if we were at liberty to disregard the statute, in this case we find that the second purpose was not fulfilled. Affirmed.

Divine v. Zarwakov (2005)

The appellant, Carla Divine, brought suit seeking rescission of her contract with Zarwakov's School of Ballet. Divine, who has an eighth-grade education and is twenty-five years old, has always dreamed of becoming a great dancer. She began taking lessons in classical ballet at Zarwakov's dance school in response to a special introductory offer of ten lessons for fifty dollars. During this time she was repeatedly told that she was a natural dancer and that she had exceptional rhythm, grace, and poise. The school told her that with minimal training she would be assured of a spot as a principal dancer in one of the national dance companies. On the basis of this encouragement,

Divine entered into a series of written contracts in which she agreed to pay $10,000 over the next five years for private dance lessons. In reality, Divine is extremely uncoordinated and has no natural aptitude for dance. The trial court held that she was bound by the terms of the contract and dismissed her suit. We disagree.

Courts in this state will not enforce an agreement when there has been a misrepresentation in the inducement to contract. The party seeking to be relieved of the bargain must establish six things: (1) false representations, (2) of material facts, (3) that the defendant knew were false, (4) that the defendant intended the plaintiff to rely on, (5) that the plaintiff was justified in relying on, and (6) the plaintiff suffered damages as a result of this reliance. There is no doubt that there were false representations, that the defendant knew they were false, that the defendant intended the plaintiff to rely on them, that the plaintiff relied on them, and that she was damaged as a result. The only questions here are whether they were material facts and whether the plaintiff was justified in relying on the representations of those facts.

We hold that while these representations were not material facts in the strict legal sense, they were sufficient to satisfy the requirement. Ordinarily, a representation is material if it would induce a reasonable person to change his or her position. When there has been some artifice or trick by the representor, or when the parties do not in general deal at arm's length, or when the representee does not have equal opportunity to become apprised of the truth or falsity of the fact represented, material facts in the strict sense are not required.

The same reasoning applies to the justifiable reliance element. The dance school held itself out to be an expert. Given the plaintiff's lack of knowledge and education, not to mention her lifelong dream, she was justified in relying on the dance school's representation of the material facts. Reversed.

1. As a starting point, what is the question stated in this problem?

2. For the Statute of Frauds rule:
   a. State the elements of the rule.
   b. Using your answer to question (a), prepare an elements chart to identify any issues and sub-issues on the Statute of Frauds in this problem.

3. For the misrepresentation rule:
   a. State the elements of the rule.
   b. Using your answer to question (a), prepare an elements chart to identify any issues and sub-issues on misrepresentation in this problem.

Common Law Analysis

The peculiar way lawyers think has been ridiculed for centuries, and often for good cause. Montaigne wrote of several men who had been executed for a crime, even though the actual culprits were discovered after their trial, because the authorities did not want the public to think the judicial process was imperfect. Charles Dickens devoted a lengthy novel, *Bleak House,* to what he described as the "foggiest and muddiest" place in London, the High Court of Chancery.

Although some legal reasoning seems unreasonable, most analysis reflects honest intellectual differences about what the law means or what direction it should take. Perceived unreasonableness also reflects limitations in the analytical process. There are few judicial opinions whose logic is airtight, whose assumptions cannot be questioned, or whose analysis addresses all of the ramifications of the decision. Dissenting opinions often bring these shortcomings (actual and perceived) into sharp relief. Justice David Souter's dissenting opinion in a 2006 United States Supreme Court decision, for example, described the majority opinion's analysis as "fallacious" and "mistaken."[1]

All these criticisms notwithstanding, there is a method to legal analysis, and it is a sensible one. Previous chapters examined some of the basic principles of legal analysis. This chapter will describe and illustrate the method of common law analysis.[2]

---

1. Garcetti v. Ceballos, 547 U.S. 410, 436 (2006) (Souter, J. dissenting).

2. Statutory analysis is described in Chapter 8. Constitutional analysis, a hybrid of common law and statutory analysis, is not specifically addressed in this book. Constitutions, particularly the United States Constitution, are similar to, but usually more general than, statutes.

The common law is the body of rules and principles found exclusively in judicial decisions. It is not created by legislatures, and it is not found in constitutions; the common law is judge-made law. The development of the common law began many centuries ago in England, when early courts were first called on to resolve disputes. These disputes were resolved according to particular principles derived from earlier decisions. Common law analysis has remained virtually unchanged since that time—judges look to earlier cases for guidance in resolving disputes.

The common law develops cautiously because the principles of precedent and *stare decisis* render it comfortable with the familiar and less comfortable with the unknown. As new cases are decided, legal rules evolve and become more complex. Although many areas of the common law have been translated by legal scholars into rule-focused restatements, the facts and policies of the cases on which these rules are based are still of great importance.

The primary methods of common law analysis are analogy and distinction. Every case involving the possible application of a common law rule involves two basic questions: (1) How are the decided cases similar to my client's case? (2) How are the decided cases different from my client's case? The more analogous the cases are, the more precedent and *stare decisis* dictate the application of their conclusions to the present case. The more distinguishable they are, the more inapplicable they should be.

Common law analysis must be undertaken on several related levels. First look at the facts of the decided cases and compare them with the facts of your case. Then examine the reasons and policies stated in the decided cases to see whether these reasons and policies apply to your case. Much of this examination will concentrate on why your significant facts are actually significant. You may find that a policy stated in the decided cases is inapplicable because the facts of your case are significantly different, or you may find that a decided case is applicable to your case for reasons the court did not state. You must always be alert to similarities and differences in both the factual situations and underlying policies.

Analogy and distinction are not simply matters of spotting obvious similarities and differences. A good lawyer will spot threads running through entire lines of cases that the courts themselves may not have made explicit, and use these threads to weave sophisticated arguments for or against the application of these cases.

Judicial decisions interpreting and applying constitutional provisions are thus highly significant because they create a body of "common law" on the meaning of these provisions. But constitutional provisions, like statutes, must also be understood in light of their language and the intent of their drafters.

A sound understanding of both sides of a controversy is the primary goal of all legal analysis. Only when you fully understand both sides can you accurately assess the strengths and weaknesses of your client's position. Even when particular cases seem to be favorable to your client, you cannot afford to ignore distinctions between those cases and your client's situation. You must be prepared to determine whether the similarities are more important than the differences, and why. If you fail to analyze both sides of the problem objectively, you may mislead your client about the strength of her legal position or be unable to properly state and defend that position. Common law analysis must not be a one-sided process.

The basic principles of common law analysis can best be stated and understood in the context of a specific problem.

Your client, Arthur Dooley, a tenant in a large apartment building, had several grievances with the building's manager, Otis Fremont. Dooley designed a one-page flier in which he asserted, "Fremont has a long record of criminal convictions as a landlord." Fremont had received three notices of violation from the local housing commission in the past two years for inadequate lighting and locks. The commission had threatened to seek a court order requiring correction of the violations, but dropped the matter when Fremont made the necessary repairs. Fremont has no criminal record.

Dooley made 200 copies of the flier to distribute to other tenants in the building. On his way back from the print shop, Dooley met Fremont by chance and, after a lengthy conversation, they settled their differences. The fliers were not mentioned. Although Dooley intended to destroy the fliers when he returned to his apartment, he was struck by a teenager riding a skateboard and the fliers were scattered by the wind. Other persons read many of the fliers, and Fremont filed suit for libel.

There are three relevant cases. All are from the highest appellate court of the state:

White v. Ball (1966)

Ball appeals from a libel judgment awarded to White and two other employees of the R&T Construction Company. Ball had hired the company to remodel his home. The judgment was based on a letter written by Ball to the company president shortly after the work was completed, in which Ball accused the employees of stealing a valuable watch.

The first issue on appeal is whether the letter was intentionally published. As a general matter, libel consists of the intentional publication of false statements about a person that humiliate the person or subject him to the loss of social prestige. All that is necessary for publication to occur is the delivery of the defamatory matter in written or other permanent form to any person other than the one libeled. It is receipt by a third person that makes the statements so damaging. Because the president of the company, a third person, received and read the letter, the trial court was correct in finding that there was intent to publish.

The second issue is whether the letter was false. On this issue, the trial court erred. A statement is false if the gist, the sting, of the matter is false. Minor inaccuracies in the statement are not sufficient to show that it is false. In this case, the accusation against the employees was, in a technical sense, false. None of the employees took the watch. But a male friend of one of the employees took the watch when he picked her up at the end of the workday. Because of the relationship between the employee and the thief, we believe that the letter was substantially accurate. Reversed.

Simmons v. Deluxe Plaza Hotel (1988)

The manager of defendant hotel wrote Simmons a letter falsely accusing Simmons of staying in the hotel, failing to pay for the room, and taking several articles from the room. The manager was mistaken as to the culprit's identity, so the letter was false. The letter was addressed to Simmons personally and sent by certified mail.

Simmons's wife signed for the letter at his residence and read it. The question on appeal is whether the trial court correctly ruled that the letter was not intentionally published. The evidence shows the manager considered it possible that some third person might receive the letter, though he did not know Simmons was married. This falls far short of a showing that he was reasonably chargeable with appreciation or knowledge of the likelihood that the letter would be opened and read by another. A mere conceivable possibility or chance of such eventuality is not sufficient to demonstrate intent. Affirmed.

Willow v. Orr (2001)

This case arises from a battle between the parties for custody of their four-year-old son, Matthew. Mr. Willow took Matthew from Ms. Orr's home without her consent or knowledge and traveled with him to another state. Ms. Orr looked for them for six weeks and, after she located them, obtained a court order compelling Matthew's return. Mr. Willow then told Ms. Orr, as part of their divorce proceeding, that he might take Matthew again. Thereafter, Ms. Orr wrote a letter to fifteen of her neighbors. The letter said, in part, "Help! Jason Willow kidnapped my child and said he would do it again." Mr. Willow sued Ms. Orr for libel. The trial court granted Ms. Orr's motion for summary judgment.

On appeal, Mr. Willow claims that the letter is false because he did not kidnap the child in the legal sense of that term. Because Mr. Willow's act did not violate any judicial custody order, he did not kidnap Matthew under the state statute. But technical errors in legal terminology and reports of matters involving violations of the law are immaterial if the defamatory charge is true in substance. Because of the nontechnical meaning that "kidnap" has acquired in the child custody context, we hold that Ms. Orr's letter is substantially true. Affirmed.

The problem lends itself to the following preliminary analysis, using the elements chart from Chapter 6 (Identifying and Selecting Issues for Analysis):

Libel ELEMENTS CHART		
Element	**Facts of Our Case**	**Element Met?**
Intent to publish	Dooley wrote and printed 200 fliers, intending to distribute them to Fremont's tenants. They were published accidentally after Dooley no longer intended to publish them.	Maybe
Publication	Fliers were read by third persons.	Yes
of false statements about a person	Fliers said Fremont had a long record of criminal convictions as a landlord. Fremont was cited three times in two years by Housing Commission and corrected violations to avoid court order. Fremont had no criminal record.	Maybe
that humiliate the person -or-	Fliers said Fremont had a long record of criminal violations.	Maybe
subject him to the loss of social prestige	Fliers said Fremont had a long record of criminal violations.	Yes

This analysis suggests that the problem contains two sub-issues: whether Dooley's publication of the fliers was intentional, and whether the fliers were false. It is given that the fliers were published. It is also given that the fourth element is met. Because the accusation of criminal convictions subjected Fremont to the loss of social prestige, it does not matter if there is some question about whether he was humiliated.

The rest of this chapter provides a method for analyzing one of these sub-issues: whether the "intent to publish" rule should be applied to these facts. (The falsity sub-issue is addressed in Exercise 7-A.) Before analyzing this or any issue, you may find it useful to identify the relevant parts of the cases you will be using. As you read in Chapter 3 (Case Analysis and Case Briefs), briefing cases will often help you understand them.

The chart below shows modified briefs of the intent sub-issue from the *White* and *Simmons* cases and includes the relevant facts of our case:

Intent to Publish CASE BRIEFING CHART			
	Our Case	**White**	**Simmons**
Facts	Dooley designed and printed copies of a flier that he intended to distribute to tenants in his apartment building. After he decided not to publish them, they were released by accident.	The defendant wrote a letter to a company president containing allegations about his employees. The company president received and read the letter.	The defendant wrote a letter that was addressed personally to the plaintiff and sent by certified mail. The plaintiff's wife read the letter. The defendant thought it possible that someone else would read the letter, but did not know the plaintiff was married.
Holding		There was intent to publish.	There was no intent to publish.
Reasons and Policies		Receipt by third person makes statements damaging.	Intent requires reasonable knowledge or appreciation that a letter will likely be read by another. Mere conceivable possibility or chance that a third person would read a letter does not constitute intent.

This case briefing chart helps focus the intent sub-issue. It extracts the facts, holdings, and reasons and policies of the cases concerning this sub-issue. The *Willow* case is not included because it is irrelevant to the sub-issue. The chart also extracts the relevant facts from Dooley's case. The case briefing chart thus contains the basic information you need to analyze the problem. You may find that using this chart, or a similar chart, will help your analysis. The following steps provide a method for analyzing this or any other common law issue.

1. Determine how the facts of the decided cases support your client's position.

Because each case is decided on the basis of unique facts, it is important to understand the facts of each case completely. First identify similarities and differences between the facts of the decided cases and those of your client's case. In each instance, ask yourself how the facts of a case lend support to your client's position. If a decision is favorable to your client's position, you should show that the decision is factually similar. If the decision is unfavorable, you should try to show that the decision involves different facts.

The holdings in the case briefing chart provide an idea of what cases are likely to be useful to your client. If possible, your client would like to show that he had no intent to publish. *Simmons v. Deluxe Plaza Hotel* is likely to be helpful because the court in that case held that the defendant had no intent to publish. You should look for ways in which the facts of *Simmons* are analogous to the facts of our case.

In *Simmons v. Deluxe Plaza Hotel*, the defendant wrote a letter to the plaintiff containing false accusations against him. The defendant attempted to ensure that only the plaintiff would read the letter by addressing it to him personally and sending it by certified mail. Despite these precautions, the plaintiff's wife read the letter. *Simmons* is like the present case because Dooley, like the defendant hotel manager, did not intend to distribute the fliers to third persons after his conversation with Fremont. He intended to destroy the fliers when he returned to his apartment, and it was only by accident that they were released. In any event, he never intended distribution to passersby, just as the defendant in *Simmons* did not intend the plaintiff's wife to read the letter.

The holdings in the case briefing chart also suggest the case your opponent will want to use. Your opponent may try to argue that Dooley intended to distribute the fliers. Because *White v. Ball* held that there was intent, your opponent will try to analogize *White* to our case. You must therefore be prepared to distinguish *White*.

In *White v. Ball*, the defendant wrote a third person—a company president—making false accusations against company employees. The court found intentional publication because the president received and read the letter. *White* is different from Dooley's case in that the release of the fliers was not intended and, unlike the defendant in *White*, Dooley did not address his accusations directly to a third person. This analysis indicates that the interpretation of *White* and *Simmons* most favorable to your client would emphasize the unintentional release of the fliers. Draw an analogy to *Simmons* and distinguish *White* to support that conclusion.

2. Determine how the facts of the decided cases support your opponent's position.

The omission of certain facts in the previous discussion suggests how your opponent will use the decided cases. To identify the facts supporting the opposing position you must think like your opponent. Actually construct the best opposing arguments. Where you try to show similarities, your opponent will try to show differences. Where you find distinctions, your opponent will find analogies.

Thus, in *White v. Ball*, the defendant prepared a false letter, fully intending to send it to a third person. Similarly, Dooley prepared a false flier with intent to distribute it to third parties. In both *White* and the present case, the defamatory material was received and read by third persons. Preparation with intent to publish makes *Simmons v. Deluxe Plaza Hotel* different from these facts. In *Simmons*, the defendant prepared a letter intending that only the plaintiff see it. That an unintended third person read the letter was not enough for publication. In Dooley's case, although passersby rather than tenants read the flier, Dooley intended to distribute it to third parties when he prepared it. These cases suggest that your opponent's strongest case would be based on Dooley's preparation and printing of the fliers with intent to distribute them. Your opponent would rely on *White* and distinguish *Simmons*.

3. Determine how the reasons and policies of the decided cases support your client's position.

The factual similarities and differences between the decided cases and the present case are significant only to the extent that they are given importance by the reasons and policies of the decided cases. Because the intent issue was of concern in both *White* and *Simmons*, the factual analysis in the present case has focused on the absence or presence of facts that indicate an intent to publish. The analysis has suggested two interpretations, one based on intent at the time of preparation and the other based on intent at the time of distribution. Neither of the decided cases specifically addresses this distinction.

The next level of analysis requires examination of the reasons and policies of the decisions. This examination could show what considerations the courts thought were important to the question of intent. Such considerations assist the analysis of the present case because the courts indicate that some principles are more significant than others, despite different factual settings. The reasons and policies in the case briefing chart provide a basis for this analysis.

The court in *Simmons* refused to find publication simply on the possibility that someone other than the plaintiff would read the letter. The court's conclusion that the defendant "was not reasonably chargeable with appreciation or knowledge of the likelihood that the letter would be opened and read by another" suggests that intent at the time of distribution is required for publication. Dooley originally intended to distribute the fliers after they were printed, but after they were printed he decided not to distribute them at all. At that point, you would reason, the possibility of the accident, just like the possibility of a third person reading the letter in *Simmons*, was speculative. The court in *White v. Ball* focused on receipt of defamatory material by a third person and the subsequent damage caused to the plaintiff's reputation. *White* must be viewed narrowly rather than broadly because, as the court said in *Simmons*, delivery of defamatory material to a third person is not enough. You would conclude that there must be an intent to publish at the time of distribution.

4. Determine how the reasons and policies of the decided cases support your opponent's position.

Your opponent will emphasize reasons that you would downplay and de-emphasize reasons you believe to be significant. Your opponent may also show that your policy arguments are inapplicable because of the different factual situation presented by this case and demonstrate why his or her policy arguments are more relevant and important. The reasons and policies in the briefing chart provide a starting point.

The court in *White v. Ball*, your opponent would argue, shows primary concern for a person's reputation. This concern is illustrated by the court's observation that receipt by a third person is what makes the defamation damaging. If intent to publish the defamatory material is what made the defendant blameworthy in *White*, then Dooley should also be held blameworthy. By intending to harm Fremont's reputation and by writing and printing a flier to do so, Dooley showed that he was prepared to go to great lengths to injure him. Even assuming his change of mind was genuine, your opponent would reason, Dooley set in motion a series of events that resulted in harm to Fremont.

Simmons is different from Dooley's situation because in *Simmons* there was an unintentional distribution of defamatory material. Dooley, on the other hand, intentionally prepared and printed the flier for distribution. Persons who print 200 copies of a flier, and who hold them so carelessly that an accident sets them loose in the wind, are not unintentionally defaming others. If Dooley had not taken his scheme of damaging Fremont's reputation as far as he did, your opponent would conclude, the fliers would not have been distributed.

You might depict the first four steps in this method by using the chart below:

	Intent to Publish **ANALYSIS CHART**	
	Why Element Is Met **(Opponent's Argument)**	**Why Element Is Not Met** **(Our Client's Argument)**
Facts	*White* is analogous. The defendant prepared a letter with intent to send it to a third person. Similarly, Dooley prepared the flier with intent to distribute it. *Simmons* is distinguishable. In that case, the defendant intended only that the plaintiff see the letter when he wrote it. In our case, Dooley intended the fliers to be read by third persons when he prepared them.	*Simmons* is analogous. The defendant in that case did not intend the letter to be read by third persons. The letter was addressed to the plaintiff personally and sent by certified mail. Similarly, Dooley did not intend anyone to read the fliers. They were disseminated by accident. *White* is distinguishable. The defendant wrote a letter to a company president, who then read the letter. In our case, by contrast, Dooley did not intend anyone to read the fliers at the time of their release.
Reasons and Policies	The *White* court stated that receipt by a third person is what makes false statements damaging. Intent to publish fliers makes Dooley blameworthy. Dooley intended to hurt Fremont's reputation, and wrote and printed fliers to do so. Even though he changed his mind, the fliers would not have been released if he hadn't prepared them. *Simmons* is different because the defendant did not intend publication.	Intent occurs when there is reasonable appreciation or knowledge that material would be read by third persons. The mere possibility or chance that a third person would read the material does not demonstrate intent. When Dooley decided not to distribute the fliers, the possibility of an accident that would release the fliers was as remote as the possibility that a third person would read the letter in *Simmons*. *White* is different because the defendant wrote a letter to the company president and had reason to believe that he would read it.

5. Evaluate the strength of your client's case.

The process of constructing and evaluating arguments runs from the technical level of comparing facts to increasingly abstract levels involving basic assumptions and values about the point at which one should be held blameworthy for damage to the reputation of another. Your conclusion should be based on a careful examination and analysis of the facts, policies, and reasons of the decided cases and their application to the present case. You might conclude that there was no publication because the fliers were distributed when Dooley no longer intended to distribute them and because they were distributed accidentally to third persons. This interpretation follows from *White* and *Simmons* and seems to be the most likely outcome here. But you might also conclude that there was publication because the fliers were written and printed for distribution to third persons and then were actually distributed to third persons. That conclusion also reasonably follows from *White* and *Simmons*.

Whatever your thoughts are about the strength of your client's case, you must draw a conclusion and you must be prepared to show that your conclusion is more reasonable than any other. This is not to say that the law will always clearly favor your client's position, or that you must always give your clients the answers they would like to hear. You must remember, however, that your client wants an answer. Whether you are writing a brief or an office memo, you cannot simply state the competing considerations or describe the relevant cases. You must scrutinize each consideration, weigh it, and then balance it against other considerations. If you cannot come to a satisfactory conclusion, think about it some more. Reaching a well-reasoned conclusion requires careful reading of the cases and thoughtful analysis. There is always a good reason, if not a definitive one, for preferring one side to another. Chapter 9 (Reaching a Conclusion) provides a framework for reaching a conclusion that you should use to check your analysis.

EXERCISES

Work through the following exercises using the analysis principles discussed in this chapter. Although the process may seem mechanical, you will become more comfortable as you gain familiarity with it.

Exercise 7-A

Use the five principles described in this chapter to analyze the sub-issue of the falsity of the fliers in the Dooley case:

1. Prepare a case briefing chart on the sub-issue.

2. Prepare an analysis chart on the sub-issue

* 3. Evaluate the strength of Dooley's position on the falsity of the fliers.

Exercise 7-B

Fourteen-year-old Andrew Quale was struck by a truck while riding his bicycle. Although his injuries seemed slight, his mother, Mary Quale, took him to the hospital. His sole complaint was a headache. After Mary described the accident, Dr. Richard Farmer ordered X-rays. The X-rays did not indicate a skull fracture. Farmer did not examine the back of the boy's head, where there was a red mark, nor did he use the other diagnostic procedures that are standard in such cases. Farmer sent the boy home and asked his mother to observe him. Andrew died early the next morning. The coroner concluded from an autopsy that the boy died from hemorrhaging due to a basal skull fracture.

Mary Quale has asked you to sue Farmer for malpractice. You contacted another doctor as a possible expert witness. He told you that there is no doubt the doctor was negligent. In answer to your question about the likelihood of the boy's survival if there had been proper treatment, he said that the mortality rate for such injuries was about 100 percent without surgery. Then he added, "There is a reasonable medical possibility, 1 chance out of 2, maybe a little higher, that he would have survived with surgery."

Assume that Farmer was negligent. Did Farmer's negligence proximately cause the boy's death? There are two relevant cases in your state:

Moulton v. Ginocchio (1996)

Craig Moulton, who is the administrator of the decedent's estate, brought this action against Samuel Ginocchio, a physician, for negligence in treating the decedent's illness. The trial court dismissed the complaint on the ground that the doctor's negligence did not proximately cause her death. We disagree and reverse. The decedent, a diabetic, went to Ginocchio's hospital with intense abdominal pain, which Ginocchio diagnosed as a stomach "bug." He gave her pain medication and released her. She died several hours later from massive hemorrhaging caused by an intestinal obstruction. Ginocchio claims that there is no basis for concluding with certainty that his negligent diagnosis and treatment caused her death. The law does not require certainty, however; a physician is answerable if he prevents a substantial possibility of survival. Moulton's experts testified categorically and without contradiction that the decedent would have survived had she undergone prompt surgery. Moulton, therefore, satisfied the "substantial possibility" requirement.

Mallard v. Harkin (1999)

Eleanor Mallard brought suit against Joseph Harkin, a physician, for Harkin's allegedly negligent failure to immediately diagnose and perform surgery to arrest a degenerative disease that has now left Mallard paralyzed. The trial court found that Harkin breached his duty of reasonable care but that his actions did not proximately cause Mallard's condition. Only the latter ruling has been appealed. We agree with the trial court and affirm.

We held in *Moulton v. Ginocchio* (1996) that a doctor is liable when his negligence "prevents a substantial possibility of survival" for the decedent. In that case, there was testimony that the decedent would have survived. Traditional standards of proximate cause similarly require evidence that the result was more likely than not caused by the act. Mallard does not meet that standard. Mallard's expert witness testified that prompt surgery would have given Mallard "a possibility" of recovery but that she "probably would not have recovered."

It is an attractive and emotionally appealing idea that a physician should be held liable for the loss of even a remote chance of full recovery from a debilitating disease or injury. But such a rule would result in an unjust situation in which the physician would be held accountable for harm that he did not cause and may not have been able to prevent. We refuse, as a matter of public policy, to hold a physician liable on a mere possibility.

1. Prepare a case briefing chart for the question in this problem.

2. Prepare an analysis chart for the question in this problem.

3. Evaluate the strength of Quale's position.

Exercise 7-C

Bradley Greenleaf just finished renovating an old house located on a busy street in Porterville. The house, which is now the office for his twelve-person architectural firm, cost $245,000. The renovations, including retrofitting the house with solar panels, cost an additional $195,000. The solar panels provide heating and cooling for the air and water in the building, but they do not provide electricity. His firm, Greenleaf Associates, which specializes in solar design for residences, uses the building as a model for persons who are interested in constructing or retrofitting homes with solar panels. Its extensive "You Can Do It" promotional campaign relies heavily on the building for that purpose.

Peter Elliot owns the property just west of Greenleaf's office. Recently, Elliot erected two large billboards that shield the sun's rays from the panels by early afternoon and force Greenleaf to rely on conventional energy sources. As a result, Greenleaf is paying substantially more than before in utility bills (about $500 per month, he estimates), and his promotional appeal is less attractive. What good is solar energy, some potential customers ask, if it can be blocked? Greenleaf talked to Elliot about this problem. Elliot apologized for any inconvenience but refused to remove the billboards because he would lose too much money.

Greenleaf has asked you if he has a basis for a lawsuit against Elliot. You have determined that there are no relevant statutes, easements, or zoning provisions. There are, however, three relevant cases from this state.

Shover v. Scott (1889)

Larry Shover brought an action against Wayne Scott, an adjoining landowner, for damage caused by Scott's excavation of adjacent land. The trial court found that the excavation caused Shover's land to cave in, destroyed a barn and some fences, and greatly devalued Shover's property. It ordered judgment for Shover. We affirm.

The maxim that landowners must so enjoy their property as not to injure the property of another has been interpreted in this state to mean that they must enjoy their property without injuring a legal right in the property of another. A landowner has the legal right to lateral support of his lot from the adjoining land. If the support is removed, the owner has a right of action against the person removing the support for the amount of the damages sustained to the land.

Blum v. Disposal Systems, Inc. (1997)

Disposal Systems, Inc. (DSI) operates a landfill adjacent to Loretta Blum's hog farm. Blum brought a nuisance action against DSI, alleging that noise and vibrations generated by DSI's trash-hauling trucks caused the conception rate of Blum's sows to decrease from 80% to 30%. The trial court found that the alleged facts were true but nevertheless entered judgment for DSI, holding that its use of the land was reasonable and therefore not a nuisance. We reverse.

Whether one's use of property is reasonable is determined by the effect such use has on the neighboring property. In private nuisance actions, therefore, we must balance the interests of the respective landowners. Although mere annoyance or inconvenience will not support an action for nuisance, a use of property that essentially confiscates or destroys the neighboring property is unreasonable and constitutes a private nuisance. The landfill operation has had that effect on Blum's hog farm.

The following case is from another state:

Cassells International v. Avery Resorts (2012)

Cassells International, which owns a large resort hotel on an ocean beach, brought suit against Avery Resorts, a neighboring hotel owner, to prevent construction of a ten-story addition to Avery's existing hotel. Cassells claims that the addition will cast a shadow on its beaches and other sunbathing areas and will render these areas unfit for the use and enjoyment of its guests. The trial court refused to enjoin construction of the addition. We agree.

   The doctrine of nuisance does not mean that a property owner must never use the property to the injury of another, but rather that the owner may not use the property to injure the legal rights of another. We have found only one American case (*Cohen v. Andrus*) establishing—in the absence of a contractual or statutory obligation—that a property owner has a legal right to the free flow of light that can be protected in a nuisance action. In that case, shade from defendant's proposed construction on adjacent property threatened to interfere with the plaintiff's solar collector. The court's decision emphasized the increasing need for solar energy. These considerations do not apply here. Affirmed.

1. For the nuisance rule, prepare an elements chart to identify any givens and sub-issue(s) in this problem.

2. For one sub-issue chosen by you or your professor:

   a. Prepare a case briefing chart for this sub-issue.

   b. Prepare an analysis chart for this sub-issue.

   c. Evaluate the strength of Greenleaf's position.

8

Statutory Analysis

Statutory analysis is the process of determining how statutes apply to a given situation and what effect they may have.[1] Statutory analysis differs from common law analysis because it focuses on the meaning of legislative pronouncements rather than judicial ones. Legislatures write rules in broad strokes. Because most statutes are enacted to cover categories of future situations, statutory analysis requires one to determine how these broad rules affect particular cases. Statutory analysis therefore focuses on the meaning of the statutory text. The purpose of the analysis is to determine whether the category described by the text does or does not apply to your client's situation.

Common law analysis, by contrast, requires one to compare and contrast factual situations. Common law rules tend to represent a synthesis of the decided cases, and these rules may change as courts decide new cases involving different factual situations. The specific facts of decided cases are thus as important as—if not more important than—the common law rules themselves. In statutory analysis, the text of the statutory rule tends to be more important than the facts of the decided cases. Statutory analysis thus tends to be deductive, while common law analysis tends to be inductive.

Statutory analysis is also different because statutes are less easily modified by courts than are common law principles. The doctrine of separation of powers—under which the legislature writes statutes and courts interpret them—limits courts to ascertaining and carrying out the legislative will. Courts may expand or contract the scope of a

---

1. The basic rules for statutory analysis also apply to the analysis of administrative regulations, local ordinances, and other public laws that contain categorical rules.

statutory rule when the statutory language permits such flexibility, but they may never disregard an applicable statute unless it is unconstitutional. On the other hand, courts are free to modify or reject common law rules, within the limits of precedent and *stare decisis,* because modifying or rejecting common law rules does not encroach on the prerogatives of another branch of government.

Predicting how a court might apply or fail to apply a statute to your client's case requires an understanding of how courts approach statutory analysis. The courts (and, in some jurisdictions, legislatures) have developed rules or canons of statutory construction. These rules are intended to help attorneys and courts interpret statutes.[2]

Despite these differences, common law and statutory analysis are similar in that both require an examination of potential weaknesses in your client's position. That is best accomplished, as explained in Chapter 7 (Common Law Analysis), by developing potential opposing positions and evaluating their strength. Every case involving the possible application of a statute or statutory provision involves these questions: (1) How is the statute or statutory provision applicable to my client's case? (2) How is the statute or statutory provision inapplicable to my client's case? The more applicable it is, the more it should dictate the outcome of the case. The more inapplicable it is, the less it should dictate the outcome.

Common law and statutory analysis are also similar when courts have decided relevant cases involving the statute. You must still examine the text of the statute to determine how it applies to your client's situation, but you must also compare and contrast the facts of decided cases with the facts of your case. This kind of statutory analysis is a hybrid of "pure" statutory analysis and common law analysis.

There are two steps in statutory analysis. The first is to determine whether the statute covers your client's situation at all. Statutes impose restrictions on certain people or activities, provide benefits to certain others, or establish procedures for the orderly accomplishment of certain goals. Your first task is to decide whether the statute covers the individual, group, or activity in your case. If the statute is applicable, the second step is to evaluate what effect application of the statute will have on your client's problem. This requires you to determine what conduct is commanded, prohibited, or regulated; whether your client's actions complied with or contravened the statute; and what the consequences of non-compliance are to your client.

---

2. There are numerous canons of construction. A standard work in this area is NORMAN J. SINGER, SUTHERLAND STATUTORY CONSTRUCTION (7th ed. 2007), which collects all of the rules with citations to representative federal and state cases and reprints selected scholarly articles on the subject.

Statutory analysis can best be understood by use of a hypothetical problem.

> Until the recent election, members of the Liberal Party held all seven seats on the Grand View City Council. The Conservatives, who promised in the recent election to significantly reorder the city's budget priorities, now outnumber the Liberals on the Council by four to three. Your client, Joshua Smith, an important member of the Liberal Party, learned that the four Conservative members plan to meet privately within several weeks to write their proposed budget. This budget will then be presented to the full Council. The budget goes into effect once it has been adopted by a majority of the Council. Council meetings require a quorum of five. The Conservatives told Smith that neither hc nor any other member of the public would be permitted to attend the private meeting. The four members do not constitute any formal Council committee.

Is the Conservatives' position lawful under the state Open Meetings Act? That Act provides:

Sec. 1. Purpose. It is vital in a democratic society that public business be performed in an open and public manner so that the citizens shall be advised of the performance of public officials and of the decisions that are made by such officials in formulating and executing public policy. Toward this end, this chapter is adopted and shall be construed.

Sec. 2. Definitions. As used in this Act:

(a) "Meeting" means the convening of a public body for the purpose of deliberating toward or rendering a decision on a public policy.
(b) "Public body" means any state or local legislative body, including a board, commission, committee, subcommittee, authority, or council that is empowered by law to exercise governmental or proprietary functions.

Sec. 3. All meetings of a public body shall be open to the public and shall be held in a place available to the general public.

The state court of appeals has decided one case concerning this statute:

Times-Journal Co. v. McPhee (1977)

The appellant, Times-Journal Co., brought an action seeking declaratory and injunctive relief against McPhee and the other members of the Bedford Board of Education, claiming that they had violated, and planned to continue violating, the state Open Meetings Act by closing a series of "preliminary" and "informal" meetings to the public. The trial court granted the defendants' motion to dismiss on the ground that no formal actions were taken at these meetings, even though they were attended by the entire board. Therefore, the court reasoned, they were not "meetings" within the meaning of the Act. We reverse.

Section 2(a) defines "meeting" as the convening of a public body "for the purpose of *deliberating toward* or rendering a decision on a public policy" (emphasis supplied). Every step in the decision-making process, including the decision itself, is necessarily part of the deliberation that the legislature intended to affect by enactment of the statute before us. "Preliminary" and "informal" meetings are necessarily part of that deliberative process.

The Open Meetings Act, like many statutes, contains a statement of purpose, definitions, and substantive provisions. To understand a statute, you need to read it carefully. Then reread the substantive provisions. These provisions state what the statute requires, prohibits, or allows. They are the central parts of the statute. In this case, the substantive provisions are in section 3 of the Act.

Section 3 would require the caucus of the four Conservative members to be open if it is a "meeting" and if these members constitute a "public body." Words in statutes are ordinarily interpreted according to their customary meaning and usage, as defined in a dictionary. But legislatures often want certain words or phrases in a statute to have a different or more specific meaning. When this occurs, the statute usually will contain its own set of definitions. The terms "meeting" and "public body" are both defined in section 2 of the Open Meetings Act. The two questions posed by the problem are whether the definitions of these terms have been met.

A "meeting" occurs under section 2(a) if there is (1) a convening (2) of a public body (3) for the purpose of deliberating toward or rendering a decision (4) on a public policy. The first and fourth elements are givens because the four Conservative members are meeting to write a budget. The third element is met because of *Times-Journal Co. v. McPhee*, which further defined the meaning of the term "meeting." In that case, the court emphasized the deliberative nature of "preliminary" or "informal" meetings to support its conclusion that they were meetings within the meaning of section 2(a). The same type of deliberation would occur at the caucus of the Conservatives. They would be deliberating toward, and possibly deciding, the budget. This construction would most likely be controlling. The second element—whether these four members constitute a "public body"—is a more difficult question. The applicability of this element is also the second question posed by the problem.

The following chart depicts this analysis:

Meeting ELEMENTS CHART		
Element	**Facts of Our Case**	**Element Met?**
Convening	Four Council members meet privately	Yes
of a public body	Four-member Conservative majority of City Council; five required for quorum	Maybe
for the purpose of: deliberating toward -or-	Will write proposed budget, which will then be presented to full Council	Yes
rendering a decision	Will write proposed budget, which will then be presented to full Council	Maybe
on a public policy	Budget	Yes

A "public body" exists under section 2(b) when there is (1) a state or local legislative body, including a board, commission, committee, subcommittee, authority, or council (2) that is empowered by law to exercise governmental or proprietary functions. The Grand View City Council is a local legislative body under the first element, but it is not clear whether a majority of the Council would be held to constitute the Council. It is also unclear whether the second element is met because these four members constitute a majority but not a quorum of the Council.

This analysis may be shown as follows:

Public Body ELEMENTS CHART		
Element	**Facts of Our Case**	**Element Met?**
State or local legislative body, including a board, commission, committee, authority, or council	Four-member Conservative majority of City Council	Maybe
Empowered by law to exercise governmental or proprietary functions	Five members of seven-member Council required for quorum	Maybe

Before analyzing a statutory issue that involves cases, you may find it helpful to develop a case briefing chart like the one shown in Chapter 7 (Common Law Analysis). In this problem, however, a case briefing chart is not likely to be helpful because there is only one relevant case, and it is based primarily on the deliberation issue.

As the above elements chart indicates, the problem has two sub-issues—whether the four members are a "local legislative body" and whether they are empowered to exercise "governmental or proprietary functions." The following principles provide a method for resolving these sub-issues, using the governmental functions sub-issue as an example. (The local legislative body sub-issue is addressed in Exercise 8-A.)

1. Determine how the language of the statute, and the facts of any cases interpreting the statute, support your client's position.

The *plain meaning* rule is a keystone of statutory construction. Courts presume that words and phrases in a statute have a meaning common to drafter and reader alike and that reasonable persons would not disagree over what the meaning is. Courts therefore tend not to stretch the meaning of a term or phrase beyond its ordinary understanding. Courts also assume that statutory drafters have followed commonly accepted rules of grammar and punctuation.

As already stated, a court will also consider previous cases construing the same or a similar statute. The court will follow the principles of precedent and *stare decisis* whenever previous decisions do not clearly conflict with the plain meaning and clear intent of the statute in question.

According to section 2(b), any entity that has the legal authority to exercise governmental or proprietary functions, including those listed, is a "public body." Although the term is defined in the statute, its applicability to the facts of your client's case is uncertain. Governmental functions would be your focus, however, because proprietary functions are based on ownership. You would argue that the four Conservative members are a public body because they control the Council, an entity that exercises governmental functions. This control exists because they have enough votes to compel adoption of any budget they draft. In that significant sense, their formulation of a budget at a secret meeting would be tantamount to the exercise of a governmental function. They do not need a quorum at this caucus because they can achieve the needed quorum when the full Council meets to consider the budget they have proposed. The *de facto* budget will then become the legal budget. For these reasons, the Conservatives can exercise governmental functions under section 2(b).

2. **Determine how the language of the statute, and the facts of any cases interpreting the statute, support your opponent's position.**

The same statutory language provides support for the opposite conclusion. Where you try to show how the language of a statute applies to your client's situation, your opponent will try to show that the language of the statute does not apply. Where you try to analogize cases interpreting the language to support your conclusion, he will show that these cases are inapplicable or that they support his position.

Your opponent will argue that "governmental functions" should not be enlarged by judicial interpretation to include a private meeting of Council members belonging to the same party. They cannot exercise any governmental functions at the secret meeting because the Conservative caucus is short of the needed quorum (even if all the other procedural requirements for calling a City Council meeting could be sidestepped). The full Council must still adopt the budget for it to have the force of law, and that Council meeting will be open to the public.

3. **Determine how the policies of the statute, and the policies of any cases interpreting the statute, support your client's position.**

Another significant statutory construction rule is that the statute should be interpreted to carry out the legislature's intent. The initial presumption is that the legislature intended to say what it actually said. When the intent is clear from the statutory language, and application of the statute unambiguously advances that intent, the court's function is straightforward. When the provision itself is unclear or could be applied in a way that is not in accord with the intent of the statute, the court is likely to engage in statutory interpretation. The overriding concern will then be to ascertain and give effect to the legislature's intent.

The task of ascertaining legislative intent is relatively easy if the purpose of the legislation is explained in a preamble or introductory section of the statute. If it is not, the court will look at the entire statute and try to discern a legislative purpose from its provisions. The legislative history of a statute (published records of hearings, debates, committee reports, proposed bills, and other materials that shed light on what the legislators did and why) can also be a valuable guide to the statute's purpose and the meaning of specific provisions. Courts interpreting federal statutes may consult legislative history because it is printed and accessible. Generally there is little, if any, legislative history for most state statutes because state legislative proceedings are rarely reduced to writing. Occasionally, the drafters will write a commentary explaining the intent of the legislation and giving some guidance on how the provisions are meant to be applied.

Be aware that some courts, particularly federal courts, believe that it is inappropriate to use committee reports, hearing records, legislative debates, and similar materials to interpret statutes. They view the law as being the text of the statute, which the legislature adopted. In their view, statements or materials written by individual legislators, committees, or their staffs should not be used to interpret or modify the statute itself.

Although there is no legislative history for the Open Meetings Act, section 1 of the Act states the legislature's intent. It declares in broad terms the importance of conducting "public business" in an "open and public manner" so that citizens can know what decisions are made, how they are made, and the reasons for these decisions. Section 1 also requires interpretation of the Act to effectuate this goal. The *McPhee* court carried out the purpose of the Act by concluding that each step in the decision-making process ought to be made public.

These policies are particularly applicable here because the most important steps in the decision-making process will occur at the caucus. The Conservative members will resolve many, if not all, of their differences at the caucus and thus foreclose full debate before the full Council. Because the Conservatives will in all likelihood be locked into their positions after the caucus, the debate at the Council meeting will be more form than substance. As a result, an important piece of "public business," the budget, will not be resolved in the "open and public manner" contemplated by the legislature. Section 1 implies that the legislature believed open meetings to be of greater importance than the privacy of political parties, and that decision should be respected.

4. Determine how the policies of the statute, and the policies of any cases interpreting the statute, support your opponent's position.

Other policies in the statute—some expressly stated, some merely implicit in the legislative scheme—support the opposing view. Your opponent will attempt to show that your policy arguments do not apply to the facts of this case or that they are simply not as important as others that support his client's position.

The statutory emphasis on "public body," "public business," and governmental functions indicates that the legislature did not intend the Open Meetings Act to reach what is essentially private behavior. The planned caucus is only for members of a private political party. *McPhee* supports this conclusion because the court in that case dealt with meetings of the full Board of Education, not with some faction of the Board. To require that private groups open their meetings to the public because of their conceivable impact on public business would stretch the Act far beyond its intended meaning. In any event, the Conservatives and Liberals will almost certainly debate each other at the Council meeting. The Conservative budget proposal and the Council's final budget will tell people what choices were made.

There is no guarantee that debate will be stifled or foreclosed at the City Council meeting. The caucus will merely provide the Conservative members, all of whom are newly elected, with a chance to discuss the budget and arrive at a consensus. No facts support the conclusion that the four members will vote as a bloc on every single budget issue debated before the City Council. They may disagree on some issues initially, or they may change their minds as they listen to the debate or receive new information. Arguments to the contrary are simply speculative.

The following chart shows the first four steps of this analysis:

Governmental Functions ANALYSIS CHART		
	Why Element Is Met (Our Client's Argument)	**Why Element Is Not Met (Opponent's Argument)**
Facts	City Council has seven members. Four Conservatives want to meet secretly to adopt a proposed budget. At the meeting, they will be able to adopt the budget they wrote secretly.	Five members are required for a quorum. The budget cannot be adopted at the meeting. The meeting is for members of the same political party to develop a budget proposal.
Policies	"Public business" should be conducted in an open and public manner so that citizens know what decisions are made and the reasons for those decisions. The Conservatives will likely resolve many or all differences in the secret meeting. The Council debate will not include much real debate. The public will not know the choices that were made or the reasons for those choices.	The statute was not intended to reach private behavior. The Conservatives may not resolve their differences at the private meeting. At the Council meeting, the Conservatives may not vote together on all issues; they may change their minds. The Liberals and the Conservatives will almost certainly debate each other. The proposed budget by Conservatives and the Council's final budget will inform the public of the choices that were made.

5. Evaluate the strength of your client's position.

Although the issue can be characterized as a technical one involving the definition of several words, it actually raises important and competing policy considerations that need to be reconciled. Ultimately, your client probably has a stronger legal position because the caucus, a majority of the Council, is likely to greatly influence, if not dictate, the budget adopted by the City Council. You should check this result using the factors in Chapter 9 (Reaching a Conclusion). Although there is room for a contrary point of view, the more important point is that you must draw a conclusion and be able to demonstrate that your conclusion is more reasonable than any other. As noted earlier, your client wants an answer. It is not enough to merely list competing considerations; you must scrutinize and evaluate their merits.

This illustration focuses on analysis of the first kind of statutory issue—whether the statute applies to the case. There may be an additional question—what effect application of the statute will have on your client. If Smith is able to obtain relief beforehand, the Conservatives likely will be required to hold an open meeting. If the Conservatives have already met, however, the question is more complicated. What remedy is appropriate? A court will look at the statute to see what guidance, if any, it includes.

The statutory construction rules used in this chapter—plain meaning and legislative intent—are relatively straightforward. Other statutory construction rules, however, are more subtle. The purpose of these other rules is also to ascertain legislative purpose from the language of the statute. They work by creating a presumption that a particular question should be resolved in a particular way unless the legislature clearly intended otherwise. A court is likely to presume, for example, that the legislature did not intend an unjust or absurd result and will construe the statute accordingly. It is likely to presume that the legislature was aware of the common law and prior statutes affecting the categories that are the subject of the statute and will harmonize the statute with prior law if it can.

A rule known by its Latin title, *ejusdem generis* (of the same kind or class), is also widely employed. This rule says that if a general term precedes or follows a list of specific terms, the general term is presumably limited to items of the same kind as those specified in the list.

Suppose your client's car and trailer containing personal items were stolen from a motel parking lot and never recovered. He consults you four months after the theft, wanting to know whether he can recover from the motel owner. In your state, there is a ninety-day statute of limitations for "the recovery or conversion of personal property, wearing apparel, trunks, valises, or baggage left at a hotel or other public lodging." This example presents a classic instance in which a court might apply the *ejusdem generis* rule. The court could reason that the enumerated items—wearing apparel, baggage, and so forth—are the kinds of personal property one might take into a hotel room. A car and trailer do not fit within the enumerated list (are not of the same kind or class) and so are not included within the general term "personal property." That means your client could recover for the loss of his car and trailer because the ninety-day statute of limitations does not apply. He could not, however, recover for the loss of his personal items. The court would reach this conclusion only after deciding that the legislature did not intend the contrary.

You should consult the law in your jurisdiction to see which rules of construction have been adopted. Because it is difficult to argue against a presumption, you should try to fit your case within one or more of the presumptions that have been recognized.

EXERCISES

Work through the following exercises with the help of the analysis principles discussed in this chapter. Try to understand the similarities and differences between common law analysis and statutory analysis, and remember that the process will get easier as you become familiar with it.

Exercise 8-A

Using the guidelines described in this chapter, evaluate the strength of Smith's position on whether the four Conservative members of the City Council constitute a "state or local legislative body."

Exercise 8-B

What arguments would you make for the motel owner in the example involving the theft of a car and trailer from a motel parking lot?

Exercise 8-C

For six months Marianne Preston was a temporary employee of Jade Enterprises, Inc. As soon as her term of employment ended, she filed a complaint with the state Fair Employment Commission accusing her former employer of sexual harassment. The Commission ordered a hearing before an administrative law judge who found that Jade had engaged in sexual harassment. The judge ordered Jade to pay Preston compensatory damages of $30,000 for humiliation and emotional pain and distress.

The Fair Employment Act provides in part:

> **Sec. 1.** The purpose of this Act is to eliminate employment discrimination based on race, sex, national or ethnic origin, or handicap by providing effective remedies to the victims of such discrimination.
> . . .
> **Sec. 6.** Upon a finding that an employer has engaged in employment discrimination, including sexual harassment, the Commission shall order the employer to take such action as will effectuate the purpose of the Act, including, but not limited to, hiring, reinstating, or upgrading employees; awarding back pay; and restoring membership in pension and other employee benefit plans.

Jade plans to appeal the administrative law judge's decision on the ground that the Commission is not authorized under the Act to require an employer to pay compensatory damages.

1. Can reasonable minds disagree over the meaning of the phrase "such action as will effectuate the purpose of the Act, including, but not limited to"? Explain how broadly or narrowly the phrase can be construed.

2. Does the *ejusdem generis* rule of construction apply here? What arguments would you make for the Commission? What arguments would you make for Jade Enterprises? Do any other rules of construction apply?

3. How do the stated and implicit purposes of the Act support the Commission's position?

4. How do the stated and implicit purposes of the Act support Jade's position?

5. How should a court decide Jade's appeal? Explain.

Exercise 8-D

The Metropolitan Social Welfare League is an organization composed of social workers and welfare recipients that advocates welfare reform. For two years, the League has urged the city of Lake Rapids to set aside an eighteen-square-block area on the city's east side for low-income housing. That area is now vacant. The League has negotiated with city, state, and federal officials on this matter because the mayor said the proposal was "worth looking into" at a news conference ten months ago.

The area is now zoned for multiple-family housing. The Swift Land Development Corporation applied eight months ago for a zoning amendment to permit the construction of an auto salvage yard on one block of that eighteen-block area. Several other companies are also interested in zoning amendments. Six months ago, the city denied Swift's proposal. Swift immediately filed suit to force approval of the amendment. Last week, the city attorney stated that he thought the city might be wrong in this case. The mayor has stated several times that "City Hall represents the people, not narrow special interest groups."

Can the League now intervene as a defendant under State Court Rule 779.1(3)? State Court Rule 779.1(3), which is codified in the state statutes, provides:

> Anyone shall be permitted to intervene in an action:
>
> . . .
>
> (3) Upon timely application when the representation of the applicant's interest is or may be inadequate and the applicant may be bound by a judgment in the action.

The Drafting Committee for the rules made this comment in drafting Rule 779.1(3):

There may be persons having interests so vital that they ought to have been made parties in the first place. They must be allowed to intervene. Therefore, the court is given no discretion in this regard.

There is one relevant case in this state:

Halsey v. Village of Elk Mound (1986)

The appellee petitioned the Elk Mound Planning Commission to rezone two adjacent parcels within the village from single-family residential to multiple-family residential. The Commission denied his request, and the Town Council agreed. The appellee brought suit against the village to prevent it from interfering with his proposed use for the parcels. The appellants, persons with homes within 300 feet of the parcels, sought to intervene. The trial court determined that the appellants could not intervene because they had not met the requirements of Court Rule 779.1(3). We reverse.

The intervention rule requires (1) timely action by the applicant, (2) possible or actual inadequacy of representation by existing parties, and (3) the possibility that the applicant may be bound by a judgment in the action. There was no unreasonable delay here, since the appellants filed their motion to intervene only three weeks after suit was brought. The appellants were not too late to protect their interests. In addition, the rule requires only that existing representation may be inadequate. The burden of satisfying this requirement must be minimal. The appellants meet this requirement because the village does not purport to represent the interests of their neighborhood. Finally, we read the term "bound" to mean that, as a practical matter, the appellants' ability to protect their interest may be substantially affected. Since the appellants have met all three requirements, they are entitled to intervene.

1. For the intervention rule, prepare an elements chart to identify any givens and sub-issue(s) in this problem.

2. For one sub-issue chosen by you or your professor:
   a. Prepare a case briefing chart for this sub-issue, if appropriate.
   b. Prepare an analysis chart for this sub-issue.
   c. Evaluate the strength of the League's position.

Exercise 8-E

Francine Odegaard was recently elected governor. She received 50.2 percent of the vote, and her opponent received 49.8 percent. A state legislative committee set up to monitor the effects of the Election Campaign Finance Act investigated the funding sources of the two candidates and learned that Odegaard's campaign committee received $41,995 from her grandfather after the election. This amount was precisely the debt with which her campaign committee ended the general election. Odegaard's natural parents died when she was very young. She was raised by her grandfather, Rolf Odegaard, although he never formally adopted her. Her grandfather made no other contributions to her campaign. The committee has drafted a report recommending that he be prosecuted for violating section 31 of the Act. The committee has hired you to review its recommendation.

The Election Campaign Finance Act provides in part:

> **Sec. 2.** This Act is intended to regulate political activity, to regulate campaign financing, and to restrict campaign contributions and expenditures without jeopardizing the ability of candidates for state public office to conduct effective campaigns.
>
> . . .
>
> **Sec. 31.** (a) Except as provided in subsection (b), a person other than a campaign committee member shall not make contributions on behalf of the winner of a primary election for the office of governor in excess of $2,500 for any purpose after the date of such primary election.
>
> (b) A contribution from a member of a candidate's immediate family to the campaign committee for that candidate is exempt from the limitation of subsection (a).
>
> (c) As used in subsection (b), "immediate family" means a spouse, parent, brother, sister, son, or daughter.
>
> . . .
>
> **Sec. 44.** A person who violates the provisions of this Act is guilty of a misdemeanor and shall be fined not more than $5,000.

The highest appellate court in the state has decided the following cases:

Alberts v. Election Commission (1987)

Section 31(a) of the Election Campaign Finance Act prohibits any person from making contributions "on behalf of the winner of a primary election for the office of governor in excess of $2,500 for any purpose after the date of such primary election." The appellant challenges the validity of a trial court determination that he violated section 31(a) by contributing $4,500 to the unsuccessful candidate for governor in the 1984 general election. He argues that he made the contribution to help retire the candidate's debt from the primary. We affirm.

Section 31(a) of the Election Campaign Finance Act was designed to reduce, if not eliminate, the improper influence a contributor gains from a large contribution near the end of the campaign. More generally, the Act was designed to help improve the integrity, and the appearance of integrity, of the election process. These policy considerations make it particularly important that the phrase "for any purpose" be read for its full meaning. We hold that the phrase includes payments for the purpose of reducing primary debts. Affirmed.

Toland v. Election Commission (1994)

Clyde Swanson lost the general election for governor after winning his party's primary election. His son Raymond handled the finances for Clyde's general election campaign. As treasurer, Raymond received funds from various sources, deposited them in his personal checking account, and then wrote checks from that account to pay for campaign expenses. Clyde's largest contribution, a $15,000 check from Alphonse Toland, was processed in this manner. Toland was convicted of a misdemeanor for violating section 31 of the Election Campaign Finance Act. We affirm that conviction.

Section 31 limits contributions to candidates for governor in a general election to $2,500 per person, unless the contributor is a member of the candidate's "immediate family." The immediate family exception is premised on a legislative desire to protect freedom of expression by candidates; donating money is a recognized way of expressing a preference. In addition, the Act's purpose of reducing the corrupting influence of outside financial sources has much less force when the contributor is from the candidate's immediate family. Although Swanson's son is a member of his "immediate family" under section 31(b), the son was a conduit, rather than a source, of the funds. The important purposes of the Act should not be undermined by such transparent schemes.

1. State the general rule and the elements of the rule in this problem.

2. Using an elements chart for the general rule and elements identified in your answer to question 1:
   a. Identify any issue(s) and sub-issue(s) you would discuss in this memorandum.
   b. Identify which of the elements, if any, are givens and explain how the facts resolve each.

3. For the one plausible exception presented by this problem, state the rule and the elements of the rule.

4. Using your answer to question 3, prepare an elements chart to identify the issue in this exception.

5. For the issue identified in question 4:
   a. Prepare a case briefing chart.
   b. Prepare an analysis chart.

9

Reaching a Conclusion

The final step in common law and statutory analysis, as we saw in Chapters 7 and 8, is evaluating the strength of your client's position. A lawyer helps clients make decisions—often painful and difficult decisions. Clients need to be fully informed of their choices and the relative strengths and weaknesses of each choice so they have all the information they need to make a sound decision. Sometimes that requires a lawyer to inform clients that their position is weak or that the law cannot provide them with the remedy they want. Regardless of their choices, clients do not want to worry about whether the lawyer is right, and no lawyer wants a client to regret taking her advice. The best way to avoid both of these undesirable results is to give clients advice that is reliable, accurate, and complete.

Evaluating the strength of your client's position requires judgment about the merits of competing considerations. There is no complete guidebook for exercising good judgment, and there is no substitute for experience with difficult problems. Three basic principles nonetheless provide valuable guidance in evaluating the strength of competing legal positions. In general, the strongest legal positions are those that (1) involve little or no extension of existing law, (2) result in a decision that furthers the policies or purposes of the law, and (3) reach a fair or just outcome for the parties. If all of these factors are in your client's favor, your client will almost certainly prevail. If all are in your opponent's favor, your client will almost certainly lose.

If some factors support your client and some factors support your opponent, drawing a conclusion becomes more difficult. Differences between the outcomes suggested by individual factors reduce the level of certainty that a lawyer can express about a particular position and must be reflected in a memorandum. To the extent that such differences exist, moreover, they will raise more questions about a particular position, requiring further legal research and analysis. This should be reflected in your writing.

Each of the three factors must be considered separately in reaching a conclusion about the strength of your client's position. One way to test each factor is to construct an argument for your client's position and your opponent's position, and then see which is stronger according to that factor. The factors are applied and analyzed in the context of the following problem. (Note that the answers used to illustrate these factors are set out in shorthand form rather than in the way that you would draft your conclusion in a memorandum.)

1. A position is stronger to the extent that it involves little or no extension of existing law.

Judges must determine how the relevant statutes, regulations, cases, and other law apply to the facts of the case. A legal position based on existing law is more likely to win than one involving substantial extension or revision of existing law.

This principle operates on a sliding scale. If no extension of the law is required to support a legal position, the position is very strong. In cases involving the common law, for example, the strongest position will be one based on existing decisions where your client's situation is plainly analogous or plainly distinguishable. In cases involving statutes, the strongest position will be one based on language of the statute that plainly includes or excludes your client's factual situation. A legal position generally is weaker to the extent that it requires a court to extend or revise existing case law, or to interpret a statute in a way that seems to depart from its plain meaning. The other factors described in this chapter may overcome this weakness, however. The most important judicial decisions, in fact, break new legal ground precisely because other factors outweigh a court's deference to existing law.

Your client, Rochelle Timmers, a retired school teacher in her eighties with a perfect driving record, has been injured in a car accident. She was driving to the hospital to visit her husband, who had recently undergone heart surgery. While rounding a corner in the city of Goshen, she unexpectedly encountered a traffic jam caused by the city's traditional St. Patrick's Day parade on a main traffic artery. Timmers was not aware that the traditional parade always traveled down that street. There were no signs, traffic control devices, or police officers to direct traffic or warn motorists. Timmers would like to recover for the damages she suffered when her car collided with another car that was waiting in traffic. Consider whether the city may be liable because the City Council granted the parade permit and knew from previous years that the parade frequently caused a traffic jam.

There are two pertinent cases:

Town of Parkview v. Simon (1993)

While riding her motorcycle, the appellee was injured when she struck the side of an automobile that pulled out into her path. The driver of the automobile was unable to see the appellee approaching because of the shrubbery and tall grass growing in the median, which had been designed and maintained by the town of Parkview. The jury found that the median had been negligently designed and maintained, and awarded the appellee damages. The town appeals the denial of its motion to set aside the verdict.

Traditionally, a private landowner has no duty to maintain his property so that it does not obstruct a motorist's view. However, when a governmental entity creates a condition it knows or should know is dangerous, it must avert the danger or warn the public. Otherwise, it must be held liable for any resulting damages. This rule strikes a balance between the government's broad right to manage public property as it sees fit and its obligations to the safety of motorists. The town of Parkview built and maintained the median and should have known that failing to properly maintain the shrubbery would create a hazard to motorists. Whether the town did so or not was a question for the jury. The trial court did not err in refusing to overturn the verdict. Affirmed.

Brockton v. City of Adrian (1981)

This is an appeal of a summary judgment granted in a wrongful death action. The appellant's decedent drowned when the car in which she was riding went straight through a "T" intersection and into a canal that ran parallel to the intersecting road. The canal is owned by the city. The driver, while approaching the intersection, apparently failed to see four signs: (1) a warning of the approaching "T" intersection; (2) a warning of the decreasing speed limit; (3) a warning of the approaching "STOP" sign; and (4) the "STOP" sign itself. The signs were not obstructed or obscured and met the state requirements for traffic signs. The appellant asserts that the appellee was negligent in failing to warn drivers of the danger posed by the canal located across from the intersection.

The duty to warn was clearly met by the signs, which satisfied the state requirements and were properly maintained. To hold otherwise would improperly penalize diligent municipalities for the negligent conduct of motorists. Judgment affirmed.

The cases show that the city's liability turns on two issues: whether the traffic jam was a hazard and whether the council failed to warn approaching motorists of the hazard. Your summary of the competing arguments might look like this:

Issue 1: Was the traffic jam a hazard?

Client: Yes. The hazard is analogous to the blind median in *Town of Parkview* and the canal in *Brockton*.

Opponent: No. A traffic jam is different from the road feature design in *Town of Parkview* and the adjacent physical hazard in *Brockton*; it is not permanent or dangerous.

Issue 2: Did the city fail to warn approaching motorists of the hazard?

Client: Yes. The failure to warn here is analogous to the failure to warn in *Town of Parkview*. *Brockton*, where warning was given, is thus distinguishable.

Opponent: No, because there was no hazard. The case is thus distinguishable from *Town of Parkview* and *Brockton*. Warning signals weren't given here because they weren't necessary.

This analytical summary indicates that resolution of the problem will turn on whether the unexpected traffic jam was a hazard. Because warning signals were not provided, the city is liable if the traffic jam is a hazard. If the traffic jam is not a hazard, it does not matter that signals were not provided. Your client would like to analogize the decided cases and state that the traffic jam was a hazard. Your opponent would like to distinguish the decided cases because they involved permanent features and state that the traffic jam was not a hazard. As you assemble arguments for each side, check to see whether the arguments made by one side are answered by the other side. If they are not answered, check to see whether they can be answered; that is, whether you can think of an answer you have not considered. In this situation, there is no answer so far to the assertion that the decided cases involve permanent features. You would likely answer that this distinction is immaterial because the parade was a hazard. Because the existing law does not clearly favor one party's position at this point, the first factor does not weigh in favor of either party. The first factor is a toss-up.

2. A position is stronger to the extent that it furthers the policies or purposes of the law.

Cases are decided to further specific purposes, and statutes are adopted for particular reasons. Courts will look to those purposes and reasons to see whether they will be advanced by their decisions. The purpose of a law does not automatically override the text of that law, but a court will test its conclusions about the result indicated by the law to see whether that result is consistent with the purposes of the law. The more clearly a particular position is consistent with the purposes of the law, the stronger it is.

In common law cases, the policies or purposes of the law are stated in previous court decisions. As noted earlier, courts tend to follow previous decisions rather than chart a new or modified course. In some common law cases, however, the result indicated by the law may be inconsistent with the purposes stated by previous courts. There is no widely accepted theory about how to resolve such differences. It is nonetheless true that in such cases courts will be tempted to modify existing case law to further the underlying purposes.

In statutory problems, the policies or reasons for the law may be expressly stated in the statute, or they may be inferred from the statute's language or structure. Committee reports and other sources of legislative history are often helpful. As with common law cases, statutory problems sometimes involve situations in which the language of the statute points to a result that is inconsistent with its underlying policies. Courts tend to respond to such cases in two ways. In some cases, courts find ways to interpret statutes to further their underlying purposes, on the theory that courts should assist in the implementation of statutes. This approach is more likely when the statutory language is flexible or general enough to accommodate such a reading. A legal position based on a general or flexible statute will be weakened to the extent that it contradicts or does not further the underlying purposes of the statute.

In other cases, courts read statutes as they are written, regardless of whether the outcome is consistent with the underlying purposes. This is true especially when the language unambiguously indicates a particular result. The federal courts—including the Supreme Court—often take this approach. A legal position based on an unambiguous statute is likely to prevail even if it contradicts or is inconsistent with the statute's purposes. The rationale is that the legislature, rather than the court, is responsible for correcting problems with statutes.

Your summary concerning the purposes of the law might look like this:

Was the traffic jam a hazard?

Client: Yes. The purpose of the law is to protect motorists from traffic hazards created by the city. The type of hazard does not matter. *Town of Parkview* suggests the purpose of the law is broad enough to extend the term "hazard" to include any danger to motorists created by the city's management of public property. Evidence of the hazard includes its unexpected nature and the accident itself.

Opponent: No. The purpose of the law is to protect motorists from hazards that could not reasonably be known or foreseeable without warning signals. A traffic jam is a foreseeable event in any driving situation, regardless of whether there is a parade.

The summary shows that there are policy arguments for each position. Look carefully, however, at the nature of these arguments. Your client's position focuses on the traffic jam as a hazard. In this part of the analysis, your opponent challenges the premise that a traffic jam is a hazard, saying instead that a traffic jam is foreseeable in any driving situation. Your client's position provides no direct answer to that assertion. Although general policy arguments supporting your client's position are appropriate, they must be sensitive to the facts of the case; otherwise, they seem abstract, even irrelevant. Is there a good answer to the assertion that traffic jams are foreseeable in any driving situation? You might argue that this traffic jam occurred in an unexpected place, but the gist of your opponent's position is that traffic jams often occur in unexpected places. Unless you come up with a better answer your case is weakened.

3. **When the law does not require a particular result, a position is stronger to the extent that it involves a fair or just outcome for the parties.**

One of the worst mistakes a lawyer can make is to assume that the logic of the law matters more than how it affects people. To be sure, there are cases in which the law, its purposes, and the logical structure of an argument dictate a result that the judge might not agree with, but that the judge nonetheless upholds. But when the legal strength of competing positions is otherwise relatively equal, the equities matter a great deal. In such cases, the position that leads to the fairest result is likely to prevail.

As will be explained in more detail in Chapter 26 (Briefs to a Trial Court), sensitivity to the equities is more pronounced at the trial court level than it may be at the appellate court level. Virtually all cases begin in front of trial judges, and trial judges are keenly aware of the facts of a particular case. Their job is to apply the law to real situations involving real people who live in their community and who often watch or participate in the proceedings.

Statements about fairness or justice must be based on particular reasons. Some fairness statements are based on policies expressed in the relevant law. Other fairness statements are based on policies expressed in other laws. Some are based on generally accepted social values.

In this case, the facts of the decided cases and their underlying reasons and policies tend to support your opponent's position, but they do not support it conclusively. Your summary on fairness and justice might look like this:

Client: Timmers had a perfect driving record, is in her eighties, and was on her way to visit her hospitalized husband. It is unfair for Timmers to bear responsibility for the city's failure to warn of the hazard, especially when the city council was aware of the traffic jam and could easily have taken measures to warn unsuspecting motorists. The city will be more careful to warn of future hazards if it is required to compensate Timmers.

Opponent: The accident occurred because of Timmers's negligence. City taxpayers should not be penalized for Timmers's failure to exercise ordinary care in the operation of her car.

The fairness arguments on each side appeal to different values and even to different emotions. Your client's position rests to some extent on sympathy for her situation. Inherent in our culture's concept of fairness is a desire to recognize the needs of people who are in special or difficult situations. But you must be careful how you use facts to gain sympathy. You may want to state that an older driver should not be held to the same standard as other drivers, for example. That statement, however, would hurt your client in two ways. It tacitly admits that your client was not driving as carefully as other drivers, and it seems to condone dangerous driving by senior citizens. You would find it very difficult to defend these positions in court. This example illustrates an important point: You should exclude from your analysis contentions that cannot be even minimally defended.

Your opponent's main fairness argument will likely rest on Timmers's actual behavior and her possible negligence. This argument appears relatively strong in this case because it fits neatly with the claim that she should have been prepared for an unexpected traffic jam. This argument also lessens sympathy for her situation. Because a traffic jam is unlikely to be considered a hazard, a court would probably not hold the city liable in any action brought by Timmers.

The analytical framework used in this chapter requires you to make decisions about the relative strengths of competing positions. It requires you to probe for strengths and weaknesses and to evaluate those strengths and weaknesses in light of the relevant law. It also requires you to develop explanations for the position you take and to be able to explain why that position is better than others.

EXERCISES

The following exercises are intended to help you use this framework.

Exercise 9-A

This exercise is based on the information contained in Exercise 6-A, pp. 89-91. For one issue or sub-issue chosen by you or your professor, evaluate the strength of McKay's position, using the principles described in this chapter.

Exercise 9-B

This exercise is based on the information contained in Exercise 6-B, pp. 91-94. For one issue or sub-issue chosen by you or your professor, evaluate the strength of the *Star City Banner Patriot*'s position, using the principles described in this chapter.

Exercise 9-C

This exercise is based on the information contained in Exercise 6-C, pp. 94-97. For one issue or sub-issue chosen by you or your professor, evaluate the strength of Hughes's position, using the principles described in this chapter.

Basic Concepts of Legal Writing

CHAPTER 10 Organization

G ood organization is fundamental to effective legal writing. No matter how well you have stated the question and the significant facts, how thoughtfully you have analyzed the problem, or how skillfully you have used language, your work will be wasted unless it is organized intelligently. As a lawyer, you will be lucky if you are simply asked to rewrite poorly organized documents. More likely, you will be ignored or misunderstood. This chapter discusses the large-scale, conceptual organization of legal analysis. Once you have decided how to organize your analysis, Chapter 14 (Drafting the Analysis) addresses how to present it in a manner that allows the reader to follow and understand your reasoning.

Poor organization happens more frequently than you might imagine; readers of legal materials are often confused or have little or no idea what the writer is trying to say. Although a writer's failure to communicate effectively can result from many causes, it is most often caused by poor organization. Even though a perceptive reader may be able to piece together the writer's ideas, doing so is not the reader's job. A writer is obligated to make his work as accessible as possible.

Just as legal thinking has its own analytical framework, it also has its own organizational requirements. Because of the complexity of legal analysis, you will not be able to produce a professional, written product using only a mental checklist of ideas or a few scribbled notes. A well-organized piece of writing requires advance planning. First, as discussed in Chapter 5 (Understanding Legal Rules), you must fully understand the governing law because the law will provide the structural framework for your analysis. Next, you need to devote time to "pre-writing." Some writers find that advance planning requires a detailed outline. Outlining may help you think through a problem and avoid omitting important points. Outlining may also help you spot organizational deficiencies. Some writers find that charts such as those in Chapters 6, 7, and 8 are more helpful than outlines and can serve the same purpose of helping you organize your thoughts. While developing a chart or an outline requires extra work at the outset, pre-writing is ultimately a time-saving method of organization. Rewriting an outline or chart is easier than rewriting a paper.

As noted in earlier chapters, good legal writing does not require the reader to figure things out for herself. Apart from careful planning, there are six basic principles of good organization that will enable you to explain your analysis in a manner that is easy for the reader to follow. These basic principles apply to both the objective analysis necessary in an office memo and the legal analysis presented persuasively for a trial or appellate brief.

1. Address "givens" at the outset of your analysis.

Any legal analysis requires a thorough explanation of how the law applies to the facts. Keep in mind, however, that not all elements of a particular rule require the same level of analysis. When you need to analyze a rule that involves multiple elements, you will often find that some of them are "givens." As you know from Chapter 6 (Identifying and Selecting Issues for Analysis), you need not analyze givens at length; one or two sentences should ordinarily be enough. If you have to analyze cases or compare and contrast the facts of the decided cases with the facts of your case, the element is not a given. Generally, givens should be addressed at the outset of your analysis. By doing so, you simplify your organization and focus the reader's attention on the elements that require detailed analysis and more careful consideration.

Rhoda Shiver is a firefighter who broke her leg when she stumbled over fallen tree limbs in the parking lot of an office building that was burning. The tree limbs had fallen during a storm several days earlier. Shiver was on her way to assist in placing hoses for the firefighters to connect to the building's fire suppression system. She would like to recover damages from the owner of the office building to compensate her for her injuries. The fire was caused by faulty wiring installed by the owner, who is not an electrician. Two weeks earlier, a city official advised the owner to bring the building's wiring into compliance with the electrical code. An affirmative defense, the public safety officer's rule, could provide a complete defense to Shiver's possible lawsuit.

Consider the following possible organizational structures for an analysis of this rule:

ANSWER A: Shiver will likely not be able to recover for her injuries. The public safety officer's rule bars recovery when (1) a public safety officer (2) was injured in the course of performing tasks relating to his or her employment, (3) the risk of injury was one that the officer could reasonably anticipate would arise in the dangerous situations that the officer's employment typically required him or her to encounter, and (4) the alleged tortfeasor was the individual responsible for bringing the officer to the scene where the injury then occurred. *Barron v. Day* (1996). Here, three of these requirements are easily established. First, Shiver, a firefighter, is a public safety officer. Second, she was injured in the course of her employment when she tripped over tree limbs and broke her leg while fighting a fire. Third, the building owner's faulty wiring caused the fire that brought her to the scene where she was injured. Thus, the only issue is whether the third element is satisfied.

Shiver's injury from tripping over the tree limbs in the parking lot of the burning building was most likely caused by a danger that she could reasonably anticipate in the situations she typically encountered as a firefighter. This case is similar to *Barron*, where the plaintiff police officer was injured when he slipped and fell on the defendant's snow- and ice-covered walkway while responding to a home security alarm at the defendant's residence. The plaintiff claimed that the defendant was negligent in failing to clear the walkway of snow and ice. The court nevertheless held that the police officer's action was barred because the injury was caused by a danger the plaintiff should reasonably have anticipated during the winter months. In this case, Shiver could reasonably have expected to encounter fallen trees and even fallen buildings in her firefighting activities. Like the snow- and ice-covered walkway in *Barron,* the risks from fallen limbs were foreseeable.

Shiver's case differs from *Barron* because the building owner was aware of the faulty wiring that led to the fire. For two weeks, he ignored a warning to repair the wiring in his building that ultimately caused the fire. However, the public safety officer's rule is focused on the risks that fire and police officers confront when responding to emergencies, not on the cause of those emergencies. Although the building owner might have been negligent in not cleaning up the limbs, Shiver should reasonably have anticipated such obstacles in the course of her work. Thus, her claim is probably barred.

ANSWER B: Shiver will likely not be able to recover for her injuries. The public safety officer's rule bars recovery when (1) a public safety officer (2) was injured in the course of performing tasks relating to his or her employment, (3) the risk of injury was one that the officer could reasonably anticipate would arise in the dangerous situations that the officer's employment typically required him or her to encounter, and (4) the alleged tortfeasor was the individual responsible for bringing the officer to the scene where the injury then occurred. *Barron v. Day* (1996).

First, Shiver, a firefighter, is a public safety officer. Second, she was injured in the course of her employment when she tripped and broke her leg while fighting a fire. Third, Shiver's injury from tripping over the tree limbs in the parking lot of the burning building was most likely caused by a danger that she could reasonably anticipate in the situations she typically encountered as a firefighter. This case is similar to *Barron*, where the plaintiff police officer was injured when he slipped and fell on the defendant's snow- and ice-covered walkway while responding to a home security alarm at the defendant's residence. The plaintiff claimed that the defendant was negligent in failing to clear the walkway of snow and ice. The court held that the action was barred because the injury was caused by a danger the plaintiff should reasonably have anticipated during the winter months. In this case, Shiver could reasonably have expected to encounter fallen trees and even fallen buildings in her firefighting activities. Like the snow- and ice-covered walkway in *Barron*, the risks from fallen limbs were foreseeable.

Shiver's case differs from *Barron* because the building owner was aware of the faulty wiring that led to the fire. For two weeks, he ignored a warning to repair the wiring in his building that ultimately caused the fire. However, the public safety officer's rule is focused on the risks that fire and police officers confront when responding to emergencies, not on the cause of those emergencies. Although the building owner might have been negligent in not cleaning up the limbs, Shiver should reasonably have anticipated such obstacles in the course of her work.

The fourth and final element is also met because the building owner's faulty wiring caused the fire that brought Shiver to the scene where she was injured. Thus, the public safety officer's rule will likely bar any recovery for damages in a negligence action against the building owner.

Answer A is better. The writer has identified which of the elements are givens, that is, easily established by the facts. For each of the givens, the writer has stated the rule and applied it to the facts in a sentence or two. Answer A ends with a detailed analysis of the element that is at issue, focusing the reader's attention on that requirement. By not differentiating between givens and issues, Answer B wrongly suggests that all four elements deserve equal attention and makes it difficult for a reader to focus on the most significant aspect of the problem. Answer B also makes the fourth element seem like an afterthought instead of a requirement under the rule, since it follows the detailed analysis of the third element. Quickly analyzing givens at the outset focuses the reader's attention on the most difficult and significant aspect or aspects of the analysis.

Be aware that not every legal analysis will have givens. In some situations, each element of the rule requires analysis or argument. In other situations, including many but not all trial or appellate briefs, the issues are framed in a way that excludes consideration of givens. The issues in most briefs, after all, require extended analysis and argument. Thus, although givens are explained at the outset of the memo in Appendix A, there is no separate explanation of givens for the trial court briefs (Appendices C and D) and appellate briefs (Appendices F and G).

2. Discuss each issue separately.

When there are two or more issues that merit analysis, you must examine each separately. Discuss and draw a conclusion about one issue before moving to the next. Distinct separation of issues helps the reader understand each one and sharpens your understanding as well.

Separating issues is especially difficult in three types of situations. First, some issues may be hard to distinguish from one another because they are similar or similar-sounding. Effective organization requires a clear understanding of the relevant law. Second, the same reasons or policy considerations are sometimes applicable to more than one issue when they are closely related. Never ignore points you have already discussed when they are relevant to a subsequent issue. Instead of completely restating a point you have already made, though, you may simply refer back to it. Finally, a particular case may deal with several issues requiring you to discuss that case several times. Set out the case's holding and underlying facts pertaining to Issue X when you are discussing Issue X, and discuss the holding and underlying facts pertaining to Issue Y when you are discussing Issue Y. Avoid the temptation to set out all the facts and holdings of the case in one place; it will only confuse the reader. This last point is simply a variation of the basic theme: Always discuss each issue separately.

Our client, Patrick Johnson, is charged with assault and rob-
bery in connection with the theft of $300 from First National
Bank. The prosecutor alleges that Johnson pointed a gun at
a teller and told him to hand over what money he had. After
Johnson's arrest, police learned that his gun was not loaded.
Does this fact provide a defense to the charges?

There are two relevant cases:

State v. Cox (1948)

Gilbert Cox was convicted of robbery for taking $15 from a small grocery. He
appeals on the ground that his "weapon," a pointed finger pressed against
the inside of his coat, was not lethal. We think he misses the real issue, and
consequently we affirm. Robbery requires that the taking be accomplished
by either violence or the threat of immediate harm to the victim. Because
Cox's act reasonably frightened the clerk into giving away the money, he
cannot claim it was only a ruse.

State v. Hines (1962)

Carol Hines appeals her conviction for assault. We affirm. Hines was convicted for placing the eraser end of a pencil against the back of a blind man
and threatening to shoot him if he did not turn over his money. He fainted
and she fled. She claims that the absence of a real gun frees her from guilt
for assault. We disagree. A person is guilty of assault if she intentionally puts
another in fear that she may cause him serious bodily injury or death. The
pencil accomplished Defendant's purpose of making the blind man fear
bodily injury if he did not comply.

Consider these discussions:

ANSWER A: Johnson cannot use the fact that his gun was unloaded
as a defense to either assault or robbery. In *State v. Hines*, the court
held that the defendant's failure to use a real gun was not a defense
to assault when she caused a blind man such fear for his life that he
fainted. The defendant had pressed a pencil against the victim's back
as if it were a handgun. The court held that reasonable fear for one's
safety makes it irrelevant that there is actually nothing to fear. Similarly, in *State v. Cox*, the court held that a person can be convicted of
robbery if the taking occurs because the defendant caused the victim to reasonably fear immediate harm. The court reasoned that the
defendant's "weapon," a hidden pointed finger, frightened a clerk into
turning over the store's money.

Johnson cannot use the fact that his gun was unloaded as a defense to assault because he intentionally put the teller in fear of serious bodily injury or death by pointing his gun at him. Just like the harmless pencil in *Hines*, the unloaded gun was sufficient to cause the victim reasonable fear for his safety. Nor is the unloaded gun a defense to robbery. Like the defendant in *Cox*, Johnson used the threat of immediate harm from what appeared to be a loaded gun to frighten the clerk into surrendering the $300.

ANSWER B: Johnson cannot use the fact that his gun was unloaded as a defense to either assault or robbery. He committed assault because he intentionally put the teller in fear of serious bodily injury or death. In *State v. Hines*, the court held that the defendant's failure to use a real gun was not a defense to assault when she had caused a blind man such fear for his life that he fainted. The defendant had pressed a pencil against her victim's back as if it were a handgun. The court held that reasonable fear for one's safety makes it irrelevant that there is actually nothing to fear. Like the defendant in *Hines*, Johnson committed assault because he intentionally put the teller in fear of serious bodily injury or death. Just like the harmless pencil in *Hines*, the unloaded gun was sufficient to cause the victim to reasonably fear for his safety.

Johnson also committed robbery because his threatened use of the gun prompted the teller to give him money. In *State v. Cox*, the court held that a person can be convicted of robbery if the taking occurs because the defendant caused the victim to reasonably fear immediate harm. The court reasoned that the defendant's "weapon," a hidden pointed finger, frightened a clerk into turning over the store's money. Like the pointed finger in *Cox*, Johnson's pointed gun frightened the teller into giving him $300. In both cases, the victim was not aware that the "weapon" was harmless; thus, it is irrelevant that Johnson's gun was unloaded.

Although the descriptions of the cases and analysis of the facts in Answers A and B are virtually identical, Answer B is preferable because it is easier to understand. Answer B shows a distinct separation of issues. It describes the assault case and its application to Johnson's situation in the first paragraph, and the robbery case and its application to Johnson's situation in the second. The transition from the description of the case law to analysis of the facts for each issue is smooth and easy to follow.

Answer A, on the other hand, is organized like this: assault, robbery, assault, robbery. It explains the law concerning assault, then explains the law concerning robbery. When it relates the facts to the law, Answer A takes the reader back to assault, then back again to robbery. The organizational pattern is disjointed and hard to follow. Answer A imposes an unfair burden on the reader and is ineffective.

3. Discuss each sub-issue separately.

Each issue, as you have discovered, often has several parts or sub-issues. Each sub-issue involves its own rule, and thus its own set of significant facts. You should deal with each sub-issue in sequence, finishing the discussion of one before continuing to the next. Discuss sub-issues as part of the issue they comprise. If Issue A involves two sub-issues and Issue B also involves two sub-issues, discuss each sub-issue under Issue A before going to any part of Issue B. As with issues, clear separation of sub-issues sharpens your presentation and helps the reader understand your position.

Burns Research Corp., a consulting firm, successfully persuaded the Salem Township Board of Trustees to grant a zoning amendment to reclassify a ninety-seven-acre parcel from agricultural (A) to research office (RO). Our client, a local landowners group known as Save Our Heritage Association, is contemplating a lawsuit challenging the amendment on a number of grounds, including spot zoning. The parcel previously was used by a home for delinquent children, whose founders believed in the therapeutic value of agricultural work. Burns plans to lease most of the land for pasture. The surrounding area is made up of homes on five-acre lots as well as farms.

There are two relevant cases in the state:

Costello v. Plainview Zoning Commission (1975)

The appellants challenge a decision by the Zoning Commission for the City of Plainview changing the classification of a one-half acre lot from RR (single family residential) to C (commercial). The appellants are homeowners and residents of the fourteen-acre RR zone surrounding the lot. The applicant for the zoning change, a trucking company which is an appellee here, sought permission to build a trucking terminal on the lot. The appellants argued unsuccessfully to the trial court that the Commission's decision constituted unlawful spot zoning.

We agree with the appellants and reverse. The essence of zoning is the division of a municipality into districts defining present or potential suitable uses for property. Spot zoning is unlawful when a parcel of land is singled out for special treatment for the benefit of the owner and to the detriment of other landowners and the community. The zoning change at issue here constituted special treatment for the trucking company because it affected only the small parcel owned by the company. Rezoning also was detrimental to the surrounding landowners and the community because the terminal would lead to a decline in property values. Under these circumstances, the Commission's action was impermissible spot zoning.

Persich v. Pole (1984)

Michael Pole, the owner of an undeveloped seven-acre tract zoned R2 (multiple family residential), successfully persuaded the Medford Zoning Commission to rezone the property to C (commercial). He plans to build a shopping center on the tract, lease the center to various retail stores, and use the remainder of the tract for a parking lot. Persich, a homeowner on adjoining property, sued to enjoin the amendment as spot zoning. The trial court agreed with the Commission and we affirm.

We ruled in *Costello v. Plainview Zoning Commission* that spot zoning is impermissible "where a parcel of land is singled out for special treatment for the benefit of the owner and to the detriment of other landowners and the community." Pole is not being unfairly benefited here because the rezoning applies to a large block of land, unlike the half-acre rezoning for the trucking company rejected in *Costello*. In addition, because the record shows the absence of any shopping centers in the area, location of the center on this property will benefit the neighborhood and the city.

Consider these discussions:

ANSWER A: The amendment was probably not improper spot zoning. "Spot zoning is unlawful when a parcel of land is singled out for special treatment for the benefit of the owner and to the detriment of other landowners and the community." *Costello v. Plainview Zoning Commission*.

The amendment is not an unfair benefit to Burns because of the large size of the tract. In *Persich v. Pole*, the court held that a seven-acre undeveloped residential tract that was rezoned commercial was large enough to preclude an unfair benefit to the owner. However, in *Costello*, the court held that rezoning did create an unfair benefit because it involved only a half-acre lot in a large residential area that was rezoned to accommodate a trucking terminal. The court reasoned that the essence of zoning is division of a municipality into districts and concluded that a half-acre lot was unreasonably small for a district. Thus, even more so than the seven acres in *Persich*, a ninety-seven-acre tract is large enough to be a zoning district and does not create the unfair benefit to the landowner that rezoning the half-acre parcel did in *Costello*.

In addition, the rezoning in the Burns case creates no detriment to the surrounding landowners. The court in *Persich* found a proposed shopping center to be beneficial to the neighborhood, rather than detrimental, because no other shopping centers were located there. Like the landowners in *Persich*, the surrounding landowners here will benefit because they can lease land formerly owned by the home for delinquent children. This case is also different from *Costello* because the trucking terminal in that case would have led to lowered property values in the neighborhood. No such problems are foreseeable here because the essential use of the parcel for agricultural purposes will remain the same.

ANSWER B: The amendment was probably not improper spot zoning. "Spot zoning is unlawful when a parcel of land is singled out for special treatment for the benefit of the owner and to the detriment of other landowners and the community." *Costello v. Plainview Zoning Commission*. The court in *Costello* concluded there was spot zoning where a half-acre lot located in a large residential area was rezoned "commercial" to accommodate a trucking terminal. The court said the essence of zoning is division of a municipality into districts, and concluded that a half-acre lot was unreasonably small for a district. The court also found that the rezoning would lead to lowered property values in the surrounding neighborhoods.

However, in *Persich v. Pole*, the court concluded that rezoning an undeveloped seven-acre lot from a residential classification to a commercial one for a shopping center and parking lot was not spot zoning. The tract owner was not "unfairly benefited," the court reasoned, because the seven-acre property was much larger than half an acre. The court also found a benefit to the neighborhood because of the absence of any shopping centers in the area.

In this case, there is no unfair benefit to Burns because of the large size of the tract and because the basic use of the property will remain the same. The ninety-seven-acre property is larger than the seven-acre tract in *Persich* and thus is a reasonable size for a zoning district. In addition, there is no unfair burden to the surrounding landowners. Like the landowners in *Persich* who would benefit from the shopping center, the surrounding landowners here will benefit from the rezoning because they will be able to lease land formerly owned by the home for delinquent children. Unlike the situation in *Costello*, no decline in property values is foreseeable because the essential use of the parcel for agricultural purposes will remain the same.

Answer A is more understandable because it is better organized. The spot zoning issue depends on two sub-issues: (1) whether there is an unfair benefit to the owner, and (2) whether there is a detriment to other landowners and the community. Answer A sets out the description and analysis of the law for each sub-issue separately, completing the discussion of one before moving to the next. Because both the description and analysis for each sub-issue are stated in the same place, Answer A more clearly reflects the governing law and is much easier to follow than Answer B.

Answer B describes both cases before analyzing either sub-issue and is organized like this: private benefit, neighborhood detriment, private benefit, neighborhood detriment, private benefit, and neighborhood detriment. Such zigzagging requires unnecessary effort simply to understand the discussion. This criticism should be familiar to you from the previous discussion on separation of issues. By describing all the law applicable to multiple points first and then trying to analyze the points, the writer risks hopelessly confusing the reader. Moreover, although it appears that the writer understands the individual cases, it is less clear that the writer understands the rule. Stated another way, the sub-issues dictate the organization in Answer A, while the cases dictate the organization in Answer B. The issues and sub-issues, not the cases, should dictate your organization.

---

4. For each issue or sub-issue, describe the applicable law before applying it to the factual situation.

Each issue or sub-issue involves the application of a legal rule to specific facts. The relevant legal rules, therefore, provide a framework for your analysis and should be stated first. If you state the facts concerning an issue or sub-issue first, without describing the applicable law, the facts will mean nothing to your reader.

Stating the applicable law first enables you to be concise. The Statement of Facts at the beginning of an office memo or brief gives the reader a complete picture of the factual situation. Stating the facts in your formal Statement of Facts in a memo or brief, then stating the facts for a particular issue or sub-issue, then stating the law, and then applying the law to the facts is inherently repetitious. When you write the discussion, therefore, avoid simply restating the facts; analyze them. Instead of writing again "Joe drove through a red light," write "Because Joe drove through a red light, he violated . . . ." The facts, in other words, must be analyzed in the discussion, not simply restated.

Ronald Jenkins owns a riparian lot on Fredda Lake, a shallow, thirty-acre body of water with no inlets or outlets. David McNulty, who also owns a riparian lot on the lake, wants to drain one-third of the lake for water for a small brewery he plans to establish. McNulty's plans would reduce the size of the lake to fourteen acres, making it difficult for Jenkins to use it for fishing or boating. Jenkins, who is your client, wants to know if he can prevent McNulty from carrying out his plans.

There is one pertinent case:

Posner v. Fox (1987)

The appellant, Duane Posner, wants to construct an apartment complex on Lake Minnesota, a 400-acre lake drained by a small stream. He has owned riparian land on the lake for several years. His plans require the diversion of 1,200 acre-feet of water annually. The appellee, Sheila Fox, who also owns riparian land on the lake, seeks to block the diversion of the water. The trial court found that the proposed diversion would permanently reduce water levels by about three feet and would interfere with boating, swimming, and fishing on the lake by Fox and other abutting landowners. The court permanently enjoined the diversion. We affirm. Each riparian owner has the right to use the lake for domestic or recreational purposes, but each owner must accommodate the others. Posner's plans would unreasonably interfere with the rights of the other owners.

Consider the following:

ANSWER A: McNulty's proposal can likely be enjoined because it is an unreasonable interference with Jenkins's use of the lake. Each riparian owner of land along a lake must not unreasonably interfere with the rights of other riparian owners to use the lake. *Posner v. Fox*. The court in *Posner* held that the defendant could be enjoined from diverting enough water from a 400-acre lake to permanently reduce water levels by about three feet. The court maintained that the reduction would unreasonably interfere with the rights of other owners to use the lake for recreational purposes. McNulty's proposal, which would reduce a thirty-acre lake to fourteen acres, would have an even more drastic effect on the lake than the comparatively slight reduction in water levels found in *Posner*. The proposal here, like the proposal in *Posner*, would have a significant adverse impact on fishing and boating by Jenkins and other riparian owners on the lake. McNulty's proposal can thus be enjoined.

ANSWER B: McNulty's proposal can likely be enjoined as an unreasonable interference with Jenkins's use of the lake. McNulty's plans would reduce Fredda Lake from thirty acres to fourteen acres in size. This reduction in size would make it difficult for Jenkins to fish or boat on the lake. The court in *Posner v. Fox* held that a similar action could be enjoined as an unreasonable use of water. The defendant in that case sought to divert water from a 400-acre lake for a proposed apartment complex, thus permanently reducing water levels by about three feet. The court held that proposal to be an unreasonable use because it interfered with recreational uses of the water by the other riparian landowners along the lake. In McNulty's case, as in *Posner*, the proposed diversion would significantly interfere with the recreational use of the lake. Reducing the size of the lake by more than one-half seems an even more unreasonable encroachment than the comparatively slight reduction in water levels found in *Posner*. McNulty's proposal can thus be enjoined.

Answer A is preferable because it describes the law from the *Posner* case prior to analyzing the facts of the McNulty situation. This method of organization avoids needless repetition, makes the significance of the stated facts immediately apparent, and clarifies the analysis. Unlike Answer A, Answer B reads like this: facts, applicable law, facts. This method of organization is confusing because the reader cannot determine the significance of the facts until the legal rules have been stated. This method is also repetitious because the facts are stated twice.

Answer A is more readable, easier to understand, and more concise than Answer B because it is better organized.

---

5. State the reasons supporting your conclusion on an issue or sub-issue before discussing counterarguments.

The result of your thinking on an issue or sub-issue should be a legal conclusion. This conclusion should be expressed in your thesis. After stating your thesis, explain the reasons for it—reasons you likely came to understand only after thoughtful analysis. The counterarguments should not be stated until you have finished explaining your position. It is at this point in the memo, and only at this point, that you should discuss why the counterarguments are not as compelling as the arguments supporting your position. This method of presentation makes your discussion easier to follow and also ensures that you will draw a conclusion on each issue and sub-issue.

This principle does not permit you to intuit a particular result and then marshal justifications for it. Rather, it requires that you distinguish your thought process from your writing and present your reader with a finished product, rather than a work-in-progress. As other chapters indicate, you should anticipate how your opponent will respond to your conclusions. This process sharpens your understanding of the issues and helps you determine the strength of your case. Your writing will become disjointed, however, if it reads "on one hand . . . but on the other hand . . . nonetheless . . . still on the other hand." Do not require your reader to follow a game of intellectual ping-pong. Writers who adopt a back-and-forth style tend to avoid drawing any conclusions, leaving the reader with only a set of considerations rather than a prediction of the probable legal outcome. When closely related arguments are discussed, this style also makes it difficult to state a precise legal conclusion or the reasons for it.

Your client, the Red Rock Fishing Club, opposes a federal agency's proposed construction of a large hydroelectric dam on the Red Rock River, which is known for excellent fishing. The purpose of the dam, according to the agency, is to provide "clean, pollution-free electricity." As required by the 1969 National Environmental Policy Act, the agency has prepared an environmental impact statement (EIS). The Act permits groups such as the Red Rock Fishing Club to bring an action in federal district court challenging the adequacy of an EIS. The adequacy of the EIS is one of three potential issues in this case.

Consider the following discussions of that issue:

ANSWER A: The agency's EIS is most likely inadequate under the National Environmental Policy Act. The Act requires that an EIS discuss as fully as possible (1) the environmental effects of a proposed project and (2) alternatives to that project. The EIS in this case discussed the environmental effects of flooding on the fish, wildlife, and plants of the river and on areas that would be affected by subsequent development. Although it did discuss the siltation issue, it did not indicate how long it will take the river bed just upstream from the dam to fill with silt. This inadequacy is not relevant, though, because courts will not scrutinize an EIS that closely. Because the EIS did not discuss alternatives, however, the agency has violated the Act. The agency did discuss the alternative of "no action," but it did not consider electricity generation from other sources or whether the electricity is even needed.

ANSWER B: The agency's EIS is inadequate under the National Environmental Policy Act. The Act requires that an EIS discuss as fully as possible (1) the environmental effects of a proposed project and (2) alternatives to that project. Because this statement did not fully discuss alternatives, particularly electricity generation from other sources or the need for the power, the agency has violated the Act. The Act does not absolve an agency because it discussed some alternatives, and it is thus irrelevant that the agency did discuss the alternative of "no action." The discussion of environmental effects of flooding, however, is probably adequate because there was full discussion of the effects of flooding on the fish, wildlife, and plants of the river, siltation behind the dam, and the areas that would be affected by subsequent development. Although there was no indication of the time necessary for large-scale siltation to occur, the courts do not subject a statement to this kind of close scrutiny.

Answer B is preferable because it is easier to understand. Answer B begins by discussing the sub-issue concerning alternatives as the basis for its thesis. The reason for the conclusion on that sub-issue is explained (no full consideration of alternatives), and then the counterargument (discussion of "no action") is refuted. Finally, Answer B draws a conclusion as to the environmental effects sub-issue, explains the basis for that judgment, and dismisses the counterargument. The procedure remains the same, even though the client loses one of these sub-issues and wins the other.

Answer A considers the sub-issues separately, but the discussion of each is muddled by its back-and-forth style. On one hand, it says, these effects have been considered. On the other hand, one effect has not been considered. Answer A concludes that the failure to consider that effect is probably not important. This awkward style follows a zigzag line of reasoning instead of a straight line. The same style is used with the sub-issue concerning alternatives.

There is another basic flaw in Answer A. Because the sub-issue concerning alternatives determines the inadequacy of the EIS in this case, that sub-issue should have been discussed before the sub-issue of environmental effects. Always remember that the points supporting your conclusion, not those supporting your client's case, should be discussed first.

6. When there is more than one issue, discuss the issues in a logical order.

If the resolution of one issue depends on the resolution of another issue, the initial or threshold issue belongs first. As illustrated in the example in Chapter 6 (Identifying and Selecting Issue for Analysis), for example, a jurisdictional issue should be addressed before the substantive issues. Because Fred Brookson wants to file suit in federal court, you would analyze the diversity of citizenship issue before addressing the merits of his claims for intentional infliction of emotional distress and battery. In court, the jurisdictional issue needs to be resolved before there can be any discussion of the merits. If you discuss the substantive issues before the diversity issue, your reader may believe you have assumed that a federal court has jurisdiction or that you simply missed the threshold issue. Even if you tell your reader you will discuss the substantive issues before the jurisdictional issue, your discussion will almost certainly appear illogical. The example below illustrates another instance when logic dictates the ordering of the issues.

> Steve Maxon has been subpoenaed to testify before a grand jury. Eli Maxon, his 17-year-old son, is the target of the investigation. Last month, Eli came home at about 10:00 p.m. in a state of great distress. He told his father that as he entered an intersection with the green light, another car ran a red light and drove right in front of him. He crashed into the other car. Instead of stopping, he drove away as rapidly as he could, a decision he now regrets. The next morning, they learned that the driver of the other car had suffered fatal injuries. A police investigation has implicated Eli.
>
> You have been asked to write a memorandum on whether Steve Maxon can assert a parent-child testimonial privilege so that he will not be compelled to testify against his son.

Your research has revealed that there is no relevant law in your state, but you have found the following federal district court opinion.

In re Vogler (2001)

Charles Vogler, his mother, and his father are targets of a drug trafficking investigation. Vogler, who is twenty years old, has been subpoenaed to testify before the grand jury and has filed a Motion to Quash the Subpoena on the grounds that he would be psychologically and emotionally damaged if forced to testify against his parents. Federal Rule of Evidence 501 provides that testimonial privileges shall be "governed by the principles of common law as they may be interpreted by the courts of the United States in light of reason and experience." Our common law has never recognized a parent-child testimonial privilege, though such a privilege was recognized in early Roman law (*testimonium domesticum*) and is currently recognized in several European countries. The justification for the privilege is that preserving and fostering family relationships is more important than compelling disclosure for the benefit of the criminal justice system.

Several federal courts of appeal have addressed this issue but none have recognized the privilege, although two district courts have done so. The courts uniformly recognize other relationship-based privileges, such as those between husband and wife, priest and penitent, attorney and client, and doctor and patient. Confidentiality and trust are at least as important in the parent and child relationship. The family unit is fundamental to our society, and it is necessary to shield the family relationship from the devastating effects likely to result from compelled testimony. Reason and experience dictate that we recognize a parent-child privilege, but we wish to avoid unduly restricting the process of ascertaining the truth in criminal proceedings. The privilege is therefore subject to the following restrictions: (1) the parties must intend that the communication be confidential; (2) the communication must be strongly related to the seeking or giving of parental advice or guidance; and (3) the need for confidentiality of the particular communication must be weighed against the need for relevant evidence in a criminal proceeding.

In this case we will not quash the subpoena because the requirements listed above have not been met. Vogler has not demonstrated that any of his testimony would involve communications intended to be confidential. More significantly, he has not demonstrated that such communications were not in furtherance of joint criminal activity rather than related to the seeking or giving of parental guidance. It is so ordered.

Consider the following outlines:

ANSWER A:
1. Will the court recognize a parent-child testimonial privilege?
2. If so, is the privilege applicable in this case?
    a. Would the testimony include communication that was intended to be confidential?
    b. Was the communication strongly related to the seeking or giving of parental advice or guidance?
    c. Is the need for confidentiality in this case stronger than the need to provide evidence in a criminal proceeding?

ANSWER B:
1. Would the testimony include communication that was intended to be confidential?
2. Was the communication strongly related to the seeking or giving of parental advice or guidance?

3. Is the need for confidentiality in this case stronger than the need to provide evidence in a criminal proceeding?
4. Will the court recognize a parent-child testimonial privilege?

In this example, the threshold issue is whether the court will recognize a parent-child testimonial privilege. If the court recognizes the privilege, it will likely consider the three limitations on the privilege required in *In re Vogler*. Answer A is best because it sets forth the threshold issue in the first question and begins the second question with "If so," which tells the reader that the sub-questions under question 2 are applicable only if the court recognizes the privilege. Answer B is poorly organized for two reasons. First, it incorrectly lists the threshold issue last. Second, it fails to categorize the issues in questions 1, 2, and 3 as limitations that the court is likely to place on the privilege. Answer B is thus misleading because it does not give an accurate picture of how the issues are logically related to each other.

EXERCISES

The following exercises should help you learn to apply these principles.

Exercise 10-A

Several months ago, Colonel Augustus P. Ferguson, who won several medals for bravery in World War II, died at age 91 in the crash of a private plane. His only surviving child is Augustus Jr. In 1952, the Colonel and his wife executed wills leaving all their property to each other, or in the event the spouse had previously died, in equal shares to their surviving children. His wife passed away in 1987. Shortly after her death, the Colonel became involved with Arizona Properties, Inc., a land development company. He was vice-president of the company at his death. Before he died, he revoked his 1952 will and executed a new will giving his entire $1.3 million estate to Arizona Properties.

Augustus Jr. has asked your senior attorney to challenge the validity of the second will in probate court. The law in this state reinstates the previous will if the later will is invalid. Junior stated that the Colonel's new attorney, also general counsel for Arizona Properties, drafted the second will. This attorney and the Colonel were both avid fishermen and went fishing together two or three weekends each month. The attorney resigned as general counsel a year ago. Junior also said that the corporation financed trips for the Colonel, "allegedly for purposes of learning foreign land development strategies," to Hong Kong, Rio de Janeiro, and Cairo. These trips occurred before he revoked the first will. Junior admitted that his father, from whom he was estranged since the death of his mother, "was not at all senile." You are to write an office memo ascertaining the validity of the second will.

There are two relevant cases in this state:

In re Estate of Steffans (1962)

This case involves the validity of the will of Maxine Steffans, a real estate broker, who left her entire $385,000 estate to her paperboy for eight years, Rodney Prentice. This court has recently required those challenging a will for undue influence to show (1) susceptibility to undue influence, (2) opportunity to influence, (3) disposition to influence, and (4) coveted result. The court below concluded that no such influence occurred, and we agree.

Mr. Prentice testified without contradiction, and the trial court found as fact, that Steffans spoke to Prentice only when he came to collect the biweekly payment for the paper and that she frequently paid him by putting a small envelope under her doormat to avoid this contact. A neighbor also testified that Steffans, who had a reputation as eccentric, told her that she, Steffans, was willing Prentice her entire estate because he brought the paper on time. Under these circumstances, the claim of undue influence is

speculative at best, particularly when the neighbor did not pass this information on to Prentice or anyone else.

In re Will of Kendall (1969)

Harriett Kendall's first will, executed when she was fifty-two, left her entire
estate to her husband, Ralph. She entered a nursing home in 1965, when she
was eighty-one. Shortly thereafter, she called an attorney to ask some questions about her will. Harriet was bedridden at the time, unable to carry on a
conversation for more than several minutes, and prone to forgetfulness.

The attorney made his first visit to the nursing home with Harriet's sister,
Mabel. Mabel suggested that she think about writing a new will. On their
second visit, about one week later, the attorney and Mabel brought a new
will for Harriet to sign. Although she was too weak to sit up to sign it, she was
able to mark it with an "X" after Mabel propped her up with some pillows.
When Harriet died in early 1966, her husband learned that the second will
left her estate to Mabel's only son, Edmund. He also learned that the attorney
who drafted the second will was not Harriet's personal attorney, but rather
was Mabel's attorney. The trial court nonetheless admitted the second will to
probate. We reverse.

There are two tests for determining whether there was undue influence
in the execution of a will. The first test, described in *In re Estate of Steffans*
(1962), need not be considered here because we find the trial court erred
under the second test. Undue influence can occur when there is a confidential relationship between the testator and the one alleged to have exercised
undue influence, and there are suspicious circumstances surrounding the
making of the will. The existence of a confidential relationship depends on
the ease with which the confidant controlled or influenced the drafting of
the will. Suspicious circumstances exist when there is a sudden and unexplained change in the attitude of the testator, activity by the beneficiary in
procuring the drafting and execution of the will, or similar circumstances.
In this situation the activity of the attorney and the beneficiary's mother in
procuring a will from an elderly woman meets both requirements.

1. For the rule in each of the cases, prepare an elements chart to:

   a. Identify any issue(s) and sub-issue(s) in this problem.

   b. Identify any givens.

2. Consider the validity of the second will under the rule in the *Kendall*
   case:

   a. Prepare an analysis chart and, if appropriate, a case briefing chart.

   b. Draw a conclusion about a probate judge's likely decision.

   c. Write an outline as if you were preparing to draft the discussion of your
      analysis in a memorandum.

3. Consider the validity of the second will under the rule in the *Steffans* case:

   a. Prepare an analysis chart and, if appropriate, a case briefing chart.

   b. Draw a conclusion about a probate judge's likely decision.

   c. Write an outline as if you were preparing to draft the discussion of your analysis in a memorandum.

Exercise 10-B

All-Rite Industries, Inc., operates a coal-fired powerhouse to generate steam and electricity at its factory in Junction City. The powerhouse has a capacity of 500,000 pounds of steam per hour and burns coal containing 0.9 percent to 1.2 percent sulfur by weight. All-Rite manufactures chemicals, inks, and dyes at this factory for a variety of commercial products. The short smokestack from the powerhouse emits about 500 pounds of sulfur dioxide per hour.

Farmers downwind of the powerhouse have complained about sulfur dioxide emissions for several years. They can show that sulfur dioxide settles on their alfalfa fields under certain atmospheric conditions, whitening the leaves and reducing the value of the crop by at least 5 percent. The tax assessor has told several of these farmers that the value of each of their properties is $5,000 to $10,000 lower because of the sulfur dioxide emissions. A physician for several of the farmers attributes their above-average number of respiratory ailments to inhalation of sulfur dioxide.

All-Rite has ignored these complaints. A spokesman for the company states that the factory employs 490 persons and provides millions of dollars of income for the community. By contrast, he says, the farmers' claims are insignificant. The *Junction City Ledger-Gazette* refuses to print letters from the farmers complaining about sulfur dioxide emissions and regularly praises the company in editorials for its "good work and solid contributions to our economy." An article published six months ago in the *Ledger-Gazette* pointed out that coal containing a lower percentage of sulfur releases less sulfur dioxide when burned than coal containing higher amounts of sulfur. The *Ledger-Gazette* cited the relatively low sulfur content of the coal burned at the powerhouse, stating, "When you compare that with the high-sulfur coal used in other states, it is clear that top management at All-Rite is dedicated to the environment."

The farmers have retained your firm to determine whether they have any causes of action against the company, and your senior attorney has asked you to draft a memorandum on the matter.

The state Air Quality Act provides in part:

> **Sec. 11.** The Department of the Environment shall promulgate regulations for classes of industries sufficient to assure the highest practicable degree of protection for public health and welfare.
>
> . . .
>
> **Sec. 14.** Any person may bring an action in the appropriate trial court to enforce the provisions of this Act and the regulations promulgated pursuant to it.

The regulations in the state Administrative Code promulgated by the Department of the Environment under the Act provide in part:

> **Sec. 405.221(a).** It is unlawful for a powerhouse that has a capacity of more than 500,000 pounds of steam per hour to burn fuel that exceeds 1.0% sulfur content by weight.

The following are three relevant cases from your state:

Neely v. Hoff Theater Co. (1970)

The appellee, Hoff Theater Co., operates an outdoor motion picture theater on a large lot adjoining the home of the appellant, Ervin Neely. Neely sued the appellee for trespass to land, claiming that light from the theater and the automobile headlights of its patrons constituted a physical invasion of his land. The trial court granted summary judgment for the appellee, and we affirm. Trespass to land requires a physical invasion—the presence of some tangible object on another's property. The appellant argues that light is a physical invasion because he can see the presence of light on his property. We think this argument goes too far. If the appellant found the light objectionable, he should have brought his action in nuisance, not in trespass.

Peters v. Hancock (1921)

William Peters sued Molly Hancock in nuisance to enjoin Hancock from operating her saloon, located on a parcel of land adjoining Peters's home. Peters alleged in his complaint that patrons of the saloon "severely disturb the plaintiff's sensibilities and sleep by loitering on the street outside the plaintiff's house and by occasionally using loud and abusive language." The trial judge granted judgment for the plaintiff. This court hesitates to reverse the judgment of the learned trial judge, but the allegations in the complaint do not constitute nuisance. Nuisance requires an unreasonable interference by the defendant landowner with the use or enjoyment of the plaintiff's land. The defendant should exercise what control she can over her patrons, but we do not think their occasional loudness or rudeness is "unreasonable" under the circumstances. Reversed.

Jacobs v. Metzger (1934)

This action arose when the defendant's motor vehicle left a one-lane dirt road to avoid colliding with another motor vehicle speeding from the opposite direction. The defendant's car stopped in the plaintiff's front yard. The plaintiff won damages for trespass in the trial court. We reverse. Although there clearly was a physical invasion of the plaintiff's land by the defendant and his automobile, the defendant was privileged by necessity. The defendant should not be penalized for attempting to save his life by avoiding a collision with a speeding car.

1. For each rule in this problem, prepare an elements chart to:

   a. Identify any issue(s) and sub-issue(s).

   b. Identify any givens.

2. Consider the farmers' situation under the trespass rule:

   a. Prepare an analysis chart and, if appropriate, a case briefing chart.

   b. Draw a conclusion about a judge's likely decision.

   c. Write an outline as if you were preparing to draft the discussion of your analysis in a memorandum.

3. Consider the farmers' situation under the nuisance rule:

   a. Prepare an analysis chart and, if appropriate, a case briefing chart.

   b. Draw a conclusion about a judge's likely decision.

   c. Outline your analysis as if you were preparing to draft the discussion of your analysis in a memorandum.

Exercise 10-C

Mary Ferguson, who is fifty-nine years old, worked for seventeen years as an office manager at Country Gardens, a lawn maintenance and landscaping business owned by Frank Currier. Several months ago, Currier decided to expand his business and move to a new location. He told Ferguson that he would manage the business himself and her employment was terminated. He said that the only available jobs at the new location involved physical labor, such as mowing, spraying, pruning, and digging, and that Ferguson had no experience in this type of work. He also said that she was "getting up there" and ought to retire and enjoy life. Currier retained all of the other employees and hired several new ones. The other employees, including those he retained, were considerably younger than Ferguson and had been employed by Currier for a shorter amount of time. Ferguson told Currier that she maintains her own private lawn and garden and was capable of doing the work. She believes Currier did not retain her because her wages were higher than those of the younger employees. You are to write an office memorandum analyzing whether Ferguson has a cause of action against Currier for discrimination because of her age.

State Code § 492 provides:

(a) It shall be unlawful for any employer, labor organization, or employment agency to discriminate with respect to any matters related to employment because of a person's race, religion, national origin, sex, marital status, physical or mental handicap, or age if the person is 18 years of age or older and under 70 years of age.

(b) Discrimination is not an unlawful practice if the discrimination is based on a bona fide occupational qualification reasonably necessary to the operation of the employer's business.

The following two cases were decided by your state's intermediate level appellate court.

Alders v. City of Oak Grove (1993)

Benjamin Alders applied for a job as a firefighter for the City of Oak Grove. He successfully completed the required examinations and was put on a waiting list. At the time of the application, he was thirty-one years old. A month later, he was removed from the waiting list. He was told that he did not qualify because of the following provision in the Oak Grove City Code:

Section 203. All firefighters shall be between the ages of twenty-one and thirty years on the date of their appointment.

Alders filed an age discrimination complaint with the Commissioner of the Oak Grove Labor Bureau. After investigating the matter, the Commissioner charged the City with unlawful employment practice and issued an order stating that the refusal to hire persons over age thirty violated State Code § 492. The City appeals, claiming that the age requirement is a bona fide occupational qualification (BFOQ) because of the demanding nature of the job and because hiring older persons would have a negative impact on pension and disability plans. We do not find these arguments persuasive. Alders presented evidence to the Commissioner that persons over the age of thirty could perform the tasks required of firefighters. Furthermore, we do not believe that the BFOQ exception was intended to include economic justifications for discrimination. Affirmed.

Hawkins v. International Brotherhood of Masons Local 397 (2004)

International Brotherhood of Masons, Local 397 (Union) appeals from an order of the State Human Rights Commission awarding Joe Hawkins damages for age discrimination, in violation of State Code § 492. The Union operates a hiring hall in which members needing employment register and the Union calls the members when jobs are available. After receiving no call for several months, Hawkins complained to the Union's international office. At the hearing before the Commission, Hawkins introduced into evidence a copy of a letter from the Union's business agent to the Union's international office that he obtained when he sent in his complaint. The letter stated that Hawkins would be called after the Union had found jobs for those members whose unemployment compensation had expired because Hawkins, who is sixty-five years old, receives social security payments and an annuity. Based on this evidence, the Commission found that the Union had discriminated against Hawkins because of his age.

To establish a prima facie case of discrimination, the complainant must show that (1) the complainant is a member of a protected class, (2) the complainant is qualified for the position, (3) the employer made an adverse decision concerning the complainant, and (4) but for the complainant's protected status, the adverse decision would not have been made. Hawkins, who was qualified for the jobs that became available, was not placed sequentially on the out-of-work list but was placed after those who were running out of unemployment benefits. Because the receipt of social security payments and retirement benefits are correlative with age, the Commission's inference that Hawkins had been discriminated against because of his age was reasonable. Affirmed.

1. For each rule in this problem, prepare an elements chart to:

   a. Identify any issue(s) and sub-issue(s).

   b. Identify any givens.

2. Consider Ferguson's situation under the general discrimination rule:

   a. Prepare an analysis chart and, if appropriate, a case briefing chart.

   b. Draw a conclusion about a judge's likely decision.

   c. Write an outline as if you were preparing to draft the discussion of your analysis in a memorandum.

3. Consider Ferguson's situation under the bona fide occupational qualification rule:

   a. Prepare an analysis chart and, if appropriate, a case briefing chart.

   b. Draw a conclusion about a judge's likely decision.

   c. Write an outline as if you were preparing to draft the discussion of your analysis in a memorandum.

Describing the Law

Regardless of whether it is presented objectively or persuasively, the description of the law must provide your reader with the essential legal rules or principles on which your discussion is based and establish the framework for the rest of the discussion. A good explanation of the law makes your analysis credible to your reader. It also improves your analysis because it requires you to identify and state the legal basis for your conclusions. This chapter sets out basic principles for describing the law.

1. Be accurate.

An accurate explanation will enable the reader to understand precisely what the law says and provide a logical and coherent basis for the analysis that follows. Your credibility will depend on whether your explanation accurately reflects the law. Real decisions will be based on the analysis presented in legal writing. The quality and defensibility of those decisions will depend on the accuracy of your explanation.

Accuracy is also important in legal writing because of the precise meaning given to many words and phrases. The difference between similar-sounding words and phrases can be substantial. Take, for example, the difference between "homicide" and "murder." Homicide is any unlawful killing of a human being, but murder is reserved for the most serious homicide. Imprecise use of legal terms can convey a meaning totally different from what you intend and can lead to an analysis of the wrong issue or an analysis that is incoherent.

As you write and rewrite a memorandum or brief, consider whether you have explained the law as accurately and precisely as possible. If you are having difficulty explaining your analysis, you may find it necessary to reread the relevant law and think about it further.

Consider the following case excerpt and descriptions of the elements of the law for specific performance of a contract:

Lopez v. Singh (1993)

Specific performance is, of course, a remedy available for breach of contract. The plaintiff must show that the remedy at law is inadequate. The remedy at law will be considered inadequate if, for example, the contract involves unascertainable damages or unique items. The plaintiff must also show that the contract is just, reasonable, and supported by adequate consideration. Finally, the plaintiff must show that there is a mutuality of remedies and that the terms of the contract are definite enough to enforce what was promised in the contract.

ANSWER A: Specific performance is available when the remedy at law is inadequate; the contract is just, reasonable, and supported by adequate consideration; there is a mutuality of remedies; and the terms of the contract are definite enough for the court to enforce what the contract promised.

ANSWER B: Specific performance is available when the following criteria exist: unascertainable damages, unique items, an inadequate legal remedy, definite contract terms, and fair consideration when the contract was made.

Both answers describe elements of a claim for specific performance. Answer A is better, though, because it states the law more accurately. As discussed in Chapter 5 (Understanding Legal Rules), it is essential that a lawyer be able to understand and describe the structure and operation of legal rules. The writer of Answer A demonstrates a full understanding of the rule by setting out all four elements of the claim. Answer B, however, properly identifies only two of the four elements: an inadequate legal remedy and just contract terms. Answer B states there must be fair consideration (which may or may not be different from adequate consideration), but it does not say the contract must be just or reasonable. Answer B also incorrectly suggests that one element (inadequate remedy at law) is really three elements (inadequate remedy at law, unascertainable damages, and unique items), rather than recognizing that unascertainable damages and unique items are *examples* rather than requirements. Whether there is an inadequate legal remedy will depend on whether the damages cannot be ascertained or whether the items in question are unique. The legal analysis that flows from Answer B will likely be incorrect or incomplete because the writer's understanding of the law is incorrect and incomplete. The legal analysis based on Answer A, however, will likely be more accurate, credible, and coherent because the writer fully understands and correctly describes the law.

When describing statutory law, quote the language in the statute that is pertinent to the issue you are analyzing. If you paraphrase, you run the risk of changing the meaning or glossing over issues raised by the statutory language. Statutory issues can hinge on the legislature's choice of one word over another, the grammatical structure of a sentence, or even the punctuation of a particular sentence. If the language at issue is part of a longer statute, set the quoted language in context by paraphrasing the rest of the statute, but make sure the paraphrase is accurate. Omission of text within a quoted sentence is indicated by a series of three points known as an *ellipsis*. Omission of text at the end of a quoted sentence is indicated by an ellipsis and then a period (four periods).

> Your client, Toy Kingdom Industries, Inc., was recently named as a defendant in a suit alleging multiple violations of the state Water Quality Act. The suit was brought under the "citizen suit" provision of the Act. The plaintiff, a local resident named Felix Thorpe, warned your client's chief executive officer of a possible suit against his "stinking operation" four weeks ago in a telephone conversation. The question is whether that conversation satisfied the notice requirement in the "citizen suit" provision.

Consider the following descriptions of the notice requirement:

ANSWER A: Section 17(b) of the state Water Quality Act provides that no action may be commenced under the citizen suit provision prior to sixty days after the plaintiff has given notice of the alleged violations to the person.

ANSWER B: Section 17(b) of the state Water Quality Act provides that "no action may be commenced under this section prior to sixty days after the plaintiff has given notice of the alleged violation to the person."

> ANSWER C: Section 17(b) of the state Water Quality Act requires the plaintiff to give the defendant sixty days' advance notice.

Answer B is best because it simply quotes the notice provision. The exact text of the provision is important here because the telephone conversation occurred only four weeks before the suit and because that conversation does not appear to have focused on violations of the Water Quality Act. In short, there may be two ways in which the plaintiff ignored the notice provision.

Answer A uses the statutory language almost verbatim but does not say so, improperly implying that the language is the writer's own. When you quote, use quotation marks.

Answer C attempts to summarize section 17(b) but is not accurate because it fails to state that the plaintiff must give notice *of the alleged violation* sixty days *before filing suit*. Even if the summary were more accurate, an exact quotation would ensure that the writer is analyzing the precise language of the statute and boost the reader's confidence in the discussion.

---

2. Describe only the relevant law.

Describe only the law that is relevant to the client's case. If a statute is relevant, describe only that portion of the statute that may apply to your client's situation. If common law is relevant, describe only the rules, facts, holdings, and reasons and policies that are relevant to the issue or sub-issue being analyzed. Do not include extraneous facts or a description of other holdings in multiple-issue cases. By describing only the relevant law, you will keep yourself and the reader focused. Long statutory quotations and unfocused case descriptions interrupt the flow of your discussion and confuse the reader. They may also obscure the relevant law. If you omit anything, however, be sure that it is immaterial to the discussion and does not change the meaning of the statutory provision or common law rule at issue.

> Your client, the Huntington Park Authority, recently purchased lakefront property to develop a new park. It then discovered that several rusting drums with hazardous chemical waste are buried on the property and are leaking into the lake. It wants to know whether it is liable for cleaning up the property under the state Superfund Act. Your memo concludes that the Huntington Park Authority is liable.

Consider these descriptions of the law:

> ANSWER A: Section 701 of the Superfund Act provides:
>
>> A person shall be responsible for the release or threatened release of a hazardous substance from a site when any of the following apply:
>>
>>> (1) The person owns or operates the site when a hazardous substance is placed on the site or comes to be located in or on a site.
>>> (2) The person owns or operates the site when a hazardous substance is located in or on the site but before it is released.
>>> (3) The person owns or operates the site during the time of the release or threatened release.
>
> ANSWER B: Section 701 of the Superfund Act provides that "a person shall be responsible for the release or threatened release of a hazardous substance from a site when . . . (3) The person owns or operates the site during the time of the release or threatened release."

Answer B is better because it quotes only the language on which liability is based. The authority did not own the property when the drums were buried, so paragraph (1) does not apply. The chemicals are already being released into the environment, so paragraph (2) does not apply. Because the chemicals are now being released, however, paragraph (3) applies. The ellipsis before paragraph (3) indicates the deletion. Answer B focuses attention on the law that decides the issue. Answer A, on the other hand, does not.

---

3. Describe the law in enough detail to enable your reader to understand the discussion.

You should be able to analyze each issue or sub-issue solely on the basis of your written explanation of the law. Likewise, your reader should be able to independently analyze the issue solely from your description of the law. You will need to add to your explanation if, as you write, you find you are drawing on parts of cases, statutes, or constitutional provisions that have not yet been included in the explanation.

The level of detail in your explanation of the law will vary with the complexity of the analysis. Your analysis of "givens" will probably require only the briefest description of the relevant law. The issues central to your memo or brief, however, will likely require a longer explanation.

A nonresident alien domiciled in New Mexico has brought an action in federal court against a permanent resident alien domiciled in Delaware. Does the court have jurisdiction?

Consider the following explanations of the law:

ANSWER A: Section 1332(a) of the Judicial Code permits federal court jurisdiction of civil actions between "citizens of a State and citizens of a foreign state." A permanent resident alien is "deemed to be a citizen of the State in which such alien is domiciled."

ANSWER B: Section 1332(a) of the Judicial Code permits federal district court jurisdiction of civil actions "between citizens of a State and citizens or subjects of a foreign state." For purposes of section 1332, "an alien admitted to the United States for permanent residence shall be deemed a citizen of the State in which such alien is domiciled." In *Salazar v. Viegas*, the court interpreted section 1332(a) to mean that diversity of jurisdiction did not exist between a permanent resident alien and a nonresident alien.

ANSWER C: Section 1332(a) of the Judicial Code permits federal district court jurisdiction of civil actions "between citizens of a State and citizens or subjects of a foreign state." For purposes of section 1332, "an alien admitted to the United States for permanent residence shall be deemed a citizen of the State in which such alien is domiciled." In *Salazar v. Viegas*, the court held that diversity of jurisdiction did not exist between a permanent resident alien and a nonresident alien. The court recognized that the "deeming provision" appears on its face to treat permanent residents the same as citizens and thus extend jurisdiction to suits between aliens. The court did not adopt that construction, however, because Article III, Section 2, of the Constitution requires that one of the parties be a citizen of the United States. *Accord Sikh v. Hudson Metalworks, Inc.; Menta v. Panamerican Corp.*

Answer C is best because it contains the most complete and understandable discussion of the law. It describes the statutory rule and the constitutional provision and then explains the judicial interpretation of the rule. Answer C gives the reader confidence because it allows evaluation of the law on which the writer's analysis will be based.

Answer B explains the statutory rule and the holding in *Salazar*, but it does not include the reason for the holding and the relevant constitutional provision. Answer B is thus incomplete and raises questions about the writer's thoroughness.

Answer A is the worst of the three answers because it contains only a description of the statutory rule. It is also misleading because it does not include the constitutional provision and an explanation of how the courts have interpreted the rule in light of Article III.

---

4. Summarize the law whenever appropriate.

In any discussion of a legal issue, you must identify the sources of the legal rules. How much information to provide about the source of a rule varies. When setting out a general and undisputed legal principle, such as in an introductory statement to move from the broad area of the law to the narrow issue under consideration, a bare citation to a case or statute is usually sufficient. As you proceed with the discussion, you should summarize the cases used in your analysis. The amount of detail required in a case summary depends on the complexity of the case and how significant it is to your analysis. A case that is complex, either in its facts or in the legal issues presented, requires a more extensive discussion than a less complex case. Similarly, a case central to your analysis should be discussed in detail, while one used only for a collateral point could be summarized in a sentence or two. When deciding how much is enough, consider how much the reader needs to know in order to understand your point.

When writing about issues involving only a handful of relevant cases, you can describe each case in some detail. Many legal problems, however, involve more relevant cases than you can reasonably include. For these problems, summarize the general legal principles and then describe several representative cases to illustrate your point. In selecting representative cases, you may examine in detail leading cases that have been followed by many other courts. Another approach is to examine cases with factual situations that are most analogous or most different. Decisions by higher courts or courts from your jurisdiction are ordinarily preferable to lower court cases or cases from another jurisdiction.

Your client, Susan Wennerberg, was seriously injured while skiing near a small town that has a private hospital. Although she had heard many times that this hospital treated injuries, she was refused emergency treatment. She wants to know whether she can successfully sue the private hospital for the aggravation of her injury that occurred during the drive to the public hospital.

Consider the following ways of describing the relevant law:

ANSWER A: Traditionally, a private hospital has had the right to select those persons who could enjoy its benefits. Private hospitals have been able to lawfully reject emergency patients because they had policies of not accepting members of certain health insurance plans, *O'Neill v. Montefiore Hospital*, or persons with contagious diseases, *Birmingham Baptist Hospital v. Crews*. This right was so well established that the *Crews* court said a private hospital needs no reason at all to refuse service to a particular emergency patient.

The principal exception to this right to refuse treatment is when there is an unmistakable emergency and the patient has relied on the well-established custom of the hospital to render aid in such cases. In the leading case for this exception, *Wilmington General Hospital v. Manlove*, a private hospital refused emergency treatment to the plaintiffs' 4-month-old infant, who had a sore throat, diarrhea, and a 102-degree temperature. The hospital did not treat the child because she was already under a physician's care. The baby died of pneumonia several hours later. In affirming the trial court's denial of the hospital's motion for summary judgment, the court stressed the importance of the time lost in fruitless attempts to obtain medical aid.

ANSWER B: Traditionally, a private hospital has had the right to select those persons who could enjoy its benefits. In *Birmingham Baptist Hospital v. Crews*, the parents of a 2½-year-old girl suffering from diphtheria brought her to the defendant hospital, where she was diagnosed and treated with antitoxin. The hospital staff told the parents that the hospital did not accept patients with contagious diseases and refused to allow her to stay. She died within five minutes of returning home. In deciding that the hospital was not liable for the child's death, the court reasoned that a private hospital can lawfully refuse service to emergency patients and that preliminary treatment should not prejudice that right of refusal.

Similarly, in *O'Neill v. Montefiore Hospital*, a private hospital refused admission to a man who complained of heart attack symptoms, because he was a member of a particular health insurance plan. The man subsequently died. Although there was some question whether the hospital undertook to aid the man initially, the court held that the hospital had no obligation to treat him in the first place.

The principal exception to this right to refuse treatment occurs when there is an unmistakable emergency and the patient has relied on the well-established custom of the hospital to render aid in such cases. In the leading case for this exception, *Wilmington General Hospital v. Manlove*, a private hospital refused emergency treatment to the plaintiffs' 4-month-old infant, who had a sore throat, diarrhea, and a 102-degree temperature. The hospital did not treat the baby because she was already under a physician's care. The baby died of pneumonia several hours later. In affirming the trial court's denial of the hospital's motion for summary judgment, the court stressed the importance of the time lost in fruitless attempts to obtain medical aid.

Answer A is preferable because it gets to the point more quickly and clearly than Answer B. Answer A summarizes the absolute right of refusal cases to provide the context for a lengthy discussion of *Manlove*. The issue is whether Wennerberg fits the exception, not whether she fits the rule. Because *Manlove* is the leading case on the exception to the rule, it deserves detailed consideration and the reader's focused attention. Answer B, however, describes in detail cases that do not need to be explained at this point, if at all. Writers who devote a paragraph to each of several cases in succession tend to ramble and fail to analyze the issues. Answer B also makes it hard for both the reader and the writer to understand what law is relevant. You can write more clearly and briefly by summarizing the relevant law when appropriate.

Similar principles apply to describing statutes. As stated earlier, you should quote the statutory provision at issue, but often it will be necessary to explain the statutory scheme into which that provision fits. It is better to summarize this part of the law than to quote it. A summary is usually more direct than a quotation, fits into the flow of your discussion better than a longer quotation, and lets the reader concentrate on the statutory text relevant to the issue.

Consider the following descriptions of the entire citizen suit provision from the problem discussed earlier:

ANSWER A: Section 17 of the state Water Quality Act provides:

(a) Authority to bring civil action—Any person may commence a civil action on his own behalf against any person who is alleged to be in violation of this Act or a regulation promulgated thereunder.

(b) Notice—No action may be commenced under this section prior to sixty days after the plaintiff has given notice of the alleged violation to the person.

ANSWER B: Section 17 of the state Water Quality Act authorizes any person to bring a civil action against any other person for violating the act or regulations adopted under the Act. Subsection (b) provides: "No action may be commenced under this section prior to sixty days after the plaintiff has given notice of the alleged violation to the person."

Answer B summarizes part of the citizen suit provision and then quotes the notice language. The summary allows the reader to understand the citizen suit provision, and the quotation focuses the reader's attention on the text relevant to the question. Answer B is the better answer. By quoting the entire section, Answer A fails to focus attention on the specific language at issue.

5. Synthesize the law whenever necessary.

Chapter 5 (Understanding Legal Rules) explained that it is sometimes necessary to synthesize two or more legal authorities in order to create a complete statement of a legal rule. Similarly, it is sometimes necessary to synthesize several authorities in order to create a complete description of the law. You will often find that several highly relevant cases support your position or that several cases need to be distinguished. Describe these cases together. Synthesizing cases gives the reader a complete understanding of the entire body of law supporting or opposing your position on a particular issue or sub-issue. Synthesizing cases is also consistent with the guideline in Chapter 10 (Organization), which states that all of the law on an issue or sub-issue should be described before it is applied to the facts. Resist the temptation to describe a case, apply it to your facts, then describe another case, apply it to your facts, and so forth. Such an approach leaves the reader with no clear understanding of the law.

Recall the rule on aggravated menacing discussed in Chapter 5 (Understanding Legal Rules). You asked your law clerk to research the meaning of the word "knowingly" as used in the statute. Which of the following descriptions of the law would be easier for you, the supervising attorney, to understand?

ANSWER A: To be found guilty of aggravated menacing, the defendant must "knowingly cause another to believe that the offender will cause serious physical harm to the person or property of the other person, the other person's unborn, or a member of the other person's immediate family." State Code § 290.30. Whether one acts "knowingly" depends on the manner in which the threat is delivered. *See, e.g., State v. Rosenby; State v. Wentz; State v. Huffman.*

In *State v. Rosenby* the defendant repeatedly called his former girlfriend, sometimes as often as twenty times a day, after she broke up with him because he physically abused her. One evening he drove to her house and screamed at her from his car, threatening to "take her to the grave with him." The defendant argued that his statement was not accompanied by any physical movement or attempt to carry out the threat. The court stated that the statute does not require that the defendant be able to carry out his threat, only that he knowingly cause the victim to believe that he will carry it out. The court concluded that the jury could reasonably find that the defendant "knowingly" caused his former girlfriend to believe he would kill her when he approached her at home and told her that he would "take her to the grave with him."

In *State v. Wentz* the defendant told a teenage boy to tell his mother that "she's messing with the wrong person and if she tries to bust him for anything, she'll be hurting." Later he asked the boy if he had relayed the message to his mother. The boy's mother testified that her son told her what the defendant had said and that she interpreted the message as a threat. The defendant appealed his conviction for aggravated menacing, arguing that he did not "knowingly cause" the victim to believe that he would harm her because he did not threaten her personally. The court affirmed the conviction, noting that the defendant knew that the boy lived with his mother, told the boy to deliver the message to her, and then verified that the message had been delivered. The defendant therefore acted knowingly when he told the boy to deliver a threatening message to a member of his own family, his mother.

Finally, in *State v. Huffman* a man told a child support enforcement worker, "I should just kill [my ex-wife], maybe that will end it all." The worker told her supervisor, who informed police and the defendant's ex-wife. The defendant's conviction for aggravated menacing was reversed. The court stated that a person acts knowingly under the statute if it is "more likely than not" that the person to whom the defendant makes a threat will deliver it to the intended victim. In this case, the caseworker did not know the defendant's ex-wife. She also testified that she did not call the police and did not think that her supervisor would. The court reversed the defendant's conviction, holding that "reasonable minds could not conclude" that the defendant knew that his statement would be conveyed to his ex-wife.

ANSWER B: To be found guilty of aggravated menacing, the defendant must "knowingly cause another to believe that the offender will cause serious physical harm to the person or property of the other person, the other person's unborn, or a member of the other person's immediate family." State Code § 290.30. The "knowingly" element is established if the defendant (1) delivers the threat directly to the victim, *State v. Rosenby*; (2) delivers the threat to a member of the victim's family, *State v. Wentz*; or (3) delivers the threat to a third party whom the defendant believes will "more likely than not" convey the threat to the victim, *State v. Huffman*.

In *State v. Rosenby*, for example, the court stated that a jury could reasonably find that the defendant "knowingly" caused his former girlfriend to believe that he would kill her when he went to her house and screamed to her from his car, threatening to "take her to the grave with him." It is not necessary, however, for a defendant to personally deliver or communicate a threat to the victim to establish the requisite knowledge under the statute. A defendant also acts knowingly if the threat is delivered indirectly, through a third party. In *State v. Wentz* the court concluded that a defendant acted knowingly when he knew that a teenage boy lived with his mother, and he told the boy to deliver a threat to her, "a member of his own family." Even when there is no family relationship between the person to whom a threat is made and the intended victim, a defendant still acts knowingly if it is "more likely than not" that the person to whom the threat is made will convey it to the intended victim. In *State v. Huffman*, the standard was not met because the defendant had no reason to believe that it was "more likely than not" that the caseworker to whom he made a threat against his former wife would report the incident to her supervisor, who would then report it to the police and to the former wife.

Both answers begin by citing the basic statutory authority. Both also flesh out the meaning of "knowingly" by citing and describing the same three cases. Answer A, however, merely presents the cases in the form of individual "mini-briefs." The cases are described in terms of their facts, holding, and reasoning, but the descriptions include some non-relevant facts that distract from the main point. Moreover, Answer A does not tell the reader what the cases mean when read together. At the end of the paragraph the supervising attorney must still figure out how the cases define the word "knowingly."

Answer B, on the other hand, explains the meaning of "knowingly" immediately; the answer to the supervising attorney's question is provided at the outset. Instead of reciting all of the details, the writer of

Answer B has synthesized the cases into a simple and straightforward explanation of the law and tells the reader exactly what "knowingly" really means. This description of the law not only gives the reader the relevant rule, but also puts it in context and identifies the kinds of facts that will satisfy the rule. The cases are used effectively to support and explain the synthesized rule. Thus, Answer A describes cases but requires the reader to do most of the analytical work, while Answer B describes the law and presents the results of the writer's analytical work.

Consider another example:

Randall Byar recently signed a contract to purchase a house in the community to which he has been relocated. He has since discovered that at certain times of the year atmospheric conditions are such that the fumes from a nearby chemical plant become trapped at ground level. The fumes smell noxious and cause watery, burning eyes. Although this problem was not apparent when Byar was shown the house, the seller, Stephen Graham, was aware of the problem. This was the primary reason Graham sold the house, but he never mentioned the problem to Byar. Byar is your client and wants to know whether he can rescind this contract.

The highest court in your state has decided the following two cases:

Stewart v. Avery (1984)

The appellee, Jessica Avery, sued to rescind a contract for the purchase of a house. The appellee contends that the appellant deceived her because he was aware, but failed to disclose, that the house contained high levels of radon—odorless and colorless radioactive particles that can cause cancer. Normally, the rule of *caveat emptor* applies to the purchase of real estate, requiring the buyer to thoroughly inspect the property before agreeing to purchase it. Here, however, such an inspection would not have revealed the high levels of radon. Such a defect is a critical factor in the transaction, affecting the value of the property and its potential resale value. Thus, rescission is appropriate to relieve the appellee from the burden of this agreement, obtained through the appellant's silence on a matter he surely knew was material to the transaction. The decision of the trial court to rescind the contract is, therefore, affirmed.

Waters v. Morton (2001)

The appellee was granted rescission of a contract for the purchase of a house. The appellee did not discover until afterwards that the septic tank and drain lines were inadequate. This deficiency resulted in the overflow of raw sewage into the front yard after every heavy rain. This condition was apparent only then.

Passive concealment of defective realty constitutes an exception to the rule of *caveat emptor.* This exception places a duty on the seller to disclose facts not apparent to the buyer that would probably affect his decision to purchase.

In this case even the most diligent of examinations would not have disclosed this defect, because the problem was apparent only after a heavy rain. The appellant knew of the deficiencies in the sewage system, yet he allowed the appellee to sign the contract without disclosing these facts. Such conduct constitutes fraud and warrants rescission of the contract. Affirmed.

Consider these descriptions of the law:

ANSWER A: Byar is entitled to rescind his purchase contract. Even a diligent inspection would not have revealed the problem with the toxic fumes, and Graham failed to disclose this problem to Byar before he signed the contract. Although the general rule in purchasing real property is *caveat emptor,* an exception exists when the defect is not discernible through a thorough inspection and the seller is aware of the defect yet fails to disclose it, knowing that such information is relevant to the buyer's decision to purchase. *Stewart v. Avery; Waters v. Morton.*

In both *Stewart* and *Waters* the sellers withheld material information regarding a defect in the property, even though they knew the purchasers could not discover the defect by inspecting the property. In *Stewart,* the seller of a house did not disclose that the house contained high levels of radon. In *Waters,* the seller did not disclose the inadequacy of the septic system, which caused the overflow of raw sewage into the front yard after every heavy rain. In both cases the sellers withheld information that the purchasers could not have discovered through a diligent inspection of the premises.

[Discussion analogizing cases to Byar's situation omitted.]

Furthermore, in each of these cases, the information withheld was material to the purchaser's decision. The radon levels and the inadequacy of the septic system affected the value of the respective properties involved. The sellers in each case had a duty to disclose the facts regarding the defect in the property. In both *Stewart* and *Waters,* concealment of the defect constituted fraud and warranted rescission of the contract.

[Discussion analogizing cases to Byar's situation omitted.]

ANSWER B: Byar is entitled to rescind his purchase contract. Even a diligent inspection would not have revealed the problem with the toxic fumes, and Graham failed to disclose this problem to Byar before he signed the contract. Although the general rule in purchasing real property is *caveat emptor,* an exception exists when the defect is not discernible through a thorough inspection and the seller is aware of the defect yet fails to disclose it, knowing that such information is relevant to the buyer's decision to purchase. *Stewart v. Avery; Waters v. Morton.*

In *Stewart,* the court granted rescission of a contract for the purchase of a house when the seller had failed to disclose that the house had high levels of radon. The court found that this information affected the value of the property and was therefore relevant to the purchaser's decision to buy the house. Reasoning that even the most diligent inspection of the premises would not have revealed the radon levels, the court placed the burden of disclosing this fact on the seller.

[Discussion analogizing case to Byar's situation omitted.]

In *Waters,* the court also granted a rescission of a sales contract because the seller failed to disclose a defect in the real estate. The seller had failed to disclose that the septic system was inadequate, causing an overflow of raw sewage into the front yard after any heavy rain. The condition was not apparent at any other time. The court reasoned that the seller's knowledge of this defect and the buyer's inability to discover it during a diligent inspection of the premises warranted rescission of the contract.

[Discussion analogizing case to Byar's situation omitted.]

Answer A is better because it summarizes and synthesizes the *Stewart* and *Waters* cases according to the two sub-issues raised. Answer A explains the law of the two cases concerning failure to disclose and then explains the law concerning information that is material to the purchaser's decision. The discussion that follows each sub-issue likely will be focused and coherent.

Answer B, by contrast, summarizes the cases sequentially. Because the cases are not integrated or related to each other, the reader must pull together the law that the cases represent. Answer B is also confusing because it does not discuss the two sub-issues separately and would require the writer to analyze both sub-issues after each case summary.

EXERCISES

The principles in this chapter address many of the most common and difficult problems you will encounter in describing the law. The following exercises will give you practice using these principles.

Exercise 11-A

This exercise is based on the information contained in Exercise 6-A, pp. 89-91. For one rule chosen by you or your professor, describe the relevant law based on the principles contained in this chapter.

Exercise 11-B

This exercise is based on the information contained in Exercise 6-B, pp. 91-94. For one rule chosen by you or your professor, describe the relevant law based on the principles contained in this chapter.

Exercise 11-C

This exercise is based on the information contained in Exercise 6-C, pp. 94-97. For one rule chosen by you or your professor, describe the relevant law based on the principles contained in this chapter.

Exercise 11-D

Philip and Julia Langford own a nursery that sells plants, trees, and gardening equipment. Last spring, they received a shipment of young dogwood trees and had no space for all of them in the nursery. They planted ten of the trees in the backyard of their residence, four feet apart, with the intention of moving them to the nursery as soon as space was available. Two months later, they sold their residence to Wilbur and Marcie Cliff, who did not plan to move in until the fall. The dogwood trees were not mentioned during the negotiations. The Langfords did not remove the trees prior to the sale because there was still no room in the nursery, but they planned to do so before the Cliffs moved in. The Cliffs assumed that the trees were part of the realty and have refused to allow the Langfords to remove them. The Langfords have consulted you regarding the ownership of the trees. You have found the following two cases.

Stafford National Bank v. Dinesen (1958)

Eric Dinesen owned property, including 30 acres of bogs, on which he grew cranberry bushes. He defaulted on a mortgage held by Stafford National Bank, which now has title to the real estate. Dinesen attempted to dig up and transplant the cranberry bushes to another tract of land he owns. The bank filed suit, claiming that the bushes are part of the real estate and no longer Dinesen's property. Dinesen appeals from the trial court's decision awarding ownership of cranberry bushes to the bank.

This is a case of first impression in this state. At common law, whatever was affixed to the land, including plants and trees, was part of the land. Crops, however, even though growing in the soil, were considered personalty if that was the intent of the owner. The cranberry bushes in this case are not crops because there is no intent to harvest them annually. The purpose is to harvest the berries, not the plants themselves. The bushes are therefore part of the realty and belong to the bank. Affirmed.

Updike v. Teague (1995)

Leslie Updike's action against William Teague for the conversion of nursery stock was dismissed by the trial court for failure to state a cause of action. Updike had entered into a contract with Teague for the sale of certain real estate. After Updike defaulted on the contract, Teague took possession of the land.

Updike owned a nursery, which was located on the property. He supplied orchards with fruit trees and used the land to grow other young trees for resale. After the default, Teague refused to allow Updike to remove the nursery stock and sold it himself. Updike claims the trees were his personal property because he did not intend for them to be part of the realty. He stated that the trees were planted close together in rows and that the planting was temporary, usually for no longer than a year, and for the purpose of maintaining them until they were sold.

The trial court applied the traditional common law rule that plants and trees growing in the soil are part of the land and belong to the landowner. We believe these trees are more properly characterized as stock in trade, which is defined as goods and chattels that a merchant obtains for the purpose of resale and is considered personal property. Trees offered for sale must necessarily be kept in the soil. Updike placed them there for the sole purpose of keeping them alive prior to sale. They were therefore the personal property of Updike. Reversed.

1. State the common law rule and the exceptions.

2. Describe the law relevant to each exception.

12 Applying the Law

After describing the law supporting your position, you must explain how the law actually supports your position. Similarly, after describing the law that might support a counterargument, you should explain how the law fails to support that counterargument. This chapter builds on the lessons in Chapter 11 (Describing the Law). It identifies particular problems in analyzing the law and explains how to resolve them.

1. Be precise.

Effective communication is directly related to the care with which words are chosen and sentences and paragraphs are structured. Theodore M. Bernstein of *The New York Times* once said: "If writing must be a precise form of communication, it should be treated like a precision instrument. It should be sharpened, and it should not be used carelessly." Bernstein's statement is perhaps more true of legal writing than of journalistic writing. Legal conclusions depend on the application of specific cases, statutes, and constitutional provisions to specific situations. Your analysis will be strengthened by your precision in analyzing problems. Precision leads to clarity and forces you to identify and correct weaknesses in your discussion.

Consider the following approaches to analyzing the citizen suit problem in Chapter 11:

ANSWER A: The court does not have jurisdiction to hear Thorpe's citizen suit. Section 17(b) of the state Water Quality Act provides: "No action may be commenced under this section prior to sixty days after the plaintiff has given notice of the alleged violation to the person." In this case, Thorpe did not meet the requirement for sixty days' advance notice. Nor did he give specific notice of the alleged violation to the defendant. His notice was too general to let the defendant know what the violations were. His citizen suit therefore can be dismissed.

ANSWER B: The court does not have jurisdiction to hear Thorpe's citizen suit. Section 17(b) of the state Water Quality Act provides: "No action may be commenced under this section prior to sixty days after the plaintiff has given notice of the alleged violation to the person." In this case, Thorpe did not meet the requirement for sixty days' advance notice because his phone call was only twenty-eight days before he filed the suit. Furthermore, given the great variety of potential violations of the Water Quality Act, the necessary notice of the alleged violation was not met by a general threat against the defendant's "stinking operation." Because the sixty day notice requirement was intended to give potential defendants an opportunity to correct specific violations, Thorpe should have identified the alleged violations more specifically and waited sixty days to file suit. His citizen suit can therefore be dismissed.

Both answers begin with a thesis sentence and a description of the relevant law. Answer B is better because it explains precisely that the court does not have jurisdiction to hear Thorpe's citizen suit for two reasons: (1) The requirement of sixty days' notice is not met by twenty-eight days' notice, and (2) Thorpe's notice was not specific enough to satisfy the statutory requirement to give "notice of the alleged violation." The reader of Answer B knows why the writer reached this conclusion.

Answer A, on the other hand, contains no specific statements about the relationship between the statutory rule and the facts of this case. Instead, it contains only general statements that the requirements were not met. Unlike Answer B, Answer A does not explain the reasons for the writer's conclusion; notice that Answer B includes the word "because," but Answer A does not. While it is sometimes possible for a reader to figure out the steps that lead the writer from rule to conclusion, you should leave nothing to chance. Make the relationship between the rule and the facts explicit.

2. Show every step in your analysis.

Because memos are written for lawyers, it is safe to assume that the reader will have a basic understanding of the law and the legal process. You should not assume, however, that the reader will understand how the cited cases or statutes support your conclusion. It is not enough to state that a particular result will occur; you must identify the analytical steps leading to that result. As discussed in Chapter 10 (Organization), if there are several "givens" and one issue, you should discuss the givens before you discuss the issue. A reader who is able to follow all the important steps of your thought process on paper will be able to evaluate the soundness of your conclusions. Failure to show all the steps of your analysis may give the reader an incomplete understanding of the issue or sub-issue and thus little or no confidence in your conclusion.

In a way, writing a memorandum or brief is like giving directions to your home. You know how to get there, but the directions you give or the map you provide must enable someone else to get there. Each important feature or turn in your analytical map must be clearly identified, or your reader is likely to get lost. Your directions should include only what is necessary—no more, but also no less. Many writers understand their subject so well that they may compress several analytical steps into one, make unexplained assumptions, or fail to define important terms. Make sure your directions are clear and complete.

Your client, Carl Norbert, was recently injured when the jeep he was driving struck a deer and ran off the road. The jeep, which was owned by the state Fish and Game Department, was signed out to Stephanie Bennett, a field biologist for the Department. She allowed Norbert to drive it because he was considering a job with the Department. He was driving through state game land at the time. Norbert believes that Bennett was negligent in not accompanying him in the jeep and for not telling him about the numerous deer on state land. He would like to recover from the Department for his injuries. You have been asked to assume the Department's negligence and determine whether the state's Sovereign Immunity Act would bar an action for his injuries.

ANSWER A: The Sovereign Immunity Act does not bar an action against the Fish and Game Department. The Act does not apply to negligence actions when a state employee is in control of the vehicle, and Bennett, a state employee, had control of the jeep.

The Act, which generally prohibits suits against "state parties" for damages caused by negligent acts, is a codification of the common law doctrine protecting the government or sovereign against suits for the government's alleged negligence. The Fish and Game Department is a "state party." Although the Act does not define the term, the courts have held other departments to be state parties. *E.g., Wold v. Department of Transportation.*

The Department is nonetheless liable for negligence because the statute contains an exception for the "operation of any motor vehicle in the possession or control of a state party." Bennett, a state employee, had control over the jeep because it was signed out to her and because she allowed Norbert to drive it without accompanying him. Under the doctrine of vicarious liability, state parties are liable for the acts of their employees. *Wold.* The only case interpreting this provision, *Hall v. Department of Banking*, is distinguishable. In *Hall*, a Department of Banking employee negligently ran Hall's car off the road. The court held that the Act did not apply. The employee had taken the Department's vehicle without permission and thus the Department did not have control or possession of it. This case is different because Bennett had permission to take the jeep and because she then authorized Norbert to drive it.

ANSWER B: The Sovereign Immunity Act does not bar an action against the Fish and Game Department because the Department had control of the vehicle. The Act generally prohibits suits against "state parties" for damages caused by negligent acts. The Department is liable for negligence because the statute contains an exception for the "operation of any motor vehicle in the possession or control of a state party." The only case interpreting this provision, *Hall v. Department of Banking*, is distinguishable. In *Hall*, a Department of Banking employee negligently ran Hall's car off the road. The court held the Department did not have control or possession of the vehicle since the employee had taken it without permission.

Answer A is better because it explains every step needed to show how the writer reached a conclusion. It explains the general rule in the statute and then explains that the statute codifies the common law sovereign immunity doctrine. This is a helpful step for readers who are unfamiliar with sovereign immunity or who understand sovereign immunity only as a common law doctrine. Answer A also explains that the Department is a state party and would be liable for the acts of its employees. These are "givens" in this case, but the discussion would be incomplete without them.

Answer A discusses the exception to sovereign immunity, showing why it is applicable, and then discusses *Hall*, a potential basis for a counterargument, showing why it is distinguishable.

Answer B is the same as Answer A, but several steps are missing that seriously undermine Answer B's effectiveness and credibility. Answer B omits the following: an explanation that the statute codifies the common law rule, an explanation of how the Department is a state party and would be liable for the acts of its employees, an explanation of precisely how the Department had control over the jeep, and an analysis distinguishing *Hall*. These omissions leave gaps in the discussion. Some readers will see these gaps as evidence that the writer has not thought through the problem or is hiding something. Other readers will simply be confused. Still others will be able to fill in the blanks, but you should not leave this to chance. A writer who leaves gaps in her analysis has not justified the conclusion.

---

3. Describe every reasonable basis for your conclusion.

In many legal problems, several reasons or legal theories may lead to the same conclusion. A particular action may have violated several laws, for example. To show your reader that you have reached the right conclusion, your discussion should reflect these reasons and theories. You should, however, include only the most persuasive or effective reasons or theories. A good test is whether each reason or theory could stand on its own without support from the others. If so, it is probably worth including. Using weak reasons or theories to support your conclusion hurts your credibility.

Your client, Theresa Clare, owns Tess's Bed & Breakfast, an elegant Victorian house in which up to seven rooms are rented to overnight guests who are served breakfast in the morning. The house is located in a residential area in the city of Nekoosa. Several neighborhood teenagers have recently formed a band they call "Slow Death." They practice each night from 9 p.m. to 1 or 2 a.m. in a garage two doors away. The noise from the band has been recorded continuously at thirty to seventy decibels at the front door of your client's house. Her business has decreased dramatically since the band began practicing, and she has been unable to persuade the teenagers or their parents to control the noise. The City Council has not taken any relevant action. She wants to know what she can do.

Section 305.5(c) of the Nekoosa Municipal Code states:

> Unless specifically authorized by the City Council, no person may cause any noise that exceeds fifty decibels. The City Council may order the cessation of any unauthorized activity under this subsection.

There is one relevant case in your jurisdiction:

Hooke v. Allen (1982)

Raymond Allen, who lives in a residential area, erected a seventy-foot tower with an old windmill at the top to save energy and reduce his electric bills. Shortly after the windmill was erected, it began to make a loud and continuous noise. His neighbor, Pearl Hooke, filed suit claiming that the windmill caused a private nuisance. The trial court ordered the windmill dismantled, and we affirm.

A private nuisance is an unreasonable interference with the use and enjoyment of land. Noise is an actionable private nuisance if the health and comfort of ordinary people in the vicinity are injured and if the injury is unreasonable under all the circumstances. The trial court found that the windmill's noise is louder, more constant, and more offensive than other noises in the vicinity. The noise occurs both during the day and at night when people are trying to sleep. The trial court also found, by contrast, that virtually all newer windmill designs make little noise. Because of these findings, we have no reason to disturb the trial court's order.

ANSWER A: The band's practice violates the city's municipal code and also constitutes a private nuisance. It therefore can be enjoined.

The band's noise level violates section 305.5(c) of the Nekoosa Municipal Code. Section 305.5(c) provides: "Unless specifically authorized by the City Council, no person may cause any noise that exceeds fifty decibels." Because the band's noise has been continuously recorded at thirty to seventy decibels in front of Clare's house, and because the City Council has not authorized the noise, the band violates the ordinance. Section 305.5(c) also provides that the "City Council may order the cessation of any unauthorized activity under this subsection." The City Council could therefore order the noise stopped.

The practice also constitutes a private nuisance because it unreasonably interferes with Clare's use and enjoyment of her land. In *Hooke v. Allen*, the court stated that noise can constitute a private nuisance if it injures the health and safety of ordinary people in the vicinity and if the injury is unreasonable under all the circumstances. In that case, the court held that noise from a nearby windmill was injurious because of its loudness, duration, offensiveness, and occurrence at night. The Nekoosa Municipal Code generally limits noise from any person to fifty decibels, and this limit may be understood as a maximum reasonable level. Thus, at thirty to seventy decibels, the band is often unreasonably loud. Like the windmill noise in *Hooke*, the band noise occurs at night when people are trying to sleep and, although not continuous as was the noise from the windmill, it lasts for four or five hours each night. That it is offensive is manifest by the dramatic decline in Clare's business since the band began practicing. The court in *Hooke* found the windmill noise unreasonable partly because moving the windmill or choosing another design would have reduced the noise. The band could have avoided unreasonably interfering with Clare's use of her land by practicing at a different time of day or in a location more removed from the neighbors. The band practice is a private nuisance and may be enjoined.

ANSWER B: The band's practice constitutes a private nuisance because it unreasonably interferes with Clare's use and enjoyment of her land. In *Hooke v. Allen*, the court held that noise can constitute a private nuisance if it injures the health and safety of ordinary people in the vicinity and if the injury is unreasonable under all the circumstances. In that case, the court held that noise from a nearby windmill constituted a private nuisance because of its loudness, duration, offensiveness, and occurrence at night. Like the windmill noise in *Hooke*, much of the band's noise occurs at night when people are trying to sleep. That it is offensive is manifest by the dramatic decline in Clare's business since the band began practicing. The band is causing a private nuisance and may be enjoined.

Answer A is better. It discusses both grounds for proceeding against the band—private nuisance and violation of the municipal code. Answer A also discusses a complete range of relevant factual analogies between *Hooke* and this case. The completeness of the answer gives the reader greater confidence in the writer's conclusion.

Answer B justifies the writer's conclusion less completely and less persuasively. By ignoring the ordinance as an independent basis for action, the writer overlooks an option that his client or the court, if properly informed, might use. By omitting several factual analogies, the writer makes the nuisance claim seem weaker than it really is. Describing every reasonable basis for your conclusion ensures that you have thoroughly analyzed the issue and communicated that analysis to the reader.

---

4. Explain the context.

When the importance of a legal issue or sub-issue to the resolution of a problem may not be apparent to the reader, you must explain how that issue or sub-issue fits into the factual situation and how it relates to your analysis. When the problem involves a single subsection of a complicated statute, for example, you should outline the statute before applying the subsection. Failure to describe the context may leave a reader guessing about the significance of an issue or sub-issue you raise.

> Ann White, an elderly woman, was detained by the clerk of a department store in which she was shopping because the clerk suspected that White had stolen several items from the store. The clerk grabbed White by the wrist as she was leaving the store and quietly said, "OK, come with me, lady." The clerk then led her by the wrist to the manager's office, told her not to move, offered her a cup of coffee, and propped a chair against the outside of the door to prevent her escape while he looked for the manager. When the clerk and the manager returned a few minutes later, they found that she had not stolen anything, even though her physical description closely fit that of a woman who in previous weeks had taken several items from the store.

State Compiled Laws § 32.01 provides:

> A merchant's employee who has reasonable grounds to believe that goods have been unlawfully taken by a person may, for the purpose of attempting to effect a recovery of said goods, take the person into custody and detain him in a reasonable manner for a reasonable length of time. Such action does not render a merchant's employee civilly or criminally liable for false imprisonment.

Consider these two ways of discussing the liability of the store for false imprisonment:

ANSWER A: The store is liable for White's false imprisonment because it did not detain her in a reasonable manner. State Compiled Laws § 32.01 provides:

> A merchant's employee who has reasonable grounds to believe that goods have been unlawfully taken by a person may, for the purpose of attempting to effect a recovery of said goods, take the person into custody and detain him in a reasonable manner for a reasonable length of time. Such action does not render a merchant's employee civilly or criminally liable for false imprisonment.

The clerk in this case grabbed the wrist of an elderly woman who was leaving the store, led her by the wrist to the manager's office, and then physically restrained her there. The clerk's quiet voice and offer of a cup of coffee do not make his excessive use of force reasonable.

ANSWER B: The store falsely imprisoned White and is not relieved of liability by state statute because the store's clerk detained her in an unreasonable manner. A person is liable for false imprisonment when he intentionally restrains another person against that person's will. There was false imprisonment here because the clerk prevented White from leaving the store and put her in the manager's office, all against her will.

The statutory defense of State Compiled Laws § 32.01 does not absolve the store of liability. Section 32.01 provides:

> A merchant's employee who has reasonable grounds to believe that goods have been unlawfully taken by a person may, for the purpose of attempting to effect a recovery of said goods, take the person into custody and detain him in a reasonable manner for a reasonable length of time. Such action does not render a merchant's employee civilly or criminally liable for false imprisonment.

The clerk had reasonable grounds to suspect White because she matched the description of an elderly shoplifter. In addition, the detention period of two or three minutes is a reasonable length of time. The clerk nevertheless failed to detain White in a reasonable manner. He grabbed the wrist of an elderly woman who was leaving the store, led her by the wrist to the manager's office, and physically restrained her there. The clerk's quiet voice and offer of a cup of coffee do not make his excessive use of force reasonable.

Answer B is preferable because it shows that the common law tort of false imprisonment has been committed, describes the statute as a defense to false imprisonment, and completely explains the application of each element of the statute—reasonable grounds, reasonable manner, and reasonable time—to White's situation. Answer A, however, incorrectly implies that restraint in an unreasonable manner is necessary for false imprisonment. By focusing only on the issue supporting that conclusion, Answer A does not give the reader a complete and balanced picture. It fails to explain how each element of the statute applies to White's situation and assumes the reader will be able to fill in the gaps.

EXERCISES

As you work through the following exercises, remember that your responsibility is to analyze the law accurately and completely.

Exercise 12-A

This exercise is based on Exercise 11-A, p. 184. For one rule chosen by you or your professor, explain your analysis of the issue and any sub-issues.

Exercise 12-B

This exercise is based on Exercise 11-B, p. 184. For one rule chosen by you or your professor, explain your analysis of the issue and any sub-issues.

Exercise 12-C

This exercise is based on Exercise 11-C, p. 184. For one rule chosen by you or your professor, explain your analysis of the issue and any sub-issues.

Exercise 12-D

Explain your analysis of any issues or sub-issues based on your description of the law in Exercise 11-D, pp. 184-85.

Signposting

Tell your reader where you are going, and then clearly and carefully guide the reader as you go. This rule is especially important when discussing multiple issues, each of which may have several sub-issues. Thinking and writing about a legal problem is like hacking through a dense jungle: As a writer you may backtrack, go in circles, or make long detours because you started in the wrong place or reached an impossible obstacle. While this process is necessary, the final product must be more direct. When putting your thoughts on paper, take the reader only where necessary and erect clear signposts along the way. Remember, the reader is not as familiar with the law and how it applies to the facts as you are.

Signposting is especially important in legal writing because of the nature of your audience and the circumstances under which your document will be read. Your audience is likely to be lawyers, who read documents in a hurry, under pressure, and for a specific purpose. Good signposts can make the structure of your analysis so clear that even hurried and impatient readers can follow your logic and understand your conclusions. Poor signposts, on the other hand, can obscure the structure of the analysis and tax the patience of your reader.

This chapter sets out the basic principles of signposting and explains how to use four types of signposts: thesis statements, paragraphs, topic sentences, and transitions.

1. Use thesis statements to set out your conclusion for each issue and sub-issue.

A *thesis statement* is a sentence in the first or second paragraph of a formal paper that states the writer's conclusion. It gives the reader a foundation for reading and understanding the paper. You should have a thesis stating your conclusion on each issue and sub-issue at the outset of the discussion of that issue or sub-issue. A clear opening thesis tells the reader what to look for while reading your memo or brief.

Your client, Alice Woodford, is considering a lawsuit against a company that has threatened to stop delivering steel to her. Her state recognizes a cause of action for business or economic duress. One element of this cause of action requires that the defendant threatened unlawful conduct. Which of the following introductions to the discussion is better?

ANSWER A: Woodford cannot recover civil damages for business or economic duress because the company with which she contracted for delivery of steel did not threaten her with unlawful conduct. In *Porter v. Falk*, the court held that a defendant was not liable for business or economic duress when it threatened to take actions that the defendant had a legal right to take.

ANSWER B: In *Porter v. Falk*, the court held that a defendant was not liable for business or economic duress when it threatened to take actions that the defendant had a legal right to take.

Answer A is better because it begins with the writer's statement of the issue and its resolution. This statement provides the context for the rule that follows. Answer B, on the other hand, gives no direction as to why the rule matters or where the writer is going.

2. Use paragraphs to divide the discussion into manageable parts.

A *paragraph* is a group of sentences relating to one discrete idea or topic. The proper use of paragraphs helps to divide the discussion into parts that can be readily understood. Proper paragraphing is especially important in legal documents because of their complexity and the circumstances in which they are read. Improper paragraphing can cause a reader to miss, or misunderstand, your analysis.

Paragraphs are the building blocks of legal analysis. They are visual cues that the writer is moving to a new idea. Paragraphs also give the reader a mental pause. The reader expects legal writing to be divided into coherent paragraphs and is likely to become frustrated and impatient with solid pages of text.

As a building block, each paragraph contains only a part of the larger unit of information you are communicating to the reader. It is important not only that the reader be able to understand each paragraph as a unit, but also that the reader be able to put all your paragraphs together to develop a complete picture. Each paragraph must play a significant role in the discussion and clearly relate to both the paragraph before and the one that follows. Good paragraphing places your ideas in logical order and ties them together.

The length of a paragraph depends primarily on how much information and reasoning you must include to develop a topic or idea fully. A typical paragraph contains four to eight sentences, including a thesis or topic sentence. A succession of two- or three-sentence paragraphs indicates one of two problems. Either you have not fully developed each idea or you have broken one discrete discussion into several parts, thus fragmenting your analysis.

To some extent, paragraph length is also a matter of discretion. An occasional short paragraph will capture the reader's attention and is an excellent device for emphasizing a point. Paragraphs that are too long may present the biggest problem for readers. Some writers use a half-page as a warning signal. When a paragraph reaches that length, review it for problems. Long paragraphs may indicate that you have not sorted out your ideas, that you have included more than one topic in each paragraph, or that you need to tighten your sentence structure and eliminate unnecessary words. If you have a paragraph longer than a double-spaced page, try to find a logical place to divide it. Sometimes more than one paragraph is necessary to develop a single idea.

Albert Sands owned an abandoned building in which he had stored highly flammable chemicals for several years. The drums in which they were stored had leaked and the floor had become saturated with the chemicals. After Sands removed the drums, several small fires occurred that were put out by the city fire department. Last week, Sands's faulty wiring of an electrical circuit breaker caused another, larger fire. Sands called the fire department for help. Although he knew of the danger the saturated floor posed to firefighters, he did not warn the fire department. Paul Romano, a firefighter called to the scene, was injured when the saturated floor suddenly burst into flames and collapsed. He wants to sue Sands for negligence. A potential obstacle is the "fireman's rule," under which emergency personnel injured in the line of duty cannot sue for negligence.

Compare the following discussions on the underlying policies for the rule:

ANSWER A: Jurisdictions recognizing the "fireman's rule" have enumerated several policies supporting the rule. Among them are fairness to the landowner and a desire to spread the cost of such injuries to the community through workers' compensation insurance.

Neither of these policies applies to this case. Fairness is not a factor here because Sands knew of the presence of the hazardous materials and his failure to warn the firefighters responding to the call was directly responsible for Romano's injuries. Some jurisdictions have applied the fireman's rule to avoid penalizing landowners for seeking help from professionals trained and employed to handle emergencies.

These professionals are aware of and assume the normal risks involved in responding to dangerous situations, including fires resulting from landowners' negligence. Romano's claim, however, would not penalize Sands for the negligence that started the fire. Rather, it would be based on Sands's failure to warn the fire department of a risk that the department could not reasonably have foreseen. The desire to spread costs of such injuries to the community is also not a factor here.

The fireman's rule recognizes that firefighters will sometimes be injured while fighting negligently caused fires and that the community should pay workers' compensation claims for such injuries as part of the community's public safety effort. This policy does not apply when injuries occur because of a landowner's subsequent negligence.

Romano was injured not because of Sands's negligence in wiring the circuit breaker, but rather because of Sands's failure to warn of the chemically saturated floor. Sands, not the community, should pay for such injuries.

ANSWER B: Jurisdictions recognizing the fireman's rule have enumerated several policies supporting the rule. Among them are fairness to the landowner and a desire to spread the cost of such injuries to the community through workers' compensation insurance. Neither of these policies applies to this case.

Fairness is not a factor here because Sands knew of the presence of the hazardous materials and because his failure to warn the fire-fighters responding to the call was directly responsible for Romano's injuries. Some jurisdictions have applied the fireman's rule to avoid penalizing landowners for seeking help from professionals trained and employed to handle emergencies. These professionals are aware of and assume the normal risks involved in responding to danger-ous situations, including fires resulting from landowners' negligence. Romano's claim, however, would not penalize Sands for the negli-gence that started the fire. Rather, it would be based on Sands's failure to warn the fire department of a risk that the firefighters could not reasonably have foreseen.

The desire to spread the costs of such injuries to the community is also not a factor here. The fireman's rule recognizes that firefighters will sometimes be injured in fighting negligently caused fires and that the community should pay workers' compensation claims for such inju-ries as part of the community's public safety effort. This policy does not apply when injuries occur because of a landowner's subsequent negligence. Romano was injured not because of Sands's negligence in wiring the circuit breaker, but rather because of Sands's failure to warn of the chemically saturated floor. Sands, not the community, should pay for such injuries.

Answer B is better because the structure of its three paragraphs is evident. The first paragraph identifies the two policies supporting the fireman's rule and states that these policies do not apply. The second paragraph describes the fairness policy and explains why that policy does not apply, and the last paragraph describes the cost-spreading policy and explains why it does not apply. Each paragraph contains a single basic point—no more and no less.

Answer A is much harder to read and understand. The first para-graph describes the policies underlying the fireman's rule, but it does not explain how the writer would apply these policies to the facts. The first paragraph thus is aimless. The second paragraph begins with the broad thesis that should have been in the first paragraph and wrongly implies that the second paragraph will discuss the reasons that neither policy applies. The second paragraph also has an incomplete discussion of the fairness policy. The third paragraph has incomplete discussions of both policies. The fourth and fifth paragraphs have a fragmented discussion of the cost-spreading policy. Each paragraph contains more or less than a single point, but none has just a single point. In short, Answer A does not make as much sense to the reader as Answer B.

3. Use a topic sentence to define the purpose of a paragraph.

Just as a thesis statement summarizes your basic point or conclusion on an issue or sub-issue, a *topic sentence* explains the basic point of a paragraph and thus provides a frame of reference for what is to follow. It is usually the first or second sentence of a paragraph. Because the paragraph is part of your discussion of a particular issue or sub-issue, the topic sentence should support your thesis. The topic sentence should also be connected to the previous paragraph. A topic sentence satisfies your reader's desire to know right away what a paragraph is about and enables a busy reader to skim through your analysis and see the key points. To test the quality of your topic and thesis sentences, extract them from your memo or brief and create a topic sentence outline. If your paragraphs are well-written, these sentences will form a coherent and logical outline of the key steps in your analysis.

Your client, Cindy Ortez, was recently discharged from her job at Packey's Toys, Inc., for filing an antitrust complaint against her employer. As a general rule, an employer can discharge an at-will employee (one who is employed for an unspecified time period) at any time, for any reason. One exception to this rule is that the employee's discharge violates public policy. Several cases illustrate what types of discharges violate public policy. Consider the following excerpts from discussions of whether public policy has been violated in Ortez's case:

ANSWER A: . . . and was discharged when he refused to lie on the witness stand. The court held this to constitute a wrongful discharge because of the necessity of truthful testimony and because perjury is a criminal offense.

Public policy can also be violated when an employer discharges an employee for exercising a statutorily conferred right. In *Frampton v. Central Indiana Gas Co.*, an employee filed a workers' compensation claim for injuries she received in the course of her employment. She was promptly fired. The court held this to be a wrongful discharge and drew an analogy to retaliatory eviction under the state's landlord-tenant law. It determined that the discharge was contrary to the purposes of the workers' compensation statute and thus violated public policy.

ANSWER B: . . . and was discharged when he refused to lie on the witness stand. The court held this to constitute a wrongful discharge because of the necessity of truthful testimony and because perjury is a criminal offense.

In *Frampton v. Central Indiana Gas Co.,* an employee filed a workers' compensation claim for injuries she received in the course of her employment. She was promptly fired. The court held this to be a wrongful discharge and drew an analogy to retaliatory eviction under the state's landlord-tenant law. It determined that the discharge was contrary to the purposes of the workers' compensation statute and thus violated public policy.

Both answers cover the same ground, but Answer A is clearer and more direct. The topic sentence in Answer A states the subject of the paragraph and connects the paragraph with the rest of the discussion before the description of the *Frampton* case begins. Answer A has a good topic sentence and guides the reader through the discussion.

Answer B is less direct. It begins the first full paragraph with a discussion of the *Frampton* case, without giving the reader any clue about the subject of the paragraph or why *Frampton* is being discussed. It directs the reader's attention to the case itself, rather than to the point the writer is using it to make. Thus, the analysis leading to the conclusion is harder to follow because it is less focused.

4. Use transitions to show the relationship between ideas.

Transitions are the directions the writer uses to guide the reader from one point in the discussion to another. Transitions signal to the reader that you have completed the discussion of one point and are proceeding to the next. A discussion that treats a second and separate point as a continuation of the first is confusing.

There is an important relationship between thesis statements and topic sentences on one hand and transitions on the other. The more clearly you have stated the thesis or topic sentence, the more obvious it will be to the reader when you move to the next point in your discussion.

To choose an effective transition, identify the precise relationship between the two ideas to be connected. Transitional words or phrases may be used to indicate a similarity or difference between the previous point and the next one, a simple enumeration of points, a causal relationship, or a temporal relationship. Here are some examples of transitional words and phrases for each of these:

Relationship Between Ideas	Transitional Words & Phrases
Similarity between the previous point and the next one	Similarly Also In addition Further Furthermore Moreover
Difference between the previous point and the next one	However Nevertheless Nonetheless Although On the other hand In contrast
Enumeration of points	First, second, third, etc. Finally Last
Causal relationship	Consequently Therefore Thus Because
Temporal relationship	Subsequently Previously Later In the meantime Then Recently

Transitions sometimes require more than a word or phrase—they may require a sentence or even a paragraph. Transitional sentences may appear at the end of one paragraph or at the beginning of the next. Transitional paragraphs generally are shorter than other types of paragraphs and are used to explain a relationship between paragraphs or ideas that is too complex to be explained in a word or sentence.

Consider the following:

ANSWER A: Under traditional property law analysis, if two people own insured property as joint tenants and one co-owner destroys the property, the innocent co-insured cannot recover insurance proceeds. . . .

The modern approach allows the innocent co-insured to recover if that person's expectations of what the policy covered were reasonable. . . .

ANSWER B: Under traditional property law analysis, if two people own insured property as joint tenants and one co-owner destroys the property, the innocent co-insured cannot recover the insurance proceeds. . . .

Most courts today treat this issue as a contract dispute, regardless of how the insured property is owned. The modern approach allows the innocent co-insured to recover if that person's expectations of what the policy covered were reasonable. . . .

Answer B is better because it constructs a bridge between traditional property law analysis and the modern approach. That bridge—a transitional sentence—tells the reader that you are now switching from a property law analysis to a contract law analysis. Answer A, by contrast, leads the reader to believe that the second paragraph continues an analysis based on property law.

Consider another illustration:

You work for the federal Equal Employment Opportunity Commission (EEOC). An employee for a company operating in Arizona has just filed a sex discrimination lawsuit against the company in federal court under Title VII of the Civil Rights Act of 1964. The case involves an interpretation of Title VII that could significantly affect the EEOC's implementation of the statute. Thus, the EEOC would like to intervene on behalf of the plaintiff to ensure that its view of the law is brought to the court's attention. Rule 24 of the Federal Rules of Civil Procedure provides two methods of intervention. One method applies when a statute provides a conditional or unconditional right to intervene. Consider the following edited discussions:

ANSWER A: Rule 24(a) permits intervention of right when a federal statute confers an unconditional right to intervene. Title VII does not give the EEOC an unconditional right to intervene because intervention is based on the court's discretion when the EEOC certifies that "the case is of general public importance." The EEOC, therefore, may not intervene of right. The EEOC should, however, be able to obtain permissive intervention. Rule 24(b) allows permissive intervention when a federal statute grants a conditional right to intervene, as this one does. . . .

ANSWER B: Rule 24(a) permits intervention of right when a federal statute confers an unconditional right to intervene. Title VII does not give the EEOC an unconditional right to intervene because intervention is based on the court's discretion when the EEOC certifies that "the case is of general public importance." The EEOC, therefore, may not intervene of right. Rule 24(b) allows permissive intervention when a federal statute grants a conditional right to intervene, as this one does. . . .

The only difference between Answer A and Answer B is that Answer A includes the sentence: "The EEOC should, however, be able to obtain permissive intervention." This sentence alerts the reader that the writer has shifted to the discussion of permissive intervention. Because the sentence also draws a conclusion, it is a particularly concise transition. The absence of an effective transition in Answer B obscures its discussion of permissive intervention. The reader of Answer B could easily miss the shift.

The two examples in this section illustrate that a transition need not be obvious to be effective. In the first example, the topic sentence at the beginning of the paragraph serves as the transition. In the second example, the thesis statement in mid-paragraph serves as the transition. If your thesis statement or topic sentence is precise and well placed, you may not need any other transitions from one point to the next.

Thesis
Topic
Rule

P /facts

EXERCISES

The following exercises will help you practice using the guidelines described in this chapter.

Exercise 13-A

You represent Timothy McGraw, who has been arrested for robbing a coin shop. During the robbery, McGraw used a cane carved and painted to look like a shotgun. Swinging the cane around in a menacing manner during the robbery, McGraw told the shop owner he would "hurt [the shop owner] bad" if the shop owner did not cooperate. McGraw motioned with the cane for the shop owner to get into a closet. The shop owner complied, and McGraw then locked the closet. The shop owner, who was unharmed, later told police he was afraid he would be shot or struck if he did not comply. McGraw has now been indicted for armed robbery.

Revise and edit the following discussion using the principles described in this chapter:

> A person commits armed robbery when, with intent to commit theft, he takes the property of another by use of an "offensive weapon." State Code § 365(b). The courts have defined "offensive weapon" as including not only a weapon per se but also anything used in a manner likely to cause death or great bodily injury. *Fann v. State*; *Meminger v. State*.
>
> In both *Fann* and *Choate v. State* the defendants used replicas of guns to commit robberies. The court held in both cases that the defendants could not be convicted of armed robbery because the legislature had specifically eliminated statutory language that would have brought replicas within the purview of the armed robbery statute. Like the defendants in *Fann* and *Choate*, McGraw cannot be convicted of armed robbery simply because he used something that looked like a gun.
>
> In *Fann* there was no evidence that the defendant tried to strike the victim. In *Choate*, the defendant was unable to do so because the victim was seated in an enclosed booth. In both cases the court noted the lack of any evidence of intent to harm the victim. Similarly, McGraw did not attempt to hit the owner, or show any intent to do so.
>
> Unlike the defendant in *Fann*, who gave no indication of intent to strike the victim, McGraw did swing the weapon back and forth menacingly and did threaten to "hurt [the shop owner] bad" unless he cooperated. Also, the shop owner stated that he was fearful of being either shot or struck, indicating that the weapon's movement implied this threat. However, the court in *Fann* did not infer an intention to harm without substantive indication of such intent. The court is unlikely to find swinging the cane back and forth sufficient to establish McGraw's intent to strike the shop owner when McGraw made no attempt to do so. Therefore, because McGraw did

not use the cane in a manner indicating intent to harm the shop owner, he
is not likely to be convicted of armed robbery.

In *Meminger* the defendant was convicted of armed robbery when he
hit the victim in the head with a liquor bottle. The court held that because
the bottle was used in a manner likely to cause harm, it was an offensive
weapon. McGraw, on the other hand, did not use the cane in a way indicating intent to hit the shop owner because he only swung the cane back and
forth and did not swing it at the owner.

Exercise 13-B

Your client, Scott Spencer, was injured when he went on his first white-
water rafting trip. Before the trip he signed a rental agreement that included
a paragraph releasing Rocky River Outfitters from liability for any damages
arising from the trip. The release did not specifically mention "negligence."
Your client thought it was merely a rental agreement and did not take the
time to read it carefully before he signed. He is now considering a lawsuit
against the company.

The issue is whether the word "negligence" must be included specifically in the release in order to bar an action for negligence. The intent of the
parties, their relative bargaining position, and the specificity of the language
of the release are all considered by the court in reaching this decision. The
Conner and *Anders* cases are from your jurisdiction. The *Sommers* and
Cabel cases are from other jurisdictions.

Revise and edit the following discussion using the principles discussed
in this chapter:

> The court in *Conner* held that a release was invalid and did not bar a
> cause of action arising from a motorcycle accident at a racetrack. The
> release purported to absolve the defendant from liability, but it mentioned
> only "automobile racing" in a list of racing activities included. The court
> reasoned that motorcycle racing was not included under the commonly
> understood definition of automobile racing. In *Anders*, the court granted
> summary judgment to the defendant after the plaintiff sued for damages
> arising from the defendant's negligence in drilling oil and gas wells. The
> contract between the parties specifically absolved the defendant from li-
> ability arising from its negligence. The court based its decision on the
> equal bargaining positions of the parties and the unequivocal language of
> the contract. *Anders* did not address the specific issue presented here.
> The contract between Spencer and Rocky River Outfitters, however, did
> not contain the word "negligence." The courts in *Sommers* and *Cabel*
> concluded that specific mention of the word "negligence" was not neces-
> sary if the intent of the parties was otherwise clearly expressed. The re-
> lease in *Sommers* absolved a parachuting school from "any and all claims,
> demands, actions, . . . whatsoever, in any way resulting from personal
> injuries . . . arising from . . . parachute jumping." In *Cabel* the release

covered "any and all losses, claims, actions, or proceedings of every kind and character . . . arising directly or indirectly from any activity . . . such as parachuting." In both cases, the actions brought by students injured in parachute jumping were barred by the releases. In the release Spencer signed, he specifically absolved Rocky River Outfitters from liability for "any and all claims I have or may acquire against RRO for any personal injury or property damage I may sustain as a result of this rafting trip." Like the releases in *Sommers* and *Cabel*, this release specifically covered all claims that might arise from the specified activity in language that was obviously intended to be all-inclusive.

Drafting the Analysis

Legal writing differs from the kind of writing you probably did as an undergraduate. The three main differences are its purpose, the process, and the audience.

Purpose

Generally, the purpose of undergraduate papers is to allow students to develop their intellectual or creative talents within limits circumscribed by the assigned topic. The purpose of a legal memo or brief is much more practical and specific: to put in writing, in a way that is both credible and convincing, how the law applies to a client's particular legal problem. Whether you succeed or fail in this purpose can have serious consequences for your client. Although writing in law practice requires both intellect and creativity, it is never merely an intellectual or creative exercise.

Process

The complexity of legal analysis makes the process of writing different from undergraduate expository writing, much of which is done using a linear approach. As the name suggests, the steps in a linear process move from beginning to end, with the tasks neatly divided into categories that are addressed in that order. Each step is independent and is performed sequentially because each builds on the previous steps. Later steps may be taken only when earlier ones have been completed, and nothing along the way should require you to return to an earlier step. The chart below illustrates this.

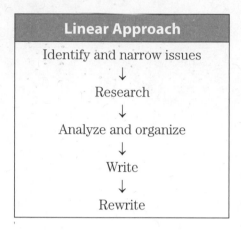

Although a linear approach is effective for some types of writing, it will not work for legal writing. Using a linear approach risks oversimplifying the issues and overlooking important authorities or legal theories. Because of its complexity, legal writing requires instead a recursive approach.

The recursive approach includes the same five components that are used in the linear approach—identifying and narrowing issues, researching, analyzing and organizing, writing, and rewriting. But under this approach, you may work on "later" steps before completing "earlier" steps, and then return again to later ones. The later steps help you refine your work on earlier ones. In essence, your writing develops as your understanding of the problem develops.

When you receive an assignment, the first step is to identify probable issues and begin the research. The order in which you will undertake the other steps will differ from assignment to assignment. Researching enables you to refine issues and may suggest others, since researching is not merely collecting sources but analyzing them to determine whether or how they are relevant. While researching, begin writing your first, tentative analysis of each issue. Beginning to draft an issue will likely reveal gaps in your research. It may also cause you to rethink the issue, requiring more research, analysis, and revision. This back-and-forth approach is not only normal but desirable.

The steps in the legal writing process can be envisioned as an inverted pyramid. The first step is understanding the question or questions and beginning the research. The last step is rewriting. This final step may be repeated several times before the final draft is completed. Notice that as you proceed, you perform progressively fewer tasks, and your focus becomes clearer. The nature and number of steps needed to progress from the first step to the last varies according to the nature of the problem. This chart illustrates a typical progression:

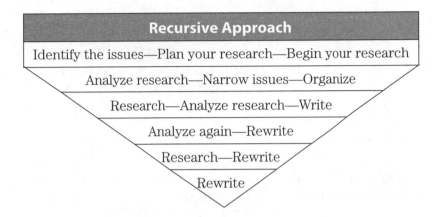

Recursive Approach

Identify the issues—Plan your research—Begin your research

Analyze research—Narrow issues—Organize

Research—Analyze research—Write

Analyze again—Rewrite

Research—Rewrite

Rewrite

Two steps in the chart need to be emphasized. First, begin writing early, as soon as you have a grasp of what the law is and how it applies to your client's case. By writing early, you will keep your focus on the final product. Second, allow plenty of time for rewriting.

Writing as soon as possible begins the process of continual definition and refinement of the issues and sub-issues; the parameters of the issues will not emerge until you have researched them and written about them. The familiar saying that writing is thinking on paper is particularly applicable to the process of legal writing. During the early stages, sometimes called *pre-writing,* write in any form that works for you. Good writers brief cases, make charts, make notes on cards or legal pads, write outlines, write pieces of the discussion, or use some combination of these methods. The worst thing you can do is delay writing until you have digested every case you plan to use and analyzed every issue and sub-issue. By then you will be so familiar with the analysis you are apt to forget that your reader is not. Think about a legal problem as a puzzle that you must solve for your reader by fitting the pieces together. Begin to construct the individual pieces as soon as you have a general idea of how the pieces will fit together. Then fit them together.

Allow plenty of time for rewriting; it is often the most difficult part of the process. During the pre-writing and writing stages, concentrate on analyzing and structuring the problem, first in your own mind and then on paper. The rewriting stage requires a shift in perspective from writer to reader.

It is a good practice to let the memo or brief "rest" for a day or two and then carefully read it again. You will often find that the organizational scheme is not working the way you intended, that analytical steps are missing, that the discussion is unclear on some points, or that you have a sentence that is ten lines long. If you do not see any such problems, you are not looking at the paper critically enough. Learn to separate the intensely personal experience of producing a memo or brief from the product itself. An old saying among film writers and directors is that you are not finished until you have cut your favorite scene. The development of your writing ability can be measured partially by your readiness to reorganize, delete, insert, or rewrite whole pages, paragraphs, or sentences.

This process, again, takes time. Those who indulge in the common undergraduate practice of writing an assignment the night before it is due will probably do poorly. The law demands precision and penalizes those whose work is rushed and sloppy.

Audience

Audience is the final difference between legal writing and many types of undergraduate writing. The audience for legal documents is usually another lawyer who is reading the document for a specific purpose—a judge or supervising attorney, for example, who needs to know how law and policy apply to a particular case. These lawyers, your readers, are a skeptical lot. They will not accept your conclusions on faith. They will expect a carefully constructed chain of logic without significant missing links. Anticipate their skepticism about each argument you make and each conclusion you draw. Write as if these hypothetical readers are looking over your shoulder.

Your audience will also expect you to present complex material clearly and coherently. Read your draft critically from the reader's perspective. Consider whether a reader without your knowledge of the law or the facts would find your analysis readable, credible, logical, and complete. This is the hallmark of effective legal writing.

This chapter pulls together the basic principles in Chapter 10 (Organization), Chapter 11 (Describing the Law), Chapter 12 (Applying the Law), and Chapter 13 (Signposting). It shows, step by step, how to construct a discussion from the common law and statutory analysis explained in Chapter 7 (Common Law Analysis) and Chapter 8 (Statutory Analysis), as well as how to apply the principles for reaching a conclusion described in Chapter 9 (Reaching a Conclusion).

The organizational structure suggested in this chapter includes all the components of a complete discussion of each issue or sub-issue. It begins with your conclusion, then follows with a description of the rule or rules involved and an explanation of how those rules apply to a particular set of facts. Unless the discussion as a whole is short, the discussion of each issue should end by re-stating the conclusion. Some writers find it helpful to remember this organizational structure with the acronym CiRAC (Conclusion to the issue, Rule, Application, Conclusion).[1] This organizational approach is effective because it provides the reader with information in a logical order, as it is needed. If there is a credible contrary analysis or counterargument, present it after the analysis explaining your conclusion, using steps that parallel the main discussion: a conclusion that the counterargument is weaker (because, for example, it is based on distinguishable cases or illogical reasoning), a description of the law or an interpretation of the law on which the contrary view would be based, an explanation of how the law could be used to reach the contrary view, and, finally, an explanation of why this approach does not change your initial conclusion. Finally, as discussed in Chapter 13 (Signposting), use signposts throughout your writing to guide the reader through your analysis.

This structure ensures that you provide everything the reader needs to understand your analysis—in a logical, straightforward manner. It can be applied to both memoranda and briefs. Using this structure will help you organize your ideas more efficiently and effectively, but it is not a formula or "fill-in-the-blanks" template. Each analysis will vary in the level and type of complexity presented by the facts and the applicable law. Be flexible in adapting this basic approach to each problem. As you gain experience in legal writing, you will learn to recognize situations in which some deviation from the structure suggested here may result in a more cogent discussion.

1. For each issue, state your conclusion and set up your discussion of the issue in an introduction.

State your conclusion on any specific issue at the outset. This is the "Ci" in your organizational structure. Stating your conclusion first serves two purposes. First, it ensures that you have actually reached a conclusion. It is difficult, if not impossible, to begin writing a discussion of a legal issue until you have sorted out how the law applies to the relevant facts. Putting your conclusion first prevents you from writing

---

1. Writers use various acronyms to describe this structure, but they all take the essentially the same approach: state your conclusion, explain the law, and then explain objectively how the law applies to your facts. Similar acronyms commonly used include CRAC (Conclusion-Rule-Application-Conclusion) and CREAC (Conclusion-Rule-Explanation-Application-Conclusion). The approach used here differs from IRAC (Issue-Rule-Application-Conclusion) because it requires that you first state your conclusion on an issue, not simply identify the issue.

a rambling discussion of law and facts that leaves the reader with only a set of considerations instead of a coherent legal analysis. If you cannot articulate your conclusion, you need to spend more time thinking. Second, putting the conclusion first enables the reader to follow your discussion more easily by pointing him in the right direction from the outset.

As explained in Chapter 13 (Signposting), your conclusion is a thesis that should be stated in terms of the issue. The introductory conclusion, therefore, should include both the relevant legal rule and the significant facts. The "Ci" reminds you to include both of these aspects of the issue in your conclusion. If the issue is relatively simple, a conclusion stated in terms of the relevant rule and relevant facts may be a single, well-written sentence, but complex issues may require two or three sentences.

If the issue you are discussing contains sub-issues or multiple points of analysis, the introductory conclusion may be part of an introductory or "roadmap" paragraph that orients your reader—one that explains where you are going and what path you will take to get there. Once you have stated your conclusion on the issue, state how relevant "givens" are resolved. As discussed in Chapter 10 (Organization), resolution of a particular issue may require, for example, discussion of three elements, only one of which is an issue. Addressing the two "givens" as part of the opening paragraph will frame the discussion for the reader and allow you to focus attention on the element in question.

The examples in this chapter are based on the libel problem discussed in Chapter 7 (Common Law Analysis), pages 101-03, as well as the charts used to analyze that problem.

Consider the following introductions:

ANSWER A: Dooley did not commit libel because he did not intend his fliers containing false statements about Fremont to be read by others. In *Simmons v. Deluxe Plaza Hotel,* the court held that a person's reading of defamatory material does not necessarily show intentional publication. The fliers were published and subjected Fremont to the loss of social prestige.

ANSWER B: Dooley did not commit libel because Dooley did not intend his fliers to be read by others. Libel is the "intentional publication of false statements about a person that humiliate that person or subject him to the loss of social prestige." *White v. Ball.* Two elements of this rule have been satisfied. The fliers were published when they were released by accident. The fliers also subjected Fremont to the loss of social prestige because they accused him of having a criminal record. The intent element has not been met, however.

ANSWER C: Dooley did not commit libel through the fliers he prepared. Libel is the "intentional publication of false statements about a person that humiliate that person or subject him to the loss of social prestige." *White v. Ball.*

Answer B is best because it states a conclusion on the issue, briefly describes the libel rule, and shows how the two "givens" are resolved. The writer concludes that Dooley did not commit libel because he did not intentionally publish the fliers, and then the writer quotes the basic libel rule. The writer addresses each "given" in sentences that identify the rule and the relevant facts and state how the "given" is resolved. Answer B thus provides a good framework for the ensuing discussion.

Answer A shows the writer's conclusion on the libel issue. The description of the law, however, focuses only on the intent element. As a result, the reader has not been informed of the basic legal framework for the discussion that follows. The two "givens" are resolved, but it is impossible to know on what basis because the significant facts are not identified.

Answer C states a conclusion but does not give the reader any indication of the legal or factual basis for that conclusion. Answer C thus does not focus the discussion for the reader. Although it does quote the libel rule, it does not show how any of the "givens" were resolved.

2. For each sub-issue, state your conclusion in terms of the rule and the relevant facts.

This step requires you to state your conclusion for each sub-issue that arises under an issue, the "Ci" for the sub-issue. Like the first step, this ensures that you have actually reached a conclusion and makes it easier for the reader to follow your discussion. Again, your conclusion should include both the relevant legal rule and the significant facts. You do not need to describe any law or analyze "givens"; merely state the thesis for the sub-issue.

For purposes of this example, this step and steps 3 through 7 are specifically applied to the sub-issue of intent to publish. The same approach is also effective in analyzing issues that contain no sub-issues.

> Consider the following conclusions on intent to publish:
>
> ANSWER A: Dooley did not intentionally publish the fliers because they were released by accident.
>
> ANSWER B: Dooley did not have the requisite intent for libel.
>
> ANSWER C: The first issue is whether Dooley intentionally published the fliers.

Answer A is best because it states the conclusion in terms of the rule and key facts and provides the reason, which helps the reader understand what will follow. Answer B states the conclusion in terms of the rule but does not provide the reason, making it harder for the reader to understand the rest of the discussion. Answer C states the issue but gives no conclusion and no reason. Sentences like this may indicate that the writer has no idea where the discussion will go.

3. Describe the law relevant to your conclusion for each sub-issue.

As Chapter 11 (Describing the Law) explains, the law provides a structure for your discussion. Therefore, a description of the applicable law supporting your position should immediately follow your conclusion. This is the "R" in your organizational structure. This description must be accurate and complete. It may be as brief as a sentence or as long as several paragraphs, depending on the complexity of the problem and the strength of potential counterarguments.

For common law problems, state the general rule first and then describe cases relevant to your conclusion that apply the rule. For statutory problems, quote or summarize the relevant provision first and then explain how any judicial decisions may have defined, extended, restricted, or modified the statute. Whether you are discussing a statutory or a common law issue, the description of a case should ordinarily require only a few sentences that focus on the facts and reasoning relevant to the issue or sub-issue. Avoid the historical approach; instead, give the reader a concise view of the current state of the law.

Consider the following descriptions of the law:

ANSWER A: Intent occurs when the defendant should reasonably be aware of the likelihood that the material may be read by others. *White v. Ball*; *Simmons v. Deluxe Plaza Hotel*. In *White*, the court held that a letter containing allegedly false accusations against company employees was published when it was read by the company president. In *Simmons*, however, the court held that a letter making false accusations against the plaintiff was not intentionally published even though it was read by the plaintiff's wife.

ANSWER B: In *White v. Ball*, the defendant wrote a third person, a company president, making allegedly false accusations against company employees. The court held that intentional publication occurred because the president, the person to whom the letter was addressed, received and read the letter. In *Simmons v. Deluxe Plaza Hotel*, the court held that a letter making false accusations against the plaintiff was not intentionally published even though the plaintiff's wife read it. The letter had been addressed to the plaintiff personally and sent by certified mail. The court noted the precautions the defendant had taken to prevent the letter from being read by third persons, and reasoned that "a mere conceivable possibility or chance" that the letter would be read by others did not demonstrate intent.

ANSWER C: Intent occurs when the defendant should reasonably be aware of the likelihood that the material may be read by others. *White v. Ball*; *Simmons v. Deluxe Plaza Hotel*. In *White*, the defendant wrote a third person, a company president, making allegedly false accusations against company employees. The court held that intentional publication occurred because the president, the person to whom the letter was addressed, received and read the letter. In *Simmons*, however, the court held that a letter making false accusations against the plaintiff was not intentionally published even though the plaintiff's wife read it. The letter had been addressed to the plaintiff personally and sent by certified mail. The court noted the precautions the defendant had taken to prevent the letter from being read by third persons, and reasoned that "a mere conceivable possibility or chance" that the letter would be read by others did not demonstrate intent.

Answer C is best because it summarizes the relevant law clearly and completely. It defines intentional publication—the element at issue here. It then describes the facts and reasoning of the *White* and

Simmons cases, thus providing a framework within which to compare the facts of Dooley's case.

Answer A summarizes some of the basic facts of *White* and *Simmons* but it does not fully describe all of the relevant facts or the courts' rationale. It will be difficult to compare the cases with Dooley's situation on the basis of this summary. Answer A, unfortunately, represents a common error in legal writing.

Answer B explains the facts and rationale of *White* and *Simmons* but omits the basic legal principles. Without the legal principles, the reader will have difficulty discerning why the facts and rationale in these cases are significant.

---

4. Explain why the law supports your conclusion for each sub-issue.

Once you have stated your conclusion and the relevant law, you must explain the reasons for your conclusion—how you think the law will likely be applied to your facts. This application of the law is the "A" in your organizational structure and is the most important part of your discussion. It should include every step in your reasoning process as well as every reasonable basis for your conclusion.

In problems involving the common law, explain your reasoning by comparing or contrasting your facts with those of the relevant cases. First explain how the facts of the decided cases support your conclusion. Generally you will analogize cases with holdings consistent with your position and distinguish cases with holdings contrary to your position. Thus, although your conclusions will often be based upon similarities between the facts of the cases and those of your case, a conclusion can be just as strongly supported by pointing out differences. Remember to base factual similarities and differences on the specific legal rule at issue. Use the reasons and policies of the decided cases to explain why the factual comparisons matter and how they support your conclusion. You may recognize this process as part of the analytical method set out in Chapter 7 (Common Law Analysis). It enables the reader to follow every step in your reasoning process.

Here are some possible explanations for the application of the cases in the libel problem. The sentence in italics is from Answer C in the previous example.

ANSWER A: *The court noted the precautions the defendant had taken to prevent the letter from being read by third persons and reasoned that "a mere conceivable possibility or chance" that the letter would be read by others did not constitute intent.* Like the defendant in *Simmons*, Dooley did not intend for a third party to read the fliers when they were knocked out of his hands in an accident. Dooley's case is distinguishable from *White*, where the defendant addressed and sent the letter to the company president.

ANSWER B: *The court noted the precautions the defendant had taken to prevent the letter from being read by third persons and reasoned that "a mere conceivable possibility or chance" that the letter would be read by others did not constitute intent.* Like the defendant in *Simmons*, Dooley did not intend for a third party to read the fliers when they were knocked out of his hands in an accident and he could not reasonably have anticipated that publication would occur. Dooley's case is distinguishable from *White*, where the defendant addressed and sent the letter to the company president.

ANSWER C: *The court noted the precautions the defendant had taken to prevent the letter from being read by third persons and reasoned that "a mere conceivable possibility or chance" that the letter would be read by others did not constitute intent.* Like the defendant in *Simmons* but unlike the defendant in *White*, Dooley could not reasonably have anticipated that his fliers would be read by third persons.

Answer B is best because it compares and contrasts Dooley's situation to the facts in both cases. Phrases such as "like the defendant in *Simmons*" alert the reader that a comparison is being made. Answer B also explains how the underlying policy in *Simmons*—to hold a defendant responsible only for harm he could reasonably have anticipated—reinforces the writer's conclusion.

Answer A compares the facts of *White* and *Simmons* with those of Dooley's case but says nothing about the underlying reasons or policies. The court's reasoning will necessarily guide the discussion about factual similarities. Answer A is deficient because it does not reveal why the factual similarities are important.

Answer C is a cryptic version of Answer B. It does not fully compare the *Simmons* facts with those of Dooley's case, nor does it clearly explain how the rationale in *Simmons* supports the writer's conclusion. In addition, Answer C says nothing at all about *White v. Ball*. The analysis is too brief to be informative.

You should handle problems involving statutory analysis similarly. First, explain how the language of the statute and the facts of any cases interpreting that statute support your conclusion. Next, use the policies of the statute and the policies of any cases interpreting the statute to further explain and support your conclusion. These statements are part of the method of analysis described in Chapter 8 (Statutory Analysis).

5. Describe any reasonable counterargument for each sub-issue and state why it is unpersuasive.

As explained in Chapter 10 (Organization), you should state your reasons for rejecting an opposite conclusion only after you have explained the reasons for reaching your conclusion. When you state your reasons for rejecting an opposite conclusion, you begin your response to potential counterarguments and signal to the reader that you are moving to a different part of the discussion. You should use a transition that serves as your thesis statement about the counterargument. Your transition should also explain or summarize the counterargument in terms of the sub-issue.

A *counterargument* is a plausible reason for arriving at a different conclusion. If no counterargument can be advanced against your conclusion, you can skip this step and also steps 6 and 7 below. If your opponent could advance one or more counterarguments, this step and steps 6 and 7 will allow you to address them. Sometimes, such as when your client is already involved in litigation, you will know the counterarguments because your opponent will already have made them. More often, you will have to predict the counterarguments based on an objective analysis of the law.

This step and steps 6 and 7 follow a pattern similar to that provided in steps 2, 3, and 4 above. You should state your conclusion concerning the counterargument, explain the relevant law, and then explain how the relevant law could be applied to the facts to support that conclusion. If more than one counterargument is possible, you should repeat these three steps for each.

> **Consider the following thesis statements for the counterargument in the libel problem:**
>
> ANSWER A: *White v. Ball* could support Fremont's argument.

ANSWER B: That Dooley intended to distribute the fliers to other tenants when he printed them is not sufficient to show intent.

ANSWER C: *White v. Ball* is analogous to Dooley's case because the defendant in *White* intended a third party to read his letter when he prepared it.

ANSWER D: Fremont could argue, relying on *White v. Ball*, that Dooley intentionally published the fliers.

ANSWER E: Fremont could argue that, because he did not intentionally publish the fliers, *White v. Ball* is inapplicable.

Answer B is best because it addresses the most logical counterargument, which is based on an analogy to *White v. Ball*. Because it also answers the counterargument, it serves as a thesis statement for the discussion that follows, as well as a transition from the previous part of the discussion.

Answer A is virtually useless because it does not even identify, much less explain, how the case supports the discussion or supports the counterargument.

Answer C is confusing because it states the counterargument from the viewpoint of the lawyer making it. When you state your thesis on the counterargument, however, you are not simply stating the opposing position; you must also summarize your answer to the counterargument. Answer B addresses the counterargument simply by denying its validity: Dooley's intent at the time he printed the fliers is not sufficient.

Answer D begins with the clause "Fremont could argue." Sentences that begin with such clauses are usually ineffective for two reasons: They often do nothing more than state the obvious, and they rarely state a thesis or specific position. Answer D is poor for both reasons. It states the obvious (Fremont will argue that Dooley intentionally published the fliers) and does not introduce the discussion to follow.

Like Answer D, Answer E begins by stating the obvious—"Fremont could argue that." Unlike Answer D, however, it states a thesis and therefore is a better answer. Stylistically, though, it is inferior to Answer B. The prefatory clause "Dooley could argue that" adds nothing but length to the sentence.

6. Describe how the law supports the counterargument for each sub-issue.

To be even minimally credible, opposing arguments require some legal basis. The description of the law that you previously provided to support your conclusion should be complete enough for the reader to understand the relevant cases or statutory provisions, but you must also explain how the law supports the counterargument. This rule may not be stated exactly as you stated the rule for your primary analysis. It may be a different interpretation of common law rule or statute or it may simply reflect a different perspective on how the cases have applied the law.

Resist the temptation to automatically divide legal authority into "for" and "against" categories. Analyzing a problem this way does not give the reader an overall understanding of the law. A court will base its decision on the law as a whole, not just on the cases with a particular outcome. Support for a counterargument most often will arise from similarities or differences in the same statutes or cases as those used in developing your conclusion, or from competing policies the court has emphasized in cases you have already described. In these situations you can simply refer to the statute or cases, describe only those parts of the law that have not already been described or, when appropriate, skip this step altogether. When you have already synthesized a rule from several authorities, as explained in Chapter 5 (Understanding Legal Rules), it may be sufficient to simply refer to that rule when addressing a counterargument.

Sometimes, however, you will find separate cases or lines of cases resolving the same legal issue differently, or you will have a choice of statutes to be applied. In these situations, the adverse law will be new to your reader because you did not use it in describing the law supporting your conclusion. You must describe the different lines of authority completely and fairly. Only then can the reader appreciate the strength of your position and the weaknesses of the counterarguments.

Consider these descriptions of how the law could support the counterargument:

ANSWER A: The court in *White* noted that "[i]t is receipt by a third person that makes the statements so damaging."

ANSWER B: In *White*, the defendant wrote and addressed the letter to the company president, making allegedly false accusations against company employees. The court held that intentional publication occurred because the president received and read the letter. Similarly, Dooley printed the fliers intending to distribute them.

ANSWER C: The court in *White* noted that "[i]t is receipt by a third person that makes the statements so damaging." Even though Dooley changed his mind, he intended to publish the fliers when he prepared them. This original intent to distribute the fliers and harm Fremont's reputation makes Dooley blameworthy and could satisfy the intent requirement.

Answer C is best because it describes the policy of *White* and explains how it could provide a framework to support the counterargument. Although the court's reasoning in that case seems more relevant to publication than intent to publish, it could provide the basis for a counterargument, minimizing the importance of intent when publication has occurred.

Answer A, by contrast, describes the policy of *White* but does not explain how it is relevant to the counterargument. Without this information, the reader will not be able to easily understand the counterargument.

Answer B compares the facts of *White* with Dooley's case, but it repeats facts that have already been explained and is silent about the court's rationale. The court's rationale would have guided the discussion about factual differences. By not stating it, however, the writer had a difficult time answering a counterargument based on the court's reasoning.

7. Explain why the counterargument does not change your conclusion for each sub-issue.

Once you have set out the law on which the counterargument would be based, you must explain why this application of the law is less convincing than your conclusion. This part of your discussion is second in importance only to your initial explanation of how the law supports your conclusion. Just as you did in your explanation of how the law supports your conclusion, you must include every reason and step in your analysis to explain why it does not. Be sure to address the strongest counterarguments. A writer gains credibility by acknowledging and refuting the most difficult counterarguments, not by constructing and rejecting weak or insupportable arguments. You and your reader need to understand the weaknesses in your position to ensure that your conclusion is indeed the most likely outcome. If you find that you cannot respond to the strongest or most persuasive counterarguments, you may want to change your conclusion.

For common law problems, explain how the decided cases do not support the opposing argument by explaining how the facts of the decided cases are distinguishable from your case or why the reasons and policies of the cases are not applicable. You should handle problems involving statutory analysis similarly. First explain how the statutory language and the facts of the decided cases do not support the counterargument. Then explain how the policies of the statute and any cases interpreting the statute fail to support the counterargument.

After you have answered the counterargument, restate your conclusion, the final "C" in your organizational structure. This restatement may be unnecessary if the discussion is relatively brief. Even in a longer discussion, this concluding statement can often be short, but it is helpful to reiterate for the reader how your analysis supports your conclusion. Otherwise, your discussion may end abruptly with your last point and force the reader to pull the various steps of your analysis together.

Here are several possible analyses of the counterarguments in the libel problem. The sentence in italics is taken from Answer C in the previous example.

ANSWER A: *This original intent to distribute the fliers and harm Fremont's reputation makes Dooley blameworthy and could satisfy the intent requirement.* The defendant's planned and intentional distribution of the letter in *White*, however, is different from Dooley's release of the fliers. In addition, Dooley's fliers were read by passersby on the street, not the apartment tenants for whom he prepared the fliers. Although the court was concerned with the damaging effect of publication, libel occurs only when there is intent to publish. Dooley did not intentionally publish the fliers.

ANSWER B: *This original intent to distribute the fliers and harm Fremont's reputation makes Dooley blameworthy and could satisfy the intent requirement.* The defendant's planned and intentional distribution of the letter in *White*, however, is different from Dooley's accidental release of the fliers after he had decided not to publish them. In addition, the company president to whom the letter was addressed in *White* was the same person who read the letter. In Dooley's case, by contrast, the fliers were read by passersby on the street, not the apartment tenants for whom he prepared the fliers.

ANSWER C: *This original intent to distribute the fliers and harm Fremont's reputation makes Dooley blameworthy and could satisfy the intent requirement.* The defendant's planned and intentional distribution of the letter in *White*, however, is different from Dooley's accidental release of the fliers after he had decided not to publish them. In addition, the company president to whom the letter was addressed in *White* was the same person who read the letter. In Dooley's case, by contrast, the fliers were read by passersby on the street, not the apartment tenants for whom he prepared the fliers. Although the court was concerned with the damaging effect of publication, libel occurs only if there is intent to publish at the time the documents are published. Dooley did not have that intent.

Answer C is best because of its completeness. The writer includes several arguments. The first two show differences between the facts of *White* and the facts of Dooley's case. The third argument is of a different kind: It directly addresses the tension between the elements of publication and intent to publish. When two cases seem to stand for somewhat different conclusions, it is important to find credible ways to reconcile them.

Answer A ineffectively states the factual differences between *White* and Dooley's case. To be understandable, a discussion must show what is being compared or contrasted. A comparison that explains the facts of one case without describing the facts of the other is impossible to understand. When the writer makes assertions with no justification, those assertions simply are not credible.

Answer B compares the facts but leaves out any discussion of the court's reasoning in *White*. By not fully addressing the counterargument, Answer B gives it more credibility than it actually deserves. Failure to restate the conclusion compounds the problem.

---

8. Edit the discussion to include signposts.

The first seven steps in this chapter provide a structure for developing your discussion. Steps 1, 2, and 5—in which you state your conclusion on the issue, your conclusion on the sub-issue, and your response to a potential counterargument—tell your reader where you are going.

But these steps, by themselves, do not necessarily ensure that your reader will understand the discussion supporting your conclusion or the discussion of the counterargument. If the reader does not understand the discussion, your memo or brief is of little value. This last step is based on Chapter 13 (Signposting) and is included here to illustrate how signposting will make your writing more understandable.

> If you put the best answer for each of the first seven steps in a separate paragraph, your discussion so far would look like this (the paragraphs are numbered for reference only):

(1)   Dooley did not commit libel because Dooley did not intend his fliers to be read by others. Libel is the "intentional publication of false statements about a person that humiliate that person or subject him to the loss of social prestige." *White v. Ball.* Two elements of this rule have been satisfied. The fliers were published when they were released by accident. The fliers also subjected Fremont to a loss of social prestige because they accused him of having a criminal record. The intent element has not been met, however.

(2)   Dooley did not intentionally publish the fliers because they were released by accident.

(3)   Intent occurs when the defendant should reasonably be aware of the likelihood that the material may be read by others. *White v. Ball; Simmons v. Deluxe Plaza Hotel.* In *White*, the defendant wrote a third person, a company president, making allegedly false accusations against company employees. The court held that intentional publication occurred because the president, the person to whom the letter was addressed, received and read the letter. In *Simmons*, however, the court held that a letter making false accusations against the plaintiff was not intentionally published even though the plaintiff's wife read it. The letter had been addressed to the plaintiff personally and sent by certified mail. The court noted the precautions the defendant had taken to prevent the letter from being read by third persons, and reasoned that "a mere conceivable possibility or chance" that the letter would be read by others did not demonstrate intent.

(4)   Like the defendant in *Simmons*, Dooley did not intend for a third party to read the fliers when they were knocked out of his hands in an accident and he could not reasonably have anticipated that publication would occur. Dooley's case is distinguishable from

White, where the defendant addressed and sent the letter to the company president.

(5) That Dooley intended to distribute the fliers to other tenants when he printed them is not sufficient to show intent.

(6) The court in *White* noted that "[i]t is receipt by a third person that makes the statements so damaging." Even though Dooley changed his mind, he intended to publish the fliers when he prepared them. This original intent to distribute the fliers and harm Fremont's reputation makes Dooley blameworthy and could satisfy the intent requirement.

(7) The defendant's planned and intentional distribution of the letter in *White,* however, is different from Dooley's accidental release of the fliers after he had decided not to publish them. In addition, the company president to whom the letter was addressed in *White* was the same person who read the letter. In Dooley's case, by contrast, the fliers were read by passersby on the street, not the apartment tenants for whom he prepared the fliers. Although the court was concerned with the damaging effect of publication, libel occurs only if there is intent to publish at the time the documents are published. Dooley did not have that intent.

Although this discussion is reasonably complete, it is still rough. It contains two one-sentence paragraphs (paragraphs 2 and 5). Although one-sentence paragraphs may occasionally be appropriate to emphasize a particular point, they are not helpful here. In addition, the point of several of the paragraphs, and the relationship between them, is not clear. Finally, the overall structure of the discussion is hard to discern.

The lead paragraph focuses on the entire question of libel, while the other six paragraphs focus on one element of libel. This difference in focus is a signal that the first paragraph should not be combined with the other paragraphs. But should it be divided? It contains six sentences—a thesis, a description of the overall legal rule, three sentences to establish the two "givens," and a sentence to focus on the specific sub-issue. It is unlikely that dividing this paragraph will improve the discussion. The first paragraph can thus be left unchanged.

Paragraphs 2, 3, and 4 discuss the conclusion on the intent-to-publish sub-issue, and paragraphs 5, 6, and 7 discuss the counterargument. The discussion of your conclusion and the discussion of the counterargument should generally be in separate paragraphs or groups of paragraphs. These two parts of your discussion are so different that combining some of each in the same paragraph would confuse the reader.

Signposts for paragraphs 2, 3, and 4 should explain the relationship of these paragraphs if that relationship is not clear from the text. Paragraph 2 states a conclusion, and the first sentence in paragraph 3 helps explain that conclusion by describing the legal rule on which the conclusion is based. What follows is a summary of the two cases that illustrate the court's application of this rule. These cases are described in detail to set the stage for the writer to analogize or distinguish them from Dooley's situation in paragraph 4.

As already suggested, paragraph 2 needs to be combined with another paragraph, which would have to be paragraph 3. Should those two paragraphs also be combined with paragraph 4? As noted in Chapter 13 (Signposting), a general rule is that paragraphs should contain between four and eight sentences. Seven sentences is not overly long for a single paragraph, but a closer look at paragraphs 3 and 4 shows that they contain different types of information. Paragraph 3 summarizes the law, while paragraph 4 shows its specific application to this situation. When summarizing the law requires a detailed explanation of the cases, it is often better to begin your factual analysis in a separate paragraph. When your summary of the law is shorter or requires less detail, you may include your factual analysis in the same paragraph. Here, since the summary of the law requires significant detail, it is logical to leave paragraph 4 as a separate but short paragraph.

Paragraphs 5, 6, and 7 also need editing. Paragraph 5 is plainly a transition sentence, and its relationship to paragraphs 6 and 7 is clearly stated.

Two of these paragraphs need to be consolidated, however. Because it is only a single sentence, paragraph 5 should be combined with paragraph 6. Paragraph 7 can stand by itself because it distinguishes the law described in paragraphs 5 and 6 from Dooley's situation. Since it is distinguishing the law, however, a transition indicating this change in perspective is needed, as is indicated below with the conjunction "However."

The final discussion looks like this:

Dooley did not commit libel. Libel is the "intentional publication of false statements about a person that humiliate that person or subject him to the loss of social prestige." *White v. Ball.* Two elements of this rule have been satisfied. The fliers were published when they were released by accident. The fliers also subjected Fremont to a loss of social prestige because they accused him of having a criminal record. The intent element has not been met, however, because Dooley did not intend his fliers to be read by others.

Dooley did not intentionally publish the fliers because they were released by accident. Intent occurs when the defendant should reasonably be aware of the likelihood that the material may be read by others. *White v. Ball*; *Simmons v. Deluxe Plaza Hotel*. In *White*, the defendant wrote a third person, a company president, making allegedly false accusations against company employees. The court held that intentional publication occurred because the president, the person to whom the letter was addressed, received and read the letter. In *Simmons*, however, the court held that a letter making false accusations against the plaintiff was not intentionally published even though the plaintiff's wife read it. The letter had been addressed to the plaintiff personally and sent by certified mail. The court noted the precautions the defendant had taken to prevent the letter from being read by third persons, and reasoned that "a mere conceivable possibility or chance" that the letter would be read by others did not demonstrate intent.

Like the defendant in *Simmons*, Dooley did not intend for a third party to read the fliers when they were knocked out of his hands in an accident and could not reasonably have anticipated that publication would occur. Dooley's case is distinguishable from *White*, where the defendant addressed and sent the letter to the company president.

That Dooley intended to distribute the fliers to other tenants when he printed them is not sufficient to show intent. The court in *White* noted that "[i]t is receipt by a third person that makes the statements so damaging." Even though Dooley changed his mind, he intended to publish the fliers when he prepared them. This original intent to distribute the fliers and harm Fremont's reputation makes Dooley blameworthy and could satisfy the intent requirement.

However, the defendant's planned and intentional distribution of the letter in *White* is different from Dooley's accidental release of the fliers after he had decided not to publish them. In addition, the company president to whom the letter was addressed in *White* was the same person who read the letter. In Dooley's case, by contrast, the fliers were read by passersby on the street, not the apartment tenants for whom he prepared the fliers. Although the court was concerned with the damaging effect of publication, libel occurs only when there is intent to publish at the time the documents are published. Dooley did not have that intent.

This chapter has thus far focused on the intent-to-publish sub-issue from the Dooley case in Chapter 7 (Common Law Analysis). As you may recall, a second sub-issue is whether the fliers were false.

Consider these discussions of that sub-issue:

ANSWER A: The fliers are false because Fremont has no record of criminal convictions. "A statement is false if the gist, the sting, of the matter is false." *White v. Ball.*

This case is different from cases in which the court held that statements with minor errors were substantially accurate. *Willow v. Orr; White v. Ball.* In *Willow*, a wife's allegation that her estranged husband had "kidnapped" their son was held to be substantially accurate. The husband took their son to another state for six weeks without her knowledge. Although he did not "kidnap" the child in a legal sense because he did not violate any judicial custody order, the court found that the allegation was substantially true because of the non-technical way that "kidnap" is used in child custody cases. Similarly, in *White*, the court held that an accusation of theft against company employees was substantially accurate because an employee's friend took a watch after the employee allowed the friend on the defendant's premises.

Unlike the statements in *Willow* and *White*, the statement about Fremont in the fliers is not substantially accurate. The fliers accused Fremont of having a "long record of criminal convictions as a landlord." In fact, he has no criminal convictions at all. Unlike the non-technical use of the word "kidnap" the court relied on in *Willow*, an accusation that someone has a record of criminal convictions is generally understood to be different from an accusation of having a record of housing violations. Even though the violations were corrected only after a threatened court order, Fremont was not convicted or even charged with any criminal offense. Unlike the substantially accurate accusation of theft in *White*, Fremont does not have "a long record of criminal convictions," as the fliers asserted. Thus, the fliers are false.

ANSWER B: The fliers are false because Fremont has no record of criminal convictions. "A statement is false if the gist, the sting, of the matter is false." *White v. Ball.* The fliers accused Fremont of having a "long record of criminal convictions as a landlord." In fact, he has no criminal convictions at all. This case is different from cases in which the court held that statements were substantially accurate. *Willow v. Orr; White v. Ball.*

In *Willow*, an ex-wife's allegation that her former husband had "kidnapped" her child was held to be substantially accurate. Although he did not "kidnap" the son in a legal sense because he did not violate any judicial custody order, the court found that the allegation was substantially true because of the non-technical way that "kidnap" is used in child custody cases. Similarly, in *White*, the court held that an accusation of theft against company employees was substantially accurate.

These cases are different from Dooley's case because the statement in the fliers is not substantially accurate. Although only technical differences exist between the public and legal understandings of kidnapping, substantial differences exist between criminal convictions and notices of housing violations.

Even though the violations were corrected only after a threatened court order, Fremont was not convicted or even charged with any criminal offense, and he certainly does not have "a long record of criminal convictions," as the fliers asserted. Nor is this a case like *White*.

ANSWER C: The other issue is whether the fliers are false. "A statement is false if the gist, the sting, of the matter is false." *White v. Ball*. The fliers accused Fremont of having a "long record of criminal convictions as a landlord." In fact, he has no criminal convictions at all.

Dooley could argue that the "gist" of the statement is accurate because Fremont received three notices of violation from the local housing commission for inadequate lighting and locks and corrected them only after the commission threatened to seek a court order. He may say that he used the term "criminal" only as a way of expressing the seriousness of the violations. That argument is likely to be unpersuasive.

This case is different from *Willow v. Orr*. In *Willow*, an ex-wife's allegation that her former husband had "kidnapped" her child was held to be substantially accurate. Although the ex-husband did not "kidnap" the son in a legal sense because he did not violate any judicial custody order, the court found that the accusation was substantially true because of the non-technical way that "kidnap" is used in child custody cases.

Although only technical differences exist between the public and legal understanding of kidnapping, substantial differences exist between criminal convictions and notices of housing violations. Even though the violations were corrected only after a threatened court order, Fremont was not convicted or even charged with any criminal offense, and he certainly does not have "a long record of criminal convictions," as the fliers asserted.

This case is also different from *White v. Ball*. In *White*, the court held that an accusation of theft against company employees was substantially accurate because an employee's friend took a watch after the employee allowed the friend on the defendant's premises. Again, a substantial difference exists between violations of the housing code and "a long record of criminal convictions as a landlord." The gist of the matter is that Fremont has no criminal convictions.

Answer A is best. It states a conclusion at the outset, describes the law on which the conclusion is based, and then shows how the law applies to Dooley's factual situation. Answer A uses the rule in *White v. Ball* to show how the rule applies. The writer concludes that the fliers are false, but both of the cases described involve factual situations in which the court held the statements to be true. Thus, there are no analogous cases to support the conclusion. So Answer A sets out the facts and holdings of both cases and distinguishes them. The cases are used together, or synthesized, because they have similar facts and the same holding.

Answer B is difficult to read and understand. It sets out the facts before describing the law, so the reader has no basis upon which to evaluate why they matter. Furthermore, the paragraph structure is choppy and hard to follow. For example, the last sentence in the first paragraph should be the first sentence of the second paragraph. Answer B also does a poor job of describing the facts of *White v. Ball*. The description of the holding in that case does not provide a full understanding of what happened. Nor does the bare statement that *White* is distinguishable explain why.

Answer C begins without giving the writer's conclusion. Like Answer B, it also sets out the facts before describing the law, so the reader cannot evaluate their significance. Readers of legal documents may be confused by such an introduction. The writer adds to the reader's confusion by describing *Willow* and distinguishing it, and then describing and distinguishing *White*. Notice the repetition in the last two paragraphs of Answer C. When cases are this similar, discussing them one at a time makes the discussion choppy and repetitious and also gives the reader an incomplete understanding of the law. Discussing several similar cases together furthers the reader's understanding of the law. Similarly, distinguishing a group of cases together is better than distinguishing one at a time, particularly when the reasons for distinguishing them are the same.

This chapter has shown how you might draft the discussion of both sub-issues in the libel problem. You should have noticed differences in the analysis of the two sub-issues. In the first sub-issue, one case is analogized and the other distinguished. In the second sub-issue, both cases are distinguished. This illustrates how the relevant law often dictates the approach a writer must take, even though both discussions use the same steps of the CiRAC organizational structure. When drafting the discussion for other problems, you will likely find other types of differences. When you do, keep in mind the underlying purposes of the steps outlined in this chapter and modify your approach to present your analysis as effectively as possible.

EXERCISES

The following exercises should help you learn to use these steps.

Exercise 14-A

Ralph Watson, a hockey fan, hired Claude Deemer to work temporarily at Watson's grocery store. Deemer had just been suspended from his semi-professional hockey team for unsportsmanlike conduct and violence. While working at the store, Deemer assaulted a customer named Allen Worthington. Worthington's family wants to know whether he can recover against Watson for his injuries. Which of the following discussions is best? Why?

ANSWER A: Watson is liable for hiring Deemer. In *Tyus v. Booth*, the court held that the plaintiff may recover only after showing that the employer knew or should have known that the employee had a propensity toward violence. In that case, the employee worked at a service station and assaulted a customer. The victim sued the employer, claiming that the employer was negligent in not finding out beforehand that the employee had previously been convicted of assault. The court held that the employer had no duty to learn of the employee's criminal record when the employer had not seen the employee behave in a manner indicating a propensity toward violence.

Tyus is different from our case because Watson knew that Deemer had a propensity toward violence. As an avid fan and season ticket holder of the hockey league in which Deemer played, Watson knew that Deemer had been suspended for twenty-one days for unsportsmanlike conduct and fighting. Watson knew that this suspension occurred in a league that is plagued with violence and unsportsmanlike conduct. Watson also knew that hockey, by itself, is a violent sport that attracts dangerous and frightening people like Deemer.

Watson may argue that violent hockey playing does not indicate a propensity toward violence off the hockey rink. The unusually violent nature of this particular hockey league, and the reason for Deemer's suspension, suggest that Watson likely will be unpersuasive. Hockey is not, after all, the Bolshoi Ballet.

In *Hersh v. Kentfield Builders, Inc.*, the court held that an employer was not liable for an employee's assault on a salesman when the employer did not know the violent nature of the employee's criminal record and had not seen the employee behave in a manner indicating a propensity toward violence. Although the employer probably knew that the employee had a criminal record, he did not know that the employee had been convicted of manslaughter and carrying a concealed weapon. The court stated that the employer had no duty to investigate the employee's criminal record in the absence of evidence of the employee's propensity toward violence.

Hersh is different from our case because, again, Watson knew that Deemer had a propensity toward violence. Watson held season tickets to the hockey league in which Deemer played. He was there the night Deemer was suspended for twenty-one days for unsportsmanlike conduct and fighting. He knew that the league had a reputation for violence and unsportsmanlike conduct. As described above, Watson will not be able to argue successfully that violent hockey playing does not indicate a propensity toward violence off the hockey rink.

Knowing that Deemer was violent, Watson hired him to work in a public place. Deemer assaulted a customer in that public place—the produce department of Watson's store—as Deemer was cleaning vegetable trays. In fact, much of Deemer's work involved contact with customers. Watson should have expected that someone like Deemer would eventually have a violent altercation with a customer. The fact that Deemer's assault was provoked by three teenage boys shows Watson's negligence, because only an employee who is prone to violence would have reacted by chasing and beating one of the boys.

This case is thus different from *Hersh*, because the employer in that case did the right thing. He had the employee work in a location that was not usually open to the public. This employee, whom the employer probably knew to have a criminal record and to have been belligerent at times, was required to clean out model homes not open to the public. After the employee injured a salesman with a knife, the employer was held not liable for negligence in hiring this employee. Deemer, however, worked in a public place. It is reasonable to expect that customers in a grocery store will frequent the produce department, will come into contact with the employer's maintenance workers, and will sometimes be obnoxious. Every business owner knows that some customers will be obnoxious. Watson is liable for hiring Deemer.

ANSWER B: Watson is most likely responsible for Deemer's assault on a customer because he hired Deemer, knowing of his violent hockey playing, and then placed him in a position involving public contact. An employer is liable for the intentional torts of an employee committed on a customer at the workplace if (1) the employer knew or should have known beforehand of the employee's propensity toward violence and (2) the employer had the employee work in a place open to the public. *Tyus v. Booth*; *Hersh v. Kentfield Builders, Inc.*

Watson satisfies the "propensity toward violence" requirement because he knew of Deemer's violent hockey playing before hiring him. In both *Tyus* and *Hersh*, the courts held that an employer was not liable for an employee's assault on a person at the workplace because the employer had no knowledge, and no reason to know, of the employee's prior conviction for a violent crime. In both cases, the employer had not seen the employee behave in a manner that suggested a propensity toward violence. In this case, however, Watson actually knew of Deemer's propensity toward violence. As an avid fan and season ticket holder of the hockey league in which Deemer played, he knew that Deemer had been suspended for twenty-one days for unsportsmanlike conduct and fighting. Watson also knew that this suspension occurred in a league that has a lot of violence and unsportsmanlike conduct.

Watson may argue that violent hockey playing does not indicate a propensity toward violence off the hockey rink. The unusually violent nature of this particular hockey league, and the reason for Deemer's suspension, suggest that Watson likely will be unpersuasive.

Deemer's lack of a criminal record does not change this conclusion. In *Tyus* and *Hersh*, the courts held that employers were not liable for the assaults committed by their employees in part because they had not seen evidence of violent behavior beforehand. Because the employers were unaware of their employees' violent criminal records, these records were irrelevant. Deemer's actual behavior before the assault—not the presence or absence of a criminal record—demonstrates Watson's negligence in hiring him.

Watson satisfies the "public place" requirement because he hired Deemer to work in areas open to the public. This case is analogous to *Tyus*, in which the employee worked in a service station and assaulted a customer, because Deemer's work also involved public contact. Deemer assaulted a customer in a public place—the produce department of Watson's grocery store—as Deemer was cleaning vegetable trays. The presence of three teenage boys in the produce department supports this conclusion.

Watson may argue that Deemer did not have regular customer contact in the same way as the employee in *Tyus*. Because Deemer did have some customer contact, however, this argument is not likely to prevail. This case is distinguishable from *Hersh*, in which the court held an employer not negligent for an employee's assault on a salesman because the employee worked in an area not usually open to the public. Unlike the employee in *Hersh*, Deemer was working in a public place—in the produce department of a grocery store, where public contact could reasonably have been expected—when the assault occurred. Although the assault was provoked by three obnoxious teenage boys, it occurred in a place open to the public. Watson likely will be held liable for Deemer's assault on Worthington.

ANSWER C: Watson most likely is responsible for Deemer's assault on a customer because he hired Deemer, knowing of his violent hockey playing, and then placed him in a position involving public contact. An employer is liable for the intentional torts of an employee committed on a customer at the workplace if (1) the employee has a propensity toward violence, (2) the employer knows or should know of that propensity, and (3) the employer had the employee work in a place open to the public. *Tyus v. Booth*; *Hersh v. Kentfield Builders, Inc.*

Deemer satisfies the "propensity toward violence" requirement because of his violent hockey playing. In *Tyus* and *Hersh*, a customer and a salesman each were assaulted by employees who previously had been convicted of violent crimes. The courts recognized that such crimes were evidence of a propensity toward violence. Similarly, Deemer's manner of playing hockey is evidence of his propensity toward violence. Deemer was suspended from his hockey team for twenty-one days for unsportsmanlike conduct and fighting. In addition, his hockey league is plagued with violence and unsportsmanlike conduct. The unusually violent nature of the league along with the conduct that led to Deemer's suspension suggest that Deemer's propensity toward violence is not limited to the game of hockey.

Watson satisfies the "knowledge" requirement because he knew of Deemer's propensity toward violence when he hired Deemer. In both *Tyus* and *Hersh*, the court held that an employer was not liable for an employee's assault on a person at the workplace because the employer had no knowledge, and no reason to know, of the employee's prior conviction for a violent crime. In both cases, the employer had not seen the employee behave in a manner that suggested a propensity toward violence. In this case, however, Watson actually knew of Deemer's propensity toward violence because Watson, an avid fan and season ticket holder of the hockey league in which Deemer played, watched the game in which Deemer was suspended.

Even if Watson did not actually know of Deemer's propensity toward violence, he *should* have known of that propensity. His familiarity with Deemer, the team, and the league gave him constructive knowledge.

Deemer's lack of a criminal record does not change the conclusion that Watson had actual or constructive knowledge of Deemer's propensity toward violence. In *Tyus* and *Hersh*, the courts held that employers were not liable for the assaults committed by their employees in part because the employers had not seen evidence of violent behavior beforehand. Because the employers were unaware of their employees' violent criminal records, these records were irrelevant. Watson's awareness of Deemer's behavior before the assault—not the presence or absence of a criminal record—establishes Watson's knowledge of Deemer's propensity towards violence.

Finally, Watson satisfies the "public place" requirement because he hired Deemer to work in areas open to the public. In *Tyus*, the court held that a service station where an employee assaulted a customer was a public place, while in *Hersh*, the court declined to impose liability where the assault took place in an area not open to the public.

Like the employee in *Tyus*, Deemer also assaulted a customer in a public place—the produce department of Watson's grocery store—as Deemer was cleaning vegetable trays. The presence of three teenage boys in the produce department supports this conclusion. Although Deemer probably did not have customer contact to the same extent as the employee in *Tyus*, customer contact was an inevitable part of his job. Thus, this case is distinguishable from *Hersh*, where the assault did not occur in a "public place." Watson will likely be held liable for Deemer's assault on Worthington.

Exercise 14-B

Draft the discussion for an office memorandum based on the facts and materials in Exercise 7-B, pp. 110-11.

Exercise 14-C

This exercise is based on Exercise 7-C, pp. 111-13. For one sub-issue chosen by you or your professor, draft the discussion for an office memorandum.

Exercise 14-D

Draft the discussion for an office memorandum based on the problem contained in the text of Chapter 8 and Exercise 8-A, p. 126.

Exercise 14-E

This exercise is based on Exercise 8-D, pp. 127-28. For one sub-issue chosen by you or your professor, draft the discussion for an office memorandum.

Revising and Editing

Almost everything you need to know about writing can be summarized in one principle: Write to communicate. You will impress the reader more with good organization, thoughtful analysis, and clear writing than with rhetorical flourishes. Language that interferes with the reader's ability to understand—no matter how good it sounds—should be revised.

Although there is little about the law that cannot be explained to a layperson, most nonlawyers are mystified by legal writing. They believe—too often with good reason—that legal writing is a careful blend of the pompous and the dull, consisting of lengthy sentences, unintelligible phrases, and plenty of legal jargon. This style of writing results from misplaced professional pride, professional insecurity, sloppy thinking, the desire to impress clients, habit, and blind repetition of previous bad legal writing. Legal writing, however, does not have to be this way. The law is a literary profession; legal writing should and often does approach the level of good literature. Many judicial opinions, for example, are remembered not only for their ideas but also for the way in which the ideas are expressed.

Revising and editing are essential to both the substance and the style of your writing. By revising and editing, you can improve the substance of your analysis as well as the style of your writing by clarifying points and including analytical steps you had previously ignored. Lawyers are professional writers; your audience will expect an acceptable level of proficiency in your use of the English language and its conventions.

1. Be direct and precise.

As stated in Chapter 14 (Drafting the Discussion), letting your writing rest before editing allows you to take a fresh look at it. To make sure that your writing is as direct and precise as possible, review your draft paragraph by paragraph, word by word. As you write and edit, you should find that your thinking—and consequently your memo or brief—becomes increasingly clear and focused.

Lack of focus is the primary reason that so much legal writing is imprecise. If you are unclear about what you want to say, obviously you cannot say it clearly and precisely. Think some more about the exact idea you want to convey and then consider the most direct way to express that idea. If you cannot find the right words, perhaps it is because you have only a vague idea of what you want to say. There is interplay between thoughts and words. Clear thinking can help you find the right words to express your idea, and the right words can help clarify your thinking.

Assume, for example, that your client's water supply wells have been contaminated by a nearby impoundment containing liquid industrial waste. In *Branch v. Western Petroleum, Inc.*, the highest court of your state held that a company that disposed of toxic industrial waste on its property in close proximity to the plaintiff's water supply wells was strictly liable for the contamination of these wells. You have written the following sentence in a draft:

When addressing this issue, the supreme court's decision in *Branch v. Western Petroleum, Inc.*, must be strongly considered.

The most basic question in editing your own writing is "What do I mean?" If the sentence you have written does not clearly answer that question, revise it so that it does. Then review it again. Precise writing results from continual self-criticism as you go through each sentence of your draft. Early drafts often include vague expressions of imperfectly formed ideas. You have not made a mistake by including such language in a draft—that is what drafts are for—but you will make a mistake if you do not recognize and correct the problem.

The sentence in question indicates that there is binding precedent in your state on this issue, but is it dispositive? The phrase "must be strongly considered" does not answer this question. Suppose you decide that it is dispositive. The revised sentence might look like this:

The supreme court's decision in *Branch v. Western Petroleum, Inc.*, will likely govern the outcome of this case.

This sentence is more definite, but the thought is still incompletely expressed. Another important question in revising your writing is "Have I completed the thought?" The sentence says that the *Branch* decision will likely govern the outcome, but it does not say why. The third draft completes the thought and forms a transition to the supporting sentence that follows:

The supreme court's decision in *Branch v. Western Petroleum, Inc.*, will likely govern the outcome of this case because the facts are virtually identical. In both cases, disposal of toxic waste contaminated water supply wells on adjacent property.

Some writers are reluctant to take a clear position, fearing they may be wrong, and so resort to the kind of vague language that the first draft of this sentence illustrates—the supreme court's decision "must be strongly considered." This timidity defeats the whole purpose of a legal memo or brief. Remember that you have analyzed the problem, whereas your reader has not, and that your job as a writer is to express your analysis as precisely as you can.

2. Blend precision with simplicity.

As you strive for precision, be careful to state your ideas as simply as possible. Avoid jargon, legalese ("said defendant," "to wit," "heretofore"), and Latin phrases (except terms of art such as *stare decisis* and *res judicata*), and scrutinize long sentences and paragraphs. Persons untrained in the law should be able to read and understand your writing.

Two equally precise statements of the same idea may vary considerably; one may be understandable to the reader, while the other may be confusing.

Consider these descriptions of a city ordinance:

ANSWER A: The ordinance forbids, *inter alia,* inhalation and exhalation of the fumes of a lighted *cannabis sativa* instrument.

ANSWER B: Among other things, the ordinance forbids marijuana smoking.

Answer B is better because it is simple, accurate, and precise. Answer A has far more words, but it probably conveys less information to the average reader. The Latin name for marijuana may make the writer seem learned, but this impression is of no value if the reader does not know what is being said. Similarly, the wordy phrase that describes smoking in Answer A, while technically correct, does not convey anything more than the word "smoking." Answer A is also obscured by legal jargon. The Latin phrase for "among other things," *inter alia*, is one of many you will encounter in the law; substitute an English translation whenever possible.

3. Use verbs whenever possible to make your writing forceful.

A. Prefer the active voice. In active voice, the subject performs the action. In passive voice, the subject is acted upon. Active voice is preferable because it is direct, leaves no ambiguity about who is doing what, and requires fewer words. Passive voice, by contrast, is detached and often ambiguous. Writers who use passive voice must either omit the actor or append it to the sentence with a prepositional phrase.

Consider these statements:

ANSWER A: The department shall disclose all relevant information to the requesting party.

ANSWER B: All relevant information shall be disclosed to the requesting party.

Answer A is clearer and more forceful than Answer B because the verb (*shall disclose*) states an action to be performed by the subject (*department*). Answer A, unlike Answer B, states who will disclose the information. If Answer B is changed to read "All relevant information shall be disclosed to the requesting party by the department" it is still less forceful than Answer A and is slightly longer. Although passive voice may be useful if you want to emphasize the object being acted upon or omit any reference to the actor, you should use it only for good reason.

B. Avoid excessive nominalizing. To *nominalize* is to express the key action with a noun instead of a verb. Nouns are static; they only state what is. Verbs state what happened. Therefore, using a verb instead of the noun form of that verb (*e.g., operate* instead of *perform an operation*) makes your writing more dynamic.

Compare these sentences:

ANSWER A: Disruption of the school board meeting by a group of angry parents caused a reconsideration of the board's plan for closure of three high schools.

ANSWER B: A group of angry parents disrupted the school board meeting and caused the board to reconsider its plan to close three high schools.

Answer B is better because it uses verbs—"disrupted," "caused . . . to reconsider," and "close"—to describe the main ideas, whereas Answer A uses nouns—"disruption," "reconsideration," and "closure." Note the weak phrase, "caused a reconsideration of," in Answer A. Such verbs often signal that a nominalization will follow: for example, *resulted in a modification of* (modified), *resulted in a solution to* (solved), *resulted in a settlement of* (settled).

Below are a few phrases that lawyers commonly use and the verbs that should replace them:

bring about a resolution	resolve
make a determination	determine
make an assumption	assume
make a proposition or proposal	propose
take under consideration	consider
state by implication	imply
reach an agreement	agree

Lawyers use other nominalizations as well. You should avoid them and use action verbs whenever possible.

4. Be concise.

One favorite maxim of the noted English professor and editor William Strunk was "Omit needless words." Strunk wrote, "This requires not that the writer make all his sentences short, or that he avoid all detail and treat his subjects only in outline, but that every word tell."[1] Every part of your memo—every word in every sentence—should be there for a reason. If not, delete it. Needless words result from repetition, fuzzy thinking, use of a long phrase when a short phrase or single word will do, and poorly structured clauses, among other things.

A. Avoid wordy phrases. Some phrases are inherently wordy and should be replaced with a single word.

> ### Compare these statements:
>
> ANSWER A: Due to the fact that the defendant had a history of driving while drunk, the judge imposed the maximum penalty.
>
> ANSWER B: Because the defendant had a history of drunk driving, the judge imposed the maximum penalty.
>
> Answer B substitutes one word, "because," for the phrase "due to the fact that," resulting in a shorter, more direct sentence. Answer B also substitutes "drunk driving" for "driving while drunk."

Here are some other wordy phrases and suggested substitutes:

despite the fact that	although
in accordance with	under
subsequent to	after
at such time as	when
until such time as	when
at the present time	now
in regard to	about
in relation to	about

B. Avoid tautological phrases. Certain phrases are often used when a single word would suffice, simply because we are accustomed to using them. Legal writers, especially, are loyal to traditional phrases. For

---

1. WILLIAM STRUNK, JR. & E.B. WHITE, THE ELEMENTS OF STYLE 23 (4th ed. 2000).

example, "cease" is almost always followed by "and desist," and "aid" by "and abet." Many of these word pairings were originally formed in early England by combining the same words from different languages (Anglo-Saxon, French, Latin) because lawyers then had a choice of languages or needed more than one word to communicate clearly. This is obviously no longer necessary, yet many legal writers continue to use traditional phrases such as "null and void," "devise and bequeath," "fraud and deceit," and "false and untrue." Scrutinize word pairings to determine whether both parts are necessary or, if not, which of the two more clearly expresses your meaning.

Some other tautological phrases are

> actual fact
> basic fundamentals
> consensus of opinion
> continue to remain
> false misrepresentation
> final result
> it is possible that he may
> next subsequent
> positive benefits
> sufficient enough
> true facts
> unexpected surprise

C. Avoid unnecessary modifiers. Unnecessary modifiers divert the reader's attention from the words they modify and make your writing less forceful.

Compare these sentences:

ANSWER A: A well-drafted complaint should set out the facts establishing that the plaintiff is entitled to the relief sought.

ANSWER B: A well-drafted complaint basically should set out the facts definitely establishing that the plaintiff is entitled to the relief sought.

The two sentences are identical except for the modifiers "basically" and "definitely" in Answer B. These words are distracting and are not necessary to explain what a well-drafted complaint should do. While it is grammatically correct to use such adverbs as modifiers, before using them you should ask yourself whether they contribute anything to the sentence. Some commonly overused modifiers are: basically, very, extremely, truly, clearly, completely, generally, virtually, obviously, essentially, and surely.

D. Scrutinize sentences beginning with "there" or "it." The following sentences are normal in English syntax:

It is raining.

There is no room for doubt.

But, do not start a sentence with "it" or "there" if it would lengthen the sentence unnecessarily or impede the reader's understanding.

Compare these sentences:

ANSWER A: There was a large bush overhanging the intersection, and it was this obstruction that blocked the driver's view of oncoming traffic.

ANSWER B: A large bush overhanging the intersection blocked the driver's view of oncoming traffic.

"There was" and "it was" in Answer A add nothing except length and delay the reader's understanding of the main ideas. Answer B is shorter and more direct.

Sentences that begin with "it" or "there" often include phrases such as "the type of," "the case that," "in the nature of," and "of the sort," which add nothing to a sentence except length.

Consider the following:

ANSWER A: Courts rarely grant summary judgment.

ANSWER B: It is rarely the case that courts grant summary judgment.

Answer A is more concise than Answer B. Streamline your writing by including only what is necessary.

___

Poor sentence structure can give the impression that a writer is not confident in his own position, conclusions, or understanding of the law.

Consider the following examples:

ANSWER A: It can be argued that the court abused its discretion when it admitted the photograph into evidence. There are many cases where less graphic photos were excluded because they might prejudice the jury.

ANSWER B: The court abused its discretion when it admitted the photograph into evidence. Less graphic photos have often been excluded because they might prejudice the jury.

Answer A is tentative and unsure; it approaches the subject matter indirectly, and the reader does not sense that the writer is committed to his position. Answer B, on the other hand, is direct and positive. Answer A suggests a possible argument in the first sentence. Answer B simply makes the argument. Answer A, when referring to the cases that support the argument, buries the key factual information in the middle of the second sentence. Answer B places the key information at the beginning of the sentence.

___

E. Avoid redundancies. A word, phrase, or concept may be repeated to provide a transition from one thought to another. Repeating a word, phrase, or concept may lead the reader smoothly to the next point. Repetition should be purposeful, however, and not merely redundant.

Compare the following:

ANSWER A: The primary problem with rejecting improperly filed documents is unfairness to the client, who had no control over how the case was handled.

> ANSWER B: The primary problem with rejecting improperly filed documents is the injustice of being unfair to the client, who had no control over how the case was handled.

Answer B is repetitive because it states that the problem is the "injustice of being unfair." Answer A is better because it simply uses "unfairness."

Other examples of redundancies include tautological phrases such as those discussed earlier in this chapter and constructions such as "large size," where the more precise word in a pair ("large") encompasses the meaning of the more general word ("size"). At best, redundancies make your writing wordy. At worst, readers might wonder if the two or three words you used carry two or three different meanings. If all of your meaning is conveyed by a single word, that one word is sufficient.

F. Avoid extraneous facts. Think carefully about the point you wish to make; omit any definitions, details, or commentary the reader does not need to understand your point.

Consider the following passages:

> ANSWER A: This jurisdiction has recognized the rescue doctrine to assure the rescuer that any slight negligence on his part will not bar recovery for his damages. In *Garber v. Radic*, the plaintiff sued a negligent driver for injuries he sustained while trying to save a victim trapped in a car. The appellate court allowed the negligent plaintiff to recover and adopted the rescue doctrine to encourage rescuers to extend aid to those in peril.

> ANSWER B: This jurisdiction has recognized the rescue doctrine to assure the rescuer that any slight negligence on his part will not bar recovery for his damages. In *Garber v. Radic*, the plaintiff sued both the railroad and the negligent driver for injuries the plaintiff sustained trying to save a victim trapped in a car stalled on railroad tracks. At trial, the jury found that the railroad had not been negligent and that the plaintiff had been contributorily negligent, thus barring his recovery. The plaintiff appealed and the appellate court reversed, adopting the

rescue doctrine in order to encourage rescuers to extend aid to those in peril.

Answer A is better because it says only what needs to be said. Answer B burdens the reader with unnecessary information about the railroad and the location of the stalled car. It also includes unnecessary procedural information. As you edit, focus on what the reader needs to know to understand your point.

---

5. Edit intrusive or misplaced words and phrases.

A reader expects the verb to follow the subject in most sentences. Do not make the reader wait for important information by inserting long phrases or clauses between the subject and the verb. This delay is irritating and possibly confusing enough to require a second or third reading of the sentence.

Compare the following:

ANSWER A: No document, that is, no contract, invoice, receipt, bill of lading, or other similar item regarding the transaction between the parties, specified the date of delivery.

ANSWER B: No document specified the date of delivery. The date was not in any contract, invoice, receipt, bill of lading, or other similar item regarding the transaction between the parties.

Answer A separates the subject (*document*) from the verb (*specified*) with the long phrase defining "document." It makes the reader wait for two lines to find out what is significant about these documents. Answer B is better because it does not burden the main sentence with the definition of "document." Instead, it tells the reader the important information first, then follows with the qualifying definition.

Modifying words and phrases should generally be as close as possible to the word or phrase they modify. The more words that come between these elements, the greater the risk that the sentence will not say what you intend. Confusion can also result when a word or phrase may modify more than one other element in a sentence.

Consider the following:

> The officer served the warrant for illegal dumping at the defendant's place of business.

In this sentence, it is impossible to determine whether the illegal dumping occurred at the defendant's place of business, or whether the warrant for this offense was merely served on the defendant at his place of business. The sentence could be rewritten to convey either meaning:

> The officer served the defendant with a warrant, charging him with illegal dumping at his place of business.

> The officer charged the defendant with illegal dumping and served him with a warrant at his place of business.

---

6. Use correct grammar, punctuation, and spelling.

Errors in grammar, punctuation, and spelling suggest that the writer is sloppy and careless—qualities that people do not want in a lawyer. Minor errors distract the reader from the message to be conveyed. Major errors may distort the message or make it unintelligible. In either case, the communication between writer and reader is interrupted.

Always proofread your sentences to make sure they are technically correct, even if you begin by using spell-checking programs on your word processor. Remember that these programs will not catch words that have been incorrectly used but correctly spelled—words such as "trail" instead of "trial" and "statue" instead of "statute"—and they will not flag omitted words or recognize legal terms whose spelling is peculiar to the law. Many lawyers customize their word processing programs so they will be more likely to catch these kinds of errors.

Any lawyer's bookshelf should include at least one good reference book on grammar and another on style. Appendix H lists selected books that address these topics.

EXERCISES

The following exercises will help you learn to write more clearly and concisely.

Exercise 15-A

Edit the following for wordiness and imprecision:

1. Canon 9 requires a lawyer to avoid even the appearance of impropriety. Despite the fact that this requirement has led several courts to disqualify attorneys even though no actual impropriety existed, clearly the appearance of impropriety is not always sufficient. For example, in *Blumenfeld v. Fusco*, the court held that the fact of the marriage of two attorneys employed by different firms did not create an appearance of impropriety sufficient to warrant disqualification of the wife in a case in which the propounder had been represented by the wife's firm at some point in the past. The case involved a challenge to a will, in which an associate in the firm representing the propounder was married to a partner in the firm retained to represent the caveator in the trial *de novo* following the trial in probate court. It was the court's finding that no actual impropriety existed since the husband worked in the real estate department and had no contact with the attorneys who were actually representing the caveator. In reversing the trial court's disqualification of the wife, the appellate court balanced the need to avoid the appearance of impropriety with the plaintiff's right to employ the counsel of his choice. In *Blumenfeld v. Fusco*, considerations relevant to the latter outweighed the former, given the improbability that any impropriety had actually occurred.

2. It is interesting to note that no court that has addressed the question of recognizing fraud in the context of an adoption has refused to do so where there was some kind of evidence of active concealment. For example, in *In re Baby J.*, the court found fraudulent concealment of the truth where the adoption agency told the parents that the birth mother was an 18-year-old unwed mother who could not care for the baby. The truth in this case, which the agency was clearly aware of, was that the mother was a 35-year-old patient in a mental institution and the father was presumed to be another patient. The truth was discovered only by the adoptive parents after their 13-year-old adopted son was diagnosed as having an inherited mental disorder. Similarly, in *Roe v. Jones*, the court awarded damages due to the fact that the adoption agency placed three school-aged children for adoption, telling the prospective parents that the children were normal, healthy children. The agency clearly knew that this was not the truth because it had test results and psychological evaluations showing that the

children had a history of dangerously violent behavior and other behavior disorders. In both cases the court placed its emphasis on the agencies' actual knowledge and active concealment of the truth.

Exercise 15-B

Edit or rewrite the sentences below as needed:

1. Due to the fact that medical malpractice lawsuits are of the type that can be lengthy and expensive, plaintiffs and their attorneys should carefully weigh the chances of a successful outcome before proceeding to file a complaint.

2. The defendant's reprehensible conduct clearly falls in the category of fraud and deceit and should be punished to the fullest extent of the law by the maximum fine allowed under the statute.

3. Being immaterial, irrelevant, and a product of hearsay, the attorney strenuously objected to the witness' testimony.

4. A view generally held by most jurisdictions is that the "fireman's rule" acts as a bar to any recovery by emergency personnel for certain injuries suffered as a result of the peril such personnel have been summoned to handle.

5. Because the deadline for answering had passed, the attorney filed a motion correctly attempting to open the default.

6. The plaintiff's allegation was that the warning given by the manufacturer in relation to the hazardous nature of the product was not sufficient enough to inform the public about the dangers involved.

7. Obviously, it was the discrepancy in the testimony of the defendant that persuaded the jury of her guilt as to all the charges.

8. It was essentially the plaintiff's contention that basic, fundamental fairness required he be given another chance to prove his case, in view of the unethical nature of the conduct on the part of the defendant's attorney.

9. Until such time as the witness makes the decision to disclose the information required by the court, he will be held in contempt of court.

10. In weighing the benefits of a recreational camp versus possible injury to the lake, it cannot be concluded that the former will compensate for the latter.

The Office Memorandum and the Opinion Letter

Elements
of an Office
Memorandum

A lawyer's most important job is advising a client how to approach a particular situation in light of the relevant law. Sound legal advice may permit a client to benefit from some situations and avoid exposure to liability in others. Even when a client seeks advice too late, proper counseling can minimize the damage. If litigation occurs—for whatever reason—good legal advice can help bring about a fruitful conclusion. For every case that goes to court, however, there are dozens of others that were never litigated, and did not have to be, because someone followed a lawyer's advice.

Legal advice to a client is often based on a formal memorandum of law, which is a basic document of legal writing. It is usually written by a clerk or junior attorney for a more experienced attorney to predict what effect application of the relevant law will have on the client's situation. Senior attorneys use memoranda to determine what advice to give a client. Three fundamental principles should guide you in researching, drafting, and writing an office memorandum:

Be objective. The hallmark of a memo is objectivity. Scrupulously examine your own arguments as well as those you anticipate from your opponent. Only then can you honestly assess the strengths and weaknesses of your client's case. Above all else, you must be honest about what the law permits and what it does not; the senior attorney or the client should not be misled by your wishful thinking or advocacy. As noted in Chapter 7 (Common Law Analysis), the law will not always favor your client's position. The lawyer-as-counselor must give a client the information he or she needs to make good decisions about important matters. After the client has made a decision, the lawyer-as-advocate can then consider how to obtain the best result for the client under the circumstances. This characteristic of a memorandum is so important that it is addressed in greater detail in Chapter 17 (Objective Writing).

Be thorough. Lawyers and clients make major decisions based on office memos. Consequently, you should make every effort to ensure that these decisions are informed by the best analysis you can provide. You can do this only if your knowledge of the relevant law is solid and your thinking is clear.

Communicate. The memo must be organized and written so that your thoughts are clearly and precisely stated. All of your effort is for nothing unless the reader understands what you are saying. People do not usually read legal writing for fun, so make the reader's job as easy as possible. Remember, too, that your reader may not be familiar with the relevant law.

The memorandum is composed of several distinct but related sections. Label each section (except the heading) by underlining or capitalizing its name on a separate line immediately preceding that section. Although there are many variations, the following format for preparing a legal memorandum is widely used. Appendix A is a sample memorandum using this format that you should read in conjunction with this chapter.

1. Heading

The Heading is the part of the memorandum that tells who wrote it, to whom it is written, what it is about, and the date. It should look like this:

MEMORANDUM

To: Cheryl Scott

From: Eli Blackburn

Re: Possible abuse of discretion by trial judge in enjoining landfill operation, Department of Environmental Resources v. Fredericks, file no. 12-104

Date: October 3, 2012

The explanation of the subject not only identifies the client and the file number but also briefly describes the general legal question. This description helps separate this memo from other memos in the same file and also provides a means of locating the memo later if a similar issue arises concerning different parties.

2. Questions Presented

This section should contain balanced and understandable statements of the legal questions you will answer in the memo. The Questions Presented will parallel the issues (and possibly the sub-issues) that you analyze in the Discussion section of the memo. When there is more than one question, identify them by number or letter (*e.g.*, "I," "II," or "A," "B"). Each question must describe the relevant legal rule and summarize the legally significant facts. Chapter 19 (Questions Presented) discusses how to formulate these questions.

3. Brief Answer(s) (optional)

This section provides a short answer to each of the questions presented in the preceding section. The Brief Answer is a conclusion and a brief explanation of the reasons for that conclusion. It is useful because it provides immediate answers to the questions. This section is optional because it serves essentially the same purpose as the Conclusion section of the memo, although it differs from the Conclusion in length and form.

Because the Brief Answer section immediately follows the Questions Presented section, it should begin with a direct reply to each of the questions, such as "yes," "no," "probably," or "probably not." Each answer should be self-contained and should be identified by the same number or letter as the question to which it pertains. The answers should not include citations to cases, regulations, or statutes except when citations are so determinative of the issue that it would be senseless to exclude them. Of course, each Brief Answer should be responsive to the corresponding question.

A judge has enjoined your client, Al Fredericks, from operating a landfill on his property because it causes odors and groundwater contamination. The Question Presented in your memo is whether the judge abused her discretion in granting the injunction. Consider these Brief Answers:

ANSWER A: No. The judge's ruling was well within her reasonable discretion. Her conclusion that the damage to nearby landowners from odors and groundwater pollution outweighs the harm caused to the defendant by the injunction is amply supported by the record.

ANSWER B: Injunctive relief is proper only when the damage being enjoined outweighs the harm to the defendant caused by the injunction. A trial court's injunction can be reversed on appeal only if the judge abused her discretion. The findings of the trial judge indicate that she did not abuse her discretion.

Answer A is better because it answers the question in a single word, "no," and then succinctly explains this conclusion by applying the legal rule to the summarized facts. Answer B fails to answer the question immediately and directly. Though it gives a bare statement of the legal rules involved, it fails to explain the conclusion. Answer A directly answers the question and explains the answer. Answer B does neither.

4. Statement of Facts

The Statement of Facts is a formal and objective description of the relevant facts in the problem. It must be accurate and complete. This section of the office memo is addressed in Chapter 18 (Statement of Facts for a Memorandum).

5. Discussion

The Discussion is the heart of the memo and draws on lessons from many of the chapters in this book, particularly Part C (Basic Concepts of Legal Writing). The Discussion is divided into sections according to the issues and sub-issues presented by the problem. As noted earlier, these sections parallel the Questions Presented. Each section may be headed by a restatement of the corresponding Question Presented. The Discussion, as already suggested, must also be objective.

6. Conclusion

The Conclusion section is a somewhat longer and slightly different version of the Brief Answer. The Conclusion is longer because it contains a more thorough description of the reasoning supporting the ultimate conclusion. For each issue, it briefly describes the relevant law and explains how the law does or does not apply to the facts in the case. It should contain enough detail so that it can stand on its own. The theory is that a busy reader will read the Brief Answer(s), a reader who has a little more time will read the Conclusion section, and a reader who has enough time will read the entire memo. The Conclusion also differs from the Brief Answer in that it is not segmented by issues. As with the Brief Answer, the Conclusion section should not include citations except in rare instances.

> **Consider these possible Conclusion sections for a memo on the landfill injunction problem:**

ANSWER A: Injunctive relief is proper when the damage being enjoined outweighs the harm to the defendant caused by the injunction. The judge found that the injunction would deprive the defendant of his only source of income, but it would substantially reduce odor and groundwater contamination problems for neighboring landowners.

ANSWER B: The judge did not abuse her discretion in granting the injunction because she carefully followed the *Redding v. Stone River Flour Co.* standards for equitable relief. The judge found that an injunction would deprive the defendant of his only source of income, and that he and his wife would have severe trouble continuing to make payments for their house and car. The court also found, however, that eighteen neighboring landowners became nauseated from the site's odors and that the wells from which they pumped household water were contaminated with a variety of harmful chemicals. There is sufficient evidence to show she did not abuse her discretion.

ANSWER C: The judge did not abuse her discretion in granting an injunction because she reasonably concluded that the damage being enjoined outweighed the harm to the defendant caused by the injunction. The judge found that the injunction would deprive the defendant of his only source of income but that it would substantially reduce odors and groundwater contamination for neighboring landowners. Although her conclusion may be debated, it has ample support in the record.

All three answers cover the same ground, but Answer C is the best. Answer C states a conclusion and then summarizes the applicable law and the relevant facts to show how they justify that conclusion. The answer is brief and to the point.

Answer A, in contrast, is not an answer at all. It describes the relevant law and the facts, but it does not draw any explicit conclusion from them. Because the purpose of a memo is to predict the likely outcome of a legal dispute, Answer A is useless.

Answer B offers a conclusion but is much too long and detailed. Only essential facts belong in the Conclusion section; other facts belong in the Discussion. In addition, the bare reference to the *Redding* rule is not helpful. The reader will probably not understand the significance of that particular case without an explanation or statement of the rule it contains. Remember that the Conclusion section must be self-contained.

Sometimes, an attorney or law clerk will be asked to include recommendations regarding the case at the end of the Conclusion. It might then be appropriate, for example, to weigh the merits of a settlement offer, to suggest that further discovery be conducted to establish the existence of certain facts, or to remind the reader that an important filing deadline is approaching.

While this memorandum format is widely used, it is not the only possible memorandum format. The Short Answers are identified as optional because some law offices do not use them. In other offices, additional portions of this format are also omitted (*e.g.,* Questions Presented). This book explains all of the traditional elements of a legal memorandum so that you are prepared to write an effective legal memo wherever you practice law.

Special Considerations for Electronic Communication

E-mail is now commonly used for many business communications, including interoffice memos. There is an ongoing debate about whether e-mail is a blessing or a curse, but it is unlikely that it will disappear. E-mail is another tool in your professional toolbox. Used skillfully, it can be an effective means of communication.

As a starting point, e-mail does not change the kind of careful writing and analysis required for a legal memorandum. The rapidity and brevity of e-mail makes it easy to think you can now give a quick legal opinion without much analysis or research. For the sake of your legal career, do not fall into that trap. Unless you already know an area of law very well and the question requires only a simple answer, there is absolutely no substitute for the traditional work of drafting a legal memorandum.

More generally, the following guidelines apply to the use of e-mail for legal memoranda and other e-mail correspondence.

A. Be professional. A lawyer's communications should always be professional, regardless of the medium. Using an electronic form of communication rather than a traditional print form does not change the nature of the communication. In personal e-mail, we might use shorthand expressions or abbreviations, reveal personal information, express casual opinions, make sarcastic or rude statements, or vent emotionally. There is an enormous temptation to carry these practices into professional e-mail correspondence. *Do not yield to that temptation.* Make sure that e-mail communications are as professional as printed communications.

E-mail correspondence should be written in standard English. An informal tone is appropriate in personal correspondence, but it is not acceptable in a professional setting. Use the same level of courtesy and formality in a memorandum sent by e-mail as you would in a printed version. This rule applies not only to the substantive content of the e-mail, but also to the salutation and form of address. For example, an e-mail to a client should open with "Dear Ms. Sweeney" or (for clients you know well) "Dear Susan," rather than a more informal "Hi, Susie."

Similarly, although the abbreviations and symbols used in personal e-mails, text messages, and chat rooms might be useful and easily understood by many users, avoid using them in a professional e-mail. Emoticons—those happy and sad little faces that appear in so many e-mails—also have no place in professional correspondence. Avoid nonstandard fonts, font sizes, and font colors; if you would not choose that font, size, or color for a printed letter, do not use it for the same correspondence sent via e-mail.

B. Proofread before sending. Many writers do not take the time to spell check or grammar check their e-mails correspondence. Use these tools on any written document before sending it. In addition, as noted in Chapter 15 (Revising and Editing), always proofread because automated programs do not catch every error. Take the same care with every document, from a two-page memo to a fifty-page brief. Printing the document and reading it carefully will help you spot errors you might have missed while reading from the screen.

C. Honor the need for client confidentiality. Rule 1.6, Model Rules of Professional Conduct, states in part, "A lawyer shall not reveal information relating to the representation of a client unless the client gives informed consent." Comment 16 to Rule 1.6 states that "[a] lawyer must act competently to safeguard information relating to the representation of a client against inadvertent or unauthorized disclosure by the lawyer or other persons who are participating in the representation of the client or who are subject to the lawyer's supervision." A responsible lawyer will ensure that any use of e-mail complies with this Rule. Before sending any e-mail message, for example, double check to make sure that it is going only to the right person(s), and not to anyone else.

Most lawyers have adopted practices designed to reduce the risk of inadvertent disclosure of confidential information. Two of the most common practices are e-mail encryption and the use of a confidentiality warning and disclaimer on every e-mail. An encrypted e-mail can be read only by the sender and the intended recipient. The following are two sample confidentiality warnings.

CONFIDENTIALITY NOTICE AND DISCLAIMER

The information in this transmission may be confidential and/or protected by legal professional privilege and is intended only for the person or persons to whom it is addressed. If you are not such a person, you are warned that any disclosure, copying, or dissemination of the information is unauthorized. If you have received the transmission in error, please immediately contact this Office by telephone, fax, or e-mail, to inform us of the error and to enable arrangements to be made for the destruction of the transmission or its return at our cost. No liability is accepted for any unauthorized use of the information contained in this transmission.

If the transmission contains advice, the advice is based on instructions in relation to, and is provided to the addressee in connection with, the matter mentioned above. Responsibility is not accepted for reliance upon it by any other person or for any other purpose.

Confidentiality Warning

The information contained in this e-mail and any attached documents may be privileged, confidential, and protected from disclosure. If you are not the intended recipient you may not read, copy, distribute, or use this information. If you have received this communication in error, please notify the sender immediately by replying to this message and then delete it from your system.

Objective Writing

The most fundamental rule of memorandum writing can be simply stated: be objective. Clients rely on memos to make choices about their lives and businesses. Senior lawyers rely on memos to advise clients and make decisions concerning strategy or procedure. When people are making decisions like this, they need to know exactly where they stand. Your role, in a fundamental way, is similar to that of a doctor or dentist—to tell someone the truth about a particular condition or situation. Neither a patient nor a client can decide effectively how to proceed without an objective assessment.

Objective writing means that you do not overestimate or underestimate; you communicate precisely your client's likelihood of success. Objective writing is harder than it may seem when you are advising a client, because your natural inclination is to believe that the judge will see it your way. You will be tempted to tell your client what he or she wants to hear, or, more subtly, to overstate the good news and understate the bad news. But an attorney for the opposing side presumably will make the best arguments she can make, and your client needs to be aware of their potential effect. On the other hand, you don't want to lean so far the other way that, in the name of objectivity, you understate your client's likelihood of success.

The Discussion in a memorandum will be based mostly on lessons described earlier, especially in Part B (Basic Concepts of Legal Method) and Part C (Basic Concepts of Legal Writing). This chapter identifies four principles concerning objectivity that are important in a memorandum.

1. Think like a judge.

To be objective, you must be able to see a particular legal problem from at least three perspectives. Your client's perspective is one, and the position opposed to your client is another. The third perspective, which includes the first two, is that of the judge who will decide your case. Put yourself in the position of the judge who will resolve this case after weighing all competing arguments. What law and what facts would you, as the judge, rely on? What would you decide as a judge? Then, shifting to your role as attorney and advisor for a particular client, explain what that judge is likely to do.

The memorandum excerpts used in Chapter 16 (Elements of an Office Memorandum) conclude that the trial judge did not abuse her discretion by issuing the injunction. It therefore does not tell the client what she wants to hear. But the attorney reached that result by putting himself in the position of the court that would hear an appeal from the trial judge's decision. This example is perhaps the most difficult form of objective writing because it gives the client almost no reason to be hopeful. Still, it provides the client with important and useful information. The unfavorable conclusion indicates that an appeal would mean a great deal of time and trouble with little likelihood of success. The lawyer should try to resolve the client's problem in some other way. Being a good lawyer means looking for every possible way to help a client and being completely honest—even when the findings are unfavorable.

To put yourself in the position of a judge, recall the six elements of a judicial opinion from Chapter 3 (Case Analysis and Case Briefs): facts, rule, issue, holding, disposition, and reasons and policies. As a judge, the facts you would employ are not limited to the facts that one side finds significant; they are the facts that each side believes to be significant. The rules you would apply, and the legal issues on which they are based, would not be only the rules that favor one side; they would be the rules that are important to each side. Your holding, disposition, and reasons and policies would all be based on the arguments from both sides. Always keep the judge's objective perspective in mind as you advise a client. Sooner or later, you may have to defend or explain your position to a court.

2. State your conclusion on each issue or sub-issue objectively and candidly.

Legal memos are written to predict outcomes, and your prediction is reflected in your conclusion. Properly stating your conclusion requires you to balance adverse interests. On the one hand, you must take a position. Clients and senior attorneys do not want a set of competing considerations. They want you to tell them how the issue will likely be resolved. They want you to make a judgment, to predict the outcome. They want your guidance, and may ask you how you would proceed if you were in their shoes. They do not want waffling statements such as "our client might or might not prevail" or "our client has a chance of successfully defending the claim."

On the other hand, as discussed previously, your obligation to be objective requires you to point out both the strengths and the weaknesses in your client's position. Statements such as "our client will prevail" or "our client definitely will lose," while stating a position, might be overly confident and thus misleading. Some legal positions are sufficiently one-sided to merit such confidence. If they are, such as when you have one or a series of "givens," you should make an unequivocal statement. Often, however, your analysis will lead you to conclude that your client's chances of success are best measured in degrees of probability, rather than absolutes. Your task then is to frame your conclusion candidly to reflect these degrees of probability.

Each case is different, and the possible ways to describe your conclusion are limited only by your creativity. Strong conclusions can be expressed as "most likely," somewhat certain conclusions can be expressed as "probably," even less certain conclusions can begin with "on balance," and so forth. The point is that you must balance competing considerations in your statement.

You represent Herbert Pearson, the owner of a fifty-two-foot sport fishing yacht that was transported by ship from Florida to Colombo, Sri Lanka. As the yacht was being unloaded at Colombo, the ship's crane malfunctioned, causing the yacht to fall into the water and sink. The yacht, worth $2.4 million, is now a total loss. Pearson wants to sue the ship owner for damages, and you have been asked to write a memo on his chances of success.

The United States Carriage of Goods by Sea Act ordinarily would limit Pearson's recoverable damages to $500. However, your research has revealed cases in which the court held that the ship owner would not be entitled to limit its liability if it failed to advise Pearson properly in the bill of lading (the legal document that accompanies the shipment) that the limitation was applicable and that the limitation could be avoided by paying a greater freight rate. The language in the bill of lading issued to Pearson is ambiguous. You nonetheless believe that the reasoning of the authorities supports Pearson's position, that a decision in Pearson's favor would be fair, and that the arguments supporting Pearson's position are significantly stronger than opposing arguments. Consider the following statements of your conclusion:

> ANSWER A: Pearson will most likely prevail in recovering full damages for loss of his yacht.

> ANSWER B: Pearson may prevail in recovering full damages for loss of his yacht, but there are strong arguments to the contrary.

> ANSWER C: Pearson will prevail in recovering full damages for loss of his yacht.

Answer A is best because it honestly and candidly conveys the writer's best judgment on Pearson's chances of success. It also lets the reader know that there is some room for doubt.

Answer C is too bold; it leads the reader to believe that a court will certainly decide the case in favor of Pearson. Answer C is not objective.

Answer B gives the reader a mixed message. It says that Pearson may succeed but, then again, he may not. This is not a prediction; it is merely a statement that the case could go either way. Conclusions such as this are confusing and do not satisfy the writer's obligation to assess the client's chances of success candidly and objectively.

---

3. Describe the law objectively.

Although there are many legitimate ways to describe the law, you must describe it objectively. Avoid the temptation to oversimplify or slant your explanation so that it favors your client's position. Objectivity in describing the applicable law is essential to your credibility. In any subsequent litigation, your client will not want to learn for the first time that there is a case or statutory provision hostile to her position. Because memos predict likely outcomes in actual or potential legal disputes, the importance of maintaining objectivity in describing the law cannot be overemphasized. Objectivity may differ from accuracy. It is possible to explain the supportive cases or statutory provisions accurately but fail to explain other cases or provisions that are relevant but damaging. Sometimes these omissions are stark, but they can also be subtle.

The new state Recycling Act requires each municipality with more than 5,000 people to set up a recycling program. Your client, the town of Elk Crossing, applied to the state Department of Environmental Quality for a grant to finance a recycling program for its population of 700. Last week, the Department denied the application, saying only that "the town's program, while very good, cannot be funded at this time." The town seeks your opinion on whether it can appeal the denial of the grant application. The Elk Crossing recycling program is one of the oldest and most successful in the state and has been featured in several national magazines. Consider these descriptions of the Act's grant provision:

ANSWER A: Section 902 of the Recycling Act provides that "the Department of Environmental Quality shall award grants for the development and implementation of municipal recycling programs, upon application from any municipality."

ANSWER B: Section 902 of the Recycling Act provides that "the Department of Environmental Quality shall award grants for the development and implementation of municipal recycling programs, upon application from any municipality. In awarding these grants, the Department shall give priority to municipalities that are required to establish a recycling program under this Act."

Answer B is better because it contains both the good news and the bad news. The good news is that grants are available to municipalities that are not required to set up a recycling program. The bad news is that these municipalities are given a lower priority than other municipalities. A description like this gives your client a much better sense of its chances than Answer A. By stating only the good news, Answer A sets up your client to learn the bad news later, probably after a lot of wasted time and expense. To judges and other attorneys, moreover, an argument based only on the law in Answer A will be seen as slipshod at best and dishonest at worst.

4. Explain the analysis objectively.

Objectivity in memorandum writing is important because the weaknesses of your position will come to light sooner or later, and it is better for that to happen sooner. An objective analysis is one that a reasonable attorney, reading dispassionately, would find to be an accurate and fair explanation of the strengths and weaknesses of your position. Even if your description of the law is objective, that does not necessarily mean your analysis will be objective. You must avoid putting a "spin" on your analysis to favor your client's position.

Consider these analyses of the recycling grant problem:

ANSWER A: The town will not succeed in an appeal. Section 902 of the Recycling Act provides that "the Department of Environmental Quality shall award grants for the development and implementation of municipal recycling programs, upon application from any municipality. In awarding these grants, the Department shall give priority to municipalities that are required to establish a recycling program under this Act." The town of Elk Crossing qualifies for a grant because "any municipality" may be awarded a grant under section 902. Municipalities required to implement recycling programs are given first priority for this grant, however, and Elk Crossing is not one of those municipalities. The Department's statement that the Elk Crossing program "cannot be funded at this time" obviously means that no funds were available after grants were awarded to municipalities required to establish a recycling program.

ANSWER B: The town will succeed in an appeal of the grant denial. Section 902 of the Recycling Act provides that "the Department of Environmental Quality shall award grants for the development and implementation of municipal recycling programs, upon application from any municipality. In awarding these grants, the Department shall give priority to municipalities that are required to establish a recycling program under this Act." The town of Elk Crossing qualifies for a grant because "any municipality" may be awarded a grant under section 902. The Department should have ensured the availability of funds for Elk Crossing because the Department is required to encourage recycling under the Act. It was absurd and inappropriate for the Department to award grants only to larger municipalities and deny a grant to a nationally prominent program with a long and successful history.

ANSWER C: The town has a small chance of succeeding in an appeal because it must first show that funds were available after the Department awarded grants to municipalities that are required to establish a recycling program. Section 902 of the Recycling Act provides that "the Department of Environmental Quality shall award grants for the development and implementation of municipal recycling programs, upon application from any municipality. In awarding these grants, the Department shall give priority to municipalities that are required to establish a recycling program under this Act." The town of Elk Crossing qualifies for a grant because "any municipality" may be awarded a grant under section 902. Municipalities required to implement recycling programs are given first priority for this grant, however, and Elk Crossing is not one of those municipalities. The Department's statement that the Elk Crossing program "cannot be funded at this time" could mean that no funds were available after it awarded grants to municipalities required to establish a recycling program. That is a likely meaning, but it is not the only possible meaning. The statement does not refer to Section 902. It could therefore be a bureaucratic way of saying that some funds were available for non-priority municipalities, but that the Department awarded the funds to municipalities other than Elk Crossing. If so, the national prominence of the Elk Crossing recycling program, coupled with its long and successful history, provide an attractive basis for claiming that Elk Crossing should have received a grant.

Answer C is best. Answer C concludes that Elk Crossing may succeed in an appeal if it can show that funds were available after the high-priority municipalities received their grants. It states that the Department's explanation for the denial of the grant could have two meanings, and explains why. Answer C then states that the national prominence and success of the Elk Crossing program provide an attractive basis for claiming that the Department should have approved a grant. Answer C explains the law and the facts and then discusses the possible effect of the program's success in objective terms. As Answer C says, Elk Crossing does not seem likely to prevail, but there is at least a plausible basis for appeal.

Answer B is wrong because it is not objective. First, it omits any legal analysis that Elk Crossing is a low-priority municipality. Second, it indulges in editorial commentary that effectively contradicts part of the statute. Answer B states that the Act requires the Department to encourage recycling and then, using that premise, states that money should have been made available to Elk crossing. The statute, however, specifically gives priority to larger municipalities. The writer is advocating when she ought to be assessing her client's chances of success.

Answer A is also wrong; it is biased against the town because its analysis is too superficial. It concludes that Elk Crossing will not succeed in its appeal because the Department's letter "obviously" means that insufficient funds were available after the high-priority municipalities received their grants. As Answer C suggests, however, the letter may actually have another meaning. If so, the national prominence and success of the Elk Crossing program—facts that are not mentioned in Answer A—may matter a great deal.

EXERCISES

The following exercises are intended to help you apply these principles.

Exercise 17-A

Assume that you are the trial judge in the Calvert County District Court for the State of Chesapeake. You are deciding the case involved in Exercise 6-A, pp. 89-91. Hugh Green has sued Neil McKay, claiming that there is a valid contract to sell McKay's yacht. Green has filed a motion for summary judgment on an issue or sub-issue chosen by you or your professor. The facts contained in Exercise 6-A are not contested. Draft an opinion on that issue or sub-issue. Use a caption like that in Appendix E on p. 471, but modify it for this problem. The docket number for the case is CV-13-671. Structure your opinion using the following headings in this order: facts, issue, rule, holding, reasons and policies, and disposition. Be sure to sign and date your opinion as shown on p. 476.

Exercise 17-B

Assume that you are the trial judge in the Humboldt County Superior Court for the State of Huron. You are deciding the case involved in Exercise 6-B, pp. 91-94. The *Star City Banner-Patriot* has sued Star City because of the police department's refusal to provide the requested information under the state Freedom of Information Act. The city has filed a motion for summary judgment on an issue or sub-issue chosen by you or your professor. The facts contained in Exercise 6-B are not contested. Draft an opinion on that issue or sub-issue. Use a caption like that in Appendix E on p. 471, but modify it for this problem. The docket number for the case is CIV-121-2013. Structure your opinion using the following headings in this order: facts, issue, rule, holding, reasons and policies, and disposition. Be sure to sign and date your opinion as shown on p. 476.

Exercise 17-C

This exercise is based on Exercise 10-A, pp. 161-163. Using the principles stated in this chapter, draft the discussion of one issue or sub-issue chosen by you or your professor. Write the discussion as if you were preparing an office memorandum.

Exercise 17-D

This exercise is based on Exercise 10-B, pp. 163-165. Using the principles stated in this chapter, draft the discussion of one issue or sub-issue chosen by you or your professor. Write the discussion as if you were preparing an office memorandum.

18 Statement of Facts for a Memorandum

An office memo structured according to the traditional pattern has a separate section for the Statement of Facts. This statement gives the reader a context for the legal problem at issue and shows what facts are important to its resolution.

Every legal problem involves the interplay of numerous facts, only some of which are relevant to its analysis. Whether you acquire these facts from interviews with clients or witnesses, from examination of documents, or from a senior attorney, you will invariably accumulate more facts than are necessary. These facts also tend to be disorganized and scattered through different interview notes and documents. You must set aside extraneous facts and work with only those necessary to understand and resolve the legal issues. You must then present these remaining facts intelligibly, accurately, and coherently. The basic principles for selecting and appropriately stating the facts of a case are best understood in the context of a specific problem.

You represent Clara Finch in a land dispute. An interview with her and a subsequent investigation have revealed the following facts:

Memo to File

Clara Finch Access Dispute, File No. 157-13

February 28, 2013

I met with Clara Finch this morning. Finch is an 80-year-old widow living on a small pension. She has a home on five acres of mostly wooded land off Highway Q. Her primary means of access to her home is on a road from Highway Q through property now owned by William Amodio. Finch and the prior owner, George Brauzakas, had an oral agreement that she could use his road as long as he owned the land. The new owner, Amodio, is a wealthy banker who bought the Brauzakas property on speculation that land prices would continue to increase. Amodio has recently felled several large trees across the road through his property to prevent Finch from using the road. Amodio has told Finch several times that he blocked the road because he does not like Finch. There is another way to get to her home, but it adds 45 minutes to her drive each way. She wants to know if she can force Amodio to reopen the road she has been using.

Ready Title Company

Property Title Summary

Clara Finch Issue

March 10, 2013

In 1991, George Brauzakas purchased a forty-acre tract of land on the north side of County Highway Q, which runs east and west. Finch purchased five acres of this tract from Brauzakas in 2009. Brauzakas sold the remainder of his land (thirty-five acres) to William Amodio in 2012. Finch's lot adjoins the Amodio property on its north side. There is no reference to Finch's use of the road in Amodio's deed to the property, and there is no recorded easement. Aerial photos show that Finch has another access to her house by a dirt road leading from another highway, but that route is thirty miles in length.

There are two relevant appellate decisions in your state:

Carson v. Dow (1944)

The appellant, Carl Carson, brought this action for injunctive relief against Edward Dow, claiming that he had an express easement to run a natural gas pipeline across Dow's property and that Dow refused him access. There is no recorded easement. The trial court held that there was no express easement because of the absence of any mention of the alleged easement in Dow's deed to the property or in any other written agreement. We agree. Absent some written contractual agreement, there can be no express easement.

Watzke v. Lovett (1990)

Andrew Watzke purchased a tract of land from Peter Lovett. The tract is located on the shore of a lake and is surrounded on the remaining sides by property owned by Lovett. The only means of access to Watzke's property is by a road that crosses Lovett's property and connects to a public highway. Lovett has recently blocked the road, claiming that Watzke has no right to use it. Watzke conceded to the trial court that there is no written agreement creating an easement across Lovett's property, but he argued that the court should imply an easement out of necessity. The trial court refused. We reverse.

When one person owns a parcel of land, and that person transfers part of that parcel to another person, access to the transferred part cannot be denied if the only means of access is through the remaining part of the original parcel. A showing of strict necessity is required before an easement will be implied. The landlocked nature of Watzke's property satisfies that requirement in this case. Watzke has an implied easement by necessity to use the road over Lovett's property.

Certain facts have special significance in light of these two cases. The following is a procedure for selecting and stating them.

1. Identify the legally significant facts.

The legally significant facts are those that will affect the legal outcome of your client's case. As explained in Chapter 3 (Case Analysis and Case Briefs), some facts of a judicial opinion are more important than others. The most important facts are those the court used to determine whether to apply particular legal rules to the case it was deciding. Writing a legal memo reverses this perspective. Instead of looking backward to determine what facts a court thought were important, you must look forward to predict what facts in your client's case a court is likely to find significant.

You can identify the legally significant facts in a case only after you have identified the relevant rules and the corresponding issues. As you research and read the law, you will discover the kinds of facts upon which the cases turn. You will then be able to recognize the analogous and distinguishable facts in your client's case and determine how those facts are likely to be seen by a court. Many legal writers do not draft the Statement of Facts until after they have completed the Discussion section and discovered which facts will have the greatest effect on the disposition of the case. Those facts are then incorporated into the Statement of Facts.

Isolating the legally significant facts is a process of eliminating extraneous facts until only those necessary to resolve the legal issues remain. This process allows a clearer understanding and analysis of the problem because it focuses the reader's, and the writer's, attention exclusively on the facts that matter. Identify all significant facts, regardless of whether they help or hurt your client's position.

When the legal rules are clear and unmistakable, you will need to identify relatively few significant facts. The ambiguity or vagueness of many legal rules, however, means that the legal significance of some facts will depend on how the rule is interpreted. These borderline facts should be included if the interpretation requiring them is plausible.

Blatant appeals to emotion are not appropriate in an objective memo. Emotional facts, therefore, should be included only if those facts have independent legal significance or are likely to influence the outcome by appealing to a judge's sympathy and sense of justice. When the law is straightforward and applies to your problem so clearly that there is little doubt concerning the outcome, emotional facts have little or no significance and should be omitted. When the law is not straightforward or the outcome is uncertain, however, emotional facts take on greater significance. Many exceptions to general rules have been made or expanded to reach a just result in light of the facts. Nonetheless, the value of emotional facts is speculative because a court may ignore them. Because a court cannot ignore legally significant facts, such facts give the best indication of the likely outcome.

The *Carson* and *Watzke* cases indicate that Finch could raise two possible legal objections. She could claim that she has an express easement and, if not, that she has an implied easement by necessity. The *Carson* court held that an express easement must be created either in a written agreement or in the deed to the property across which the easement runs. It is thus legally significant that there is no provision in Amodio's deed permitting Finch to use the road across Amodio's property and that there is no recorded easement. These facts will make it difficult for Finch to claim an express easement, but they must nonetheless be included in the Statement of Facts.

The claim that Finch has an implied easement by necessity involves a somewhat different set of legally significant facts. The court in *Watzke* held that when the only means of access to a person's property is through the property of the person who originally transferred the land, the person seeking access is entitled to an implied easement by necessity. In Finch's case, it is legally significant that there is a road across the Amodio property which Finch uses to get to her home, that there is another route to Finch's house, and that Brauzakas sold part of his property to Finch and the remainder to Amodio.

Although the significance of many facts will be immediately apparent, the significance of others will depend on how the legal rules are interpreted. For example, the *Watzke* court indicated that an easement would be implied only out of strict necessity. As a result, the existence of the second road may work to Finch's disadvantage. It may thus be significant that Finch is 80 years old and that the other road would take her thirty miles and forty-five minutes out of her way (facts which may have appeared at first to be emotional ones) because these facts tend to show that Finch's use of Amodio's road is more a necessity than a convenience. These facts should be included in a Statement of Facts because they may have a bearing on the strict-necessity rule, even though there was no other access in *Watzke*.

Finch's problem involves emotionally significant facts you should exclude from analysis—particularly those suggesting that the wealthy banker Amodio is spitefully imposing a hardship on the poor widow Finch. Although these facts might influence how a judge would perceive the fairness of the situation, they have nothing to do with either of the legal rules concerning easements. Similarly, it is not significant that Amodio bought the property on speculation. Identify only the facts that are relevant to the possible application of a legal rule.

2. Identify key background facts.

Legally significant facts tell part of the story, but these facts alone may not tell the whole story. Background facts are often needed to make the factual situation understandable and to put the legally significant facts in context. Include as many background facts as the reader needs to understand the problem, but no more.

In Finch's case, for example, it probably would help the reader to know that Brauzakas's tract was forty acres, that Finch's parcel is five acres, and that Amodio's is thirty-five acres. This information provides background for the implied easement question by clarifying Brauzakas's original ownership and subsequent division of the property. The dates on which Finch and Amodio bought their property from Brauzakas may be helpful, although the date on which Brauzakas purchased the land is not. In addition, it is useful to state that Brauzakas and Finch had an oral agreement because this fact highlights the absence of a written agreement. The name of the highway, however, is not relevant. Nor is it necessary to state that Amodio blocked the access by felling several trees; the statement that he blocked the access will do.

3. Organize the facts intelligibly.

The statement of legally significant and key background facts should tell your client's story completely and coherently. In most cases, the most sensible and convenient method of organization is to relate the facts in chronological order. Chronological order is easy for the reader to understand because it is the usual way a story is told; it is convenient for the writer because the facts are stated as they occurred. Some cases might lend themselves to a different method of organization, though. If a case involves multiple business transactions, for example, it might be easier to track each transaction separately. Although you may organize facts in a number of ways, you should never organize them according to issues, even though you separately analyze the issues in the Discussion. Such segmentation invariably results in repetitious and disjointed factual statements. You must also be able to pull these facts together from different sources and describe them in a coherent whole. That requires you, in this case, to pull together facts from a memo to the file and the realty company's summary of the state of title of the two properties.

In writing a Statement of Facts for this problem, you should begin with Finch's purchase of the property from Brauzakas and their oral agreement permitting her to use the dirt road across his tract. This chronological beginning of the problem sets the stage for the events that follow. You should then state that Brauzakas sold the rest of his land to Amodio. Amodio's deed for the property contains no reference to Finch's use of the road, and there is no recorded easement. Recently (you would continue), Amodio has blocked the road to prevent Finch from using it. You should then add that Finch is 80 and that, while there is another access to her house, this alternative route takes her thirty miles and forty-five minutes out of her way. This last statement is difficult to place chronologically, but it fits here because it suggests the possible consequences of the blocked access. The reader would easily understand a statement drafted along these lines.

4. Describe the facts accurately and objectively.

Describe legally significant facts precisely, for they are crucial to the outcome. It is improper and misleading, for example, to say simply that Brauzakas and Finch had an agreement concerning her use of the dirt road because it matters whether that agreement was oral or written. It is also improper to say simply that Finch has another access to her property because her age and the circuitous route are relevant to the legal rule concerning implied easements by necessity. These are legally significant facts, and you must describe them precisely. You may summarize background facts, but only if you do so accurately.

Be careful to describe the facts rather than evaluate, analyze, or characterize them. It is one thing to say that Amodio blocked the road, but it is quite another to say that Amodio *wrongfully* blocked the road. The latter is an evaluative statement that belongs only in the Discussion or Conclusion. Similarly, it is one thing to say that the alternate route takes her thirty miles and forty-five minutes out of her way, but another to conclude that this route is impossibly difficult for a person of her age. State the facts objectively in the Statement of Facts; you can analyze and characterize them in the Discussion.

Consider these factual statements:

ANSWER A: George Brauzakas, who owned a forty-acre tract, sold Clara Finch five acres of that tract in 2009. Her her home is on this land. They agreed orally that Finch could use an old road through his property for access to her home because her lot was separated from the highway by the remaining part of his tract. In 2012, Brauzakas sold this thirty-five-acre tract to William Amodio. There is no reference to Finch's use of the road in Amodio's deed to the property, and there is no recorded easement. Amodio has now blocked the dirt road across his property. Finch, who is 80, has access to her house through a dirt road leading from another highway. That route takes her thirty miles and forty-five minutes out of her way.

ANSWER B: Clara Finch's land is separated from the highway by William Amodio's land. Finch had a deal with the previous owner that she could use an old road through the tract for access to her five-acre lot. Amodio, whose property is thirty-five acres in size, has blocked Finch's access to her property. There was no mention of Finch's easement in the agreement, and the easement is not recorded. There is another road Finch could use, but that route takes her a considerable distance out of her way, and she is 80 years old. Both Amodio and Finch bought their land from the same person. She bought five of his forty acres in 2003; Amodio bought the remaining thirty-five acres in 2012.

ANSWER C: Clara Finch is an 80-year-old widow living on a meager pension. She has a house on a small tract separated from the highway by property owned by William Amodio, a wealthy banker, who bought the land from the previous owner on speculation that prices would rise. The previous owner had long permitted Finch to use the dirt road through the property, but Amodio has refused access out of dislike for Finch. Although there is another road that Finch could use, it takes her thirty miles and forty-five minutes out of her way.

Answer A is best because it is a neutral and accurate description of the facts, stated in chronological order. Answer A includes the legally significant facts and just enough background facts for the reader to understand the problem.

Answer C is biased. The income or motives of the parties involved are not legally relevant. Answer C also omits such legally significant facts as the absence of a written agreement, a separate recorded easement, or a reference to an easement in Amodio's deed.

There are three problems with Answer B. First, it tries to describe separately the facts pertaining to two closely related issues. The result is repetitious and disjointed. Second, it uses vague terms such as "land," "deal," and "considerable distance" instead of more precise terms, thus raising unnecessary questions and perhaps changing the meaning of the statement. Third, it draws a legal conclusion by describing the road as an easement. Legal conclusions belong in the Discussion, not in the Statement of Facts.

EXERCISES

The following exercises will give you practice with the Statement of Facts in particular problems.

Exercise 18-A

The following documents are in your file:

> Gotham City Times
>
> April 5, 2013
>
> Page D-4
>
> ### Apartment for Rent
>
> New, beautiful, spacious, one-bedroom apartment; recently redecorated; extremely clean; nice neighborhood; walking distance to university; immed. occupancy; no pets. $600 per mo. Resistance Realty Co. 5911001.

From: Stephen Farley

Date: April 7, 2013

Re: Help Needed Right Away!

I need your help. I have lived on my parents' melon farm for twenty-two years, I am tired of the country life, and I want to get a fresh start. So I recently moved to Gotham City. When I arrived, I spent several days trying to find an apartment that suited my needs. Living in hotels was quickly consuming my meager savings. Finally, I saw an ad in the newspaper.

I called the number and talked to a rental agent who confirmed all the statements in the ad. He told me the place was perfect for my needs. The agent further told me that several people were interested in the apartment and that I should sign the lease at the realty office and then go see the apartment. Taking the agent at his word, I went to the realty company, paid a $600 security deposit, and signed the lease. I then went to look at my new apartment and received the shock of my life.

The neighborhood was the worst one in town. Two vagrants were asleep on the front steps and several of the apartment windows were broken. The toilet did not work and there was no hot water. The kitchen sink had a pile of dirty dishes. Two rats were sitting on the sofa, roaches were scurrying everywhere, and there were large holes in some of the walls outside the kitchen area. The floors were grimy. When I went out to my car to leave, I found that all of my hubcaps had been stolen.

I went back to the realty office and demanded that the agent tear up the lease and refund my money. The agent refused, saying "A deal is a deal." What should I do?

Memo to File

Stephen Farley Apartment Matter, File No. 13-91-LT

April 9, 2013

    I met with Stephen Farley after receiving his e-mail message and a copy of the newspaper notice advertising the apartment he rented. He was very upset. Based on the ad, I asked him if any part of the apartment had been "recently redecorated." He said the kitchen area had just been renovated, and contained a new refrigerator, new stove, and a new microwave, all in working order.

Assume the rule of law and issue below are the only ones that apply to Farley's case.

Rule of Law: Every sale of a leasehold estate carries with it an implied covenant that the leased property is fit for human habitation. A lease is unenforceable if the covenant is breached.

Issue: Whether the leased apartment was so unfit for human habitation that the realty office breached the covenant of habitability.

    1. List the legally significant facts.

    2. List any key background facts.

    3. Draft a Statement of Facts based on your answers to the previous questions.

Exercise 18-B

The following documents are in your file:

To: Law Clerk

From: Supervisor

Re: Raleigh Wilkins, File # 13-0382

    I met with Raleigh Wilkins, a speech therapist, on Friday. She is extremely upset about a letter she received from her former employer, accusing her of violating a covenant not to compete. Ms. Wilkins worked for Sterling Speech & Hearing Center, located in Tylerville, for approximately one year; about sixty percent of her patient case load consisted of children in the Ross City school district, one of Sterling's major clients. Ms. Wilkins married Justin Brill last February, and they bought a house on the north side of Ross City. The house is on three acres, where the couple is developing a large organic garden and hope to start a small kennel to breed Norfolk terriers.

In mid-May Ms. Wilkins declined an offer to renew her contract with Sterling Speech & Hearing Center because the twenty-mile commute from her new home to Tylerville cuts into her time with her husband and the time they want to spend fixing up their new house and garden. Sometime in August she began working with her husband, who is the director of the Ross City Speech Clinic. Ms. Wilkins reports that Sterling Speech & Hearing Center is about fourteen-and-one-half miles away from Ross City Speech Clinic. Tylerville and Ross City are a little more than sixteen miles apart, from city center to city center.

Please look at the attached documents and do a little research. Plan to sit down after I get back from court tomorrow afternoon to tell me what you think.

Agreement Not to Compete

Employee expressly agrees that: (a) all Clients and Patients and related confidential records remain the exclusive property of Sterling Speech & Hearing Center and shall not be taken by the Employee if this Agreement is terminated, with or without Cause, by the Employee or by Sterling Speech & Hearing Center or by mutual agreement of both Parties; and (b) during the eighteen-month period following termination, the Employee will not perform or offer speech and/or hearing therapy services within 15 miles of Sterling Speech & Hearing Center, nor shall he provide speech and/or hearing therapy services to any of Sterling Speech & Hearing Center's Clients or Patients.

August 6, 2013

Dear Ms. Wilkins:

Dr. Brandt, Superintendent of the Ross City school system, just called to tell me that he is not going to renew the system's contract with Sterling Speech & Hearing. Dr. Brandt said he is convinced that your husband's business, the Ross City Speech Clinic, will provide better service for the dollar. He also told me that he liked your work and rapport with the students, and was glad that you would continue to work with them.

Frankly, Raleigh, I am shocked and disappointed by your actions. You know perfectly well that the employment contract you signed put limits on where you could work when you left us. While I have no actual proof, I believe you probably told Mr. Brill things that helped him underbid us for the Ross City school system contract, and by changing jobs you have helped steal away a substantial part of our business. I expect you to inform Dr. Brandt and your husband that you cannot subvert Sterling Center's business and cannot work for Ross City Speech Clinic for eighteen months. If you refuse to adhere to your contractual obligations, I will have no choice but to sue you and prevent you from continuing to breach our agreement.

Kathleen M. Sterling, Ph.D., C.C.C.
Director, Sterling Speech & Hearing Center

August 11, 2013

Dr. Sterling:

I was amazed when I got your letter last week. I thought our relationship was satisfactory and you know I did a great job for you. I did not expect to be threatened and treated this way, especially after I spent an additional two months with you training my replacement.

My husband never talked to me about his bid for the school contract, and you know very well I had no access to your business records and no idea what the terms were between Sterling Center and the school system. I am hurt and insulted that you would accuse me of these things when you know they are false and libelous.

I want to work for Ross City Speech Clinic so I can be close to Justin and to our home. If Sterling Center was anywhere except on the very north edge of Tylerville, there wouldn't be a problem. And Ross City isn't the only school district in the area. I just don't understand why you're making such a fuss. Can't you just be reasonable and forget the matter?

Raleigh Wilkins

Assume the rule of law and issue below are the only ones that apply to the case.

Rule of Law: A covenant not to complete is reasonable if it is narrowly tailored in geographic scope and duration to protect the employer's legitimate interests.

- The geographic scope of the restriction generally must be limited to that area in which the employee had client contact, as that is usually the extent of the area in which the employer's good will is subject to appropriation by the employee.
- A covenant not to compete should last no longer than necessary for the employee's replacements to have a reasonable opportunity to demonstrate their effectiveness to customers.

Issue: Whether the agreement not to compete is narrowly tailored to protect the employer's legitimate interests.

1. List the legally significant facts.

2. List any key background facts.

3. Draft a Statement of Facts based on your answers to the previous questions.

Questions Presented

A basic principle of legal education and legal practice is that you receive answers only to the questions you ask. The exactness of the question determines the precision and usefulness of the answer.

An office memorandum usually begins with a section stating the questions presented by the problem. This section alerts the reader to the specific issues addressed. It is, therefore, important to frame the questions in this section as precisely as possible. A question that is too broad or too narrow misrepresents the scope or focus of your analysis.

Properly framing a legal question is a two-step process requiring you to combine the lessons from Chapter 6 (Identifying and Selecting Issues for Analysis) and Chapter 18 (Statement of Facts for a Memorandum). First, you must identify precisely the legal rules that might apply to your problem. Second, you must identify the legally significant facts—the facts that determine how, in light of the rule, the situation will be resolved. The Questions Presented section has its origins in the beginning of your research and analysis. As you work through a problem using the recursive approach as explained in Chapter 14 (Drafting the Analysis), your understanding of the rules and the legally significant facts and how they relate to each other will become more refined and complete. The Questions Presented section, therefore, is the link between your initial work and the final product.

The formula for framing a question is simple: How does the relevant law apply to the significant facts? Both the law and the facts should be included in a succinct, one-sentence question. The question should be precise and complete. Generally, the legal rule should precede the facts.

Traditionally, each question began with the word "whether"—*e.g.,* "Whether the defendant is liable under [relevant rule] when [significant facts]." Notice that this form ends with a period instead of a question mark. A legal question may also be stated as an interrogative sentence, introduced with words such as "Is," or "Can," or "Does" and punctuated with a question mark—*e.g.,* "Is the defendant liable under [relevant rule] when [significant facts]?" The two examples below are based on the jurisdictional issue in Chapter 6:

Example 1: Whether there is diversity of citizenship for purposes of federal jurisdiction when one of the parties is a resident of Oregon and the other party has been a college student in Oregon for the past three years but previously resided in another state.

Example 2: Is there diversity of citizenship for purposes of federal jurisdiction when one of the parties is a resident of Oregon and the other party has been a college student in Oregon for the past three years but previously resided in another state?

Either style is appropriate, although you should obviously be responsive to the preference of your professor or senior attorney.

Finally, when you have formulated a question by combining the relevant law with the significant facts, check to be sure that it conforms to the following principles.

1. Be understandable.

A question should be as precise and complete as possible without being so complex that your reader cannot understand it. When a problem involves so many facts relevant to a single issue that including them in the question would make it too long and awkward, you should examine the significant facts and choose only those most relevant to the case at hand. You may be able to summarize or condense closely related facts, but you should do so only with great care. Whenever you generalize about the facts, you risk distorting them or making the issue seem broader than it really is. When in doubt, err on the side of being specific and awkward—but not so specific and awkward that the question is difficult to understand.

When a legal issue has several sub-issues, you should have a separate question for each. To make sure your reader understands that they are sub-issues, you may want to use a brief introductory question to identify the broad issue and set the sub-issues in context. The Questions Presented in the legal memorandum in Appendix A provide an example.

2. Be objective.

Because an office memo should predict how a court is likely to decide a particular case, you must avoid advocating or anticipating a certain result. Include the significant facts favoring each side of the case. If you paraphrase facts to make the question more readable, do so objectively. You should also state the law objectively and not take a partisan approach. If the legal rule has several reasonable interpretations, state the rule so that you can discuss all of these interpretations. When the interpretations differ greatly, present separate questions for each.

Your client, Eric Vosberg, is a frail, chronically ill, 13-year-old boy. Deborah Starsky is a 17-year-old girl who has a reputation as a neighborhood bully. Vosberg and others know that she picks fights and has been found guilty of several misdemeanors in juvenile court. Two weeks ago, Starsky confronted Vosberg while he was on his way to a violin recital. She told Vosberg to put his nose against a nearby telephone pole. Vosberg complied. Starsky instructed Vosberg not to move until she gave him permission and then walked away. At no point did Starsky explicitly threaten Vosberg, touch him, or prevent him from continuing down the sidewalk. Vosberg remained at the pole for two hours and then ran home. He missed the recital and has suffered severe emotional problems as a result of the incident. Vosberg's parents want to know whether they can sue Starsky.

Your research has revealed only one relevant case:

Palmer v. Woodward (1960)

After making several purchases in Schwenson's Department Store, the appellant, Roger Palmer, left. He began to walk down the sidewalk when the appellee, Troy Woodward, a store detective, ran from the store and yelled, "Stop!" Palmer stopped. Woodward approached Palmer, stood in his way, and put his hand on Palmer's chest. After telling Palmer he had to go back and see the store manager, Woodward gently grasped Palmer's elbow and led him back into the store. Palmer, sixty-eight, has failing health and a heart condition. He did not resist. As a result of the incident, Palmer suffered a mild heart attack and severe emotional distress.

Palmer filed suit for false imprisonment. The trial court dismissed Palmer's complaint, holding that restraint, a necessary element of false imprisonment, had not occurred. The trial court reasoned that Palmer voluntarily complied with Woodward's demands because he did not resist or make any attempt to free himself. We disagree.

The trial court correctly stated that false imprisonment requires the defendant to actually confine or restrain the plaintiff. The restraint must be obvious, and the plaintiff must be aware that he is being restrained. But the restraint does not have to be forceful; threats, express or implied, can be sufficient. In this case, the appellant is a frail, elderly man. The appellee is a six-foot, five-inch, 220-pound, semiprofessional football player who works part time as a store detective. Blocking another person's way is restraint when the aggressive person is obviously stronger, as he was here. In addition, the appellee touched the appellant by taking his arm and guiding him into the store. We hold that under the facts of this case, particularly the great disparity of physical strength, there was sufficient restraint. Reversed.

Consider the following attempts to state the question:

ANSWER A: Whether Vosberg can recover damages for false imprisonment.

ANSWER B: Whether Vosberg was sufficiently restrained to support a cause of action for false imprisonment.

ANSWER C: Whether the apparent strengths of Vosberg and Starsky were so unequal that Vosberg can recover damages for emotional distress.

ANSWER D: Whether sufficient restraint to support an action for false imprisonment exists when a 17-year-old juvenile delinquent with a police record and a reputation of being a bully instructs a frail, chronically ill, 13-year-old boy who plays violin to remain in one place.

ANSWER E: Whether the fact that a 17-year-old female delinquent, who has been convicted several times and who has a reputation of being a bully and a fighter, gave instructions to a frail 13-year-old boy, on his way to a violin recital, to put his nose against a phone pole and stay there until told otherwise, but never touched the boy or blocked his path and walked away immediately after the boy complied with the instructions, though the boy did not move from the pole for two hours, constitutes sufficient restraint to support an action for false imprisonment, when the boy missed the recital and suffered severe emotional problems as a result.

ANSWER F: Whether restraint sufficient to support an action for false imprisonment exists when a 17-year-old girl known as a juvenile delinquent and bully instructs a frail 13-year-old boy to remain in one place, and he does so for two hours after she has walked away, even though the girl neither touched him nor blocked his path.

The *Palmer* case indicates that your problem concerns what type of force, if any, is required to satisfy the restraint element of false imprisonment. Answer F is the best way of stating that question. It correctly identifies the relevant law, includes the facts of the problem that a court is likely to find legally significant, and states the law before it states the facts. The question in Answer F identifies the precise legal question presented; it is neither unduly narrow nor overly broad. It is also readable and objectively stated.

Answer A, by contrast, is of no help to the reader. The question is too broad. It does not identify the restraint element in false imprisonment or the legally significant facts. The writer might just as well have stated the question as "Whether the law has been violated."

Answer B does pinpoint the legal question of restraint, but it fails to place that question in context because it omits the facts that will provide the basis for its resolution. A question framed this way is too unfocused to be of much value to the reader.

Unlike Answers A and B, which are too broad, Answer C is too narrow. By limiting the legal question to whether the strength of the parties is unequal, it fails to consider other factors that contribute to restraint. In addition, the mention of damages for emotional distress mistakes the real issue. Whether the plaintiff can recover damages for emotional distress is a different question from whether there has been restraint. In this respect, Answer C illustrates an important reason to ask the right question; if you ask the wrong question, you are likely to get the wrong answer. Even if your discussion covers the right issue, you have seriously misled the reader about the direction of the memo. Finally, Answer C, like Answers A and B, omits the significant facts of the case.

Answer D is not objective. The question exaggerates the strength of the client's case because the facts included are relevant to only one side of the question. Answer D fails to note that Starsky did not touch Vosberg or block his path. Whenever you state a question, you must include those facts that hurt your case as well as those that help it. Answer D also includes some irrelevant facts, such as Vosberg's being a violinist.

Answer E is complete enough. It includes all the significant facts and properly states the issue of law. It is so complete, however, that it is awkward and unreadable. Answer E does not sort out the most relevant facts. Answer E also includes several facts that are not legally significant, such as those concerning the violin recital and telephone pole. While you may want to include some background facts in the Statement of Facts, do not include them in the Questions Presented.

EXERCISES

As you complete the following exercises, remember that your questions must combine the relevant law with the significant facts. They form the basis for the rest of the memorandum, and you should focus them as sharply as possible.

Exercise 19-A

This exercise is based on Exercise 6-C, pp. 94-97, and focuses on the Statute of Frauds rule:

1. State the issue(s) and any sub-issues (question 2 in Exercise 6-C).

2. What are the legally significant facts, both favorable and unfavorable to Hughes, for each issue and sub-issue?

3. Draft the Questions Presented for an office memorandum based on your answers to questions 1 and 2 above.

Exercise 19-B

This exercise is based on the facts and cases from Exercise 10-B, pp. 163-65, and focuses on the trespass rule:

1. State the issue(s) and any sub-issues (question 2 in Exercise 10-B).

2. What are the legally significant facts, both favorable and unfavorable to your clients, for each issue and sub-issue?

3. Draft the Questions Presented for an office memorandum based on your answers to questions 1 and 2 above.

CHAPTER 20

Opinion Letters

Lawyers write many types of letters. Some simply set a time and date for a meeting. Others report the status of a client's case. Still others are demand letters requesting payment of an outstanding debt or engagement letters outlining the terms of a lawyer's employment with the client. Many simply request information or some type of action. This chapter addresses only one type of letter: the opinion letter.

Opinion letters most often are written to provide a lawyer's legal advice on a given situation. They communicate advice on the chances of successfully pursuing or defending a claim or case in litigation. They also can provide advice on the legal (or tax) implications of contemplated actions or transactions. The opinion letters discussed in this chapter are probably the most common type in the practice of law.

As noted in Chapter 16 (Elements of an Office Memorandum), a lawyer's most important job is advising a client in light of the applicable law. This advice is often based on a legal memorandum. When the reader is law-trained, the memorandum of law may be forwarded directly, with only a cover letter to explain its purpose. When the reader is not law-trained, however, an opinion letter explains the law and its application in terms the reader can understand. Although opinion letters are not as thorough as legal memoranda, the same fundamental principles apply: be objective, be thorough, and communicate clearly and precisely.

Opinion letters often supplement the oral advice that a lawyer may provide in a telephone call or in a face-to-face meeting with the client. Because recollection of oral advice can be imprecise or selective, opinion letters provide a permanent record to which lawyers, clients, and others can later refer. Opinion letters are generally written to clients but can also be written for other audiences. Opinion letters are business letters, and they should follow the standard format for such letters. That is, they should be written on letterhead stationery with the appropriate inside address identifying to whom the letter is sent; an appropriate "Re" or "Regards" line identifying the client, subject matter, and file or tracking number; and the date of the correspondence.

1. Begin by addressing your client's question or concern.

As you have already seen, a client, whether an individual or multinational corporation, generally consults a lawyer to seek advice on a legal question. An opinion letter should state and respond to that inquiry at the outset. It should begin by referring to the meeting, issue, or circumstance that prompted the communication and then provide the lawyer's answer or evaluation in clear, concise terms. The client seeks an answer to a question. Thus, simply providing an evaluation of both sides is not helpful. Just as a patient expects a doctor to make a recommendation as to treatment, a client expects a lawyer to offer advice. And lawyers, like doctors, must be careful never to guarantee an outcome unless the situation only allows for one result. Thus, the lawyer's answer to the client's question, like the doctor's, should be phrased in terms of likely outcomes or probabilities of success.[1]

Your client, Susan Sweeney, has a neighbor, Todd Pimm, who recently replaced the four-foot chain link fence that enclosed his backyard with a five-foot wooden fence. The fence runs along the property line between their adjacent beachfront lots. Sweeney wants the fence removed because it blocks her view of the ocean on that side, and she can no longer sit on her patio and watch the sun set. She and her neighbor have argued bitterly for years because Sweeney keeps her yard and patio neat and well-groomed, while Pimm does not mow his grass regularly or trim his bushes or trees. Pimm owns a small dog that he sometimes lets out into his backyard, but it is primarily kept inside. The dog roamed around the neighborhood before Pimm built his first fence. Sweeney asserts that Pimm changed the fence "just to spite her." She wants the wooden fence removed. She asked him to remove the wooden fence, but in her words he "just got ugly about it." Sweeney is a retired school teacher and moved to the coast to enjoy her retirement and spend time with her grandchildren.

---

1. Another issue is whose opinion is being rendered. In a solo practice, the opinion will be that of the lawyer signing the letter. In a law firm or other law organization, by contrast, the opinion has historically often been stated as the opinion of the firm or organization rather than simply the individual signing the letter.

There are two relevant cases in your jurisdiction.

Tinker v. Walden (1997)

Paul Tinker alleges that Lee Walden constructed a fence between their two adjoining properties for the sole purpose of disrupting Tinker's truck repair business. The fence bisects the land between their businesses—an area they had previously shared. The fence also impedes access to Tinker's garage by leaving only a narrow lane for his customers to use. Tinker alleges that Walden did this in retaliation for Tinker's refusal to buy Walden's property at Walden's asking price.

This state recognizes that a defendant may not construct a fence or other structure for the sole purpose of annoying his neighbor. A plaintiff is entitled to removal of such a "spite fence" and to compensation for any damages caused thereby. Here, there is evidence that Walden was displeased that Tinker would not purchase the property at the desired price. Yet there is also evidence that the fence was intended to secure Walden's business premises, which had been broken into on at least one occasion. The chain link fence erected by Walden lets in both light and air. It also precisely encloses Walden's property—part of which he had previously allowed Tinker to use. Since erecting the fence serves a valid purpose for Walden, it is not a "spite fence" and Tinker is not entitled to its removal.

Loren v. Bell (2008)

Jessica Loren brought suit seeking to force Otis Bell, the owner of the property adjacent to hers, to remove a fence he erected between the two properties. Bell erected a ten-foot wooden fence on his property line after the city council denied Bell's proposal to build additional condominium units on the property. Loren, who serves on the city council, did not participate in the review of Bell's proposal. She alleges that the fence was built in retaliation for the denial of Bell's proposal. She also alleges that the fence blocks her view of the Peaceful River and restricts sunlight onto her property.

This Court has previously held that a plaintiff is entitled to the removal of a spite fence that has no beneficial use to the owner and is erected and maintained for the sole purpose of annoying the adjoining landowner. While Bell alleges the fence was built to prevent trespassers from gaining access to his property through Loren's lot, he has produced no evidence that trespassers have ever used such access. Nor has he provided any rationale for installing a ten-foot fence when the original plans for his development called for the security fence around the property to be only six feet tall. We find no reason other than spite to support the construction of Bell's ten-foot fence. Thus, Loren is entitled to its removal.

Compare these introductions in a letter to Sweeney:

ANSWER A: I enjoyed meeting with you last Tuesday and discussing your ongoing disagreement with your neighbor. Your situation presents an interesting problem and the court could really go either way regarding the fence.

ANSWER B: I enjoyed meeting with you last Tuesday. I have considered the situation you presented to me and have concluded that Pimm's fence will have to come down.

ANSWER C: I enjoyed meeting with you last Tuesday and I have considered your goal of requiring your neighbor, Todd Pimm, to remove his wooden fence. In my opinion, for the reasons stated below, the court will likely order Pimm to remove the wooden fence and allow him to replace it with a chain link fence similar to the one that was there previously.

Answer C is the best alternative. Answer C immediately states and responds to the question Sweeney asked: "Can I make Pimm take down his wooden fence?" Although it states a likely outcome, it does so in terms of probability, not certainty. Answer A does not restate her question or help Sweeney understand whether she can make Pimm remove the fence. Answer B restates her inquiry in the form of a conclusion, which is fine for now but might raise concerns later if someone is looking for a record of what Sweeney actually wanted in that meeting. It also asserts the outcome with a degree of certainty not warranted by the situation.

---

2. Summarize the facts upon which your opinion is based.

Lawyers evaluate specific factual situations, and the legal advice given in an opinion letter will be based on the lawyer's understanding of that situation. Like the Statement of Facts in the legal memorandum, a summary of the relevant facts at the outset of your letter ensures that you have understood the situation correctly and that your evaluation and advice addresses the question posed by the client. Unlike the memorandum, however, the factual summary in an opinion letter gives the client the opportunity to correct any misunderstanding of the facts. A summary of the relevant facts also defines the scope of the analysis of the client's situation, which should prevent misunderstanding of that advice. Like the Statement of Facts, this summary should include all relevant facts but should not include any inferences or assumptions based on those facts. If the facts are relatively brief and straightforward, they can be summarized and included as a paragraph or two within the body of the letter. If the facts are lengthy or complex, however, it may be more effective to create a separate "Facts" section following the introduction. Sections of your fact summary may come from or sound a great deal like the Statement of Facts in the legal memorandum, but the fact summary in the opinion letter should be finely tuned to direct the reader's attention to the most significant facts in light of the attorney's analysis of the situation.

Consider the following fact summaries for an opinion letter to Sweeney.

ANSWER A: As I understand your situation, you and your neighbor, Todd Pimm, have had a difficult relationship over the years because he does not keep his yard well maintained. Pimm previously had a four-foot chain link fence surrounding his property that enclosed his backyard, where he sometimes allows his small dog to play. He recently took down the chain link fence and replaced it with a five-foot wooden fence that now blocks your view of the ocean so you can no longer watch the sunset. You believe Pimm changed the fence only to spite you and would like it removed, but he has been unresponsive to your requests that he do so.

ANSWER B: As I understand your situation, your neighbor, Todd Pimm, has built a five-foot wooden fence to block your view of the ocean in retaliation for your complaints about his overgrown yard. You want him to remove the fence because its purpose is to annoy you by preventing you from being able to watch the sun set from your back patio. To this point, he has not done so.

ANSWER C: As I understand the situation, you wish to force your neighbor, Todd Pimm, to remove the wooden fence he has constructed on the property line between your properties.

Answer A is the best answer. It summarizes the facts relevant to the question and carefully characterizes the allegation regarding Pimm's motive as Sweeney's opinion. Answer B misstates the facts by assuming that Pimm built the fence only to annoy Sweeney. It does not even mention the purpose of fencing in the neighbor's dog, which arguably provides a useful purpose for the fence. Answer C is the least helpful because it merely restates Sweeney's original question as a statement.

3. Explain the law and its application.

To allow the reader to understand a lawyer's recommendation, an opinion letter must explain the law and how it applies to the facts at hand. This requires a lawyer to explain the legal rule or rules involved in a clear and straightforward manner appropriate for the reader. Just as a patient does not expect a doctor to use medical jargon in explaining his diagnosis or course of treatment, a client does not expect his lawyer to use legal terms of art unless they are explained. Similarly, the opinion letter should not contain references to case analysis or legal citations unless the reader already has some understanding of the law. Thus, the summary of the law need not be as thorough as that in a memorandum. It need not explore all of the court's interpretations of the rule or go into detail about aspects of the rule not applicable to the client's situation.

In addition, the opinion letter must explain how the law applies to the facts of the client's situation. Like the summary of the law, the explanation of the law's application will likely not be as thorough or detailed as a discussion in a memorandum. Comparing the client's facts with the facts of the relevant cases will not be helpful to a lay reader. At the same time, explaining how the law applies to specific facts of the client's case is necessary for the reader to understand how the lawyer reached his conclusion or recommendation. Broad generalizations will not enable the reader to understand the logic or reasoning on which the recommendation is based.

Consider the following explanations of the law and its application to Sweeney's situation.

ANSWER A: The courts of this state have previously held that a plaintiff is entitled to removal of a "spite fence" that has no beneficial use to the owner but has been erected solely to annoy an adjoining or adjacent landowner. A court has previously ordered a defendant to remove a fence that had purportedly been erected for security purposes, where no security concerns had been entered into evidence. Thus, we can force Pimm to remove his "spite fence" because there is little, if any, evidence that it serves a useful purpose because his dog only comes out occasionally. Your testimony will be crucial here to establish that Pimm acted only to block your view of the ocean.

ANSWER B: A fence that has been built only to annoy a neighbor has come to be known under the law as a "spite fence." But a spite fence cannot be helpful to the person who built it; if it is helpful to the owner, then it is not a spite fence. A spite fence is not legally allowed, so if the fence built by Pimm is a spite fence, we can ask the court to direct him to take it down. The question we need to ask is whether the fence is helpful to Pimm. Because it keeps his little dog safe in his yard, we might not be able to prove it is a spite fence, but your disagreements with him over the years might help us to convince the judge that he is just trying to make you angry.

ANSWER C: The law does not allow someone to put up a fence that serves no purpose other than to annoy a neighboring landowner. The neighboring landowner is entitled to have such a "spite fence" removed. Pimm seems to have a legitimate need for a fence to keep his dog in his backyard. However, the previous chain link fence, which was shorter, kept his dog enclosed. Because your difficult relationship seems to be at the root of Pimm's building the taller wooden fence, we have a good chance of convincing the court that the wooden fence is a "spite fence." If we can do so, the court will likely direct Pimm to take down the wooden fence and allow him to replace it with one like the original chain link fence, which serves his purposes without impeding your view.

Answer A does not clearly explain either the law or its application. It uses the legal term "defendant" and refers to the facts and holding of a previous case. Clients who are not lawyers probably will not understand legal terms or the importance of prior cases because they are generally not familiar with the doctrines of precedent and *stare decisis*. Answer A also does not adequately explain the law's application to Sweeney's situation. It overstates the client's case by dismissing the importance of Pimm's dog and stating unequivocally that the client "can force Pimm to remove" his fence. Answer A could also intimidate Sweeney by implying, wrongly, that the outcome will rest on her testimony. The tone of this example is legalistic and seems intended to impress rather than communicate.

Answer B, on the other hand, goes too far the other way. The explanation of the law is condescending, and its treatment of the facts glosses over the issue. Although intended to reassure Sweeney, it oversimplifies so much that it does not adequately explain her position.

Answer C is the best. It provides a straightforward and understandable explanation of the law without using any legal terms or references. It also explains how the law is likely to be applied to Sweeney's situation, carefully distinguishing between the purpose of the original chain link fence and the evident purpose of the wooden fence that replaced it.

4. Be objective.

An opinion letter is not an appropriate forum to be an advocate for the client. Its purpose is to objectively advise the client about how the law is likely be applied to his or her situation. As in a legal memorandum, a lawyer should not gloss over any potential difficulties or downplay any weaknesses in the client's position. Knowing of potential weaknesses is critical in allowing the client to make an informed decision. As the client's advocate, a lawyer should be as creative and positive as possible in finding a way to help the client succeed, while remaining honest and realistic in advising the client. Neither unrealistic optimism nor false pessimism will best serve the client.

> ### Consider the following summary paragraphs:
>
> ANSWER A: Thus, because Pimm has a legitimate need for the fence and his backyard was previously enclosed with a fence, we face an uphill battle to convince the court that he only built the fence to annoy you. In the end, it all depends on what the judge thinks. But if you want to go forward with this, please give me a call so I can file the papers.
>
> ANSWER B: Thus, the outcome ultimately depends on the court's conclusion about Pimm's motive for building the taller wooden fence. That his yard was previously enclosed with a fence to contain his dog cuts against a contention that he built a fence only to annoy you. Because the original fence was sufficient to contain his dog, however, the court is likely to conclude he built the new fence to retaliate against you for your complaints about his yard. Please let me know if you have any questions, and whether you would like to discuss pursuing this matter further.
>
> ANSWER C: Thus, I am confident that we will be able to resolve the conflict you are involved in with your adjacent landowner and obtain a favorable outcome from your lawsuit. I await your approval to file the papers so we can get this matter resolved in an expeditious manner.

Answer B is the best answer. It specifically defines the potential weaknesses in Sweeney's case and also explains how these weaknesses can be addressed. It gives an objective view of both the strengths and the weaknesses, along with the lawyer's evaluation of which is stronger. Answer A, on the other hand, focuses only on the negative points and does not give the client a clear basis on which to make a decision, or even a good idea of what the lawyer is advising. Answer C goes too far the other way by providing an overly optimistic view of the outcome, with no explanation as to potential weaknesses. Its tone seems to push the client toward litigation without providing sufficient information on which to evaluate that option.

---

5. Adopt a style and tone appropriate for your reader.

Although opinion letters are professional communications, they are not office memoranda or court filings. As pointed out in Chapter 14 (Drafting the Discussion) with regard to drafting memoranda, you should keep the audience in mind and adopt a style and tone suitable to communicate effectively with the reader. The tone of a letter can be more conversational than that of a formal document. It can include the use of first-person pronouns where appropriate, as well as contractions and other forms or conventions appropriate in less formal writing. And it should communicate effectively by using appropriate vocabulary, sentence structure, and complexity. A letter to a layperson will differ from one written to a reader who is law-trained. A letter to a corporate executive will differ from one written to a high school coach or a retired professional cellist. At the same time, you should not be condescending or "folksy." A lawyer's work product should always be the unmistakable work of a professional. A client relies on his lawyer because of the lawyer's legal training and experience. Thus, the lawyer should always present herself as a legal professional.

In this case, Sweeney is a retired school teacher. Thus, she has a college degree but is likely not familiar with the legal theories involved or the process of litigation. The tone of your letter to Sweeny should take into account her educational level in terms of vocabulary and content in explaining how the law will apply to her situation.

The final letter to your client looks like this:

Dear Ms. Sweeney:

I enjoyed meeting with you last Tuesday and I have considered your goal of requiring your neighbor, Todd Pimm, to remove his wooden fence. In my opinion, for the reasons stated below, the court will likely order Pimm to remove the wooden fence and allow him to replace it with a chain link fence similar to the one that was there previously.

As I understand your situation, you and your neighbor, Todd Pimm, have had a difficult relationship over the years because he does not keep his yard well maintained. Pimm previously had a four-foot chain link fence surrounding his property that enclosed his backyard, where he sometimes allows his small dog to play. He recently took down the chain link fence and replaced it with a five-foot wooden fence that now blocks your view of the ocean so you can no longer watch the sunset. You believe Pimm changed the fence only to spite you and would like it removed, but he has been unresponsive to your requests that he do so.

The law does not allow someone to put up a fence that serves no purpose other than to annoy a neighboring landowner. The neighboring landowner is entitled to have such a "spite fence" removed. Pimm seems to have a legitimate need for a fence to keep his dog in his backyard. However, the previous chain link fence, which was shorter and less obtrusive, kept his dog enclosed. Because your difficult relationship seems to be at the root of Pimm's building the taller wooden fence, you have a good chance of convincing the court that the wooden fence is a "spite fence." If the court is convinced of that, it will likely direct Pimm to take down the wooden fence and allow him to replace it with one like the original chain link fence that serves his purposes without obstructing your view.

Thus, the outcome ultimately depends on the court's conclusion about Pimm's motive for building the taller wooden fence. That his yard was previously enclosed with a fence to contain his dog cuts against a contention that he built a fence only to annoy you. Because the original fence was sufficient to contain his dog, however, the court is likely to conclude he built the new fence to retaliate against you for your complaints about his yard. Please let me know if you have any questions, and whether you would like to discuss pursuing this matter further.

6. Additional considerations for e-mail correspondence.

Lawyers often send electronic copies of opinion letters to clients and then send a paper copy by regular or express mail. These e-mail letters often lead to subsequent e-mails about the meaning and scope of legal advice that might otherwise be handled through a telephone call. Follow the guidelines for electronic communication explained in Chapter 16 (Elements of an Office Memorandum)—especially the need to honor client confidentiality—and the following additional guidelines.

A. Consider whether e-mail is appropriate for this particular communication. E-mail may not be the best way to communicate legal advice on highly sensitive information, including legal matters that involve a person's mental health or a person's reputation. In many cases, it is simply better to mail a letter to the client or speak privately to the client in person or by telephone.

B. Take your time. E-mail allows us to communicate more quickly and sometimes more efficiently than we can when using traditional "snail mail." The speed that e-mail affords, however, makes it easy to send a message in the heat of anger, or to hit "Reply all" rather than "Reply," sending a response to many unintended recipients. E-mail never dies. Even if deleted, it can be retrieved, forwarded, or broadcast to the world; it has a life of its own. Every e-mail user should be aware of the harm that can be done by one hasty keystroke. Put bluntly, do not put anything in an e-mail message unless you would be willing to have it published on the front page of the newspaper and attributed to you.

A few simple precautions will allow you to take advantage of the convenience that e-mail affords while avoiding the hazards. First, prioritize your e-mails as you read them. If the e-mail requires more than a simple response, set it aside until you have the time to deal with it thoughtfully. Second, do not insert the recipient's e-mail address until you are ready to send the message. If you are drafting a new e-mail, leave the address line empty. If you are replying to an e-mail, delete the sender's name temporarily. If the message is complex, use your word processing program to draft your message and insert the sender's name into the e-mail when the message is finished. Finally, for all but the most simple, uncontroversial messages, let your message "rest" for a while before you send it. Then, and only then, insert the recipient's address and send the message.

EXERCISES

The following exercises will help you practice writing effective opinion letters.

Exercise 20-A

Draft an opinion letter to your client, Allen Worthington, advising him of the likelihood that he can recover against Ralph Watson for his injuries, based on the facts and materials in Exercise 14-A, pp. 238-42.

Exercise 20-B

Draft an opinion letter to your client, Mary Quale, advising her of the likelihood that she can successfully sue Dr. Richard Farmer for malpractice, based on the facts and materials contained in Exercise 7-B, pp. 110-11.

Briefs and Oral Argument

Elements of a Brief

The lawyer is a counselor to her client, but an advocate to the outside world. As an advocate, the lawyer exercises persuasion in a variety of ways to achieve results favorable to the client. A lawyer may help a client avoid a lawsuit by convincing an adversary that the client's position is solid or avoid a government agency proceeding by persuading the agency to adopt a more favorable attitude toward the client's position. And if the dispute must be litigated, the lawyer assists the client by persuading a tribunal to decide the dispute in the client's favor. Effective advocacy thus can help keep a dispute out of court and can increase the likelihood of success if litigation is necessary.

The *brief* is the formal document a lawyer uses to persuade a court to adopt the client's position. Many of the principles that apply to office memos also apply to briefs. Both must clearly, concisely, and honestly state the law, the facts of the case, and the reasons for their conclusions. Briefs differ from memos, however, in two important respects. The first difference is the tone of the documents: briefs argue; memos discuss. The writer of a memo is developing a legal strategy with other attorneys; the writer of a brief is submitting a legal argument to opposing counsel and a tribunal, both of whom will scrutinize it. Open and honest assessment of the client's position, essential for memos, is absolutely wrong for briefs. The brief presents the client's position as strongly as possible, emphasizing favorable arguments and minimizing the force of opposing arguments. The client's position must appear more than logical or even desirable; it must seem compelling.

The second difference is the thinking process used in drafting. The brief writer knows the conclusions in advance. He searches for arguments and materials supporting those conclusions and showing that his client's position should prevail. The memorandum writer, by contrast, is concerned with objectively determining whose position is most sound and usually will not come to a conclusion until relatively late in the research and analysis.

There are two kinds of briefs. A brief to a trial court (sometimes called a *memorandum of law* or *memorandum of points and authorities*) is presented to convince the court to decide a motion or the merits in a particular way. A brief to an appellate court is presented to challenge or defend a trial court's decision.

Trial and appellate court briefs differ in several ways. Trial court briefs tend to focus more on the facts and binding precedent because trial courts are closer to the parties and are responsible for deciding cases according to established precedent rather than establishing new law. Appellate briefs discuss allegations of trial court error but focus more on policy because appellate courts are concerned with establishing and applying rules that will work in many situations. An edited transcript of the record from the trial court usually accompanies appellate briefs. Appellate briefs also have more elements and tend to be more formal than trial court briefs. These differences are described in more detail in Chapter 26 (Briefs to a Trial Court) and Chapter 27 (Briefs to an Appellate Court).

Following are generally accepted formats for both trial and appellate briefs:

Brief to a Trial Court	Brief to an Appellate Court
Caption	Title Page
	Table of Contents
	Table of Authorities Cited
	Opinion(s) Below
	Jurisdiction
	Constitutional Provisions, Statutes, Regulations, and Rules Involved
	Standard of Review (required by some courts)
Introduction	
Questions Presented (optional)	Questions Presented
Statement of Facts	Statement of Facts
	Summary of Argument
Argument	Argument
Conclusion	Conclusion
	Appendix(es)

The name of each section (except the Caption and Title Page) should be underlined or capitalized and placed immediately above that section.

When drafting a brief you should be aware of three things. First, trial and appellate courts have specific rules concerning the format and content of briefs. These rules ensure some uniformity and make it easier to compare arguments made in opposing briefs. Always consult the rules for the court to which you are submitting the brief, as those rules may vary from the general rules given here. Second, the importance of many of the elements of an appellate brief may seem obscure at first, and many of the court rules will concern seemingly minor items such as length, page size, and citation form. Although some of these elements and rules may seem tedious and overly technical, you must take them seriously. Many courts impose sanctions on lawyers who do not comply with the court's rules, including rejection of incorrectly presented briefs. Third, briefs are rarely drafted in the order in which these elements appear. You will usually write the Argument, Summary of Argument, Statement of Facts, and Questions Presented before you write the other elements.

The following is a description of each element of a brief. The discussion focuses primarily on appellate briefs because they have more elements than trial court briefs. The discussion also explains when and why an element is presented differently in trial and appellate court briefs. Examine Appendices F and G (sample appellate court briefs) and Appendices C and D (sample trial court briefs) in conjunction with this chapter.

1. Caption or Title Page

The first page of the brief to a trial court has a Caption, which looks like this:

UNITED STATES DISTRICT COURT
FOR THE DISTRICT OF CHESAPEAKE

WESTBROOK NEIGHBORHOOD ASSOCIATION,
Plaintiff,

Civ. Docket No. CZ-8071-13
Hon. F. A. Hollender

vs.

ELLISON RECYCLING, INC.,

Defendant.

MEMORANDUM OF LAW
IN SUPPORT OF DEFENDANT'S MOTION TO DISMISS

The Caption identifies the court, the name of the case, the docket number, the motion or other matter under consideration, the judge, and the side represented. Appendices C and D illustrate another type of caption for a trial court brief, based on somewhat different court rules.

The Title Page of an appellate brief is comparable to the Caption of a trial court brief. It identifies the court, the docket number, the name of the case, the side represented, and the names and addresses of counsel. The Title Page of briefs filed in the highest state appellate court or the Supreme Court of the United States also identifies the term of the court and the court from which the appeal is taken. The Title Page distinguishes the brief from many others received by the court and ensures that the brief will be placed in the proper file. Appendices F and G show a standard Title Page for appellate briefs, although there can be minor stylistic variations.

2. Table of Contents

The Table of Contents of an appellate brief lists each element of the brief and the page on which that element begins. In addition, the point headings used in the Argument should be stated in full in the order they appear, with page numbers corresponding to their locations. The point headings, described in detail in Chapter 24 (Point Headings), are specialized thesis sentences that introduce parts of your argument. This outline of the point headings gives the reader a concise and easily understood summary of your argument. The briefs in Appendices F and G show a basic format for the Table of Contents.

3. Table of Authorities Cited

This section, sometimes called simply *Table of Authorities* or *Citations,* lists all of the legal and other materials used to support the Argument in an appellate brief and shows every page on which those materials are cited. This list of authorities permits the reader to determine quickly where specific cases, statutes, or other materials are addressed, and provides a quick reference for complete citations to that authority.

The Table of Authorities is usually divided into several basic categories, including cases, constitutional provisions, statutes, and miscellaneous materials. Each of these categories can be subdivided. Subdividing is for the reader's benefit. It often is helpful to have a separate section for cases decided by the court to which the brief is addressed. For example, you might list cases under the headings "Michigan Cases" and "Other Cases," or you might list them under "United States Supreme

Court Decisions," "Sixth Circuit Court of Appeals Decisions," and "Other Federal Decisions." You might also create categories to emphasize specific statutes, administrative rules, secondary authorities, or the legislative history of a particular act. Avoid cluttering the brief, however, with numerous subcategories that have only a few citations.

Cases, secondary authorities, and other materials should be listed in alphabetical order in each category. Statutory sections, constitutional provisions, and other materials that cannot be listed alphabetically should be listed in numerical order. The briefs in Appendices F and G show how to list Authorities Cited.

4. Opinions Below

This section, also often called *Statement of the Case,* indicates where the decisions of the lower courts or government agencies that have decided this case can be located, so that the reviewing court can find them easily. Provide a citation for these previous decisions if they have been reported; if they have not yet been reported, say so, and show their location in the record. For example:

> The opinion of the Court of Appeals for the District of Columbia Circuit is unreported and is reprinted at pages 1a–2a of the appendix to the petition for certiorari (Pet. App.). The opinion invalidated a rulemaking order of the Federal Communications Commission. The Commission's rulemaking order is reported at 27 FCC Rcd. 14989 (2011) and is reprinted at Pet. App. 3a–36a.

5. Jurisdiction

This section of an appellate brief, also called a *Jurisdictional Statement* or *Statement of Jurisdiction,* provides a short statement of the jurisdictional basis for the appeal. Because jurisdiction itself is often an issue in trial courts and is also asserted in the complaint, this section is unnecessary for briefs to a trial court. Some state appellate courts require a Jurisdictional Statement only in limited circumstances. The Jurisdiction section should briefly inform the court of the factual circumstances, court rules, or statutory provisions on which appellate jurisdiction is based. For example:

> The judgment of the United States Court of Appeals for the Seventh Circuit affirming the decision of the United States District Court was entered on September 7, 2012. The petition for a writ of certiorari was filed on November 27, 2012, and this Court granted certiorari on January 18, 2013. The jurisdiction of this Court is invoked under 28 U.S.C. § 1254(1).

6. Constitutional Provisions, Statutes, Regulations, and Rules Involved

This section tells the court what codified provisions are relevant to the determination of the case and where in your brief the judge can scrutinize the exact language of these provisions. The name of this section varies according to the materials included. When you have one or two provisions that are relatively short, you should state the exact language in full. When you have many provisions or the provisions are lengthy, you should provide the name and citation in this section and indicate that the provisions are stated in full in one or more appendices at the end of your brief. For example:

Section 29 of the Mobile Home Commission Act, Mich. Comp. Laws Ann. § 125.2329 (West 2006), provides as follows:

A utility company shall notify the department ten days before shut-off of service for nonpayment, including sewer, water, gas, or electric service, when the service is being supplied to the licensed owner or operator of a mobile home park or seasonal mobile home park for the use and benefit of the park's tenants.

Or:

The texts of the following statutes relevant to the determination of the present case are set forth in the Appendix: Sections 3(c)(2)(6) and 10(b) of the Federal Insecticide, Fungicide, and Rodenticide Act, 7 U.S.C. §§ 136a(c)(2)(6), 136h(b) (2006); Tucker Act, 28 U.S.C. § 1491 (2006 & Supp. V 2011).

7. Standard of Review

This section contains a concise statement of the appropriate standard of review to be exercised by the appellate court, with citations to authority supporting the applicability of that standard. The location of the standard of review within the brief may be specified by court rules. The appellate court's standard of review will vary, depending on the legal issues involved and the procedural posture of the determination being appealed. The various standards of review are generally not contained in the court rules, but are developed in case law. They are discussed in greater detail in Chapter 27 (Briefs to an Appellate Court). A typical standard of review section reads as follows:

The issue before this Court is whether the trial court erred in dismissing the complaint for lack of personal jurisdiction. The court's review of the grant of a motion to dismiss is *de novo*. *Larkin v. Smith Realty Co.*

If a dispute exists over the applicable standard, your discussion will be more detailed. You will have to demonstrate why your position on the appropriate standard is correct and why your opponent's is wrong.

8. Introduction

Trial court briefs commonly include a short statement identifying the parties and explaining the reason for the brief. For example:

> Defendant Dwight Sanders submits this memorandum in support of his Motion to Exclude Evidence. The evidence was seized during a warrantless search of Sanders's automobile after he was stopped for a traffic violation. The search, which was without probable cause, violated Sanders's Fourth Amendment right to be free from unreasonable searches and seizures, and the evidence seized during the search is therefore inadmissible.

Appendices C and D offer other examples of an Introduction.

9. Questions Presented

This section, sometimes called *Issues* or *Issues on Appeal,* states the legal issues involved in a trial or appellate brief and tells the court the matters you intend to address. The Questions Presented section in a brief is similar to the same section in a memorandum. Both must include the legal rule and a summary of significant facts. Both must be precise and understandable.

Unlike the Questions Presented in an office memorandum, the questions in a brief should be slanted toward your client's position and should reflect your interpretation of the law. If you are using that interpretation to emphasize certain facts in your Argument, your questions should contain these facts. In addition, the questions should be stated so that the reader sees your answer as the correct one. As Chapter 22 (Structure of an Argument) and Chapter 23 (Persuasive Writing) describe in detail, your brief should project a positive tone; it should argue for a particular conclusion rather than simply against the contrary conclusion. If you are appealing an unfavorable trial court decision, for example, your questions might begin, "Whether the trial court erred . . . ." Your opponent, appealing the same decision, might begin, "Whether the trial court properly held . . . ." Both questions suggest an affirmative answer.

There are two styles of presenting the questions in a brief, and these styles differ principally in their argumentative tone and completeness. The better style, which you should use, is to state the question so completely and so persuasively that it answers itself.

Whether the trial court deprived the defendant of his right to due process of law under the Fourteenth Amendment by admitting into evidence a confession that was extracted from the defendant after twenty-two consecutive hours of interrogation by rotating teams of detectives.

This way of presenting the question combines the relevant legal rule and the significant facts so that the only reasonable answer seems to be "yes." This style is very effective, although you should not risk your credibility by overstating or distorting your position. The other style states the question in its barest form.

Did the trial court's decision admitting the defendant's confession into evidence violate his right to due process under the Fourteenth Amendment?

This question does not provide significant facts, nor does it make the answer obvious, although it does frame the issue in a way that would be acceptable to both sides.

Many briefs to a trial court are so short or straightforward that the Questions Presented section is unnecessary. The section is necessary, however, in long or complex trial court briefs, which often contain multiple issues, and it is always required in an appellate brief.

10. Statement of Facts

The Statement of Facts in a brief, sometimes also known as *Statement of the Case* or simply *Statement,* is a descriptive account of the facts from your client's point of view. Although this statement cannot omit any damaging facts, you should write it to promote the court's understanding of and sympathy for your client's situation. Many lawyers and judges believe that the Statement of Facts, which is discussed in detail in Chapter 25 (Statement of Facts for a Brief), is the most important section of any brief.

11. Summary of Argument

This section of an appellate brief is a concise statement of your major conclusions and the most important reasons supporting them. It conveys to a judge the essence of your argument in case the judge has not had time to read the entire brief before oral argument. For this reason the summary should be specific to your case and not merely a list of general legal principles. The Summary of Argument should be self-contained; the reader should not have to look elsewhere to understand the gist of your argument. Like the Conclusion in an office memorandum, the Summary of Argument should contain no citations to cases, statutes, or regulations unless the authority is well known or absolutely essential to the reader's understanding. Each major conclusion should be in a single paragraph. The briefs in Appendices F and G show examples of the Summary of Argument.

12. Argument

The Argument is the foundation on which the brief is constructed and, like the Discussion in an office memorandum, it is the heart of the document. Although the Statement of Facts and Summary of Argument are important, and sometimes decisive, your client generally wins or loses on the quality and substance of the Argument. An effective Argument in a brief is developed using the basic concepts of legal writing described in Part C. The Argument should be clear and compelling; it should reflect a sound understanding and thoughtful analysis of the relevant law.

Although the Argument is similar to the Discussion, it is different from the Discussion in two important ways. First, as noted earlier, the Argument should be an argument rather than an objective discussion of the law. You should first state, in forceful and affirmative language, your strongest arguments and issues and present your client's position on each issue or sub-issue before you refute the position of your opponent. These and other principles of advocacy presented in Chapters 22 and 23 will help you present your case more convincingly.

Second, the Argument should contain point headings. Point headings are conspicuous thesis statements that preface each logical segment of your Argument. Because they are capitalized, underlined, or formatted in a prominent way, point headings make it easier for the reader to understand the structure and content of your Argument. Point headings are always included in appellate briefs, but their use in trial court briefs is optional. As with Questions Presented, point headings should be included in trial court briefs that are lengthy or complex. Point headings are discussed in detail in Chapter 24 (Point Headings).

The guidelines given in previous chapters, combined with those concerning advocacy and point headings, should help you prepare an effective Argument. Appendices F and G show sample Arguments for appellate briefs, while Appendices C and D show sample Arguments for trial court briefs.

13. Conclusion

This section describes what you want the court to do. It precisely states what relief you are requesting from the court—particularly if the relief you seek is more complicated than affirming or reversing the lower court's judgment. The request for relief is usually one sentence in length. In trial court briefs with complex arguments, you may include a brief summary of the arguments supporting your conclusion. Immediately following, you should include the name, address, phone number, and signature of at least one of the attorneys who prepared the brief. You should also include the date. The Conclusion section in a trial court brief should look like this:

> For the foregoing reasons, the plaintiffs respectfully request that the defendant's motion for summary judgment be denied.

> Respectfully submitted,

> Charles McGrady
> Attorney for Plaintiffs
> Smith, Dunmore & Coffin
> 420 Brookshire Commons
> Greensboro, NC 27402
> (919) 423-0706

March 1, 2013

The Conclusion section in an appellate brief is presented in the same form but requests different relief from the court. For example:

> For all the foregoing reasons, the judgment of the Ingham County Circuit Court should be reversed and the case remanded for a new trial.

> Respectfully submitted,

> Charles McGrady
> Attorney for Appellants
> Smith, Dunmore & Coffin
> 420 Brookshire Commons
> Greensboro, NC 27402
> (919) 423-0706

March 1, 2013

14. Appendices

This section contains the quoted statutes from the section of your brief called Constitutional Provisions, Statutes, Regulations, and Rules Involved. There can be a separate Appendix for each major category of statutes in the brief. There should also be an Appendix for any diagrams or charts you include. If you use more than one Appendix, give each a short descriptive title. Each of the sample briefs in Appendices F and G contains its own Appendix showing the relevant statutes.

This chapter has identified and described each component of a brief. Although assembling a brief may seem complicated, everything in a brief is for the court's convenience or for the purpose of presenting your client's position as persuasively as possible.

CHAPTER
22 Structure of an Argument

Advocacy is the craft of persuasion. It is the means by which an attorney persuades a court to adopt her client's position. An effective advocate will show a court that deciding for her client would be logical and desirable, and that deciding for the opponent would not. Courts in an adversary system depend on advocates to illuminate the strengths and weaknesses of competing positions and thereby assist the court in deciding a case. Many times, the arguments, cases, and even the language of the winning brief will appear in the court's opinion. For better or worse, the skill and resources of counsel are often as important to a decision as the relevant law.

Coherence and credibility are essential to effective advocacy. The analytical, writing, and organizational principles from Parts B and C also apply to writing a brief. The advocate's research must be complete, the analysis sound, and the conclusions sensible. Clear organization, thoughtful analysis, and a logical progression are essential. A writer who is not understandable is ineffective.

In general, written advocacy has two key components. This chapter addresses the first component: how to structure your Argument. Chapter 23 (Persuasive Writing) focuses on the second and equally important component: persuasive writing.

The structure of your Argument concerns the order of the various arguments or lines of reasoning in your brief—what is said first, second, and so on. Two key considerations must be kept in mind. First, more than one issue, sub-issue, or line of reasoning may support your client's position. If so, you should include each of them in your brief. Never assume that one issue, sub-issue, or argument is dispositive, and therefore you do not need to address any others. Second, you can improve the effectiveness of your brief by the order in which you place various issues, sub-issues, or lines of reasoning. The following principles will help you structure your overall Argument.

1. Present your strongest issues, sub-issues, and arguments first.

When your client's case involves several independent issues, present the strongest issue first, followed by the remaining issues presented in descending order of strength. Similarly, when several arguments support your client's position on an issue or sub-issue, present them in descending order of strength. The "strongest" issues, sub-issues, or arguments are those most likely to persuade a court to rule in favor of your client.

Applying this principle will make your brief more persuasive for several reasons. First, the beginning of the Argument sets the tone for what follows. Because the strongest issues or arguments are necessarily the most compelling ones, beginning with them enhances your credibility and captures the court's full attention. Second, less persuasive issues and arguments are more compelling when used to buttress stronger issues and arguments than when presented strictly on their own merits. Conversely, stronger issues and arguments seem less compelling when you present them after weaker issues and arguments. Third, crowded dockets—even at the appellate level—can mean that a brief will not necessarily be read in its entirety by all the judges or clerks. If you present the strongest issues and arguments first, they are much more likely to be read.

There is a corollary to this guideline: omit weak arguments and issues. In pre-writing and drafting briefs, think of as many arguments and issues as possible. Some of these arguments will be weak because there is scant authority to support them or because the rule in question has never been applied to your facts. Sometimes you will have to include such arguments in your brief because you have nothing stronger. When you do have stronger arguments, however, you should omit weak ones. Weak arguments undermine your credibility and detract from more persuasive arguments.

If you have arguments of nearly equal strength, consider which arguments will have the strongest appeal to the court to which you are submitting your brief. If you are writing to an appellate court, look for decisions in which that court has treated a similar issue or cases with similar policy considerations. If you are writing to a trial court, remember that trial courts are bound by decisions of the appellate courts within their jurisdiction. As previously noted, a trial court is more likely to base a decision on settled law than on unsettled law. Thus, in most cases, the better strategy is to base your first argument on settled law within the jurisdiction.

Consider the following situation:

On November 5, Paula Jennings was elected to her first term as Justice of the Peace for Monroe County, a position that enabled her to perform civil weddings and hear small claims cases. Immediately after her election, she reversed her previous support for a highly controversial court reform proposal—one that was an issue in many of the election races, including hers. After she took office on January 2, a group of citizens circulated petitions for her recall. The petitions, filed with the appropriate county official on March 15, included a statement that the basis for the recall was her "opposition to the court reorganization plan." Section 5 of the State Elections Act provides:

> The petition or petitions, which shall clearly state the reason or reasons for the recall, shall not be filed against an officer until the officer has actually performed the duties of that office to which he or she has been elected for a period of six months during the current term of that officer.

After filing a suit to prevent Jennings's recall, her attorney filed a motion for summary judgment. Relying on Section 5, he prepared two outlines of a brief in support of that motion:

ANSWER A: Summary judgment is appropriate because the petitions fail to meet the requirements of the Elections Act. The petitions do not meet the Section 5 requirement of a clear statement of the reasons for recall. The statement on the petitions that Jennings opposes the court reorganization plan does not clearly inform voters whether it is her position, her change of position, or both, that motivates the recall.

The petitions are also invalid because, contrary to Section 5, they were submitted before Jennings had been in office for six months. The petitions were submitted on March 15, less than two-and-one-half months after Jennings took office on January 2. Therefore, the six-month requirement was not fulfilled.

ANSWER B: Summary judgment is appropriate because the petitions fail to meet the requirements of the Elections Act. The petitions are invalid because, contrary to Section 5, they were submitted before

Jennings had been in office for six months. The petitions were submitted on March 15, less than two-and-a-half months after Jennings
took office on January 2. Therefore, the six-month requirement was
not fulfilled.

The petitions are also invalid because they do not meet the Section 5 requirement of a clear statement of the reasons for recall. The
statement on the petitions that Jennings opposes the court reorganization plan does not clearly inform voters whether it is her position,
her change of position, or both, that motivates the recall.

Answer B is better because the six-month argument is stronger than
the clear-statement argument. The six-month argument addresses an
unmistakable error; Section 5 is explicit and leaves little doubt about
what is required. The clear-statement argument addresses a more
debatable issue. In the absence of any relevant case law, "opposition
to the court reorganization plan" may or may not be reasonably understood as a clear statement. Beginning with that argument, as Answer
A does, is a less forceful way of presenting the case.

2. When issues are of equal strength, present the most significant issues first.

The most significant issues are not necessarily the strongest ones. The
most significant issues are those that, if resolved favorably, would help
your client most. In a criminal case involving two equally strong issues,
for example, first discuss the issue that would exonerate the defendant, and then discuss the issue that would merely win the defendant
a new trial.

This principle is subordinate to principle 1 because a strong but
less significant argument is more persuasive than a weak but more significant argument. Likelihood of success should be your main consideration. Assume, for example, that a convicted pickpocket could raise two
issues on appeal. He could argue with strong precedent that the judge
erred in permitting him to be convicted solely on the basis of hearsay,
and he could argue with tenuous support that the statute under which
he was convicted is unconstitutionally vague. The hearsay issue should
be presented first, even though it is less significant than the constitutional question, because it is more likely to succeed. If, however, the
vagueness issue were at least as strong as the hearsay issue, it should
be presented first. Winning on the vagueness issue would result in his
release rather than just a new trial.

Presenting the most significant issues first is important for the same reasons as presenting the strongest issues first. The court is more likely to take the entire brief seriously if you present a serious issue first than if you begin the brief with an issue concerning a technical violation of an obscure law. Less significant issues also seem more compelling when used to buttress important issues than when used to introduce an Argument.

Consider again the Jennings example discussed earlier:

The petition drive against Paula Jennings garnered 7,850 signatures. In the previous election, 32,000 people in Monroe County voted for a candidate for governor. The State Elections Act further provides:

Sec. 2. Every elective officer in the state except a judicial officer is subject to recall by the voters of the electoral district in which the officer is elected.

Sec. 6. The petitions shall be signed by a number of qualified and registered voters equal to not less than 25% of the number of votes cast for candidates for the office of governor at the last preceding general election in the electoral district of the officer sought to be recalled. The person or organization sponsoring such recall shall have ten days to file additional signatures after any determination that the petitions submitted contain an insufficient number of qualified and registered voters.

Jennings's attorney has prepared two outlines of a brief to the trial court concerning these sections:

ANSWER A: The petitions are invalid because they challenge an officer specifically exempted from recall by the Elections Act. Section 2 expressly exempts "a judicial officer" from the Act, a term that necessarily includes a justice of the peace performing such judicial activities as deciding small claims cases.

Even if there were no such exemption, the petitions would still be invalid because, contrary to Section 6, they do not contain signatures equal to 25 percent of the votes for governor in Jennings's electoral district in the previous election. Because the petitions have only 7,850 signatures and 32,000 people in the district voted for a candidate for governor in the last election, they are 150 signatures short of the Section 6 requirement.

ANSWER B: The petitions are invalid because, contrary to Section 6 of the Elections Act, they do not contain signatures equal to 25 percent of the votes for governor in Jennings's district in the previous election. Because the petitions have only 7,850 signatures and 32,000 people in the district voted for a candidate for governor in the last election, they are 150 signatures short of the Section 6 requirement.

Even if there were enough signatures, the petitions would still be invalid because they challenge an office specifically exempted from recall by the Elections Act. Section 2 expressly exempts "a judicial officer" from the Act, a term that necessarily includes a justice of the peace performing such judicial activities as deciding small claims cases.

Answer A is better because it places the issue of the substantive validity of the petitions before the issue of sufficient signatures, even though both issues are very strong. A favorable decision on the exempt-officer issue would foreclose the recall effort altogether, but the sufficient-signature issue might only delay the recall because Section 6 allows ten days for the filing of additional signatures. Answer A emphasizes the more significant issue and gives the less significant issue more strength by discussing it after—and therefore in light of—the more significant issue. Answer B, by contrast, emphasizes the less significant issue and obscures the more significant issue.

Answer A also shows a more logical progression of thought than does Answer B. Answer A states, in effect, that the Elections Act does not apply, and even if it did apply, the requirements of the Act were not met. Each issue is independent of the other. Answer B, on the other hand, illogically states that the requirements of the Elections Act were not met, and even if they were, the Act did not apply. Answer B assumes that the Elections Act applies to this situation when discussing the first issue but not when discussing the second. Answer A is better because it arranges the issues both logically and in order of significance.

How should the arguments and issues for Sections 2, 5, and 6 of the Elections Act be combined?

3. Present your client's position on each issue or sub-issue before answering counterarguments.

This principle is a slight modification of the rule in Chapter 10 (Organization) requiring you to state the reasons *for* a conclusion before responding to reasons *against* it. Your conclusion in a memo may support your client or your opponent. In a brief, however, your conclusion must convince the court to decide *for* your client and convince the court to decide *against* your opponent. Your client's position should define the order and tone of argument on any given issue or sub-issue. Your position will be much clearer if you state and justify it before answering counterarguments. Two potential problems result from attacking your opponent's arguments before advancing your own. First, you risk not stating your position intelligibly or, worse yet, not having your main argument read at all. Second, you sound defensive and imply that your opponent's point of view is more interesting or important to the court.

If there are several arguments opposing your client's position on an issue or sub-issue, address the strongest ones immediately after presenting your client's position. Your opponent's strongest arguments are likely to be the most interesting to the court, and you gain credibility by promptly confronting them.

Ian LeVasseur was convicted of second-degree murder on the basis of a voiceprint identification made possible because the victim had been playing with the voice recording function on her cell phone just before the crime occurred. LeVasseur has appealed on the ground that voiceprint identification is inherently unreliable.

Although courts in LeVasseur's state have not decided this issue, courts in two neighboring states with identical rules of evidence have decided the following cases:

State v. Decker (1963)

Alan Decker was convicted of arson on the basis of a voiceprint identification from the recording of a wiretapped telephone conversation. The sole issue on appeal is the propriety of the trial judge's ruling that permitted the voiceprint to be admitted into evidence. Our law does not permit evidence of a scientific test to be admitted unless its scientific basis and reliability are generally recognized by competent authorities. Voiceprint analysis, however, is not so recognized; there is little literature on the subject and great disagreement among experts as to its accuracy. For that reason, we reverse and remand for a new trial.

State v. Manning (1983)

Margerita Manning was convicted of second-degree murder in connection with the bombing of an office building that led to the death of a secretary employed there. Some twelve minutes before the explosion, local police received a phone call warning that the building should be evacuated. That call was taped and was used in a subsequent voiceprint identification that formed the evidentiary basis for Manning's conviction. Her appeal challenges the reliability of voiceprint identification. We affirm.

The record before this court indicates that voiceprint analysis is a widely accepted and scientifically accurate method of identification that has the support of many experts. Because its scientific basis and reliability are generally recognized, the trial judge committed no error in admitting the voiceprint identification into evidence.

The prosecutor's brief on appeal might be organized in either of the following ways:

ANSWER A: The voiceprint analysis was properly admitted into evidence. In this state, scientific tests are admissible when their reliability and scientific basis are generally recognized by competent authorities. *People v. Greene.* Although this state's courts have not addressed the admissibility of voiceprints under this rule, other states' courts have. In *State v. Decker,* the court held that a voiceprint analysis was improperly admitted because of the lack of scientific literature and disagreement among experts as to its accuracy. *Decker* is distinguishable because it was decided in 1963 when voiceprint analysis was at an early stage of development. In the 1983 case of *State v. Manning,* however, the court held that a voiceprint was properly admitted into evidence because by that time the reliability and scientific basis for voiceprint analysis were widely recognized by experts. *Manning* reflects significant developments in the field over twenty years and underscores the correctness of the trial judge's ruling in this case.

ANSWER B: The voiceprint analysis was properly admitted into evidence. In this state, scientific tests are admissible when their reliability and scientific basis are generally recognized by competent authorities. *People v. Greene.* Although this state's courts have not addressed the admissibility of voiceprints under this rule, other states' courts have. In a 1983 case, *State v. Manning,* the court held that the reliability and scientific basis for voiceprint analysis are widely recognized by experts and, hence, that voiceprints can be admitted into evidence. *Manning* reflects significant developments in this field and underscores the correctness of the trial judge's ruling in this case. Although a 1963 case, *State v. Decker,* held to the contrary, it was decided before voiceprint analysis had become a widely accepted and scientifically reliable identification technique.

Answer B is preferable because it describes the favorable case before it responds to the unfavorable case. Answer B states that voiceprint analysis is widely accepted and was thus proper in this case, and then distinguishes *Decker* as out of date. This response to *Decker* is consistent with the prior analysis of *Manning* and is persuasive in that context. Answer A is less clear because the older case is distinguished before the affirmative argument is even stated. Even when *Manning* is discussed, the analysis is not as sharply focused as it is in Answer B. In addition, Answer A is defensive and gives greater weight to the counterargument.

EXERCISES

The exercises that follow provide an opportunity to apply these principles.

Exercise 22-A

Arnold Jones, the driver of a fuel oil truck, was charged with driving on the left side of a two-lane highway. He said that he did so to avoid a large and unexpected patch of ice. It was rush hour. No one was forced off the road.
State Law § 117.01 provides:

> It shall be a misdemeanor for any person to drive in the left lane of a two-lane highway.

The following four cases from the state court of appeals interpret this statute:

Cain v. State (1969)

The defendant was convicted for driving on the wrong side of the road. The defendant was joyriding with friends and was intoxicated. Two cars were forced off the road. We reject his appeal. Traffic safety is of paramount concern. There can be no exceptions, for exceptions would undermine any confidence the reasonable person would have in highway safety.

McKinney v. State (1975)

The defendant was convicted for driving on the wrong side of a two-lane highway when he swerved to avoid hitting a child. There was little traffic, and the incident occurred during the day. We reverse. Although every reasonable person has a right to expect other cars to stay in their appropriate lanes, it would be intolerable for the law to put a driver in this kind of dilemma.

Shoop v. State (1981)

The defendant was convicted for driving on the wrong side of a two-lane highway when he swerved to avoid hitting a pothole. The defendant is a mechanic, and he testified that the pothole was clearly visible. He also testified that the pothole was likely to have irreparably damaged a tire and bent the tie rod on his car. The road was generally rough, and there was light traffic. We affirm. Financial self-interest is not enough to outweigh highway safety.

Gordon v. State (1998)

The defendant, a volunteer fireman driving to a fire station for an emergency call, was convicted of violating State Law § 117.01. He was not using flashing lights or a siren, and there was nothing about his car to distinguish it as an emergency vehicle. The defendant was passing long lines of cars to get to the station. We affirm the conviction. An exception to section 117.01 would be permissible when there is a clear public necessity, but this is not the proper case for such an exception.

The attorney for Jones has filed a motion with the trial court to dismiss the charge.

1. Using the statute and cases, list the arguments for Jones and identify his strongest argument.

2. Using the statute and cases, list the arguments for the state and identify its strongest argument.

Exercise 22-B

Yvonne Hardy, an employee of Tri-State Fuel Co., was driving a fuel tanker truck loaded with an expensive and highly flammable grade of oil. She had been following a pickup truck filled with pumpkins for several miles on a two-lane highway when the latch on the back of that truck suddenly came loose, spilling pumpkins on the right side of the highway. The driver of the pickup immediately pulled over. Hardy swerved into the left lane to avoid the pumpkins, forcing a car driven by Ted Hansen off the road. Hansen, who was coming from the opposite direction in the correct lane, suffered severe injuries.

Hansen sued Tri-State for negligence and claimed that Hardy (and thus Tri-State) was negligent *per se* under State Code § 98.01. Hardy testified at trial that she had driven fuel trucks for eight years. She stated that she did not think she could maintain control of the truck if she struck the pumpkins and that she did not have time to stop. She also testified that there was an extremely narrow shoulder on the right side of the highway and that it dropped off sharply into a small river valley. She said she had reason to believe the truck would explode if she went off the road or lost control, and that she did not see Hansen's car until just before he drove off the road. The driver of the pickup truck testified that he recovered eleven pumpkins, ranging from fifteen to twenty pounds in size, from the road. Other pumpkins shattered when they struck the road, he said, and several cars ran over unbroken pumpkins after the incident. The trial court found Tri-State negligent *per se* and awarded Hansen $175,000 for his injuries. Tri-State has appealed.

State Code § 98.01(c) provides:

> Upon all roadways of sufficient width, a vehicle shall be driven upon the right half of the roadway except as follows:
>
> . . .
>
> (c) When an obstruction exists making it necessary to drive on the left half of the roadway.

The highest appellate court in the state has decided the following cases:

Meekhof v. Golden (1939)

Meekhof brought an action against Golden for injuries Meekhof sustained when the automobile Golden was driving forced Meekhof off the road. Golden, who was intoxicated, was in the left lane of a two-lane highway at the time. The trial court awarded Meekhof $6,100 in damages, and we affirm. State Code § 98.01 requires all vehicles to be driven on the right side of the roadway except in specifically defined situations. The obvious purpose of this statute is to protect persons and property on the left side of the road-way. Golden's violation of the statute constitutes negligence *per se,* and the trial judge so instructed the jury. None of the exceptions stated in the statute is applicable here.

Yerrick v. Boughton (1956)

The appellee, Cecelia Boughton, was seriously injured when Bruce Yerrick's Model T automobile, which was fast approaching hers in the same lane, forced her off the road to avoid an accident. Boughton brought an action for negligence to recover for her injuries and argued that Yerrick's violation of State Code § 98.01 constituted negligence *per se.* The trial court agreed and awarded judgment to Boughton. Although Yerrick admitted that he was driving in the left lane of the highway, he argued pursuant to subsection (c) that an obstruction made it necessary for him to drive in the left lane. The obstruction was a bumpy and somewhat uneven forty-yard stretch of the right lane, which Yerrick told the trial court "might have severely damaged my antique car." We agree with the trial court.

   The purpose of § 98.01, as we said in *Meekhof v. Golden* (1939), is protection of persons and property on the left side of the roadway. There is no obstruction within the meaning of § 98.01(c) unless there is an obstacle that prevents, or is likely to prevent, the driver's safe passage on the right side of the roadway. In any case, it is not intended simply for the convenience of drivers who claim for financial or other reasons that their vehicle is somehow special. A bumpy and uneven road in itself does not meet that test. Affirmed.

James v. Strange (1964)

Alton Strange was driving about twenty miles per hour on a two-lane street in a residential neighborhood when a child suddenly ran in front of him, chasing a ball. Knowing he did not have time to stop, Strange swerved suddenly and sharply into the left lane. In so doing, he crashed into Kristine James's vehicle, which was traveling in the opposite direction. Neither the child nor James was injured. James sued Strange for damages to her vehicle, arguing that Strange was negligent *per se* under State Code § 98.01. Strange admitted that he did not see the other car until he struck it. The trial court dismissed the suit.

This court has often stated that § 98.01 is designed to protect persons and property on the left side of the roadway. *E.g., Yerrick v. Boughton* (1956). Drivers have a right to believe that the statute will be observed. At the same time, it would offend the conscience to force a driver to choose between killing a child and subjecting himself to a negligence lawsuit. Section 98.01(c), which permits travel on the left side of the road when an obstruction makes such travel necessary, encompasses small children who run into the roadway. There is no negligence *per se* here. Affirmed.

For this exercise, you or your professor will decide which client you represent.

1. Assume you are representing Tri-State:
   (a) Will your argument emphasize the general rule in the statute or the exception? Explain.
   (b) Affirmatively state your client's position in one sentence.
   (c) What argument(s) will you use to support that position?
   (d) Identify and refute the strongest argument against your client's position.
   (e) Outline the argument for Tri-State based on your answers to these questions.

2. Assume you are representing Hansen:
   (a) Will your argument emphasize the general rule in the statute or the exception? Explain.
   (b) Affirmatively state your client's position in one sentence.
   (c) What argument(s) will you use to support that position?
   (d) Identify and refute the strongest argument against your client's position.
   (e) Outline the argument for Hansen based on your answers to these questions.

Persuasive Writing

A brief writer's goal is twofold: to inform and to persuade. To inform, the writer must present a clear and complete picture of the facts and the law. To persuade, she must explain why the law and policy favor a decision in her client's favor, showing every link in her chain of logic, and use persuasive writing techniques to present her client's case in the most favorable light possible. The effective brief writer views her work from the judge's perspective. She knows that the judge's time is valuable and keeps her briefs as short as possible by editing out unnecessary words, sentences, and paragraphs. She writes with clarity and precision and avoids grammatical and typographical errors that can distract the judge from the substance of her argument.

The principles in Chapter 22 (Structure of an Argument) focus on the logical and orderly progression of the arguments in your brief. This chapter focuses on substance and style: how to construct arguments that are clear, credible, and persuasive. The following principles will help you present the Argument persuasively and honestly.

1. Be professional and honest.

A lawyer does not just perform a job. "A lawyer, as a member of the legal profession, is a representative of clients, an officer of the legal system and a public citizen having special responsibility for the quality of justice."[1] The ability to conduct yourself professionally and honestly will be critical to your success in the law. Good persuasive writing exemplifies both.

---

1. Preamble, Model Rules of Prof. Conduct ¶ 1 (2007).

A. Maintain a professional tone and manner. According to the Preamble to the Model Rules of Professional Conduct, which have been adopted in most jurisdictions, "A lawyer should demonstrate respect for the legal system and for those who serve it, including judges, other lawyers, and public officials."[2] As this admonition suggests, a lawyer should maintain a respectful tone when writing a brief. A court is much more likely to be persuaded by a brief that exhibits proper respect than by a brief that employs rude or insulting language, disparaging remarks about your opponent or the court below, and overblown rhetoric. A strident and offensive tone not only detracts from your argument, but is also viewed with great disfavor by the courts.

The Armed Career Criminal Act, 18 U.S.C. § 924(e) (2006), provides for enhanced sentences for persons who have been convicted of three violent felonies. A violent felony includes any crime involving "conduct that presents a serious potential risk of physical injury to another." *Id.* § 924(e)(2)(B)(ii). Daniel Akin was recently convicted of driving while under the influence of alcohol (DUI) for the fourth time, a felony under state law. His criminal record also includes two convictions for armed robbery, which are felonies. During the sentencing hearing, the government argued that Akin's sentence should be enhanced because all three felony convictions were for violent felonies. The trial court disagreed, holding that DUI is not a violent felony. The government appealed. Consider these introductions to the government's argument.

ANSWER A: Driving while intoxicated is conduct that "presents a serious potential risk of physical injury to another." The statute does not require that an injury is certain to occur but that the conduct poses a serious risk to others. The dangers of drunk driving are well known and well documented. It is conduct that "by its nature presents a substantial risk of harm to others." *State v. Crenshaw* (2003). Because the defendant's act of driving while drunk greatly increased the probability that he would cause injury to other persons on the roadway, it was a violent felony as defined in section 924(e).

ANSWER B: The defendant's argument is based on the absurd notion that drunk driving does not present a serious risk of physical injury to another. This far-fetched and illogical argument, which the trial court adopted, is based on the theory that because an injury did not occur there was no serious risk. Obviously, the trial court left its common sense by the wayside when it decided this case.

---

2. *Id.* ¶ 5.

Answer B is unacceptable. It includes language that is insulting to the other party and to the trial court. Also, the focus is on the alleged ineptitude of the other party and the court rather than on the gist of the government's argument. Because Answer B fails to provide the appellate court with a logical or legal reason to overturn the trial court's decision, it is not only unprofessional but ineffective. Answer A, on the other hand, maintains a respectful tone and focuses on the reasons for reversing the trial court. A court is more likely to be persuaded by an argument based on reasoning and logic than one based on offensive language.

Professional behavior, however, encompasses far more than tone. Professionalism, in its purest sense, is a general habit of civil conduct: civil conduct not just in your written work, but in *all* of your work and in *all* of your professional relationships, including those with the court and its officers, with fellow members of the bar, and with all parties to any legal matter in which you are involved. In the context of persuasive writing, you demonstrate your professionalism not only by treating your colleagues with respect but also by showing respect for the truth.

B. Be honest about the law and the facts. Honesty about the law and the facts is essential to effective advocacy. A brief should rely on shading, emphasis, and overall strength of argument for its persuasive value, rather than on omission or distortion of the relevant law or misstatement of facts. The subtlety of this distinction in certain cases makes it no less important.

The Model Rules of Professional Conduct prohibit an attorney from knowingly making "a false statement of fact or law to a tribunal" and from knowingly failing "to disclose to the tribunal legal authority in the controlling jurisdiction known to the lawyer to be directly adverse to the position of the client and not disclosed by opposing counsel."[3]

The Model Rules of Professional Conduct and the Federal Rules of Civil Procedure also establish a minimum standard for the arguments an attorney can make. The Model Rules state that a lawyer may not "bring or defend a proceeding or assert or controvert an issue therein, unless there is a basis in law and fact for doing so that is not frivolous, which includes a good faith argument for an extension, modification or reversal of existing law."[4] Rule 11 of the Federal Rules of Civil

---

3. Model Rules of Prof. Conduct R. 3.3(a)(1) & (2) (2007).
4. *Id.* R. 3.1.

Procedure and parallel state rules reinforce this ethical rule by requiring that briefs, motions, and other papers presented to a court have a reasonable factual and legal basis. Rule 11(b) provides:

> By presenting to the court a pleading, written motion, or other paper—whether by signing, filing, submitting, or later advocating it—an attorney or unrepresented party certifies that to the best of the person's knowledge, information, and belief, formed after an inquiry reasonable under the circumstances,
>
> (1) it is not being presented for any improper purpose, such as to harass, cause unnecessary delay, or needless increase in the cost of litigation;
> (2) the claims, defenses, and other legal contentions are warranted by existing law or by a nonfrivolous argument for extending, modifying, or reversing existing law or for establishing new law;
> (3) the factual contentions have evidentiary support or, if specifically so identified, will likely have evidentiary support after a reasonable opportunity for further investigation or discovery; and
> (4) the denials of factual contentions are warranted on the evidence or, if specifically so identified, are reasonably based on belief or a lack of information.

Courts may impose sanctions against lawyers who violate Rule 11. Sanctions include reasonable expenses incurred by the opposing party because of the filing of the paper as well as reasonable attorney fees. Court sanctions also expose the lawyer to public embarrassment, damage the lawyer's professional reputation, and cause clients and potential clients to lose confidence in the lawyer. The importance of honesty to your professional future cannot be overstated. Federal Judge Lynn N. Hughes puts it plainly:

> *Honesty* in fact and law determines not only the outcome of the case but also your future as a lawyer. If you appear before me well prepared and if you present your case with integrity and class, I will forget you by dinner. But if you misrepresent your facts or law or if you try cute evasions, I will remember you after you have turned gray. Do not sell off your integrity for any client. No matter how smart you may be, if I cannot approach your presentation with trust, you are but half heard at best.

Honesty about the facts requires you to inform the court of all facts relevant to the issues. Mischaracterization of facts or omission of relevant facts is dishonest. Honesty about the law requires you to accurately relate all law that is relevant to your case. A brief that includes only cases that favor the client's position and ignores unfavorable precedent, takes language out of context, or misrepresents the holding or reasoning of a case is unprofessional and fails in its primary purpose—to inform. Mischaracterization or omission of relevant facts or law is also poor strategy. Once the court recognizes that you have presented an inaccurate picture of the case, it is unlikely to be persuaded by the rest of your argument.

Consider the following example:

Lynn Monroe sued Amy Breyer for intentional infliction of emotional distress after Breyer made a series of telephone calls to local residents accusing Monroe of having an affair with Breyer's husband, Sam. Breyer stated that Monroe "won't be smiling much longer," and that she "would get even" with Monroe for trying to break up the Breyer's marriage. In this state the tort of intentional infliction of emotional distress is defined as "extreme and outrageous conduct that intentionally or recklessly causes severe emotional distress to another." The trial court granted summary judgment to Monroe, holding that Breyer's conduct was extreme and outrageous. Breyer has appealed. The attorney for Breyer has drafted two possible arguments.

ANSWER A: The court in *Grant v. Zeller* (1998) emphasized that "extreme and outrageous conduct" requires either offensive language or threats of violence by the defendant. In that case, the plaintiff accused a building contractor of fraud and threatened to sue him. The defendant, the contractor's wife, called the plaintiff seven times in one hour, yelled at her, threatened to come over, and stated repeatedly that the plaintiff "would pay" if she sued the defendant's husband. The plaintiff sued the defendant for intentional infliction of emotional distress, and the court affirmed a grant of summary judgment for the defendant, finding that she had used neither offensive language nor threats. The court construed her statement to mean that the plaintiff would pay for the defendant's medical bills and for the distress she had suffered as a result of the plaintiff's accusations against her husband. Similarly, Breyer's statements that she "would get even" and that Monroe "won't be smiling much longer" imply that Monroe would suffer the consequences of her action, but neither statement contains offensive language or a threat of physical violence.

ANSWER B: The court in *Grant v. Zeller* (1998) emphasized that "extreme and outrageous conduct" requires either offensive language or threats of violence by the defendant. In that case, the plaintiff accused a building contractor of fraud and threatened to sue him. The defendant, the contractor's wife, called the plaintiff seven times in one hour, yelled at her, threatened to come over, and stated repeatedly that the plaintiff "would pay" if she sued the defendant's husband. The plaintiff sued the defendant for intentional infliction of emotional distress, and the court affirmed a grant of summary judgment for the defendant, finding that she had used neither offensive language nor threats. If the vague statement that the plaintiff "would pay" is not a direct threat of physical violence then neither is Breyer's similarly vague statement that she "would get even" with Monroe.

Answer A is better because it accurately and honestly states both the law and the relevant facts. Answer B does neither. Answer B omits the court's interpretation of "would pay" in *Grant v. Zeller*, implying that the court construed the statement as a vague threat of violence. This is a misleading description of the court's reasoning. Answer A, on the other hand, correctly explains that the court interpreted "would pay" to be a warning that the defendant would pay for medical bills and emotional distress, not a threat of violence. Answer B also omits a relevant fact. Although the phrase "would pay" in *Grant v. Zeller* is similar to the phrase "would get even" in the present case, Breyer also said that Monroe "won't be smiling much longer." This phrase is arguably threatening. By omitting this key unfavorable fact, Answer B gives a misleading picture of the situation between the parties, and asks the court to reach a conclusion based on incomplete information. It also gives opposing counsel the opportunity to draw attention to the omission and give the fact more emphasis than it deserves. Answer A sets out all of the relevant facts and does not seek to hide anything from the court. Answer A is more credible and therefore more persuasive.

2. Fully argue your client's position.

A legal argument is a series of logical or analytical steps which is informative and persuasive only if all steps are expressly stated. If your brief omits even one of these steps, you risk losing your reader as well as your case. Don't count on the court to know or understand the things you failed to say. For example, be sure to include the holding and significant facts of any case that is central to your position. Similarly, if you want the court to recognize analogies and distinctions, you must draw explicit comparisons yourself. Do not leave this task to the court even if you think the analogy or distinction is obvious.

Because the brief is a statement of reasons for adopting a certain position, these reasons should be stated as completely as possible. The principle in Chapter 12 (Explaining the Analysis) requiring an explicit statement of all the analytical steps needed to reach a conclusion takes on a new dimension in advocacy. A brief that includes all legitimate arguments and fully explains how the facts and the applicable law and policy lead to the desired conclusion is both informative and persuasive. The following are some guidelines.

A. Emphasize helpful facts and de-emphasize unhelpful facts. As Chapter 25 (Statement of Facts for a Brief) shows in more detail, the facts have both logical and emotional value. The application of law to facts is the essence of legal reasoning, but the facts can also be used to gain empathy for the client. By marshaling and emphasizing the appropriate facts, you can overcome a weak legal position and persuade a court that the desired outcome is compelling. Similarly, you can minimize the strength of your opponent's position by de-emphasizing damaging facts—explaining them, summarizing them, or describing them blandly. Always use the facts to your client's advantage in briefs to both trial and appellate courts.

Edgar Brown was convicted of first-degree murder. Defense counsel has two drafts of the brief on appeal:

ANSWER A: The trial judge erred by not charging the jury with the lesser included offense of voluntary manslaughter. A defendant is entitled to a jury charge for manslaughter whenever there are enough facts to convince a reasonable person that the homicide was committed under the influence of an irresistible passion caused by an insult or provocation sufficient to excite a reasonable person. *People v. Valentine.* The defendant in that case was convicted of first-degree murder for killing a man who repeatedly insulted the defendant during a quarrel by calling him a window peeper and a liar, among other things. The court held that these facts could justify a verdict of voluntary manslaughter and that the trial court erred by giving jury instructions that precluded conviction for that crime.

Brown's case is similar to *Valentine* because the record shows that Brown committed the homicide after being taunted about a sensitive personal matter. Brown described the decedent as "my best friend from army days," even though the decedent had broken Brown's nose in a fight the previous year. Brown was depressed and unemployed, and the killing occurred during a weekly poker game after the decedent called him a "welfare bum" and a "loser." Any reasonable person in Brown's position would have been similarly provoked.

ANSWER B: The trial judge erred by not charging the jury with the lesser included offense of voluntary manslaughter. A defendant is entitled to a jury charge for manslaughter whenever there are enough facts to convince a reasonable person that the homicide was committed under the influence of an irresistible passion caused by an insult or provocation sufficient to excite a reasonable person. *People v. Valentine.* The defendant in that case was convicted of first-degree murder for killing a man who repeatedly insulted the defendant during a quarrel by calling him a window peeper and a liar, among other things. The court held that these facts could justify a verdict of voluntary manslaughter and that the trial court erred by giving jury instructions that precluded conviction for that crime.

Brown's case is similar to *Valentine* because the record shows that Brown committed the homicide after being taunted about a sensitive personal matter. Brown was extremely depressed after his layoff from an auto plant, where he had worked for seventeen years. He had been unable to find other work because of the local high unemployment rate. Both he and his wife testified that he had trouble concentrating after he was laid off, that he frequently forgot things, and that their marriage was strained. The homicide was committed during a weekly poker game with friends. Like the decedent in *Valentine* who repeatedly insulted the defendant, the decedent in this case, Brown's "best friend from army days," began to taunt Brown about being a "loser," a "welfare bum," and a "social parasite." Although Brown and the decedent had engaged in a brief fistfight a year earlier, several persons, including the decedent's wife, testified they had long since made up. After the decedent ignored repeated warnings to quit, Brown suddenly lunged at him with a paring knife used to make sandwiches. Brown later could remember nothing of the homicide except experiencing blind rage. A reasonable person in Brown's position would have been similarly provoked.

Answer B is better because its vivid detail forces the court to see the issue from Brown's viewpoint. The additional facts place the incident within the manslaughter rule and paint a sympathetic portrait of a harassed man pushed to the breaking point. The facts are set out in chronological order, showing Brown's growing frustration and unhappiness. Answer A's analysis of the facts, by contrast, is poorly organized, omits important facts, and does not describe precisely what happened. Answer A mentions the fistfight in a damaging way, whereas Answer B carefully excuses and blends this point into the argument. Answer A is unpersuasive because it does not provide insight or foster empathy for Brown's situation. Effective advocates recognize the most valuable facts and weave them strategically into their legal arguments.

B. Use policy arguments to support your legal analysis. The relationship between rules and policies is important in brief writing. Policies are the reasons for the legal rules in question. The result you advocate must be significant from a policy standpoint; technical infractions of the law are usually not enough. Policy arguments are also important when the legal rules or the facts do not provide you with a strong position, particularly at the appellate level. As discussed in Chapter 26 (Briefs to a Trial Court) and Chapter 27 (Briefs to an Appellate Court), policy arguments are generally more important in appellate briefs than in briefs to trial courts; appellate courts do not simply apply the law, they may also shape it.

Policy arguments allow you to explain why the result you advocate furthers important social goals or is consistent with the law's purpose. They can be particularly persuasive when there is unfavorable precedent that cannot easily be distinguished or when you are asking the court to modify or overturn existing law.

Section 23 of the Township Rural Zoning Act requires a public referendum on the "adoption of a zoning ordinance" when 8 percent of the registered voters in the township sign petitions requesting a referendum. Seymour Township adopted its zoning ordinance in 1962. Several weeks ago, the Township Board rezoned an eighty-acre tract from agricultural to residential use. Township residents gathered sufficient signatures to request a referendum, but a trial court ruled that section 23 applied to the initial decision to zone, not to subsequent zoning amendments. The citizens' brief to the court of appeals could be summarized in the following ways:

ANSWER A: Section 23 of the Township Rural Zoning Act requires the requested referendum. Section 23 applies to the "adoption of a zoning ordinance," a term that includes not only the initial decision to zone but also subsequent amendments. Because such amendments become part of the ordinance, they should be treated in the same manner.

ANSWER B: Section 23 of the Township Rural Zoning Act requires the requested referendum. Section 23 applies to the "adoption of a zoning ordinance," a term that includes not only the initial decision to zone but also any subsequent amendments. Because such amendments become part of the ordinance, they should be treated in the same manner.

This conclusion furthers the underlying purpose of section 23: to ensure that the ordinance is acceptable to a majority of those living in the township. Because zoning amendments might make the ordinance unacceptable to those citizens, the referendum requirement should apply equally to zoning amendments and the original ordinance. Zoning amendments, moreover, significantly affect the quality of life of township residents by prescribing the existence, location, and density of new developments. The public ought to be able to vote on these important decisions. Finally, because the right to vote is a fundamental one, any perceived ambiguities about the scope of a legislative grant ought to be resolved in favor of that fundamental right.

Answer B's completeness makes it far more compelling than Answer A. Answer A is merely an argument based on the language in section 23, an argument that sounds uninspired because it does not make effective use of the underlying policies. Answer B reaches the same conclusion, but it relies far more on the underlying policy of majority approval for zoning decisions than on the meaning of the words. It states that the legislative intent requires that section 23 be applied to zoning amendments, regardless of the ambiguous language of the law.

---

3. Present arguments from your client's point of view.

A. Emphasize the correctness of your client's position. The tone of your argument should be positive rather than simply negative or defensive. You therefore should frame both your arguments and counterarguments in terms of why your client should win rather than why the opposing party should lose. Rebut your opponent's position only *after* you have explained your client's position. By presenting arguments from your client's point of view, you show control over the issues and write a more persuasive brief.

The plaintiffs brought an action under the federal Noise Control Act of 1972, alleging section 1337 of the Judicial Code as the sole basis of jurisdiction. The defendant has filed a motion to dismiss on the ground that the plaintiffs did not allege an amount in controversy of more than $75,000. The plaintiffs' argument to the federal district court might be stated in either of the following ways:

ANSWER A: The defendant incorrectly contends that the plaintiffs' failure to allege more than $75,000 as an amount in controversy deprives the Court of jurisdiction. Section 1337 of the Judicial Code provides original jurisdiction to the federal courts of "any civil action or proceeding arising under any Act of Congress regulating commerce," but it does not require an allegation of an amount in controversy. Because the federal Noise Control Act, under which the plaintiffs brought this action, is a congressional regulation of commerce, the defendant's contention is untrue. Section 1332 requires an allegation of an amount in controversy for federal jurisdiction, but the plaintiffs do not rely on section 1332.

ANSWER B: The Court has jurisdiction to hear this case. Section 1337 of the Judicial Code provides original jurisdiction to the federal courts of "any civil action or proceeding arising under any Act of Congress regulating commerce," but it does not require an allegation of an amount in controversy.

The plaintiffs have alleged jurisdiction under the federal Noise Control Act, a congressional regulation of commerce. Because the plaintiffs do not rely on section 1332, which requires an allegation of amount in controversy for federal jurisdiction, this Court has jurisdiction.

Both answers cover the same ground, but they convey different messages. Answer B says the court has jurisdiction; Answer A says the defendant's claim is untrue, but it never clearly says the federal district court has jurisdiction. Answer B is better because it is more positive and lucid. It turns a refutation of the defendant's denial of jurisdiction into an affirmative argument and demonstrates control over the direction and tone of the argument. Answer A, which is dominated by the defendant's viewpoint, does not.

B. Present the law from your client's point of view. Balanced descriptions of the law, required in office memos, have no place in legal briefs. The law should be characterized to favor, and be consistent with, the client's position. The legal rules and principles, of course, determine what arguments can be made. They should also be an integral part of the Argument, stated with the same forcefulness and tone as the application of the law to the facts. The description of the law would otherwise disrupt the flow and direction of the Argument.

Consider this illustration:

Mary Elston brought an action against Jan Guerrero, the driver of a car that struck her van from the rear, causing Elston a serious back injury. At trial, Guerrero's attorney attempted to introduce evidence to show that most, if not all, of Elston's injuries could have been avoided had she been wearing a seat belt. The trial judge refused to admit that evidence. The state's appellate courts have not addressed this question. The case was tried under the state's comparative negligence rule, and Guerrero's attorney was attempting to mitigate damages. The jury returned a verdict for Elston and awarded $225,000 in damages. On appeal, Guerrero's attorney might characterize the relevant law from other states in two ways:

ANSWER A: When seat belts are available to the plaintiff in an auto negligence action and the plaintiff 's failure to use them caused or contributed to her injuries, the defendant in a growing number of states is entitled to have the damage award reduced accordingly. *E.g., Bentzler v. Braun*. This rule is based on the reasonable view that the use of seat belts reduces serious injuries and fatalities from automobile accidents and that those riding in cars should know of this additional safety factor. *Bentzler.* Cases to the contrary are based on the questionable premises that the duty to fasten seat belts arises only if the plaintiff anticipates the accident and that not all people use them. *E.g., Kopischke v. First Continental Corp.* When seat belts are available, though, it is manifestly unfair to penalize a defendant for the plaintiff's failure to exercise a simple precaution that is surely in the plaintiff's best interest.

ANSWER B: The courts of other states are divided on whether a defendant in an auto negligence action is entitled to have the damage award reduced when seat belts are available to the plaintiff and the plaintiff's failure to use them caused or contributed to her injuries. Most courts, however, deny mitigation. A minority of the courts have held that the use of seat belts reduces serious injuries and fatalities from auto accidents and that those riding in cars should know of this additional safety factor. *E.g., Bentzler v. Braun.* The majority of cases are premised on the view that the duty to fasten seat belts arises only if the plaintiff anticipates the accident and that not all people use them. *E.g., Kopischke v. First Continental Corp.* The issue is which party should bear the cost of the plaintiff's failure to use seat belts. *Bentzler* probably represents the better reasoned view because the use of seat belts reduces injuries.

Answer A is better because it is confident and forceful, and presents the law in the light most favorable to Guerrero. Answer B, by contrast, is detached, focusing on a division among the courts rather than a legal perspective that strongly supports Guerrero. The writer does not sound convinced and thus is not convincing. Answer A shows the court how to decide in Guerrero's favor; it states the position favoring mitigation, presents that position as if it were clearly better, and encourages the court to select *Bentzler* as preferable policy. Unlike Answer B, it de-emphasizes the division of the courts and the minority position of the *Bentzler* case by merely implying these facts. In short, Answer A's description of the law advances the Argument.

C. State your client's position so that it appears objective. Because courts generally do not like to innovate, try to present your client's position as reflecting the existing law. Even when a decision in your client's favor would break new legal ground, try to show that a favorable decision is required by law, justice, and common sense. Avoid wordy references to your client's position, suggestions that your client's position is merely an interpretation of the law, and explicit indications that it diverges from the law. Conversely, characterize the opposition's case as distant from the existing law or as mere interpretation.

Consider the following:

A complaint filed with the State Bar Association charged Lee Gibbon, an attorney, with depositing in his personal checking account the funds of several estates for which he was doing probate work and converting $147,000 of these funds to his personal use. A hearing panel of the State Bar Association agreed with the complaint after an evidentiary hearing and voted to suspend Gibbon from the practice of law for five years. Gibbon appealed to the State Bar Grievance Board, which affirmed the panel's findings and increased the suspension to a lifetime disbarment. Gibbon appealed the Board's disbarment decision to the state's highest appellate court. The State Bar Association's attorney might characterize its position on appeal in either of these ways:

ANSWER A: The State Bar Association interprets the State Bar Grievance Rules to provide the Grievance Board with discretionary authority to increase a five-year suspension to a disbarment. The State Bar Association agrees with the Grievance Board's conclusion, after reviewing the detailed records, that "the uncontradicted evidence of serious violations of the state Rules of Professional Conduct warrants disbarment." The Board's failure to make a detailed statement of the reasons for disbarment is therefore irrelevant, notwithstanding the obvious importance of this matter to Gibbon.

ANSWER B: The State Bar Grievance Board has discretionary authority to increase a five-year suspension to disbarment. After reviewing the detailed record, the Board concluded that "the uncontradicted evidence of serious violations of the state Rules of Professional Conduct warrants disbarment." In light of that conclusion, a more detailed statement of reasons would serve no useful purpose.

Answer A emphasizes the State Bar Association's position, but Answer B emphasizes the correctness of the Grievance Board's decision. Answer B is better because it sounds more objective than Answer A. Answer A is also verbose and less forceful because it begins with "The State Bar Association interprets . . . ." Finally, it suggests more weakness in the State Bar Association's position than is necessary ("Board's failure," "obvious importance of this matter to Gibbon," and "interprets the . . . Rules"). The difference between the two answers is one of emphasis; the skillful use of emphasis makes a more persuasive argument.

4. Craft sentences and choose words to persuade.

Word choice and placement are as important as structure in an argument. Words can make an argument seem confident or defensive, bold or halting, credible or dubious. They can make a position seem conservative or radical. Sentence structure can also influence the reader's perception of the point conveyed. Writing techniques cannot substitute for a good argument, but they can greatly enhance it. The following guidelines are illustrative.

A. Write positive assertions rather than negative ones. Negative assertions are less forceful than positive ones. They may also be less clear than positive ones because they do not state what is true; they simply tell the reader what is not. Although negative assertions are sometimes necessary, you should avoid them if the same idea can be stated positively.

Positive: The defendant ignored the warning signs.

Negative: The defendant did not pay attention to the warning signs.

The positive assertion is clear and forceful because it tells the reader precisely what the defendant did. The negative assertion, "did not pay attention," is weaker than "ignored."

Positive: A brief search incident to a traffic citation is minimally intrusive.

Negative: A brief search incident to a traffic citation is not a significant intrusion upon a person's right to privacy.

The positive assertion states the point directly. The negative assertion is not as direct and is less persuasive. That the intrusion was not significant does not necessarily mean that it was minimal.

B. Use placement of words, phrases, and sentences to emphasize or minimize points. Writing becomes persuasive by the careful placement of words in each sentence and by careful ordering of sentences in a paragraph. The first and last positions in a sentence or paragraph are the most prominent and most likely to capture the reader's attention. For example, suppose you want to emphasize the wrongful conduct of a defendant. "He stabbed the victim repeatedly" is more emphatic than "He repeatedly stabbed the victim."

Unfavorable rules and precedent must not be omitted if they are necessary for an accurate description of the law, but their impact can be minimized by careful drafting. Consider the following two examples.

ANSWER A: Evidence of a defendant's prior convictions is generally inadmissible, but in this case it should be admissible to show that the defendant acted with criminal intent.

ANSWER B: Evidence of the defendant's prior convictions, although generally inadmissible, should be admitted in this case to show that the defendant acted with criminal intent.

Answer B is better. The assertion that the evidence should be admitted is emphasized and the general rule unfavorable to his client's position is buried in midsentence. Answer A begins with the general rule, giving it more prominence than the point the writer is making.

Consider the following two drafts of an introductory paragraph on the right to the free flow of light from a brief based on Exercise 7-C.

ANSWER A: The court in *Cassells v. Avery* (2012) refused to recognize a legal right to the free flow of light in a case in which a hotel owner's proposed ten-story addition would cast a shadow on the adjoining hotel owner's sunbathing areas. The court cited a lack of precedent, as only one American court has recognized a legal right to the free flow of light. *Id.* The reasons for the rule in *Cassells* continue to be valid because recognizing such a right would infringe on individual property rights. In addition, requiring that every property owner allow the free flow of sunlight onto neighboring property would make building construction in high-density areas economically unfeasible.

ANSWER B: Only one American court has ever recognized a legal right to the free flow of light. *Cassells v. Avery* (1959). Citing this lack of precedent, the court in *Cassells* refused to recognize a legal right to light in a case in which a hotel owner's proposed ten-story addition would cast a shadow on the adjoining hotel owner's sunbathing areas. The reasons for this rule continue to be valid. Requiring that every property owner allow the free flow of sunlight onto neighboring property would make building construction in high-density areas economically unfeasible. It would also infringe on individual property rights.

Both paragraphs include the same information, but the placement of two sentences makes Answer B more persuasive. It begins with the strongest point—that only one American court has recognized the right to the free flow of light—and ends with a short, emphatic sentence regarding individual property rights, which is likely to be of greater concern to the court than the economic impact the right would have. In Answer A, these two forceful points are in the middle of the paragraph and are less likely to engage the reader's attention.

C. Use short sentences for emphasis. Short sentences are usually more emphatic than longer sentences and are useful to emphasize an important point. A well-known example is Justice Benjamin Cardozo's statement, "Danger invites rescue."[5] In the following examples, note that the more concise sentences are also more effective.

> Failure to post warnings can have consequences of a serious nature to the public at large.
>
> Failure to post warnings poses a danger to the public.

> Sometimes it is impossible to ascertain the plain meaning of a statute because whether it is plain or not often depends on whether the reader thinks it is plain.
>
> "[P]lain meaning, like beauty, is sometimes in the eye of the beholder."[6]

This technique is effective only if used sparingly. Vary your sentence structure and length, combining short sentences with longer ones, so the short sentences achieve your goal of emphasizing a point.

D. Be subtle rather than openly manipulative. As previously noted, you should make your client's position appear objective. The selection of adjectives and adverbs most often determines whether your brief appears objective and measured or has crossed the line to blatant argumentation. For this reason you should avoid using modifiers such as "clearly" and "obviously." If a particular point is in contention, the conclusion will not be clear or obvious to the court. Your task is to explain *why* your position is supported by the law and policy and *why* your client should prevail, not to draw conclusions for the court about how obviously correct your position is. Language that is openly manipulative is inappropriate in a brief and can detract from your argument. Few issues before the court are clear or obvious.

Consider this example:

> The plaintiff sued her employer after she was fired for marrying her supervisor, in violation of the company's "no-spouse" rule that forbids a married couple from working in the same department. She claimed that the employer had violated the state's Human Rights Act, which forbids an employer from discriminating against an employee because of, among other things, marital status. The

---

5. Wagner v. International Railway Co., 232 N.Y. 176, 180 (1926).
6. Florida Power & Light Co. v. Lorion, 470 U.S. 729, 737 (1985).

employer's argument is that the plaintiff was not fired because of her marital status but because she married someone who worked in the same department. Therefore, the issue in this case is the definition of "marital status." Consider which of these two arguments for the employer is most effective.

ANSWER A: The legislature did not define "marital status" in the Human Rights Act, which raises the presumption that it intended the phrase to have its ordinary meaning—whether one is legally married. When one is asked about one's marital status the expected answer is "married" or "single," not the identification of one's present or former spouse and certainly not the spouse's occupation. *City Cafe v. Jensen* (1990). The plaintiff was not fired because of her marital status but because of whom she married.

ANSWER B: The legislature did not define "marital status" in the Human Rights Act, which raises the obvious presumption that it intended the phrase to have its ordinary meaning—whether one is legally married. Clearly, when one is asked about one's marital status the expected answer is "married" or "single," not the identification of one's present or former spouse and certainly not the spouse's occupation. *City Cafe v. Jensen* (1990). Therefore, the only logical conclusion is that the plaintiff was not fired because of her marital status but because of whom she married.

Answer A uses logic to persuade. Answer B uses the same reasoning, but tries to manipulate the reader by including such terms as "obvious presumption," "clearly," and "the only logical conclusion." This language could damage your credibility with the court, especially if it is inclined to rule the other way, and lessens the effectiveness of the argument.

EXERCISES

The exercises that follow provide an opportunity to apply these principles.

Exercise 23-A

This exercise is based on the facts and cases in Exercise 22-A, pp. 332-33.

1. Draft the argument for Jones.

2. Draft the argument for the state.

Exercise 23-B

This exercise is based on your answers to Exercise 22-B, pp. 333-35. In this exercise, as in Exercise 22-B, you or your professor will decide which client you represent.

1. Assume you are representing Tri-State:
   (a) How does the case law support Tri-State's position?
   (b) What facts will you emphasize and why?
   (c) What policies will you emphasize and why?
   (d) Draft the argument for Tri-State.

2. Assume you are representing Hansen:
   (a) How does the case law support Hansen's position?
   (b) What facts will you emphasize and why?
   (c) What policies will you emphasize and why?
   (d) Draft the argument for Hansen.

CHAPTER 24

Point Headings

Point headings are statements of the legal conclusions the writer is asking the court to adopt. Like the Brief Answers in an office memo, the point headings in a brief respond directly to the Questions Presented and correspond to the issues, sub-issues, and other salient points in the brief. Point headings serve two important purposes; one relates to organization and the other to advocacy.

Point headings serve a useful organizational purpose because they help a court understand the direction and content of the brief. They are located within the body of the Argument where they serve as conspicuous thesis statements for the arguments presented. They are also listed in the Table of Contents of an appellate brief where they provide a complete and concise summary of the Argument. A judge interested in reading only about a particular point can scan the Table of Contents and then turn to the appropriate page. In addition to assisting the court, point headings assist the advocate in drafting the brief. They magnify organizational flaws and provide a useful check on the content of the argument under each heading.

Point headings are also an important part of advocacy. They are basic statements of the advocate's contentions and, as such, make the Argument more understandable to the court. Because judges are required to decide a variety of complicated matters, they are more likely to be persuaded by briefs that are easily understood. In addition, the placement of point headings in the Table of Contents and their treatment in the Argument impresses the structure of your argument more sharply in the reader's mind.

The logic of the argument in the brief unfolds in the point headings. You should arrange point headings in outline form from the most general to the most specific. State your primary arguments in capitalized point headings known as *major* headings. If there is more than one major heading, preface them with Roman numerals. State the significant points supporting each primary contention in *minor* headings. Preface minor headings with capital letters. (Some advocates underline minor headings to distinguish them from subheadings that may follow.) Finally, state the significant points supporting a minor heading in subheadings. Preface subheadings with Arabic numerals. Only rarely are headings required for the arguments supporting a subheading.

The basic rules of outlining apply to point headings. Never use minor headings or subheadings under a heading unless you use two or more of them. If you have only one minor heading or subheading under a broader heading, consolidate it with the broader heading.

For example:

    I. **FIRST MAJOR HEADING**
        A. **<u>First minor heading</u>**
        B. **<u>Second minor heading</u>**
            1. **First subheading**
            2. **Second subheading**
            3. **Third subheading**
   II. **SECOND MAJOR HEADING**

The following are the basic principles for formulating and placing point headings.

1. State your legal conclusions and the basic reasons for these conclusions.

Point headings are an integral part of the Argument section. They should be confident, forceful sentences cast in terms most favorable to your client. Because they are thesis statements for parts of your Argument, each point heading should indicate the issue being discussed (including the relevant legal rule), your position on this issue, and the basic reasons for that position. Major point headings should state your principal arguments, and minor point headings may contain the arguments or reasons that support them. When subordinate headings are used under a major heading, however, the major heading need contain only your position concerning the application of a particular legal rule. The subordinate headings will provide the reasons for that position. A major heading, for example, may draw a general legal conclusion whose underlying rationale is provided by several minor headings. Each minor heading, then, will contain a legal rule, a conclusion concerning its application to your case, and your basic reasons for that conclusion. Case or statutory citations usually should not be used as a shorthand reference to the applicable legal principle because a bare citation rarely gives the reader enough direction.

Consider the following situation:

The Williams Act is a federal statute that specifies disclosure requirements and imposes restrictions concerning tender offers. A tender offer is the term used to describe an offer by an individual or group of individuals to purchase a certain percentage of the outstanding stock of a corporation. The State of Huron has enacted a similar statute regulating tender offers that has more stringent requirements than the Williams Act. You represent a client seeking to make a tender offer who would like to avoid the requirements of the Huron statute. Your research indicates that state statutes sometimes can be declared unconstitutional if a federal statute governs the same subject. Because of your research, your client has filed a lawsuit in federal court challenging the constitutionality of the Huron statute. The supremacy clause makes the federal Constitution or statutes "the supreme law of the land." This "preemption doctrine" may be invoked when the congressional purpose in enacting the federal law is frustrated by the operation of the state statute. You might frame a major point heading on this issue in any of these ways:

ANSWER A: THE PREEMPTION DOCTRINE REQUIRES THAT A STATE LAW NOT FRUSTRATE THE PURPOSE OF CONGRESS.

ANSWER B: THIS CASE IS GOVERNED BY *HINES V. DAVIDOWITZ, PEREZ V. CAMPBELL, KEWANEE OIL CO. V. BICRON CORP.,* AND THEIR PROGENY.

ANSWER C: THE HURON STATUTE IS PREEMPTED UNDER THE SUPREMACY CLAUSE BECAUSE IT CONFLICTS WITH THE OBJECTIVES OF THE WILLIAMS ACT, THEREBY FRUSTRATING THE PURPOSES OF CONGRESS.

Answer C is best because it is an assertive and positive statement of your client's position. It states a legal conclusion and provides a reason for that conclusion, introducing the court to the argument that follows. It also incorporates the basic legal rule.

Answer A is merely a statement of a legal principle without any explanation of how that principle applies to the present case. The heading draws no conclusions and provides no reasons supporting the client's position. Although a conclusion might be implied from the argument that follows, the writer of Answer A has wasted an opportunity to advance the client's position.

Answer B is worse because it does not even describe the basic legal principle involved. If the reader is not familiar with the cases cited, the point heading is useless. Even if the reader is familiar with the cases, the point heading provides no more than the applicable legal rule. To this extent, Answer B is simply another way of stating Answer A.

---

2. Structure point headings to be both specific and readable.

Point headings must relate legal rules to specific factual situations. The more specifically these rules and facts are stated, the more persuasive the point headings will be. There is a limit, however, to how much information you can compress into a single sentence without making a heading incomprehensible. Framing a point heading is a balancing act. When deciding how general or specific to be, remember that point headings must both adequately summarize your argument and be readable.

> The state Environmental Protection Act provides in part that any person may bring a lawsuit for injunctive relief against any other person whose actions are "likely to pollute, impair, or destroy the air, water, or other natural resources, or the public trust therein." A sportsmen's club brought a lawsuit under that Act to prevent oil drilling in a state forest. After a bench trial, the court granted judgment for the defendants. Counsel for the plaintiff might use one of these point headings on appeal:

ANSWER A: The plaintiff presented uncontradicted evidence of likely pollution, impairment, or destruction of the air, water, or other natural resources, or the public trust therein because the plaintiff showed that oil development activities at the proposed sites, including seismic survey work, exploratory drilling, new roads, and other activities would substantially diminish elk populations in the forest by diminishing their habitat and would also adversely impact bear and bobcat populations, and that it would take these species at least forty to fifty years to recover from these effects.

ANSWER B: The plaintiff presented uncontradicted evidence of likely pollution, impairment, or destruction of natural resources by showing that oil drilling activities would have a substantial and prolonged adverse impact on elk, bear, and bobcat populations in the forest.

ANSWER C: The plaintiff presented uncontradicted evidence that oil drilling activities would adversely affect the forest.

Answer B is best because it states and applies the statutory rule, summarizes the relevant facts, draws a conclusion, and is readable. It is a persuasive introduction to the argument that supports and develops the conclusion stated in the point heading. Answer A is unhelpful as a persuasive or organizational tool because it is too detailed. It gives a more complete statement of the applicable law and the relevant facts, but it is difficult to read and understand. The additional details contribute nothing significant. Answer C is the other extreme; it is easy to read but too vague to be of much use. It does not state the statutory rule concerning the likelihood of pollution, impairment, or destruction of the environment, nor does it state how the forest is likely to be adversely affected. Answer B reconciles the two extremes.

3. Place headings at logical points in your brief.

Point headings must reflect your organizational scheme. Generally, you should include a separate point heading for each issue and sub-issue. If necessary, you should add another level of headings for the major points under each issue or sub-issue. In addition to point headings that make the Argument more specific, you may need point headings to divide your issues or sub-issues into categories. For example, when you have two or more broad categories of issues, such as several objections to the constitutionality of a statute and several jurisdictional issues, include a separate point heading for each category.

Placement of headings is a matter of balance and good judgment. As a rule, point headings should provide logical breaks in your Argument. A well-written brief carries the reader smoothly from one point to another. Too few point headings may make your brief more difficult to understand and lead to a long-winded, poorly organized Argument. Too many point headings can cause your brief to lose momentum and persuasive force. They can interrupt the Argument's flow, make the organizational scheme confusingly complex, and draw excessive attention to relatively insignificant points. Although it may be logical to divide the arguments under a heading into subheadings, doing so may not be prudent. You can often strengthen several weak arguments by combining them rather than by presenting them individually. Each will lend support to the others and give the appearance of a stronger overall Argument.

The State Radiation Control Act provides for the licensing of persons and medical establishments using X-rays and other sources of ionizing radiation. It also provides that a court "may grant temporary and permanent equitable relief" against persons who have violated the Act. Your client, Health Scan Associates, specialized in providing X-rays. A trial court has enjoined your client from providing X-rays until its equipment and technicians are licensed under the Act, even though they meet nearly all of the safety and training requirements of the Act. The licensing process could take six months or more. The trial court has held that "an injunction is automatically required when the Act is being violated." Traditionally, injunctions are issued only when the harm they will prevent outweighs the harm they will cause to the defendant. In addition, injunctions may be issued automatically, with no balancing of interests, when there are significant or continuing violations of the statute. You are drafting a brief supporting your motion for a stay of the injunction pending appeal and plan to argue that the injunction was wrong under both theories. Your point headings might be drafted in the following ways:

ANSWER A:

II.   THE TRIAL COURT ERRED WHEN IT ENJOINED HEALTH SCAN FROM PROVIDING X-RAYS UNTIL IT COMPLIES WITH THE TECHNICAL REQUIREMENTS OF THE RADIATION CONTROL ACT.

    A.   <u>The Act requires the automatic issuance of an injunction only for significant and continuing violations, not for minor violations such as those committed by Health Scan.</u>

    B.   <u>The harm to Health Scan from its loss of income while awaiting proper licensing, its possible bankruptcy, and the dismissal of its thirty-four trained workers outweighs the state's interest in technical compliance with the Act.</u>

ANSWER B:

II.   THE TRIAL COURT ERRED WHEN IT ENJOINED HEALTH SCAN FROM PROVIDING X-RAYS UNTIL IT COMPLIES WITH THE TECHNICAL REQUIREMENTS OF THE RADIATION CONTROL ACT.

    A.   <u>The injunction should not have been issued automatically because the appellant did not commit significant and continuing violations of the Act.</u>

B. <u>Even if the Act purported to make injunctive relief mandatory, it could not do so because such relief is always within the trial court's discretion.</u>

C. <u>The injunction should not have been issued because the Act makes such relief discretionary rather than mandatory.</u>

D. <u>The injunction should not have been issued because the harm to the appellant far outweighs the state's interest.</u>

   1. The injunction will greatly injure the appellant by causing a total loss of income for six or more months, possible bankruptcy, and unemployment of thirty-four workers.

   2. The injunction will only slightly accelerate the time by which the appellant technically complies with the Act.

ANSWER C:

II. THE TRIAL COURT ERRED WHEN IT GRANTED THE INJUNCTION BECAUSE THE INJUNCTION WAS NOT MANDATORY UNDER THE RADIATION CONTROL ACT AND BECAUSE THE BALANCE OF EQUITIES FAVORS THE APPELLANT.

Answer A provides a straightforward yet complete outline of the client's position and is the best of the three answers. The organizational scheme is smooth and understandable. Each of the client's basic contentions is summarized in a single minor heading.

Answer B is too choppy to be effective. It has too many headings and thus obscures the basic thrust of the Argument. The second minor heading (B) should be incorporated with the first minor heading (A) because the two points are closely related and more forceful when made together. Similarly, the third and fourth minor headings (C and D) should be combined, as in Answer A. Moreover, subheadings 1 and 2 after the fourth heading (D) add little to the single heading on that issue in Answer A. (Answer B also refers to Health Scan in different places as "Health Scan" and "the appellant," which wrongly suggests that Health Scan is not the appellant. It is better to use the same designation throughout—a proper name, a descriptive label (*e.g.*, licensee), or the trial court designation (*e.g.*, defendant).)

Answer C represents the other extreme by omitting the minor headings. The organizational scheme of the Argument is not explained and its persuasive value is diminished accordingly.

EXERCISES

Working through the following exercises should improve your understanding of these concepts.

Exercise 24-A

This exercise is based on Exercise 22-B, pp. 333-35. For this exercise, as in Exercise 22-B, you or your professor will decide which client you represent.

1. Assume you represent Tri-State on appeal. Using the principles described in this chapter, draft Tri-State's point headings.

2. Assume you represent Hansen on appeal. Using the principles described in this chapter, draft Hansen's point headings.

Exercise 24-B

Edward Hinkle is appealing an order of the State Industrial Commission denying his claim for workers' compensation benefits. Hinkle was employed by the Goff Medical Supply Co. to deliver medical supplies to clinics, doctors, and hospitals. The boxes containing the supplies were secured by rubber bands about twelve inches long and one-half inch wide. There was testimony before an administrative law judge that Hinkle and several other Goff employees engaged in rubber band "fights" at least two or three times a week. Hinkle's supervisor said he observed such fights several times each month and discouraged them on at least one occasion.

One day, when Hinkle was loading supplies in his truck as part of his regular work, two other employees flipped rubber bands at him. Hinkle immediately flipped a rubber band back at them. One of these employees then found an eighteen-inch sliver of wood and stepped toward Hinkle, brandishing it like a sword. Hinkle took the wood from her and used a rubber band to shoot the wood through the air at the employee. The other employee batted the sliver with a trash can lid she had been using as a shield, and the deflected sliver struck Hinkle in the face, blinding him in the right eye. The entire episode lasted about two minutes. Section 45 of the State Workers' Compensation Act provides for compensation of injuries that are not self-inflicted to "every employee who is injured by accident arising out of or in the course of his employment."

There is one pertinent appellate decision:

Sperry v. Industrial Commission (1989)

The petitioner asks this Court to review an order of the State Industrial Commission denying him workers' compensation benefits for serious injuries he sustained when he fell from a truck that a co-worker was driving around the parking lot at the warehouse where they worked. The petitioner testified that the incident occurred during regular working hours, that they were using the truck to make "figure eights" in the light snow that had just fallen, and that they had never done this before. The petitioner and his co-worker worked in the shipping department at the warehouse, and neither drove nor loaded trucks as part of their regular work. We affirm the Commission's order and we hereby adopt the following four factors for determining whether a particular act of horseplay arises "out of or in the course of" employment and thus is compensable under Section 45 of the Workers' Compensation Act.

1. Extent and seriousness of the deviation. We fully recognize the value of a little nonsense in any employment situation, and we understand that workers cannot be expected to attend strictly to their jobs every minute. The injury here, however, resulted from a lengthy and serious departure from the petitioner's job.

2. Completeness of the deviation. It is one thing for an employee to engage in a bit of horseplay as part of the performance of his duty. It is another to completely abandon the employment and concentrate one's energies on something unrelated to one's job, as occurred here.

3. Extent to which horseplay has become a part of the employment situation. The act of horseplay here occurred only once. It was not a custom in the warehouse.

4. Extent to which the nature of employment may be expected to include some horseplay. Relevant considerations here include the existence of things in the work environment that are readily usable for horseplay and the presence of lulls in the work. We do not believe that, given petitioner's work environment, a truck especially lends itself to horseplay.

For all of these reasons, the Commission's order is affirmed.

For this exercise you or your professor will decide which client you represent.

1. Assume you represent Hinkle on appeal. Using the principles described in this chapter, draft Hinkle's point headings.

2. Assume you represent the Industrial Commission on appeal. Using the principles described in this chapter, draft the Industrial Commission's point headings.

Statement of Facts for a Brief

The Statement of Facts in an office memorandum relates the facts necessary to understand and resolve the legal issues presented. The Statement of Facts in a brief does that and more; it subtly persuades the court that fairness requires a decision in your client's favor. Many advocates believe that the Statement of Facts is the most significant part of a brief because it defines the setting in which the case will be decided.

Factual statements in office memos and briefs are similar in many respects and, therefore, many of the basic rules are the same. The Statement of Facts must be an honest and accurate description of the events that gave rise to the litigation. All legally significant facts must be included and stated precisely, whether they are favorable to the client or not. Key background facts should also be included, but distracting details should not. The facts must be stated logically and understandably.

The Statement of Facts in a brief contains three additional kinds of information not found in the office memo. First, it contains emotionally significant facts. These facts, which are omitted from an office memo unless they are also legally significant, should be included in a brief because they can have a substantial effect on a court's decision-making process by appealing to its sympathies and sense of justice. The strongest cases are both emotionally appealing and soundly based on the relevant law. Cases that are weak on the law can often be strengthened by a factual situation that arouses sympathy.

Second, the factual statement in a brief describes the procedural background of the case—including the major events that led to this point in the litigation and, for an appellate brief, the decisions of any lower courts that heard the case. These procedural facts give both trial and appellate courts a better understanding of the case and the relief requested.

Third, the Statement of Facts in a brief must contain references to the record. The record is a complete history of the proceedings in a case and includes the pleadings, affidavits, exhibits, and other documents submitted to lower courts, and the decisions of those courts. The record also includes the transcribed oral proceedings before the courts, such as arguments on motions and testimony at trial. The Statement of Facts in a brief must show the place or page in the record where the stated facts can be found.

At the lower-court level, you will usually refer to specific docket entries or documents in the court file. For example: "Mrs. Henderson signed the lease on August 31, 2012. (Complaint ¶ 7.)" This citation plainly identifies the source of support for the writer's assertion. If there is support for a fact in more than one document, especially a key or disputed fact, you may cite to multiple sources. For example: "Complaint ¶ 7; Henderson Dep. 3:12." The latter citation indicates that the fact also can be found at page 3, line 12, of the Henderson deposition. At the appellate level, the entire record in the case may be combined and numbered, in which case you will refer to the relevant page in the consolidated record. For example: "The police found the pistol under Anderson's pillow. (R. at 33.)" This citation shows that the source of this fact is on page 33 of the record. Generally, a single fact, or group of related facts, should be followed immediately by a citation to the record. When you are paraphrasing or summarizing facts spread throughout several pages, such as pages 13, 14, 15, and 16, you can group them together and cite them as follows: "(R. at 13–16.)". At other times, you will need to mention several separate pages: "(R. at 11, 28, 30.)". Once you have provided a citation to the record in your Statement of Facts, you usually do not need to refer to the record again when using those facts in other sections of the brief.

The basic principles for persuasively stating the facts are best set forth in the context of a hypothetical problem.

> You represent Iris Magaro in a sex discrimination case. The trial court dismissed her complaint, and she is appealing that decision.

The following excerpts are taken from the transcript of the record in *Magaro v. Shannon Development Co.*:

Excerpt from Complaint of Iris Magaro

(Page 6 of the record)

III.

The plaintiff was employed by the defendant from August 2010 to January 30, 2012, when she resigned her position.

IV.

During her employment the plaintiff advanced from a Class IV secretary to a Class II secretary and consistently received excellent job evaluations.

V.

From September 2011 to the time of her resignation, the plaintiff was subjected to severe, excessive, and inexcusable sexual harassment by her supervisor, Clarence Dudley. Specific instances of this sexual harassment include making obscene jokes to other male employees in the plaintiff's presence, making loud remarks about personal parts of her anatomy, suggesting to other employees that he had engaged in sexual relations with her, asking her to have sexual relations with him during lunch hour, placing his hands on her, and calling her "my little girl."

(Page 8 of the record)

VIII.

The plaintiff is thirty years of age, divorced, and the sole provider for her two young children. The plaintiff has exhausted her savings, and the defendant has refused to reinstate her to her former position.

IX.

On January 15, 2012, the plaintiff filed a sexual discrimination charge with the Equal Employment Opportunity Commission (EEOC). As of the date of this complaint, the EEOC has taken no action except to inform the plaintiff that it would be unable to process her charge until November 2012.

WHEREFORE, the plaintiff prays that this Court grant a preliminary injunction requiring the defendant to reinstate the plaintiff to her former position pending the EEOC investigation of her charge.

Excerpt from Affidavit of Earl Shannon

(Page 20 of the record)

I am Earl Shannon, and I am the sole owner and manager of Shannon Development Company. My company has branch offices in four states and employs more than 150 persons. Clarence Dudley was a supervisor in my design department for six years, and he had always performed satisfactorily. I was unaware of the situation between Magaro and Dudley until February 20, 2012, when Magaro informed me of the true reasons for her resignation. At that point I questioned Dudley and promptly fired him when he confirmed Magaro's story. My purpose in firing Dudley was to make an example of him. I refuse to tolerate such immoral activity in my company.

(Page 21 of the record)

Since her discharge I have written a letter to Magaro informing her of my deep regret over the incident and her treatment by Dudley. Also, when Magaro approached me and informed me of her hardships, at two consecutive times, I offered to rehire her, but she would have had to start at a lower position than her previous one. I cannot reinstate her to her previous position because a new employee has filled that position, and it would be unfair to discharge that employee.

Excerpt from Deposition of Clarence Dudley

(Page 42 of the record)

Q: Do you admit that you committed the acts of harassment that the plaintiff enumerated in Paragraph 5 of her complaint?
A: I don't think it was harassment but I did them, yes.
Q: If it was not harassment, how would you classify such actions?
A: Mostly, I was just joking around and sometimes I was honestly showing my appreciation. For example, when I touched her and called her "my little girl," it happened like this: She would do a good job for me on something. I would pat her on the shoulder to show my appreciation for her good work. And I did call her "my little girl," but it was just another way of showing my appreciation.
Q: Did you always treat her like this?
A: No.
Q: Why did you treat her like this after September of 2011?
A: I guess I was just hurt and angry.
Q: Why? Could you explain further?
A: Well, when Magaro came to work we really hit it off, if you know what I mean. We started dating and things got serious between us. We became very intimate and we even talked of marriage. I was going to divorce my wife, of course, when all this was going on. Then all of a sudden, in September, she told me she wanted to break off the relationship. I felt hurt and used.

Trial Court Order

(Page 50 of the record)

This action was heard on the defendant's motion to dismiss for want of subject-matter jurisdiction. The parties filed documents in support of and in opposition to the motion.

The court being fully advised, it is ORDERED that the motion be granted, and that the plaintiff's complaint be and hereby is dismissed.

Excerpt from Trial Court's Memorandum Opinion

(Page 52 of the record)

A litigant filing suit based on Title VII must first follow certain procedures. Specifically, the litigant must present a "right to sue" letter to the court or satisfy the court that 180 days have expired since the filing of the charge with the Equal Employment Opportunity Commission. A federal district court lacks subject-matter jurisdiction unless one of these prerequisites is satisfied. The plaintiff has shown neither in this case. The waiting period was imposed by Congress and serves the beneficial function of resolving many claims of discrimination outside of court. This conciliation process must be protected. Therefore, this court refuses to allow a litigant to circumvent the statutory requirements.

The following federal court of appeals opinion is from this circuit:

Knowles v. Armond Tool & Die Co. (1978)

The appellant, Sheila Knowles, worked as a press operator in the appellee's plant for more than five years. Since she began her employment in January 1972, she was continually paid one dollar less per hour than the male employees with the same seniority who were doing the same work. She complained several times to the management that she should be paid the same wage, and these complaints eventually led to her discharge on April 18, 1977. She filed a sex discrimination complaint pursuant to Title VII of the Civil Rights Act of 1964 with the Equal Employment Opportunity Commission (EEOC) on April 30, 1977. On May 30, she wrote the EEOC inquiring about the status of her complaint. The Commission informed her that because it was backlogged it could not process her claim for at least six months. The company refused to reinstate her to her former position or give her any job at all, saying that she was a "liberal and a troublemaker" and that "we don't want this kind of person working for us." She is married and is the only source of support for her husband, who has been unemployed for two years. The appellant filed suit on June 9, 1977, seeking an injunction reinstating her to her former position. The district court dismissed the case for lack of subject-matter jurisdiction. We reverse.

Title VII of the Civil Rights Act of 1964 prohibits employers from discriminating against employees on the basis of sex. A Title VII plaintiff normally must satisfy the procedural provisions of the Act to be heard in federal court. First, the person must file a charge with the EEOC. Second, the complainant must receive a "right to sue" letter from the EEOC or permit 180 days to elapse from the filing of the charge. Although the congressional purpose of encouraging conciliation must be respected, it makes little sense to force a complainant to wait 180 days when the EEOC has indicated it will not attempt conciliation prior to the expiration of that period. This is especially true when, as here, it appears unlikely that the parties will voluntarily resolve their differences. In such situations, allowing the suit to proceed will undermine no congressional policy. In fact, a valuable congressional purpose—elimination of invidious discrimination based on sex—will be preserved. In this case, the company refused to attempt negotiation or other resolution of the problem. A district court has implied jurisdiction in such situations to issue a preliminary injunction ordering reinstatement of the plaintiff and preserving the *status quo* pending the EEOC investigation of the matter. Reversed.

The following principles should help you draft a persuasive Statement of Facts for a brief.

1. Describe the facts from your client's point of view.

The old adage that there are two sides to every story assumes a new meaning in advocacy. Show the court how your client saw the events unfold and describe them in a way that arouses sympathy for your client's position. This does not mean that you only include facts that favor your client, but rather that you help the court see the situation from your client's perspective. You should never omit or distort legally significant facts, whether they help or hurt your position, nor should you include any argument or argumentative statements.

In the Magaro case, your Statement of Facts should emphasize the injustice of her situation and her innocence in the matter. This characterization will make it easier for the court to decide in her favor. You might start by highlighting her early promotions with the company and then describe how intolerable her working conditions became, placing the supervisor and the company in as poor a light as possible. After showing that Magaro was forced to resign because of her supervisor's behavior, you should show the extreme hardship she is suffering as a result of the company's actions. You should detail that she has unsuccessfully tried to find other work, has exhausted her savings, and has two small children to support. You should also convey the idea that it would be insulting for her to accept a lesser position with the same company. This is how Magaro sees it, and this is how the court should see it.

2. Vividly describe favorable emotional facts and neutralize your opponent's emotional facts.

Facts that are emotionally favorable to your client are valuable persuasive tools when used effectively. The more vividly you describe these facts, the more likely a court will be sympathetic to your client.

Be careful, however, to avoid overstatement and emotionally charged language. An overwrought style detracts from the genuine emotional weight of your client's story. Present favorable emotional facts directly and clearly, but without hyperbole.

You cannot ignore unfavorable emotional facts, because the other side is sure to raise them. But you can blunt their force and reinforce your own credibility by raising them in your Statement of Facts. As discussed in Chapter 23 (Persuasive Writing), maintain a professional tone when discussing unfavorable emotional facts. Acknowledge them briefly and dispassionately. You can bleach hostile facts of their color by summarizing, explaining, paraphrasing, or otherwise minimizing them.

In Magaro's case, you should describe all the facts relating to Magaro's suffering and the conditions that prompted her resignation exactly as they occurred. Be as detailed and graphic as space will allow. Summarizing favorable facts will make your statement less persuasive. On the other hand, matter-of-factly summarizing the facts regarding Shannon's reasons for firing Dudley, and Magaro's relationship with Dudley will make your argument more persuasive. Be honest and state, for example, that Magaro and Dudley had a social relationship, but you need not and should not provide the details. While it is preferable to raise unfavorable emotional facts, you have no obligation to make your opponent's emotional appeals.

3. Organize your statement to emphasize favorable facts and de-emphasize unfavorable facts.

Emphasize, de-emphasize, and shade legally and emotionally significant facts by artfully arranging them in the Statement of Facts. This principle differs from the previous ones in that it concerns location rather than description of specific facts, and it is particularly important when your case involves few emotionally favorable facts.

Begin and end the Statement of Facts with favorable facts, burying unfavorable facts in the middle. The most helpful facts are often those that tend to show how wrong the other party's actions were, how right your client's actions were, and the significant consequences of these actions to your client. Placing these facts at the beginning will immediately invoke the court's sympathy toward your client. Placing facts that explain, mitigate, or justify your client's actions at the end of the statement is often, but not always, appropriate. This method of organization minimizes the force of unfavorable facts and ends the statement on a favorable note. Placing unfavorable facts in the middle makes them less likely to attract the reader's attention. Other ways to minimize unfavorable facts are to place them next to facts that favor or explain your client's position, or to hide them in a group of favorable facts. When possible, background facts should be placed where they will enhance the persuasiveness of your factual statement, but never where they would detract from its persuasiveness.

In your zeal to give facts the appropriate emphasis, be careful not to make your statement illogical or hard to follow. Your first priority is to tell a story the reader can understand.

In Magaro's case, you should begin with facts that show the degree of sexual harassment to which she was subjected. By showing how severe and inexcusable the harassment was, you place her supervisor and her employer in as poor a light as possible. Only then should you say that Magaro had been involved with her supervisor in a non-professional capacity. By placing the facts of the discrimination first, you minimize any importance the court might give the affair with her supervisor. In the same way, you should emphasize that Magaro had sought and been denied reinstatement to her former position before you state that Shannon had investigated the discriminatory treatment, fired Dudley, written Magaro an apology, and twice offered her another position. All of these facts are legally relevant, according to the federal court of appeals' opinion in *Knowles*, because they tend to prove that Magaro and Shannon might have reconciled their differences. These facts also tend to put Shannon in a favorable light, and you should make sure that the court sees these facts only in the shadow of the company's refusal to reinstate Magaro.

You should include the necessary background facts about the Shannon Company after you have described Shannon's refusal to reinstate Magaro. You can further minimize Shannon's honest-appearing intentions by showing that Magaro is the sole supporter of two children, that she has been unable to find other work, and that she has exhausted her savings. This will end your statement on a note of sympathy for Magaro and minimize Shannon's conciliatory actions by hiding them between two blocks of favorable facts.

Arranging the facts in this way highlights the unfair treatment and helplessness of Magaro and places the company and Dudley in an unfavorable light. A persuasive factual statement is especially important in Magaro's case because of the questionable strength of her legal position on the conciliation issue. In *Knowles*, the lack of effort to resolve the matter was much greater than here.

Now that you have seen the techniques for drafting a persuasive Statement of Facts, examine the following:

ANSWER A: The appellant, Iris Magaro, accepted a position with the appellee, Shannon Development Company, in August 2010. On January 30, 2012, she was forced to resign because of sexual harassment by her supervisor, Clarence Dudley. (R. at 6.) Dudley made obscene jokes and crude comments about personal parts of Magaro's anatomy to other male employees in Magaro's presence.

In addition, he often implied or suggested to others that he had engaged in sexual relations with Magaro, frequently touched Magaro, and called Magaro "my little girl." He also repeatedly asked her to have sexual relations with him during the lunch hour. This behavior, which was prompted by Magaro's refusal to continue seeing her supervisor socially, led to her resignation. (R. at 6, 42.) Magaro's work had always been satisfactory; in one year she had advanced from a Class IV to a Class II Secretary. (R. at 6.)

On January 15, 2012, Magaro filed a complaint with the Equal Employment Opportunity Commission (EEOC) alleging a violation of Title VII of the Civil Rights Act of 1964 due to her supervisor's sexual harassment of her at her job. On March 1, 2012, Magaro contacted the EEOC and was informed that her charge would not be processed until November 2012. (R. at 8.) Magaro twice asked the appellee to reinstate her to her former position. The appellee refused to reinstate her, although Earl Shannon, the company's sole owner, apologized for Dudley's actions. The appellee claimed that Magaro's former position was filled and offered Magaro a lower position at a lower rate of pay, which she refused. (R. at 8, 20–21.) Shannon Development Company has offices in four states and employs more than 150 people. Dudley was fired after Shannon learned of his activities. (R. at 20.)

Magaro, who is divorced and the sole provider for two children, is in dire financial straits. She has been unable to find work, has tried unsuccessfully to obtain credit, and has exhausted her meager savings. (R. at 8.) She filed suit in federal district court on March 15, 2012, alleging a violation of Title VII and seeking a preliminary injunction ordering Shannon to reinstate her to her former position pending the EEOC determination of her charge. (R. at 8.) The court held that it lacked jurisdiction and dismissed the case. (R. at 50.) Magaro appealed to this Court.

ANSWER B: The appellant, Iris Magaro, accepted a position with the Shannon Development Company in August 2010. Her supervisor was consistently satisfied with her work, and she advanced from a Class IV to a Class II secretary in a very short period of time. Shannon Development Company has offices in four states and employs more than 150 people. Earl Shannon is the sole owner of the company. Magaro filed a complaint on January 15, 2012, with the Equal Opportunity Employment Commission (EEOC), alleging sexual harassment on the part of her employer. She resigned from her job on January 30, 2012, because she could no longer tolerate the situation. Her supervisor was subjecting her to verbal and physical abuse. Magaro is currently in a precarious position. She twice requested reinstatement to her former position and both times Shannon refused her request. He offered her a lesser position, but she refused. After learning of Dudley's harassment of Magaro, Shannon fired him to make an example of him because Shannon stated he would not tolerate such immoral activity in his company. He also wrote a letter of apology to the appellant expressing his sympathies for Dudley's abuse of the appellant.

Magaro filed suit in federal district court on March 15, 2012, alleging a violation of Title VII and seeking a preliminary injunction ordering Shannon to reinstate her to her former position pending the EEOC determination of her complaint. The court held that it lacked jurisdiction and dismissed the case.

Answer A is better. It relates Magaro's story from her perspective in a concise and understandable way, and it references where the facts are located in the record. Answer A highlights the sexual harassment by vividly describing how Magaro was treated and closes on a sympathetic note by describing Magaro's desperate financial position. In addition, it neutralizes the legally significant and emotional facts that favor Shannon by placing them in the middle of the statement—after the facts concerning the harassment and Shannon's refusal to reinstate Magaro and before the facts of Magaro's financial condition. The emotional facts favoring Shannon's position, such as Magaro's relationship with Dudley, are mitigated by the bland description. Shannon's desire to eliminate immoral activity in the company and his reasons for firing Dudley are not detailed. Answer A, in short, has applied the three principles of perspective, description, and organization to make a forceful and persuasive factual statement.

Answer B, on the other hand, is not persuasive at all. Several introductory sentences include unimportant background facts instead of facts that advance Magaro's position. And Answer B concludes by showing the sincerity of Shannon's efforts to correct the problem. Facts showing the severity of sexual harassment and Magaro's financial condition are summarized and therefore used ineffectively. On the other hand, the facts showing Shannon's willingness to remedy the problem are described in detail placing Shannon in a more favorable light. In addition, Answer B includes no citations to the record and fails to include all the procedural facts.

EXERCISES

The following exercises should help you learn to write a persuasive Statement of Facts for a brief.

Exercise 25-A

Draft the Statement of Facts for the Shannon Development Company brief to the federal court of appeals.

Exercise 25-B

Ellen Brummer is appealing a trial court decision refusing to declare void a release and settlement agreement executed between her and Ivan Pearce. The following information is extracted from the transcript of the record.

Direct Examination of Ellen Brummer

(Page 41 of the record)

Q: Could you refresh the court's memory about how this matter started?

A: Sure. About two years ago, now, April 14, 2011, my daughter, Nancy, was hurt in a car accident. She was twelve at the time and already a very good violin player. Her tutor said that with normal development she might be able to play for a major symphony orchestra. Mr. Pearce's car collided with the one I was driving and Nancy was thrown against the back of the front seat. She was sitting in the back seat. Her face was severely lacerated, and the doctor said there was a chip fracture in her nasal bones. Well, we were able to settle with Mr. Pearce and his insurance company shortly after we filed a lawsuit. The agreement was for about $17,500, which we thought would cover the extent of her injuries.

Q: Then what happened?

A: We settled on August 18, 2011. Then in October, on the 14th, we had another doctor, Dr. Dion, perform an electroencephalogram on her. He said she had severe brain damage. We didn't know that when we signed the agreement.

Cross-Examination of Ellen Brummer

(Page 45 of the record)

Q: Did you read the settlement before you signed it?

A: Yes.

Q: You read it so that you would know what you were signing, is that correct?

A: Yes.

Q: Did you think you understood the settlement when you signed it?

A: Well, I thought so at the time, but I didn't think much about it.

Direct Examination of Dr. Francis Dion

(Pages 56–57 of the record)

Q: Could you describe what you found from your tests?

A: Well, to summarize, Nancy is suffering from a posttraumatic seizure disorder. Her brain was physically damaged in the accident. I will probably be able to control the disorder, but there is no question in my mind that she will require the care of a physician for seizures her entire life. I might add that she has impaired reading and hand-eye coordination and will require special help for her education.

Cross-Examination of Dr. Francis Dion

(Page 63 of the record)

Q: An electroencephalogram taken immediately after the accident would have disclosed this abnormality, would it not?

A: I think there is a reasonable medical probability of that, yes.

Release and Settlement Agreement between Ellen Brummer and Ivan Pearce

(Page 88 of the record)

FOR THE SOLE CONSIDERATION of Seventeen Thousand Five Hundred and 00/100 Dollars ($17,500.00), the receipt and sufficiency whereof is hereby acknowledged, the undersigned, Ellen Brummer, individually and as a parent and natural guardian of Nancy Brummer, a minor, hereby releases and forever discharges Ivan Pearce and Ajax Insurance Company, their heirs, executors, administrators, agents and assigns, and all other persons, firms or corporations liable or who might be liable, none of whom admit liability but all expressly deny any liability, from any and all claims, demands, damages, actions, causes of action, or suits of whatsoever kind or nature, and particularly on account of loss or damage to the property and on account of bodily injuries, known and unknown, and which have resulted or may in the future develop, sustained by Nancy Brummer, a minor, or arising out of damage or loss, direct or indirect, sustained by the undersigned in consequence of an automobile accident occurring on April 14, 2011.

Oral Opinion of Judge Miles Maloney

(Page 92 of the record)

Well, I think I've heard enough to decide this matter. The briefs of counsel and the testimony of the witnesses paint the picture pretty well. Because there is no controlling law in this state, I find the case of *Nokovich v. Myles Insurance Exchange* persuasive. That case says, in essence, that the words of a settlement agreement mean what they say. The agreement the parties signed is airtight, as near as I can tell. I sympathize with Ms. Brummer, but she signed the agreement. The defendant's motion for a directed verdict is granted.

The following cases are from different states:

Nokovich v. Myles Insurance Exchange (1982)

Helen Nokovich signed a settlement relieving Myles Insurance Exchange of "any and all claims" that "have resulted or may in the future develop" from injuries Nokovich sustained when she was struck by an automobile whose driver was insured with Myles. She now claims that she intended to release only her claim under the liability section of the insurance policy and not her claim under the section concerning medical payments. The trial court disagreed with her, and we affirm.

Settlement agreements are contracts and are governed by the law of contracts. When the language is clear and unambiguous, the test is not what the parties intended the contract to mean, but what a reasonable person would have thought the language meant. The language of the settlement here plainly bars all subsequent claims, and we so hold.

Brooks v. Pingel (1971)

Theodore Brooks learned of a severe brain injury suffered by his eight-year-old son several months after he had signed a settlement agreement with Keith Pingel holding Pingel "forever harmless" of any further claims arising from a fight between his son and Pingel's son. This injury is so severe that Brooks's son is now permanently paralyzed on his right side. The trial court refused to void the contract on the ground of mistake, but we reverse.

Settlements for personal injury claims are much different from normal contract matters. Brooks has shown here that neither party to the release knew about the hidden injury. This is not a case in which there is lack of knowledge of unexpected consequences of a known but apparently negligible injury. The parties knew that Brooks's son had been struck on the head and back, but they did not know about the brain injury. The release clause is therefore inapplicable.

For this exercise, you or your professor will decide which client you represent.

1. Assume you represent Brummer on appeal. Using the principles stated in this chapter, draft the Statement of Facts for Brummer's brief.
2. Assume you represent Pierce on appeal. Using the principles stated in this chapter, draft the Statement of Facts for Pierce's brief.

Exercise 25-C

This exercise is based on Exercise 22-B, pp. 333-35. For this exercise, you or your professor will decide which client you represent.

1. Assume you represent Tri-State on appeal. Using the principles stated in this chapter, draft the Statement of Facts for Tri-State's brief.

2. Assume you represent Hansen on appeal. Using the principles stated in this chapter, draft the Statement of Facts for Hansen's brief.

Briefs to a Trial Court

Lawyers submit briefs to a trial court to persuade the court to decide some aspect of litigation in their client's favor. They write briefs in a variety of contexts and at many stages of litigation. All briefs have one thing in common: their audience is the trial judge.

The principles for good legal writing set forth in Part C and the advocacy principles in Chapter 22 (Structure of an Argument) and Chapter 23 (Persuasive Writing) apply to briefs filed in all courts. The tactical considerations discussed in this chapter apply specifically to briefs written to a trial court. Although the examples in this chapter involve civil cases, the principles described also apply to criminal cases.

Briefs to a trial court fall into four categories:

1. Briefs submitted in connection with motions that are dispositive of some or all of the issues in the case. These briefs are generally filed either before or after discovery. Civil cases begin when the plaintiff files a complaint alleging that the defendant has done or is about to do something that violates the plaintiff's rights and requesting relief. If the defendant believes that the complaint is not based on a valid legal theory, that the court lacks personal jurisdiction, or that there is some other fundamental defect on the face of the complaint, it may file a motion to dismiss based on Rule 12(b) of the Federal Rules of Civil Procedure or the parallel state rule. The defendant will submit with this motion a "Memorandum of Law in Support of Motion to Dismiss," which is a brief explaining why the motion should be granted. (As noted in Chapter 21, a brief to a trial court, particularly one that supports or opposes a motion, is often titled a "Memorandum of Law" or "Memorandum of Points and Authorities.") The plaintiff will then file a brief opposing the motion. After reading the arguments of both parties, and perhaps hearing oral argument, the trial court will grant or deny the motion.

If the case is not dismissed, it proceeds to discovery. During this period, the Federal Rules of Civil Procedure and their counterpart state rules allow each side to learn more about the facts of the case. After discovery is complete, either side may file a motion for summary judgment (or partial summary judgment) under Rule 56 of the Federal Rules or the parallel state rule. A party filing a summary judgment motion claims that a trial is not necessary because the material facts are not in dispute and that she is entitled to judgment as a matter of law. Again, each party will file a brief supporting its position, and the judge will decide the motion.

2. Briefs submitted in connection with discovery disputes. The basic methods of discovery are written questions to opposing parties or potential witnesses (interrogatories), written requests to the other side to admit certain facts (requests for admission), written requests for the production of documents, and oral questions to potential witnesses (depositions). Trial courts expect that discovery will be conducted in a fair and responsible manner. Frequently, however, a party will claim that the other side is asking for privileged information, is making an overly burdensome request for the production of documents, is not responding to proper discovery requests, or is in some other way violating the rules governing discovery. If the dispute cannot be resolved by agreement, a party may file a motion for relief with the trial court, and each party will file a brief in support of its position on the motion.

3. Briefs submitted in connection with evidentiary or procedural disputes. Before or during trial, disputes often arise about whether particular evidence should be admitted, or how the case should proceed. When that happens, a party may file a motion and brief with the trial court to exclude the evidence in question or order other appropriate relief. The other side will then file a brief in opposition, and the judge will decide how to proceed.

4. Briefs submitted on the substantive issues in the case before and after trial. The trial is the main event in litigation. The plaintiff must present evidence to establish all of the facts necessary to prove its claims. The defendant must present evidence to rebut the plaintiff's proof or establish the facts necessary to support any affirmative defenses. The evidence presented generally consists of witnesses' testimony and documents. Some trials are finished in a few hours. Others continue for months. After all evidence has been received, the judge or jury (depending on the case) renders a decision.

Briefs may be submitted at the beginning and at the end of trials to provide the court with each party's view of the facts and how the issues should be resolved. A pre-trial brief defines the issues for the judge and demonstrates how the law applies to facts a party hopes to establish. In nonjury trials, a post-trial brief ties together all of the evidence (with citations to the record) and urges the court to reach certain conclusions based on the application of the law to that evidence. In jury trials, a post-trial brief is usually limited to presenting arguments that support a motion for judgment notwithstanding the verdict or a motion for a new trial.

Each type of brief has different requirements. Pre-trial and post-trial briefs in nonjury cases are generally the longest because they contain a full rendition of the relevant facts and complete discussion of the issues. Briefs written on discovery, procedural, or evidentiary issues, on the other hand, are usually short and generally include only an abbreviated discussion of the facts and law. Briefs on dispositive motions fall in the middle. They tend to be longer and more detailed than briefs on procedural or evidentiary issues, but shorter than pre-trial or post-trial briefs. The legal analysis, however, can be as detailed as the analysis in a pre-trial or post-trial brief, primarily because of the importance of these motions.

The following problem will help illustrate the basic tactical considerations that apply to briefs filed with trial courts:

Peter Miller was a passenger in a small private plane that crashed in a swamp in the state of West Florida. The pilot, Dennis Chisolm, who was Miller's friend, owned the plane. The crash was caused by a defective fuel pump that, because of Chisolm's neglect in maintaining the plane, was not corrected. Chisolm, who is 67 years old and retired, escaped with minor injuries. Miller suffered serious injuries, including permanent spinal damage that has left him confined to a wheelchair. Since the crash, Chisolm has become extremely depressed from guilt for having injured his friend. Psychiatric counseling has not helped.

Your firm represents Chisolm. Shortly after the crash, Miller settled with Chisolm for $1.5 million, the limit of Chisolm's insurance policy, plus one-half of Chisolm's life savings. He decided to settle based on your firm's advice that the settlement would end the matter as far as he was concerned and that he would have no further liability arising from the accident. Chisolm is living off his remaining savings of $500,000. He has no other source of income. Miller has recently commenced suit against Aaron Industries, the manufacturer of the engine and fuel pump, seeking $10 million in damages. Aaron has filed a third-party complaint against Chisolm, seeking contribution for any liability Aaron may have to Miller. Miller has offered to accept the same settlement from Aaron of $1.5 million, but Aaron has refused to discuss settlement at any figure. You have been requested to prepare a brief in support of a motion for summary judgment against Aaron's third-party complaint on the grounds of the "settlement bar" rule.

Your research has revealed these West Florida cases:

Sarasota Pools v. Buccaneer Resorts (W. Fla. 1989)

Paula Jensen, a guest at Buccaneer Resorts, was injured when the pool's diving board cracked, causing Jensen to strike the side of the swimming pool. The diving board had been improperly installed by the pool contractor, Sarasota Pools, and then improperly maintained by the resort. Jensen settled with Buccaneer for $75,000 and filed suit against Sarasota. She obtained a judgment of $50,000. Sarasota has brought this suit against the resort for contribution. The trial judge dismissed the complaint. The district court of appeals affirmed. We affirm.

Much disagreement exists in the various states and among the lower courts in this state concerning the rights of contribution between joint tortfeasors when the plaintiff has settled with one or more of them. Two leading views have emerged.

Under the first, all tortfeasors may recover against one another for each one's percentage of fault regardless of the settlement, but the settling tortfeasors receive credit against their liability for settlement funds paid to the plaintiff. Under the second, settling tortfeasors cannot recover from non-settling tortfeasors for contribution; neither can non-settling tortfeasors sue settling tortfeasors. The second view is called the "settlement bar" rule. A settling tortfeasor has literally "bought his peace" by settling and is entitled to freedom from any further litigation arising out of the incident. The plaintiff's claim against the non-settling tortfeasors is reduced to reflect the settlement proceeds received.

After much consideration we are persuaded that the settlement bar rule is the better alternative. We find this rule to be much easier to enforce and fairer because it provides more predictability so parties can know the consequences of their conduct in advance. We also find that the settlement bar rule has the salutary effect of encouraging settlements and avoiding litigation, which is much needed relief, given the congestion in our courts. Accordingly, we adopt the settlement bar rule for all contribution actions in this state.

Raseen v. Harrison Construction Co. (W. Fla. Dist. Ct. App. 2007)

Ahmad Raseen's house in Silver Lake, West Florida, collapsed during Hurricane Katrina. He sued Harrison Construction Co., the contractors that built the house, claiming that they were negligent in construction, and Designs for Living, the architects, claiming negligent design. Harrison and Designs cross-claimed against each other. After commencement of the trial, Raseen settled with Designs for $30,000. Designs then moved to dismiss Harrison's cross-claim against it. The trial court granted the motion on the basis of the court's decision in *Sarasota Pools v. Buccaneer Resorts*. The jury subsequently returned a $150,000 verdict against Harrison. Harrison appealed, claiming that the trial court erred in dismissing Designs. We agree.

Designs' settlement in this case appears grossly disproportionate to the liabilities involved. The record suggests that Designs is primarily liable for the collapse of the plaintiff's house. The court should hear the evidence, determine the percentage of liability each should bear for Raseen's damages, and enter judgment accordingly. The settlement bar rule thus far has been applied in this state only to personal injury cases, which present special difficulties in proving damages and assessing fault. We see no reason to extend it to a case such as that before us now involving only property damage. In addition, it is difficult to understand how any public policy of reducing litigation would be served because the trial had commenced when the settlement with Designs occurred. Reversed.

Sunshine Health Care, Inc. v. Rollins (W. Fla. Dist. Ct. App. 2000)

Dr. Alfred Rollins is licensed to practice medicine in this state. Sunshine is a health maintenance organization that employed the doctor. The genesis of this case was Rollins's treatment of Ina Rivkind at the Sunshine Clinic for a dog bite. There is little question that Dr. Rollins was negligent in treating the wound, which caused the bite to become infected. Ms. Rivkind subsequently was required to have a serious operation to cure the infection, which has left her with permanent disfiguring marks on her arm. Ms. Rivkind threatened to sue Dr. Rollins for malpractice and the clinic for negligence in hiring the doctor because there is a serious question about the doctor's credentials. In separate negotiations before any suit was filed, Ms. Rivkind agreed to a $90,000 settlement with the clinic and a $5,000 settlement with the doctor. The clinic brought this action against the doctor for contribution arising out of the settlement. The trial court dismissed. We affirm.

There is a strong policy in this state of upholding settlements and holding parties to the terms of their bargain. *Sarasota Pools v. Buccaneer Resorts*. This policy is especially strong where, as here, both wrongdoers have settled with the plaintiff. It makes no difference that each party had not known how much the other was settling for. They both received the benefit of their respective bargains—the end of litigation. The settlement bar rule precludes either of them from now reopening the dispute in an attempt to redistribute the liability.

You have also located a pertinent law review article, portions of which appear below:

Elizabeth B. Burns, *The Settlement Bar Rule: Tough Choices, Tough Answers,* 89 Tallahassee L. Rev. 135 (1993)

Great disagreement exists about the problem of contribution among joint tortfeasors when the plaintiff has settled with one or more of them. The question most often arises in cases of personal injury, but not exclusively so. Many instances of property damage occur in which two or more potential defendants share responsibility, making the rule just as applicable as in personal injury cases. In addition, many property damage cases involve personal injury or are cases in which an injury just as easily could have occurred. Although some cases have drawn a distinction between personal injury and property damage, applying certain rules of contribution in the former and not in the latter, there is no rational basis for doing so. The problem is highlighted in a case involving both personal injury and property damage. Is there any logic to applying two different rules to such a case? The answer is no.

. . .

Courts have taken a variety of approaches to the contribution question and each has merit. Each also requires courts to make tough choices among competing considerations. In *Sarasota Pools v. Buccaneer Resorts*, the West Florida Supreme Court selected the settlement bar rule as the law in West Florida. Under this rule a settling tortfeasor literally buys his peace with the world. He cannot be sued by anyone who may also be liable to the plaintiff but neither can he sue anyone. The incident and the litigation are over as far as a settling tortfeasor is concerned.

The settlement bar rule has much to commend it and serves many valuable policy goals. First, it is easy to enforce. The only legitimate question is whether there has been a *bona fide* settlement. If the settlement is collusive or a sham, the court can disregard it and rule on the contribution claim as if no settlement occurred. Second, the settlement bar rule is fairer to the settling tortfeasor in that it gives him the benefit of his bargain. Any settling tortfeasor certainly believes that once he settles with the plaintiff, his obligations with respect to the incident are at an end. The settlement bar rule enforces that expectation. Third, the settlement bar rule provides predictability and certainty in this troublesome area of the law. A defendant knows that he can either litigate or settle. If he chooses the latter he can do so with confidence that he will not later be drawn into any subsequent litigation arising out of the incident. Finally, and perhaps most importantly, the settlement bar rule encourages settlements, thus reducing litigation. This is perhaps the greatest policy consideration supporting the rule. The cost of litigation today is enormous and is a social cost that we all share. Significant resources are conserved every time a dispute is settled short of litigation. Because encouraging settlements is the primary policy underpinning the rule, there would seem to be no justification for applying the rule when that policy is not served.

. . .

The settlement bar rule does not come without cost. The major cost is potential unfairness to other non-settling defendants. The plaintiff is permitted to proceed against them for the full amount of the plaintiff's claim, less what the plaintiff received from the settling tortfeasor. The non-settling tortfeasor who is barred from contribution, therefore, may be held to a greater share of liability than he should legitimately have to bear. For example, if the plaintiff's damages are $100,000 and the plaintiff settles with Defendant A for $10,000, Defendant B would be fully liable for the balance of $90,000, even if Defendant B's share of responsibility for the plaintiff's damages may only be 20%.

The short answer to this dilemma, however, is that the non-settling tortfeasor could have settled but chose not to do so and instead risked litigating the claim. Presumably, the non-settling tortfeasor did this knowing he had no contribution rights. One would imagine that the lack of contribution rights would be a significant incentive for a non-settling tortfeasor to settle.

---

1. Focus more on the applicability of legal rules than on policy.

Trial judges must decide cases in accordance with the applicable legal rules. Therefore, they focus more on the application of the law to the cases before them than on the effect their decisions will have on subsequent cases or on the policies underlying the rules. Trial judges favor a straightforward application of the law to the facts before them.

Briefs to trial courts therefore should focus more on the applicable legal rules contained in statutes and cases than on the policies supporting them. Include the text of any relevant statute and the rules from cases on point, and explain their importance. If a judge believes a rule or a statute covers a particular issue, he will be less inclined to make the effort to follow an argument that policy considerations compel a different conclusion. Focusing on the legal rules is especially important in procedural, discovery, and evidentiary disputes, because these areas are comprehensively governed by codifications. This is not to say that policy has no place in a brief to a trial court. Policy is important to trial judges, especially when the law is unclear or in transition. But given a trial judge's caseload, policy generally takes a back seat to the hard legal rules.

Consider these drafts from the brief in support of the motion for summary judgment:

ANSWER A: The settlement bar rule precludes Aaron's contribution action against Chisolm. *See Sarasota Pools v. Buccaneer Resorts.* The facts in *Sarasota* are virtually identical to those presented here. In *Sarasota*, the plaintiff settled with one tortfeasor and then brought suit against the non-settlor and obtained a judgment. The non-settling tortfeasor then sued the settling tortfeasor for contribution. The supreme court, holding that a joint tortfeasor who settles is insulated from further liability, affirmed the trial court's dismissal of the non-settling tortfeasor's action. Similarly, this Court should dismiss Aaron's contribution action because Aaron, a non-settling tortfeasor, is seeking contribution from Chisolm, a settling tortfeasor. The *Sarasota* court reasoned that precluding these actions would encourage settlements, and that reasoning applies to this case.

ANSWER B: Aaron's third-party action against Chisolm should be precluded under *Sarasota Pools v. Buccaneer Resorts*, in which the court held that the settlement bar rule applied in a suit virtually identical to that presented here. Barring such an action in this case would serve the social good by encouraging settlements. It would also fulfill the parties' expectations that the amounts they have settled for represent their total liability. Finally, it would ease the burden of congestion in our courts. In *Sarasota*, the court recognized all of these policies.

Answer A is better. Answer A emphasizes the applicable rule and applies the rule in a straightforward manner to the facts. Answer A focuses primarily on the similarities between *Sarasota Pools* and our case, and only incidentally on policy.

Answer B provides only the barest explanation of the rule and how it applies to this case. The otherwise compelling effect of the case is therefore substantially diminished. The policy discussion, moreover, is much more extensive than the discussion concerning the applicability of *Sarasota Pools*. The applicability of the case will be of more interest to the trial judge than the underlying policies.

2. Emphasize that fairness requires a decision in your client's favor.

Some cases should not be filed at all, and some legal arguments are not plausible. In situations like this, where the law is clear and the trial court has no discretion, a brief based on the legal rules alone should be sufficient to prevail. The "issues" in such cases are actually givens, which are described in Chapter 6 (Identifying and Selecting Issues for Analysis). But when the adversary system is working properly, each party has a plausible legal basis for its position. The facts then assume great importance.

You should generally focus on the justice of a decision in your client's favor. To the extent possible, you must try to convince the trial judge that your client has behaved prudently and fairly, that the other party has behaved imprudently or unfairly, and that a decision for your client would work justice. You can accomplish this in a number of ways. One way is to show that your client is innocent of any wrongdoing or overreaching. Another is to demonstrate that your opponent took advantage of your client or otherwise engaged in some deceptive practice. A third is simply to point out the unfair negative consequences that a decision adverse to your client would have without an appropriate benefit to the winner.

Trial judges are close to the litigants, at least much closer than judges sitting on courts of appeals. Most people bring genuine disputes into the courtrooms, and many are very complex. Trial judges are acutely aware that each decision they make has real-world consequences and can drastically affect people's lives. Within the confines of the applicable legal rules, therefore, trial judges tend to strive for just or fair results. This principle should sound familiar to you; it is discussed as an important consideration in Chapter 9 (Reaching a Conclusion).

Using facts to your advantage requires subtlety. You must bring the facts to the court's attention without giving the impression that you are trying only to play on the judge's sympathy. Simply arguing that a result would be unjust, without legal grounds to support a decision in your client's favor, is likely to fail. The best approach is to weave facts favorable to your client into your legal argument.

Consider the following:

ANSWER A: Aaron's suit against Chisolm should be dismissed. Chisolm settled shortly after the incident for the limits of his insurance policy plus one-half of his retirement savings, acknowledging his responsibility and doing what he could to make the plaintiff whole. Aaron, however, has refused to discuss settlement with Miller, choosing instead to gamble by litigating a case it might lose and exposing itself to greater liability. Aaron should not now be permitted to involve Chisolm in such a gamble and risk eventually undoing Chisolm's settlement—particularly because Chisolm's insurance limits are exhausted, and his savings would be required to pay any judgment in favor of Aaron, which would leave Chisolm destitute. This is the very hardship the settlement bar rule was intended to remedy.

ANSWER B: Aaron's suit against Chisolm should be dismissed. The law precludes contribution from a settling tortfeasor. *Sarasota Pools v. Buccaneer Resorts*. Chisolm has settled. Aaron has not. Chisolm has "bought his peace" and is insulated from further liability.

ANSWER C: Aaron's suit against Chisolm should be dismissed. Chisolm is retired. The settlement with Miller exhausted the limits of Chisolm's insurance and consumed one-half of his life savings. Chisolm would be left destitute if he were now required to pay a judgment in favor of Aaron. Chisolm has suffered enough for injuring his friend. Allowing the suit to proceed would be grossly unfair and unjust because Chisolm may be required to pay twice, thereby penalizing Chisolm for settling his dispute with Miller.

Answer A is best because it emphasizes the facts favorable to Chisolm, and because it demonstrates to the court that justice would not be served by a decision in Aaron's favor. Answer A also weaves the facts into the legal context of the settlement bar rule to demonstrate that the rule was intended to address the very situation presented here.

Answer B makes no use of the facts favorable to Chisolm and is thus lifeless. It correctly states the legal rule but fails to animate it by placing the rule in the context of the human situation. Answer B also does not indicate how a decision in Chisolm's favor would work justice.

Answer C, while using many favorable facts, does so ineffectively. It does not artfully blend the facts with the legal principles. Answer C also goes too far in describing Chisolm's grief, which by itself is not compelling because it has no bearing on the legal rules. Chances are you have already lost if you must throw yourself upon the mercy of the court.

3. Be brief.

Trial judges usually have large caseloads, and the sheer volume of paper filed in connection with motions and trials is formidable. Most trial judges and their clerks therefore do not have the luxury of time to read, much less appreciate, extended arguments, no matter how sophisticated, well reasoned, or compelling they may be. Short, focused, and cogent briefs that make only the points necessary to prevail are more likely to be read, and the arguments in them more often understood and appreciated, than longer briefs that attempt to cover all points in great detail. Although trial courts generally place a word or page limit on briefs, you should resist the temptation to fill the number of pages permitted unless absolutely necessary. Your "brief" should be as brief as possible.

This principle requires you to make important judgments about what is important enough to include in the brief. Several considerations assist in exercising this judgment. First, if you have cases directly on point, discuss only those. A discussion of other cases that may be analogous is unnecessary and tends to muddle an otherwise clear presentation. Second, avoid extended discussions of policy. If the policy supporting a decision in your client's favor cannot be stated in one or two sentences, then it is probably too complex to be included in the brief. Third, keep your argument and analysis as straightforward and simple as possible. Try to include only arguments that compel the conclusion you seek, not ones that simply support it. Fourth, spend as little time as possible distinguishing the authority relied on by your opponent. This does not mean that you should ignore it. Rather, you should tell the court in the fewest possible words why it is inapplicable and then not discuss it again. Similarly, address one or two major flaws in your opponent's argument rather than every one. A trial court is more interested in understanding your position and learning your basic reasons for not accepting your opponent's position than it is in reading your conclusive refutation of every argument advanced by your opponent.

Consider the following:

ANSWER A: Aaron's third-party complaint against Chisolm should be dismissed. In *Sarasota Pools v. Buccaneer Resorts*, the West Florida Supreme Court adopted the settlement bar rule, which precludes any non-settling tortfeasor from recovering contribution from a settling tortfeasor. *Sarasota* is directly on point. In that case, the injured party settled with the resort and filed suit against the non-settling pool contractor. The court held that the settlement bar rule precluded such a suit. The court reasoned that its ruling would further the policies of encouraging settlements and providing settling wrongdoers with the benefit of a bargain. Other decisions are in accord. *E.g., Sunshine Health Care, Inc. v. Rollins.*

The facts of the present case are virtually identical. Chisolm settled with the plaintiff shortly after the incident. The plaintiff then sued Aaron, and Aaron brought this claim against Chisolm. The settlement bar rule should preclude Aaron's suit just as it did the claim against *Sarasota Pools.* The policy articulated in *Sarasota Pools* of encouraging settlements would be served by such a ruling.

Raseen v. Harrison Construction Co. is of little precedential value. In *Raseen,* the non-settling tortfeasor and the settling tortfeasor were both sued at the same time and cross-claimed against each other. Raseen settled with one defendant, and during trial the court dismissed the second defendant's cross-claim against the first. The court of appeals reversed, holding that the settlement bar rule did not require dismissal. *Raseen* is contrary to the West Florida Supreme Court's holding in *Sarasota Pools* and was therefore incorrectly decided. Moreover, *Raseen* is distinguishable because it did not involve personal injury and the settlement did not occur until after the trial had commenced. Accordingly, the public policy articulated in *Sarasota* of avoiding litigation through settlements would not be served.

ANSWER B: Aaron's third-party complaint against Chisolm should be dismissed. In *Sarasota Pools v. Buccaneer Resorts,* the injured plaintiff settled with one tortfeasor, then brought suit against the other. The court considered the competing rules concerning contribution among joint tortfeasors and concluded that it would adopt the settlement bar rule, which precludes an action for contribution against a settling tortfeasor. The court articulated several policies favoring this rule. The court observed that the rule was easier to enforce, fairer, and provided more predictability, allowing the parties to know the consequences of their conduct in advance. The court also held that the settlement bar rule has the salutary effect of encouraging settlements and avoiding litigation, providing much-needed relief from the congestion in our court system.

The court in *Sunshine Health Care, Inc. v. Rollins* reached a similar result. In that case an injured plaintiff settled with the medical clinic where she was negligently treated, as well as with the doctor. Both defendants settled prior to suit being filed. The clinic, which paid a much greater amount in settlement than the doctor, subsequently brought an action against the doctor for contribution. The court dismissed the action based on *Sarasota,* citing the strong policy of encouraging settlements and holding parties to the terms of their bargain.

The applicability of the settlement bar rule as the law in this state was recently recognized in a well-written article on contribution, Elizabeth B. Burns, *The Settlement Bar Rule: Tough Choices, Tough Answers,* 89 Tallahassee L. Rev. 135 (1993). The writer acknowledged the policies served by application of the rule, observing that the most important policy fostered by the rule is that of encouraging settlements.

The present case is analogous to *Sarasota* and *Rollins*. The plaintiff settled with Chisolm and then brought suit against Aaron. Aaron now attempts to seek contribution from Chisolm. The settlement bar rule as expressed in *Sarasota* and *Rollins* expressly precludes such an action.

Raseen v. Harrison Construction Co. is of little precedential value. In that case the plaintiff sued both the construction company and the architect, Designs for Living, for the collapse of the plaintiff's house as a result of Hurricane Katrina. Harrison and Designs cross-claimed against each other. The plaintiff settled with Designs for $30,000. Judgment was eventually obtained against Harrison Construction Co. in the amount of $150,000. The court of appeals reversed the trial court's dismissal of Designs, holding that the settlement bar rule did not preclude Harrison from continuing to litigate its cross-claim against Designs. The court held that the settlement bar rule applied only in personal injury cases and saw no reason to extend the doctrine to cases involving only property damage. The *Raseen* case directly conflicts with *Sarasota Pools* and therefore was incorrectly decided by the court. In any event, *Raseen* is distinguishable because it involved property damage only. Moreover, in *Raseen* both parties were named defendants and the trial was proceeding when one party settled. Accordingly, the policies of discouraging litigation and relieving congestion in the court system would not have been served.

Answer A is better because it says everything that needs to be said, and in fewer words. Answer A states the rule, tells the court that there is a case from the West Florida Supreme Court directly on point, summarizes the policy in one sentence, and concisely disposes of the opposing authority.

Answer B, while a complete and well-reasoned answer, is too long for a brief to a trial court. It needlessly discusses all of the cases in detail and thereby extends the discussion without adding force. This extended discussion actually detracts from the inherent forcefulness of the leading case on point. Similarly, the discussion of the law review article is unnecessary, especially because cases directly support Chisolm's position. References to law review articles in a brief to a trial court are unnecessary except when the law is unclear or no analogous authority can be found. Answer B also spends too much time discussing the policy considerations supporting the settlement bar rule and distinguishing the one case that tends to support Aaron's position. In short, although Answer B has the makings of a good appellate brief, it is simply too detailed for a brief to a trial court.

---

4. Write for the court.

Writing for the court involves two considerations: the local court rules and the temperament of the judge. Most federal district courts and many state trial courts have rules that dictate the form and content of briefs, including requirements for the font, margins, and maximum number of pages or words. Judges frequently have their own individual rules as well. As stated in Chapter 21 (Elements of a Brief), you must know and follow these rules. Many courts simply refuse to read briefs that do not comply with local rules.

Writing for the court also means tailoring your writing to the interests and temperament of the judge who will decide whether your client wins or loses. Judges strive to be impartial and to decide cases based on the applicable law and the relevant facts. Trial judges nonetheless have individual judicial philosophies and attitudes, which can influence their decisions.

A judge can become known as strict, lenient, a stickler, or policy oriented. You can learn about a particular judge's philosophies and attitudes from reading legal journals or other publications, from discussions with other attorneys, from personal observation of the judge in court, or from the judge's published opinions.

Your brief will be more effective if it is sensitive to the judge's particular leanings. For example, you would concentrate more on the wording of court rules for the stickler and focus more on policy for the policy-oriented judge. If the judge has written an opinion on or close to the issue in your case, you should refer to it in your brief.

Writing for the court requires a light touch—a judge who suspects that you are attempting to flatter or manipulate will not be persuaded. You therefore should always follow the basic principles of advocacy, writing, and analysis described in this book. Any brief, even a brief written with an individual judge in mind, must be able to stand on its own merits. Sometimes another judge is assigned to the case at the last minute and sometimes, particularly in busy courts, the judge's law clerk (not the judge) reads the briefs and recommends a decision. Judges may resent being perceived in a certain way, and sometimes they decide cases in ways that are inconsistent with their reputations. In addition, an appellate court can reverse the trial judge's decision if the decision has an inadequate factual or legal basis. If you know who the judge is, however, you can write with that audience in mind and shade your brief in ways that enhance the likelihood that your client will prevail.

Assume that the trial judge assigned to the case is an outspoken advocate of reducing congestion in the courts and is known to exert considerable pressure on litigants to settle. Consider the following:

ANSWER A: Aaron's third-party complaint against Chisolm should be dismissed. In *Sarasota Pools v. Buccaneer Resorts*, the West Florida Supreme Court held that a non-settling tortfeasor is precluded from asserting a claim for contribution against a settling tortfeasor. *Sarasota* is controlling here. Chisolm settled with the plaintiff and therefore is not liable to Aaron, the non-settling tortfeasor, for contribution.

Raseen v. Harrison Construction Co. is contrary to the holding in *Sarasota* and therefore should be disregarded as wrongly decided. In any event, *Raseen* is a different case because the plaintiff there sued both wrongdoers and it was only after trial commenced that the plaintiff settled with one wrongdoer.

ANSWER B: Aaron's third-party complaint against Chisolm should be dismissed. In *Sarasota Pools v. Buccaneer Resorts*, the court held that a non-settling tortfeasor is precluded from recovering contribution from a settling tortfeasor because of the settlement bar rule. The court stated that the settlement bar rule served the laudable public policy purpose of encouraging settlements, thereby easing congestion in the court system. The policy underlying the settlement bar rule fully supports its application here. Chisolm settled soon after the incident. If he had believed that a settlement would not insulate him from further liability, he might not have settled. Moreover, enforcing the settlement bar rule would preclude the additional action that Aaron, the non-settling tortfeasor, now seeks to bring against Chisolm.

Raseen v. Harrison Construction Co. is a very different case. In *Raseen* the plaintiff sued both wrongdoers, and it was only after trial commenced that the plaintiff settled with one. The policy of encouraging settlements and thereby avoiding litigation would not be served by imposing the settlement bar rule under those circumstances.

Answer B is better because it is tailored to the judge's disposition. Answer B emphasizes that application of the settlement bar rule would encourage settlements and help relieve court congestion, arguments to which the judge is known to be receptive. Answer A misses this opportunity to appeal to the judicial philosophy of the judge and is therefore inferior. Answer A would be appropriate if the judge were known for deciding cases strictly in accordance with the letter of the law, but it is not as persuasive to a judge who has already expressed a view on the policies underlying the relevant rule. Both answers communicate Chisolm's argument, and both are persuasive. Answer B, however, is more likely to impress the judge who has been assigned to this case.

EXERCISES

The following exercises should help you apply the principles outlined in this chapter.

Exercise 26-A

This exercise is based on the facts and cases in Exercise 7-B, pp. 110-11. Mary Quale has sued Dr. Farmer for the negligent death of her son. All of the facts in Exercise 7-B were brought out during discovery, and they are not in dispute. There is no dispute that Farmer was negligent. Farmer's lawyer has filed a motion for summary judgment with the trial court, claiming that Farmer's negligence did not proximately cause Andrew Quale's death.

For this exercise, you or your professor will decide which client you will represent.

1. Assume you represent Farmer. Write the argument portion of Farmer's brief supporting the motion for summary judgment, based on the principles contained in this chapter.

2. Assume you represent Quale. Write the argument portion of Quale's brief opposing the motion for summary judgment, based on the principles contained in this chapter.

Exercise 26-B

This exercise is based on the facts and cases in Exercise 8-D, pp. 127-28. The Metropolitan Social Welfare League filed a motion to intervene in the lawsuit brought by the Swift Land Development Corporation. For this exercise, you or your professor will decide which client you will represent. Focus only on the element of the intervention rule concerning adequacy of existing representation.

1. Assume you represent the League. Write the argument portion of the League's brief supporting its motion to intervene, based on the principles contained in this chapter.

2. Assume you represent the city. Write the argument portion of the city's brief opposing the motion to intervene, based on the principles contained in this chapter.

Exercise 26-C

Assume you are representing Aaron Industries. Prepare a detailed outline of the argument for the brief in opposition to the motion for summary judgment.

27 Briefs to an Appellate Court

Once the trial court enters a judgment, whether it is a judgment of dismissal, summary judgment, or judgment on the merits after a trial, the case is finished unless one of the parties appeals. To appeal a case, the party bringing the appeal (called the *appellant*) must allege that the trial court committed a specific reversible error. Some examples of trial court error include failing to admit certain evidence, misinterpreting or failing to follow a rule of procedure, not applying the proper legal rule, incorrectly interpreting the rule, or failing to properly instruct the jury. If there is conflicting evidence at trial, the appellant may also challenge the trial court's determination of which version of the facts is correct. Appeals challenging factual findings, however, are rarely successful.

Generally, a party may appeal only from a final judgment. The purpose of this rule is to prevent piecemeal appeals until a matter has finally been resolved by the trial court. Under very limited circumstances, appeals are permitted from orders entered by the trial court prior to the entry of final judgment. These are known as *interlocutory appeals.* In federal courts some interlocutory appeals are brought as of right, but most are heard only if the trial court, in its discretion, certifies the order for interlocutory appeal and the appellate court, in its discretion, decides to hear the appeal. Rules governing interlocutory appeals in state courts vary significantly. State rules of appellate procedure should always be consulted.

Litigants have a right of appeal from final judgments to an intermediate appellate court in the federal and in most state systems. The losing party in the intermediate appellate court has a right in some instances and in some states to appeal to the highest state court or, in the federal system, to the United States Supreme Court. In the over-whelming majority of appeals, however, the highest court has discretion whether to hear the case. If the court declines to hear the case, the decision of the intermediate appellate court is final.

A litigant appeals by filing a notice of appeal with the appellate court. The appellate court notifies the trial court that an appeal has been filed, and the trial court transmits the record to the reviewing court. Each party then submits a brief arguing why the trial court did or did not commit reversible error. Appellate briefs are subject to extensive rules concerning content, length, and style, which often differ from court to court. Each appellate court requires litigants to follow its own rules.

Appellate briefs tend to be longer and more formal than briefs to trial courts. The rules for style and advocacy, however, remain the same. Several tactical considerations should be kept in mind when preparing appellate briefs.

1. Focus on the claimed errors of the lower court.

A litigant cannot appeal simply because he does not like the trial court's decision. Nor can he prevail on appeal simply by demonstrating that the trial court made a mistake. An appellant must convince the appellate court that the trial court erred *and* that the error adversely affected the outcome of the case. The opposing party (usually called the *appellee*) attempts to persuade the appellate court that the trial court ruled correctly on all points claimed to be error and that, even if any rulings were erroneous, they were harmless because they did not affect the outcome of the trial.

Because an appellate court is responsible for correcting mistakes made by the trial court, you should frame your argument in terms of the error you or your opponent alleges the trial court made. The appellate court from the outset must fully appreciate the nature of the error and the procedural context in which it occurred.

Consider this principle in the context of the *Miller v. Aaron Industries* case from the previous chapter. You were unsuccessful in obtaining summary judgment in Chisolm's favor. The trial judge denied Chisolm's motion with the following opinion and order:

Third-party defendant Chisolm has filed a Motion for Summary Judgment with this Court, requesting an order of dismissal based on the settlement bar rule. Chisolm, relying on the decisions in *Sarasota Pools v. Buccaneer*

Resorts and *Sunshine Health Care, Inc. v. Rollins*, contends that he is entitled to dismissal because he settled with Miller, the plaintiff in this case.

The Court disagrees. *Sarasota* is a very different case and not controlling. In *Sarasota*, the plaintiff settled with one tortfeasor, Buccaneer Resorts, and then litigated against the other, Sarasota Pools, obtaining a judgment. Sarasota afterward brought suit against Buccaneer for contribution. The court concluded that the settlement bar rule should apply and affirmed the lower court's dismissal of the suit.

The decision in *Raseen v. Harrison Construction Co.* relied on by Aaron Industries, is more instructive. The court there refused to dismiss for two reasons. The first was that the trial had already commenced when the settlement with one tortfeasor occurred and that tortfeasor sought dismissal. Although the court attempted to distinguish *Sarasota* for the second reason that *Raseen* did not involve personal injury, the real distinction is in the timing.

That brings us to Chisolm's case. Suit is now pending between Miller and Aaron. The case appears unlikely to be settled. Granting Chisolm's motion will not conserve judicial resources or encourage settlements. This Court is not convinced that the rule even persuaded Chisolm to settle. The present case therefore is not the same as the wholly independent second trial sought by the non-settling tortfeasor in *Sarasota*. It is more like the situation in *Raseen*. IT IS THEREFORE ORDERED that third-party defendant Chisolm's Motion for Summary Judgment is hereby DENIED.

The trial judge subsequently certified his order for an immediate interlocutory appeal, and the court of appeals accepted the appeal. You are handling the appeal. Consider the following:

ANSWER A: The trial court should have dismissed Aaron's third-party complaint. In *Sarasota Pools v. Buccaneer Resorts*, the West Florida Supreme Court held that a settling tortfeasor is not liable to a non-settling tortfeasor in contribution. The *Sarasota* case is controlling here.

ANSWER B: The trial court erred in denying Chisolm's Motion for Summary Judgment. The West Florida Supreme Court held in *Sarasota Pools v. Buccaneer Resorts* that a settling tortfeasor is not liable in contribution to a non-settling tortfeasor. The *Sarasota* case is controlling, and the court's failure to follow the mandate of the supreme court is reversible error.

Answer B is better. Answer B firmly focuses the appellate court on the trial court's mistake, which Chisolm claims is reversible error. Answer B also correctly describes the procedural setting of the trial court's decision and thus provides a framework for the remainder of the argument.

Answer A has a thesis sentence and properly states the law, but it does not do so in terms of the alleged trial court error. Answer A is too abstract and thus lacks the persuasiveness of Answer B.

---

2. Base your argument on the appropriate standard of review.

Appellate courts exercise different standards of review, depending on the nature of the case and the judgment being appealed. The standard of review determines the appellate court's latitude to substitute its judgment for that of the trial court. Textbooks have been written on the subject of appellate standards of review, but the three most common standards of review are *"de novo,"* "clearly erroneous," and "abuse of discretion."

Generally, appellate courts exercise *de novo* review of all legal conclusions. This means the court is free to substitute its judgment for that of the trial court on legal conclusions without giving any deference to the trial court's decision or reasoning. Review of the trial court's findings of fact, however, is usually limited to a clearly erroneous or similarly restricted standard. This restricted review accords great deference to trial judges, who observe the witnesses first hand, to determine credibility when conflicting versions of the same event are introduced into evidence. In jury trials, it reflects the deference given to the jury in its role as the finder of fact.

Trial court decisions on non-dispositive matters, such as the admission or exclusion of evidence, are also subject to a fairly deferential standard of review. An appellate court usually will not disturb a trial court's decision on such issues unless it finds that the trial court abused its discretion. Moreover, appellate courts generally exercise *de novo* review of summary judgments and dismissals granted on the pleadings. The standard of review for such decisions varies from state to state, however, and you should always check the law in your jurisdiction to determine the applicable standard.

Frame your argument to an appellate court in terms of the appropriate standard of review. You should state the standard of review at the beginning of the brief and, if it furthers your argument, periodically remind the court of the appropriate standard. Many appellate courts require a statement of the applicable standard of review in the opening sections of the brief. Even when such a statement is not required, draft your main arguments with the applicable standard in mind.

Consider the following examples:

ANSWER A: The trial court erred in denying Chisolm's Motion for Summary Judgment. The standard of review of a grant or denial of summary judgment is *de novo*. This court therefore is not bound by the trial court's conclusions.

[Sections of argument omitted.]

The trial court incorrectly concluded that applying the settlement bar rule in this case would not conserve judicial resources or encourage settlements. To the contrary, Chisolm's dismissal from the case would constitute a significant savings of judicial energy. If Chisolm's action is not dismissed, the court must consider issues of Chisolm's negligence in order to apportion the liability between Chisolm and Aaron. The issue of Chisolm's negligence will inevitably extend the trial and consume greater resources than if it were not in question. Moreover, enforcement of the settlement bar rule may encourage Aaron to settle, because Aaron will know that if it loses, it must bear full responsibility for the plaintiff's damages without recourse against Chisolm. In any event, the policy is to encourage settlements in the first instance. Chisolm was encouraged to settle in the first instance on the belief that he would have no further liability. This Court should reject the trial court's conclusions to the contrary.

ANSWER B: The trial court erred in denying Chisolm's Motion for Summary Judgment.

[Sections of argument omitted.]

The trial court was wrong in concluding that no judicial savings would accrue by applying the settlement bar rule. Judicial economy would be served by trying only the issue of whether Aaron was negligent as opposed to the issues of whether Aaron and Chisolm were both negligent and the percentage of fault each should bear for Miller's damages. The court was also wrong in concluding that application of the settlement bar rule would not encourage settlements. The court's focus is too narrow. Enforcement of the policy encourages settlements generally even if it does not encourage Aaron to settle in the present case. Chisolm certainly was encouraged to settle based on the belief that he would have no further liability.

Answer A is better. Answer A states the standard of review at the outset and again as part of the argument when the trial court's findings are discussed. Answer A thus reminds the appellate court that it is considering a denial of a motion for summary judgment and that it may therefore freely substitute its judgment for that of the trial court.

Answer B, on the other hand, does not remind the court that its standard of review is *de novo*. Even though appellate judges are presumed to know the standard of review, the failure to expressly remind the court of its standard of review risks the appellate court's inadvertently or subconsciously giving undue weight to the trial court's conclusions.

---

3. Emphasize that a decision in your client's favor would further the policies underlying the law.

As explained in Chapter 9 (Reaching a Conclusion), Chapter 22 (Structure of an Argument), and Chapter 23 (Persuasive Writing), an argument that incorporates policy is stronger than one based solely on the law. Appellate briefs should contain a more extensive discussion of policy than trial court briefs. Appellate courts are responsible for providing guidance to the trial courts and for determining the direction of the law within their jurisdictions. Appellate judges, therefore, are very interested in understanding the policies that support the applicable legal rules and in determining whether those policies would be served by applying the rules to the case before them. This is especially true of the highest appellate court in a jurisdiction. A good appellate brief should clearly articulate the policies underlying the key legal rules and demonstrate how a decision in your client's favor would or would not further those policies.

Consider the following:

ANSWER A: The trial court erred in denying Chisolm's Motion for Summary Judgment. In *Sarasota Pools v. Buccaneer Resorts*, the West Florida Supreme Court adopted the settlement bar rule, which precludes any action for contribution by or against a settling tortfeasor. *Sarasota* is controlling. In that case, the injured party settled with the resort. She afterward filed suit against the non-settling pool contractor and obtained a judgment. The pool contractor then commenced an action for contribution against the resort. The court held that the settlement bar rule precluded such a suit. The court reasoned that such a ruling would further the policy of encouraging settlements and providing parties who settle with the benefit of their bargain. Other decisions are in accord. *E.g., Sunshine Health Care, Inc. v. Rollins*.

The facts of the present case are virtually identical. Chisolm settled with the plaintiff shortly after the incident. The plaintiff then sued Aaron, and Aaron brought this claim against Chisolm. The settlement bar rule should preclude Aaron's suit just as it did the claim in *Sarasota Pools*. The policy articulated in *Sarasota Pools* of encouraging settlements would be served by such a ruling.

ANSWER B: The trial court erred in denying Chisolm's Motion for Summary Judgment. In *Sarasota Pools v. Buccaneer Resorts*, the West Florida Supreme Court adopted the settlement bar rule, which precludes any action for contribution by or against a settling tortfeasor. *Sarasota* is controlling. In that case, the injured party settled with the resort and filed suit against the non-settling pool contractor, obtaining a judgment. The pool contractor then commenced an action for contribution against the resort. The court held that the settlement bar rule precluded such a suit. Other decisions are in accord. *E.g., Sunshine Health Care, Inc. v. Rollins*.

The court in *Sarasota* articulated several policies fostered by the settlement bar rule. The court stated that the rule was much easier to enforce and much fairer than the alternatives. The court further observed that the rule provided more predictability, allowing the parties to know the consequences of their conduct in advance. The court also said that the settlement bar rule had the salutary effect of encouraging settlements and providing much-needed relief for the congestion in our court system. Legal commentators have agreed. In her article, *The Settlement Bar Rule: Tough Choices, Tough Answers,* 89 Tallahassee L. Rev. 135 (1993), Elizabeth B. Burns pointed to the rule's tendency to encourage settlements as its single most beneficial policy.

The facts of the present case are virtually identical to those in *Sarasota*. Chisolm settled with the plaintiff shortly after the incident. The plaintiff then sued Aaron, and Aaron brought this claim against Chisolm. The settlement bar rule should preclude Aaron's suit just as it did the claim in *Sarasota*.

The policies underlying the settlement bar rule would be well served by its application to this case. Chisolm would not have settled but for the belief that doing so would end his liability. The trial court erred in concluding that the rule did not encourage Chisolm's settlement. This Court exercises plenary review in this manner and should disregard the trial court's erroneous determination. Moreover, to look at the current situation and determine whether the policy of encouraging settlements would be served is myopic. The proper question is whether the settlement bar rule encourages settlements generally, not whether the rule should be disregarded after one tortfeasor settles if the remaining tortfeasors refuse to settle. The policy of conserving judicial resources would also be served by applying the settlement bar rule to this case. The difficult issue of apportionment of fault between Aaron and Chisolm would be removed from the case, leaving for trial only the issue of Aaron's negligence.

Answer B is better. It effectively explains the key policies underlying the rule and demonstrates that the supreme court and a legal commentator have recognized the rule. Answer B then demonstrates how application of the rule to Chisolm's case would further the policies underlying the rule. It fleshes out the bare legal rules, making the argument much more compelling and significant to an appellate judge.

Answer A should look familiar. It is similar to the better answer under the third principle in Chapter 26 (Briefs to a Trial Court). Answer A is good for a trial brief but deficient for an appellate brief because it includes no meaningful discussion of policy. While Answer A correctly states the rules of law and mentions the supporting policy, it does not explain the underlying policy considerations and demonstrate how they would be served by applying the settlement bar rule to Chisholm's case.

---

4. Explain how a decision in your client's favor would foster harmony or consistency in the law.

Appellate courts are concerned with the orderly development of the law. They want to ensure that the policies supporting the rules are being served and that their decision will not create disharmony in the law or set bad precedent. The most convincing briefs therefore demonstrate that the decision sought is consistent with previous decisions and that it would foster, rather than discourage, a rational development of the law.

Consider the following:

ANSWER A: The West Florida Supreme Court's decision in *Sarasota Pools v. Buccaneer Resorts* is controlling.
[Argument on law and policy omitted.]
A decision reversing the trial court would therefore be in complete accord with *Sarasota* and *Rollins*. To the extent that *Raseen* was cor-

rectly decided, it is not to the contrary. The trial in *Raseen* had already commenced when the settlement was reached. The public policies of encouraging settlements and conserving judicial resources would not have been furthered by application of the settlement bar rule in that case.

ANSWER B: The West Florida Supreme Court's decision in *Sarasota Pools v. Buccaneer Resorts* is controlling.
    [Argument on law and policy omitted.]
    The trial court's decision therefore should be reversed. Its decision is contrary to *Sarasota* and *Rollins*. For the reasons given, *Raseen* was incorrectly decided and should be disregarded.

Answer A is preferable because it clearly articulates how a decision in Chisolm's favor would be consistent with the uniformity or harmony in this area of the law. Even the troublesome *Raseen* decision is harmonized. Answer B is little more than a summary. It fails to demonstrate how a decision in Chisolm's favor would contribute to the orderly development of the law. It does not attempt to harmonize the *Raseen* decision, leaving the court to choose between two divergent lines of authority. Answer A therefore is more persuasive than Answer B.

EXERCISES

The following exercises should help you learn to apply these principles.

Exercise 27-A

This exercise is based on the facts and cases in Exercise 7-C, pp. 111-13. Bradley Greenleaf brought a nuisance action against Peter Elliot. The case was tried before Judge Claudia Shea. All of the facts stated in the exercise are included in the record of the trial. Afterward, Judge Shea delivered an opinion from the bench. The transcript of that opinion is as follows:

> I find that Greenleaf was damaged sufficiently for a nuisance action, but that his case has one fatal flaw. The law in this state does not give Greenleaf a legal right to the free flow of light. Without such a right, I must decide this case in favor of Peter Elliot.

For this exercise, you or your professor will choose which client you represent.

1. Assume you represent Greenleaf. Draft the argument portion of Greenleaf's brief on appeal, using the principles contained in this chapter.

2. Assume you represent Elliot. Draft the argument portion of Elliot's brief on appeal, using the principles contained in this chapter.

Exercise 27-B

Assume you are the lawyer representing Aaron Industries. Prepare a detailed outline of the argument for the appellate brief supporting the trial court's decision on the motion for summary judgment.

28 Preparing and Presenting an Oral Argument

When you have filed your brief with a trial or appellate court, you may not have finished presenting your case. Trial and appellate courts often schedule a time when the attorneys for both sides appear in person to argue their case and answer questions from the court. This is called *oral argument*.

Oral argument gives the attorneys one last chance to present their arguments (which may be presented differently from the way they were presented in the briefs), address arguments advanced by their opponents, and focus the court on why their client should prevail. It also gives the judge or judges the opportunity to ask questions that the briefs did not fully answer. These questions may be on minor points or they may go to the heart of the case, such as when the court is inclined to decide the matter in your client's favor but requires clarification on a particular issue before it can do so.

Oral argument is "a Socratic dialogue" between the bench and the bar.[1] In that dialogue, you must highlight key aspects of your case, answer the court's questions about your position, and respond to your opponent's arguments. Oral argument is not simply an oral presentation of your brief—nor should it be. In most cases, the court will already have read your brief, and you will not have time to raise and argue every point you have included in your brief. In fact, the Federal Rules of Appellate Procedure state that "[c]ounsel must not read at length from briefs, records, or authorities."[2] Nor is oral argument simply a

---

1. Justice William Brennan, *Harvard Law School Occasional Pamphlet* No. 9, 23 (1967).

2. Fed. R. App. P. 34(c).

debate in which each side is given the opportunity to present a position and rebut opposing arguments. Oral argument is first and foremost a conversation between the lawyers and the court.

Does oral argument matter? By the time oral argument takes place, judges often have already reached a tentative decision about which side should prevail based on the briefs. Still, former United States Chief Justice William Rehnquist captured the experience of many judges when he wrote that "in a significant minority of the cases in which I have heard oral argument, I have left the bench feeling different about the case than I did when I came on the bench."[3] You can also lose a case in oral argument that you might otherwise have won, particularly if you are not well prepared. Many courts are deciding an increasing number of cases on the briefs, in part to reduce workload and in part to limit oral argument to those cases where it might truly matter. When a court does schedule oral argument, you should assume the court is interested in hearing from you and that your argument could make a difference in the outcome.

We include a chapter on oral argument in a legal writing book because oral and written advocacy are linked. Oral argument is an extension of the brief, and many of the principles that apply to effective legal writing apply equally to effective oral advocacy. The better your brief, the more focused and compelling your oral argument is likely to be.

This chapter is divided into two parts. The first part addresses your preparation for oral argument. Just as a well-written memorandum or brief conceals the hard work of preparing it, a strong oral argument requires thoughtful preparation. The second part focuses on presenting the oral argument.

This chapter continues using the Chisolm problem from Chapters 26 (Briefs to a Trial Court) and 27 (Briefs to an Appellate Court). The trial court denied the motion for summary judgment filed on behalf of your client, Dennis Chisolm. The West Florida Court of Appeals has scheduled oral argument in your appeal of that decision.

Preparing for Oral Argument

The goal of oral argument is to present a coherent and compelling explanation of the case, your client's position, and the reasons why your client should prevail—all within the limited time allowed by the court. You also need to be prepared to respond to whatever questions the judges may ask. In that respect, the key to successful oral argument is mental and oral agility.

---

3. WILLIAM H. REHNQUIST, THE SUPREME COURT: HOW IT WAS, HOW IT IS 276 (1987).

The following steps provide a way to prepare your presentation and answer whatever questions are asked.

1. Know your case.

Oral argument normally occurs some weeks or even months after you have submitted your brief. You knew your case well when you submitted the brief; now you have to relearn it. A well-prepared oral argument requires you to do more than just know your case. You must be fully conversant with the facts and the relevant law and have a complete understanding of your argument's strengths and weaknesses.

Begin by rereading your brief. Then reread the relevant cases and your research notes and update your research to make sure there are no new developments in either the facts or the law that change your argument or that of your opponent. Reread your opponent's brief as well to ensure you fully understand the other side's arguments. If your opponent cited cases, statutes, or other authority you did not cite, read that authority. Make sure you can state where in the record or trial court pleadings all legally significant facts can be found.

2. Know your audience.

Because oral argument is essentially a dialogue with the court, its success depends on how well you communicate with the court. One of the most effective ways to learn about your audience is by observing oral arguments in other cases before your judge or court. You will learn a great deal about particular judges—their perspective, demeanor, which issues they consider important, and how many and what type of questions they ask. You can also learn a great deal about courtroom etiquette and how lawyers are expected to behave.

As explained in Chapters 26 and 27, how you present the facts, law, and policy in a brief depends on your audience. A trial court will focus more on the facts of the case and the law as it has been interpreted by the appellate courts. An appellate court will review the case in the context of the standard of review, will be concerned with the claimed errors of the lower court, and will be more open to policy arguments and persuasive authority. These considerations apply equally in determining which aspects of the case are most important to highlight in the limited time available for oral argument and which should be left to your brief.

It is also important to understand the rules that govern oral argument before the court in which you will appear. Court rules regulate many aspects of oral argument, including whether oral argument must be requested in writing, how much time you will be allowed, and even where you should sit in the courtroom. Knowing and following these rules will minimize distractions from the merits of your case and increase your credibility with the court. Finally, you will be more effective if you know the resources available to the court. A judge with several clerks and a smaller docket of cases is likely to be better prepared for oral argument than a judge with a larger docket of cases and only one clerk or none at all.

> The Chisolm case is an appeal to an intermediate appellate court, the West Florida Court of Appeals. This court hears appeals of trial court decisions, but it is subordinate to the West Florida Supreme Court. In this case, two of the key decisions are by the Court of Appeals, and one is by the Supreme Court. The Court of Appeals will be inclined to decide your case within the framework of all three cases, and is unlikely to be persuaded by an argument that *Raseen*, a Court of Appeals decision, should be overruled.

3. Plan within the court's time limit for oral argument.

Most courts impose some time limit on oral argument. In the federal appellate courts, "[t]he clerk must advise all parties whether oral argument will be scheduled, and, if so, the date, time, and place for it, and the time allowed for each side."[4] Thirty minutes per side is common, but the court may shorten or extend that time based on the court's view of the number and complexity of the issues presented. Time limits vary in the state appellate courts. In Minnesota, for example, the appellant is given thirty to thirty-five minutes, and the appellee twenty to twenty-five minutes.[5] Oral argument on trial court motions in federal and state trial courts is often determined by the local rules of the court in question, the individual judge, or both. When allowed, oral arguments on a motion may be as short as five or ten minutes per side. Given this lack of uniformity, you should consult with the court and with experienced practitioners to determine what to expect if no published time limits exist.

Prepare your oral presentation based on the amount of time you will be allowed. The time limit is not a guideline that you can ignore because you think you have something important yet to say. You usually cannot exceed the limit without the court's permission, at least without risking the court's ire. Plan to use no more than one-half to two-thirds of your allotted time for your argument, leaving the balance

---

4. Fed. R. App. P. 34(b).

5. Minn. R. Civ. App. P. 134.03.

of time for responding to the court's questions and following up on the issues the court considers important. Remember that the purpose of oral argument is to engage in a dialogue with the judges who will decide your client's fate, not to rush through a prepared script.

In this case, the rules for the West Florida Court of Appeals state: "The time for argument of cases shall be limited to not more than 30 minutes for each side." You should therefore prepare to speak for fifteen to twenty minutes, not including questions. However, if both Aaron Industries and Peter Miller are opposing your appeal of the trial court's decision, they would have to divide their thirty minutes between them.

4. Develop a theme when appropriate.

A theme is the central "truth" of your case—the point of view on which the case rests. It is a point around which to organize the entire argument, a point to which each argument you raise can return, and the idea that ties everything together. Not all cases lend themselves to a theme. When a motion or appeal involves a straightforward application of the controlling law to undisputed facts, or the issue is otherwise uncomplicated and one-sided, a theme will contribute little to the argument. But when a case or issue is more complex, and policy is likely to play a role in the decision, a theme can be a highly persuasive tool.

Your theme should be both simple and compelling, and it may have a logical, moral, or emotional basis. A theme might focus, for example, on how your client has been treated unjustly, how public policy compels a decision in your client's favor, how your opponent is seeking an unfair advantage or undeserved reward, or simply how the law is clear and not open to interpretation.

A theme should allow the court to see the case from your client's perspective, to understand why your client should prevail, and to allow the judge to tie all of the pieces of your argument together. In that respect, developing a theme is like solving the Rubik's cube puzzle, which requires you to turn the differently colored squares in various ways until all of the squares on each side are of the same color. In preparing for oral argument, you need to turn the different sides of your argument in various ways until you find a compelling way to succinctly state your client's position that captures and accounts for all sides of the argument.

Developing your theme refines your understanding of the case. It may evolve from a compelling phrase or visual image and leave the judge with a mental picture or catchphrase that summarizes your argument. But be careful not to be too creative or too cute. Do not risk offending the court by seeming to trivialize the issues. Also, think defensively; make sure your opponent cannot turn your theme against you.

One approach to developing a theme is to begin by writing your case in twenty-five words or less, exactly as you would explain why your client should win during oral argument. Begin by writing down all the phrases you think describe the important aspects of your facts, the law, or the underlying policy. Then evaluate, omit those that are less significant, combine similar concepts, and refine those that capture the essential ideas. When you are finished, cut it down to ten or fewer words. Another approach is to draw a picture or write a newspaper headline that captures the essence of your case. Try a variety of approaches to help you to identify and focus on the essential "truth" of your case.

> **Consider several possible themes for an oral argument to the court of appeals in the Chisolm case:**
>
> ANSWER A: Parties who settle should not be used as insurance against a potential damage award by tortfeasors who choose to "roll the dice" in litigation.
>
> ANSWER B: Allowing Aaron Industries to prevail is like handing them a winning lottery ticket.
>
> ANSWER C: The settlement bar rule is a "win" for both parties here, since Chisolm gets his peace of mind and Aaron Industries knows it will be solely liable if it "rolls the dice."
>
> ANSWER D: Chisolm did the right thing; he has "bought his peace."

Answer D is the best example of a theme. It is direct and straightforward and states a principle that few people would find fault with, yet places it in the context of this case. The phrase "did the right thing" can be used to tie every argument together, whether focused on the positive outcome of favoring Chisolm or the negative aspects of a decision in favor of Aaron Industries. Since it states a positive idea that few people could disagree with, it is likely to appeal to the court. It also directly ties to the underlying policy previously recognized by the court that settling tortfeasors have "bought their peace."

Answer A does not have the flexibility of Answer D. While it incorporates a familiar phrase ("roll the dice") it focuses only on the negative aspect of your argument—the unfairness of allowing non-settling tortfeasors to force parties who have already settled to contribute even more. It is also too abstract because it is not related to your facts. Answer B uses a visual image—a lottery ticket—but oversimplifies the argument and seems to trivialize it. Answer C, while positive and incorporating a sports analogy, does not really define the issue in any meaningful way from your perspective.

---

5. Select for presentation your strongest and most essential arguments.

You must distill your case down to a relatively small number of legal arguments to present—ordinarily no more than two or three. These arguments must directly support your theme, allowing the court to follow your logic and reasoning without effort or confusion. If the arguments you have determined to be the strongest or most significant cannot be related to your theme, you need to reconsider the theme.

The following considerations are important in selecting which arguments to include.

- *Arguments regarding issues on which the case is likely to turn.* Most cases have one or more fundamental issues that determine the outcome. These are issues on which you must prevail to win. Such issues should be addressed in your argument.
- *The strongest and most significant arguments.* The principles discussed in Chapter 22 (Structure of an Argument) are also relevant in selecting which arguments to include in oral argument. The strongest arguments are those most likely to persuade the court. From all of the strong arguments you included in your brief, use the strongest in oral argument. The most significant arguments are those that will help your client the most. When several arguments are of equal strength, it is usually better to choose the most significant one. The examples in Chapter 22 illustrate each type of argument.
- *Arguments and authority not addressed in your brief.* Sometimes arguments will arise or be presented that you have not yet had an opportunity to address. These may be new arguments or new authority raised in a reply brief or they may simply be based on cases that were decided after your brief was filed. If the arguments

are important, they should be considered for presentation at oral argument.

Next, you must determine the order in which to present them. Since the court will likely ask questions, present your best and most essential arguments first to make sure you do not run out of time to discuss them all. Just as presenting the strongest arguments first sets the tone for your brief, presenting the most important and compelling arguments first sets a strong and forceful tone for the rest of your oral argument.

The process for selecting and prioritizing arguments for inclusion in your oral argument can be illustrated by examining several from the Chisolm case. Consider the following:

ARGUMENT 1: Fairness requires that the settlement bar rule be applied in order to give Chisolm the benefit of his bargain. Chisolm has compensated Miller by settling for $1.5 million. Aaron Industries, on the other hand, refuses to discuss any settlement and is attempting to use Chisolm's remaining resources as insurance against a potential damage award if the case is tried. In *Sarasota Pools*, the court recognized the settlement bar rule encourages settlement by protecting tortfeasors who have "bought their peace." Applying the rule here is not only fair but furthers this policy.

ARGUMENT 2: Chisolm's settlement with Miller is not a sham nor will dismissing Chisolm as a codefendant leave Aaron Industries with a disproportionate financial burden. First, even though Miller and Chisolm are friends, nothing indicates collusion in their settlement. Second, Miller has offered to settle with Aaron Industries for the same amount he received from Chisolm, thus placing no greater liability on Aaron Industries unless it proceeds with litigation.

ARGUMENT 3: The trial court erred in not applying the rule from *Sarasota Pools* that a settling tortfeasor cannot be sued for contribution by non-settling tortfeasors. The court recognized that the settlement bar rule conserves judicial resources by encouraging plaintiffs to settle; they have thus "bought their peace" and are free from future litigation. Under *Sarasota Pools*, Chisolm has bought his peace and should not be subjected to further litigation.

ARGUMENT 4: The trial court erred in applying *Raseen* here, since it was an action for property damage while this case involves damages for personal injury.

Argument 1 portrays Chisolm as a responsible party who has compensated Miller for the harm he caused, while emphasizing Aaron Industries' refusal to do so. While these compelling facts highlight the fairness of Chisolm's position, the argument also incorporates both a legal and a policy foundation for applying the settlement bar rule. As noted in Chapter 27, an appellate court is concerned with creating precedent and will often be receptive to a policy argument, unlike a trial court that will focus more on applying the law. Since Argument 1 incorporates compelling facts, law, and policy, it would be a strong issue that you might want to present first.

Argument 2 also defines the case in terms of fairness and incorporates facts sympathetic to Chisolm, but its tone is defensive. Instead of asserting Chisolm's position, it attacks an argument Aaron Industries might raise. Neither of the points it addresses has been addressed in the precedent cases. Sham settlements were addressed in the law review article but have not been addressed by the court and disproportionate damage awards did not concern the court in *Sunshine Health Care*. Thus, since Argument 2 is weaker you should be prepared to address it, but only if your opponent or the court raises it.

Argument 3 asserts that the trial court improperly ignored *Sarasota Pools*. It is a strong argument both because it relies on precedent and because it incorporates policy. The relevant facts are similar to those used in Argument 1, but it focuses on precedent and the error by the trial court. It should be one of the issues included in your oral argument.

Argument 4, while accurately distinguishing *Raseen* on a point the court specifically addressed, is not very strong. Even the trial court noted this distinction but did not rely on it. Thus, there is little reason to include it in your argument, but you should be prepared to answer a question on this issue should it arise.

---

6. Plan and practice your argument.

Your overarching goal at oral argument is to present your main arguments and respond to questions in the time allocated. To accomplish this, you will find it helpful to prepare an outline that includes the key points under each issue. You should also have an annotated list of relevant cases and statutes that you intend to refer to in your argument or that you may be questioned about. The cases should be listed alphabetically and the annotations should include the citation and a brief summary of the facts and holding. One way to organize this material is to write your argument outline on the right side of a manila folder and tape note cards containing your annotated list of authorities on the left side.

Prepare to be flexible. You may intend to discuss points A, B, and C, in that order, but the court may be interested only in B and C. You may be asked so many questions about B and C that you never get a chance to address A, or at least not in any detail. An outline helps you adapt your argument to cover the points that interest the judges by providing a quick reference to your main points under each argument. This will help you navigate through your argument while minimizing the chances you will inadvertently omit a key point.

Sometimes you will address a "hot bench"—a court that asks a lot of questions. At other times, you will have a "cold bench"—a court that asks few questions. One approach is to prepare a shorter outline that has all your critical arguments (for the hot bench) and a longer outline (for the cold bench).

The court may or may not want you to present the facts at the beginning of your argument, and you may not know the court's preference until you start to speak. Although many judges do not want to hear a recitation of the facts—they have read the briefs and are acquainted with the facts—you should find a way to focus the court's attention not only on the legally significant facts, but also on the facts that most compellingly support a decision in your client's favor. There are two possible approaches to use:

1. Be prepared to give a statement of facts. Even if the court does not want a formal statement of the facts, your preparation will ensure the relevant facts are at your disposal and can be used when the opportunity arises.
2. Be prepared to weave the key facts into the appropriate points of your argument. If you presented the facts at the beginning of the argument, referring to them later will remind the court of those that are most important to your side. If you did not present the facts initially, referring to them throughout the argument will establish that the facts of the case support a decision in your client's favor.

Be ready for questions. The best way to answer questions effectively during oral argument is to anticipate those questions beforehand. Make a list of the questions you would ask if you were the judge. Put yourself in your opponent's position and think of the questions she would ask you during oral argument if she had the chance. These generally will probe the weakest parts of your case or focus on issues that have not been addressed in the briefs. Then write your answer to each question and practice stating the answer out loud. Your answers should be honest about the law and facts, while still making the strongest argument that you can for your client. You will not likely think of all significant questions initially; add to your list as questions occur to you and prepare answers to them.

> In the Chisolm case, you are asking a court of appeals to reverse the trial court's decision. The court will likely ask questions about the trial court's reasoning, so review the trial court's order and be prepared to respond to specific questions about it. Because collusion in the original settlement between Chisolm and Miller would provide a compelling reason not to apply the settlement bar rule, your opponent will likely raise this issue and the court may have questions about it. What other questions would you expect?

Practice your argument with your colleagues or friends, using the time limit to which you will be subject. It may be helpful to write out your main arguments under each point and study them prior to practice. As you practice, question and critique each other. This will enable you to determine whether you have presented each point clearly and persuasively, whether your argument flows well, and whether there are points that should be omitted or further developed. Practice also allows you to gauge the timing of each portion of your argument so you can allocate enough time to fully develop each of your major points. As you practice, keep track of the questions that are asked and evaluate the effectiveness of your answers, revising them as necessary.

In addition to practice in answering questions, you need to practice transitioning back to your argument after answering a question. At oral argument, you do not want a long pause after you have answered a question while you try to figure out what to say next. If you had not finished an important point when you were interrupted, go back to that point. If you were essentially finished with that point when you were asked a question, go on to the next important point you planned to make. If one or more questions consumed a lot of time, and you no longer have time to say many of the things you planned to say, go to the most important point or points you still have time to make.

When practicing your oral argument, keep in mind the guidelines for presenting an effective oral argument stated below. These include, for example, the manner of your presentation and your closing. Be sure to address each of these in practice; you are not likely to effectively present them at oral argument unless you do.

If you follow these suggestions—if you know your law and your facts, if you have reviewed the briefs and updated your research, if you have identified a compelling theme and strong arguments that support it, and if you have practiced—you will be prepared for oral argument.

Presenting an Oral Argument

The following guidelines will assist you in presenting your argument effectively.

1. Begin with a strong opening.

The opening is the court's first impression of you as an advocate. Unless you regularly appear before that court, the judges will be curious and interested in observing you and hearing what you have to say. You will have their complete attention for the first few minutes at the podium. Make the most of this opportunity to set a strong, persuasive tone for your entire argument.

A good opening has three components: a formal introduction, a few sentences summarizing your theme and key arguments, and a roadmap for the court. The formal introduction usually is a respectful greeting to the court. In an appellate argument, advocates often open by saying, "If it please the Court," or "May it please the Court." If you are arguing to a trial judge, a less-formal greeting, such as "Good morning, Your Honor," may often be used. Follow the opening salutation by introducing yourself and your co-counsel, if you have one, and state the party or parties you represent. If you are the appellant before an appeals court or the moving party in a trial court (having filed, say, a motion for summary judgment), make sure you reserve rebuttal time; some judges will not allow rebuttal if you fail to expressly reserve time at the beginning of your argument. Finish your introduction with a clear and affirmative statement of the relief you are requesting.

If the case or issues are complex, you should provide the court with a brief "roadmap" or outline of your argument. The roadmap will allow the court to determine whether you are going to address its most important concerns. A judge is more likely to defer a question if he or she knows that you will address a particular issue later in the argument.

Immediately after the opening, an advocate usually is expected to address the facts of the case. This can be one of the more challenging moments in your argument. On the one hand, you do not want to spend valuable argument time reciting the facts of the case; on the other hand, you are expected to address the facts in some respect. As explained above, many advocates simply ask the court if it would like to hear a summary of the facts. If the answer is "yes," provide a brief recitation of the facts; if the answer is "no," proceed with your argument but emphasize the key facts during the argument. Be prepared for both possibilities. A third approach, particularly if the case turns on straightforward and uncontested facts, is to begin your main argument by stating those facts in the context of the governing law. For example: "To be valid, a will must be signed by two witnesses. Mrs. Johnson's will is valid because the parties agree that it was signed by her husband, Wayne Johnson, and her daughter, Jess Johnson Young." In any event, careful planning and practice of alternatives is the best way to avoid an awkward moment.

You should draft your opening as part of your preparation, then read it aloud to see how it sounds. Revise and practice your opening until it sounds both compelling and natural. At oral argument, you should be able to deliver your opening without notes.

Consider these ways of beginning an argument to the court of appeals in the Chisolm case.

ANSWER A: If it please the Court, my name is Marva Kelly, and I represent the third-party defendant, Mr. Dennis Chisolm, in this matter. I would like to reserve two minutes for rebuttal.

The trial court erred when it failed to apply the settlement bar rule from *Sarasota Pools* in this case. As a result of that error Mr. Chisolm will be penalized for doing the right thing: accepting his share of responsibility for a terrible accident and entering into a settlement to compensate the plaintiff, Peter Miller. I will proceed with my argument unless the court would prefer a brief summary of the facts.

[Chief Judge instructs counsel to proceed with the argument.]

Thank you, Your Honor. This case turns on two key points. First, the settlement bar rule is applicable in this case. Under *Sarasota Pools*, Mr. Chisolm has "bought his peace." The trial court's reliance on *Raseen* rather than on *Sarasota Pools* was incorrect.

Second, enforcing the settlement bar rule in this case will recognize that Mr. Chisolm did the right thing. As previously recognized by this Court, enforcing the rule will encourage parties to settle and promote judicial efficiency.

ANSWER B: Good morning, and if it please the Court, my name is Marva Kelly and I represent Dennis Chisolm in this case.

Peter Miller was paralyzed when the private plane in which he was a passenger crashed. It crashed because of a defective fuel pump made by the defendant, Aaron Industries, and because Dennis Chisolm—my client, Mr. Miller's friend, and the owner and pilot of the plane—had neglected some of the maintenance of his plane and thus failed to recognize and replace the defective fuel pump.

My client was devastated by the injury to his friend, Mr. Miller. But Mr. Chisolm did the right thing and admitted his fault. He agreed to pay as much as he could to compensate Mr. Miller for his share of the harm he caused. He therefore settled with Mr. Miller for the limits of his insurance policy—one million dollars—and paid Mr. Miller one-half of his life savings—another half million dollars. At age sixty-nine, my client has only half his life savings left to live on. He has no other source of income.

The settlement bar rule must be enforced. Mr. Chisolm has "bought his peace" and should be allowed to enjoy the benefit of his bargain. The trial court committed reversible error when it failed to dismiss Aaron Industries' third-party complaint against him. Finally, it is only fair—to Mr. Chisolm and to all the other parties in the case—to enforce the settlement bar rule in this case.

Both openings begin with a formal salutation and introduce the advocate and her client, but that is where the similarities end. Answer A identifies the client not only by name but by his relationship to the underlying dispute, which helps orient the judges to the case. Answer A also reserves rebuttal time. Counsel in Answer B has probably waived the right to rebuttal by failing to reserve it at the beginning of the argument.

After the introduction, Answer A also sets out a clear and affirmative statement of the advocate's conclusion. The conclusion is stated in terms of the trial court's error and includes a reference to the theme of the case: that Mr. Chisolm "did the right thing." Answer B does not include a statement of the advocate's conclusion but moves directly into a short recitation of the facts.

The two answers take two different approaches to the facts. In Answer A the advocate asks the judges if they would like to hear the facts and proceeds as they prefer. In Answer B the advocate does not ask for guidance from the court but simply begins to recite the facts. The emphasis, however, is on background and emotional facts, rather than on legally significant facts. It is not wrong to try to humanize your client, but that should not be done at the expense of the facts upon which the case will turn.

Finally, both answers end with a "roadmap" that informs the court of the points that the advocate will discuss, but Answer A does this far more successfully than Answer B. Answer A provides cues for the judges: "two points . . . first . . . second." These cues provide a clear framework that makes the argument easy to follow. Answer A also states each point in affirmative terms, providing enough detail to draw a line directly from the policy behind the law to the source of the trial court's error to the appellate court's power to ensure a just result. Answer B mentions the same two points, but much less clearly. They are not enumerated and include far less detail. If the advocate could only deliver her introduction, Answer A has outlined her complete case, but Answer B has not.

---

2. Make your basic arguments as simple and direct as the material allows.

When you write a legal argument, you are putting on paper something that can be read, reread, and studied. When you talk, though, your words cannot so easily be studied. To make sure you are understood at oral argument, explain your argument as simply and basically as you can. If there are two ways to explain something—a more complicated way and a simpler way—use the simpler way. Use examples or illustrations when appropriate to make your explanation easier to understand.

Your theme is an important tool for keeping your argument as simple and direct as possible. It provides a way for the court to understand and remember your case. During your argument, be prepared to demonstrate how each argument leads back to that central "truth" of your case. If it works, the theme becomes the central principle around which the judge or the court can organize a decision and opinion on your client's behalf. Your theme, in other words, is the simplifying explanation for your entire argument.

Consider the following ways of making part of the argument in the Chisolm case.

ANSWER A: Both fairness and the policy underlying the settlement bar rule support its application here. Chisolm accepted responsibility for the harm his negligence caused to his friend by settling for the limits of his insurance policy and one-half of his savings, for a total of $1.5 million. Chisolm has "bought his peace" at the cost of half of his life savings, permanently decreasing his standard of living. Applying the rule in this case is fair because it allows Chisolm the "benefit of his bargain." It also supports the policy of encouraging settlement by tortfeasors by guaranteeing that they need fear no future litigation. This reduces the burden on the court system by decreasing the number of lawsuits that are litigated. In addition, Aaron Industries and all future non-settling tortfeasors can decide whether to settle or litigate, knowing that there will be no contribution to offset any potential damage award.

ANSWER B: Applying the settlement bar rule here is not only fair but will encourage parties to do the right thing and take responsibility for their actions by ensuring that they need fear no future litigation. Chisolm did the right thing in accepting responsibility for the harm his negligence caused by settling at significant personal cost. He contributed half of his life savings in addition to all his insurance would cover. Encouraging parties to do the right thing also directly supports the policy of encouraging settlement by tortfeasors. It thus decreases the burden on the judicial system by reducing the number of lawsuits that are litigated.

Answer B is a simple and straightforward statement of the argument. Although it includes both the fairness of applying the rule to Chisolm and the underlying policy of encouraging settlement to conserve judicial resources, it presents these arguments clearly and directly ties them to the theme of "do the right thing."

Answer A begins by defining both the fairness and policy aspects of the argument but then includes unnecessary factual detail that only obscures the argument about fairness. It also includes Aaron Industries without explaining how it fits into the fairness argument. Although there is an argument that applying the rule is not unfair to Aaron Industries and other non-settling tortfeasors, it presents a subtle shift in point of view from "fair" to "not unfair." Even this minor shift in perspective can confuse a listener. Finally, the argument is not tied to the main theme, but instead introduces another memorable phrase—"benefit of his bargain." This phrase, while applicable, dilutes the effectiveness of the theme by giving the audience another catchy phrase to apply to the case.

3. Make effective use of questions.

Judges ask many different types of questions. Some are friendly; some are not. Some are easy to answer, and some are not. But whatever the question, you can be sure of one thing: judges want to know your answer. Welcome questions, respond directly to them, and never show a reluctance to answer them. They are an enormous opportunity to help your client because you are addressing exactly what most interests the court. If a question requires a yes or no answer, begin your answer with "Yes, Your Honor" or "No, Your Honor," and then explain your answer more fully. Never answer a question by saying that you will get to it later; this indicates you are more interested in following your outline than in providing the information the judges need to make a sound decision.

Judges may ask questions about the facts or the authorities cited in your brief or your opponent's brief. Be prepared to answer these questions by knowing the record and reviewing the relevant cases and statutes. Other types of questions, however, can be more difficult to handle.

A court is likely to ask questions challenging a point that you have made. Lawyers often refer to these as "unfriendly questions." Yet it would be wrong to automatically assume that the judge is opposed to your position; to the contrary, this may be the one remaining issue the judge needs to resolve in your favor before he writes an opinion for your client. A court is also likely to ask questions about the weak points in your argument. As explained earlier, prepare and practice your answers in advance. Remember to tie your answers back to your theme.

Consider these responses to the following question:

QUESTION: As the trial court pointed out in its very well-reasoned order, the real distinction between this case and *Sarasota Pools* is the timing. The parties are already in trial on this case, like the parties were in *Raseen*, so I'm not sure why you're arguing about the settlement bar rule. Those policies just aren't relevant now, are they?

ANSWER A: I understand, Your Honor. We've got a trial going on in both cases, that's true, but it's our position that Mr. Chisolm did the right thing and is entitled to the benefit of his bargain. Also, *Raseen* was not a personal injury case, like our case and like *Sarasota Pools*, but a property damage case.

ANSWER B: Yes, Your Honor, those policies are relevant. The trial court's reliance on *Raseen* was misplaced because that case differs from ours in one crucial respect. In *Raseen*, the plaintiff sued *both* tortfeasors and the trial against *both* tortfeasors had begun. Only *after* the trial began did Mr. Raseen settle with one of the two defendants. The court in *Raseen* was therefore correct when it said that the public policy of reducing litigation would not be served by dismissing the settling tortfeasor; *all* of the parties were already involved in the trial. The present case is distinguishable because the settlement with my client happened *before* trial; in fact, it happened before a lawsuit had even been filed.

Here, Mr. Chisolm stepped up, accepted responsibility for his own negligence, and entered into a settlement with the plaintiff. The present suit was filed only against the non-settling tortfeasor, Aaron Industries. Mr. Chisolm's dismissal from the case will therefore conserve judicial resources because the court will not need to apportion liability between the defendants, and neither the plaintiff nor Aaron Industries will have to extend the trial by presenting a case against Mr. Chisolm. Mr. Chisolm did the right thing by acknowledging the case against him without complaint; there is no purpose to be served by dragging him into court to revisit the matter.

Answer A more or less concedes the point made by the judge: that the present case is analogous to *Raseen* because the parties in both cases are in trial. The advocate makes some additional points, but they are not responsive to the question asked. The judge may agree that Mr. Chisolm did the right thing by trying to settle the case, and there is no dispute that *Raseen* involved property damage rather than a personal injury claim. Neither point, however, explains how the timing of the settlement distinguishes *Raseen* from the present case.

Answer B is better. It begins with a strong statement of the advocate's position and explains in detail why the trial court's reliance on *Raseen* was incorrect. The advocate demonstrates a thorough mastery of the law and the facts by making explicit and relevant distinctions between *Raseen* and the present case. Answer B emphasizes public policy, explaining how the policies supporting the settlement bar rule will be undermined by the trial court's approach to the case but advanced by the advocate's approach. Answer B also ties the answer to the advocate's theme. The phrases "stepped up," "accepted responsibility," "did the right thing," and "acknowledged the case against him without complaint" all reinforce the theme that Mr. Chisolm "did the right thing" and implies that "dragging him into court" will undermine the very conduct that the court should encourage and reward.

Courts may ask you to clarify or further explain a point in your favor. This, of course, is a "friendly question." Sometimes, however, lawyers are convinced that all questions are hostile or unfriendly, and do not take full advantage of the opportunity being offered.

Consider these responses to the following question:

QUESTION: But Counsel, isn't there a downside for Aaron Industries here? If one party settles, doesn't that leave the non-settling party—Aaron Industries—with all the risk?

ANSWER A: Well, I guess that's right, Your Honor, but . . . but there's always that risk when you don't settle, isn't there? That's one of the risks that litigators take; sometimes it's better to settle and sometimes it's not, but unfortunately you don't always know that unless—and until—you go to trial and find out you should have settled in the first place.

ANSWER B: That's correct, Your Honor, there can be a downside for the non-settling party, but that is not the case here. First, there is no risk that Aaron Industries will be left with a greater share of the liability than it should have to bear because Mr. Miller has offered to enter into the very same agreement with Aaron Industries that he made with Mr. Chisolm. That's a 50/50 split, even though Aaron Industries manufactured the defective part that caused this crash and Mr. Chisolm merely failed to discover it. If anything, Mr. Chisolm's settlement has *reduced* the risk to Aaron Industries.

Second, Your Honor, even if there is a risk to the non-settling party, it is not unfair because the non-settling party chose to accept that risk. As the court said in *Sarasota Pools*, the settlement bar rule allows parties to "know the consequences of their actions in advance." There is no downside for either party on that score—both Mr. Chisolm and Aaron Industries "knew the consequences of their actions in advance." Mr. Chisolm knew that he would "buy his peace" by taking responsibility for his actions, and Aaron Industries knew that there was a risk in deciding to roll the dice at trial. Both parties had the same opportunity to consider the consequences before deciding on a course of action.

The advocate in Answer A seems thrown off balance by the question and fails to recognize that the question gives her the opportunity to discuss a potentially troubling point: whether the settlement bar rule exposes the non-settling party to an unreasonable amount of risk. By agreeing with the judge the advocate concedes an essential point, thus weakening her argument.

The advocate in Answer B recognizes the question as an opportunity to explore an issue that may concern one of the judges and provides two alternative responses, one factual and one legal, both of which favor her client's position. She begins by acknowledging that the settlement bar rule may sometimes seem unfair to the non-settling party but explains why, under the facts of *this case*, there is no unfairness. She does not concede the point. She then reminds the court that the settlement bar rule actually *is* fair to all parties because all parties know what their options are before choosing a course of action. A judge who is concerned with fairness now has two reasons to conclude that enforcing the settlement bar rule here is fair.

Judges sometimes ask questions about issues or aspects of the case other than the ones you are addressing at the moment. For example, you may be in the middle of an argument regarding point B when a judge asks a question about point C. When this happens, be prepared to alter your prepared outline to address what interests the judges. If the question is material to point C, take the opportunity to fully address the considerations relating to point C so your specific answer to the judge's question is cast in the context of your planned presentation on that point. Depending on where you are in your argument and how important point C is to your overall argument, it may be most effective to fully present your argument on point C once you are led there by the court's questions.

Making effective use of questions involves more than just appropriately answering the question. The skilled advocate will use questions to smoothly transition to another argument, perhaps the argument she was addressing when interrupted by the judge's question or to another point or argument not yet addressed. This requires you to understand the connections between your arguments and to use those connections to move around within your argument. For example, once you finish answering a question on point C or perhaps even finish the arguments you had intended to make on point C, lead the court back to one of your other arguments. Make this transition by relating a point in the argument on point C to an argument you want to make on point B. Your theme can be a useful tool for making this transition.

Assume, for example, that the advocate is making an argument similar to the one above, that the possible risks to Aaron Industries should not deter the court from enforcing the settlement bar rule in the Chisolm case. As she begins to discuss that point, the court interrupts with a question on an unrelated topic. Read the question below and consider the following responses:

QUESTION: Wait a minute Counsel. I am troubled by the fact that your client and the Plaintiff, Mr. Miller, are friends. How do we know that this was a *bona fide* settlement and not a sham? I noticed that your client still has plenty of money left for his retirement—something like half a million dollars?

ANSWER A: Yes, Your Honor, they are friends, but this was not a sham settlement. I'll discuss that in a minute, but as I was saying, there is no downside for Aaron Industries here. First, . . .

ANSWER B: Yes, Your Honor, they are friends, but there is no evidence that this is anything but a *bona fide* settlement. The heavy price Mr. Chisolm paid in exhausting his savings confirms this. Now, as I was saying about the possible downside risks to Aaron Industries . . .

ANSWER C: Yes, Your Honor, they are friends, but there is no evidence that this is anything but a *bona fide* settlement. Mr. Chisolm has exhausted his insurance and, at the age of sixty-nine, permanently diminished his standard of living. That's a heavy price to pay. My client didn't get off easy; the bargain he made left him far less well off than one would expect if he and Mr. Miller planned to take advantage of Aaron Industries to enrich themselves.

Now it is true that by permitting a defendant to buy his peace, as Mr. Chisolm did here, the settlement bar rule can expose the non-settling party to some risk. But the risk to Aaron Industries is very limited. In fact, there is no risk that Aaron Industries will be left with a greater share of the liability than it should have to bear because Mr. Miller has offered . . .

Answer A will not be well received by a judge. Instead of fully answering the judge's question, the advocate brushes the question aside with a cursory answer and says she'll "get to it." The advocate sounds annoyed and disrespectful ("as I was saying"), as if the advocate's planned remarks are more important than the judge's question. This advocate forgot that oral argument is a conversation with the people who will decide what is going to happen to her client.

Answer B is better, but not by much. The advocate answers the question but does not do so completely. This suggests to the court that the advocate has nothing further to say on the point, thereby squandering a good opportunity to further advance the client's position. It also leaves her vulnerable to follow-up questions on the same point, which if asked will require her to spend even more time giving additional explanation.

Answer C gives a complete answer to the question. The advocate does not simply deny that the settlement is a sham, but makes a logical factual argument against that conclusion. The advocate then uses the phrase "now it is true that" and her theme to smoothly transition back to a stronger argument. This phrase respectfully acknowledges the judge's concern that the non-settling party be treated fairly. It also leads directly into a complete explanation of why enforcement of the settlement bar rule is not only fair to Aaron Industries but that "fairness" actually compels a decision in favor of Mr. Chisolm.

4. Manage your time.

When you first begin to speak, your allotted time may seem like an eternity. This is true regardless of how much time you have been given. As you begin to develop your arguments, however, and especially as you begin to respond to questions and engage in a conversation with the court, time will pass quickly. The following tips will help you manage your time well, so you can sit down after your argument confident that you gave the court the information it needs to rule in your client's favor.

First, pay attention to the time as you speak. Most courtrooms have a timekeeping system of some kind. A modern courtroom may have a clock at the podium that counts down the time remaining, or a system of lights that switch from green to yellow to red. In older buildings a clerk or bailiff may give time signals to the advocates, or attorneys may bring a cell phone or watch and monitor their own time. Regardless of the system, make use of it. Respect the court's time and be respectful of the time of those who may be scheduled to argue after your case has been heard. Be prepared to adapt your planned presentation as you go. The ability to manage your time is perhaps the best demonstration of the mental agility, preparation, and practice required for a successful oral argument.

In preparing your oral argument, you identified your essential points. As you progress through your oral argument, keep track not only of the remaining time but also of the points you have made and those you still need to make. If you realize that your time is running out, and you still have one or more important points to make, you can often do so quickly. For example:

> I see my time is almost up, but before I close I would like to draw the court's attention to an opinion issued last week by our supreme court. In *Smith v. Greene Tractor Corporation*, the court analyzed a case that is factually very similar to my client's case and came to the same conclusion that I ask you to reach today . . . .

This approach allows you to mention one last important point in the context of your closing. You are not likely to be interrupted by the court once it is clear that you are being respectful of the time limits for the argument.

Do not be overly concerned about covering all of the points in your outline. It is better to cover a few points thoroughly and fully respond to the court's questions than to rush through every point in your outline. If you finish your argument early and there are no more questions—sit down.

5. Present your argument in a professional manner.

Although the oral argument is a dialogue, it is not a fireside chat. Rules of etiquette and appropriate public speaking apply. The following techniques should help you become a more confident, effective, and accomplished speaker and provide a framework for developing a style that is comfortable and effective for you.

Courtroom Etiquette

Part of your preparation is becoming familiar with the norms and expectations of the courtroom. Observe these norms. If the judge is distracted by your behavior, dress, or lack of professionalism, you are not serving your client's interests. It is not about you or your ideals. The "star" of the argument is your client; do not do or say anything that could detract from or undermine your client's case.

Oral argument, especially at the appellate level, can be formal, and the level of formality tends to increase with the level of the court.

When in doubt, err on the side of formality. Advocates in every court are expected to be punctual, respectful to judges and court personnel, and civil to opposing counsel. Address judges as "Your Honor" or by name and title—for example, "Judge Anderson," or "Justice Ginsberg." Address and refer to co-counsel and opposing counsel by their last names, using either "Ms." or "Mr."

Rise promptly when the bailiff calls the court to order and when the judge or judges enter the courtroom. Sessions often begin with the bailiff's call, "oyez, oyez, oyez" (meaning "hear ye, hear ye, hear ye"). Remain standing until the presiding judge or justice invites you to be seated. Stand when you address the court and any time the judge or judges rise, such as when they leave the courtroom after an argument. The bailiff will often say "all rise" when it is time for the attorneys and others in the courtroom to stand.

Physical Techniques

Your oral argument, or at least your opportunity to persuade, begins when you take your seat at counsel table. Practice standing and moving in a way that conveys confidence and calmness. Whether sitting or standing, maintain good posture and a professional demeanor. When opposing counsel is speaking, do not do anything that could be construed as disrespectful or disinterested. Do not slouch or lean back in your chair; do not sigh, rustle your papers, drop your pencil, or roll your eyes. Do not talk to co-counsel; write a note on a legal pad if you need to communicate with co-counsel. Keep the counsel table organized and neat at all times.

When it is your turn to speak, take a stance at the podium that allows you to maintain your balance easily, even if you are nervous and a little shaky. Remain behind the podium during your argument. Learn to control large, expansive gestures if that is your natural speaking style. Instead, keep your hands and arms relatively still, using modest, natural gestures in a way that will emphasize important points and enhance your argument. Never point at a judge. If you have a tendency to fidget with your pen, jangle the change in your pocket, or twist a ring or bracelet, do not take those objects with you to the podium.

Your ability to make and maintain eye contact with the judges is the most effective way to communicate confidence, enhance your credibility, and strengthen your argument. You may have to glance at your notes occasionally, but if you are well prepared you will not have to rely on your notes. Instead, you will be able to make eye contact with each judge as you speak. Similarly, speak directly to each judge when you answer a question; do not look only at the judge who asked the question.

Vocal Techniques

As emphasized throughout this chapter, oral argument is a conversation with the court. You should therefore speak in a conversational manner, not as if you were delivering a speech, performing in a play, or engaged in a debate.

Recognize that, as a lawyer, your voice is a tool that you can and should learn to handle well. If you are not used to public speaking, learn to support your voice by breathing slowly and deeply. Practice using tone, inflection, and intensity to emphasize words and phrases. Practice your articulation and phrasing by reading aloud, or practice vocal exercises and tongue-twisters to strengthen your vocal skills and build confidence.

Take your time when you speak. You know what you intend to say, but your listener is hearing the words for the first time. He or she needs time to hear and understand your words. As a general rule, if you think you are speaking at a "normal" rate, you are probably going too quickly. When you sound to yourself as if you are speaking a little too slowly, the rate is probably appropriate for your listener. Practicing your argument with a friend or colleague will help you discover the proper rate of delivery that will be most effective for your listener.

Finally, do not forget the power of silence. Many oralists are afraid of silence, fearing that any pause implies that they have forgotten or do not know what to say next. In fact, a silence seems far longer to the speaker than it does to the listener. A pause to consider a question, collect your thoughts, or choose the right word conveys thoughtfulness and care to your listener, not incompetence. Pauses can also be used to give your listener time to catch up with your thoughts, or to let the meaning of a fact or argument to sink in.

6. Close with confidence.

Listeners tend to remember only about a third of what they hear, but they remember best what they hear first and last. Your closing is therefore one of the most important parts of your oral argument. Ideally, your closing should parallel and reinforce the points that opened your argument, delivering the same message to the judges. To achieve maximum effect from your closing, follow these guidelines.

- ■ Keep your closing short—you should not need more than a minute to wrap up.
- ■ Request the relief that you want from the court. Keep the request clear and precise.

■ Tell the court why that relief is necessary and should be granted. Summarize your essential case in as few words as possible, emphasizing the theme of your case.

■ When you have said what you need to say, stop. Thank the court and sit down. Do not pause after you finish, and do not ask the court if it has any further questions.

The following examples illustrate different ways of using these guidelines to close the argument in the Chisolm appeal.

ANSWER A: If I may take a minute to conclude Your Honors? Mr. Chisolm accepted responsibility for his role in this accident and entered into a fair settlement to compensate Mr. Miller for his injuries. Under the settlement bar rule in *Sarasota Pools,* he is entitled to the benefit of his bargain: to be free of the risk of litigation and further liability. Aaron Industries, however, wants to take a risk; it wants to roll the dice at trial and force Mr. Chisolm to share that risk by acting as the corporation's insurer in case it loses that gamble. Mr. Miller is ready and willing to settle with Aaron Industries on the same terms as his settlement with Mr. Chisolm. But the corporation that manufactured the defective part that caused this crash won't even discuss settlement; it would rather waste the court's time by going to trial.

In closing, unless you have any further questions, we respectfully request that the trial court's decision be reversed. Thank you.

ANSWER B: In conclusion, Your Honors, the trial court's misplaced reliance on *Raseen* will allow Aaron Industries to roll the dice at trial and force Mr. Chisolm to act as the corporation's insurer in case it loses that gamble. That result is not fair, and it is not consistent with the controlling law. Mr. Chisolm did the right thing, accepted responsibility for his role in the accident, and compensated Mr. Miller for his injuries. Under the settlement bar rule he has "bought his peace."

Mr. Chisolm therefore respectfully requests that this court reverse the trial court and dismiss Aaron Industries' third-party complaint.

Thank you, Your Honors.

Answer B is a stronger, more confident closing than Answer A. Answer B begins by identifying the trial court's error—its reliance on the wrong case and consequent misapplication of the governing law. This focus reflects an understanding of the judges' role: to correct trial court errors. Answer B also uses language that echoes the theme of the case and the differences between the parties: "roll the dice" and "gamble" for Aaron Industries; "did the right thing," "accepted responsibility," and "compensated Mr. Miller for his injuries" for Mr. Chisolm. This part of the conclusion is brief, but it creates a stark contrast between the two parties. Answer B ends with a clear request for relief; the advocate tells the court exactly what it is being asked to do: reverse the trial court and dismiss the complaint.

Answer A also uses language that echoes the theme of the case and ends with a clear request to reverse the trial court. Answer A, however, demonstrates several common mistakes that can undermine an otherwise strong argument. First, Answer A does not clearly identify the trial court error that requires reversal and does not make a specific request for dismissal of the third-party complaint. Because it is the appellate court's job to correct errors in the court below, the closing should remind the court one more time exactly where and how the trial court erred and what the proper remedy is. Answer A also contains some unnecessary information, giving it a less-focused, somewhat meandering tone. For example, that Aaron Industries has refused to discuss settlement with Mr. Miller paints a negative picture of the opposing party, but it does not relate directly to the legal foundation for the request for relief. The appellate court will reverse because the trial court erred, not because it dislikes the opposing party. Answer A also has a more emotional tone than Answer B, created by phrases such as "defective part that caused this crash" and "waste the court's time."

Finally, Answer A encourages the court to interrupt the closing by (1) beginning the closing with a request for permission to conclude, and (2) creating an opening for further questions at the end. Unless your time has already run out, it is not necessary to ask permission to conclude; simply make a smooth transition from your final argument to the conclusion. Similarly, it is not necessary to give the court a final opening for questions. If a judge has a question, you can be sure that it will be asked, whether you invite the question or not. More importantly, you should end the argument with the words and thoughts that *you* have chosen, so that the judges will remember your essential points.

7. Use rebuttal time effectively.

In an appellate court, the appellant normally argues first. In a trial court, the moving party normally argues first. The appellant (and sometimes the moving party at the trial court level) is then given a brief time for rebuttal, if counsel has reserved the time.

Rebuttal is the appellant's or the moving party's last chance to influence the court's decision. It presents great opportunities and equally great risks. If your side has the opportunity for rebuttal, pay close attention to concerns raised by the court during your opponent's argument, questions asked by the court, and points made by opposing counsel that weaken your argument. Choose no more than two or three responses that address the most significant concerns of the court or weaknesses of your argument. The points should be chosen carefully to shore up your argument, should be simple to state, should be legally strong, and should not repeat statements you have already made. You may also use rebuttal to correct factual or legal misstatements by opposing counsel. Done correctly and confidently, rebuttal can remove significant doubts from the court's mind about whether your client should prevail.

Done poorly, rebuttal weakens your position. If you simply repeat prior points, present arguments that are complicated and relatively weak, say things that are not responsive to the central points made by opposing counsel, or have a long laundry list of quibbles, you will likely hurt your client's chances. Weak or marginal arguments in rebuttal invite sharp questions from judges that are hard to answer effectively within a limited time and create a last impression of you and your client as defensive.

Due to these risks, it is sometimes better to waive rebuttal, even when you have reserved it. When the court's leanings are clear, or there is nothing of consequence to say, or the risks are too great, then stand up from your seat and tell the court that you are waiving your rebuttal time. The court will be grateful.

Species of Oral Advocates

Chief Justice William Rehnquist once categorized the various oral advocates before the U.S. Supreme Court as including the following "species":*

The lector. "He reads his argument." He treats questions as interruptions to his argument, receives fewer questions, and is less effective as a result. "The ultimate purpose of oral argument, from the point of view of the advocate, is to work his way into the judge's consciousness and make the judge think about the things that the advocate wishes him to think about." Reading doesn't accomplish that.

The debating champion. "He has an excellent grasp of his theory of the case and the arguments supporting it," but he is so interested in demonstrating his knowledge that "he doesn't listen carefully to questions" or answer them carefully. As a result, he does not convince judges who are doubtful of his position.

Casey Jones. This advocate, also knowledgeable, is "like an engineer on a nonstop train" who "will not stop to pick up passengers along the way." He speaks rapidly and tries to cover as much material as possible within the allowed time, not realizing that judges "require a little time to assimilate what he saying." This advocate will not be truly effective until he slows down and focuses on a small number of key points.

The spellbinder. This species of advocate is rare. He has a good voice and is able to "talk *with* rather than talk *to* the Court." But he lets his eloquence substitute for careful analysis. "A florid peroration, exhorting the Court either to save the Bill of Rights from the government or to save the government from the Bill of Rights," is unlikely to work well in any Court.

The "All American oral advocate." This advocate combines the strengths of the others but not their weaknesses. "If the essential element of the case turns on how the statute is worded, she will pause and slowly read the crucial sentence or paragraph." She has planned her argument and focuses only on significant issues. She treats all questions seriously and answers them carefully, regardless of whether the judge's question is "ignorant, stupid, or both."

* Rehnquist, *supra* note 3, at 278-281.

EXERCISES

The following exercises will give you practice in preparing for and presenting an oral argument.

Exercise 28-A

Assume you are representing Aaron Industries in the Chisolm appeal.

1. Draft your theme.

2. Select and summarize your strongest and most essential arguments.

Exercise 28-B

This exercise is based on Exercise 22-B, pp. 333-35. For this exercise, you or your professor will decide which client you represent.

1. Assume you are representing Tri-State on appeal:
   a. Draft your theme.
   b. Select and summarize your strongest and most essential arguments.

2. Assume you are representing Hansen on appeal:
   a. Draft your theme.
   b. Select and summarize your strongest and most essential arguments.

Exercise 28-C

Assume you have been given fifteen minutes for oral argument. Using Exercise 28-A (representing Aaron Industries) or 28-B (representing Tri-State or Hansen):

1. Prepare an outline of your argument.

2. Draft at least three questions the court is likely to ask you, and draft your answers to those questions.

Exercise 28-D

Using Exercise 28-A (representing Aaron Industries) or 28-B (representing Tri-State or Hansen):

1. Draft an opening and a closing for your oral argument.

2. Practice delivering your opening and closing by yourself and with a partner.

3. Prepare to deliver your opening and closing to the class.

Exercise 28-E

This exercise is based on Exercise 28-B and requires a partner. Each of you will represent one of the parties—Tri-State or Hansen.

1. Draft three questions that you would like a judge to ask *your opponent* (partner). Exchange questions with your opponent and draft answers to the questions you are given.

2. Play the role of judge for your opponent, asking the questions you prepared and giving your opponent the chance to practice answering the questions.

3. Let your opponent play the role of judge for you, and repeat question 2 with your roles reversed in this way.

Appendices

Appendices A through G include an office memorandum, an opinion letter, two trial briefs addressing a motion for summary judgment filed by the defendant, a trial court opinion granting the defendant's motion, and two appellate briefs filed by the parties regarding the trial court's grant of summary judgment. Each of these documents concerns the same dispute regarding a claim for negligent misrepresentation.

The dispute is governed by California law, but the action was filed in federal court based on the parties' diversity of citizenship. Thus, for the most part, the trial briefs were formatted according to the local rules for the Federal District Court for the Northern District of California, and the appellate briefs were formatted for the Ninth Circuit Court of Appeals. The hearing date and time information on the first page of Appendices C and D, for example, is required by the Northern District rules. Under the Ninth Circuit rules, the appendices for the appellate briefs would be much longer and would contain relevant portions of the record or of documents from the lower court. For the sake of brevity, much of this material has been omitted from the appellate brief appendices. While we have tried to make these documents resemble their real-world counterparts, the documents are neither double-spaced nor printed on only one side of the page, as they most likely would be in practice. Finally, the Bluebook (19th edition) and Federal Rules of Appellate Procedure allow case names in memos and briefs to be either underlined or italicized. In these appendices, one side's documents as well as the trial court opinion use italics for case names; the other side's documents underline case names.

Appendix H contains a list of useful books on writing style, grammar, and punctuation.

MEMORANDUM

TO: Maria Hernandez
FROM: Loren Taylor *LT*
DATE: September 8, 2012
RE: Tyler's possible fraud claim against Eastern Pacific University, file no. P12–37

QUESTIONS PRESENTED

I.   Can a student recover damages for negligent misrepresentation by a university recruiter regarding a preferential graduate admissions policy?

A. Did the recruiter make a positive assertion of an existing fact rather than a statement of opinion when he told a student that, as a graduate of the university, the student would have a "better chance" of being admitted to a graduate degree program at that university?

B. Did the recruiter lack a reasonable basis to believe that his statement was true when the recruiter based his statement only on his knowledge that five of the university's twenty-three other graduate programs had preferential admissions policies?

C. Was the student's reliance on the recruiter's statement reasonable when the student did not investigate the statement despite his student employment in the graduate program's office and discovered there was no preferential admissions policy only after his application for admission was denied?

II.   Is an action for negligent misrepresentation allowed by the three-year statute of limitations when the alleged misrepresentation concerning a graduate admissions policy occurred five years ago, the student did not learn of it until he was denied admission six months ago, and the student worked in the graduate program office during the intervening four years but had no contact with the admissions decisions during that time?

BRIEF ANSWERS

I.   The student can probably recover in an action for negligent misrepresentation.

A. Probably yes. The recruiter's misrepresentation regarding the preferential admissions policy was most likely a statement of fact rather than an opinion. The statement was asserted as a fact and was made by one holding himself out as having superior knowledge or who was presumably in a position to know such information.

B. Probably yes. The recruiter misrepresented the university's policy without any specific factual basis for believing that the program had a preferential admissions policy. His personal belief that such a policy existed because five of the university's twenty-three other graduate programs had such a policy does not provide a reasonable basis for the statement.

C. Probably yes. The student could reasonably have believed that the university recruiter was in a position to know about the admissions process for the university's graduate programs. Although the student did not investigate the recruiter's statement, he heard nothing that contradicted it or put him on notice to conduct further investigation.

II. Probably yes. The action is probably allowed because the student did not discover the misrepresentation until six months ago, when he was denied admission to the graduate school. Even though he performed clerical work for the graduate program, he was never put on notice that the policy might not exist and thus had no reason to investigate or otherwise discover the truth earlier.

STATEMENT OF FACTS

When Timothy Tyler began his senior year of high school in September 2007 he considered attending either Eastern Pacific University in San Francisco or the smaller, less prestigious Crater Lake College in his home state of Oregon. At that time he spoke with representatives of Eastern Pacific's small but well-known Global Policy Studies (GPS) program, which he wanted to attend after obtaining an undergraduate degree. The representatives told Tyler that he would need excellent credentials to be admitted and pointed out that many of their students were honor graduates of major universities. There was no discussion about whether Eastern Pacific graduates received priority in admissions to the GPS program. The financial assistance office at Eastern Pacific told him that he did not qualify for a scholarship. A short time thereafter, he decided to accept a full, four-year athletic scholarship to attend and play soccer at Crater Lake College. He planned to graduate from Crater Lake and then pursue a graduate degree from that college's International Environmental Protection Program.

In April 2008, before Tyler accepted Crater Lake's offer, Richard Cramer, a recruiter from Eastern Pacific, approached Tyler about playing soccer for Eastern Pacific. Tyler told Cramer he was interested in Eastern Pacific's GPS program. Cramer then suggested that the GPS program gave Eastern Pacific graduates priority in the admissions process by stating, "You'll have a better chance of getting into the GPS program as an Eastern Pacific graduate than coming in as a graduate from somewhere else." No such policy or preference exists; in fact, no Eastern Pacific graduates have been admitted to the GPS program since 2002, although at least three have applied.

Cramer later said he believed Eastern Pacific had such a policy because he had recruited students for five of Eastern Pacific's twenty-three other graduate programs. Because these five programs had preferential admissions policies, Cramer said, he assumed all of Eastern Pacific's programs, including the GPS program, had such a policy. No one had ever told him that the GPS program had a preferential admissions policy, and Cramer never investigated the existence of this policy or the admission requirements for the GPS program. Cramer freely admitted that he had made the statement to recruit Tyler for Eastern Pacific.

Tyler gave up his scholarship at Crater Lake to enroll at Eastern Pacific University in 2008. Because he received only a nominal athletic scholarship to play soccer at Eastern Pacific, he incurred substantial debt to pay his educational and living expenses. While an undergraduate, he worked part-time in the GPS department, assisting the admissions secretary by performing clerical work such as handling routine inquiries for applications and mailing letters. He was not involved with admissions decisions, and the existence of a preferential admissions policy was never discussed.

In October 2011, when Tyler was a senior at Eastern Pacific, he applied for admission to the GPS program. In March 2012, Eastern Pacific's GPS program denied the application. Tyler then learned that Eastern Pacific graduates received no preferential admission to the GPS program. Tyler has since applied to several other graduate programs and reapplied to Crater Lake. He has not been admitted to any of these programs. Tyler would like to know if he can recover damages from Eastern Pacific for his financial losses caused by Cramer's misrepresentation.

DISCUSSION

I. Negligent Misrepresentation

Timothy Tyler can probably recover damages for harm caused by Richard Cramer's negligent misrepresentation that Eastern Pacific's GPS program had a preferential admissions policy for Eastern Pacific University graduates. Damages for misrepresentation are recoverable under Cal. Civ. Code § 1709 (West 2009): "One who willfully deceives another with intent to induce him to alter his position to his injury or risk, is liable for any damage which he thereby suffers." Deceit is defined to include: "The assertion, as a fact, of that which is not true, by one who has no reasonable ground for believing it to be true." Cal. Civ. Code § 1710(2) (West 2009). One type of deceit or fraud is negligent misrepresentation. *B.L.M. v. Sabo & Deitsch*, 64 Cal. Rptr. 2d 335, 342 (Ct. App. 1997). A plaintiff making a negligent misrepresentation claim must prove each of the following elements: "(1) A misrepresentation of a past or existing material fact, (2) without reasonable grounds for believing it to be true, (3) with intent to induce another's reliance on the fact misrepresented, (4) ignorance of the truth and justifiable reliance thereon by the party to whom the misrepresentation was directed, and (5) damages." *Id.* (quoting *Fox v. Pollack*, 226 Cal. Rptr. 532, 537 (Ct. App. 1986)).

In this case, two elements are easily established. First, Cramer freely admitted that he made the statement to induce Tyler to enroll at Eastern Pacific, thereby establishing intent to induce reliance. Second, Tyler suffered damages in giving up his full scholarship at Crater Lake College to attend Eastern Pacific. He received only a nominal scholarship amount and had to pay most of Eastern Pacific's tuition himself. He also suffered damages because he was not given priority in his application to the GPS program. Therefore, three questions remain: A) whether Cramer's statement was a misrepresentation of an existing fact or only his opinion, B) whether Cramer lacked reasonable grounds for believing his statement to be true, and C) whether Tyler was justified in believing the statement to be true and relying on it.

A. Cramer's statement will probably be considered a statement of fact rather than an opinion because he held himself out as a trained professional on this subject. A misrepresentation must be one of existing fact; a statement as to value or other casual expression of belief is not actionable. *See Gentry v. eBay, Inc.*, 121 Cal. Rptr. 2d 703, 718–19 (Ct. App. 2002). However, a statement made by one who possesses or holds himself out as possessing superior knowledge or information regarding the subject of the statement may be treated as one of fact where the statement, although in the form of an opinion, is "a deliberate affirmation of the matters stated." *Bily v. Arthur Young & Co.*, 834 P.2d 745, 768 (Cal. 1992) (quoting *Gagne v. Bertran*, 275 P.2d 15, 21 (Cal. 1954)).

The courts have applied this rule to conclude that an opinion by a trained professional may be a statement of fact in an action for negligent misrepresentation, while a casual opinion offered by one speaking outside of his expertise is not. For example, in *Shafer v. Berger, Kahn, Shafton, Moss, Figler, Simon & Gladstone*, 131 Cal. Rptr. 2d 777, 793 (Ct. App. 2003), the court held that a statement by legal counsel for an insurance company regarding exclusions in a policy was a statement of fact. Similarly, in *Anderson v. Deloitte & Touche*, 66 Cal. Rptr. 2d 512, 516–17 (Ct. App. 1997), the court concluded that inaccurate financial projections in an accountant's report were positive assertions of fact sufficient to create a triable issue of negligent misrepresentation. However, where a principal in an accounting firm stated his opinion as to the appraisal value of real estate, the court held that his statement constituted only his opinion because he was not an appraiser and had never represented himself as such. *Neu-Visions Sports, Inc. v. Soren/McAdam/Bartells*, 103 Cal. Rptr. 2d 159, 163–64 (Ct. App. 2000).

The defendants in *Shafer* and *Anderson* were professionals providing information regarding a matter about which they were known to have specific information. Similarly, Cramer was a professional who asserted the existence of a preferential admissions policy, a matter within his professional expertise. His situation is markedly different from the accountant's in *Neu-Visions Sports*, who asserted his opinion regarding appraisal value. As a recruiter, Cramer is presumed to know the admissions policies of the university that employed him. Even if his assertion that Eastern Pacific's GPS program gave priority to its own graduates was an opinion, it was a statement related specifically to his profession. Therefore, like the statements in *Shafer* and

Anderson, Cramer's statement should be regarded as a statement of fact rather than a statement of opinion.

It is worth noting that recent cases concerning the distinction between fact and opinion in this context have concerned statements by defendants trained in recognized professions like law and accounting, not university recruiters. However, in *Gagne*, an earlier case, the court concluded that a statement regarding soil composition on a lot being tested for fill was one of fact even though the defendant had not held himself out as an engineer or geologist. The court so held because the defendant represented that he was in the business of testing soil for fill and because he had asserted his findings as fact rather than as a statement of his opinion. *Gagne*, 275 P.2d at 21. That Cramer was a recruiter rather than an attorney or accountant thus is not likely to make a difference in the court's determination of this question. A court is likely to conclude that Cramer's statement was a positive assertion of fact, rather than an opinion.

It is possible, but not likely, that the court will regard Cramer's statement as an opinion rather than a statement of fact. His statement that Tyler would have "a better chance of getting into the GPS program as an Eastern Pacific graduate" is not as clearly factual as the attorney's statements regarding exclusions in the insurance policy in *Shafer* or the accountant's financial projections in *Anderson*. This may lead a court to view his statement less as a professional opinion constituting a statement of fact and more as an expression of his personal view of the situation. However, by telling Tyler that he would have a better chance of being admitted as an Eastern Pacific graduate, Cramer asserted the existence of a preferential admissions policy as a fact. Therefore, his assertion is likely to be regarded as a statement of fact, rather than his personal opinion.

B. A court would likely conclude that Cramer had no reasonable grounds for making the statement because he had no specific information about the GPS admissions policy and based his statement only on the existence of such a policy in five other graduate programs. The courts have required persons making such representations to have a reasonable factual basis for them, generally grounded in personal inspection or investigation or in standard industry practice. In *Wilbur v. Wilson*, 3 Cal. Rptr. 770, 773 (Ct. App. 1960), for example, the court held that the seller of a 79-acre farm had no reasonable basis for his belief that his farm had 94 acres, when he based his representation solely on statements from the previous owner. Similarly, it was unreasonable for the seller of a lot containing substantial fill to tell the purchaser that the lot was solid when he had no factual basis for the statement, even though neither the seller nor the previous owner had put fill on the lot. *Gagne*, 275 P.2d at 15. However, in *Diediker v. Peellee Financial Corp.*, 70 Cal. Rptr. 2d 442 (Ct. App. 1997), a trustee who sold property subject to foreclosure reasonably believed the property was unencumbered because he had received a report from a title insurance company that did not show an

IRS lien. The court noted that it was standard industry practice to rely on such reports to disclose the existence of any liens. *Id.* at 448.

In light of these cases, Cramer's representation is most likely unreasonable because he did not personally investigate the factual basis for what he represented. Like the defendant in *Gagne*, who wrongly assumed that the lot had not been filled, Cramer wrongly assumed that the GPS program had a preferential admissions policy. Cramer's statement may be more egregious than the statement in *Wilbur*, because the defendant in that case based his representation about the size of the property on a statement by the previous owner. In Tyler's case, no one told Cramer that GPS had a preferential admissions policy. And, unlike the trustee in *Diediker*, who relied upon the title report, Cramer had nothing beyond his personal assumption regarding the existence of the admissions policy. That Cramer knew five other graduate programs had preferential admissions policies does not make his belief reasonable in light of his lack of information specifically regarding the GPS program.

To be sure, Cramer based his assertion on accurate information regarding the preferential admissions policies of five other graduate programs at Eastern Pacific for which he had previously recruited students. He is therefore unlike the defendants in *Wilbur* and *Gagne*, who based their misrepresentations on inaccurate information. Nevertheless, because Cramer was in a position that would have easily allowed him to obtain information regarding admissions policies at Eastern Pacific, his awareness that he had no specific information regarding the GPS program probably makes his belief unreasonable.

C. Finally, Tyler was probably justified in believing Cramer's statement about the preferential admissions policy and relying on it. The courts evaluate the reasonableness of a plaintiff's reliance "in light of his own intelligence and information." *Seeger v. Odell*, 115 P.2d 977, 980–81 (Cal. 1941). The plaintiff may recover for damages based on a reasonable-sounding representation even if he did not conduct his own investigation. *Ashburn v. Miller*, 326 P.2d 229, 234–35 (Cal. Ct. App. 1958). When the plaintiff has not conducted his own investigation, the courts consider two factors in determining the reasonableness of the plaintiff's reliance: the position or experience of the person making the representation and the existence of facts that should make the plaintiff suspect the truth of the representation. *See Carroll v. Gava*, 159 Cal. Rptr. 778, 780–81 (Ct. App. 1979). Cramer's position as a recruiter for Eastern Pacific University and the absence of any facts contradicting his representation likely justify Tyler's reliance.

The court will likely conclude that Cramer held himself out as an expert on Eastern Pacific's admission policies since, as a recruiter, it was his job to represent the university and provide information to potential students. When the person making the representation holds himself out as an expert on the subject of the representation, the courts have held that the plaintiff has acted reasonably in relying on the representation.

In *Shafer*, for instance, the court held that the plaintiffs' reliance was reasonable when the misrepresentation regarding exclusions to the insurance policy was made by the attorney representing the insurance company. 131 Cal. Rptr. 2d at 793. Similarly, in *Carroll*, the court held that it was reasonable for the buyers of a mobile home park to rely on the seller's statement concerning zoning because the seller had experience with real estate generally and mobile home parks specifically. 159 Cal. Rptr. at 780–781. Finally, in *Gagne*, the court held that the plaintiffs were justified in relying on misrepresentations about fill on the property they purchased because the defendant held himself out as an expert in soil testing, 275 P.2d at 15. Like the defendants in these three cases, Cramer also held himself out as an expert in his field and made a statement about the existence of a preferential admissions policy for the GPS program. Providing such information was within the scope of his expertise as a recruiter for Eastern Pacific and likely makes Tyler's reliance reasonable.

Moreover, Tyler's reliance was probably reasonable because he had no information that called into question the truth of Cramer's representation, even though he was employed in the GPS office as a student. The reasonableness of the plaintiff's reliance is questionable only when the plaintiff is given information that contradicts the representation. In *Harper v. Silver*, 19 Cal. Rptr. 78 (Ct. App. 1962), the seller of a boat told the buyer that the boat had matching 275 horsepower engines when in fact it had one 250 and one 275 horsepower engine, causing the boat to run erratically. Even though the buyer talked to the mechanic who had replaced one of the original engines prior to the sale, he never asked about the horsepower of the new engine and did not discover any information that contradicted the original misrepresentation. As a result, the court held that the buyer's reliance on the original misrepresentation was reasonable. *Id.* at 81. Likewise in *Clement v. Smith*, 19 Cal. Rptr. 2d 676, 680 (Ct. App. 1993), the court found that, absent some notice or warning, an insured could reasonably rely on his agent's broad assertions regarding the coverage of his policy without verifying the accuracy of the statement. Like the plaintiffs in these cases, who had no reason to doubt the truth of the matter represented, Tyler had no reason to doubt Cramer's assertion since nothing he learned from Cramer or through his employment with the GPS office called the matter into question.

The court could conclude that Tyler's reliance was not reasonable since his employment with the staff responsible for admissions gave him easy access to information regarding admissions policies. But, like the plaintiff in *Harper*, Tyler received no information that contradicted the misrepresentation he relied on. He had no reason to make further inquiries until he applied for and was denied admission to the GPS program. Thus, Tyler can likely establish all the elements for negligent misrepresentation and recover damages for Cramer's misrepresentation regarding the GPS admissions policy.

II. Statute of Limitations

Tyler's claim probably is not barred by the statute of limitations even though his suit would be brought more than three years after the misrepresentation. Negligent misrepresentation is a species of fraud and is subject to the statute of limitations for fraud. An action is to be brought "[w]ithin three years after all of the elements of fraud have been met." Cal. Civ. Proc. Code § 338(d) (West 2006). The statute also contains an exception: "The cause of action in that case is not to be deemed to have accrued until the discovery, by the aggrieved party, of the facts constituting the fraud." *Id.* The term "discovery" has been defined as the point at which the plaintiff has sufficient information to put a reasonable person on notice that the injury was caused by wrongdoing. *Kline v. Turner*, 105 Cal. Rptr. 2d 699, 702 (Ct. App. 2001).

Tyler probably did not have information sufficient to make him suspect the truth regarding the admissions policy until six months ago. Courts have tolled the statute when a plaintiff was deceived as to the truth, but not when a plaintiff had sufficient information to put a reasonable person on notice to inquire further. For example, in *Watts v. Crocker-Citizens National Bank*, 183 Cal. Rptr. 304, 307 (Ct. App. 1982), a property owner's action for misrepresentation concerning the installation of a water line was not barred by the statute of limitations. The court held that the defendant had failed to disclose during ongoing communications with the plaintiff that there was no water flowing through the pipeline or that the defendant was no longer operating the water system. However, in *Bedolla v. Logan & Frazer*, 125 Cal. Rptr. 59 (Ct. App. 1975), the court held that a claim brought by the limited partners of a business against the general partners was barred where the plaintiffs knew of some financial mismanagement by the defendants during the three years following the fraud. The court stated that this financial mismanagement should have alerted them, as reasonably prudent men, to suspect the other wrongdoing and therefore to discover the fraud earlier than they did. *Id.* at 69–70.

Tyler's case is more similar to *Watts* than to *Bedolla*. Like the plaintiff in *Watts*, who had no notice of any problems with the water line, Tyler had no notice that the information regarding the admissions policy was false. Unlike the plaintiffs in *Bedolla*, who knew of wrongdoing by the defendants that should have prompted inquiry, Tyler had no reason to investigate the admissions policy until his application was denied six months ago.

Nor is it likely that Tyler's part-time job in the GPS program put him in a position where he should have discovered the misrepresentation. Having access to information regarding a misrepresentation is not sufficient to trigger the statute unless a duty to inquire is imposed by law or the circumstances are such as to put a reasonably prudent person on notice to inquire further. *Vega v. Jones, Day, Reaves & Pogue*, 17 Cal. Rptr. 3d 26, 38 (Ct. App. 2004). In *Vega*, the court held that the statute did not bar an action based on fraud concerning the terms upon which a merger and stock issuance were based, even though the terms of the transaction were a matter of public record in documents filed in Delaware. Although the means of learning about the fraud were available to the plaintiff earlier, the court concluded that the statute did not begin to run unless and until the terms of the transaction or other circumstances would have made a reasonable person suspicious enough to inquire further. *Id.* By contrast, in *National Automobile & Casualty Insurance Co. v. Payne*, 67 Cal. Rptr. 784, 789 (Ct. App. 1968), the court held that an action alleging the fraudulent sale of stock options was barred when the plaintiff corporation had two representatives on the defendant corporation's board of directors for eight years before filing the action. The court found that their duties on the board of directors and their access to records were sufficient to show that the plaintiff should have discovered the fraud earlier. *Id.*

Because Tyler had the means to obtain the relevant information, but he had no reason to do so, his situation is more like that in *Vega*, where the plaintiffs could have located the information but were under no duty to do so. His job responsibilities in the GPS program did not involve admissions policy or admissions decisions, and the preferential admissions policy was never mentioned during his employment. Unlike the corporate officers in *Payne*, who had a duty to discover the corporate fraud, Tyler had no duty to investigate the admissions policies of the GPS program.

Although less likely, a court could conclude that Tyler should have discovered the truth sooner. Unlike the information in *Vega*, which was filed in another state, Tyler could have easily verified the existence of such a policy given his employment in the GPS office. Tyler's employment was similar to the directors' position in *Payne*, whose access to records put them in a position to discover the fraud. But while the directors in *Payne* had a legal duty to inquire further, Tyler had no such duty, and no factual circumstances put him on inquiry notice. The policy was never discussed during his employment, and his duties did not involve any matters related to the admissions process. Thus, because he never had a reason to inquire about the truthfulness of Cramer's representation, his claim is probably not barred under the statute of limitations.

CONCLUSION

Tyler's claim against Eastern Pacific University is likely to succeed because Cramer's representation that Eastern Pacific's GPS program gives priority admission to Eastern Pacific graduates likely satisfies all the elements of negligent misrepresentation and the statute of limitations was probably tolled until Tyler discovered the truth. Negligent misrepresentation requires proof that the defendant, with no reasonable grounds for believing the statement to be true, misrepresented a past or existing material fact in order to induce the plaintiff to rely on the statement to his detriment. The law further requires that the plaintiff's reliance was reasonable. Here, Eastern Pacific's recruiter intended that Tyler rely on the false statement regarding the admissions policy in deciding to play for Eastern. Tyler, relying on the statement, declined a scholarship to another college, yet was not given any priority in his application to the GPS program. Thus, the only elements likely to be contested are 1) whether Cramer's misrepresentation was a statement of fact or opinion, 2) whether Cramer lacked a reasonable basis for making the statement, and 3) whether Tyler was justified in believing the statement and relying on it. All three are probably met in this case.

Cramer's statement was most likely a statement of fact, not opinion. Statements by those who hold themselves out as having special knowledge are actionable as statements of fact. Cramer, a recruiter for Eastern Pacific, asserted the existence of a preferential admissions policy while acting as a professional with expertise in the subject matter and in the course of his professional responsibilities to recruit Tyler. Despite the somewhat general nature of Cramer's assertion that Tyler's chances would be "better" as an Eastern Pacific graduate, the statement is probably one of fact in light of Cramer's special expertise and because an improved chance of admission is the defining characteristic of a preferential admissions policy.

Further, Cramer probably had no reasonable grounds to believe his statement to be true because he had no factual information that directly supported it. Although he knew that five of Eastern Pacific's twenty-three other graduate programs had preferential admissions policies, he did not know whether the GPS program had such a policy. Cramer's knowledge regarding the other graduate programs provides some support for his belief, but is unlikely to convince a court that as a university recruiter his ignorance of the university's admissions policies is reasonable.

Finally, Tyler's reliance on Cramer's misrepresentation was probably justified in light of Tyler's own intelligence and information. Cramer's position and experience in providing students with information about the university, together with Tyler's lack of any information that contradicted the misrepresentation made it reasonable for Tyler to believe Cramer's statement. Even though his employment in the GPS office gave him easy access to the truth, Tyler's belief was likely still reasonable because he had no reason to suspect the falsity of the statement and had no duty to verify it.

Nor should the three-year statute of limitations bar Tyler's claim even though he would file suit approximately five years after the misrepresentation occurred. The statute begins to run when a reasonably prudent person would have discovered the fraud. Tyler received no information that contradicted Cramer's original misrepresentation until his application to the GPS program was denied six months ago. The easy access to the truth provided by his employment did not trigger the statute since Tyler had no information to prompt him to inquire further and no duty to do so. Thus, the court will likely find that the statute was tolled until he was denied admission and therefore conclude that Tyler's claim is not time-barred.

Hernandez & Cruz

334 Mission Street
San Francisco, California 94133

September 20, 2012

Mr. Timothy Tyler
420 Oakview Avenue
San Francisco, CA 94135

RE: Possible lawsuit against Eastern Pacific University, file no. P12-37.

Dear Mr. Tyler:

We have considered the potential misrepresentation claim against Eastern Pacific University. In our opinion, based on the facts set forth in this letter, you are likely to prevail should you decide to pursue this claim.

You indicated during our meeting that even though you were interested in attending Eastern Pacific in 2008 and ultimately obtaining a graduate degree from its Global Policy Studies program, you did not qualify for a scholarship there. Thus, you decided to attend Crater Lake College because of its offer of a full soccer scholarship. Subsequently, you were contacted by Mr. Richard Cramer, a recruiter for Eastern Pacific, about playing soccer for Eastern. In order to convince you to attend Eastern, Mr. Cramer told you that you would have a better chance of being admitted to the Global Policy Studies (GPS) program as a graduate of Eastern Pacific. Mr. Cramer admits that he had no specific information regarding the admissions policies of the GPS program and that he based his assertion on knowledge that five other graduate programs at Eastern Pacific gave such a preference to Eastern graduates.

Relying on Mr. Cramer's statement, you declined your full scholarship at Crater Lake and enrolled at Eastern Pacific. During your four years there, you incurred substantial debt because you received only a nominal athletic scholarship. As a student, you also worked part-time in the GPS office but had no contact with the admissions process. No one ever mentioned the preferential admissions policy for Eastern Pacific graduates and you never inquired about it since you assumed Mr. Cramer's statement was true. However, when you applied for admission to the program during your senior year, you were turned down and discovered that the program gave no priority to Eastern Pacific graduates.

Mr. Cramer's false statement that you were more likely to be admitted to the GPS program as a graduate of Eastern Pacific can likely be the basis for a successful claim of negligent misrepresentation. To succeed, you need to prove five things: 1) Mr. Cramer made the statement in order to induce you to play soccer for Eastern Pacific; 2) you suffered substantial financial harm as a result of relying on his statement; 3) Mr. Cramer made a false statement of fact and did not merely express an opinion; 4) Mr. Cramer had no reasonable basis on which to believe his statement was true; and 5) you had no reason to know the statement was false when you decided to decline the scholarship at Crater Lake and enroll at Eastern Pacific.

Since Mr. Cramer admits that he told you that Eastern Pacific graduates were more likely to get into the GPS program in order to recruit you to play soccer for Eastern Pacific, we can prove the first requirement. Further, since you have incurred substantial debt in attending Eastern Pacific for four years, but did not obtain the promised priority in applying to the GPS program, we can prove the second requirement, that you were harmed as a result of your reliance. We are also likely to be able to establish the remaining three requirements.

As to the third requirement, there is no question that Mr. Cramer's statement was false. To support a legal claim, however, the statement must also be one of fact and not just his opinion. This will be one of the most difficult aspects of your case. A statement made by an expert regarding his area of expertise is generally considered to be a statement of fact rather than opinion, since a lay person will assume an expert knows what he's talking about. Because Mr. Cramer was a recruiter for Eastern Pacific, he will probably be considered an expert on Eastern's admissions policies. Therefore, his statement will likely be considered to be one of fact rather than just his opinion. This rule has previously only been applied to members of recognized professions, like lawyers or accountants, but because of Mr. Cramer's position of recruiting potential students for Eastern Pacific, he is likely to also be considered an "expert" in his field.

Further, it is probable that Mr. Cramer had no reasonable basis for believing that the GPS program had a preferential admissions policy, thereby meeting the fourth requirement. His knowledge that five other graduate programs had such a policy provides some basis for his belief regarding the GPS program. Yet he had no specific information regarding the GPS program and made no effort to confirm his belief.

Finally, you can likely prove that you had no reason to know or suspect that Mr. Cramer's statement was false when you made your decision to attend Eastern Pacific. Your employment in the GPS office during your undergraduate career raises a significant question as to whether you should have realized sooner that there was no preference given to Eastern Pacific graduates. The court may look unfavorably on your working in the GPS department for four years and never asking about the priority admissions policy. But since your work did not concern admissions decisions and you learned nothing to contradict your belief that such a policy existed, a court probably will conclude you had no reason to ask about the policy.

There is some question as to ~~whether you can sue Eastern Pacific at this point, for Mr. Cramer's misrepresentation, since it has been more than four years since he made the statement to you.~~ The law limits the length of time during which an injured party can bring an action. In your case, that limit is three years. However, the three-year period is measured from the point at which you either discovered there was no priority admissions policy or had information that should have led you to ask about it. Thus, we must be able to convince the court not only that you did not know Mr. Cramer's statement was false, but also that you had no reason to ask about the admissions policy before your application was rejected.

As I mentioned before, your job with GPS raises some significant questions as to whether you should have asked about the admissions policy sooner. The court only imposes a responsibility to discover the truth where some information raises a question about the matter. We can argue that although you worked in the GPS office, you had no reason to ask about the policy; you did not work with anyone involved in the admissions process, and nothing you came across in your job raised any question about the existence of the preferential admissions policy. Unless Eastern Pacific can show that you had some information that should have prompted you to investigate further, the court will likely conclude that you had no reason to ask about the policy before your application was denied in March of 2012. Under this reasoning, you discovered the misrepresentation only a few months ago—well within the three-year limit.

In closing, I think you will probably succeed should you decide to sue Eastern Pacific for Mr. Cramer's misrepresentation. Since your employment in the GPS department will be a key element in Eastern Pacific's defense of your suit, the court's perception of your demeanor and credibility as a witness will be crucial to your success. You can anticipate very detailed questions in any deposition or trial regarding your job responsibilities and any conversations you had with other people in the department regarding admissions. If your testimony is credible and is consistent with the facts stated above, you will likely succeed in your claim. I look forward to hearing from you.

Sincerely,

Maria Hernandez

Maria Hernandez

Julia P. Chan, State Bar No. 71038
SAMUEL, PARKS & RIORDAN
485 Battery Street, 8th Floor
San Francisco, California 94111
Telephone: (415) 722-5454
Attorneys for Defendant EASTERN PACIFIC UNIVERSITY

UNITED STATES DISTRICT COURT FOR
THE NORTHERN DISTRICT OF CALIFORNIA

TIMOTHY TYLER,	)	CASE NO. CV 13-1532 THB
	)	
Plaintiff,	)	MEMORANDUM OF POINTS
	)	AND AUTHORITIES IN SUPPORT
	)	OF EASTERN PACIFIC
vs.	)	UNIVERSITY'S MOTION FOR
	)	SUMMARY JUDGMENT
	)	
EASTERN PACIFIC UNIVERSITY,	)	
	)	
Defendant.	)	
	)	

Hearing Date: April 15, 2013
Time: 9:30 a.m.
Courtroom 10

INTRODUCTION

Defendant Eastern Pacific University submits this memorandum in support of its motion for summary judgment in Plaintiff Timothy Tyler's diversity action for negligent misrepresentation. Tyler's action is barred by the three-year statute of limitations. The alleged misrepresentation occurred more than four years ago, in 2008. Tyler did not file this suit until 2012. Tyler should have discovered the alleged misrepresentation in 2007 or 2008 but did not do so because he failed to act diligently. Tyler's action therefore is time-barred. Moreover, the alleged misrepresentation was a statement by Richard Cramer, a university recruiter, of his personal belief as to a future event and is not actionable under California law.

STATEMENT OF ISSUES TO BE DECIDED

I.   Whether the plaintiff's claim is barred by the three-year statute of limitations for fraud when his complaint was filed more than three years after he obtained employment in the very office where admissions decisions are made and could easily have discovered accurate information regarding the graduate school admissions policy.

II.   If not, whether the plaintiff can maintain an action for negligent misrepresentation based on the university recruiter's evaluation of the likelihood that plaintiff would be admitted to the university's graduate program at some future point in time, when the tort of negligent misrepresentation must be based on a statement of fact, not opinion.

STATEMENT OF FACTS

Eastern Pacific University (Eastern) is a private university located in San Francisco. In April 2008, Eastern recruited Timothy Tyler, a high school senior residing in Oregon, to play soccer for the university. (Joint Stipulation of Facts ¶ 4.) Tyler matriculated at Eastern in September of 2008 and worked part-time as a work-study student in the Global Policy Studies (GPS) program while he completed his undergraduate education. During his freshman year, Tyler assisted the GPS admissions secretary. His duties included sending packets containing the program's handbook and application to prospective graduate students and assisting in sending out letters either accepting or rejecting applicants to the program. (Joint Stip. ¶¶ 5–6.) In October 2011, Tyler, who was then a senior at Eastern, applied for admission to the GPS graduate program. He was denied admission in March 2012. (Joint Stip. ¶ 11.)

After he was denied admission, Tyler asserted that he had been misled in April of 2008 about an alleged policy of Eastern to give priority to its own graduates for admission to its GPS program. Richard Cramer, the recruiter who approached Tyler about playing soccer for Eastern, believed that such a policy existed and admits telling Tyler that he would have a better chance of being admitted to the program as an Eastern graduate. Cramer did not make any specific promise or guarantee. (Joint Stip. ¶ 9.)

Tyler had also been told by university representatives during his own investigation of the GPS graduate program that excellent credentials were required for admission and that many of the GPS graduate students were honor graduates of major universities. No one in the GPS program has ever mentioned the preferential admissions policy, since no such policy has ever existed. During the four years that Tyler was employed by the GPS program, 2008–2012, no Eastern graduate was admitted to the GPS program. In fact, no Eastern graduate has been admitted to the program since 2002. (Joint Stip. ¶¶ 10, 13–14.)

In October 2012, Tyler filed this diversity action against Eastern, alleging that he had been fraudulently induced to attend Eastern by Cramer's negligent misrepresentation regarding the preferential admissions policy. Tyler asserts that he declined a scholarship at another college to attend Eastern and, as a result, he has incurred debt in excess of $75,000 to attend Eastern.

ARGUMENT

Summary judgment is appropriate in this case. Under Rule 56, summary judgment should be granted where there is no genuine dispute of material fact and the moving party is entitled to judgment as a matter of law. Fed. R. Civ. P. 56. Here, there are no material facts in dispute. The parties agree and have stipulated to most of the material facts. Further, there is no dispute as to the applicable law. Defendant is entitled to summary judgment because this claim is barred by the three-year statute of limitations and because Plaintiff has failed to establish each of the elements required for a claim of negligent misrepresentation under California law.

I.   TYLER'S CLAIM IS BARRED BY THE STATUTE OF LIMITATIONS BECAUSE HE FILED HIS COMPLAINT MORE THAN THREE YEARS AFTER HE KNEW OR SHOULD HAVE KNOWN THAT THE RECRUITER'S OPINION REGARDING THE PREFERENTIAL ADMISSIONS POLICY WAS INCORRECT.

This diversity action is governed by the law of California. See Erie R.R. Co. v. Tompkins, 304 U.S. 64 (1938). In California, negligent misrepresentation is a type of fraud. B.L.M. v. Sabo & Deitsch, 64 Cal. Rptr. 2d 335, 342 (Ct. App. 1997). The statute of limitations for fraud requires that an action be brought within three years after all the elements have been met. Cal. Civ. Proc. Code § 338(d) (West 2006). The statute further provides that the limitation period is tolled until after discovery, by the aggrieved party, of the facts constituting the fraud or mistake. Id. A plaintiff seeking to rely on the "discovery" exception of section 338(d) must prove that with reasonable diligence he could not have discovered the fraud earlier. See Nat'l Auto. & Cas. Ins. Co. v. Payne, 67 Cal. Rptr. 784 (Ct. App. 1968). The alleged fraud here occurred in 2008, when Tyler declined the scholarship to another college and decided to attend Eastern at his own expense. The statute of limitations on the plaintiff's claim therefore expired in 2011.

Tyler cannot rely on section 338(d) to extend the limitations period because he failed to act with reasonable diligence in discovering the fraud earlier. The test for determining whether a plaintiff's delay in discovering the fraud was reasonable is an objective one. The limitation period begins to run when the plaintiff has information "sufficient to make a reasonably prudent person suspicious of fraud, thus putting him on inquiry." Payne, 67 Cal. Rptr. at 788; accord Bedolla v. Logan & Frazer, 125 Cal. Rptr. 59 (Ct. App. 1975).

Not only was Tyler's failure to investigate the admissions policy unreasonable in April 2008, when he had reason to suspect Cramer's statement was not true, he most certainly should have discovered the truth when he began working in the GPS office in the fall of 2008. In Bedolla the court held that a fraud claim against an accounting

3

firm was barred where, in the three years following the alleged fraud, the plaintiff general partners knew of irregularities in the way the defendants had been keeping the financial records for several limited partnerships. The court concluded that this financial mismanagement should have alerted the general partners, as reasonable men, to suspect other wrongdoing. It held that the statute began to run when the plaintiffs received information sufficient to put them on notice to inquire further. 125 Cal. Rptr. at 64. On the other hand, in Watts v. Crocker-Citizens National Bank, 183 Cal. Rptr. 304, 308 (Ct. App. 1982), the court held that a property owner's action for misrepresentation in the installation of a water line was not barred by the statute of limitations. Because the defendant had not mentioned any problems in ongoing communication with the plaintiff, the plaintiff had no notice that the defendant was no longer operating the system or that there was no water available in the line.

Tyler's failure to exercise reasonable diligence, given his knowledge about the GPS program, is more striking than that of the plaintiffs in Bedolla. While the general partners in Bedolla knew of financial mismanagement regarding other limited partnerships, Tyler knew in 2008 that the recruiter's statement was inconsistent with the specific information he had learned about the GPS program during his own investigation—that excellent credentials were required for admission and that many of the students in the program were honor graduates from major universities. No one with whom he had previously spoken had mentioned anything regarding a preferential admissions policy. Unlike the plaintiff in Watts, whose ongoing communications with the defendant discouraged the plaintiff from investigating, Tyler had specific information that should have prompted him to ask about the admissions policy. These facts were sufficient to make a reasonably prudent person suspicious and placed Tyler under a duty to inquire further. Even if this information did not put Tyler on inquiry in April of 2008, he was put on notice after September 2008 when he actually began working in the office of the GPS program. Unlike those cases in which the defrauded parties had no easy access to the correct information and no reason to suspect fraud before the three-year period expired, Tyler's duties included assisting the admissions secretary in handling inquiries and sending out letters accepting and rejecting applicants. During this entire time, no one ever mentioned the preferential admissions policy, nor were any Eastern graduates admitted to the program. These additional facts were sufficient to make a reasonably prudent person suspicious and placed Tyler under a duty to inquire further. Tyler's failure to do so precludes him from relying on section 338(d) to extend the limitations period.

Not only did the information Tyler had impose a duty to investigate further, he also had ready access to the correct information about the admissions policy. He literally had access to the truth every time he went to work. In Payne, the court held that an action regarding the fraudulent sale of stock options was barred when the plaintiff corporation had two representatives on the board of directors of the defendant corporation for eight years prior to the filing of the action. The court found that the directors' participation in the management of the defendant corporation and their access to the books that disclosed the truth about the options were sufficient to make a reasonably prudent person suspicious of fraud earlier. 67 Cal. Rptr. at 789. However, in <u>Vega v. Jones, Day, Reaves & Pogue</u>, 17 Cal. Rptr. 3d 26 (Ct. App. 2004), the court held the cause of action was not barred where a party to a merger asserted he had been misled regarding the "toxic" stock provisions of the transaction. The court held the filing of a stock certificate in Delaware with the details of the financial restructuring was not sufficient to put the plaintiff on notice where there was no other information to make the plaintiff suspicious.

Like the members of the board of directors in <u>Payne</u> who had access to the corporate books to discover the fraudulent sale, Tyler went to work every day in the GPS office. He easily could have asked why no one in the office mentioned a preferential admissions policy, or why Eastern graduates were not admitted to the program during his time as an employee there. The conclusion that the statute of limitations bars Tyler's cause of action is even more compelling than in <u>Payne</u> because Tyler was actually aware of information sufficient to trigger inquiry notice. Tyler's case differs from <u>Vega</u>, where the plaintiff had no reason to suspect there was anything questionable about the transaction and thus was not placed on inquiry notice by the routine filing of a stock certificate, even though it contained the details of the transaction. Unlike those plaintiffs, Tyler had the information at his fingertips. No one attempted to conceal the true admissions policy; all he had to do was ask. Given his access to the truth, Tyler's failure to do so establishes a lack of reasonable diligence that, when combined with his easy and ongoing access to the truth, prevents his using section 338(d) to toll the statute.

Thus, the three-year period for bringing a complaint expired in 2011. Tyler's complaint, filed in 2012, is barred by the statute of limitations. Therefore, Defendant is entitled to judgment as a matter of law.

II. THE RECRUITER'S OPINION REGARDING THE LIKELIHOOD THAT TYLER WOULD BE ADMITTED TO THE GRADUATE PROGRAM IS NOT SUFFICIENT TO SUPPORT TYLER'S CLAIM FOR NEGLIGENT MISREPRESENTATION BECAUSE SUCH A CLAIM MUST BE BASED ON A STATEMENT OF FACT, NOT OPINION.

Negligent misrepresentation requires a statement of existing fact, not opinion; a casual expression of belief is not actionable. <u>Vega v. Jones, Day, Reaves & Pogue</u>, 17 Cal. Rptr. 3d 26, 32 (Ct. App. 2004). In <u>Vega</u>, the plaintiff alleged the defendant had misrepresented the terms of a merger transaction, hiding the so-called "toxic" stock provisions. The court concluded that an attorney's statements regarding the financing of the merger as "standard" and "nothing unusual" were not actionable because they were casual statements of the attorney's opinion and not affirmations of any fact. Id. Similarly, in Gentry v. eBay, Inc., 121 Cal. Rptr. 2d 703, 718 (Ct. App. 2002), the court concluded that the defendant's assertion that a positive rating on its website was "worth its weight in gold" was not a statement of fact that would support an action for negligent misrepresentation.

In this case, Cramer's assertion that Tyler would "have a better chance of getting into the GPS program as an Eastern graduate" was an accurate statement of Cramer's personal belief. Cramer did not assert that Tyler would be admitted to the program, but rather asserted his opinion as to the likelihood of Tyler's future admission. Like the statements in Vega and Gentry, his statement expressed his opinion of the situation and was not a positive assertion of fact.

Such a statement of opinion is fundamentally different from the concrete, factual assertion found actionable in Shafer v. Berger, Kahn, Shafton, Moss, Figler, Simon & Gladstone, 131 Cal. Rptr. 2d 777 (Ct. App. 2003). In that case, the court held that an insurance company attorney's statements regarding exclusions from a company insurance policy were statements of fact. Id. at 793. Representations about the actual content of an insurance policy are not the same as an opinion regarding the likelihood of a future event.

Nor was his statement the kind of professional opinion that may be taken as one of fact. While an opinion by one employed to provide a professional evaluation may be actionable, a casual statement of one's personal belief as to future events is not. The statement in Shafer was made by a lawyer employed to provide his legal evaluation regarding coverage of an insurance policy. By contrast, in Neu-Visions Sports, Inc. v. Soren/McAdam/Bartells, 103 Cal. Rptr. 2d 159 (Ct. App. 2000), an accountant gave his opinion regarding the likely appraisal value of a parcel of real estate. The court held this to be a casual statement of his opinion, not a fact, noting that he was not a professional appraiser. Id. at 163–64. Like the opinion of the accountant in Neu-Visions Sports regarding the value that an appraiser could attach to a particular parcel, Cramer's statement was no more than his opinion about the likelihood Tyler would be admitted to a graduate program at some future point after he obtained an undergraduate degree from Eastern.

Thus, since Cramer's statement was an opinion rather than a statement of fact, Tyler cannot show all of the elements necessary to recover in this action, and Eastern Pacific University is entitled to judgment as a matter of law.

CONCLUSION

Defendant is entitled to judgment as a matter of law. Tyler's claim is time-barred, and the facts do not establish a statement of fact as required to support an action for negligent misrepresentation. Defendant's motion for summary judgment therefore should be granted.

Dated: March 12, 2013

SAMUEL, PARKS & RIORDAN

By: *Julia P. Chan*
Julia P. Chan
Attorneys for Defendant
Eastern Pacific University

Maria Hernandez, State Bar No. 68223
HERNANDEZ & CRUZ
334 Mission Street
San Francisco, California 94133
Telephone: (415) 429-6848
Attorneys for Plaintiff TIMOTHY TYLER

UNITED STATES DISTRICT COURT FOR
THE NORTHERN DISTRICT OF CALIFORNIA

TIMOTHY TYLER,	)	CASE NO. CV 13-1632 THB
	)	
Plaintiff,	)	MEMORANDUM OF
	)	POINTS AND AUTHORITIES IN
	)	OPPOSITION TO EASTERN
	)	PACIFIC UNIVERSITY'S
	)	MOTION FOR SUMMARY
	)	JUDGMENT
EASTERN PACIFIC UNIVERSITY,	)	
	)	
Defendant.	)	
	)	

Hearing Date: April 15, 2013
Time: 9:30 a.m.
Courtroom 10

INTRODUCTION

Plaintiff, Timothy Tyler, submits this memorandum in opposition to Defendant Eastern Pacific University's Motion for Summary Judgment. Summary judgment is only proper where there is no dispute of facts and the moving party is entitled to judgment as a matter of law. The court considers the facts in the light most favorable to the non-moving party. Fed. R. Civ. P. 56. The statute of limitations was tolled in this action because Tyler had no reason to suspect fraud or to inquire further until he discovered Cramer's misrepresentation in March 2012. This action therefore has been timely filed. Furthermore, under California law, Richard Cramer's statement regarding admission to a graduate program was a statement of fact sufficient to support an action for negligent misrepresentation. Thus, summary judgment is not appropriate in this action because Defendant has not established it is entitled to judgment as a matter of law.

QUESTIONS PRESENTED TO THE COURT

I.   Was the statute of limitations tolled when the plaintiff did not discover that he had been misled by the university recruiter regarding the university's graduate school admissions policy until he was denied admission to a graduate program in March 2012 since, although he had access to information regarding the admissions policy, he had no reason to investigate the veracity of the recruiter's statement prior to being denied admission?

II.   Can the plaintiff bring this action for negligent misrepresentation, which requires that the misrepresentation be one of fact rather than opinion, based on the recruiter's false statement that the plaintiff would be given preferential status when applying to a graduate studies program if he obtained his undergraduate degree from the university?

STATEMENT OF FACTS

Plaintiff Timothy Tyler, an Oregon resident, was a member of his high school's varsity soccer team and was named to the state's All Star team. (Joint Stipulation of Facts ¶ 2.) In 2008, during the spring of his senior year, Tyler was recruited to play soccer for Defendant Eastern Pacific University (Eastern) by Richard Cramer, a recruiter for Eastern. Eastern is a private university located in San Francisco, California. Tyler had already been offered a full athletic scholarship to attend Crater Lake College in Oregon after graduation. (Joint Stip. ¶¶ 3, 5.)

In the course of their discussion, Cramer learned of Tyler's desire to obtain a graduate degree from the Global Policy Studies (GPS) program at Eastern. Cramer led Tyler to believe that Eastern had a policy of giving priority to its own graduates in admission to the GPS program, stating that he would have a better chance of being admitted to the program as an Eastern graduate. Cramer admits that he had no idea whether the GPS program had such a policy and made this statement only to induce Tyler to play soccer for Eastern. (Joint Stip. ¶ 9.) Tyler had previously spoken with the staff of the GPS program and no such policy had been mentioned. The discussion with GPS staff had concerned the excellence of the program and the high caliber of student the program was able to attract. (Joint Stip. ¶ 10.)

Tyler subsequently declined the scholarship to Crater Lake College and enrolled at Eastern. Since he received only a small scholarship, he financed his education by working part-time and taking out substantial loans. Tyler was able to obtain a position as a student assistant in the GPS office. (Joint Stip. ¶ 5.) Although he assisted the admissions secretary, his responsibilities were primarily clerical and included handling routine inquiries for applications and mailing letters as instructed by the secretary. Tyler was not involved in admissions decisions and was not aware of how they were made. The preferential admissions policy was never mentioned during the course of his employment. (Joint Stip. ¶ 6.)

In October 2011, Tyler applied for admission to the GPS program. When his application was denied in March 2012, Tyler discovered for the first time that Cramer had deceived him regarding the admissions policy. (Joint Stip. ¶ 11.) Tyler promptly filed this diversity action in October of 2012 to recover the damages incurred as a result of Cramer's deception.

ARGUMENT

I. TYLER'S ACTION FOR FRAUD WAS FILED WITHIN THE THREE-YEAR PERIOD ALLOWED BY THE STATUTE OF LIMITATIONS BECAUSE HE DID NOT DISCOVER UNTIL MARCH 2012 THAT HE HAD BEEN MISLED AND COULD NOT REASONABLY HAVE DISCOVERED THE FRAUD EARLIER.

Summary judgment is only properly granted where there is no genuine issue of material fact and the moving party is entitled to judgment as a matter of law. Further, the court must consider the facts in the light most favorable to the non-moving party. *PhotoMedex, Inc. v. Irwin*, 601 F.3d 919 (9th Cir. 2010). The facts, when viewed in the light most favorable to Timothy Tyler, establish that he was not sufficiently put on notice of the falsity of Cramer's misrepresentation. Thus, summary judgment is not appropriate in this case.

Because this is a diversity action, California law governs. *See Erie R.R. Co. v. Tompkins*, 304 U.S. 64 (1938). Under California law, negligent misrepresentation is a species of fraud. *Balfour, Guthrie & Co. Ltd. v. Hansen*, 38 Cal. Rptr. 525, 536 (Ct. App. 1964). Thus, any action for negligent misrepresentation must be brought within three years. Cal. Civ. Proc. Code § 338(d) (West 2006). The statute of limitations for fraud does not begin to run until "the discovery, by the aggrieved party, of the facts constituting fraud." *Id.* Discovery occurs when the plaintiff obtains information "sufficient to make a reasonably prudent person suspicious of fraud, thus putting him on inquiry." *Nat'l Auto. & Cas. Ins. Co. v. Payne*, 67 Cal. Rptr. 784, 788 (Ct. App. 1968). When a plaintiff has no reason to suspect fraud, however, the statute of limitations does not begin to run. *Watts v. Crocker-Citizens Nat'l Bank*, 183 Cal. Rptr. 304 (Ct. App. 1982).

In this case, the statute did not begin to run until Timothy Tyler was put on notice in March of 2012 that the Global Policy Studies (GPS) program did not give Eastern graduates priority in its admissions process. When a plaintiff relies on information provided by one in a position to know such information, the statute is tolled. For example, in *Watts*, the plaintiff property owner was misled by the owner of a water system regarding the installation and operation of a water line. Because ongoing communications between the parties failed to disclose any difficulties, the plaintiff had no notice to inquire further into potential problems with the system. *Id.* at 307. However, in *Bedolla v. Logan & Frazer*, 125 Cal. Rptr. 59 (Ct. App. 1975), the court held that the plaintiff general partners should have suspected more wrongdoing on the part of the defendant accounting firm when the partners were already aware of other discrepancies in the books kept by the firm. 125 Cal. Rptr. at 68. In each case, the court held that the statute was tolled until the plaintiffs obtained information indicating that the defendants had lied. *Id.*; *Watts*, 183 Cal. Rptr. at 304.

Tyler was misled by Richard Cramer, someone on whom Tyler reasonably believed he could rely. Tyler, a high school senior, had no reason to suspect that a recruiter employed by Eastern would lie to him about its admissions policy, just as the plaintiff in *Watts* had no reason to suspect that the defendant would lie about the water lines. And, unlike the general partners in *Bedolla*, Tyler had no reason to inquire further; during the time of his employment as a student worker, the admissions policy was never mentioned. Believing he had been given correct information, he had no reason to make any further inquiry prior to his application to the program. Thus, the statute did not begin to run until Tyler discovered Cramer's misrepresentation in March of 2012.

Nor did Tyler's job at the GPS office put him on notice earlier than March 2012. Access to information does not put the plaintiff on notice unless he is aware of other wrongdoing by the defendants that should have aroused suspicion and imposed a duty to investigate. In *Vega v. Jones, Day, Reaves & Pogue*, 17 Cal. Rptr. 3d 26 (Ct. App. 2004), the court held the cause of action was not barred when a party to a merger asserted he had been misled regarding the "toxic" stock provisions of the transaction. The court held the filing of a stock certificate containing the details of the financial restructuring was not sufficient to put the plaintiff on notice when there was no other information to make the plaintiff suspicious. The court noted that "the means of knowledge are equivalent to knowledge" only where there is information sufficient to put a reasonable person on notice to inquire further. *Id.* at 38. On the other hand, in *Payne*, the court held that an action regarding the fraudulent sale of stock options was barred because the plaintiff's representatives on the defendant's board of directors had a duty to discover the fraud. They had access to corporate books that disclosed the truth, the court reasoned, and their participation in managing the plaintiff corporation was sufficient to make a reasonably prudent person suspicious of fraud earlier. 67 Cal. Rptr. at 791.

Tyler had no reason to suspect that Cramer had lied to him and no reason to inquire further. His previous discussion with the staff of the GPS program had disclosed only that many of its students were honor graduates from major universities. There was no discussion regarding the preferential admissions policy. Like the plaintiffs in *Vega*, Tyler had no information that led him to suspect fraud. Tyler's situation is significantly different from that of the directors in *Payne*, who had a fiduciary responsibility to know the contents of the corporation's books. Tyler, whose job as a part-time student worker was to complete the various clerical tasks assigned to him by the secretary in the GPS program, had no information that contradicted Cramer's statement. Thus, he had no duty to learn how admissions decisions were made.

Tyler has been harmed by the false statements Cramer used to induce him to attend Eastern for the benefit of its soccer team. He should not be barred from recovering for the damages he has incurred because it took four years for the truth to come to light. As observed by the court in *Twining v. Thompson*, 156 P.2d 29, 34 (Cal. 1945), "[t]he courts do not lightly seize upon small circumstances in order to deny an award to an innocent victim of a fraud upon the ground that he did not discover the fraud sooner." Since Tyler had no reason to suspect the lack of a preferential admissions policy before his application was rejected, the statute of limitations began to run only in March 2012. This action therefore is timely and summary judgment is not appropriate.

II. TYLER IS ENTITLED TO RECOVER DAMAGES FOR NEGLIGENT MISREPRESENTATION BECAUSE EASTERN PACIFIC'S RECRUITER'S FALSE REPRESENTATION THAT THE UNIVERSITY HAS A PREFERENTIAL ADMISSIONS POLICY WAS A STATEMENT OF FACT.

A misrepresentation must be one of existing fact. *Gentry v. eBay, Inc.*, 121 Cal. Rptr. 2d 703, 718–19 (Ct. App. 2002). A statement made by a person who possesses or holds himself out as possessing superior knowledge or information regarding the subject of the statement may be treated as one of fact when the statement is "a deliberate affirmation of the matters stated." *Bily v. Arthur Young & Co.*, 834 P.2d 745, 768 (Cal. 1992) (quoting *Gagne v. Bertran*, 275 P.2d 15, 21 (Cal. 1954)). Although a casual statement of belief will not support an action for negligent misrepresentation, *Vega v. Jones, Day, Reaves & Pogue*, 17 Cal. Rptr. 3d 26, 32 (Ct. App. 2004), Cramer's statement was a deliberate and positive affirmation of a fact—that Eastern graduates are given priority in GPS program admissions. Further, his statement was made as a professional in his field, while he was acting in his official capacity representing Eastern.

This case is similar to other cases imposing liability when the speaker is a professional who is presumed to be in a position to know the fact asserted. For example, in *Shafer v. Berger, Kahn, Shafton, Moss, Figler, Simon & Gladstone*, 131 Cal. Rptr. 2d 777, 789 (Ct. App. 2003), the court imposed liability for a statement by counsel representing an insurance company regarding exclusions in a company policy. Similarly, in *Anderson v. Deloitte & Touche*, 66 Cal. Rptr. 2d 512, 517 (Ct. App. 1997), the court held that an accountant's inaccurate financial projections in a report were positive assertions of fact.

Like the professionals in those cases, Cramer was representing his employer in his official capacity as a recruiter at the time he made the false statement regarding information he was in a position to know. The statement that Tyler's chances of admission to the GPS program would be greater if he were a graduate of Eastern Pacific University is an assertion of fact concerning the existence of a preferential admissions program.

This case differs from those in which a defendant has offered his casual opinion on matters outside the area of his expertise. Where a principal in an accounting firm stated his opinion as to the appraisal value of real estate, for example, the court declined to impose liability since the defendant was not an appraiser and had never represented himself as such. *Neu-Visions Sports, Inc. v. Soren/McAdam/Bartells*, 103 Cal. Rptr. 2d 159 (Ct. App. 2000). Cramer, however, is a professional who was in a position to know the information asserted.

Cramer's statement was also more definite and substantive than statements the courts have previously determined were only opinions. For example, the courts have declined to hold a defendant responsible for vague statements that financing for a merger was "standard" and "nothing unusual," *Vega*, 17 Cal. Rptr. 3d at 32, or for the assertion that a positive rating on a website was "worth its weight in gold," *Gentry*, 121 Cal. Rptr. 2d at 7018. Cramer's statement was much more specific. He asserted unequivocally that Tyler would have a better chance of being admitted to the GPS program as a graduate from Eastern than as a graduate from another institution.

Cramer's statement that Eastern graduates are given priority in admissions to the GPS program was made in his official capacity as a recruiter for Eastern. It was information he held himself out as being in a position to know and was asserted as a statement of fact. It is therefore sufficient to support an action for negligent misrepresentation and Defendant is not entitled to judgment as a matter of law.

CONCLUSION

For the reasons stated herein, Eastern's motion for summary judgment should be denied.

Dated: March 17, 2013

HERNANDEZ & CRUZ

By: *Maria Hernandez*

Maria Hernandez
Attorneys for Plaintiff
Timothy Tyler

UNITED STATES DISTRICT COURT FOR
THE NORTHERN DISTRICT OF CALIFORNIA

TIMOTHY TYLER,	)	CASE NO. CV 13-1632 THB
	)	
Plaintiff,	)	
	)	
v.	)	ORDER RE SUMMARY
	)	JUDGMENT MOTION
EASTERN PACIFIC UNIVERSITY,	)	
	)	
Defendant.	)	
	)	

Defendant, Eastern Pacific University, has moved this Court for summary judgment in Plaintiff Timothy Tyler's diversity action for negligent misrepresentation. Eastern so moves on two grounds. First, Eastern contends it is entitled to summary judgment because Tyler's claim is time-barred. Second, Eastern contends that Tyler has failed to establish all necessary elements of his negligent misrepresentation cause of action. For the reasons that follow, Defendant's motion is granted.

Facts

In his senior year of high school, Oregon resident Timothy Tyler applied for and was granted admission to Eastern Pacific University (Eastern) in San Francisco and Crater Lake College in Oregon. His preference was to obtain his undergraduate degree from Eastern and then attend Eastern's graduate Global Policies Studies Program (GPS). To that end, Tyler spoke with representatives of Eastern's GPS program, who told Tyler that he would need excellent credentials for admission and that many of their students were honor graduates from major universities. Tyler did not inquire and Eastern did not offer any information concerning whether Eastern graduates received preferential admissions to the GPS program.

Tyler subsequently was advised by Eastern's financial assistance office that he did not qualify for a scholarship. Crater Lake College, however, offered Tyler a four-year athletic scholarship to play soccer. Tyler decided to accept this scholarship and attend Crater Lake.

In April 2008, before Tyler paid his deposit to Crater Lake, Richard Cramer, a recruiter from Eastern, approached Tyler about playing soccer for Eastern. When Cramer learned that Tyler was interested in Eastern's GPS Program, Cramer told Tyler,

"You'll have a better chance of getting into the GPS Program as an Eastern graduate than coming in as a graduate from somewhere else."

Based on his conversation with Cramer, Tyler declined his scholarship at Crater Lake and enrolled at Eastern in May 2008. He received only a nominal scholarship for playing soccer and incurred substantial debt to pay his educational and living expenses. As an undergraduate student, Tyler worked part-time in the GPS Department assisting the admissions secretary by performing clerical work, including handling routine inquiries for applications and mailing letters. He was not involved with admissions decisions, and he never discussed or inquired regarding the preferential admissions policy at any time. During the time Tyler worked in the GPS Department, no Eastern graduates were accepted in the GPS Program.

Tyler applied for admission to the GPS Program in October 2011 during his senior year at Eastern. He was denied admission in March 2012. He learned at that time that Eastern graduates received no preferential admission to the GPS Program and that Eastern never had such a policy. This suit was filed shortly thereafter.

Tyler has since admitted in these proceedings that he was never told by anyone other than Cramer that Eastern or the GPS Program had such a preferential admissions policy and that he never investigated the existence of any such policy. Cramer has admitted that he made the statement solely to recruit Tyler to play soccer for Eastern.

I. Statute of Limitations

The Court finds that Tyler's suit is time-barred. California Civil Procedure Code §338(d) (West 2006) requires an action for negligent misrepresentation to be brought within three years after all the elements of the cause of action have been satisfied. The statute, however, provides an exception; the cause of action is not deemed to have accrued, and therefore the limitation period does not begin to run, "until discovery, by the aggrieved party, of the facts constituting the fraud or mistake." *Id.* Discovery occurs when a plaintiff has sufficient information to put a reasonable person on notice that an injury was caused by wrongdoing. *Klein v. Turner*, 105 Cal. Rptr. 2d 699, 702 (Ct. App. 2001). A plaintiff seeking to invoke the "discovery" exception must prove that with reasonable diligence, he could not have discovered the fraud earlier. *Nat'l Auto. & Cas. Ins. Co. v. Payne*, 67 Cal. Rptr. 784, 788 (Ct. App. 1968).

The cause of action in the present case "accrued" in May 2008 when Tyler gave up his scholarship at Crater Lake and enrolled at Eastern. All elements of negligent misrepresentation were allegedly satisfied at that time. The statute of limitations thus ran on Tyler's claim in May 2011, and Tyler's suit was time-barred as of that date unless the facts bring it within the discovery exception.

The Court further finds that Tyler's claim does not fall within the discovery exception. Tyler not only had information sufficient to put a reasonable person on notice to inquire further, his employment in the GPS office provided him ample opportunity to do so. Thus, at the latest, the statute began to run in September of 2008 when he began working in the GPS office and this action is time-barred.

The test for determining whether a plaintiff's delay in discovering a fraud is reasonable is an objective one, and the limitation period is no longer suspended when the plaintiff has information "sufficient to make a reasonably prudent person suspicious of fraud, thus putting him on notice of inquiry." *Payne*, 67 Cal. Rptr. at 788. In *Bedolla v. Logan & Frazier*, 125 Cal. Rptr. 59 (Ct. App. 1975), the court held that a fraud claim against an accounting firm was barred by the statute of limitations. There, the general partners knew of mismanagement and irregularities in the financial records for several limited partnerships managed by the defendant. The court concluded that this information should have alerted the general partners, as reasonable men, to suspect other wrongdoing. *Id.* at 71. On the other hand, in *Watts v. Crocker-Citizens National Bank*, 183 Cal. Rptr. 304 (Ct. App. 1982), the court found that the discovery exception preserved the plaintiffs' claim. In *Watts*, the plaintiffs had no reason to suspect a fraud, given their ongoing communications with the defendant, and therefore had no reason to inquire further.

Tyler's actions are strikingly similar to those of the plaintiffs in *Bedolla*. Tyler has not demonstrated due diligence in investigating the GPS admissions policy and discovering the fraud, despite having information that should have prompted him to do so. Tyler had reason to be suspicious of Cramer's statement since his own inquiries in 2008 had disclosed that students in the GPS program had excellent credentials and many were honor graduates from major universities. Tyler simply accepted Cramer's representation at face value without requesting any confirmation of the preferential admissions policy or otherwise making any effort to determine whether Cramer's representation was accurate. Tyler's situation is markedly different from that of the plaintiff in *Watts*, who had no reason to suspect fraud, because Cramer's statement was inconsistent with the information Tyler had obtained during his prior inquiries. Therefore, Tyler failed to exercise reasonable diligence to discover the fraud.

Moreover, Tyler's failure to make any inquiry regarding the alleged preferential admissions policy after he began working in the GPS office is not reasonable given the additional information he acquired and the ease with which he could have verified the policy. In *Vega v. Jones, Day, Reaves & Pogue*, 17 Cal. Rptr. 3d 26 (Ct. App. 2004), the court held the cause of action was not barred where a party to a merger asserted he had been misled regarding the "toxic" stock provisions of the transaction. The court held the filing of a stock certificate with the details of the financial restructuring was not sufficient to put the plaintiff on notice where there was no other information to make the plaintiff suspicious. *Id.* at 38. However, in *Payne*, the court held that an action alleging the fraudulent sale of stock options was barred. The court concluded that the plaintiff's representatives on the defendant's board of directors had a duty to discover the fraud earlier. Their participation in managing the plaintiff corporation was sufficient to make a reasonably prudent person suspicious and they had access to corporate books that disclosed the fraud. 67 Cal. Rptr. at 791.

Tyler's situation is similar to that of the plaintiff corporation in *Payne*. Knowing that no graduate from Eastern received preferential admissions treatment during his tenure as an employee, a fact that would have aroused suspicion in the mind of any reasonable person, Tyler made no effort to investigate the admissions policy despite his ongoing employment in the GPS office. Although access to the truth does not necessarily put a plaintiff on notice, the information Tyler had as well as what he learned while working in the GPS office imposed a duty to at least inquire about the admissions policy. The ease with which he could have discovered the truth makes his failure to do so unreasonable under the circumstances. Tyler's situation is quite different from the facts of *Vega*, where the plaintiffs had had no information about problems with the stock transaction and therefore no duty to investigate the stock certificate. As Eastern urges, "all he had to do was ask." (Eastern's Mem. of Points and Authorities 6).

Tyler has been seriously harmed by Cramer's deliberate deception. But Tyler's argument that he should not be barred from recovering damages because it took four years for him to discover the truth is an argument against the statute of limitations itself, not against its application in this case. The discovery exception is not applicable here and, because the statute expired no later than September 2011, this action is barred.

II. Negligent Misrepresentation

Even if Tyler's claim were not barred by the statute of limitations, the Court finds that Eastern is entitled to summary judgment as a matter of law because Tyler has failed to establish all the elements of his cause of action. Negligent misrepresentation is a form of fraud. To prove a claim for negligent misrepresentation a plaintiff must establish each of the following elements: "(1) A misrepresentation of a past or existing material fact, (2) without reasonable grounds for believing it to be true, (3) with intent to induce another's reliance on the fact misrepresented, (4) ignorance of the truth and justifiable reliance thereon by the party to whom the misrepresentation was directed, and (5) damages." *B.L.M. v. Sabo & Deitsch*, 64 Cal. Rptr. 2d 335, 342 (Ct. App. 1997) (quoting *Fox v. Pollack*, 226 Cal. Rptr. 532, 536 (Ct. App. 1986)).

Defendant argues that Tyler cannot establish the first element in this case. The issue, precisely stated, is whether Cramer's statement about the priority admissions treatment given to Eastern undergraduates was a representation of fact or a casual statement of belief or opinion. If it is the former, then plaintiff has established this element of the tort of negligent misrepresentation. If it is the latter, as Eastern contends, then this action must be dismissed. *See Gentry v. eBay, Inc.*, 121 Cal. Rptr. 2d 703 (Ct. App. 2004).

The record supports the conclusion that Cramer's statement was nothing more than a casual statement of his belief or opinion that Tyler's chances of admission to the GPS Program would be better if he attended Eastern as an undergraduate. There is no fundamental difference between Cramer's statement and what the California courts have heretofore considered an "opinion" or "casual expression of belief." *See Vega v. Jones, Day, Reaves & Pogue*, 17 Cal. Rptr. 3d 26 (Ct. App. 2004) (attorney's statements that merger was "standard" and "nothing unusual" were casual statements of belief and not assertions of fact); *Gentry*, 121 Cal. Rptr. 2d 703 (assertion that positive rating on website was "worth its weight in gold" was not a statement of fact). Significantly, Cramer did not guarantee that Tyler would be accepted into the GPS Program, nor did he represent that Eastern had a formal policy of giving priority to Eastern undergraduate applicants. Thus, while Cramer's statement was misleading, it falls short of the positive, substantive assertion of fact necessary to support a cause of action for negligent misrepresentation. *See Shafer v. Berger, Kahn, Shaftner, Moss, Figler & Gladstone*, 131 Cal. Rptr. 2d 777 (Ct. App. 2003); *Anderson v. Deloitte & Touche*, 66 Cal. Rptr. 2d 516 (Ct. App. 1997).

Nor does the Court accept Tyler's argument that even if Cramer's statement was an opinion, it nonetheless should be considered an assertion of fact given Cramer's position as a college recruiter. A statement of a professional can be considered "a deliberate affirmation of the matter stated," even though it is in the form of an opinion. *Bily v. Arthur Young & Co.*, 834 P. 2d 745, 768 (Cal. 1992) (quoting *Gagne v. Bertran*, 275 P. 2d 15, 21 (Cal. 1952)). Cramer, however, is a college recruiter, not a professional. Accordingly, the standard applicable to opinions expressed by professionals is not applicable here.

The Court further rejects Tyler's suggestion that the professional opinion rule should be expanded beyond trained professionals, such as lawyers and accountants, to include Cramer. There is no justifiable reason for such an expansion, nor would the rule's underlying policy be served by applying it to non-professionals such as college recruiters. Lawyers and accountants are trained professionals having special knowledge, whose fiduciary obligations place them in a relationship of trust with their clients. It is this fiduciary relationship that holds such professionals to a more exacting standard and justifies imposing liability on them for misrepresentations in their "opinions." The same fiduciary relationship does not exist between college recruiters and prospective students.

Moreover, it has not been demonstrated anywhere in the record that Cramer, although a recruiter for Eastern's sports programs, had any detailed knowledge of Eastern's admission policy. In fact, the representation at issue here strongly suggests he did not. Thus, even if Cramer could be considered a "professional" recruiter, he was not a professional admissions officer. Accordingly, his opinion regarding Eastern's admission policy was outside his field of expertise and therefore not actionable. *See*

Neu-Vision Sports, Inc. v. Soren/McAdam/Bartells, 103 Cal. Rptr. 2d 159 (Ct. App. 2000) (statement regarding the likely appraisal value of real estate by accounting firm principal was only his opinion as he was not a professional appraiser and never represented himself as such).

In sum, Cramer's statement was not a misrepresentation of fact. Eastern's motion for summary judgment based on Tyler's failure to establish all elements of his cause of action therefore must be granted.

Conclusion

For the reasons given above, it is hereby ORDERED that defendant Eastern Pacific University's Motion for Summary Judgment be and hereby is GRANTED.

IT IS SO ORDERED this 13th day of July, 2013.

Thomas H. Belknap

THOMAS H. BELKNAP, JR.
United States District Judge
Northern District of California

UNITED STATES CIRCUIT COURT OF APPEALS
FOR THE NINTH CIRCUIT

CIVIL CASE NO. 13-16702

TIMOTHY TYLER,
                               Appellant,

v.

EASTERN PACIFIC UNIVERSITY,
                               Appellee.

ON APPEAL FROM THE UNITED STATES DISTRICT COURT
FOR THE NORTHERN DISTRICT OF CALIFORNIA
(Case No. CV 13-1632 THB)

BRIEF FOR THE APPELLANT

Maria Hernandez, State Bar No. 68223
HERNANDEZ & CRUZ
334 Mission Street
San Francisco, California 94133
Telephone: (415) 429-6848

TABLE OF CONTENTS

Table of Authorities Cited..ii

Jurisdictional Statement...1

Statutes Involved...1

Standard of Review..1

Statement of Issues Presented..1

Statement of the Case..1

Statement of Facts...2

Summary of Argument...3

Argument 4

I.   THE DISTRICT COURT ERRED IN HOLDING THAT PLAINTIFF'S
      ACTION FOR NEGLIGENT MISREPRESENTATION WAS BARRED
      BY THE STATUTE OF LIMITATIONS BECAUSE THE STATUTE WAS
      TOLLED UNTIL PLAINTIFF DISCOVERED THE RECRUITER HAD
      MISLED HIM AND PLAINTIFF FILED THIS ACTION WITHIN
      MONTHS OF DISCOVERING THE TRUTH. 4

      A.   Plaintiff was entitled to rely on information provided by Defendant's
            recruiter without further investigation because, as a professional
            representative of Defendant Eastern, the recruiter was in a position to
            know the information he asserted regarding admissions policies...................5

      B.   Plaintiff had no duty to investigate further regarding the preferential
            admissions policy because he had no information that called the
            recruiter's statement into question. 6

II.   THE DISTRICT COURT ERRED IN HOLDING THE UNQUALIFIED
      ASSERTION THAT DEFENDANT EASTERN HAD A PREFERENTIAL
      ADMISSIONS POLICY FOR ITS GRADUATES WAS NOT A
      STATEMENT OF FACT SUFFICIENT TO SUPPORT AN ACTION FOR
      NEGLIGENT MISREPRESENTATION, BUT WAS MERELY A CASUAL
      STATEMENT OF THE RECRUITER'S OPINION. 7

      A.   The statement regarding the graduate program's preferential
            admissions policy was a statement of fact since it was made by a
            university recruiter who was in a position to have superior
            knowledge regarding university policies. 8

      B.   The recruiter's statement regarding the existence of a preferential
            admissions policy was a concrete assertion of fact, not a casual or
            general statement of personal opinion. 9

Conclusion 10

Appendix...a-1

TABLE OF AUTHORITIES CITED

Federal Cases:

Buono v. Norton, 371 F.3d 543 (9th Cir. 2004) 1

Erie R.R. Co. v. Tompkins, 304 U.S. 64 (1938) 5

Laws v. Sony Music Entm't, Inc., 448 F.3d 1134 (9th Cir. 2006) 1

PhotoMedex, Inc. v. Irwin, 601 F.3d 919 (9th Cir. 2010) 5

California Cases:

Anderson v. Deloitte & Touche, 66 Cal. Rptr. 2d 512 (Ct. App. 1997) 8

Balfour, Guthrie & Co. v. Hansen, 38 Cal. Rptr. 525 (Ct. App. 1964) 5

Bedolla v. Logan & Frazer, 125 Cal. Rptr. 59 (Ct. App. 1975) 5

Bily v. Arthur Young & Co., 11 Cal. Rptr. 2d 51 (Ct. App. 1992) 8

B.L.M. v. Sabo & Deitsch, 64 Cal. Rptr. 2d 335 (Ct. App. 1997) 7

Fox v. Pollack, 226 Cal. Rptr. 532 (Ct. App. 1986) 7

Gagne v. Bertran, 275 P.2d 15 (Cal. 1954) 8

Gentry v. eBay, Inc., 121 Cal. Rptr. 2d 703 (Ct. App. 2002) 7, 9

Nat'l Auto. & Cas. Ins. Co. v. Payne, 67 Cal. Rptr. 784 (Ct. App. 1968) 5, 6, 7

Neu-Visions Sports, Inc. v. Soren/McAdam/Bartells, 103 Cal. Rptr. 2d
   159 (Ct. App. 2000) 8

Parsons v. Tickner, 37 Cal. Rptr. 2d 810 (Ct. App. 1995) 5

Shafer v. Berger, Kahn, Shafton, Moss, Figler, Simon & Gladstone,
   131 Cal. Rptr. 2d 777 (Ct. App. 2003) 8

Twining v. Thompson, 156 P.2d 29 (Cal. Ct. App. 1945) 7

Vega v. Jones, Day, Reaves & Pogue, 17 Cal. Rptr. 3d 26 (Ct. App. 2004) 6, 7, 9

Watts v. Crocker-Citizens Nat'l Bank, 183 Cal. Rptr. 304 (Ct. App. 1982) 5

Statutes:

28 U.S.C. § 1291 (2006) 1

28 U.S.C. § 1332(a)(1) (2006) 1

Cal. Civ. Proc. Code § 338(d) (West 2006) 1, 5

Fed. R. Civ. P. 56 4

JURISDICTIONAL STATEMENT

This diversity action was brought in the United States District Court for the Northern District of California under 28 U.S.C. § 1332(a)(1) (2006). Plaintiff is a citizen of the State of Oregon and Defendant is a private educational institution located in San Francisco, California. The amount in controversy exceeds $75,000.

This Court has jurisdiction over this appeal from a final order of the district court pursuant to 28 U.S.C. § 1291 (2006). The district court's grant of summary judgment in favor of Defendant on July 13, 2013, was a final order as to all claims. The Notice of Appeal was filed on July 20, 2013, and is thus timely under F.R. App. P. 4.

STATUTES INVOLVED

The text of § 338(d) of the California Civil Procedure Code (West 2006) relevant to this case is reproduced in the Appendix.

STANDARD OF REVIEW

The standard of review for a grant of summary judgment by the district court is *de novo*. *Buono v. Norton*, 371 F.3d 543, 545 (9th Cir. 2004). That is, the Court must view the evidence in the light most favorable to the nonmoving party and determine whether there is any genuine issue of material fact and whether the district court properly applied the relevant substantive law. *Laws v. Sony Music Entm't, Inc.*, 448 F.3d 1134 (9th Cir. 2006).

STATEMENT OF ISSUES PRESENTED

I.   Did the district court err in holding that the three-year statute of limitations barred Plaintiff's fraud claim, where the statute is tolled until Plaintiff reasonably should have discovered the fraud and Defendant university's recruiter misrepresented the graduate school admissions policy in April 2008 to recruit Plaintiff to play soccer for the university, but Plaintiff had no reason to question the truth of the recruiter's statement until his application to graduate school was denied in March 2012?

II.   Did the district court err in holding that the university recruiter's unqualified statement that Defendant gave priority to Eastern graduates in its graduate admissions process was not a statement of fact sufficient to support a cause of action for negligent misrepresentation, but was merely a statement of opinion and thus not actionable?

STATEMENT OF THE CASE

Plaintiff Timothy Tyler filed this diversity action on October 10, 2012, in the United States District Court for the Northern District of California, seeking to recover damages he suffered as a result of the negligent misrepresentation of Defendant Eastern Pacific University's ("Eastern's") athletic recruiter. The university filed a motion for Summary Judgment on March 12, 2013, alleging that the action was barred by the applicable statute of limitations and that the recruiter's statement was a statement of opinion insufficient to support a cause of action. Tyler opposed the motion on March 17, 2013, asserting that the statute of limitations was tolled until he discovered the falsity of the recruiter's statement in March 2012 and that this action was therefore timely filed. Tyler further asserted that the recruiter's statement was a factual statement asserting the existence of a specific preferential admissions policy. The district court heard the motion on April 15, 2013, and on July 13, 2013, the court granted summary judgment for the university on both issues. Order re Summ. J. Mot., July 13, 2013. (R. at 51-57.) The decision is not reported.

STATEMENT OF FACTS

Plaintiff Tyler filed this action for negligent misrepresentation against Defendant Eastern, a private university located in San Francisco, California. Tyler, an Oregon resident, was a member of his high school's varsity soccer team and was named to the state's All Star team. (R. at 2.) In 2008, during the spring of his senior year, Tyler was recruited to play soccer for Defendant by Richard Cramer, a recruiter for Eastern. At that point, Tyler had been offered a full athletic scholarship to attend Crater Lake College in Oregon after graduation. (R. at 3, 5.)

In the course of their discussion, Cramer learned of Tyler's desire to obtain a graduate degree from the Global Policy Studies ("GPS") program at Eastern. Cramer led Tyler to believe that Eastern had a policy of giving priority to its own graduates who applied to the GPS program, stating that Tyler would have a better chance of being admitted to the program as an Eastern graduate. Cramer admits that he had no idea whether the GPS program had such a policy and made this statement only to induce Tyler to play soccer for Eastern. (R. at 9.) Tyler had previously spoken with the staff of the GPS program and no such policy had been mentioned. The discussion with the GPS staff had concerned the excellence of the program and the high caliber of student the program was able to attract. (R. at 10.)

Tyler subsequently declined the scholarship to Crater Lake College and enrolled at Eastern. Since he received only a small scholarship, he financed his education by working part-time and taking out substantial loans. To meet his financial obligations, Tyler obtained a position as a student assistant in the GPS program. (R. at 5.) Although one of his duties was assisting the admissions secretary, his responsibilities were primarily clerical, such as handling routine inquiries for applications and mailing letters as he was instructed by the secretary. Tyler was not involved in admissions decisions and was not aware of how they were made. The preferential admissions policy was never mentioned during the course of his employment. (R. at 6.)

In October 2011, Tyler applied for admission to the GPS program. When his application was denied in March 2012, Tyler discovered for the first time that Cramer had deceived him regarding the admissions policy. (R. at 11.) Tyler promptly filed this diversity action in October of 2012 to recover damages incurred as a result of Cramer's deception. Eastern thereafter was granted summary judgment by the district court on July 13, 2013. Tyler filed a Notice of Appeal on July 20, 2013, and brings this appeal to challenge the district court's Order.

SUMMARY OF ARGUMENT

The district court improperly granted summary judgment because Timothy Tyler's action for negligent misrepresentation was timely filed and Cramer's statement regarding the admissions policy was a statement of fact and therefore sufficient to support this cause of action. Since Tyler brought this action within months of discovering that Richard Cramer, a recruiter employed by Eastern, had misled him in order to recruit him to play soccer for Eastern, it is not barred by the statute of limitations. This diversity action must be decided under California law, which generally imposes a three-year statute of limitations in fraud cases. The statute is tolled, however, when 1) the false information was provided by one in a position to know the truth of the matter asserted, and 2) the plaintiff had no information that called the defendant's statement into question. Here, Tyler, a high school senior, was told by a recruiter for Eastern that he would have a better chance of being admitted to the Global Policies Studies graduate program at Eastern if he obtained his undergraduate degree from Eastern. The information regarding Eastern's admissions policies was provided to Tyler by Eastern's representative—an athletic recruiter. Because it is a recruiter's job to provide information to prospective students, he had a responsibility to provide accurate information about Eastern's programs and the means to investigate any information about which he was unsure.

Tyler did not learn anything during the four years of his undergraduate education that cast any doubt on the recruiter's assertion, contrary to the district court's opinion. He was aware that the GPS program was well regarded and admitted highly qualified students. This was not inconsistent with the recruiter's assertion that Eastern graduates receive priority in the GPS admissions process. Moreover, Tyler's employment in the GPS office did not provide him with any information inconsistent with the recruiter's statement. The district court incorrectly equated Tyler's access to information with a duty to investigate. His employment as a student worker assisting the departmental secretary, while giving him access to information about admissions policies, did not impose upon him a duty to investigate the policies. In the course of his running errands and stuffing envelopes, he learned nothing that caused him to question what he had been told. That information only came to light when his application was denied in March 2012. At that point the statute began to run. Because this action was filed in October of that same year, the district court erred in holding that this action was barred by the statute of limitations.

The tolling provision in the statute of limitations for fraud is intended to prevent defendants who are successful in perpetrating fraud upon their unsuspecting victims from using the passage of time to protect them from liability. Instead, the tolling provision allows the plaintiff to hold the defendant responsible for his actions as soon as the fraud comes to light. Here, to find Tyler's action barred by the statute would be to allow the outcome that the tolling provision specifically seeks to prevent; Eastern will be protected from liability by the success of the recruiter's misrepresentation. Such an outcome is not supported by California law or policy. The district court's grant of summary judgment should be reversed.

Moreover, the recruiter's misrepresentation that the GPS program gave priority in its admissions process to graduates of Eastern is a statement of fact, not merely an opinion, and is sufficient to support an action for negligent misrepresentation. California courts have recognized that statements by professionals in a position to know the information asserted are statements of fact, rather than mere opinions. Contrary to the district court's opinion, this rule is not limited to lawyers and accountants. The Eastern recruiter, as one employed to convince prospective students to attend Eastern, was in a position to know whether a preferential admissions policy existed. He made this statement in his official capacity, as a representative of Eastern, not as a friend or advisor. Further, he asserted the existence of such a policy as a fact, not as his evaluation of the situation. His statement was not intended nor understood to be merely his opinion.

The essence of an action for negligent misrepresentation is to make defendants liable for the harm caused by falsehoods carelessly thrown around to induce another's action. Here, the recruiter's statement benefited Eastern exactly as it was intended—it induced Tyler to forego his scholarship from another college and play soccer for Eastern. The law does not allow Eastern to avoid responsibility for the actions of its recruiter by asserting that his statement was only a casually-given opinion. The district court erred in so concluding and its grant of summary judgment should be reversed.

ARGUMENT

I.   THE DISTRICT COURT ERRED IN HOLDING THAT PLAINTIFF'S ACTION FOR NEGLIGENT MISREPRESENTATION WAS BARRED BY THE STATUTE OF LIMITATIONS BECAUSE THE STATUTE WAS TOLLED UNTIL PLAINTIFF DISCOVERED THE RECRUITER HAD MISLED HIM AND PLAINTIFF FILED THIS ACTION WITHIN MONTHS OF DISCOVERING THE TRUTH.

Summary judgment was improperly granted because Defendant Eastern failed to establish that there is no genuine dispute as to any material fact and that it is entitled to judgment as a matter of law. *See* Fed. R. Civ. P. 56. The court must consider the facts in the light most favorable to the non-moving party. *PhotoMedex, Inc. v. Irwin*, 601 F.3d 919 (9th Cir. 2010). When viewed in the light most favorable to Timothy Tyler, the facts establish that he was not put on notice before March 2012 that Cramer had misled him.

California law governs this diversity action. *See Erie R.R. Co. v. Tompkins*, 304 U.S. 64 (1938). Under California law, negligent misrepresentation is a species of fraud. *Balfour, Guthrie & Co. Ltd. v. Hansen*, 38 Cal. Rptr. 525, 536 (Ct. App. 1964). Thus, any action for negligent misrepresentation must be brought within three years. Cal. Civ. Proc. Code § 338(d) (West 2006). However, the statute of limitations for fraud does not begin to run until "the discovery, by the aggrieved party, of the facts constituting fraud." *Id.*

When a plaintiff has no reason to suspect fraud, the statute of limitations is tolled. *Watts v. Crocker-Citizens Nat'l Bank*, 183 Cal. Rptr. 304 (Ct. App. 1982). The tolling provision is supported by the underlying policy of protecting a plaintiff who, due to the circumstances, does not know he has been harmed, and the corollary that the defendant should not benefit from the plaintiff's ignorance. *Parsons v. Tickner*, 37 Cal. Rptr. 2d 810, 817 (Ct. App. 1995). The courts have defined "discovery" as the point at which the plaintiff obtains information "sufficient to make a reasonably prudent person suspicious of fraud, thus putting him on inquiry." *Nat'l Auto. & Cas. Ins. Co. v. Payne*, 67 Cal. Rptr. 784, 788 (Ct. App. 1968).

A. <u>Plaintiff was entitled to rely on information provided by Defendant's recruiter without further investigation because, as a professional representative of Defendant Eastern, the recruiter was in a position to know the information he asserted regarding admissions policies.</u>

The statute began to run only when Tyler discovered in March of 2012 that the GPS program did not give Eastern graduates priority in its admissions process. In defining what constitutes "discovery," the courts have held that where a plaintiff relies on information provided by one in a position to have such information, the statute is tolled until the plaintiff is put on notice to inquire further. For example, in *Watts* the plaintiff property owner was misled by the owner of a water system regarding the installation and operation of a water line. The court noted that ongoing communications between the parties failed to mention any difficulties and held that the statute was tolled until the plaintiff obtained information indicating that the defendant had lied. *Watts*, 183 Cal. Rptr. at 307. However, in *Bedolla v. Logan & Frazer*, 125 Cal. Rptr. 59 (Ct. App. 1975), the court held the statute was not tolled where the plaintiff general partners were aware of other discrepancies in the books kept by the defendant accounting firm and thus, were put on notice to inquire further about the firm's wrongdoing. *Id.* at 68.

Like the plaintiff in *Watts*, Tyler was misled by someone who held himself out to be knowledgeable. Tyler, a high school senior, had no reason to suspect that a recruiter employed by Eastern would mislead him about its admissions policy, just as the plaintiff in *Watts* had no reason to suspect that the defendant would lie to him. And, like that plaintiff, Tyler had no reason to inquire further; the information regarding the preferential admissions policy was provided by a person in a position to know the information asserted—a recruiter who represented Eastern. This situation is distinguishable from *Bedolla*, where the plaintiff general partners had specific information that should have led them to investigate the defendant's wrongdoing. Since Tyler had no reason to suspect that the recruiter had lied to recruit him to play soccer for Eastern, he was not put on notice to investigate the recruiter's statement. Thus, the statute did not begin to run until Tyler discovered the recruiter's misrepresentation when his application was denied in March of 2012.

B. Plaintiff had no duty to investigate further regarding the preferential admissions policy because he had no information that called the recruiter's statement into question.

Unless a plaintiff is aware of information sufficient to arouse suspicion of wrongdoing, merely having access to the information does not impose a duty to investigate. In *Vega v. Jones, Day, Reaves & Pogue*, 17 Cal. Rptr. 3d 26 (Ct. App. 2004), the court held the cause of action was not barred where a party to a merger asserted he had been misled regarding the "toxic" stock provisions of the transaction. Because there was no information to arouse the plaintiff's suspicions regarding the transaction, the court held that the filing of a stock certificate containing the details of the financial restructuring did not put the plaintiff on notice or impose a duty to investigate. The court noted "the means of knowledge are equivalent to knowledge" only where there is information sufficient to put a reasonable person on notice to inquire further. *Id.* at 38. In contrast, the court in *Payne* held the statute was not tolled. The court concluded that two representatives of the plaintiff corporation who were members of the defendant's board of directors had a duty to discover a fraudulent sale of stock options because they had participated in decisions regarding the management of the corporation and had access to the corporate books that disclosed the fraud. 67 Cal. Rptr. at 791.

Tyler had no reason to suspect that Cramer had lied to him and no duty to investigate further. His previous discussion with the staff of the GPS program had disclosed only that many of its students were honor graduates from major universities; there was no discussion regarding the preferential admissions policy. Like the defendants in *Vega*, Tyler had no information that should have led him to suspect fraud. The admissions policy was never mentioned and, believing he had been given correct information, he had no reason to inquire further at any point prior to his application to the program. Unlike the directors in *Payne*, who had a fiduciary responsibility to know the contents of the corporation's books, Tyler, as a part-time student worker assigned to complete clerical tasks, had no responsibility to learn how admissions decisions were being made.

The district court improperly equated access to information with the duty to investigate, concluding that Tyler should have discovered the truth merely because he could have done so. This is inconsistent with the case law that imposes a duty to investigate only where the plaintiff had either actual or constructive knowledge of wrongdoing by the defendant. *See Vega*, 17 Cal. Rptr. 3d at 26; *Payne*, 67 Cal. Rptr. at 784. Contrary to the district court's assertion, nothing that Tyler learned regarding the caliber of students admitted or the lack of admission of other Eastern graduates was in any way inconsistent with the recruiter's assertion that Eastern graduates were given priority. Tyler had no duty to verify the recruiter's statement and no reason to do so until his own application was denied in March 2012. It was at this point he discovered the fraud, and it was at this point the statute began to run.

As the district court acknowledged (Order at 5), Tyler has been harmed by the deliberate deception the recruiter used to induce him to attend Eastern for the benefit of its soccer team. He should not be barred from recovering for the damages he has incurred because it took four years for the truth to come to light. As observed by the court in *Twining v. Thompson*, 156 P.2d 29, 34 (Cal. Ct. App. 1945): "The courts do not lightly seize upon small circumstances in order to deny an award to an innocent victim of a fraud upon the ground that he did not discover the fraud sooner." Since Tyler had no reason to suspect the lack of a preferential admissions policy before his application was rejected, the statute of limitations began to run only in March 2012. This action therefore is timely and the decision of the district court should be reversed.

II.   THE DISTRICT COURT ERRED IN HOLDING THE UNQUALIFIED ASSERTION THAT DEFENDANT EASTERN HAD A PREFERENTIAL ADMISSIONS POLICY FOR ITS GRADUATES WAS NOT A STATEMENT OF FACT SUFFICIENT TO SUPPORT AN ACTION FOR NEGLIGENT MISREPRESENTATION, BUT WAS MERELY A CASUAL STATEMENT OF THE RECRUITER'S OPINION.

Under California law, the tort of negligent misrepresentation requires proof of: "(1) A misrepresentation of a past or existing material fact, (2) without reasonable grounds for believing it to be true, (3) with intent to induce another's reliance on the fact misrepresented, (4) ignorance of the truth and justifiable reliance thereon by the party to whom the misrepresentation was directed, and (5) damages." *B.L.M. v. Sabo & Deitsch*, 64 Cal. Rptr. 2d 335, 342 (Ct. App. 1997) (quoting *Fox v. Pollack*, 226 Cal. Rptr. 532, 537 (Ct. App. 1986)). The misrepresentation must be one of existing fact, *Gentry v. eBay, Inc.*, 121 Cal. Rptr. 2d 703, 718–19 (Ct. App. 2002); a casual statement of belief will not support an action for negligent misrepresentation. *Vega v. Jones, Day, Reaves & Pogue*, 17 Cal. Rptr. 3d 26 (Ct. App. 2004). Because the facts establish that the recruiter's statement was a statement of fact, Defendant Eastern is not entitled to judgment as a matter of law.

A. <u>The statement regarding the graduate program's preferential admissions policy</u> <u>was a statement of fact since it was made by a university recruiter who was in a position</u> <u>to have superior knowledge regarding university policies.</u>

In explaining what constitutes a "statement of fact," the court of appeals has held that a statement made by a person who possesses or holds himself out as possessing superior knowledge or information regarding the subject of the statement may be treated as one of fact when the statement is "a deliberate affirmation of the matters stated." *Bily v. Arthur Young & Co.*, 11 Cal. Rptr. 2d 51, 74 (Ct. App. 1992) (quoting *Gagne v. Bertran*, 275 P.2d 15, 21 (Cal. 1954)). In this case, the recruiter's statement was a deliberate and positive affirmation of a fact—that Eastern graduates have a better chance of being admitted into the GPS program. A better chance of admission is the defining characteristic of a preferential admissions program. Moreover, Cramer made that assertion while he was acting in his official capacity as a recruiter representing Defendant Eastern. Thus, the recruiter's statement is one of fact and is sufficient to support an action for negligent misrepresentation.

This case is similar to other situations where the court has imposed liability, finding that a statement by a professional presumed to be in a position to know the fact asserted is a statement of fact. In *Shafer v. Berger, Kahn, Shafton, Moss, Figler, Simon & Gladstone*, 131 Cal. Rptr. 2d 777, 793 (Ct. App. 2003), the court imposed liability for a statement by counsel representing an insurance company regarding exclusions in a company policy. Similarly, in *Anderson v. Deloitte & Touche*, 66 Cal. Rptr. 2d 512, 515 (Ct. App. 1997), the court held that an accountant's inaccurate financial projections in a report were positive assertions of fact. The recruiter's statement differs markedly from those in which a defendant has offered a casual opinion on matters outside his area of expertise. When a principal in an accounting firm stated his opinion as to the appraisal value of real estate, for example, the court declined to impose liability because the defendant was not an appraiser and had never represented himself as such. *Neu-Visions Sports, Inc. v. Soren/McAdam/Bartells*, 103 Cal. Rptr. 2d 159, 163 (Ct. App. 2000).

The district court incorrectly concluded that a college recruiter is either not a professional or does not occupy a position of trust and held that the recruiter should not be held accountable for misleading Tyler. (Order at 6–7). Neither conclusion is supported by the facts or the law. The California Supreme Court did not impose the restriction adopted by the district court, but rather stated:

> [W]hen a party possesses or holds himself out as possessing superior knowledge or special information or expertise regarding the subject matter and a plaintiff is so situated that it may reasonably rely on such supposed knowledge, information, or expertise, the defendant's representation may be treated as one of material fact.

Bily, 11 Cal. Rptr. 2d at 74 (citing *Gagne v. Bertran*, 275 P.2d 15 (Cal. 1954)). Indeed, the *Gagne* case cited in *Bily* for this proposition and relied upon by the district court concerned neither lawyer nor accountant, but rather an untrained individual who represented himself as being in the business of soil testing. The circumstances defined by the court aptly describe the situation here—where a college recruiter was sent to recruit and, in so doing, to provide information to a high school senior. Under the court's holding in *Bily*, the recruiter's statement was a statement of fact.

Further, like the professionals in *Shafer* and *Anderson*, Cramer was acting in his official capacity as a college recruiter when he asserted as fact information he was in a position to know. Unlike the accountant in *Neu-Visions* who speculated on appraisal values, the recruiter was in a position to know the information asserted and held himself out to be an expert on information regarding Eastern. Contrary to the district court's decision, Cramer's responsibility as a recruiter necessarily includes the duty to provide accurate information about the university's programs, including its admissions policies. A college recruiter holds no less a position of trust than other professionals, including lawyers and accountants. Our system of higher education depends on a high level of trust by prospective students in the claims made by college recruiters, including recruiters for athletic programs. The district court's decision that recruiters can be held to a lower standard of truthfulness weakens that trust and is inconsistent with California law.

B. <u>The recruiter's statement regarding the existence of a preferential admissions policy was a concrete assertion of fact, not a casual or general statement of personal opinion.</u>

The recruiter's statement was also more definite and substantive than statements the court has previously determined were only opinions. The court has declined to hold a defendant responsible for vague statements that financing for a merger was "standard" and "nothing unusual," *Vega*, Cal. Rptr. 3d at 26, or for the assertion that a positive rating on a website was "worth its weight in gold," *Gentry*, 121 Cal. Rptr. 2d at 703. The recruiter's statement, however, was a far cry from these general, unspecific opinions. He asserted unequivocally that Tyler would have a better chance of being admitted to the GPS program as a graduate from Eastern than as a graduate from another institution. This was a statement of fact and it was false.

The recruiter's statement contained no guarantee and did not mention a formal admissions policy. Contrary to the district court's conclusion, however, the statement was nonetheless a statement of fact rather a mere statement of opinion. Tyler has not alleged that the recruiter guaranteed his admission. And while the recruiter might not have designated the preferential admissions policy as a "formal admissions policy," he stated without qualification that as an Eastern graduate Tyler would have an increased chance of being admitted. This is markedly unlike the vague, general statements the court concluded were opinions in *Vega* and *Gentry*. His flat statement regarding preferential admissions did not indicate that it was his personal assessment of Tyler's chances or that such an advantage was in any way qualified or questionable. It would be manifestly unfair to allow the university to avoid responsibility for the harm caused by its recruiter's negligent misrepresentation now, after having received the benefit of Tyler's athletic talents, with the excuse that "it was just his opinion."

The tort of negligent misrepresentation protects a plaintiff from the harm caused by a false statement carelessly made by a defendant to induce the plaintiff to rely upon it. Eastern's recruiter knew how important admission to the GPS program was to Tyler. He asserted the existence of a preferential admissions policy for the sole purpose of convincing Tyler to forego the scholarship he had already been offered and attend and play soccer for Eastern instead. (Joint Stip. ¶ 9.) Under California law, his unequivocal assertion that as an Eastern graduate Tyler would have a better chance of being admitted to the GPS program was a statement of fact and is sufficient to support this cause of action. Since the district court incorrectly concluded that Eastern was not responsible for the harm caused by its recruiter's negligent misrepresentation, its decision should be reversed.

CONCLUSION

For the reasons set forth above, Plaintiff respectfully requests the Court to reverse the summary judgment granted by the district court and remand this case for a trial upon the merits.

Respectfully submitted, this 10th day of August, 2013.

Maria Hernandez

Maria Hernandez, State Bar No. 68223
HERNANDEZ & CRUZ
Attorneys for Appellant
Timothy Tyler
334 Mission Street
San Francisco, California 94133
Telephone: (415) 429-6848

Appendix

California Civil Procedure Code (West 2006)

Chapter 3 Time of Commencing Actions Other Than for the Recovery of Real Property

§ 338(d):

Within three years:

. . .

(d) An action for relief on the ground of fraud or mistake. The cause of action in that case is not to be deemed to have accrued until the discovery, by the aggrieved party, of the facts constituting the fraud or mistake.

UNITED STATES CIRCUIT COURT OF APPEALS
FOR THE NINTH CIRCUIT

CIVIL CASE NO. 13-16702

TIMOTHY TYLER,

Appellant,

v.

EASTERN PACIFIC UNIVERSITY,

Appellee.

ON APPEAL FROM THE UNITED STATES DISTRICT COURT
FOR THE NORTHERN DISTRICT OF CALIFORNIA
Case No. CV 13-1632 THB

BRIEF FOR THE APPELLEE

Julia P. Chan, State Bar No. 71038
SAMUEL, PARKS & RIORDAN
485 Battery Street, 8th Floor
San Francisco, California 94111
Telephone: (415) 722-5454

TABLE OF CONTENTS

Table of Authorities Cited ii

Jurisdictional Statement 1

Statutes Involved 1

Standard of Review 1

Issues Presented for Review 1

Statement of the Case 1

Statement of Facts 2

Summary of Argument 2

Argument 4

I.   THE DISTRICT COURT PROPERLY CONCLUDED THAT
      PLAINTIFF'S CLAIM IS BARRED BY THE STATUTE OF
      LIMITATIONS BECAUSE IT WAS FILED MORE THAN THREE
      YEARS AFTER HE KNEW OR SHOULD HAVE KNOWN THAT
      THE RECRUITER'S OPINION REGARDING THE ADMISSIONS
      POLICY WAS INCORRECT. 4

      A.   Plaintiff was put on notice of potential fraud in the spring of 2008
            because the recruiter's statement was not consistent with previous
            statements to Plaintiff by other representatives of the Defendant
            university. 5

      B.   Plaintiff was put on notice to investigate admissions policies in the
            fall of 2008 and throughout his undergraduate career because of
            information he was provided or could have obtained while working
            in the admissions office. 5

II.   THE DISTRICT COURT PROPERLY GRANTED SUMMARY
      JUDGMENT BECAUSE THE RECRUITER'S OPINION REGARDING
      THE LIKELIHOOD OF PLAINTIFF'S FUTURE ADMISSION TO THE
      GRADUATE PROGRAM WAS NOT A STATEMENT OF FACT
      SUFFICIENT TO SUPPORT A CLAIM FOR NEGLIGENT
      MISREPRESENTATION. 6

Conclusion 8

Appendix A-1

TABLE OF AUTHORITIES CITED

Federal Cases:

Buono v. Norton, 371 F.3d 543 (9th Cir. 2004) 1

Erie R.R. Co. v. Tompkins, 304 U.S. 64 (1938) 4

California Cases:

Anderson v. Deloitte & Touche, 66 Cal Rptr. 2d 512 (Ct. App. 1997).............................. 7

Bedolla v. Logan & Frazer, 125 Cal. Rptr. 59 (Ct. App. 1975) 5

B.L.M. v. Sabo & Deitsch, 64 Cal. Rptr. 2d 335 (Ct. App. 1997) 4

Gentry v. eBay, Inc., 121 Cal. Rptr. 2d 703 (Ct. App. 2002)... 7

Nat'l Auto. & Cas. Ins. Co. v. Payne, 67 Cal. Rptr. 784 (Ct. App. 1968)................. 4, 5, 6

Neu-Visions Sports, Inc. v. Soren/McAdam/Bartells, 103 Cal. Rptr. 2d 159
    (Ct. App. 2000) 7-8

Shafer v. Berger, Kahn, Shafton, Moss, Figler, Simon & Gladstone,
    131 Cal. Rptr. 2d 777 (Ct. App. 2003)... 7

Vega v. Jones, Day, Reaves & Pogue, 17 Cal. Rptr. 3d 26 (Ct. App. 2004) 6, 7

Watts v. Crocker-Citizens Nat'l Bank, 183 Cal. Rptr. 304 (Ct. App. 1982) 5

Statutes:

Cal. Civ. Proc. Code § 338(d) (West 2006) 1, 4

28 U.S.C. § 1332(a)(1) (2006).. 1

28 U.S.C. § 1291 (2006) 1

JURISDICTIONAL STATEMENT

Plaintiff Timothy Tyler filed this diversity action pursuant to 28 U.S.C. § 1332(a)
(1) (2006) in the United States District Court for the Northern District of California.
Diversity jurisdiction is appropriate because Plaintiff is a citizen of Oregon and
Defendant Eastern Pacific University is located in San Francisco, California. The
amount in controversy is alleged to exceed $75,000. This appeal was brought pursuant
to 28 U.S.C. § 1291 (2006) as an appeal of a final order granting Defendant summary
judgment as to all claims.

STATUTES INVOLVED

The text of § 338(d) of the California Civil Procedure Code (West 2006) relevant to
this case is reproduced in the Appendix.

STANDARD OF REVIEW

The standard of review for an appeal from a grant of summary judgment is de novo.
Buono v. Norton, 371 F.3d 543, 545 (9th Cir. 2004).

ISSUES PRESENTED FOR REVIEW

I.   Whether the district court properly granted summary judgment to Defendant,
concluding that the statute of limitations was not tolled by Plaintiff's failure to discover
that he had received inaccurate information regarding the graduate school admissions
policy, when Plaintiff had ready access to information that would have revealed the truth
for more than four years prior to the filing of the suit.

II.   Whether the district court properly granted summary judgment in this action for
negligent misrepresentation, concluding that Defendant's recruiter's general statement
regarding the likelihood of Plaintiff's future admission to a graduate degree program was
a statement of opinion, not fact, and therefore could not form the basis for this action.

STATEMENT OF THE CASE

Plaintiff Timothy Tyler filed this action in federal court on October 10, 2012,
seeking damages for an alleged negligent misrepresentation made by a recruiter from
Defendant Eastern Pacific University (Eastern) in April of 2008. The United States
District Court for the Northern District of California granted summary judgment to
Defendant on July 13, 2013, concluding that the action was barred by the three-year
statute of limitations and that the alleged misrepresentation was a statement of opinion
and therefore could not form the basis for this tort claim. Order re Summ. J. Mot.,

July 13, 2013. (R. at 51–57.) The decision is unreported. Tyler now appeals the district court's judgment.

STATEMENT OF FACTS

Defendant Eastern Pacific University is a private university located in San Francisco, California. In April 2008, Eastern recruited Timothy Tyler, a high school senior residing in Oregon, to play soccer for the university. (R. 19.) Tyler matriculated at Eastern in September of 2008 and obtained part-time employment as a work-study student in the Global Policy Studies (GPS) program. During the four years of his undergraduate studies, Tyler assisted the GPS admissions secretary, sending packets containing the program's handbook and application to prospective graduate students and assisting in sending out letters either accepting or rejecting applicants to the program. (R. 17.) In October 2011, Tyler, who was then a senior at Eastern, applied for admission to the GPS graduate program. He was denied admission in March 2012. (R. 18.)

After he was denied admission, Tyler asserted that he had been misled in April of 2008 about an alleged policy of Eastern to give priority to its own graduates for admission to its GPS program. Richard Cramer, the recruiter who approached Tyler about playing soccer for Eastern, believed that such a policy existed and admits telling Tyler that he would have a better chance of being admitted to the program as an Eastern graduate. Cramer did not make any specific promise or guarantee. (R. 17.)

Tyler had been told by university representatives during his own investigation of the GPS graduate program in 2008 that excellent credentials were required for admission and that many of the GPS graduate students were honor graduates of major universities. (R. 8.) No one in the GPS program has ever mentioned the preferential admissions policy, since no such policy has ever existed. During the four years that Tyler was employed by the GPS program, 2008–2012, no Eastern graduate was admitted to the GPS program. In fact, no Eastern graduate has been admitted to the program since 2002. (R. 1, 17.)

In October 2012, Tyler filed this diversity action against Eastern, alleging that he had been fraudulently induced to attend Eastern by Cramer's statement regarding Tyler's chances of being admitted to the GPS program as an Eastern graduate. Tyler asserts that, based on the recruiter's statement, he declined a scholarship at another college to attend Eastern. Since he received only a nominal scholarship at Eastern, Tyler alleges that he incurred debt in excess of $75,000 to attend Eastern. (R. 4.)

SUMMARY OF ARGUMENT

Summary judgment was appropriately granted in this case. There is no disagreement as to the facts and, under California law to be applied in this diversity action, Defendant Eastern Pacific University is entitled to judgment as a matter of law. The statute of limitations for negligent misrepresentation in California is three years. The alleged misrepresentation occurred in April 2008; this action was not filed until October 10, 2012, and is barred by the statute. In addition, Plaintiff Timothy Tyler cannot recover for negligent misrepresentation because such an action cannot be based on a statement of opinion like Richard Cramer's prediction regarding Tyler's chances of being admitted to a graduate degree program at some indefinite point in the future.

The district court correctly concluded that the statute of limitations was not tolled in this case by Tyler's failure to discover the truth for more than four years. Under California law, the statute of limitations may be tolled in an action for fraud when the plaintiff did not discover, and in the exercise of ordinary diligence could not have discovered, the truth. While the statute seeks to protect plaintiffs who have been the innocent victims of fraud, it imposes a duty on plaintiffs to be diligent. If plaintiffs have information that should have prompted further inquiry or are in a position to discover the truth, the law imposes a duty that they be diligent in doing so.

In this case, Tyler was given information that should have prompted inquiry; the truth was literally right in front of him for four years. Tyler investigated the admissions criteria for the GPS Program while he was still in high school and discovered that the program required top credentials and many of its students were honor graduates of major universities. No preferential treatment for graduates of any institution was mentioned because there was no such policy. This omission should have put him on notice that he should inquire further. The statute was not tolled under the discovery exception because his failure to inquire was not reasonable.

Moreover, for the ensuing four years while he studied at Eastern, Tyler was physically present in the offices of the GPS program, working as a work-study student assisting the secretary. His duties included sending admissions information to prospective students. He worked on an ongoing basis with the very people who could have cleared up his misconception. The exercise of reasonable diligence in these circumstances required that he at least ask. As the district court noted, a single question at any point would have been enough to disclose the true state of affairs. Thus, under California law, the district court correctly concluded that Tyler did not exercise reasonable diligence in discovering the truth and that the statute was not tolled. This action is therefore barred by the three-year statute of limitations.

Summary judgment was also properly granted because Cramer's opinion regarding the probability that Tyler would be admitted to the GPS program at some future time cannot support an action for negligent misrepresentation. Such an action must be based on a misrepresentation of existing fact; an opinion is not sufficient. In this case, Tyler seeks to recover damages for an opinion expressed by a college recruiter to a high school senior as to the likelihood of his future admission to a graduate program. The recruiter in this case made no promise or guarantee regarding Tyler's future admission to the GPS program. His assertion that Tyler's chances would be "better" if he obtained his degree from Eastern was merely his personal evaluation of the situation. The district court correctly concluded that the recruiter's opinion in no way qualifies as the concrete, factual statement necessary to support this cause of action.

The district court also declined to categorize the recruiter's statement as a professional opinion. Although California courts have held attorneys and accountants liable for their professional opinions issued in the course of their employment, they have declined to impose liability when the matter was outside the professional's area of expertise. The district court correctly concluded that a college recruiter is not the type of trained professional to whom this exception applies. The court further noted that an undergraduate recruiter is not in the business of giving professional opinions regarding admissions to specific graduate degree programs. Thus, the recruiter's opinion regarding Tyler's chances of future admission to the GPS program was not a "statement of fact" required to support this cause of action.

Therefore, because this action is barred by the statute of limitations and Tyler cannot establish all the elements necessary to bring an action for negligent misrepresentation, the district court properly granted Eastern's Motion for Summary Judgment. Its decision should be affirmed.

<u>ARGUMENT</u>

I.   THE DISTRICT COURT PROPERLY CONCLUDED THAT PLAINTIFF'S CLAIM IS BARRED BY THE STATUTE OF LIMITATIONS BECAUSE IT WAS FILED MORE THAN THREE YEARS AFTER HE KNEW OR SHOULD HAVE KNOWN THAT THE RECRUITER'S OPINION REGARDING THE ADMISSIONS POLICY WAS INCORRECT.

This diversity action is governed by the law of California. See Erie R.R. Co. v. Tompkins, 304 U.S. 64 (1938). Under California law, negligent misrepresentation is a type of fraud. B.L.M. v. Sabo & Deitsch, 64 Cal. Rptr. 2d 335, 342 (Ct. App. 1997). The statute of limitations for fraud requires that an action be brought within three years after all the elements have been met. Cal. Civ. Proc. Code § 338(d) (West 2006). The statute further provides that the limitation period is tolled until after discovery, by the aggrieved party, of the facts constituting the fraud or mistake. Id. A plaintiff seeking to rely on the "discovery" exception of section 338(d) must prove that with reasonable diligence he could not have discovered the fraud earlier. See Nat'l Auto. & Cas. Ins. Co. v. Payne, 67 Cal. Rptr. 784 (Ct. App. 1968). The alleged fraud here occurred in 2008, when Plaintiff Timothy Tyler declined the scholarship to another college and decided to attend Eastern Pacific University at his own expense. The district court correctly concluded that the statute of limitations on Tyler's claim expired in 2011.

A. Plaintiff was put on notice of potential fraud in the spring of 2008 because the recruiter's statement was not consistent with previous statements made to Plaintiff by other representatives of the Defendant university.

The test for determining whether a plaintiff's delay in discovering the fraud was reasonable is an objective one. The limitation period begins to run when the plaintiff has information "sufficient to make a reasonably prudent person suspicious of fraud, thus putting him on inquiry." Payne, 67 Cal. Rptr. at 788. In Bedolla v. Logan & Frazer, 125 Cal. Rptr. 59 (Ct. App. 1975), the plaintiff general partners brought a fraud claim against an accounting firm. The plaintiffs had known of irregularities in the way the defendant accountants kept financial records for several limited partnerships. The court concluded that this knowledge of financial mismanagement should have alerted the general partners, as reasonable men, to suspect other wrongdoing. The court held that their claim was barred by the statute of limitations because it began to run when the plaintiffs had information sufficient to put them on inquiry. 125 Cal. Rptr. at 64. However, in Watts v. Crocker-Citizens National Bank, 183 Cal. Rptr. 304 (Ct. App. 1982), the court held that a property owner's action for misrepresentation concerning the installation of a water line was not barred because the plaintiff had no reason to suspect that there were problems with the water system. The plaintiff had not been put on notice because ongoing communications with the defendant had raised no problems. Id. at 308.

Tyler's lack of reasonable diligence is even more egregious than that of the plaintiff in Payne. As noted by the district court, Tyler had been provided with information that would have prompted any reasonably diligent person to inquire further. Tyler should have realized in the spring of 2008 that the recruiter's statement was inconsistent with the information he had previously received. He knew that excellent credentials were required for admission and that many of the students in the program were honor graduates from major universities. He also knew that no one with whom he had previously spoken had mentioned anything regarding a preferential admissions policy. Unlike the plaintiff in Watts, who not only had no information regarding potential fraud but had been discouraged from inquiring by his ongoing communications with the defendant that raised no problems, Tyler had been given specific information by Cramer that was inconsistent with what he had previously learned from the GPS program. The district court properly concluded that his failure to discover the truth at that point was not reasonable and therefore the statute was not tolled.

B. Plaintiff was put on notice to investigate admissions policies in the fall of 2008 and throughout his undergraduate career because of information he was provided or could have obtained while working in the admissions office.

Even if Tyler was not put on inquiry in April of 2008, he was in September 2008 when he began working in the office of the GPS program, assisting the admissions secretary in handling inquiries and sending out letters accepting and rejecting applicants. Where information has placed the plaintiff on notice of the fraud and the truth is easily accessible, the law requires the plaintiff exercise reasonable diligence in discovering the truth. Payne, 67 Cal. Rptr. at 790. In Payne, the court held that an action regarding the fraudulent sale of stock options was barred when the plaintiff corporation had two representatives on the defendant's board of directors for eight years prior to the filing of the action. The court found that not only was the directors' participation in the management of the defendant corporation sufficient to make a reasonably prudent person suspicious of fraud, but the directors also had access to corporate records that disclosed the truth. Id. at 791. On the other hand, in Vega v. Jones, Day, Reaves & Pogue, 17 Cal. Rptr. 3d 26 (Ct. App. 2004), the court held the cause of action was not barred where a party to a merger asserted he had been misled regarding the "toxic" stock provisions of the transaction. The filing of a stock certificate in another state that contained the details of the financial restructuring was not sufficient to put the plaintiff on notice where there was no other information to arouse suspicions of wrongdoing.

Tyler's situation is like that of the plaintiffs in Payne because facts in front of him were sufficient to make a reasonably prudent person suspicious, and placed a duty on him to inquire further. During the four years Tyler worked in the GPS office, no one ever mentioned the preferential admissions policy, nor were any Eastern graduates admitted to the program. Also like the plaintiffs in Payne, Tyler had the means to discover the truth—it was literally at his fingertips. No one attempted to conceal the true admissions policy. As the district court observed, "all he had to do was ask." This case is distinguishable from Vega, where, even though the defrauded parties could have investigated the stock certificate and discovered the fraud, they had no reason to suspect any wrongdoing.

The law requires plaintiffs to exercise diligence in finding out the truth once they have been put on notice that further inquiry is needed. Tyler's failure to make even the simplest inquiry once he had notice that there was no preferential admissions policy for Eastern graduates precludes him from relying on section 338(d) to toll the statute of limitations. Therefore, the three-year period for bringing a complaint expired in 2011. Tyler's complaint, filed in 2012, is barred by the statute of limitations. The district court properly granted summary judgment.

II.   THE DISTRICT COURT PROPERLY GRANTED SUMMARY JUDGMENT BECAUSE THE RECRUITER'S OPINION REGARDING THE LIKELIHOOD OF PLAINTIFF'S FUTURE ADMISSION TO THE GRADUATE PROGRAM WAS NOT A STATEMENT OF FACT SUFFICIENT TO SUPPORT A CLAIM FOR NEGLIGENT MISREPRESENTATION.

Negligent misrepresentation requires a statement of existing fact, not opinion; a casual expression of belief is not actionable. Vega, 17 Cal. Rptr. 3d at 26. In Vega, the plaintiff alleged the defendant had misrepresented the terms of a merger transaction, hiding the so-called "toxic" stock provisions. The court concluded that an attorney's statement regarding the financing of a merger as "standard" and "nothing unusual" were not actionable as they were casual statements of the attorney's opinion and not affirmations of any fact. Id. at 32. Similarly, in Gentry v. eBay, Inc., 121 Cal. Rptr. 2d 703, 718 (Ct. App. 2002), the court concluded that the defendant's assertion that a positive rating on its website was "worth its weight in gold" was not a statement of fact that would support an action for negligent misrepresentation.

In this case, the recruiter's assertion that Tyler would "have a better chance of getting into the GPS program as an Eastern graduate" was an accurate statement of the recruiter's personal belief. As the district court noted, the recruiter did not guarantee Tyler's future admission, nor did he represent his personal evaluation as a formal admissions policy. Instead, he asserted his opinion as to the likelihood of Tyler's future admission. Like the statements in Vega and Gentry, his statement expressed his opinion of the situation and was not a positive assertion of fact.

Such a statement of opinion is different from the concrete, factual assertion found actionable in Shafer v. Berger, Kahn, Shafton, Moss, Figler, Simon & Gladstone, 131 Cal. Rptr. 2d 777 (Ct. App. 2003). In that case, the court held that an insurance company attorney's statements regarding exclusions from a company insurance policy were statements of fact. Id. at 793. A lawyer's representations about the actual content of an insurance policy are much different from the recruiter's opinion about the likelihood of a future event. Thus, the district court correctly concluded that the recruiter's statement could not form the basis for this cause of action.

While an opinion by one employed to provide a professional evaluation may be actionable, a casual statement of one's personal belief as to future events is not. In Shafer, the court held that a statement made by a lawyer employed to provide his legal evaluation regarding coverage of an insurance policy was sufficient to support the cause of action. Id. In a similar case, the court found that financial projections provided by an accounting firm were statements of fact. Anderson v. Deloitte & Touche, 66 Cal. Rptr. 2d 512, 515 (Ct. App. 1997). The district court correctly declined to expand this doctrine beyond the court's application to trained professionals. As noted by the court, a college recruiter does not provide the same type of professional opinion expected of attorneys and accountants, who are specially trained and specifically employed to provide such evaluations. (Order at 6–7.) The casual evaluation provided by the recruiter regarding Tyler's chances of future admission to the GPS program was not the kind of professional opinion that courts have treated as statements of fact.

Even assuming the recruiter could be held to the same standard as attorneys and accountants, the opinion he offered to Tyler was outside of his area expertise and therefore cannot be treated as a statement of fact. In Neu-Visions Sports, Inc. v. Soren/

McAdam/Bartells, 103 Cal. Rptr. 2d 159 (Ct. App. 2000), an accountant gave his opinion regarding the likely appraisal value of a parcel of real estate. The court held that the statement was only a casual opinion, not a fact, noting that the defendant was not a professional appraiser. Id. at 163. Like the accountant in Neu-Visions Sports, who gave his opinion of matters outside of his expertise, Cramer, who was an undergraduate college recruiter and did not work in the GPS admissions office, stated his opinion about the likelihood of Tyler's future admission to that specific graduate program. The district court correctly concluded that even if a college recruiter is considered a trained professional, the opinion offered by Cramer concerning graduate admissions was outside his area of expertise. Cramer's knowledge of undergraduate programs and admissions standards does not include familiarity with the specific admissions requirements and policies of all the various graduate programs at Eastern.

Therefore, the district court properly concluded that Cramer's statement regarding Tyler's chances of being admitted to the GPS program was his opinion, not a statement of existing fact. Because Tyler cannot show all of the elements necessary to recover in this action, summary judgment in favor of Eastern was proper and should be affirmed.

CONCLUSION

For the reasons stated above, the district court's grant of summary judgment in favor of Defendant Eastern was proper. Tyler's claim is time-barred, and the alleged misrepresentation was a statement of opinion, not of fact as required to support an action for negligent misrepresentation. The judgment of the district court should be affirmed.

Respectfully submitted this 31st day of August, 2013.

By: *Julia P. Chan*

Julia P. Chan, State Bar No. 71038
SAMUEL, PARKS & RIORDAN
Attorneys for Appellee
 Eastern Pacific University
485 Battery Street, 8th Floor
San Francisco, CA 94111
(415) 722-5454

Appendix

California Civil Procedure Code (West 2006)

Chapter 3 Time of Commencing Actions Other Than for the Recovery of Real Property

§ 338(d):

Within three years:

. . .

(d) An action for relief on the ground of fraud or mistake. The cause of action in that case is not to be deemed to have accrued until the discovery, by the aggrieved party, of the facts constituting the fraud or mistake.

Selected Books on Style and Grammar

Stephen V. Armstrong & Timothy P. Terrell, *Thinking Like a Writer: A Lawyer's Guide to Effective Writing and Editing* (3d ed., Practising Law Institute 2009).

Gertrude Block, *Effective Legal Writing for Law Students and Lawyers* (5th ed., Foundation Press 1999).

Anne Enquist & Laurel Currie Oates, *Just Writing: Grammar, Punctuation, and Style for the Legal Writer* (4th ed., Aspen Law & Business 2013).

Bryan A. Garner, *Garner's Dictionary of Legal Usage* (3d ed., Oxford University Press 2011).

Bryan A. Garner, *Legal Writing in Plain English* (2d ed., University of Chicago Press 2013).

Bryan Garner et al., *The Redbook: A Manual on Legal Style* (2d ed., Thomson/West 2006).

Tom Goldstein & Jethro K. Lieberman, The Lawyer's Guide to Writing Well (2d ed., University of California Press 2002).

C. Edward Good, *Mightier Than the Sword: Powerful Writing in the Legal Profession* (Lel Enterprises 1989).

Diana Hacker & Nancy Sommers, *A Writer's Reference* (7th ed., Bedford/St. Martin's Press 2011).

Muriel Harris, *Prentice Hall Reference Guide to Grammar and Usage* (5th ed., Prentice Hall 2003).

Edward D. Johnson, *The Handbook of Good English* (rev. ed., Washington Square Press 1991).

Terri LeClercq & Karin Mika, *Guide to Legal Writing Style* (5th ed., Aspen Law & Business 2011).

Mary Bernard Ray & Jill Ramsfield, *Legal Writing: Getting It Right and Getting It Written* (5th ed., West Group 2010).

William Strunk, Jr. & E. B. White, *Elements of Style* (4th ed., Longman Publishing Group 2000).

Texas Law Review, *Manual on Usage & Style* (12th ed., Texas Law Review Association 2011).

Lynn Truss, *Eats, Shoots and Leaves: Illustrated Edition* (Gotham Books 2008).

Joseph M. Williams & Joseph Bizup, *Style: Lessons in Clarity and Grace* (11th ed., Pearson Longman Publishing Group 2013).

Richard C. Wydick, *Plain English for Lawyers* (5th ed., Carolina Academic Press 2005).

Bibliography
Sources of Law

The cases and statutes in this book are used only to illustrate specific principles of legal writing and legal method. Although they are not intended to teach substantive rules of law, they are based on or inspired by real cases and statutes which are too lengthy to be reproduced in full. This section is provided to show from where the ideas for the illustrations and exercises were derived. When an exercise or example is based on an earlier one, no additional authority is provided.

Chapter 1

Exercise 1-B is inspired by *People v. Utica Daw's Drug Store Co.*, 225 N.Y.S.2d 128 (App. Div. 1962), and *People v. Walker*, 200 N.E.2d 779 (N.Y. 1964).

Chapter 2

The evidentiary rule in Exercise 2-A is based on Model Rule of Evidence 404. Case examples are based on *Lovely v. United States*, 169 F.2d 386 (4th Cir. 1948); *Commonwealth v. Minor*, 591 S.E.2d 61 (Va. 2004); and *State v. Cox*, 787 P.2d 4 (Utah Ct. App. 1990). A representative law review article is Dana Berliner, *Rethinking the Reasonable Belief Defense to Rape*, 100 Yale L.J. 2687 (1991).

The case examples in Exercise 2-B are drawn from *Assicurazoni General v. Neil*, 160 F.3d 997 (4th Cir. 1998); *American States Insurance Co. v. Netherby*, 79 F.3d 473 (5th Cir. 1996); *Stoney Run Co. v. Prudential-LMI Commercial Insurance Co.*, 47 F.3d 34 (2d Cir. 1995); *Owners Insurance Co. v. Farmer*, 173 F. Supp. 2d 1330 (N.D. Ga. 2001); *Quadrant Corp. v. American States Insurance Co.*, 110 P.3d 733 (Wash. 2005); and *MacKinnon v. Truck Insurance Exchange*, 73 P.3d 1205 (Cal. 2003). The references to secondary authority are drawn from various sources, including Thomas K. Bick & Lisa G. Youngblood, *The Pollution Exclusion Saga Continues: Does It Apply to Indoor Releases?*, 5 S.C. Envtl. L. J. 119 (1997), and Claudia G. Catalano, Annotation, *What Constitutes "Pollutant,"*

"Contaminant," "Irritant," or "Waste" Within Meaning of Absolute or Total Pollution Exclusion Clause in Liability Insurance Policy, 98 A.L.R. 5th 193 (2002 & Supp. 2012).

Chapter 3

The first case in the text, *State v. Jones,* is based on *United States v. Castillo,* 524 F.2d 286 (10th Cir. 1975), and *State v. Baxter,* 208 S.E.2d 696 (N.C. 1974).

The burglary case under Part 2 is based on *State v. Crawford,* 80 N.W. 193 (N.D. 1899).

The case under Part 3 is based on *Jackson v. Brown,* 164 N.W.2d 824 (Iowa 1969).

The wills case under Part 4 is drawn from *Brown v. Union Trust Co.,* 98 N.E.2d 901 (Ind. 1951).

The corporation case under Part 4 is based on the reasoning in *Decker v. Juzwik,* 121 N.W.2d 652 (Iowa 1963), although the court in that case concluded the promoters were not liable because there was a novation of the contract by the corporation.

The found property case in Part 4 is based on *Corliss v. Wenner,* 34 P.3d 1100 (Idaho Ct. App. 2001).

The case under Part 5 is drawn from *Stratton v. Mt. Hermon Boys' School,* 103 N.E. 87 (Mass. 1913).

The case and sample case brief after Part 8 are based on *Jones v. City of Atlanta,* 363 S.E.2d 254 (Ga. 1988).

Exercise 3-A is derived from the principles stated in *Missouri Federation of the Blind v. National Federation of the Blind,* 505 S.W.2d 1 (Mo. Ct. App. 1973), and *Powell v. Zuckert,* 366 F.2d 634 (D.C. Cir. 1966). Exercise 3-B is drawn from W. Page Keeton et al., *Prosser and Keeton on the Law of Torts* § 70 (5th ed. 1984).

Exercise 3-C was inspired by *State v. Glover,* 50 S.W.2d 1049 (Mo. 1932), and *Commonwealth v. Redline,* 137 A.2d 472 (Pa. 1958). *But see Commonwealth v. Lang,* 426 A.2d 691 (Pa. Super. Ct. 1981).

Chapter 4

The cases in the text are based on *Johnston v. Harris,* 198 N.W.2d 409 (Mich. 1972), and *Samson v. Saginaw Professional Building,* 224 N.W.2d 843 (Mich. 1975).

Exercise 4-A is modeled on a trilogy of Rhode Island decisions: *State v. Welford,* 72 A. 396 (R.I. 1909); *State v. Scofield,* 138 A.2d 415 (R.I. 1958); and *State v. Lunt,* 260 A.2d 149 (R.I. 1969).

Exercise 4-B is drawn from *Ellis v. Butterfield,* 570 P.2d 1334 (Idaho 1977), and *Skendzel v. Marshall,* 339 N.E.2d 57 (Ind. 1975).

Exercise 4-C was inspired primarily by *Williams v. Walker-Thomas Furniture Co.,* 350 F.2d 445 (D.C. Cir. 1965).

Exercise 4-D is based on a line of cases typified by *Wyman v. Newhouse,* 93 F.2d 313 (2d Cir. 1937). *See generally* H.H. Henry, Annotation, *Attack on Personal Service as Having Been Obtained by Fraud or Trickery,* 98 A.L.R.2d 551 (1964 & Supp. 2006 & Supp. 2009).

Chapter 5

The aggravated menacing example is based on Ohio Rev. Code Ann. § 2903.21 (West 2006) and on adaptations of the following cases: *State v. Schwartz*, 602 N.E.2d 671 (Ohio Ct. App. 1991); *State v. Striley*, 488 N.E.2d 499 (Ohio Ct. App. 1985); and *State v. Richard*, 718 N.E.2d 508 (Ohio Ct. App. 1998).

The hate crime cases in the second example in the text are based on *People v. B.C. (In re B.C.)*, 680 N.E.2d 1355 (Ill. 1997); *People v. Vladimir P. (In re Vladimir P.)*, 670 N.E.2d 839 (Ill. App. Ct. 1996); *People v. Davis*, 674 N.E.2d 895 (Ill. App. Ct. 1996); and *People v. Rokicki*, 718 N.E.2d 333 (Ill. App. Ct. 1999).

The rule in Exercise 5-A is from *In re Fickert's Estate*, 337 A.2d 592, 594 (Pa. 1975).

The rule in Exercise 5-B is based on *Hubbard v. United Press International, Inc.*, 330 N.W.2d 428 (Minn. 1983), and other cases adopting and applying Restatement (Second) of Torts § 46(1) (1965).

The cases in Exercises 5-C and 5-D were based in part on *Rappaport v. Nichols*, 156 A.2d 1 (N.J. 1959); *Soronen v. Olde Milford Inn, Inc.*, 218 A.2d 630 (N.J. 1966); and *Linn v. Rand*, 356 A.2d 15 (N.J. Super. Ct. App. Div. 1976).

Chapter 6

The statutes in the text are 28 U.S.C. §§ 1332(a) and 1333 (2006).

The cases in the text were inspired by *Sisson v. Ruby*, 497 U.S. 358 (1990) (admiralty jurisdiction); *Executive Jet Aviation, Inc. v. City of Cleveland*, 409 U.S. 249 (1972) (admiralty jurisdiction); *Taylor v. Vallelunga*, 339 P.2d 910 (Cal. Ct. App. 1959) (emotional distress); *Whitley v. Andersen*, 551 P.2d 1083 (Colo. Ct. App. 1976) (battery); and Restatement (Second) of Torts § 13 (1965).

The authority in Exercise 6-A is based on *Soldano v. O'Daniels*, 190 Cal. Rptr. 310 (Ct. App. 1983); *Timmons v. Bostwick*, 82 S.E. 29 (Ga. 1914); *Olson v. Rasmussen*, 8 N.W.2d 668 (Mich. 1943); and *Lucy v. Zehmer*, 84 S.E.2d 516 (Va. 1954). The principles find some support in John Calamari & Joseph Perillo, *The Law of Contracts* §§ 2-3, 2-20(e), 4-4 (4th ed. 1998).

Exercise 6-B is derived from Mich. Comp. Laws. Ann. §§ 15.231–.246 (West 2004 & Supp. 2012); Tex. Gov't Code Ann. §§ 552.021, .108 (Vernon 2012); *Ayers v. Lee Enterprises, Inc.*, 561 P.2d 998 (Or. 1977); and *Houston Chronicle Publishing Co. v. City of Houston*, 531 S.W.2d 177 (Tex. Civ. App. 1975).

Exercise 6-C is based on the English Statute of Frauds entitled "An Act for the Prevention of Frauds and Perjuries," 29 Charles II, c.3 (1677). The sale of land case is based on the principles contained in John Calamari & Joseph Perillo, *The Law of Contracts* §§ 19-26, 19-35 (3d ed. 1987). The dance case is inspired by *Vokes v. Arthur Murray, Inc.*, 212 So. 2d 906 (Fla. Dist. Ct. App. 1968).

Chapter 7

The cases in the text are based on *Ball v. White*, 143 N.W.2d 188 (Mich. 1966); *Barnes v. Clayton House Motel*, 435 S.W.2d 616 (Tex. Civ. App. 1968); *Anderson v. Cramlet*, 789 F.2d 840 (10th Cir. 1986); and Bruce W. Sanford, *Libel and Privacy* §§ 6.2–.3 (2d ed. 1993).

Exercise 7-B is drawn from *Jones v. Owings*, 456 S.E.2d 371 (S.C. 1995); *Hicks v. United States*, 368 F.2d 626 (4th Cir. 1966); and *Walden v. Jones*, 439 S.W.2d 571 (Ky. 1968).

The cases in Exercise 7-C are based on *Prah v. Maretti*, 321 N.W.2d 182 (Wis. 1982); *Fontainebleau Hotel Corp. v. Forty-Five Twenty Five, Inc.*, 114 So. 2d 357 (Fla. Dist. Ct. App. 1959); *Moellering v. Evans*, 22 N.E. 989 (Ind. 1889); and *Sherk v. Indiana Waste Systems, Inc.*, 495 N.E.2d 815 (Ind. Ct. App. 1986).

Chapter 8

The open meetings example in the text is drawn from Mich. Comp. Laws Ann. §§ 15.262(a)–(b), 15.263(1) (West 2004) and the *News-Journal Co. v. McLaughlin*, 377 A.2d 358 (Del. Ch. 1977). The example illustrating *ejusdem generis* is taken from *Martin v. Holiday Inns, Inc.*, 245 Cal. Rptr. 717 (Ct. App. 1988).

Exercise 8-C was suggested by *Peralta Community College District v. Fair Employment & Housing Commission*, 801 P.2d 357 (Cal. 1990).

Exercise 8-D is based on Mich. R. 2.209 and *D'Agostini v. City of Roseville*, 240 N.W.2d 252 (Mich. 1976).

Exercise 8-E was inspired by Mich. Comp. Laws Ann. §§ 169.252, .269 (West 2005); N.J. Stat. Ann §§ 19:44A-29 (West 1999); *Buckley v. Valeo*, 424 U.S. 1 (1976); and *Common Cause v. New Jersey Election Law Enforcement Commission*, 377 A.2d 643 (N.J. 1977).

Chapter 9

The cases in the text came from *Payne v. Palm Beach County*, 395 So. 2d 1267 (Fla. Dist. Ct. App. 1981), and *Town of Belleair v. Taylor*, 425 So. 2d 669 (Fla. Dist. Ct. App. 1983).

Chapter 10

The case in the text under Part 1 is based on *Day v. Caslowitz*, 713 A.2d 758 (R.I. 1996).

The cases in the text under Part 2 are based on Wayne R. LaFave & Austin W. Scott, *Criminal Law* §§ 7.16, 8.11(d) (2d ed. 1986).

The cases in the text under Part 3 are drawn from *Bartram v. Zoning Commission*, 68 A.2d 308 (Conn. 1949); *Rodgers v. Village of Tarrytown*, 96 N.E.2d 731 (N.Y. 1951); *Thomas v. Town of Bedford*, 214 N.Y.S.2d 145 (Sup. Ct. 1961); and *D'Angelo v. Knights of Columbus Building Association*, 151 A.2d 495 (R.I. 1959).

The case under Part 4 is drawn from *Thompson v. Enz*, 154 N.W.2d 473 (Mich. 1967), and *In re County Ditch No. 34*, 170 N.W. 883 (Minn. 1919).

The problem used under Part 5 is based on section 102(2)(C) of the National Environmental Policy Act of 1969, 42 U.S.C. § 4332(2)(C) (2006).

The example in Part 6 was suggested by *In re Grand Jury Proceedings*, 103 F.3d 1140 (3d Cir. 1997), and *In re Grand Jury Proceedings, Unemancipated Minor Child*, 949 F. Supp. 1487 (E.D. Wash. 1996), and sources cited therein.

Exercise 10-A was inspired by *In re Estate of Kamesar*, 259 N.W.2d 733 (Wis. 1977), and *In re Estate of Malnar*, 243 N.W.2d 435 (Wis. 1976).

Exercise 10-B was inspired by sections 109 and 304 of the Clean Air Act, 42 U.S.C. §§ 7409, 7604 (2006); Mich. Admin. Code r. 336.1401(1), MI ADC R. 336.1401(1) (Westlaw); *Jost v. Dairyland Power Coop*, 172 N.W.2d 647 (Wis. 1969); *Amphitheaters, Inc. v. Portland Meadows*, 198 P.2d 847 (Or. 1948); and W. Page Keeton et al., *Prosser and Keeton on the Law of Torts* §§ 88-89 (5th ed. 1984).

Exercise 10-C is based on *Jarman v. Deason*, 618 S.E.2d 776 (N.C. 2005); *Civil Service Board v. Bureau of Labor & Industries*, 692 P.2d 569 (Ore. 1984); and *United Brotherhood of Carpenters Local 261 v. Pennsylvania. Human Relations Commission*, 693 A.2d 1379 (Pa. Commw. Ct. 1997).

Chapter 11

The common law illustration under Part 1 was inspired by the principles in *Henderson v. Fisher*, 46 Cal. Rptr. 173 (Ct. App. 1965). The statutory illustration is based on Federal Water Pollution Control Act § 505, 33 U.S.C. § 1365 (2006).

The illustration under Part 2 is drawn from section 107 of the Comprehensive Environmental Response, Compensation, and Liability Act of 1980, 42 U.S.C. § 9607(a) (2006), and section 701(a) of the Hazardous Sites Cleanup Act, 35 Pa. Cons. Stat. Ann. § 6020.701(a) (West 2003).

The illustration under Part 3 is based on 28 U.S.C. § 1332(a) (2006), *Saadeh v. Farouki*, 107 F.3d 52 (D.C. Cir. 1997), and *Chavez-Organista v. Vanos*, 208 F. Supp. 2d 174 (D.P.R. 2002).

The cases cited under Part 4 are based on *Chandler v. Hospital Authority*, 500 So. 2d 1012 (Ala. 1986); *Birmingham Baptist Hospital v. Crews*, 157 So. 224 (Ala. 1934); *Wilmington General Hospital v. Manlove*, 174 A.2d 135 (Del. Super. Ct. 1961); *O'Neill v. Montefiore Hospital*, 202 N.Y.S.2d 436 (App. Div. 1960); and *Valdez v. Lyman-Roberts Hospital*, 638 S.W.2d 111 (Tex. Ct. App. 1982).

The illustration under Part 5 is drawn from *Wilhite v. Mays*, 235 S.E.2d 532 (Ga. 1977), and *Stambovski v. Ackley*, 572 N.Y.S.2d 672 (App. Div. 1991).

Exercise 11-D is based on *First Wisconsin National Bank v. Federal Land Bank of St. Paul*, 849 F.2d 284 (7th Cir. 1988), and *Story v. Christin*, 95 P.2d 925 (Cal. 1939).

Chapter 12

The illustration under Part 1 is based on Federal Water Pollution Control Act § 505, 33 U.S.C. § 1365 (2006).

The illustration under Part 2 is drawn from *Walters v. Department of Transportation*, 474 A.2d 66 (Pa. Commw. Ct. 1984). *But see Capuzzi v. Heller*, 5558 A.2d 596 (Pa. Commw. Ct. 1989), which required that a government employee actually be driving in order for the vehicle exception doctrine of governmental immunity to apply.

The illustration under Part 3 was inspired by *Rose v. Chaikin*, 453 A.2d 1378 (N.J. Super. Ct. Ch. Div. 1982).

The illustration under Part 4 is drawn from *Meadows v. F.W. Woolworth Co.*, 254 F. Supp. 907 (N.D. Fla. 1966), and *Coblyn v. Kennedy's Inc.*, 268 N.E.2d 860 (Mass. 1971).

Chapter 13

The illustration under Part 1 is loosely based on *Machinery Haluing, Inc. v. Steel of West Virginia*, 384 S.E.2d 139 (W. Va. 1989).

The illustration under Part 2 is based on *Ingram v. Peachtree South, Ltd.*, 355 S.E.2d 717 (Ga. Ct. App. 1987), and *Furstein v. Hill*, 590 A.2d 939 (Conn. 1991).

The illustration under Part 3 is based on *Frampton v. Central Indiana Gas Co.*, 297 N.E.2d 425 (Ind. 1973), and *Petermann v. International Brotherhood of Teamsters, Local 396*, 344 P.2d 25 (Cal. Ct. App. 1959).

The first illustration under Part 4 was suggested by a line of cases including *Dolcy v. Rhode Island Joint Reinsurance Association*, 589 A.2d 313 (R.I. 1991); *Morgan v. Cincinnati Insurance Co.*, 307 N.W.2d 53 (Mich. 1981); and *Cooperative Fire Insurance Association v. Domina*, 399 A.2d 502 (Vt. 1979).

The second illustration under Part 4 is based on Fed. R. Civ. P. 24 and *McElrea v. Volt Information Sciences, Inc.*, 119 F.R.D. 630 (E.D. Pa. 1987).

Exercise 13-A is based on *Meminger v. State*, 287 S.E.2d 296 (Ga. Ct. App. 1981), *rev'd on other grounds*, 292 S.E.2d 681 (Ga. 1982); *Choate v. State*, 279 S.E.2d 459 (Ga. Ct. App. 1981); and *Fann v. State*, 266 S.E.2d 307 (Ga. Ct. App. 1980). *Choate* and *Fann* were superseded by a statutory amendment that is now codified at Ga. Code Ann. § 16-8-41 (2011).

Exercise 13-B is based on *ANR Production Co. v. Westburn Drilling, Inc.*, 581 F. Supp. 542 (D. Colo. 1984); *Cain v. Cleveland Parachute Training Center*, 457 N.E.2d 1185 (Ohio Ct. App. 1983); *Phibbs v. Ray's Chevrolet Corp.*, 357 N.Y.S.2d 211 (App. Div. 1974); and *Schutkowski v. Carey*, 725 P.2d 1057 (Wyo. 1986).

Chapter 14

Exercise 14-A is based on *Tyus v. Booth*, 235 N.W.2d 69 (Mich. Ct. App. 1975), and *Hersh v. Kentfield Builders, Inc.*, 172 N.W.2d 56 (Mich. Ct. App. 1969), *rev'd on other grounds*, 189 N.W.2d 286 (Mich. 1971).

Chapter 15

The illustration under Part I is based on *Branch v. Western Petroleum, Inc.*, 657 P.2d 267 (Utah 1982).

Exercise 15-A(1) is based on *Blumenfeld v. Borenstein*, 276 S.E.2d 607 (Ga. 1987).

Exercise 15-A(2) is based on *Roe v. Catholic Charities*, 588 N.E.2d 354 (Ill. Ct. App. 1992), and *Burr v. Board of County Commissioners*, 491 N.E.2d 1101 (Ohio 1986).

Chapter 16

The injunction rule alluded to several times in the chapter is drawn from cases such as *People v. Black's Food Store*, 105 P.2d 361 (Cal. 1940).

Chapter 17

The illustration under Part 1 is based on *Komatsy Ltd. v. Staton Steamship Co.*, 674 F.2d 806 (9th Cir. 1992).

The illustration under Parts 2 and 3 was inspired by the Municipal Waste Planning, Recycling and Management Act § 902, 53 Pa. Cons. Stat. Ann. § 4000.902 (West 2011).

Chapter 18

The illustration in the text is derived from the principles stated in *Canell v. Arcola Housing Corp.*, 65 So. 2d 849 (Fla. 1953) (express easement), and *Romanchuk v. Plotkin*, 9 N.W.2d 421 (Minn. 1943) (implied easement by necessity).

Exercise 18-A is similar to *Kline v. Burns*, 276 A.2d 248 (N.H. 1971).

Exercise 18-B is based on *Moore v. Dover Veterinary Hosp.*, 367 A.2d 1044 (N.H. 1976); *Technical Aid Corp. v. Allen*, 591 A.2d 262, 265 (N.H. 1991); and *Concord Orthopedics Prof. Ass'n v. Forbes*, 702 A.2d 1273 (N.H. 1997).

Chapter 19

The illustration in the text is based on W. Page Keeton et al., *Prosser and Keeton on the Law of Torts* § 11 (5th ed. 1984).

Chapter 20

The illustration in the text is based on *Austin v. Bald II, L.L.C.*, 658 S.E.2d 1 (N.C. Ct. App. 2008), and *Tedder v. Alford*, 493 S.E.2d 487 (N.C. Ct. App. 1997).

Chapter 21

The quotation under Part 4 is adapted from the "opinions below" section in the petitioner's brief in *MCI Telecommunications Corp. v. American Telephone & Telegraph Co.*, No 93-356 (U.S. filed Sept. 2, 1993).

The quotation in Part 5 is adapted from the "jurisdiction" section in the petitioner's brief in *Griffin v. United States*, 502 U.S. 46 (1991) (No. 90-6352).

Chapter 22

The statute described under Parts 1 and 2 is drawn from Mich. Comp. Laws Ann. §§ 168.951, .952, .955 (West 2005). *See also Woods v. Clerk of Saginaw County*, 264 N.W.2d 74 (Mich. Ct. App. 1978).

The cases under Part 3 are based on the discussion in *People v. Kelly*, 549 P.2d 1240 (Cal. 1976), and *State v. Coon*, 974 P.2d 386 (Alaska 1999).

Exercises 22-A and 22-B were inspired by 75 Pa. Cons. Stat. Ann. § 3301(a) (West 2006); *Hamilton v. Glemming*, 46 S.E.2d 438 (Va. 1948); and *Stoll v. Curry*, 175 A. 724 (Pa. Super. Ct. 1934).

Chapter 23

The illustration in Part 1 is based on *Gable v. Curtis*, 673 N.E.2d 805 (Ind. Ct. App. 1996). Representative cases in which the court has reprimanded lawyers for using rude or offensive language in their briefs include *Cox v. Wood*, 247 U.S. 3 (1918); *Anderson v. Federal Cartridge Corp.*, 156 F.2d 681 (8th Cir. 1946); *Mt. Sinai Hospital v. Borg-Warner Corp.*, 527 F. Supp. 922 (S.D.N.Y. 1981); *Gregoire v. National Bank*, 413 P.2d 27 (Alaska 1966); and *WorldCom Network Services v. Thompson*, 698 N.E.2d 1233 (Ind. Ct. App. 1998).

The illustration under Part 2(a) is inspired by *People v. Valentine*, 169 P.2d 1 (Cal. 1946).

The illustration under Part 2(b) is based on *Stadle v. Township of Battle Creek*, 77 N.W.2d 329 (Mich. 1956) (construing Mich. Comp. Laws Ann. § 125.282 (West 1986) (repealed 2006)). *See also Hilltop Realty, Inc. v. City of South Euclid*, 164 N.E.2d 180 (Ohio Ct. App. 1960).

The illustration under Part 3(a) is based on 28 U.S.C. § 1337 (2006) and the Federal Noise Control Act, 42 U.S.C. §§ 4901–4918 (2006).

The cases cited under Part 3(b) are *Kopischke v. First Continental Corp.*, 610 P.2d 668 (Mont. 1980), and *Bentzler v. Braun*, 149 N.W.2d 626 (Wis. 1967).

The illustration under Part 3(c) is inspired by *State Bar v. Geralds*, 263 N.W.2d 241 (Mich. 1978), and *State Bar v. Williams*, 228 N.W.2d 222 (Mich. 1975), modified, 240 N.W.2d 246 (Mich. 1976).

The illustration under Part 5 is based on *Miller v. C.A. Muer Corp.*, 362 N.W.2d 650 (Mich. 1985).

Chapter 24

The Williams Act cited under Part 1 is located at 15 U.S.C. §§ 78m(d), (e), 78n(d)–(f) (2006). The cases are *Kewanee Oil Co. v. Bicron Corp.*, 416 U.S. 470 (1974); *Perez v. Campbell*, 402 U.S. 637 (1971); and *Hines v. Davidowitz*, 312 U.S. 52 (1941).

The illustration under Part 2 is based on Mich. Comp. Laws Ann. §§ 324.1701–.1706 (West 2007), and *West Michigan Environmental Action Council, Inc. v. Natural Resources Commission*, 275 N.W.2d 538 (Mich. 1979).

The illustration under Part 3 was inspired by Mich. Comp. Laws Ann. §§ 333.13501–.13536 (West 2012). It is based on *Tennessee Valley Authority v. Hill*, 437 U.S. 153, 193–95 (1978), and *Hecht Co. v. Bowles*, 321 U.S. 321 (1944).

Exercise 24-B is based on *Prows v. Industrial Commission*, 610 P.2d 1362 (Utah 1980).

Chapter 25

The statute in the text is the Equal Employment Opportunity Act of 1972, 42 U.S.C. §§ 2000e–2000e-17 (2006).

The case in the text was inspired by and is a combination of *Berg v. Richmond Unified School District*, 528 F.2d 1208 (9th Cir. 1975), *vacated*, 434 U.S. 158 (1977), and *Drew v. Liberty Mutual Insurance Co.*, 480 F.2d 69 (5th Cir. 1973).

Exercise 25-B is based on *Bernstein v. Kapneck*, 417 A.2d 456 (Md. Ct. Spec. App. 1980); *Thomas v. Erie Insurance Exchange*, 182 A.2d 823 (Md. 1962); *Hall v. Strom Construction Co.*, 118 N.W.2d 281 (Mich. 1962); and *Le Francois v. Hobart College*, 31 N.Y.S.2d 200 (N.Y. Sup. Ct. 1941), *aff'd*, 39 N.E.2d 271 (N.Y. 1941).

Chapters 26, 27, and 28

The Miller/Chisholm/Aaron problem in the text was inspired by the following cases: *Cook v. Stansell*, 411 S.E.2d 844 (W. Va. 1991); *Reager v. Anderson*, 371 S.E.2d 619 (W. Va. 1988); *Board of Education v. Zando, Martin & Milstead, Inc.*, 390 S.E.2d 796 (W. Va. 1990); *Cline v. White*, 393 S.E.2d 923 (W. Va. 1990); *Missouri Pacific Railroad Co. v. Whitehead & Kales Co.*, 566 S.W.2d 466 (Mo. 1978); *Iowa v. Norfolk & Western Railway Co.*, 753 S.W.2d 891 (Mo. 1988); and *Greenstreet v. Rupert*, 795 S.W.2d 539 (Mo. Ct. App. 1990).

Index

Accuracy
  importance of, 169-72, 282-84, 339-42
Advocacy generally, 323-31, 337-54
Analogy and distinction, 100, 105-06
Analysis
  common law analysis, 99-109
  describing basis for conclusion,
    191-94, 222-23
  explaining objectively, 271-74
  showing all steps in, 189-91
  statutory analysis, 115-25
Annotations, 18-19
Appellate brief
  generally, 311-12, 399-407
  basing argument on appropriate
    standard of review, 402-04
  difference from office memorandum,
    311-12
  focusing on reversible errors, 400-02
  format and elements of, 312-20
    Appendix, 320
    Argument, 319, 323-31, 337-54,
      399-407
    Authorities Cited, 314-15
    Conclusion, 319-20
    Constitutional Provisions, Statutes,
      Regulations, and Rules Involved,
      316
    Jurisdiction or Statement of
      Jurisdiction, 316
    Opinions Below, 315
    Point Headings, 357-63
    Questions Presented, 317-18
    Standard of Review, 316
    Statement of Facts, 318, 367-76
    Summary of Argument, 318-19
    Table of Contents, 314
    Title Page, 314
  harmonizing argument with existing
    law, 406-07

organization of arguments
    See Structure of an Argument
    See also Point Headings
  policy arguments in, 345-46, 404-06
  using forceful and affirmative language,
    346-54
  See also Persuasive Writing
Appendix in brief, 320
Argument section of briefs, 319
Audience, 199, 216-17, 305, 394-96, 411-12
Authorities Cited in brief, 314-15
Authority
  binding, 16
  persuasive, 16
  primary and secondary, 16-19

Background facts, 281
Brevity
  importance of in brief to trial court,
    391-94
Brief Answer in office memorandum,
    261-62
Brief to a trial court
  generally, 311-13, 381-96
  caption, 313
  format and elements, 312-13, 315
Briefs
  case briefs, 24-39
  See also Appellate brief, Brief to a trial
    court

Caption in brief to a trial court, 313
Cases
  case analysis, 23-39
  publication of decisions, 17-18
  See also Common law
Client letter
  See Opinion letter
Common law
  analysis of, 99-109

Common law *(continued)*
    defined, 12, 23
    summarizing case law, 175-78
    synthesizing case law, 61-68, 178-83
Concise writing, 248-53
    redundancy, 251-52
    sentences begun with "there" or "it,"
        250-51
    tautological phrases, 248-49
    unnecessary modifiers, 249-50
    wordy phrases, 248
Conclusion
    explaining reasons for, 155-57, 191-94,
        222-24
    in appellate brief, 319-20
    in brief to trial court, 319-20
    in office memorandum, 362-64
    reaching one, 109, 124-25, 131-38
    stating at the outset, 217-19
    stating objectively, 267-70
Concurring opinions, 45
Constitutional Provisions, Statutes,
        Regulations, and Rules involved
        in a brief, 316
Constitutions
    generally, 11-13
    publication of, 17
Counterarguments
    describing argument, 224-25
    describing law on which based, 226-27
    explaining reasons for rejecting,
        224-25, 227-29
    placement of, 155-57, 328-31
    presentation in briefs, 346-47

Describing the law
    generally, 153-55, 169-83, 220-22
    in a brief, 347-50
    in an office memorandum, 270-71
    in an opinion letter, 302-03
    summarizing case law, 175-78
    synthesizing case law, 178-83
Dicta, 45, 47
Discussion in office memorandum, 262,
        267-74
    drafting, 213-37
Dissenting opinions, 45, 47
Distinction
    See Analogy and distinction

Editing
    importance of, 243-46
    proofreading for errors, 254, 265-66
    proofreading to include signposts,
        229-36
Ejusdem generis, 124-25
Electronic communication
    confidentiality, 265-66, 306-07
    office memorandum, 264-66
    opinion letter, 306-07
    professionalism, 264-65
    proofreading, 265
Elements
    See Rules of law
E-mail
    client confidentiality, 306-07
    correspondence by, 306-07
Emphasis
    by placement of words, phrases, and
        sentences, 351-52
    by positive assertions, 351
    by short sentences, 353
    on favorable facts in a brief, 343-45,
        372-76
Encyclopedias, legal, 18
Evaluating strength of client's case, 109,
        124-25, 131-38

Facts
    background, 281
    describing favorably, 372-76, 389-90
    describing objectively, 282-84
    effective use of in argument, 342-45,
        389-90
    emotionally significant, 280, 372-73
    in oral argument, 418
    legally significant, 279-81
    omitting extraneous, 252-53
    organization of in brief, 373-76
    organization of in office memorandum,
        281-82
    relevant facts in judicial opinion,
        32-34
    Statement of Facts in brief, 318,
        367-76
    Statement of Facts in office
        memorandum, 262, 277-84
    summarizing in an opinion letter,
        300-01

Federal Rule of Civil Procedure 12,
        339-40
Federal Rule of Appellate Procedure, 409

"Givens"
    defined, 85
    placement of, 144-47
    treatment of, 85-86

Hierarchy
    of courts, 13-16
    of jurisdictions, 13
    of laws, 11-13
Holding of a court
    contrasted with court's reasoning,
        27-28
    identifying and stating, 26-28
    implied holding, 26-27
Hornbooks, 19

Intrusive words and phrases, 253-54
Issues
    defining and narrowing, 76-85, 214
    explaining the context, 194-96
    identifying and selecting, 73-88
    in judicial opinions, 28-30
    organizing, 87-88, 147-53
"It," sentences begun with, 250-51

Judicial opinions
    concurring, 45
    dicta, 45, 47
    dissenting, 45, 47
    reporting of, 17-18
    study of, 23-39
Jurisdiction
    of courts generally, 13-16
    statement of in appellate brief,
        315
    subject-matter jurisdiction, 15-16

Legal periodicals, 19
Legal rules
    See Rules of law
Legally significant facts, 279-81
Linear approach to writing, 213-14

Memorandum of law
    See Office Memorandum

Model Rules of Professional Conduct,
        338, 339
Modifiers
    ambiguous, 253-54
    unnecessary, 249-50

Nominalizations, 247

Objectivity
    in memos 259-60, 267-74
        in framing Questions Presented,
            293-95
        in stating facts, 282-84
    in opinion letters, 304-05
Office Memorandum
    confidentiality, 265-66
    electronic communication, 264-66
    elements of, 259-64
        Brief Answer, 261-62
        Conclusion, 262-64
        Discussion, 261-62, 265-70
        Heading, 260
        Questions Presented, 261, 291-95
        Statement of Facts, 262, 277-84
    objectivity in, 259-60, 267-74, 282-84
    scope, 76-77
Opinion letter, 297-307
Opinions
    publication of judicial opinions,
        17-18
Opinions Below in appellate brief, 315
Oral argument
    generally, 409-37
    formality, 431-32
    importance of, 409-10
    preparation, 410-20
        develop a theme, 413-15
        know your audience, 411-12
        know your case, 411
        outline the issues and key points,
            417-18
        plan your strongest and most
            essential arguments, 415-17
        practice, 417-20, 433
    presentation, 420-37
        closing, 433-35
        facts, 418, 421-22
        flexibility, 418
        opening, 420-23

Oral argument, presentation *(continued)*
   professional tone and manner,
      431-33
   rebuttal, 435-36
   simple and direct arguments,
      423-24
   time management, 430-32
  questions from the bench
   effective use of, 425-30
   friendly and unfriendly, 425, 427
  request for relief, 420, 433-35
  Socratic dialogue, 409
  "species" of oral advocates, 437
  time management, 412-13, 430-31
Organization
  generally, 143-60
  CiRAC, 217
  "givens," 144-47
  of arguments in a brief, 323-31
  of facts, 281-82
  paragraphs, 200-03, 227-34
  separation of issues and sub-issues,
      86-87, 147-53
  See also Emphasis; Signposts;
      Structure of an argument

Paragraphs, 200-03, 229-36
  as organizational signpost, 200-03
  defined, 200-01
  length, 201
Persuasive writing, 337-54
  emphasis on helpful facts, 343-45
  honesty about the law and facts,
      349-42
  persuasive writing techniques, 350-54
  policy arguments, 345-46
  presentation from client's point of
      view, 346-50
  professional tone and manner, 338-39
Point Headings in brief, 357-63
Policy
  generally, 3-7
  distinguished from court's reasoning,
      35-36
  in common law analysis, 106-08
  in evaluating client's case, 135-36
  in statutory analysis, 121-22
  underlying judicial decisions, 4-7,
      35-36, 106-07

  underlying statutes, 4-7, 121-22
  use in analyzing issues, 106-08,
      121-22, 135-36
  use in briefs, 345-46, 387-88, 404-06
Precedent
  generally, 43-48
  binding and persuasive, 16, 43-44
  "strict" vs. "loose" view, 44
  welcome and unwelcome, 44, 47
Precision, 187-88, 244-45
  blending simplicity with, 245-46
Primary authority, 16, 17
Process of legal writing, 213-15
  pre-writing, 215
  recursive method, 214-16
Professional conduct, 264-65, 337-42

Questions Presented
  in appellate brief, 317-18
  in office memorandum, 261, 291-95
Quotations
  ellipsis indicating omission, 172-73
  when to quote, 171-73

Reasoning of courts
  generally, 35-36
  distinguished from policy, 35-36
  use in common law analysis, 106-08
Recursive approach to legal writing,
      214-16
Redundancy, 251-52
Regulations
  generally, 3-7
  publication of, 17
Repetition, 251-52
Restatements, 19
Revising and editing, 243-54
Rules of law
  generally, 3-7
  conjunctive construction, 58
  disjunctive construction, 58
  elements of, 58
  explaining the context of, 194-96
  identifying in judicial opinions, 30-32
  identifying rules applicable to legal
      problem, 76-79
  quoting and paraphrasing, 171-73
  result, 59
  sub-elements, 60-61

synthesis, 61-68
where to include, 153-55, 220-22

Secondary authority, 16, 18-19
Signposts, 199-208, 229-33
    See also Transitions
Simplicity, writing with, 245-46
Sources of law, 11-19
Standard of Review
    element in appellate brief, 316
    basing appellate argument on proper
        standard, 402-04
Stare decisis, 43-48
Statement of Facts
    in appellate brief, 318, 367-76
    in office memorandum, 262, 277-84
    See also Facts
Statement of Issues
    See Questions Presented
Statement of the Case
    See Statement of Facts
Statutes
    generally, 12
    analyzing and construing, 115-25
    explaining the context, 194-96
    publications of, 17
    quoting and paraphrasing, 171-72,
        177-78
    See also Rules of law
Statutory analysis, 115-25
    canons of construction, 116, 124-25
    defining statutory terms, 118-19
    ejusdem generis, 124-25
    judicial interpretation of statutes,
        115-16, 120-22, 124
    judicial presumptions, 121, 124
    legislative intent
        ascertaining, 121-23
        giving effect to, 121-22
    plain meaning rule, 120

Structure of an argument, 323-31
    presenting the strongest or most
        significant argument first, 324-28
    presenting the client's position first,
        328-31
    See also Organization
Style
    See Revising and editing; Persuasive
        writing
Sub-issues
    defined, 86-87
    organization of, 87, 150-53
Summary of Argument in appellate brief,
    318-19
Synthesis, from multiple sources, 61-68,
    178-83

Table of Authorities
    See Authorities Cited
Table of Contents, in appellate brief, 314
Tautological phrases, 248-49
"There," sentences begun with, 250
Thesis and topic sentences
    conclusion as a thesis, 200
    thesis sentence defined, 200
    topic sentence defined, 204
Title Page in appellate brief, 313
Transitions, 205-08
    thesis or topic sentence as, 205-08
    transitional words and phrases, 205-06
Treatises, 19

Verbs
    preferred over nominalizations, 247
    preferring active voice, 246

West reporter system, 17-18